THE CHALLENGE OF MANAGEMENT

William G. Dyer

Robert H. Daines

William C. Giauque

J. Willard and Alice S. Marriott School of Management
Brigham Young University

Harcourt Brace Jovanovich, Publishers

San Diego   New York   Chicago   Austin   Washington, D.C.
London   Sydney   Tokyo   Toronto

To our families, to Brigham Young University, and to our students

William G. Dyer

Robert H. Daines

William C. Giauque

PREFACE

During the last half of this century, tremendous changes have occurred in almost every society, in every phase of life, and in every field of study. The world in which our children and grandchildren will live will be so different that the world that produced us will seem like ancient history.

One major change has been American businesses' declining worldwide market share. The phonograph, color television, audiotape recorder, video cassette recorder, telephone, transistor, integrated circuit were all invented in the United States, yet American manufacturers currently account for only a small percentage of the international market, despite the fact that America is also the world's greatest consumer of these products. Something has obviously gone wrong. In a special issue devoted to innovation, *Business Week* points out that American managers have found many excuses for their lack of competitiveness with other countries, including lower foreign labor costs, unfair overseas trade practices, cheaper overseas capital, and Wall Street's lack of patience. "But while there may be some truth in all those complaints, there's no escaping one fundamental fact: U.S. companies are being outmanaged by their toughest competitors."[1]

The major challenge for the next generation of managers is to lead and manage more effectively than in the past. This is not only an important challenge, but an exciting one as well. Based on decades of combined experience in teaching and practicing management, we can attest that nothing is more exciting than making an organization work effectively. Results happen only with management and leadership, and profits come only when these functions are performed well. This textbook is our attempt to capture the important lessons we have learned in management and pass them on to the next generation.

Besides the technical challenge of managing an effective organization, managers must also be concerned with ethical considerations. This volume is dedicated to the proposition of "principled management"—people working for the success of organizations, but guided by personal principles and integrity.

We hope that this book will challenge students to think about, plan, and prepare for careers as leaders in the management field. The American psychologist, Abraham Maslow, used to ask his students, "Which of you plans to be the next Albert Schweitzer, the next Florence Nightingale, the next president of the United States, the writer

---

1. Russell Mitchell, "Nurturing Those Ideas," *Business Week*, 1989 Special Issue, p. 106.

of the next great book in psychology?" Students would stammer and hang their heads, and Maslow would challenge them, "Why not you? If not you, who?"

This is our challenge to students. Which of you will be the next president of General Motors, the next CEO of a Fortune 500 company, the founder of a new enterprise, the next governor of a state, or the next secretary of defense? If not you, who? And why not you?

ORGANIZATION

The traditional functions of planning, organizing, leading, and controlling provide the central foundation for *The Challenge of Management*.

Part I introduces the field of management, traces the history of its development, and examines the environment in which today's managers work. The inclusion of Chapter 4, The Ethics of Free Enterprise, at the end of Part I underlines the importance of this topic to students and offers a frame of reference for the material that follows.

Part II explores the scope and dimensions of planning at all levels within an organization. Chapter 6, Strategic Planning, stresses the importance of directional planning in today's increasingly complex business environment and includes a summary of the most current planning models. Chapters covering managerial decision making and decision-making tools present the means and methods used by managers to make effective and informed choices.

Part III examines the organization itself—its nature and culture, its structure and design, and the factors contributing to its development and change. An understanding of group dynamics and a mastery of team-building skills are viewed as pivotal components of a manager's organizational effectiveness.

Part IV focuses on the critical role of leadership. The qualities and experiences that make and form leaders are discussed along with leadership styles and values. The abilities to motivate and to communicate effectively are presented as key elements of good leadership. The placement of Chapter 16, Human Resources Management, in this section acknowledges that the human resource function is integral to the concerns of managers. Chapter 17, The Manager, Stress, and the Family, examines the interrelationship between the home and the workplace and explores options for reducing the stress that sometimes arises through the conflicting demands of each environment.

Part V presents a discussion of the role and purpose of control and its relationship to other management functions. Various aspects of operations management are introduced, and the function of information systems and systems design in assisting and refining the control process is addressed.

Part VI expands the arena of management to international dimensions and extends it toward the future. An understanding of the world's political and economic environment, along with a knowledge of the strategies used for global production and foreign market penetration, are essential for today's managers and will continue to gain importance as we move into the twenty-first century.

SPECIAL FEATURES AND PEDAGOGY

Integrated Cases

One of the major features of *The Challenge of Management* are numerous thought-provoking cases that integrate the management concepts under discussion with real-world situations. Every chapter has a beginning case, one or two middle cases, and an ending case. Many of the cases are international in scope, such as the discussion of the organizational innovation at Volvo (Chapter 10); some deal with timely matters, such as quality control in the airline industry (Chapter 19); others pose ethical questions, such as the hiring of illegal immigrants (Chapter 3); and still others examine individual concerns, such as the problems of relocating the dual-career couple (Chapter 17).

Boxed Inserts

Important topics are often highlighted by special boxed inserts, such as a comparison of capitalism and communism (Chapter 4) or a look at overcoming resistance to change (Chapter 12). Many boxes deal with very recent events, such as the discussion of the Alaskan oil spill (Chapter 3).

Chapter Outlines and Learning Objectives

To help students focus on the important points in their reading, each chapter opens with a chapter outline and a list of learning objectives. The learning objectives can also serve students as a self-test of their comprehension of the material.

Figures and Tables

To enhance the discussion of chapter topics there is ample use of full-color figures, tables, and color photographs.

Chapter Summaries and Key Terms

The discussion in each chapter closes with a summary of the major themes and a review list of the key managerial terms that students should be able to recognize and define.

End-of-Chapter Questions

Three sets of questions are provided at the end of every chapter: (1) Review Questions, which cover the fundamental chapter concepts; (2) Challenge Questions, which deal with more complex issues and require analytical skills; and (3) Case and Related Questions, which apply management theory to real business situations discussed in the chapter.

Glossary

As a quick reference for students who want to review their management vocabulary, a complete glossary of key terms is provided at the end of the book.

SUPPLEMENTS

Instructor's Manual

To assist the instructor in preparing the most complete and effective management course, the *Instructor's Manual* provides lecture outlines with additional real-world examples and teaching tips, annotated learning objectives, and suggestions for leading class discussions of the cases. It also contains definitions for key terms, answers to Review, Challenge, and Case and Related Questions, plus one additional case study per chapter.

Testbook and Computerized Test Bank

A comprehensive *Testbook* supplies 2,100 test questions (30 true-false and 70 multiple-choice per chapter) of varying scope and levels of difficulty. The computerized version allows instructors to vary the order of questions and to modify or add to the test item file.

Study Guide

Designed as a helpful, handy aid to students, the *Study Guide* provides the following for every chapter: topical overview, study outline, review of key managerial terms, and self-test section with true-false, multiple-choice, and fill-in questions. An answer key is provided at the back of the book.

Management Transparencies

A set of 125 transparencies (100 two-color and 25 full-color acetates) is available to instructors. These transparencies, drawn from *The Challenge of Management* and other outside sources, cover the full range of management topics.

Videotapes

Adopters of *The Challenge of Management* will have the opportunity of choosing from a wide selection of videos that help illustrate key management concepts and make the field come alive for students.

Software

Schools adopting *The Challenge of Management* will also have the opportunity of selecting from management simulation software programs designed to help students better understand the complexities of management and sharpen their decision-making skills.

Acknowledgments

We would be remiss if we did not express appreciation to the many people who helped us produce this volume. These include our families, our secretarial support, and many student research assistants. Special recognition and appreciation must be given to Kirk Hart, of Brigham Young University, who provided much of the foundation of Chapter 4, The Ethics of Free Enterprise, and to Lee Radebaugh, also of Brigham Young University, who is the author of Chapter 21, International Dimensions of Management.

Special thanks should be given to Peggy Keele, who managed the several revisions of this book. Jeff Holmes, Bill McCann, Scott Hammond, and Rob Daines provided invaluable service as research assistants, and Michelle Holmes and Howard Bolton also contributed greatly. Without the help of Julie LeMaster, the massive amount of word processing would not have been completed.

We also appreciate the excellent editorial support of Harcourt Brace Jovanovich: Mickey Cox and Scott Isenberg, acquisitions editors; Jon Preimesberger, manuscript editor; Paula Bryant, production editor; Martha Roach, designer; Avery Hallowell, art editor; and Lesley Lenox, production manager.

Paul Thompson, former dean of the Brigham Young University Marriott School of Management, was a constant provider of encouragement and resource support. We owe him special thanks.

Finally, we would like to thank the following management scholars for reviewing the book and providing us with many helpful comments and suggestions: Steve Barr, Oklahoma State University; Lester Digman, University of Nebraska; Robert Findley, Northwest Missouri State University; R. E. Green, Georgia Institute of Technology; Paul Harmon, University of Utah; James W. Klingler, Villanova University; James McElroy, Iowa State University; Alan N. Miller, University of Nevada; Stuart Rosenkrantz, University of Central Florida; Nick Sarantakes, Austin Community College; Charles B. Shrader, Iowa State University; Kenneth Thompson, De Paul University; and C. E. Wooldridge, Central State University.

CONTENTS

PART 1

THE CHALLENGE OF MANAGEMENT

CHAPTER 1

AN INTRODUCTION TO CHALLENGES IN MANAGEMENT

CHAPTER OUTLINE

LEARNING OBJECTIVES

■ Answer common questions students have about management.

■ Understand the growth of management as a new profession.

■ Identify some of the problems in management.

■ Explain the importance of planning and decision making.

■ Appreciate the need to build organizations that will help achieve goals.

■ Discuss the importance of the manager as a leader of people.

■ Understand the meaning of controls as tools for managers.

■ Identify the need for managerial familiarity with computers.

■ Appreciate the scope of the challenge of management in the organizations of the next decade.

By way of introduction to the study of management, the following are answers to the questions most asked of professors about a management career.[1]

Question: I'm interested in a career in business. But what is the difference between being a manager and being a businessperson?

Answer: Years ago, the two terms were often used interchangeably. In the United States, most private businesses are still small, family-run firms. A person who operates a small business must be a businessperson whether that business is a barbershop, a corner grocery store, or any kind of business operation. This owner must be ultimately concerned about making a profit and must manage and coordinate all of the functions that contribute to profit or loss. He must purchase materials, see that production is achieved or service is provided, keep track of all expenses, advertise and sell, do all the work or hire others, and set a price that allows a profit to be made.

When businesses expand, each of their special functions (purchasing, operations, and finance, for example) become so large it takes trained people to manage individual parts of the total enterprise. Certain top-level, general managers coordinate all of the organization's activities while leaving the responsibility for individual activities to the lower-level managers. Managers, then, are those responsible for achieving goals in specific or general areas primarily by ensuring that work gets accomplished through the efforts of others.

Question: If I were to go to work as a manager for an oil company, a high-tech firm, or a big chemical corporation would I need to be a specialist in petroleum, computers, or chemistry?

Answer: Certainly it will help to know something about the industry in which you work. But most companies expect to give managers the needed background in the work of the company. It is generally agreed that despite industry variations, most management processes are the same regardless of the overall business. Whether you manage at General Foods or General Motors, you still have to develop plans, make decisions, motivate people, and communicate ideas. All companies must develop strategies or plans to market or sell the product, and all have to keep careful control of financial matters. Therefore, you prepare for a management career by learning the basic activities or processes of management first.

Question: You have made some reference to this, but exactly what do managers do?

Answer: Basically, managers make and implement decisions to achieve specified results in their assigned area of responsibility. The types of decisions you make are dependent on the area or function you manage and on your level in the organization. If you manage a production unit, where the product is actually built, you make and implement decisions about the people and the work flow that creates the finished

Managers must communicate effectively with employees to achieve management goals.

product—a car or TV set. If you are a sales manager, you make and implement decisions about the people who contact customers to sell a product.

Usually a manager will have an assigned work area with goals to achieve. The manager is responsible for getting the people together to achieve the goal, for devising a plan to get the work done, and for following through to see that the objectives are in fact achieved.

Question: How much money can I expect to make as a manager?

Answer: Again this will depend on several factors: training and education, industry, function, and location. Generally, an advanced degree—Master of Business Administration (MBA) or Master in Public Administration (MPA)—pays more than a bachelor's degree. And a bachelor's degree pays more than a high school degree. Managers can have any level of education, but the more education you have the more complex the area you will probably be allowed to manage.

A person with an MBA from a reputable university can probably expect to start with a company at around $35,000 to $45,000 a year. This will probably be higher if you live in the East but lower if you live in the Plains or Rocky Mountain areas. A bachelor's degree student will probably start at around $20,000 to $24,000. The upper levels of compensation can be staggering. The best-paid chief executive officer (CEO) in the United States has received more than $20 million per year in recent years. Many CEOs top $1 million per year with top-level executives receiving well over six figures. But the top jobs require you to be well trained, highly motivated, and able to perform effectively.

Question: What kind of educational program should I follow in college if I want to have a career in management?

Answer: That depends on whether you expect to go to graduate school and what your areas of interest are. If you decide to get an MBA or MPA degree, you could pursue an undergraduate major in a number of different areas: English, social science, engineering, sciences, economics, computer science, or accounting. All good master's degree programs will cover the basics of business administration over what is usually a two-year program.

Since all managers must excel at both oral and written communication, a mastery of English is important. It also helps to know something about economic systems, computers, and human behavior. If you do not want to go on for a master's degree, then a degree in some aspect of business management is usually desirable. All good bachelor programs impart the fundamentals of economics, computers, business communications, accounting, financial management, organization behavior, and marketing. This knowledge will allow the person to understand the nature of the business world, the language, and the usual approaches to handling business problems and solutions. However, companies also are looking for bright, competent people and will recruit people from many majors and train them in the management procedures in the specific company. General Motors, for example, hires about 20 percent liberal arts majors.

Question: I know some businesses sometimes put pressure on people to compromise ethical standards or even break the law in order to make a profit. How prevalent is this problem?

Answer: Undoubtedly some firms and individuals behave unethically, but they are few in number compared to the vast majority who insist on impeccable ethical behavior. Every reputable business school teaches ethical behavior, and most companies pride themselves on their high standards and principles. People in management will face moral dilemmas, as will every person, but management as a profession generally has very high moral and ethical standards.

Question: If I go into management will I be expected to sacrifice everything for the company? Will I be expected to put in lengthy hours, travel a lot, and put the needs of my family after the demands of the firm?

Answer: It would be a mistake to assume that a successful manager would only have to work 40 hours a week. The work of management is demanding and most companies expect managers to put in the time necessary to get the job done. Hours can be flexible and people generally have some control over their workdays. Most managers work as much as 50 to 60 hours a week. If time is managed well, though, a manager may have good family relationships and a satisfying social and cultural life.

Some management positions require extensive traveling but they are the exception. Most managers probably do not spend more than two or three nights a month away from home. Moving is another matter. In large companies managers can expect to move every two or three years as the company grows and careers change. ▼

Lee Iacocca, former general manager and president of Ford and currently chief executive officer of Chrysler—hard worker and big dreamer.

THE CHALLENGE OF MANAGEMENT

My years as general manager of the Ford Division were the happiest of my life. For my colleagues and me this was fire-in-the-belly time. We were high from smoking our own brand—a combination of hard work and big dreams.

In those days, I couldn't wait to get to work in the morning.

At night I didn't want to leave. We were continually playing with new ideas and trying out models on the test track. We were young and cocky. We saw ourselves as artists, about to produce the finest masterpieces the world had ever seen.[2]

LEE IACOCCA

We deliberately chose "The Challenge of Management" as the title for this text because we like the definition of "challenge" as applied to the field of management. One dictionary definition of challenge is "the quality of requiring the very best of one's abilities and efforts." With this orientation clearly in mind, this book was written to show the student the challenges in management—a profession that certainly requires the very best of one's abilities and efforts in a wide arena of activities. Management is one of the newest professions, and successfully guiding and directing the efforts of others in order to achieve important goals in today's organizations requires a range of attitudes and skills that is almost mind-boggling in its scope.

It has not been too long since most universities had as a major academic unit—a college, division, or department—with the sole title of "Business"—hence a College of Business. The inference was that the graduate from a program in this unit was to be a businessperson. This orientation has changed dramatically in the last decade and more and more programs are now identified as being a School of Management, or a Department of Business Management or Public Sector Management.

THE CHALLENGE OF A NEW PROFESSION

Management has emerged in the space of about 25 years as the most sought-after new profession not only in the United States but almost worldwide. In the 1950s, American universities graduated about 5,000 Master of Business Administration (MBA) students each year. By the 1980s, nearly 700 institutions were graduating over 60,000 MBA students each year, and many more thousands were getting graduate degrees in public administration, hospital administration, education administration, and a range of other management-related specialized degree programs.

In this same period the undergraduate interest in management also grew rapidly. In the 1950s about 50,000 students enrolled in undergraduate programs in business and management in the U. S. By the 1980s that number had increased to over 200,000. Many of these undergraduates will go on to get a graduate degree in some area of management, but the largest percentage will seek immediate employment, with the ultimate goal of becoming a professional manager.

Why this exploding interest? A survey conducted by *Business Week* in 1988 showed that the average starting pay for the top 20 MBA programs in America was $49,418 with salaries ranging from a high of $65,176 for Stanford MBAs to a low of $38,407 for Indiana Graduates.[3] Certainly the high amount of pay and compensation for a two-year graduate program has been one incentive that has attracted people into the management field.

Another incentive certainly must be the huge financial rewards given to top-level corporate executives. According to the consulting firm of Booz, Allen and Hamilton, Inc., today's chief executives average approximately $750,000 in annual income, including bonuses. This is triple that of fifteen years ago.[4] It is also roughly fifty times the wages of an average factory worker. In 1980, only four top managers received seven-digit compensation packages. However, in 1987 one had to make over $2.5 million to even qualify among the top twenty-five paid professionals. In 1985 Victor Posner, Chairman of DWG, received $12.7 million in compensation followed by Lee Iacocca, head of Chrysler, who pulled down $11.4 million, which was topped in 1986 when Iacocca received $20.5 million. In American society only entertainers—movie stars, singers, athletes—are paid higher than corporate executives.[5]

This tremendous growth in management coupled with huge financial rewards has attracted tens of thousands of bright, energetic young people into the management field. With this growth have come some disturbing manipulations and dubious practices that have cast a dark cloud over this new profession and now requires managers to work towards transforming this field into a mature profession with high moral and ethical standards.

Organization analysts, Meek, Woodworth, and Dyer have rather clearly shown that American corporations have undergone a marked shift from being owned and controlled by original owners, often families, to large, bureaucratic, impersonal systems operated by executives who, all too often, have their own career and financial interests at heart. These authors claim that managers have moved from being persons who were involved in creating and expanding an enterprise with their own sweat and innovation into a new breed.

> Today's manager, by contrast, professes to be a cool, calculating executive who "goes by the numbers" and is more interested in "doing deals" than achieving excellence in a particular industry. Competence is now based on credentials, college degrees, and fast-track career strategies. In fact, contemporary managers usually have a contempt for physical labor. Their hands are clean, their collars are white, and they are dressed-for-success. They seldom have roots in the local communities where their businesses are located. They control the corporation through asset management and high finance, having little shop experience or comprehension of the businesses they oversee. Disdaining the details of manufacturing and distribution, today's professional managers measure success in terms of return on investment, executive perks, and their personal investment brackets.[6]

The year 1988 was a year filled with scandals in the investment field. Investment banking has been one of the most attractive areas for people interested in the fast track for success. Here people manage "assets" rather than build a product, and the rewards are given to those who can manipulate corporate stock deals and realize tremendous profits. One of the biggest scandals centered on the investment firm of Drexel, Burnham, and Lambert, which was fined $300 million and required to put another $350 million into a restitution fund because of shady dealings in handling stocks in the marketplace.

The quote at the beginning of the chapter from Lee Iacocca exemplifies the orientation of this book. A person who sees the real challenge in management will find in this emerging profession an almost all encompassing excitement—a "fire-in-the-belly" experience. Iacocca felt that his time as a manager was filled with hard work and with dreams—a time of creativity, experimenting, taking some risk, and creating a product that would be a masterpiece, something to be proud of.

The standards of conduct, of ethics, of moral behavior, of excellence in performance are still in the process of being developed. Those students who read this text and choose to enter the management field will help forge the basic conditions that will be the basis of this profession for years to come. In order to see the multifaceted possibilities in management, the book covers the major areas of challenge.

THE CHALLENGE OF PLANNING

When Iacocca was a manager at Ford he and his colleagues planned on building a new kind of automobile. Much of the excitement in management is in this planning process. While there are some products that are discovered by pure chance, almost everything that has been produced in our high technology age is the result of careful, intense planning. Thoughtful managers begin the journey by seeing the end from the beginning. Part of the skill development in any successful manager is to learn to think through every project or task and develop as complete a plan as possible. One of the popular management orientations during the 1960s and 1970s was Management by Objectives (MBO). The emphasis here is to think of management as a series of inter-locking objectives with managers at every level encouraging the participation of every worker in setting the objectives. Managers and subordinates together think through what is needed, set objectives and plans, and then evaluate performance to the degree that objectives are achieved. This is not to be confused with another popular formula—Managing by Wandering Around (MBWA). The emphasis here is the encouragement of managers to be out and about—seeing, talking, sharing, and consulting with others involved in the enterprise rather than isolating themselves in their offices. If managers are to plan well, then they need to see how well the plans are being carried out.

As challenging as planning is, the adoption of the planning processes suggested in this text will not ensure success. In our constantly changing environment, a key to success for a firm lies not only in good operational planning but also in the quality of strategic thinking. It is essential to understand what business the organization wants to be in and then decide how to get to the desired objectives. It is the "getting there" responsibility that is aided by good planning and decision-making processes. Thus an essential part of planning is decision making. In fact, Herbert Simon, a prize-winning economist, makes a convincing argument that decision making is the central activity of all of management.[7] Management is decision making. Without decision making nothing gets done. The key is to make decisions that are both high in quality and also are highly accepted by those who must implement the decision. Competency in deci-sion making also means knowing when to make decisions alone and when to consult with others or even join with others in a consensus.

THE CHALLENGE OF ORGANIZATION

All over the civilized world, human work is done as individuals band together in collective action and form an organization—an integrated connection of people, re-sources, processes, and structures for achieving goals. Managers are faced with the challenge of organizing these elements in the most effective and efficient way. For many years, American Telephone and Telegraph (AT&T) was organized around the functions it performed—customer relations, service and maintenance, handling local and long distance calls, and financial accounting. AT&T had a regulated monopoly— that is the government allowed it to be the only communications company in exis-tence (except for a few small, isolated areas) since the mode of communication was via telephone poles and wires and no one wanted competing companies to put up a

The advent of satellite technology marked the end of the AT&T monopoly.

tangle of wires. With this monopoly it made sense to organize around the various functions facing the organization. Then new technology changed the world for AT&T. It became possible to send messages via the open air waves by satellite and telephone lines became essentially obsolete. New companies were formed to use the new technology and the government rescinded its monopoly rights to AT&T. AT&T was faced with fierce competition for customers as MCI, Tel America, SPRINT, and other companies offered the same service at a lower rate. Top management of AT&T saw that their current organization was not geared up to meet this new challenge, so they made a major organizational change and shifted to a market-oriented company. People and resources were formed around market segments—commercial, residential, professional, governmental, etc. They wanted to be able to quickly assess the needs of people in these segments and offer services and rates consistent with the competition.

Managers must know how to organize all resources and look at such issues as: how many people can effectively work together; how many people can one person manage (span of control); and what units should be clustered together and which should be kept separate. These are factors operating inside the system or business. But as in the case of AT&T, managers must also be aware of the forces outside the system. Managers must understand that all organizations are open systems, and a new technology emerging from outside the system may have serious implications for the organization inside the system.

Additionally much research has shown that when people work closely together as a team, there is a synergistic effect, and productivity and morale are increased. The question is how to build effective work teams and tap into the additional increase of effectiveness a team produces. And when the current organization is affected in such a way that the goals of the system are no longer being met, the manager must know how to create a change or redesign the system. To be effective in change, the manager should know how to alter the system in such a way that people both inside and outside the company (employees and customers) are not alienated and demotivated because of sudden disruptive actions.

So the challenge is to understand the nature of organization structures and how to build teams and work units that collaborate. It also means understanding the external world—the competition, government regulations, world affairs, new discoveries and inventions, labor unions, and a host of other factors. And when changes must be made, it is a major challenge to know how to make changes that increase, not decrease, the productive efforts of those who will be affected by the change.

THE CHALLENGE OF LEADERSHIP

Lest anyone falsely think that management is just a pure analytic process of developing plans and systems, it should be quickly pointed out that any effective manager must be in a real sense a practicing social psychologist. Managers must manage people. Some managers are like the first-grade teacher who when asked how she liked teaching said, "It would be a wonderful work if I just didn't have to deal with those kids!" In teaching, "kids" are what it is all about, and in management people are probably the most important ingredient in success or failure.

Leadership is another key issue in the managerial role. Leaders are those who are able to create a vision of what needs to be done and then communicate that vision to others so they are motivated to work with the manager to achieve that vision. The evidence seems to be clear that leaders are not born (although some are born with certain traits that make being a leader in our culture easier) but that a person can develop certain behaviors and attitudes that are essential in organizational leadership. Almost every organization of any size has a program of some type that will help supervisors and managers improve in the key skills needed in working with others.

The people challenge is everywhere. Not only must a manager learn how to deal with subordinates, current organization structures make it necessary to work with colleagues in other departments—a kind of interteam relationship. Managers must also develop some skill in dealing with their own boss. Every manager finds that the day is filled with people making requests and demands, and needing help, instruction, support, counsel, and assistance. The manager must assess each person individually and then handle each situation differently depending on the dynamics operating in that person.

The basic process through which a manager deals with people is communication. We must learn to share our intentions clearly and effectively with others so they

Managers are players in an interteam relationship.

understand not what we say but what we mean. Some managers are very effective in their own personal work—they work long and hard. But no manager can get the work of an organization done alone—others must be involved. It is a significant challenge to learn how to talk to people, listen to them, and be open and honest in dealings to gain their trust.

In this people area as in the matter of organizations, a manager is an open system. Each manager not only faces people in the workplace but also deals with a range of people outside the organization. These important people—spouse, children, friends, relatives—all have an impact on how a manager feels and responds. So a manager must not only manage those inside the organization, but must learn something about family dynamics and support systems.

Almost every organization has a formal administrative unit variously called personnel, employee relations, or human resources that is assigned the task of handling certain recurring people concerns—medical benefits, retirement, pay, grievances, and unfair practices. This unit also helps people get oriented to the company when they are hired and trains them in certain important competencies. Every manager must be a personnel expert to some degree and especially be aware of legal and company policies that guide the interaction of employee and organization.

THE CHALLENGE OF CONTROL

One of the strong positions of this book is that managers, as a result of their work, will add value to an organization and ultimately to the total society. To do this managers must do more than plan and work with people. They must be responsible for results. In order to attain results it is critical to put mechanisms in place that will allow a manager to know when a product or service is completed, at what level of quality, and at what cost. In a profit-making company, these mechanisms, found in an accounting or financial department, are essential. You do not need to know much about business to appreciate that you cannot stay in business unless income exceeds expenditures to a level that an appropriate profit is realized. Likewise, a nonprofit organization usually operates against a budget or allocation where, again, it is important to provide the service within the constraints of the budget.

The term control often has a negative connotation. To some it means that someone or something is going to be held back, inhibited, or restricted. Control measures to a manager should mean a method of tracking performance, ensuring that the goals are being achieved. The lack of adequate financial controls becomes a stumbling block to many businesses when the control system used is not sophisticated enough to cover all costs. Hence the profit picture becomes an illusion.

This chapter began with a discussion about the need for managers to be more than finance or stock manipulators. If one is to manage in a firm that builds computers or cars, or makes soap or jello, or produces oil or motion pictures, the manager needs to know the product and the business. How do you develop a realistic control system if you do not know what you are producing? This leads us to the issue of operations management—understanding in some detail what actually goes on in the producing of any product. This area of management has sometimes been overlooked with dangerous consequences, for the design of the whole method of production can be the biggest capital expense an organization may incur, and if the operation system is flawed no amount of effectiveness with people can compensate.

Control and operation systems have been heavily impacted by one of the marvelous inventions of the age—the microchip and the computer. We now have the ability to gather, store, and utilize quantities of data at an astonishing rate. It is now possible to use the computer to ensure that control measures automatically are available at whatever interval of time desired. Whole operation systems have been computerized to handle with precision every complex task. Today's managers would be seriously handicapped if they did not understand the many uses of the computer. Computer literacy is a must in modern management and one of the challenges in management is to become proficient in this most important tool.

If management is decision making as Simon suggests, then the quality and quantity of accurate data available is a key to effective decision making. The computer, or automatic or electronic data processing system, is the vehicle for quickly gathering large amounts of data before important decisions have to be made. It is not necessary for a manager to be a computer programmer, but this technology demands a familiarity with the range of uses and applications that are now available.

THE CHALLENGE OF THE FUTURE

Is the world of tomorrow—the twenty-first century—going to be more or less of an organization world than what we have now? The pessimist might foretell an atomic holocaust and predict that the next century will belong to the cave dweller again. However barring such an unthinkable event, the evidence is that the organizations of the future will be even more complex than they are now and the challenges facing managers will increase, not decrease, in kind and amount. Already most businesses of any size are developing joint ventures with foreign countries, working out complex arrangements to finance, produce, and market a product in several different countries. At the time of this writing, both China and Russia are opening their borders to the West and allowing new ventures to enter. America is forming a common market with Canada and the issue of open or closed markets is contentious all around the world.

Old organization and management concepts are being challenged and are either dropped or revised constantly. No one knows what the "best" span of control is. Some companies have managers looking after ten subordinates while other companies expand the number to forty. We have flextime—allowing people to come to and go from work at all different hours. Couples are sharing a job so both husband and wife can work and both rear the children. In Japan government, banks, labor unions and businesses have already formed a kind of partnership where they cooperate with each other and are not caught in an adversarial relationship. There are some signs of this developing in the U.S.

For the student interested in international affairs, new technology, working with people, producing results, innovating new products or services, and creating change, certainly the challenge is in management.

ENDING CASE
Overcoming the Limitations of Classroom Managing[8]

 J. Sterling Livingston was a professor of business administration at Harvard Business School when he wrote the following: "Preoccupation with problem solving and decision making in formal management education programs tends to distort managerial growth because it overdevelops an individual's analytical ability, but leaves his ability to take action and get things done underdeveloped."

Livingston said the ability to solve problems and make decisions is "respondent behavior," and managers must excel in "operant behavior"—finding problems and opportunities, initiating actions, and following through to attain desired results—that must be acquired through direct personal experience on the job. "Guided practice in real business situations is the only method that will make a manager skillful in identifying the right things to do."

Livingston claims that managers can learn a critical aspect—their own personal management style—only through "firsthand experience on the job." Studying management theory is worthless, since a manager "cannot become effective by adopting the practices or the managerial style of someone else. . . . What all managers need to learn is that to be successful they must manage in a way that is consistent with their unique personalities."

If the requirements for successful management are so contingent on the individual and his or her circumstances, can we trust any generic model of management knowledge and skills? According to Esther Lindsey of the Center for Creative Leadership the answer is yes. Lindsey, who participated in the center's extensive research on how executives learn, grow, and change throughout their careers, interviewed fast-track executives to determine what knowledge, skills, and characteristics contributed to their success. Lindsey and her fellow researchers discovered 16 common "events" for managers that offered 31 possible managerial "lessons." Excelling at these "lessons" led to successful management careers.

The 31 lessons can be grouped into 4 basic areas in which effective managers must be competent:

- Technical or business knowledge.
- People skills. ("A tremendous array," according to Lindsey. "There's not just one interpersonal skill.")
- Meeting the demands of assignments (accepting responsibility, making decisions, and getting the job done).
- Surviving hardships and growing as a result of them.

For the student pursuing a successful management career, the lessons to be learned are found both inside and outside of the classroom. ■

REVIEW QUESTIONS

1. How did the need for management emerge?
2. How would you define the role of a manager?
3. What are some of the basic challenges facing a manager?
4. What are some of the technical areas a manager should be familiar with?
5. What can you do to prepare for a career in management?

CHALLENGE QUESTIONS

1. How are planning and decision making connected?

2. Is leadership the same as management?

3. Why should management be concerned with human resource development?

4. What does it mean to think of management as a profession?

5. How do you think the "status" level of a manager in our society compares to that of other professions, for example, doctor, lawyer, teacher? Do you see this changing? If so, why?

6. How do you account for the increasing numbers of MBA and undergraduate business students?

7. How can a manager develop his or her human relations skills?

ENDNOTES

1. Student interviews with William G. Dyer, 1988.

2. Lee Iacocca, *Iacocca* (New York: G. K. Hall, 1985), p. 65.

3. "The Best B-Schools," *Business Week,* November 28, 1988, p. 77.

4. Robert Johnson, "Big Executive Bonuses Now Come with a Catch: Lots of Criticism," *Wall Street Journal,* May 15, 1985.

5. Christopher Meek, Warner Woodworth, and W. Gibb Dyer, Jr., *Managing by the Numbers: Absentee Owners and the Decline of American Industry* (Reading, MA: Addison-Wesley, 1988), p. 22.

6. Ibid., p. 16.

7. Herbert Simon, *Administrative Behavior*, 2nd ed. (New York: Macmillan, 1957).

8. "Can Management Skills Be Learned?" *Business Week,* September 24, 1984.

CHAPTER 2

THE DEVELOPMENT OF
MODERN MANAGEMENT

CHAPTER OUTLINE

LEARNING OBJECTIVES

■ Discuss the changes in organizational and management practices brought about by the development of modern management theories.

■ Trace the development and influence of the various historical schools of management thought.

■ Identify the contributions of the major contemporary schools of management thought.

■ Describe a manager in terms of function, role, and skill.

■ Understand why management theories and practices have changed over time.

■ Discuss why contingency theory is currently an attractive management orientation.

■ Understand why Fayol's original fourteen principles of management do not all apply to current situations.

■ Describe the nature of an "open" system.

■ Explain the complex nature of the roles of a modern manager.

■ Identify the mix of skills required in management today.

■ Understand what leadership is as a part of the manager's role.

The Changing Role of Management at General Motors[1]

William Durant established General Motors in 1908 as a holding company (later becoming an operating company) into which Durant brought his old Buick car company and in 1909 added Olds, Oakland, and Cadillac. The concept of General Motors from the beginning was that of a diversified automobile manufacturer that did not depend on the success of one model for its future.

Durant was a brilliant promoter and brought such figures as Walter Chrysler, Charles Nash, Alfred Champion, and Charles S. Mott into prominence, but he was not a good administrator and he lost control of the company to those who brought the discipline of modern management techniques to the largely autonomous divisional structure. Centralized financial controls and cost accounting were among the techniques introduced by these modern managers.

Alfred P. Sloan, who became chairman of the company in 1923 and guided the company until 1954, is one of the greatest management geniuses of the twentieth century. It was during his tenure that GM became a manufacturing and marketing juggernaut. Sloan devised the plan for centralized control of GM's decentralized operations and the bonus plan for management. He transformed GM's marketing efforts, introducing the concepts of the complete product line, the yearly model changeover, and mass advertising to the automobile industry.

Sloan organized General Motors into divisions based on product lines. This **divisional structure** forced the various product lines—Chevrolet, Pontiac, Buick, Oldsmobile, and Cadillac—to compete with one another as well as with Ford, Chrysler, and GM's other competitors. Marketing, design, and the day-to-day operation of the automobile plants was left at the divisional level.

The structure was held together by a strong central control system with functional specialists in finance, legal services, labor relations, accounting, etc. The control system allowed GM to pool information from the divisions and set financial targets, to use common accounting and control systems, and otherwise to assure that profit and other financial objectives were met by each division. Overall corporate strategies were also formulated at GM headquarters on West Grand Boulevard in Detroit.

GM Today: The Structure of a Modern Business

General Motors provides an excellent illustration of how sound management principles enabled an upstart competitor in a new industry to become the largest industrial enterprise in the history of the world. From the moment he took command of GM,

Alfred Sloan's grand strategy transformed GM into an industrial giant.

Alfred Sloan began to implement a grand strategy based on the segmentation of the automobile industry into a number of buying publics. By designing cars to fulfill the needs of relatively small segments of the buying public, GM was able to take a large part of the automobile market away from Ford and eventually pass the industry leader.

GM's strategy had the additional advantage of making the company less cyclical as sales of one model might be hot while those of another might be cold. Diversification of its product line led GM to organize itself along divisional lines. The divisional structure enabled the company to deliver cars uniquely suited to the needs of consumers. While marketing provided the initial impetus for the divisional structure, the structure itself dictated a divisional need for personnel, finance, production, information systems, and other divisional units.

Although GM's divisional structure was along product lines, it would have been just as easy to organize the divisions along geographic lines—U. S., Europe, etc.— or functional lines—production, distribution, marketing, etc. The product line divisional structure had the advantage of emphasizing the company's desire to serve a number of market segments simultaneously. Thus, the structure fit the strategic plan of the company.

The coordination of the various divisions required that Sloan have up-to-date information on which to base corporate decisions. A strong system of accounting and control was required and implemented. The information gathered by this system enabled Sloan and the Board of Directors to make effective resource allocation decisions (putting money where it is needed the most), enabled them to react quickly to competitive moves, and generally resulted in improved decision making.

Modern Management at Today's GM Can Mean Many Things

As GM grew, the time horizon covered by its planning process became longer and the number of variables affecting its corporate decisions increased dramatically. Today, GM must take virtually all major societal issues into account as well as the more mundane business considerations. For example, its 1986 decision to divest itself of its South African operations reflected, in part, concern with a growing public perception that only strong action would result in the elimination of apartheid. The decision also reflected a hard business look at the long-term viability of its South African business and the effect that maintaining that business would have on its world-wide operations.

Management at GM can mean a number of things. At the corporate level, the chairman and the executive committee formulate the overarching strategies employed by the corporation. Operating managers must then implement the strategic plans by developing products, marketing them, and making sure that the various projects they undertake earn a sufficient return for the stockholders. Management can also mean overseeing a staff function such as legal, personnel, and labor relations. ▨

INTRODUCTION

All societies and cultures have forms of social, political, and economic organization. Organizations require management. National managers are called presidents, pharaohs, kings, czars, emperors, chancellors, chairmen, etc.

Max Weber, the brilliant German social economist traced the evolution of organizations from the old despotic form of organization to the modern **bureaucracy**.[2] Organizations evolved from being administered by a favored class made up of those who had appropriate family connections, to being run by a group of people who handled the affairs of the organization based on their competencies. Most organizations in the Western world, whether political, economic, or business related, were operating as "rational" bureaucracies by the start of the twentieth century. It was in the 1900s that notions of how to manage began to be developed and were considered as appropriate targets of research, writing, and scientific understanding.

MODERN MANAGEMENT SCHOOLS OF THOUGHT

The act of managing, while still complex and sometimes divergent, is made up of strains of management practice produced over many decades. As social and economic conditions changed, the ways managers helped accomplish the goals of the organization also changed. The development of current management practice might best be understood by looking at the sequence of schools of management thought that have emerged since the beginning of the twentieth century.

The Classical or Rational School

The **rational school** of management thinking began in the early 1900s and was led by French writer Henri Fayol, whose *General and Industrial Management* was published in 1916. Fayol saw management as a rational system and believed that all business organizations needed to manage certain activities, such as technical, commercial, financial, security, and accounting ones. To handle these activities, managers needed to be aware of the basic principles of management.[3] Fayol identified the fourteen principles of management listed in Box 2-1.

The usefulness of Fayol's principles in the early industrial environment is clearly seen. For example, the assembly line at Sloan's General Motors is a particularly apt demonstration of the division of labor. However, from today's perspective some of these principles seem to apply while others now appear to be outdated.

More recent research has shown that management is not just the step-by-step, rational, follow-the-principles process these early writers envisioned. Dr. Rensis Likert, a former director of the Survey Research Center at the University of Michigan, researched management principles for over twenty-five years and came up with only one principle. He called this "the principle of supportive relationships." This principle states, "The leadership and other processes of the organization must be such as to ensure a maximum probability that in all interactions and in all relationships within the organization, each member, in the light of his/her background, values, desires, and expectations, will view the experience as supportive and one which builds and maintains his/her sense of personal worth and importance."[4]

The Scientific School

The orientation of management as a science was developed in the United States most strongly by Frederick Taylor, known as the father of "**scientific management**." Taylor emphasized the need for empirical observation (examination of real phenomena),

> Box 2-1
> Fayol's Fourteen Principles of Management
>
> 1. **Division of work (labor)**   The specialization of workers, including management, to improve efficiency and increase output.
>
> 2. **Authority and responsibility**   The right to give orders and the power to exact obedience.
>
> 3. **Discipline**   Obedience, application, energy, and behavior given to the organization, depending on the leaders.
>
> 4. **Unity of command**   No person should have more than one boss.
>
> 5. **Unity of direction**   An organization should have only one plan for accomplishing goals (an extension of the unity of command principle).
>
> 6. **Subordination of individual to general interest**   The concerns of the organization placed ahead of individual concerns.
>
> 7. **Pay**   Arrangements for compensation that are fair and satisfactory to all with competence rewarded but not overrewarded.
>
> 8. **Centralization**   The consolidation of the management function according to the circumstances surrounding the organization.
>
> 9. **Hierarchy**   The lines of authority should run clearly from the top of the organization to the lowest level.
>
> 10. **Order**   People and materials should be in the right place at the right time and people should be in the jobs most suited to them.
>
> 11. **Equity**   Loyalty should be encouraged by justice, kindliness, and fairness.
>
> 12. **Stability**   High employee turnover both causes and is the result of inefficiency; good organizations have stable managements.
>
> 13. **Initiative**   The necessity of "thinking out a plan and ensuring its success" and of giving subordinates the opportunity to perform.
>
> 14. **Esprit de corps**   Oral communication should be used to keep teams together.
>
> SOURCE: Adapted from Henri Fayol, *General and Industrial Management,* trans. J. A. Conbrough (Geneva: International Management Institute, 1929).

analysis, and experimentation. He believed that it was the role of the manager to discover the one best way to perform all work under the manager's direction.[5]

Taylor's basic approach was to analyze each job to determine the separate elements or motions that made up the actual physical work. The task was then to see how these elements could be redesigned or altered in some way to develop the best or

Frederick W. Taylor, father of "scientific management."

quickest method to get the work accomplished. This emphasis on efficiency became the basis for much of what is still present in time-and-motion studies.

In light of later research, Taylor did not fully understand the human needs (as explained by Maslow and Aldefer) for social interaction, self-esteem, and self-fulfillment. The application of Taylor's methods tended to result in a mechanistic system where everything was gauged by the efficiency of operation. Others picked up on Taylor's work, notably Frank and Lillian Gilbreth,[6] but this emphasis in management on scientific systems began to fade with the rise of the succeeding school of management thought.

An interesting variant of Taylorism still exists, however, in contemporary management. Frederick Herzberg developed a management theory based on job enrichment.[7] He, like Taylor, went back to looking at the basic elements of the job. While Taylor wanted to make work simpler—more work with less effort—Herzberg believed it is the challenging aspects of a job that motivate workers. Workers who are challenged in their jobs feel that they are making a real contribution, which leads to their growth and development. Herzberg was one of the first in more recent times to stress the necessity for managers to look closely again at the basic conditions of work.

The Human Relations School

Elton Mayo of Harvard was asked to conduct some initial studies at the Western Electric plant in Hawthorne, Illinois. The results of these "Hawthorne Studies" gave rise to the **human relations school** of thought, which emphasized the importance of the relationship between management and workers in obtaining productivity.[8]

The initial Hawthorne investigation looked at the output of workers under different conditions of lighting. In the 1920s, electric lights were just coming into wide use and the electric companies claimed that workers could produce more under conditions of improved lighting. The results of the study were puzzling. No matter what happened to lighting, productivity continued to rise. Even when workers were reduced to working at what was the equivalent of moonlight, production continued to improve. Obviously something else was affecting productivity, and lighting was not the key factor.

The analysis of this original study has given rise to the term "Hawthorne effect." Those who analyzed the situation felt the reason workers continued to improve their productivity was the workers' knowledge that they were an important part of the experiment. They worked harder as a result of knowing they were being observed and the outcome of the experiment depended on them. Since then all experimental researchers try to guard against the "Hawthorne effect."

However, others argued that the increase in productivity was due to the workers experiencing a change in management style. During the experiments, management paid a great deal of attention to the workers, and some people believed it was this change that was responsible for the increased output.

The initial illumination study led to a series of in-depth research studies into what happens to workers under a variety of conditions. Six operators were selected to work in a special test group whose job it was to assemble telephone relays. Data were collected on this group for five years under a variety of conditions—rest periods and methods of pay were varied, refreshments and a shortened workweek were tried, and so on.

Output seemed to ultimately be a function of something more than rest periods, incentives, or refreshments. The researchers generally agreed that the most significant factor was the building of a sense of group identity, a feeling of social support and cohesion that came with increased worker interaction. The superior or management leader was also observed to behave differently toward the workers in the experimental group, and this, too, appeared to enhance the "team" spirit. The following are some of the observations from the study:

1. The boss (chief observer) had a personal interest in each person's achievement.
2. He took pride in the record of the group.
3. He helped the group set its own conditions of work.
4. He faithfully posted the feedback on performance.

5. The group took pride in its achievement and had the satisfaction of knowing outsiders were interested in what they did.

6. The group did not feel they were being pressured to change.

7. Before changes were made, the group was consulted.

8. The group developed a sense of confidence and candor.

An excerpt from Mayo's own interpretation of what happened is contained in Box 2-2. The Hawthorne studies, carried out in the late 1920s and early 1930s, set the pattern for much research over the next twenty years—before and after World War II. The emphasis in the management field was no longer on efficiency, but on the needs and feelings of workers and the impact of social relations in groups. The current interest in teamwork and team building and concern for the individual stem largely from these early studies.

Contemporary Schools of Management Thought

Since World War II, the field of management has grown and diversified rapidly. A single overarching management school of thought does not dominate as in earlier periods. The field is now so complex that it was referred to in one article as "The Management Theory Jungle."[9] The emphasis now is on weaving all of the various areas of emphasis into a coherent whole. The major schools or perspectives currently are as follows.

THE MANAGEMENT PROCESS SCHOOL   This school carries on something of the tradition of Henri Fayol since it emphasizes the functions of management—those activities that characterize the manager's job such as planning, organizing, staffing, directing, and controlling. Included in this school of thought is the need to study the managers' roles—finding out what managers do.

THE HUMAN BEHAVIOR SCHOOL   While this school still refers to the early Hawthorne studies, it now tries to include much of the current research from the behavioral sciences and has given rise to a discipline called "organizational behavior." Management style, participative management, teamwork, group dynamics, individual behavior, motivation, and communications are emphasized. This school believes that a wide range of research needs to be integrated into a whole.

THE SOCIAL SYSTEM SCHOOL   This school, which has had an important impact on management, suggests that managers must see the organization as a total system—an "open" system that interacts with the environment and has linked, internal subsystems. The internal subsystems include the technical, social, and administrative systems. A change or disturbance in one part of the total system will affect the other parts. Additionally, managers must look at what comes into the system from the outside environment (laws, regulations, union contracts, economic conditions, labor

Box 2-2
Elton Mayo's Analysis of the Changes
Experienced at the Hawthorne Plant

These original provisions were effective largely because the experimental room was in charge of an interested and sympathetic chief observer. He understood clearly from the first that any hint of "the supervisor" in his methods might be fatal to the interests of the inquiry. So far as it was possible, he and his assistants kept the history sheets and the log sheet faithfully posted. In addition to this he took a personal interest in each girl and her achievement; he showed pride in the record of the group. He helped the group to feel that its duty was to set its own conditions of work, he helped the workers to find the "freedom" of which they so frequently speak.

In the early stages of development, it was inevitable that the group became interested in its achievement and should to some extent enjoy the reflected glory of the interest the inquiry attracted. As the years passed this abated somewhat, but all the evidence—including the maintenance of a high output—goes to show that something in the reconditioning of the group must be regarded as a permanent achievement. At no time in the five-year period did the girls feel that they were working under pressure; on the contrary, they invariably cite the absence of this as their reason for preferring the "test room."

Undoubtedly, there had been a remarkable change of mental attitude in the group. This showed in their recurrent conferences with high executive authorities. At first shy and uneasy, silent and perhaps somewhat suspicious of the company's intention, later their attitude is marked by confidence and candor. Before every change of program, the group is consulted. Their comments are listened to and discussed; sometimes their objections are allowed to negate a suggestion. The group unquestionably develops a sense of participation in the critical determinations and becomes something of a social unit.

SOURCE: Elton Mayo, *The Human Problems of an Industrial Civilization* (Boston: Harvard University, 1933), pp. 34–35.

supply, etc.) and look at ways of influencing the environment and effectively processing the inputs.

THE CULTURE SCHOOL   One of the most recent developments in management thought is to look at the organization as a small culture or subculture. This frame of reference distinguishes between the material and nonmaterial aspects of culture. The material culture in any organization includes the physical factors—building, lay-out, equipment, and technology. The nonmaterial culture includes the values, norms, symbols, and goals that define how people should live and behave, such as what is right and wrong, or important or unimportant, and identifies what goals people work for.

THE MATHEMATICAL SCHOOL   This school emphasizes the use of quantitative methods in management. The rise of the computer and mathematical and statistical models have made this an important field of understanding in most graduate schools of business. Certain fields of business—accounting, finance, and economics—are so complex that they are best handled by mathematical models. Planning, forecasting, and decision making that are based on rational analysis of the data are important features of this school.

THE CONTINGENCY SCHOOL   During the period 1960–70 the emphasis was on trying to discover the one, universally effective style of management. MIT's Douglas McGregor felt managers could be classified as having either a negative view of people (Theory X) or an optimistic view of people (Theory Y) with an accompanying set of behaviors towards people.[10] Theory Y was seen as *the* best way to manage. Rensis Likert, Blake and Mouton, and Abraham Maslow all advocated their own universal ways to manage.[11] In contrast to these positions, research started in the United Kingdom by Woodward, and Burns and Stalker[12], and then in the U. S. at Harvard by Lawrence and Lorsch, began to show that the type of management needed in an organization was influenced by the task and the technology used.[13] For example, large-scale continuous-process technologies, like those used in oil refineries, require a different kind of management than that needed in a small machine shop doing custom work in small batches. The type of management needed is contingent on the nature of the task, the kind of people involved, the time frame, and the goals.

The contingency approach asserts that no one universal effective management style is best in all situations. It is necessary to look at all the factors in the situation and then either select a person with a style that matches the situation or give people situationally specific management training.

Discussion of the Schools of Management

With all of the different orientations to understanding management, how does one determine which has the greatest value when trying to decide what course of action to take?

It should be immediately clear that no one school of thought covers all of the areas that are of concern to the manager. Some of the schools merged as an appropriate adaptation to the conditions of the times and as the times changed so did the management orientation. For example, Taylor developed his scientific management approach when the United States had a large number of immigrant workers with relatively low levels of education and industrial experience. In the new factories where the assembly line was being perfected the workers accepted a management style which was authoritarian in nature. The managers told workers exactly the "best" way to work.

Later on in this century as workers became better educated, they no longer were satisfied with authoritarian management and the human relations orientation became more prevalent. With the advent of the computer and other high technology advances in information systems and telecommunications, managers had to become more technically oriented. The contingency school is the attempt to say that management must be flexible and able to adapt to a wide range of work situations. But while this is probably true, it does not tell managers how they need to perform to be most effective. There seems to be a core of important management actions that apply to almost every situation (listening, taking people into account, using all resources available), while there are other actions peculiar to each unique situation. This means that successful managers need to be highly knowledgeable about management generally, while also understanding the special features of the organization and work situation in which they are located. Most management programs in universities try to teach as many general skills and as much broad knowledge as possible, and presume that the student will be able to become well acquainted with the peculiar features of the industry and organization where they accept employment.

The following case examines General Motors' plan of management for its new Saturn project. Which of the management approaches discussed already applies to this case?

CASE

GM's Revolutionary Pact at Saturn Corporation[14]

For all of Alfred Sloan's management innovations, he mirrored his peers in his determination to maintain management prerogatives. GM opposed the efforts of workers to organize with a vehemence that earned it the enmity of much of its work force, and its relationship with the United Automobile Workers (UAW) union remained highly adversarial for a decade or more. For example, the bitter 1945 strike resulted in the derisive nickname "Generous Motors."

However, the structure that Sloan had established and the professionalism of the management team he assembled allowed GM to gain industrial peace sooner than its major rivals. The company soon became an innovator in labor relations with the introduction of the cost of living allowance (COLA), providing automatic wage increases as the cost of living rose, and the annual improvement factor, providing automatic wage increases as productivity rose. Both proposals were accepted by the UAW and became models on which hundreds of other such proposals were patterned.

Now GM and the UAW have embarked on the most ambitious worker participation project ever undertaken. GM has formed the Saturn Corporation to market its new Saturn automobile. The details of the GM–UAW Saturn pact recently have become available.

Instead of being cogs in the system, Saturn's workers are full partners. Old job titles have been replaced, workers earn a salary and bonuses just like managers, and

Unlike these early assembly-line workers, "team members" working for GM's new Saturn Corporation are not mere cogs in the system.

the union even has a say in managerial salaries. The management system is based on consensus, a system requiring that all parties on a committee agree before an action is taken. Representatives of the UAW are on all committees, including the strategic advisory committee. The union has given up 20 percent in guaranteed wages and restrictive work rules for these new prerogatives, although it has retained the right to strike.

Basic work groups are teams of between six and fifteen members, who together decide who will be new team members and who does which job. The teams are responsible for controlling variable costs and doing quality inspections and have the authority to request that the finance and purchasing departments study proposals for new equipment. Teams maintain equipment, order supplies, and maintain relief and vacation schedules. Each team has a personal computer for keeping track of business data.

The next level, the work unit module, consists of up to six team units. GM assigns an adviser, Saturn's version of a foreman, to each module to act as a liaison with company experts in engineering, marketing, etc. These advisers act as conduits to and from the committee that runs the entire plant—the business unit. The business unit includes Saturn's version of the plant manager plus an elected UAW representative.

The manufacturing advisory committee runs the entire Saturn complex and consists of high company and UAW business unit officials as well as the manager of the

Saturn complex and an elected UAW official. This committee reaches consensus on wage and salary issues and reports to the strategic advisory committee, the highest committee in the company. This top committee consists of Saturn's president and his staff and a top UAW official, and is responsible for long-term and strategic planning.

UAW members are given three to six months of company-paid training in problem solving, decision making, business methods, and job skills. In addition, they are given classes in labor history at company expense.

Most workers (80 percent) are guaranteed jobs for life and are also protected from layoffs barring "catastrophic events." Even in that case joint committees can reject layoffs in favor of worksharing or a temporary shutdown. The seniority system, which formerly determined who was laid off, has been scrapped altogether.

The potential for problems still exists. Pay disparities may occur as a result of the bonus plan. Work teams may decide to discriminate. Favoritism in granting promotions may result in an effort to bring back the seniority system.

Saturn's framers, however, think that the potential gains are worth the risks. The group spent two years studying operations in Japan and Europe before designing the plan. They learned that flexibility is a must if they are to succeed; hence, they have vowed to drop whatever they find to be unworkable.

If the project is successful, the ideas implemented at Saturn could be adapted to other GM divisions. In addition, Ford and Chrysler have already shown interest in negotiating a Saturn-like pact. Many companies are sure to be watching with great interest.[15]

Chapter 1 presented the strong argument that management is essentially a decision-making process. Hence, it is not necessary to discover the one best way to manage. All management principles and ways of thinking about management problems have their place in a decision-making model since all provide useful input into improving the quality of decisions.

MODERN MANAGEMENT ACTIONS

Key Management Functions

A useful method of understanding management is to determine what managers are expected or need to do to meet corporate goals and what they actually do—how they really spend their time.

A modern management theorist, Luther Gulick, looked at what managers need to do to accomplish organization objectives. He came up with a widely-used list of seven **management functions**:

1. **Planning**   Determining both *what* needs to be done, and *how* things will be done to achieve the organization's objectives.
2. **Organizing**   Identifying the necessary activities and setting up the formal structure of work units and authority through which goals are accomplished.
3. **Staffing**   The process of selecting, training, and maintaining the personnel needed to run an organization.
4. **Directing**   Setting the goals, making decisions, and conveying these decisions and instructions to subordinates.
5. **Coordinating**   Ensuring the interconnections of the various parts of the organization are achieved so work is accomplished smoothly.
6. **Reporting**   A process that allows the leaders in the organization to know what is being done by means of information sharing through records, reports, research, or inspection.
7. **Budgeting**   Systematically planning for the use and control of financial resources.

The reporting and budgeting functions are often combined into what is known as the controlling function.

This list of functions describes most of what a manager is responsible for and expected to do. You can see some similarity between these functions and the principles developed by Fayol. But Gullick's list makes it appear that the manager rationally and systematically handles all work in a neat, orderly fashion, performing each function as it appears. Such is not the case. While managers may not perform these functions as systematically as presented, most management analysts agree that these activities must be handled if the organization is to be effective. Gulick provides us with a useful framework for determining what needs to be done.

Management Roles

Henry Mintzberg and other researchers have spent considerable time watching managers and recording what they actually do with their time during the regular workday.[16] Their findings are very revealing: most managers move very quickly from one activity to another and engage in a number of work functions not identified by Gulick. Guest found that a foreman engaged in between 237 and 1073 incidents a day without a break in the pace (about 48 seconds per activity).[17] Rosemary Stewart found that only during nine periods per day were managers able to work for one-half hour or more without interruption.[18]

Mintzberg's analysis shows that managers spend a great deal of time in meetings, talking on the phone, working at their desks, and handling mail—in other words,

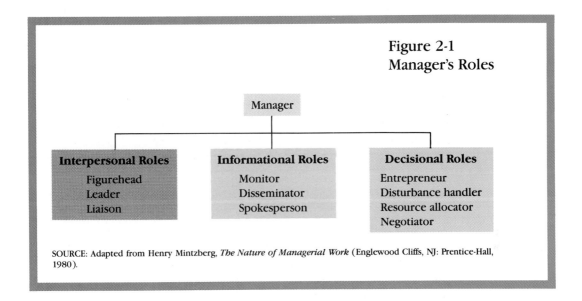

Figure 2-1
Manager's Roles

SOURCE: Adapted from Henry Mintzberg, *The Nature of Managerial Work* (Englewood Cliffs, NJ: Prentice-Hall, 1980).

communicating with others.[19] He found that these activities fell into three major roles: interpersonal roles, informational roles, and decisional roles. Each of these three groups can be further divided into subroles. See Figure 2-1.

INTERPERSONAL ROLES   In this area, the manager's interpersonal contact with others is of major importance. Mintzberg qualifies the instances when a manager, while interacting with others, functions as a leader, liaison, or figurehead:

Leader   Mintzberg sees leadership as very important to the manager's role. Leadership involves direct interaction with others; the manager tries to create energy and enthusiasm for a vision that he conveys to others. Alfred Sloan's genius as leader for GM was largely his ability to articulate his vision of GM and to get others to support him as he changed the company. As a leader, the manager attempts to motivate subordinates by acting as mentor, by helping with problems, and by integrating the needs of individuals with the goals of the organization so both can move ahead. Finally, the manager uses the power of the position to influence people to work together for the good of the enterprise. As will be discussed in a later chapter, this is the beginning of building an effective work team.

Liaison   Liaison refers to the coordination managers perform in maintaining cooperative relationships with people and units outside their part of the organization. One analysis of managerial power is that it is gained only to the extent that others support and allow the manager to take action. If the manager is going to have power and influence outside his own unit, it is important to have strong liaison relationships and support from others.

Figurehead This activity centers on the manager as a symbol. A wide variety of situations require this function—representing the company at a meeting, giving a message at someone's retirement, being present at a recognition banquet, etc. Often this role of figurehead is "window dressing"—the event requires the person as a position to be present, not the person as a resource. While this role is not a critical function in the growth and change of an organization, it is an important activity that maintains the smooth operation of a business.

Informational Roles

The manager also acts as a dispenser and receiver of information. It has already been observed that much of a manager's time is spent in getting or giving information. Mintzberg subdivides this role into three areas:

Monitor Since a manager is bombarded with data—reports, rumor, gossip, analyses from meetings, phone calls, mass media, mail, and face-to-face contacts—he or she must decide what information to hold and act on and what to ignore. Managers who do not handle this role well are easily influenced by unreliable sources of information or spend their time working on lower priority projects. In either case their resulting decisions are inappropriate.

Disseminator In this role the manager passes information to people—both information gained from outside and inside the organization. This information can either be fact or opinion or an expression of values (hopes, ideals, or aspirations). The manager is the key figure in the organization for passing information from the top down and from down up. If the manager does not provide a clear communication link, those in the lower positions do not understand where the organization is going and those at the top do not hear the concerns of the employees.

Spokesperson As a disseminator, the manager's main role is to pass on information *inside* the organization. As a spokesperson the manager shares information with the world or environment *outside* the organization.

DECISIONAL ROLES A set of key managerial activities involves managers making decisions that will affect themselves, others, and the organization. Mintzberg lists four such functions under this category:

Entrepreneur In this capacity, the manager must look at opportunities and make decisions that involve risk and change. As the manager decides to move into a new area or project, he or she may decide to delegate responsibility for a certain part of the new activity to someone else. Consider Alfred Sloan's decision to change models on a yearly basis and to offer different cars for different consumer tastes. This decision revolutionized the industry since GM's major competitor, Ford, at that time was only producing one car in one color—black. Sloan could not possibly keep up with changing consumer tastes himself, so he delegated the task of implementing the changeover to the divisional managers.

Disturbance handler   Common to any organization is the unforeseen event which triggers a crisis or disturbance in the organization. At these critical times the manager must make decisions and take action, such as during equipment failures, fires, losses of clients or customers, or wildcat strikes. Because it is virtually impossible to anticipate all of the possible disturbances that could occur, a manager needs to have a basic orientation on how to deal with any disturbances that arise. In an organization as far flung as General Motors, disturbances are part of everyday experience. During Sloan's tenure labor problems predominated and he and his staff had to become adept at resolving labor problems or risk failing to meet production requirements.

Resource allocator   For many, the ability to allocate resources is at the heart of a manager's power base. These resources include money, time, equipment, manpower, and space. Managers allocate resources, make decisions about the use of time, authorize actions, and establish programs as to who will do what and with what resources. Without the right to allocate resources, the manager's ability to get work done is reduced. Managers sometimes have responsibility without authority; this usually occurs when a manager does not have the right to make key resource allocation decisions. Sloan and his team of managers had to decide, for example, which divisions would be able to build new plants or introduce new models, a power without which the divisional structure would have degenerated into chaos.

Negotiator   In connection with the roles as figurehead, spokesperson, and resource allocator, the manager may also be required to make decisions regarding negotiations with outside organizations. These decisions bind the organization and include such situations as negotiations of government or labor contracts, mergers, acquisitions, etc. For example, General Motors' management must negotiate with the United Automobile Workers (UAW) every three years and negotiate with federal or local governments regarding pollution control, foreign imports, and auto safety standards.

Do all managers perform these roles equally? Obviously not. The mix of roles for any manager will depend on the level the manager occupies in the organization, the current assignment, the nature of the task, and the stage of the manager's career.

Management Skill Mix

Another way to think about management action is to examine the skills a manager needs. Differing levels of management require different skills to be successful. Katz developed the **skill mix model** shown in Figure 2-2. He saw management skills as a blend of **interpersonal**, **cognitive**, and **technical skills**.[20] In Figure 2-2, the mix on the right-hand side of the diagonal line represents the usual skill mix of the first-level

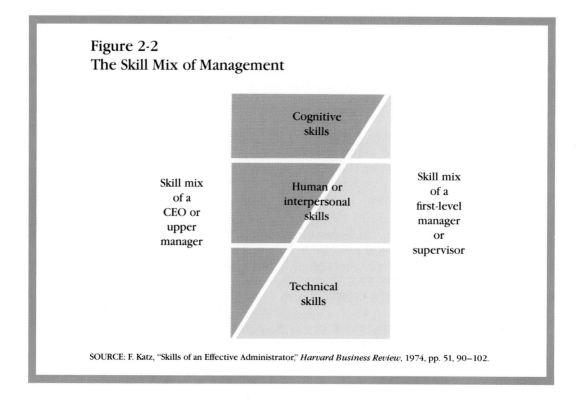

Figure 2-2
The Skill Mix of Management

SOURCE: F. Katz, "Skills of an Effective Administrator," *Harvard Business Review*, 1974, pp. 51, 90–102.

supervisor or manager. This mix is heavily oriented toward the technical aspects of the job, with a strong emphasis on interpersonal skills (dealing with people), and less concern for cognitive skills (dealing with more administrative matters such as determining the organization mission, seeing relationships with the external environment, and developing plans for markets, finances, and other resources and services).

A person entering the management field usually falls somewhere on the right-hand side of Figure 2-2. The new manager or supervisor will usually be responsible for a technical activity—actually supervising a production or sales group, working out a marketing plan, or preparing a budget. This involves working directly with people one on one or in a team. There is some need for cognitive skills but these come into play more as the manager moves up.

High-level managers require a skill mix more on the left side of Figure 2-2. They move away from direct technical activities and are more involved in planning, organizing, and handling key interfaces with the external environment—customers, government, unions, market possibilities, and foreign influences.

All of the above show clearly that modern management is an extremely complex profession requiring a person to be prepared to be effective in a wide variety of activities.

ENDING CASE
A New Kind of Business Leadership

Michael Useem, a professor and director of the Center for Applied Social Science, Boston University, has proposed that: "A new kind of business leadership has emerged in the United States during the past decade. It is a leadership of managers of large companies who are devoted not just to promoting the concerns of their own firms but also to creating an improved social and political climate for all major corporations. These leaders offer a broader vision of the public policies required if American business is to prosper. It is a vision that transcends firm, region, and sector, one that expresses a kind of nationwide business outlook. It is a public leadership on behalf of the broader business community."

Because of unprecedented challenges to the position of business during the 1970s, new business leaders entered the 1980s determined to bring their ideas to the public. Separate lobbying pressures by thousands of corporations on behalf of their separate needs has continued, but a powerful new voice has been added as well. It is a voice shorn of the sometimes parochial, often competitive needs of the separate companies. As a result, the government now hears a more general voice from business, and one that is expressed with special forcefulness by the new corporate leadership.

Entry into this leadership can be important for company managers, for it provides access to the highest circles of government. Information flows two ways: Government hears from business, but in the course of the dialogue companies also learn the inside thinking of top government. The pulse of public thinking and social trends affecting the firm are better appreciated. Thus, many corporations encourage their senior managers to participate, and they groom promising middle managers to learn the role of public leadership as well. Peter Drucker reports that one of the two vice-chairmen at Citicorp devotes two days per week to the Business Roundtable, a group of top executives dedicated to developing broad based policy papers for submission to top government officials.[21]

SUMMARY

Modern management involves a variety of skills and orientations, many of which involve the quantitative skills of statistics, computers, accounting, and mathematics. Management places a strong emphasis on rational problem solving and logical thinking. Since management necessarily involves people, a premium is also placed on interpersonal skills—the ability to work with individuals and groups. Managers must take many roles and perform many functions if they are to be successful.

The field of management cuts across many disciplines—the social sciences, logic, philosophy, mathematics, computer technology, international relations, languages, and culture. To be well prepared, a future manager needs a broad and rich background in a variety of areas and the skills to perform in a range of functions. This background and preparation will improve the quality of decisions and the ability of the future manager to carry them out.

In this chapter we reviewed the development of modern management from the early forms of social, political, and economic organization, through the emerging schools of management thought. We presented the rational, scientific, human relations, and contemporary models of management, and discussed the basic concepts of each model in conjunction with the key theorists and reported research. We presented the various roles and functions of modern management, and developed the notion that management consists of both rational systematic procedures and the ability to work with individuals and groups.

KEY TERMS

Divisional structure
Bureaucracy
Rational school
Scientific management
Human relations school
Management process school
Human behavior school
Social system school
Culture school
Mathematical school

Contingency school
Management functions
Interpersonal roles
Informational roles
Decisional roles
Skill mix model
Interpersonal skills
Cognitive skills
Technical skills

REVIEW QUESTIONS

1. What is meant by the "rational school" of management? The "scientific school," the "human relations school," and contemporary schools?

2. What are the basic differences between these schools?

3. Who are the key persons associated with each school?

4. How did the Hawthorne Studies influence the field of management?

5. Explain the Hawthorne effect.

6. What was Frederick Taylor known for?

7. What is a bureaucracy?

8. What are Fayol's fourteen principles of management?

9. Briefly explain Gulick's seven functions of management.

10. What were the basic findings of other researchers, for example, Guest, Stewart, and Mintzberg?

11. Summarize in your own words Mintzberg's major roles of management.

12. What is time management and how does it differ from the time studies used in scientific management?

13. How can a manager make meetings effective?

14. What are some keys to effective delegation?

CHALLENGE QUESTIONS

1. Why was Taylor's system perceived by unions as a means to exploit workers?

2. Why should a manager be concerned with needs like social interaction, self-esteem, and self-fulfillment, if profit is the bottom line upon which he or she is judged?

3. Why was scientific management accepted so well during its era?

4. How do Fayol's fourteen principles of management hold up in light of modern theories of management?

5. How was the scientific school of management an extension of the rational school?

6. What characteristics of the scientific school led to the development of the human relations school?

7. How do you think the principles of scientific management would be received by today's work force? By the next generation of workers?

8. What do you see as the future trends in management theory and philosophy?

9. In assessing yourself in relationship to the various roles and functions presented in this chapter what are your strengths and weaknesses?

10. Can a manager be effective without possessing a broad variety of skills? How?

CASE AND RELATED QUESTIONS

1. What are some of the chief differences between Will Durant, the founder of General Motors, and Alfred Sloan, the management genius credited with making it into the world's largest corporation?

2. What advantages accrued to GM because of Sloan's adoption of the divisional structure?

3. What stresses and information requirements did the divisional structure place on General Motors? How were these handled?

4. How does the labor-management agreement at Saturn Corporation differ from traditional labor-management agreements?

5. What advantages can Saturn expect to receive as a result of adopting what has been called the cooperative model of labor relations? What are some of the disadvantages? Do the advantages outweigh the disadvantages in your estimation? Why?

6. What did Mayo conclude to be the major reason for increased production by the experimental group at the Western Electric Hawthorne plant? How do the Hawthorne experiments relate to the Saturn Agreement?

ENDNOTES

1. Adapted from William Serrin, *The Company and the Union* (New York: Alfred A. Knopf, 1973), pp. 70–114; and Marilyn Edid, "How Power Will Be Balanced on Saturn's Shop Floor," *Business Week,* August 5, 1985, pp. 65–66.

2. Max Weber, *The Theory of Social and Economic Organization* (New York: Free Press, 1947).

3. Henri Fayol, *General and Industrial Management,* trans. J. A. Conbrough (Geneva: International Management Institute, 1929).

4. Rensis Likert, *The Human Organization* (New York: McGraw Hill, 1967), p. 47.

5. Frederick Taylor, *Principles of Management* (New York: Harper & Row, 1911).

6. Frank Gilbreth, *Motion Study* (New York: D. Van Nostrand, 1911); and Lillian M. Gilbreth, *The Psychology of Management* (New York: Sturgis & Walton, 1914).

7. Frederick Herzberg, *Work and the Nature of Man* (Cleveland: World Publishing, 1966).

8. Elton Mayo, *The Human Problems of an Industrial Civilization* (Boston: Harvard Graduate School of Business Administration, 1933).

9. H. Koontz, "The Management Theory Jungle," *Journal of the Academy of Management,* December 1961, pp. 174–88.

10. Douglas McGregor, *The Human Side of Enteprise* (New York: McGraw-Hill, 1960).

11. Characteristic works of these authors are Abraham Maslow, "A Theory of Human Motivation," *Psychological Review,* July 1943, pp. 370–96; Rensis Likert, *New Patterns of Management* (New York: McGraw-Hill, 1961); and Blake and Mouton, *The Versatile Manager* (Homewood, IL: Richard D. Irwin, 1982).

12. Joan Woodward, *Industrial Organization: Theory and Practice* (London: Oxford University Press, 1965); and Tom Burns and G. M. Stalker, *The Management of Innovation* (London: Tavistock Publication, 1961).

13. Paul R. Lawrence and Jay Lorsch, *Organization and Environment: Managing Differentiation and Integration* (Boston: Harvard Graduate School of Business Administration, 1967).

14. Adapted from Marilyn Edid, "How Power Will Be Balanced on Saturn's Shop Floor," *Business Week,* August 5, 1985, p. 65.

15. When this case was written, there was a wave of optimism about the Saturn Project. As events actually unfurled, the program has not been as successful as planned. People at all levels were not ready for so many new practices.

16. Henry Mintzberg, *The Nature of Managerial Work* (Englewood Cliffs, NJ: Prentice-Hall, 1980).

17. Robert H. Guest, *Organizational Change: The Effect of Successful Leadership* (Homewood, IL: Dorsey Press, 1962).

18. Rosemary Stewart, *Managers and Their Jobs* (London: Macmillan, 1967).

19. Mintzberg, pp. 45–53.

20. F. Katz, "Skills of an Effective Administrator," *Harvard Business Review,* 1974, pp. 51, 90–102.

21. Peter F. Drucker, *Managing in Turbulent Times* (New York: Harper & Row, 1980).

CHAPTER 3

THE EXTERNAL ENVIRONMENT

LEARNING OBJECTIVES

■ Understand how external forces influence a firm, and the implications of these forces for managers.

■ Identify some of the major social movements in the United States, and business's ethical and social responsibilities.

■ Understand the different viewpoints summarized in the Walters grid, and be able to formulate appropriate roles of government and business in addressing social issues.

■ Explain how values, norms, and religious beliefs affect management decisions, and be able to use the Kluckhohn value grid to characterize businesses and societies

■ Understand the basic legal environment in which businesses operate, and describe some of the business and ethical implications that increasing litigation has for managers.

■ Describe important economic contexts found in modern markets, and understand how the economic context of a firm affects management decision making.

■ Understand some of the motivations which drive entrepreneurs, and how entrepreneurship relates to economic development.

■ Explain the importance of international markets and economies on modern business, and identify key skills needed to succeed in international management.

"I'm a notorious character, all right," said Bill Norris, president of Melody Homes in 1985. Norris did not believe it was right for employers to demand documentation from Hispanic workers when blacks, whites, and others were not required to offer proof of legal residence. "Anybody who walks in the front door of our factory—we should be able to rely on them as a citizen of our country," he added. The fact that undocumented workers were a cheap supply of labor might have also explained Norris' attitude.

But the passage of the Immigration Reform and Control Act of 1986, the first major revision of U.S. immigration laws in decades, has forced Norris and other employers like him to retrench their positions. The new law requires all U.S. employers to verify the citizenship or legal-residence status of all new employees hired after November 6, 1986. Employers who knowingly hire or keep in employment illegal workers now face stiff fines and penalties. Illegal workers can get around the new act in two ways: (1) by keeping a job that they held before November 6, 1986; or (2) by acquiring false documentation.

The flood of largely illegal immigration from Mexico has sparked hot debate in the U.S. Unions contend that cheap foreign labor robs their workers of jobs. State and local governments strain under the burden of supplying health care and education for illegal residents. On the other side of the coin are businessmen who say they would have to close shop if the supply of illegal workers was cut off. Farmers across the U. S. would be short of workers to harvest crops, and the prices that consumers pay for everything from food to computers would increase.

For a look at the dimensions of the impact of illegal immigrants on the nation's economy consider the following:

1. Nearly two-thirds of the workers in Los Angeles' $3 billion garment industry are estimated to be illegal. Bernard Brown, regional vice-president for Levi Strauss & Co., says "Without these people from south of the border, we wouldn't have an industry. It would be a catastrophe."

2. Illegal workers constitute 10 to 20 percent of the work force in Silicon Valley. "We'd have a revolution" if all were deported, according to John Senko, an Immigration and Naturalization Service (INS) official in San Jose.

3. One-third of all construction workers in Houston are estimated to be illegal immigrants. They do the jobs most citizens refuse to do: lugging pots of hot tar to roof tops, pulling nails from concrete forms, and clearing debris.

4. Illegal workers are credited with keeping the shrimp industry in Brownsville, Texas, afloat. "They're what make this impoverished economy tick," says David Eymard, president of the Texas Shrimp Association.

5.   During the oil boom of the early 1980s, the INS estimates that as many as one in five residents in Louisiana were in the state illegally.

Companies, especially those in the Southwest, face an ethical and business dilemma: If they hire undocumented workers, they are breaking the law; if they do not hire them, they may break their company. Because of the new immigration reform act, employers can no longer avoid the issue by leaving enforcement of the immigration laws to the Immigration and Naturalization Service. But employers can avoid looking closely at the fake documentation that is proliferating.

The problem is exacerbated by two related phenomena: the dire poverty that faces most Mexicans since the peso was devalued as a result of falling oil prices in 1982, and the shortage of manual laborers in many parts of the U. S., particularly for jobs seen as dirty by Americans. The Mexican minimum wage of $3.75 per *day* is not enough to feed a family. The result is a flood of Mexicans moving north, an average of two thousand a day, and a labor shortage in Mexico as farm fields all across central Mexico lie fallow.

To complicate matters, the INS is still understaffed. The target of budget cuts during the 1970s and most of the 1980s, the INS has only recently begun to increase the number of its border patrol officers and investigative agents. INS paper work is also a major problem. Documents are so confusing that even the INS has trouble keeping them straight. For example, since 1946 fifteen different versions of the green card (which allows foreign workers to be employed in the U. S. legally) have been issued. The documents are also printed at different locations, each with slight variations that counterfeiters are able to exploit. The confusion makes it difficult for a company that wants to obey the law. If a company mistakenly fires a documented worker, believing the documentation is counterfeit, it could face accusations of discrimination and even lawsuits. This possibility of increased discrimination has prompted the INS to move slowly in enforcing the new law.

Government policy can be confusing. Some observers see the combination of lax, low-budgeted enforcement and tough legislation as a means for the U. S. government to have it both ways: It can maintain a public posture of being tough on illegal immigrants while unofficially implementing a quite liberal immigration policy.

Most unions prefer to stem the tide of illegal workers for the simple reason that cheap illegal labor is displacing union help on a large scale, especially in the Southwest. When the workers at Mission Foods, a tortilla maker for Taco Bell and Safeway Stores, went on strike, the union was forced to accept a $1.50 per hour wage cut after seven months because the company successfully hired replacement workers at $3.75 per hour (the old rate was $5.25). "The thing that scared us was that they hired these people so fast," said a union official. The company says that it did not deliberately hire illegal workers, but the president of the firm's corporate parent adds, "I wouldn't be surprised if 50 percent of them were."

Illegal residents spend an estimated $1 billion a year to get and protect their status in the U. S. Blatant exploitation often occurs as they are not in a position to go to the authorities to report abuse. Some farm and ranch operators have actually been charged under peonage statutes designed to prohibit various activities associated

Migrant workers from Mexico respond to higher U.S. wages by moving north to harvest California crops.

with slavery. In addition to poor working conditions some employers and landlords have extracted blackmail. Inflated rents at "safe houses," excessive prices for documentation, and an average $450 payment to a "coyote," one who guides them across the border, are among the most common expenses.

Thus Bill Norris and other employers can still obtain labor at rates most of us would laugh at. Even the minimum wage is often misleading as a representation of what illegal workers actually earn because some employers simply refuse to credit them with the hours actually worked. Who is going to report the violation? Norris is a hero or a villain depending on whom you talk to. ▼

INTRODUCTION

Bill Norris, like all managers, is affected by external factors—factors outside his company. Some of the factors which he must therefore be aware of, whether he likes it or not, are:

■ The international environment. The price of oil, the dollar-peso exchange rate, and social conditions in Mexico all help determine the supply and cost of labor.

- The legal environment in the United States, including laws which govern employment (such as minimum wage laws), and others which regulate his business (such as building codes). Bill had also better know his legal rights if INS authorities accuse him of hiring illegal workers, and what he could do if half his work force were carted off one day.

- The economic environment. Interest rates and economic conditions obviously affect both the demand for homes and the availability and cost of construction loans.

- The political environment, since political conditions affect the economy in several profound ways, and in Bill's case, because the immigration issue is highly political.

- The moral climate. Bill is concerned not only about what is practical and legal, but what is right. Is it ethical to hire an illegal immigrant—who may be desperately poor—very possibly saving him and his family from starvation? By paying an honest minimum wage, crediting workers their full hours, and treating them decently, isn't Bill giving his work force a better deal than do several shady employers—not to mention vastly better conditions than they would have in Mexico? But it is against the law! What about the American workers displaced by illegal immigrants? They have needs and families too. Just what is "the right thing to do" in this case?

The world of modern management is very complex and ever changing. And whether for good or bad, the modern manager must increasingly look outside the firm. It is not enough to do an excellent job of building houses; today's managers must be aware of and be able to react to the world about them. In this chapter we introduce and examine the major external factors affecting modern management.

THE SOCIAL ENVIRONMENT

In American business, there has been a growing recognition since World War II that businesses operate in and affect the societies about them. Businesses, then, are seen as having obligations to society—obligations not just to avoid harmful actions, but to take positive actions to correct injustices and inequities in society.

The Civil Rights Movement

Perhaps the most dramatic example of a social problem concerns the **civil rights movement**. While its origins go back, in one form or another, to the inception of the United States, the more immediate demands can be traced back to the impact of

Affirmative action in employment is an outgrowth of the civil rights movement.

Brown v. Board of Education, in 1954. In that case, the U. S. Supreme Court declared that the rights of black people were violated by the existence of racially segregated schools. The old formula of "**separate but equal**" educational facilities for white and black students was unacceptable and was declared "inherently unequal." With that hallmark decision, the various civil rights groups intensified their crusade to eliminate all racial barriers, whether in education, voting rights, transportation, public facilities, or employment.

The civil rights groups began to put pressure upon American businesses to hire and promote black people in the same way that they hired and promoted white people. Unfortunately, too many businesses were either timid or overtly racist and eventually the federal government had to step in. A host of laws were passed, compelling businesses to treat all people the same, regardless of race. Other minorities, from Hispanics to women, became active and American business leaders had to spend increasing amounts of time meeting the demands of such groups. This effort to improve the employment opportunities of minorities and women is called **affirmative action**. The result has been the gradual elimination of discriminatory policies in American business, although the process is far from complete. Along the way, management attitudes may now have changed fundamentally. As detailed in Box 3-1, business has found good social practice to be good business.

Box 3-1
Businessmen Prefer to Keep Affirmative Action

Clarence Thomas, the current chairman of the Equal Employment Opportunity Commission (EEOC) has been outspoken in his belief that companies should not be held to statistical standards to prove that they are hiring enough minorities and women. In his view, taking account of race and gender in hiring decisions violates Title VII of the Civil Rights Act of 1964: "Title VII says you can't consider race or sex in hiring decisions, period. It doesn't say *which* race or sex it's okay to favor."

There is a movement about to make Mr. Thomas' views public policy. A proposed Executive Order would revoke all regulations and guidelines issued pursuant to Executive Order No. 11246 (the order creating the Office of Federal Contract Compliance to enforce rules against discrimination in the award of federal contracts) if they require businesses doing business with the government "to use numerical quotas, goals, ratios, or objectives." The proposed Executive Order would do much to undermine the legality of voluntary goals and timetables and could even subject employers to lawsuits by white male employees or job applicants claiming that an affirmative action program discriminated against them.

Would such an order mean the end to affirmative action? You might expect businessmen to stand up and cheer, but strong evidence suggests that many of America's largest businesses do not want an end to affirmative action and will continue their programs with or without the government's support. In a recent survey of Fortune 500 companies by Organization Resources Counselors, more than 95 percent (122 of 128) of respondents said that they planned to continue to track the progress of women and minorities regardless of government requirements, and more than 90 percent (116 of 127) said that numerical objectives in their affirmative action programs were established to meet objectives unrelated to government regulations.

While opponents of affirmative action claim that goals and timetables amount to quotas, much of corporate America disagrees. These executives also oppose quotas, but simply do not see voluntarily agreed to targets as a form of

(continued)

Evidence thus exists that there has been a fundamental change in attitudes; equal opportunity is now seen as a right of every human being, in business as well as society. Sadly, however, the real impetus for change came from the external environment—from civil rights groups. When groups did not succeed in obtaining voluntary commitments, they turned to the federal government and equality was enforced by federal rule. How much better would it have been had business leaders not only

(Box 3-1 continued)

quota system. As William S. McEwen, director of equal opportunity affairs at Monsanto, says, "Business sets goals and timetables for every aspect of its operations—profits, capital expenditures, productivity increases. Setting goals and timetables for minority and female participation is simply a way of measuring progress." The National Association of Manufacturers even went on record in May of 1985 in a statement supporting affirmative action as good business policy saying that, ". . . goals, not quotas, are the standards to be followed in the implementation of such programs."

Companies have some sound business reasons for continuing affirmative action programs: (1) affirmative action results in a larger pool of talent to draw from; (2) the larger talent pool and increased expectations of minorities and women and the increase in competition leads to higher productivity; (3) better customer relations, especially for consumer products firms for whom minorities and women are large markets; and, somewhat more negatively, (4) withdrawal from present affirmative action programs could result in lower morale for the groups affected.

Making numerical measures entirely voluntary could mean trouble for companies. Employees are likely to be less patient with a voluntary program than one that operates under government rules and scrutiny. Title VII litigation is likely to proliferate as employees test the new system, especially white males who hope to receive a favorable hearing for their contention that affirmative action discriminates against them. Says a labor attorney who represents employers in affirmative action cases: "Getting rid of the Johnson executive order would turn the corporation into a battlefield. Again." Judith Vladek, a senior partner in a New York labor law firm, agrees: "Without the Labor Department involvement, employees with grievances would have fewer options, and they'd be a lot more confrontational. The number of lawsuits, which has been declining, would probably shoot up again."

SOURCE: Anne B. Fisher, "Businessmen Like to Hire by the Numbers," *Fortune,* September 16, 1985, pp. 26–30.

made the changes freely, but had led the way in guaranteeing the rights of all Americans, when it came to employment. If this had happened, all of the talk of goals, timetables, and reverse discrimination would probably not even be a part of the American vocabulary.

The civil rights movement is, of course, just one of the many externalities that now require major attention and effort from business leaders. A long list, from the problems of air pollution to the dumping of toxic wastes, commands the attention of management. These environmental problems are growing and show signs of becoming even more difficult. The result is that more and more time is required to deal with these problems, which business leaders can no longer ignore. Effective managers of the future must understand the origins and implications of such problems if they are to manage their businesses effectively. This will require a breadth of vision not required in the past.

What Responsibilities Does Business Have?

In response to the issues raised by the race problem, several scholars and business observers have articulated the responsibilities business should have in society. The thrust of many such recommendations is that corporations should be "good citizens"—in the words of a familiar oath—they should be loyal, trustworthy, helpful, and kind.

But as businesses move to meet these social responsibilities, many business scholars and practitioners have argued against the movement. For them, it is an illegal waste of the stockholders' money. In a very famous argument, the economist Milton Friedman contends that the only social responsibility of business is to make a profit and in that way, society receives its greatest benefits. For Friedman, and those of his persuasion, everything is reduced down to the individual and the assumption that each individual can make free choices:

> In an ideal free market resting on private property, no individual can coerce any other, all cooperation is voluntary, all parties to such cooperation benefit or they need not participate. There are no "social" values, no "social" responsibilities in any sense other than the shared values and responsibilities of individuals. Society is a collection of individuals and of the various groups they voluntarily form.[2]

Friedman, of course, also postulates an "ideal type" of market system and constructs his own theory of society around it.

While Americans believe in a free enterprise business system, it does seem to be terribly shortsighted to dismiss all notions of "society" as having no relevance. Because individuals claim rights for their corporations (the right to own property, for example), they must respect the duties that go with rights, particularly the duty not to use that ownership to harm others. Friedman's analysis is overly simplistic. For instance, he argues that minorities should not seek governmental aid in overcoming prejudice, but should fight it out in the market.[3] Yet from the Civil War to the early 1960s, scarcely any businesses at all responded to the needs of black people. It was not until the government intervened that they began to get a fair chance for significant employment.

For too many years, Americans have argued about the **social responsibilities** of business without ever achieving a consensus about what the term means. At a primary level, it means that every individual or organization that does business in a society thereby incurs obligations to that society. That is not the problem. The problem is at a secondary level: What are the specific obligations that a firm incurs?

Most analysts of modern management hold that businesses have social responsibilities. At the highest level, they are responsible for the observance of the intent of the Founding Fathers of this nation: that all people are born equal and have an inalienable right to life, liberty, and the pursuit of happiness. Unless businesses take this responsibility seriously, the government will continue to intervene and society will become even more dominated by governmental rules.

What, exactly, are the moral obligations of an organization doing business in the United States? To illustrate, assume that a business moves into a small community and finds that 80 percent of the people believe that poor eyesight is a divine curse and that those who are so afflicted should not be allowed to associate with the normal people. Obviously, no laws protect those with poor eyesight and the problem of vision is not one that is important to your firm. Does "society" require the firm to protect the minority or to follow the will of the majority? The answer cannot be found in the concept of "society."

The Walters Grid

The term "social responsibilities of business" has been used in so many ways that it is hard to come to grips with its meaning. In an excellent essay, the lawyer and business scholar Kenneth D. Walters outlined the various interpretations of the term, by linking it to political ideology.[4] He developed a grid upon which the various interpretations were laid out. As Box 3-2 illustrates, the Walters grid contrasts the ideologies of "conservatism" and "liberalism" with the arguments for and against corporate social responsibility. The issue is ". . . the proper relationship between the profit motive and government regulation [as] the focal point of the social responsibility debate."[5]

The "conservatives against" argue that the managers of firms are the employees of the shareholders. Since the sole reason for the purchase of shares is to maximize return on investment, any expenditures of time, effort, or funds on anything other than profit maximization represents an abdication of their responsibilities. Furthermore, such activities violate the integrity of the free market system which, as a result, does not work as well. Therefore, if the people want specific conditions, such as cleaner air or minority hiring, they must go through the government, which will then instruct the businesses what they must do.

Walters points out the immediate fallacy in this argument: conservatives dislike governmental regulation, yet they ask for it in the same breath. To force the government into the economic process is both shortsighted and unwise.

> Management is admonished to focus only on the financial well-being of shareholders, yet the firm that takes a "public-be-damned" attitude toward nonshareholders is a likely target for harsh and perhaps even punitive legislation. The firm that ignores the interests of society in a pell-mell pursuit of profit neglects the long-run consequences of such a strategy, consequences that could prove to be costly or even suicidal.[6]

Box 3-2
Corporate Responsibility and Political Ideology

ATTITUDES TOWARD SOCIAL RESPONSIBILITY	POLITICAL IDEOLOGY	
	CONSERVATIVE	LIBERAL
Against Corporate Responsibility	Only profit-maximizing firms are efficient.	Corporate social responsibility is antidemocratic and subverts the political process.
	Social responsibility is a self-imposed tax, which reduces profits.	Managers are not qualified to set broad social priorities.
	Social responsibility is theft—managers are giving away what is not theirs to give.	Greater government regulation of business is necessary to achieve social goals; it cannot be done through corporate social responsibility.
	Only monopolists can afford to be socially responsible; the firm that claims to be socially responsible should be prosecuted, not praised.	Social responsibility advocates an increase in corporate power and authority, when the need is for not more but less corporate power.

(continued)

The case of the "liberals against" is also seriously flawed. Essentially, they contend that business managers have neither the mandate nor the expertise to make social judgments. Managers should, in short, stay out of the process and let the government make such decisions. The problem here, of course, is that this assumption imperils the American belief that the political system and the economic system should be separate entities. Without straining the analogy too far, the "liberals against" are recommending something similar to a state-sponsored economic religion. That is anathema to a people believing in the values of pluralism.

The two commitments in favor of social responsibility are of greater interest and practicality. The "conservatives for" argue that since the government should stay out of the marketplace, it is in the long-range interests of business to anticipate, and then

(Box 3-2 continued)

ATTITUDES TOWARD SOCIAL RESPONSIBILITY	POLITICAL IDEOLOGY	
	CONSERVATIVE	LIBERAL
For Corporate Responsibility	Business operates more efficiently than government, and hence can solve problems more cheaply.	Resolving social ills is necessary if business is to have a healthy environment in which to operate, even if resolving social ills expands the role of government.
	The alternative to social responsibility is over-regulation of business or even socialism.	Social responsibility includes political responsibility; many problems can best be solved through business-government cooperation.
	Social responsibility is in the firm's long-run best interests.	Cooperation with government in finding solutions to social needs is in the long-run best interests of individual firms and of business generally.
	Social responsibility is in the long-run best interests of the free-market system.	

SOURCE: Kenneth D. Walters, "Corporate Social Responsibility and Political Ideology," *California Management Review* 19, Spring 1977, p. 41.

act upon, the social needs of society. Furthermore, they contend that since business can do things more "efficiently" that the costs to everyone will be lessened if business takes the initiative. The "liberals for" envision a division of labor, a partnership between business and government that would more effectively solve the problems of society. Walters favors either of the above positions as enhancing the future freedom of the economic system:

> A significant fact is that the conservative and liberal arguments for corporate responsibility are in agreement on the fundamental concept and goals of social responsibility. Social responsibility is not a non-market goal, but is a set of business policies to most effectively achieve profitability and to assure further profitability.[7]

The questions of business and governmental responsibilities can move from theory to the practice very quickly when problems occur. In March, 1989, the Exxon Valdez, an oil supertanker, ran aground in pristine Alaskan waters, causing an ecological and economic disaster of unprecedented proportions (see Box 3-3 on pages 60–61). Was business or government responsible for the disaster? Who should manage the cleanup? Who should be responsible for preventing and managing future oil spills?

THE CULTURAL ENVIRONMENT

The cultural environment of a nation is closely related to the social environment. Race relations in America have been so poor partly because cultural prejudice encouraged bigotry. Bill Norris is somewhat free to hire illegal immigrants with the boundaries of the law because of our cultural and legal presumptions of innocence and the feeling that those willing to work should be able to do so.

The concept of culture is so vast that it almost defies definition. For instance, in the early 1950s, two prominent anthropologists who looked at the way that "culture" was defined found 164 definitions.[8] With due recognition of the limitations of a single definition, we define **culture** as the total system of justificatory values, with their resultant behaviors, which are obtained principally through symbolic learning.[9]

Values

At the base of every culture, whether American, Japanese, or Mexican, are specific **values** that give shape and definition to that culture (the **value context**). The anthropologist Clyde Kluckhohn has defined the term "value" as follows:

> A value is a conception, explicit or implicit, distinctive of an individual or characteristic of a group, of the desirable which influences the selection from available modes, means, and ends of action.[10]

Values are important to a manager because values underlie everything the manager—or any person, for that matter—says or does. They are central to *every* human action, even the most practical. As the great American philosopher, John Dewey, wrote:

> But, on the other hand, all deliberate, all planned human conduct, personal and collective, seems to be influenced, if not controlled, by estimates of value or worth of ends to be attained. Good sense in practical affairs is generally identified with a sense of relative values. . . .[11]

Figure 3-1
The Kluckhohn Value Grid

Innate Human Nature	Evil	Neutral	Good
The Individual's Relation to Nature	Subjugation to Nature	Harmony with Nature	Mastery over Nature
The Time Focus	Past	Present	Future
Preferred Mode of Human Activity	Being	Being-in-Becoming	Doing
Preferred Relationship among Individuals	Lineality	Collaterality	Individuality

SOURCE: This table is adapted from Florence Rockwood Kluckhohn, "Some Reflections on the Nature of Cultural Integration and Change," *Sociological Theory, Values, and Sociocultural Change*, ed. Edward Tiryakin (London: Free Press, 1963), pp. 217–47.

Thus, even the most practical and commonsense actions are determined by the underlying **foundation values**, which are the basic values held by society in general. Unless the modern manager can comprehend such foundation values, he or she will be increasingly ineffective in making those necessary judgments about stability and change in the external environment.

For example, important foundation values in the United States are that individuals are important, and individual rights and freedoms are fundamental. These values motivate much of the civil rights movement; it "just isn't right" to advantage or disadvantage a person because of age, gender, or race.

To assist in the task of understanding foundation values, the value grid designed by the anthropologist, Florence Rockwood Kluckhohn, is most useful. This value grid (Figure 3-1) helps illustrate the way in which underlying values affect societies and business organizations. For example, suppose a society believes that humanity is innately evil. According to the Kluckhohn value grid human beings are then believed to be subject to nature—they are but intelligent animals, naturally subject to all forces other animals are. Thus, there is no innate reason not to use force or intimidation on humans; the survivors are those who are most fit. The time focus under this orientation is towards the past. Humans never have changed and never will, so what has worked well before will work again. Humans just exist, like any other natural phenomenon, and ideally should take their appointed roles in a structured, well-ordered society. Societies that believe that individuals are innately evil usually have political systems that are authoritarian. Likewise, some management theories assume that all

Box 3-3
The Alaskan Oil Spill

Just after midnight on Friday, March 24, 1989, the supertanker Exxon Valdez was steaming through Alaska's Prince William Sound, an area of incredible beauty and great economic and ecologic importance. The third mate, Gregory T. Cousins, was illegally in command of the ship—he had not been licensed to pilot a ship through Alaskan coastal waters. The captain, Joseph Hazelwood, was reportedly asleep in his cabin below. Later investigation indicated that Captain Hazelwood was apparently intoxicated at the time.

At 12:04 A.M. the Exxon Valdez executed what investigators now describe as an unusual series of hard right turns attempting to dodge floating ice. Suddenly, the ship was jolted by a series of violent bumps. Cousins ordered a hard left rudder, but to no avail. The ship shuddered to a stop atop Bligh Reef.

Thus began the worst oil spill in North American history. Eventually over 10 million gallons of crude oil leaked from the injured tanker, affecting an area of over 900 square miles. Elaborate plans for containment and cleanup of such a spill, detailed in a 1,800-page plan filed with the state of Alaska, proved to be a mockery. What went wrong?

The containment plan called for a slick to be encircled by booms within five hours. The Alyeska Pipeline Service Co., formed by the seven firms that pump oil from Alaska's Prudhoe Bay, stockpiled an arsenal of equipment to fight spills. Yet when the need came, much of the equipment was in disarray. Alyeska's boom-deployment barge, although seaworthy, was being repaired, and about 7,000 feet of containment boom had to be reloaded before deployment. Although Alyeska was required to notify the Coast Guard if vital equipment was taken out of service, a company official conceded that had not been done. The plan also called for an emergency crew of at least 15 to be on hand at all times. At the time of the spill, only 11 were on duty to monitor standard operations. On the Easter holiday weekend it took hours to assemble crews and equipment. It was not until 11:00 A.M. on March 25—35 hours after the accident, when the Exxon Valdez was finally encircled by an Alyeska containment boom.

Exxon planned to apply chemical dispersants to dissolve and break up the slick, but permission to use it was not given by the Coast Guard and state of Alaska until Sunday evening. By then gale force winds had sprung up, spreading the slick and destroying much of the dispersant's effectiveness. In any case, there were major questions about how much dispersant was on hand, whether the equipment to apply it was available, and how effective it would have been in the calm waters of the first two days of the spill.

In a sense, the Valdez tragedy began four years earlier, when Captain Hazelwood was convicted of drunken driving. Exxon sent him to an alcohol rehabilitation program, but was apparently not aware that his drinking problem continued. *(continued)*

(Box 3-3 continued)

In a five-year span his automobile license was revoked three times. At the time of the accident he was still not permitted to drive a car, but he retained his license to command a ship.

Two years earlier the Coast Guard had replaced a radar set at Valdez with a less powerful unit. Although the Exxon Valdez was outside the Coast Guard control area when it went aground, a more powerful radar would have allowed the Coast Guard to warn the ship that it was over a mile from the shipping lane and approaching the reef.

The short-term effects of the spill on wildlife and the local economy were devastating—damages to the fishing industry alone were estimated to total several hundred million dollars. Long-term effects are anyone's guess. The closest comparisons, slicks released by the Torrey Canyon off England in 1967 and the Amoco Cadiz off Brittany in 1978, involved very different conditions. Only few signs remain of those disasters, but nature's ability to heal itself in the cold, enclosed waters of Prince William Sound may be much less than in the warmer, open waters off France.

There is obviously plenty of blame to spread among Exxon, Alyeska, the ship's officers, the Coast Guard, and the state of Alaska. However, perhaps the most meaningful questions revolve around future responsibilities. How should management of the cleanup operation be shared between government and business? Who should bear responsibility for preventing future disasters? Or is the process unmanageable, and should all oil exploration and shipping in such sensitive areas be halted, as recommended by some environmentalists?

SOURCE: "The Future of Big Oil," and "In Ten Years You'll See 'Nothing,'" *Fortune*, May 8, 1989, pp. 46–54; "Smothering the Waters," *Newsweek*, April 10, 1989, pp. 54–57; "The Big Spill," *Time*, April 10, 1989, pp. 38–41; "Out of Control: How Unpreparedness Turned the Alaska Spill into Ecological Debacle," *The Wall Street Journal*, April 3, 1989, p. A1.

individuals are innately evil—or at least, innately lazy and indifferent. Managers adopting these theories rigidly control the working environment.

By contrast, according to the Kluckhohn value grid societies that believe that individuals are innately good believe that mankind can master nature, eventually overcoming all physical and social ills. The orientation here is towards a better, brighter future, which everyone can help to bring about by being actively involved in positive action. Human beings do not simply passively exist, they take action to control and improve their world. This orientation sees people as individuals who are best utilized by being free to exploit their individual strengths for the betterment of all. Societies based on these values usually have political institutions based upon trust and minimal rules. Managers who assume that people are inherently good create open environments in which workers are trusted and their input is valued.

Finally, Kluckhorn lists societies that view human nature as neither good nor evil. Societies that believe individuals are neutral, the product of their environment, usually have political institutions that try to create a desired cultural type. In business, managers who believe in theories which assume the neutrality and malleability of the human personality try to create an environment in which workers will want to achieve company goals or, at a minimum, not engage in counterproductive behavior.

Which of the three different assumptions is true? There are persuasive arguments in favor of each, and powerful, successful societies and companies have been built upon each set. While further discussion is deferred to a later chapter, the intelligent modern manager must understand these issues if he or she is to be a responsible and effective manager.[12] Otherwise, it is hopeless to try to understand different societies or companies.

Religious Beliefs

Closely related to the value context is the religious context, both of individuals and sometimes of a nation. In some countries, a dominant religion defines all institutions and behaviors, such as in the modern Islamic republics. In most nations religious values have been taken out of the public sphere. Religious values are generally seen as a matter for individual rather than national conscience, and thus are not subject to public scrutiny and debate. Nevertheless, if widely held, religious values affect the cultural context.

In the United States, the dominant religions are Judaism and Christianity, but they take as many different forms as can be imagined. Some important values are common to all Judeo-Christian religions, and have played a role in shaping the American sense of social responsibility discussed earlier. Other values are peculiar to specific denominations, and are important in dealing with individuals. For example, an intelligent manager would not assign a devout Catholic to superintend an abortion clinic, nor ask an evangelical to write ads for R-rated movies, nor ask a practicing Mormon to be a wine taster. Furthermore, the religions (and nonreligions) of all Americans are protected by the Constitution. Thus, there are legal as well as personal reasons to be sensitive to religious values.

Norms

Behavior **norms** are derived from the foundation values and the religions of a nation. Norms tend to be associated with fairly trivial things, such as modes of dress, speech, and such. In fact, norms involve a great deal more. They determine, among other things, the status of the various minority groups in a society and the comparative status of men and women.

Sometimes norms violate the foundation values themselves, making it very difficult to determine where the aberrant behavior comes from. For instance, in spite of three Constitutional amendments, innumerable court decisions, and a plethora of laws, racism is still a problem in the United States. Blacks, Hispanics, and Orientals are still discriminated against within organizations. Such discrimination is not only unlawful, it violates the foundation values and norms of the United States. The exploitation of illegal immigrants in the opening case is generally conceded to stem in part from prejudice against Hispanics.

Furthermore, sexism still exists, as does ageism—all in violation of foundation values. The modern manager must understand both the foundation values and the norms that are derived from them, including the deviations from those norms. However, the conduct of managers in the United States must always honor the foundation values—any attempt to compromise the basic rights of the American people will be met by stiff resistance from employees, possible civil suits, and even criminal charges (such as the peonage charges brought against some employers in the opening case).

THE LEGAL ENVIRONMENT

Values, religious beliefs, and norms are thought of most as affecting individual actions, and, if widely held, the social environment. However, pervasive assumptions and beliefs are often given the force of law, and become part of the legal environment of a society. In the United States, values regarding individual rights were part of the fabric of the Constitution—the basic law of the country. To illustrate, in the famous Federalist Paper No. 10, James Madison applies the theory of checks and balances to democratic pluralism. Recognizing that "the most common and durable source of factions, has been the various and unequal distribution of property," Madison concludes:

> The regulation of these various and interfering interests forms the principal task of modern Legislation, and involves the spirit of party and faction in the necessary and ordinary operations of government.[13]

Thus, right from the outset it was recognized that our government would be intimately involved in the amelioration of economic disputes.

What is forgotten, however, is that in the same essay Madison made a pointed reference to *what* exactly must be protected:

> The diversity in the faculties of men from which the rights of property originate, is not less an insuperable obstacle to a uniformity of interests. The protection of these faculties is the first object of Government.[14]

In other words, the primary responsibility is not the protection of property, but rather the protection of the talents by which individuals might acquire property. This means, then, that all legislation should be directed at freeing individuals to express themselves more adequately in the economic process. While that has obviously not always been the case; nonetheless, it has been of primary concern to governments through the decades.

Legal Rights and the Liability Crisis

However, the legal environment in modern America has moved far beyond the basic protection of individual and property rights. In recent years there has been an intense debate about whether liability laws in particular have gone too far. All parties concede the justice of liability laws. If an individual or company acts maliciously to harm another, whether by direct action or by making a defective product (**product liability**), the individual or company at fault obviously should be held responsible for their action. However, spurred on by what some businesses characterize as greedy lawyers searching for someone (or some company) to sue, regardless of actual fault, there has been an enormous growth of liability lawsuits and a corresponding growth of the cost of liability insurance.

David Holbrook, an executive vice-president of Marsh & McLennan, the world's largest insurance brokerage, is quoted by *Fortune* as saying: "Managers throughout U. S. industry now know that legal liabilities for potentially hazardous products may exceed not only a corporation's insurance but its total assets." The result is a reassessment by many corporations as to whether the potential profit in a product line is worth the resulting potential liability. Merrell Dow, for example, has withdrawn from the market Bendectin, the only prescription drug available to pregnant women suffering from extreme nausea. Despite successful legal defenses of the product, lawsuits continued to flood the company and the potential liability from just one courtroom loss could easily wipe out the $13 million per year in revenue from the product. Legal costs from just eight suits cost the company $1.5 million, more than 10 percent of product revenues. And these were successful defenses—the $1.5 million is just the cost of preparing and arguing the cases.

The vaccination of American children is also endangered. Only Merck & Co. continues to make the combined measles, mumps, and rubella (MMR) vaccine; only the Lederle Laboratories division of American Cyanamid and Connaught Laboratories continues to sell diphtheria, tetanus, and pertussis (DTP) vaccine; and Lederle is the only maker of polio vaccine. With the number of children decreasing as the result of birth control and demographic factors, the market for vaccines does not provide enough profit to cover potential liabilities. Merck's counsel states: "A good business-man would not be in this business. The potential liability risk is too high. But Merck is committed to manufacturing vaccines from a social responsibility standpoint."

High school athletics are also endangered. School districts hard-pressed for cash are not in a position to pay million-dollar damage awards as a result of injuries. Even rich school districts will not be able to field teams if sports equipment cannot be purchased. Only two companies dominate the market for football helmets, Bike Athletic Co. (part of Colgate-Palmolive) and Riddell (part of MacGregor Sporting Goods). The cost of insurance on the helmet line may exceed the cost of manufacturing for these companies. Despite its size, an attorney for the industry says that Bike would not be able to obtain insurance on the product line if it was not part of the larger corporation. "The bigger the parent, the better the chances of obtaining insurance."

Related effects of the explosion in product liability claims include the loss of markets to foreign manufacturers who are harder to sue and face much smaller insurance costs, the inclusion of lawyers in every phase of the design process, the inclusion of warnings covering every conceivable type of product misuse both on products themselves and in their packages and instruction booklets, the development of product failure data bases, and legal audits to identify products, procedures, manufacturing operations, or services that could trigger lawsuits. Companies have also experimented with procedures to avoid litigation, such as minitrials and no-fault claims that award actual damages only. Most companies, however, have joined the move for a reform of state and federal liability laws and favor limits on actual damages and either the elimination of or strict limitation of punitive damages.

Product liability is an area calling for the application of the best creative abilities of business managers. Any solution must take into account the needs of consumers, workers, and business alike. The concerns of trial lawyers, opponents of reform who tend to treat the "insurance crisis" as a myth based on exaggerated stories of jury awards (which fail to mention the award reduction on appeal) and insurance company greed, must also be addressed. Whether exaggerated or not, the fears surrounding product liability suits have resulted in substantially higher insurance costs for U. S. manufacturers (up to twenty times their European and Japanese counterparts).

The Need for Self-Regulation in Business

It must be recognized at the outset that today's concept of the corporation is a most modern invention and one that is uniquely American. As Hurst wrote:

> In sum, when we began making important use of the corporation for business in the United States from about 1780, there was little relevant legal experience on which to

draw. For 100 years, we proceeded to use the corporate instrument on a scale unmatched in England. In that development we built public policy toward the corporation almost wholly out of our own wants and concerns, shaped primarily by our own institutions. The one definite inheritance was the idea that some positive act of the sovereign was necessary to create corporate status. But we gave our own content to that idea.[15]

Thus, the regulation of the corporation grew as the corporation itself grew. Policy was developed as both the government and the corporation developed. But what is most evident is that governmental control must be kept to a minimum, which means that the corporation must assume to itself a larger, voluntary role toward issues of social and political concern.[16]

Regardless of the position taken in regard to legal obligations of business, it is almost self-evident that the wheels of commerce would grind to a halt if businesses fail to observe some basic ethical principles, especially those of acting in good faith, honesty in fact, and full disclosure of pertinent information needed by customers, shareholders, and suppliers. The following case illustrates the need for self-regulation in business. Some of the practices involved are illegal and would be condemned by the adherents of all of the philosophies regarding corporate social responsibility. It is in the area of legal, yet unethical practices that the approach of the parties would differ. Regardless of which philosophy is held, however, it is evident that failure to act will lead to setting laws or the failure of the business.

CASE
Scandal Rocks Lloyd's of London[17]

 The world's largest and most prestigious casualty insurer, Lloyd's of London, still conducts most of its business as it has for centuries. Lloyd's is not actually a company but rather an association of underwriters that writes its business by dividing the premium and risk among the backers of individual underwriters. Contracts are seldom used in the agreement between the broker and the underwriter; business is conducted in face-to-face meetings in which the broker presents a slip outlining the desired coverage and disclosing details that might prejudice coverage. If the underwriter agrees, he initials the slip and the deal is consummated.

If the broker fails to outline the true nature of the risk or the underwriter denies the contract when a claim is placed, it is not difficult to see that the entire system would break down. Backed by 23,435 wealthy investors from Britain, America, and 60 other countries, Lloyd's conducts business on the basis that it will insure anything. Lloyd's wrote the first automobile insurance policy as an extension of marine insurance [a ship that navigates on land], it has insured satellites, and it is well known for the policies it has issued on the voices, legs, hands, and other physical assets of entertainers.

The confidence of Lloyd's backers is slipping, however, after some of the worst financial scandals in its history. The *Economist* magazine estimates that agents and underwriters have siphoned off $500 million over the past 15 years. It has also been discovered that an "old boy" network existed inside Lloyd's that tipped off insiders to lucrative deals and left outsiders exposed to tremendous losses. Some members of a syndicate might reap profits of 50 percent or more while others lost up to three times their stake.

The loss of trust has forced Lloyd's to take vigorous action. Modern practices of disclosure, accountability, rigorous solvency tests, elimination of conflicts of interest, and aggressive internal regulation have all been instituted. Critics are not convinced that the syndicates are able to regulate themselves because a recent audit by Lloyd's managers found that 130 of the 430 syndicates could not provide "true and fair" accounts. The company is determined to avoid government regulation and most analysts are convinced that Lloyd's will withstand the scandal and painful reforms and continue to function much as it has in the past. Failure to respond appropriately could bring an end to one of the world's most interesting institutions, loss of insurance coverage to some of the world's riskiest ventures, and the loss of a $6 billion insurance market. ▨

Of course, business must obey the law of the land if it is to survive; in fact, obedience to the laws of the land may well be their primary responsibility. The secondary responsibility is to make a profit by offering goods and services for sale. As the Lloyd's case illustrates, failure to obey the law, including the spirit of the law, can lead to the inability to make a profit.

The morality of the profit motive is defended in Chapter 4. Suffice it to say here that a business firm can do only so much in dealing with the problems of society. The top executives of a business must be able to make appropriate judgments about how far they can and should go in the alleviation of social problems. They have a moral obligation to the shareholders and democracy is ill-served by the unreasonable diminution of the shareholder profit.

THE ECONOMIC CONTEXT

Several times, we have touched upon differing economic conditions in different parts of the world. Some differences arise from various levels of natural resources, industrialization, and prosperity. Other differences arise from differing economic systems themselves, and still others from different competitive environments in various industries.

Market Structures

Market structures have a strong effect on business practice. Some companies work under **perfect competition**, characterized by many customers and many suppliers of an identical product. Under perfect competition, customers shop primarily for the lowest price, so suppliers are successful only if they can produce and sell as efficiently as possible. **Imperfect competition** is characterized by fewer buyers or sellers with the possibility of some market leverage depending on the relative market strengths of the buyers and sellers.

Some markets are **monopolies**, where only one firm supplies a product. In practice, monopoly products often compete with similar products where features other than price are considered. For example, only one company produces Coca-Cola, so Coca-Cola Inc. has a monopoly on Coke. Many other products satisfy thirst, so Coke, Pepsi, 7-Up, and other soft drinks compete on the basis of taste, image, availability, and many other factors. Price is not the only competitive factor, and may not even be the most important. If the holder of a monopoly succeeds in producing a markedly superior product or succeeds in differentiating the product in the minds of the consumers, extraordinarily high profits can result, a major motivation for innovation and entrepreneurship. A new product or service has a monopoly for at least a short period of time. If the product can be patented, the developer has, in effect, a government-backed monopoly for an extended period of time.

An **oligopoly** is characterized by a few, dominant suppliers. Now the interdependencies and interactions among the supplying companies becomes important. Suppliers can act in concert to support high-price levels and profits, but the coalition is often a fragile one which can be destroyed by any of the participants. The Organization of Petroleum Exporting Countries (OPEC) was effective for several years in supporting extraordinarily high prices, thus generating enormous profits for member countries. By the mid-1980s, however, several OPEC countries were routinely violating OPEC price and production guidelines, greatly weakening its power.

Monopsonies and **oligopsonies** are similar to monopolies and oligopolies, except they have one or few customers, rather than one or few suppliers.

Economic Structures

Some economic systems are capitalist, as in the United States and Hong Kong. Under **capitalism**, individuals are free to own and profit from ideas and productive goods. The profit motive is viewed as wholesome and desirable, and strongly encourages entrepreneurship, innovation, risk taking, and efficiency. Laws and social customs reinforce the sanctity of private property. Supporters of capitalism point out that capitalism works—that profits are needed to reward innovation and risk taking, which lead to entrepreneurship, employment, improvements, and ultimately, more prosperity for everyone. There is also a strong underlying belief in the worth of the individual, and sense that all are better off when individuals are free to develop their gifts for the good of all.

Critics point out that under pure capitalism, the greedy and the strong may eventually accumulate all property, leading to a permanent idle class who live in luxury by exploiting the masses. Far from leading to freedom and enlightenment, such a system could degenerate into economic feudalism. Such concerns lead to modified forms of capitalism in practice. In the United States, for example, antitrust laws control the formation and operation of monopolies. Other laws and agencies regulate conditions of employment, including the right of workers to organize and bargain collectively, define and prohibit illegal competitive practices, and exert direct control over economic conditions.

Marxist economies are built upon a different premise. Under **Marxism**, all productive goods are owned and shared equally by everyone. There are no classes—no aristocratic few who eat cake while the masses starve for bread. All donate to the common good according to ability, and all share in the common wealth according to need. Profits are seen as evil—as the unearned skimmings of the privileged from the exploited workers, and thus are abolished. Instead of entrepreneurship, society plans for all needs centrally, setting rational plans for production and distribution of goods, defining equitable prices, and encouraging innovation in those areas most needing improvement.

Critics of Marxism point out that it simply does not work in practice. Lacking the profit incentive, human beings become risk-averse and unproductive. Rather than donating according to ability, most people donate the minimum required, since all still share according to need. Also, modern economies (perhaps all economies—ancient as well as modern) are so complex they are all but impossible to plan centrally. No matter how beautiful and complete a plan looks on paper, people will find ways to modify and exploit it for their own self-interest. Food production plans—to cite an example common in Marxist countries—generally go awry because of inadequate fertilizers, insecticides and herbicides, and machinery. Those farm supplies, in turn, are often in short supply because of inadequate or poor quality materials from other parts of the supply chain. And so on. Since, in general, everything is affected by everything else, it is impossible to overcome problems by correcting individual factors. In capitalist economies a tractor manufacturer who has a bad experience with a supplier—either with deliveries or quality—will find a new supplier. If a material is in short supply the price will rise, causing everyone in the economy to look for more efficient ways to use that material, or perhaps find an alternate material. In Marxist economies those avenues of correcting problems are closed; both supply lines and prices are set centrally.

For these reasons there are no pure Marxist economies in the world, just as there are no pure capitalist economies. All Marxist countries tolerate and depend on capitalistic subeconomies to provide some important goods, particularly foods, and all allow limited investments and partnerships with companies in capitalist economies, at least as long as there is direct and obvious benefit to them from doing so. However, Western business managers can never forget that they are essentially tolerated only as expediencies, not necessarily welcomed as beacons of things to come.

The Marxist economy will often tolerate capitalistic sub-economies that can supply goods it cannot provide from within.

Socialist economies combine many aspects of the two extremes summarized above. Most are based on the capitalist ideas of private ownership, individual initiative, and the profit motive—for the most part. However, most also believe that some important segments of the economy (often utilities, transportation, and sometimes basic industry and financial institutions) should be owned publicly and operated primarily for the public good, rather than for private profit. Even private firms must generally be operated in such a manner as to meet important social goals in such areas as employment and employee benefits. In many European countries, employee associations must, by law, have representatives in top management committees. In such countries it is generally all but impossible to fire workers or close plants, even if workers are grossly incompetent or plants obviously unprofitable.

The Entrepreneurial Environment

One of the important conditions in the economic environment involves the conditions that allow a person the opportunity to create a new product or service and exploit the opportunities available to make a profit: the **entrepreneurial environment**. Those persons who find a challenge in creating new business ventures are called entrepreneurs. Entrepreneurship is the act of starting new firms, introducing new products and technological innovations, and in general, taking the risks that are necessary in seeking out business opportunities. Of course, the concept of risk taking is strongly linked to the possibility of reward or profit as a motivating force in entrepreneurship.

The people of the United States and of other open economic and political countries have been fortunate in that opportunity for entrepreneurship exists. Countries that are more economically and politically restrictive do not easily allow people to create new enterprises. There are certain factors in the capitalistic economic environment that encourage people desiring to create something new for possible profit and economic advantage. Three of these factors are:

THE POSSIBILITY OF EXERCISING MONOPOLY POWER   If an entrepreneur can, even for a short time, create a new product or service, it may be possible to establish a monopoly. This monopoly will allow the entrepreneur to earn and enjoy the profits that are generated from the sale of the product or service. It is the attraction of the possibility of profit (the **profit motive**) that motivates most entrepreneurs to engage in new activities.

RISK TAKING   Trying to establish something new in the marketplace involves risks. Entrepreneurs usually have a risk-taking mentality and are willing to risk their time and financial resources because of the possible gains if the risk pays off.

For example, the entrepreneur may take a risk and invest in a new oil field. If, on the average, only one in ten shafts drilled pays off, financing a new oil field involves considerable risk. But entrepreneurs like the excitement of the risk, particularly if they can get sufficient data to forecast that the risks of failure to find oil are minimal and the profits for taking the risks are exceptional. These profits are the rewards or payment one receives for taking the risk. It is important to remember that the opportunity must be available in the economic environment that allows risk to be taken, and that people must be willing to take such personal risk.

INTRINSIC REWARDS OF INNOVATION   If the entrepreneur is the first to innovate some new product, or to develop a new machine or method of working, then profit may reward the effort and risk taken. However, **innovation** is different from invention. Invention is the act of generating a new idea. Innovation is the next step, and is the act of putting the new idea into practical use. Entrepreneurs are more likely to be innovators than inventors. They will take an idea and develop a new use of it with potential for personal profit.

Usually the reward for innovation is short-lived. As soon as the success of the innovation is demonstrated, others will begin to imitate it. Entrepreneurs are forced to keep searching for new ideas and to keep innovating. This constant push for something newer and better is at the heart of the growth of the capitalist system. It is one of the secrets of its extraordinary dynamism.[18]

The economic system in the United States has been such that the opportunities for people to exert their entrepreneurial tendencies have been exceptional, probably more than any other country. Most of our major companies began with the new idea of a single person. Edwin H. Land and Polaroid, John D. Rockefeller and Standard Oil, J. Willard Marriott and the Marriott Hotels, Hewlett and Packard of the company bearing their name, and J. C. Penney and his retail chain, are just a few of the companies that began with a person with an idea willing to work hard and take a risk. Since 90 percent of businesses are small, family-run firms, great opportunities still exist for those interested in managing their own enterprise.

Countries vary greatly in how entrepreneurship is rewarded. Some countries attempt to block private entrepreneurship altogether. Other countries may have tax and regulatory structures that act to check the rewards that entrepreneurs earn. Still other countries treat foreigners differently than citizens. Managers must not only be aware of the various laws and regulations of the countries that they do business in, they must also be aware of the underlying policies and possible changes that could affect the returns to entrepreneurial activities.

A natural extension of the work of the entrepreneur is the development of the small business. The new enterprise often involves the entire family as parents and children work together to get the business established. When the family is involved, many unique problems can occur. For example, do all children have equal rights to a position in the company? What about a son-in-law or a daughter-in-law? If a son-in-law holds a position in the family firm and the daughter obtains a divorce, is the son-in-law's position in jeopardy? Who takes over the firm when the father dies or retires? What if some children do not want to work in the family business—do they still have any rights in the decision making? What effect do family relationships have on business relationships and vice versa? For many family firms a time comes when the family, for many reasons, must relinquish managerial control and get nonfamily professional managers to run the enterprise.

Managing in a small business, whether family-owned or not, involves a different set of conditions than if one manages in a large organization. Usually in the small firm, anyone who manages must be involved in a much wider range of decisions and actions than is the case in the bigger organization. A few individuals often run the entire operation, and they are often involved in almost every decision—how to get capital to develop the business, how and when to market the product, pricing, hiring and firing of personnel, and formulating overall plans and goals. In the large firm all of these functions are segmented to a degree and specialists manage in each area.

For the prospective manager, it makes sense to get a broad background in many subject areas. Not only is it impossible to predict the career you will follow, thus impossible to decide which areas can safely be omitted, but you can never predict the size of the business you may enter and the demands that will be imposed.

THE INTERNATIONAL ENVIRONMENT

The opening case on illegal immigrants illustrates how international issues and politics, far from being remote and inconsequential to modern managers, strike at the very survival of a business—even at the personal freedoms of managers, since they can be jailed if they are found guilty of violating laws governing the hiring of immigrants. And this is in homebuilding—an industry which would seem to be immune from international influence if any is! Suppose you are in a business dealing directly with international markets. Obviously the international environment would be of critical importance to you.

Lorne Hehn, president of United Grain Growers Ltd. of Winnipeg, Canada, presented some unique insights into how international economics, politics, and social trends affect his business. He told the Canadian Seed Growers Association that, "We seem to have entered a new era in the grain business—not a particularly happy one."

The basis for Hehn's remarks is his interpretation of a number of recent events:

1. The Bonus Incentive Commodity Export Program (BICEP) of the United States rewards foreign buyers of U. S. wheat with free wheat out of government surpluses. This program has had the effect of lowering international grain prices and making it harder for Canada to compete in world markets.

2. The continued growth of U. S. wheat stocks despite the giveaway program.

3. Strong competitive moves by the wheat growing members of the European Economic Community (Common Market) threaten to initiate a trade war with the U. S. which can only hurt Canada.

4. Protective tariffs in the Common Market have the effect of closing this market to Canadian wheat.

5. A strong U. S. dollar during the mid-1980s had the effect of encouraging traditional grain importers, such as China and India, to increase production. China, Canada's largest export customer after the Soviet Union, increased production by 42 percent in the eight years from 1976 to 1984. India expanded its production and the Soviet Union is also expected to harvest larger crops, decreasing its need for imports.

6. Canadian farmers faced a severe drought in 1984 and conditions threatened a repeat performance in 1985 while other nations were experiencing greater harvests. The result was lower amounts available for export at lower prices.

7. The relative strength of the Canadian dollar in relation to the U. S. dollar meant a competitive advantage for Canada's chief competitors, the countries of the Common Market, Australia, and Argentina.

Given the competitive situation, Hehn believed that the government of Canada should help Canadian grain growers by assisting research and development of higher yield, cheaper to produce grain, by fostering an environment that allows efficient farmers to prosper, and by helping Canadian producers to overcome tariff and non-tariff barriers in other countries.

Hehn identified the Pacific Rim as the key area for future Canadian trading growth in grains. The Pacific Rim countries present some unique problems for Canada; however, the principal one is the need for a competitive price.

Hehn's list of political and economic factors affecting his business could obviously be expanded to include several others. The major point, however, should be apparent: Modern businesses are inherently global in nature. The prices we pay for labor, lima beans, and lumber today in Sacramento, San Antonio, or Secaucus are affected by decisions and events that occur half a world away. As managers, we need to be aware of the world about us.

The Challenge of Operating in Other Countries

Many businesses, of course, deal directly with and operate in foreign countries. International business is now a fact of life. In 1978 nearly one-third of the world's total output was represented by international business activities. Growth in trade has significantly outpaced the world growth in GNP for many years, and that trend seems likely to continue.[19] As shown by all the factors affecting the Canadian wheat growers, the statistics tell only part of the story.

In a world where all are affected by international trade, some firms are more deeply involved than others in foreign countries. Some firms are **international** in that they buy or sell abroad while keeping most facilities and people in the home country. Others are **multinational** in that they operate in several countries, and typically have substantial investments in plants and facilities in many different countries. It may be difficult, in fact, to identify a "home" country in the traditional sense for these firms. No matter what the structure and scope of international operations, people involved in international management face some unique problems.

- Language and cultural differences are obvious. In some cases, cultural differences can destroy the effectiveness of managers who are not sensitive to them. Gift giving, for example, is a potential mine field for the uninformed. In Arab countries it is in poor taste to give liquor, or to give gifts to a man's wife. In West Germany, red roses imply that the sender is in love with the recipient. In Japan or China, expensive gifts can cause great embarrassment.[20]

- Financial systems and monetary systems vary from country to country. In Japan, for example, the relationships between banks and their corporate customers are much closer and more cooperative than in the United States, where an "arms distance" relationship is required.

- Many foreign countries have restrictive requirements on local ownership of production facilities, on imports, and on how much of each product must be produced locally. It is difficult to transfer money out of some countries. Some countries suffer from severe inflation, so exchange rates with other currencies are unpredictable. Thus, financial and political risks can be much higher than in the United States.

■ Production and marketing conditions vary with the general educational level, income level, and political unity of the host country. Costs of labor, conditions of work, and productivity differ from country to country. Some countries have poor transportation, housing, and communications systems. In building a smelter in Mexico, for example, a copper producer was able to take advantage of lower wage rates and looser environmental restrictions, but had to build a hydroelectric dam and housing for workers.

■ The political structure and social aims of some governments favor social goals. In Belgium and France, for instance, it is difficult and expensive to lay workers off once they are hired. Some countries are socialist or Marxist, and tolerate capitalist enterprises only in cases of obvious and immediate social benefit. Taxes and legal environments can overtly favor local business at the expense of multinationals. Governments in some countries are unstable, and the political risk of coups from either the political left or right is real.

These examples indicate only some of the complexities of this area. Managers face a myriad of factors in actual business situations, and managers need to be aware of much more than matters of war and peace. For instance, many governments directly support favored economic systems, and sometimes companies. Thus, when one deals with a Japanese business, one also deals with the Japanese political system—and such interdependencies must be understood. Likewise, Canadian wheat growers are certainly affected by U. S. subsidies to support wheat exports.

International and Multinational Businesses

Many companies are international in scope, while others are multinational. To be truly multinational, a company should meet the following conditions:

1. The parent company is owned and managed by the nationals of one country. Exxon is a multinational company and its national headquarters are in New York. Top management comes primarily from the United States. In the various countries where it does business, Exxon appoints most of its managers from among its local employees.

2. Its production system is integrated over all its international operations. The multinational company can shift materials and products from one country to another to ensure successful functioning.

3. Control is based on equity—that is, managerial control is based primarily on ownership of the firm's assets (except when local law prohibits alien ownership).

4. It has legal residence in the country of most of the major owners and managers.[21]

A manager in a multinational firm would probably live in a foreign country and would be expected to understand the culture, customs, and language of that country. Even if he or she did not live abroad, such a manager would be managing activities that cut across national boundaries. In any case such managers must be aware of some of the following factors:

1.   What are the differences in the economic systems from one country to another?
2.   What is the tax structure in each country?
3.   How stable is the currency and what are the exchange rates of currency in the various countries?
4.   What kind of political environment is in each country and how stable is the political climate?
5.   What are the labor conditions in each country—labor supply, wages, union activity, level of education, and skills of workers?
6.   What are the laws in each country that will regulate the business enterprise?
7.   How receptive is each country to foreign investments?
8.   What are the social, political, religious, and economic environments?

Clearly, to manage in a multinational or international firm, one must have a broad grasp of many factors dealing with other countries. The international environment includes such a wide range of conditions that it usually is not possible for one person to become an expert in more than one area of the world—perhaps only one country.

Some people try to gain **area expertise** in an area of the world—Africa, the Middle East, Europe, the Far East. Others concentrate on developing countries. Still others focus their attention on one activity across many international boundaries—looking at international financial operations in many countries, for example. This area of management is a great challenge for those interested in the international scene.

ENDING CASE
Football Entrepreneurs Seek Solutions from Congress[22]

 One of the National Football League's chief problems is control of its franchises. What is good for the individual franchisee may be bad for the league and, consequently, the league would like to restrict the freedom of franchisees to move to a new city when the going gets tough. The NFL sees itself as a sort of mediator between the interests of the fans and those of the owners.

Two recent cases illustrate the league's difficulties. The Oakland Raiders moved to Los Angeles from Oakland, California, and the Baltimore Colts left late one night without warning for Indianapolis, Indiana. The cities of Oakland and Baltimore were incensed. The cities argue that franchises belong as much to the fans as the owners and should be regulated like public utilities. The mayor of Baltimore, William D. Schaefer, testified before a U.S. Senate committee: "A vital element in our community—the Baltimore Colts—was jerked from our midst. We stand before you mistreated and insulted by an owner with no regard for us." The NFL sympathizes with the mayor but is powerless to do much because the last time it tried—by attempting to stop the Raiders from leaving Oakland—it lost a $50 million antitrust suit launched by the club owner Allen Davis.

Major league baseball has not had similar problems because Congress granted it antitrust immunity in 1921. The NFL and other professional sports would also like such immunity so that they can set rules in the best interests of their sport without worrying about lawsuits. The leagues would like to prevent other midnight departures such as that of the Colts. The owners, on the other hand, feel that because it is their money that is tied up in the franchise, they should be able to act as they see fit. Tougher relocation rules could force them to accept long-term losses and diminish the value of the franchise.

Major league sports have become big business and the environment in which they exist requires that many constituencies be dealt with—the fans, the cities that have invested in facilities for the franchise, the business people who depend on the presence of the team for some or all of their own business. Like many businesses facing multiple constituencies, the professional sports leagues seek to establish stability in their environment. Recruiting Congress to remake the rules is one way to achieve the desired result.

Clearly, if the NFL is successful in gaining antitrust exemption, an important new factor must be weighed by anyone considering an NFL franchise. The public mood, if aroused, could result in legislation having a significant effect on the prerogatives of entrepreneurs. Such a change could even open an opportunity for an astute entrepreneur to challenge the NFL by creating a new league with fewer restrictions. ◼

SUMMARY

This chapter provides an overview of several external environments within which modern business must operate. Every organization exists within a society, and must shoulder responsibilities to that society. In this country, the civil rights movement provides an illuminating example of how failure to assume social responsibilities can lead to political and legal action. The Walters grid provides a valuable paradigm to define and discuss what responsibilities business has to society.

Each society has its own culture, values, and norms. Religious beliefs can play a major role in actions of individuals, and sometimes of societies.

The legal environment defines the legal and political forces that face an organization within a given society. In the United States, individual freedoms and property rights arise from the fundamental values behind the founding of the country, and are carefully defined and protected. The liability crisis, whether real or imagined, has led to questions about the fundamental role and limits of legal recourses. It is clear from the Lloyd's of London case that businesses must have internal standards, and practice self-regulation beyond legal requirements.

The economic environment was discussed first on the level of the firm and the industry, then on the level of the society. Capitalist, Marxist, and socialist economies have widely varying goals and methods of achieving goals; understanding those fundamental aims is essential in doing business in such countries. The role of entrepreneurship is critical, particularly in capitalist economies.

Finally, all firms are affected by the international economy, thus management must understand how global events and decisions will provide both threats and opportunities. Many firms deal directly in international business, either as international or multinational firms, and all such firms operate in at least one other country.

KEY TERMS

Civil rights movement	Monopoly
Separate but equal	Oligopoly
Affirmative action	Monopsony
Social responsibilities	Oligopsony
Culture	Capitalism
Values	Marxism
Value context	Entrepreneurial environment
Foundation values	Innovation
Norms	International businesses
Product liability	Multinational businesses
Perfect competition	Area expertise
Imperfect competition	

REVIEW QUESTIONS

1. What are some ways that organizations differ that affect their interaction with the environment?

2. What is the basic risk that a manager takes in failing to understand the value context of the society in which he or she works?

3. What assumptions did Kluckhohn make from her observation of the foundation values of various societies?

4. What are the three basic conceptions of human nature expressed in various management theories?

5. What are some of the current expressions of population dynamics and how might they affect organizations?

6. Name three major areas of impact that the political and legal system of a country has on how organizations are managed?

7. What are the major differences in management objectives between profit and not-for-profit organizations?

8. What is the difference between international and multinational businesses?

9. What are some of the major differences that managers should be aware of when operating in foreign countries?

10. What are the four identifying characteristics of a truly multinational firm?

11. List three factors in the external environment that are generally seen to be encouraging to entrepreneurs and entrepreneurial activity?

12. What are some of the unique problems faced by family-owned firms?

CHALLENGE QUESTIONS

1. What basic theory or assumption about the basic nature of people do you subscribe to? Be prepared to defend your belief in class.

2. Some people believe that you should never discuss religion or politics, especially on the job. From what foundation value is a norm such as this derived? Do you agree with it?

3. If you were assigned to sell the virtues of the free market to Ethiopia, what values within the free market system would you stress and why? Keep in mind the physical context for that country described in the chapter.

4. What effect do you think that the 'baby boom' had on economic growth in the period after World War II in the free world? What effect do you think that increased longevity will have? Will the businesses that thrive be the same?

5. What are some of the pressing political and legal questions facing organizations today? Do you think that their resolution will result in greater regulation of the management decision-making process? What should organizations do?

6. Which of the three basic theories of the nature of humanity are most strongly reflected in the American legal system? What does this say about the foundation values of the United States?

7. Why is it important for managers to project the kinds of laws they think will be passed?

8. Of all the trends in the workplace that you are aware of, which do you think are most likely to favor a resurgence of unionism? Which are likely to change the nature of the management-labor relationship for the better?

9. From your knowledge of world events, rank the following countries in terms of financial and political risk: United States, Argentina, South Korea, the Philippines, Canada, South Africa, France, England. What does this ranking imply about the return on investment required to get you to invest?

10. What does your answer to Question 9 imply about the return investors would expect from multinational companies? Would investors expect higher returns from Exxon (operations in 80 countries) or from an oil company dependent mainly on the Persian Gulf for its sources of supply? Why?

11. Explain the linkage between invention, innovation, risk, and economic growth.

CASE AND RELATED QUESTIONS

1. List at least three advantages and three disadvantages to the large influx of illegal immigrants into the United States. What are some of the implications of a company's open recognition of the rights of illegal workers?

2. What would be the short- and long-term economic effects of a successful effort to close the U. S.–Mexican border to illegal immigrants: in the United States? in Mexico? What political repercussions are likely to follow?

3. If you were the boss of Exxon, what would you have done differently? *Fortune* published an interview with Lawrence Rawl, Exxon's Chief Executive Officer, shortly after the Exxon Valdez spill.[23] Rawl suggested:

   ■ Keeping people with substance abuse problems, such as Captain Hazelwood, from piloting ships.

   ■ Keeping an emergency crew ready to go at all times.

   ■ Having a preplanned public relations strategy ready to go.

   Are you satisfied with these suggestions? If not, what would you do? Why?

4. The Walters grid summarizes several arguments for and against corporate responsibility in social issues. But what is appropriate in the Exxon oil spill? What are Exxon's and Alyeska's responsibilities? The federal government's? The state of Alaska's? Have your ideas on the Walters grid changed as a result of the Exxon case?

5. Exxon has announced that in the future, employees with substance abuse problems will be prohibited from filling positions of liability and responsibility, such as piloting tankers, even if they voluntarily undergo rehabilitation. This has raised concerns among groups worried about the civil rights of such employees. Do you agree? What would your policy be towards people like Captain Hazelwood?

6. If you were a U. S. wheat farmer, what would you like or dislike about the Bonus Incentive Commodity Export Program?

7. What effects would you expect a falling U. S. dollar to have on U. S. wheat exports? How might this help or hurt Canada?

8. What does it mean to "foster an environment that allows efficient farmers to prosper" in relation to the following: export subsidies, minimum price programs, government subsidized farm loans, government transportation policy. Do you really think Hehn had these kinds of effects in mind when he made this statement? Why or why not?

9. What case would you make on behalf of a city that a National Football League franchise is, at least in part, public property? Consider the investment in a stadium, police protection, added roads, etc.

10. As a fan, do you think that professional football is any different from other businesses?

11. Why should NFL owners pay attention to the various constituencies that clamor for their attention? Of what relevance are their concerns to profitability? In particular, is the NFL owner obligated to:
    A. Produce a winner if the stadium is filled without one?
    B. Repay the taxpayers for providing facilities?
    C. Remain in a city if the team is losing money?

ENDNOTES

1. This case is based on a series of articles appearing in the *Wall Street Journal* as follows: George Getschow, "Heading North: Upheaval in Mexico Is Prompting Millions to Resettle in U. S.," May 1, 1985; Matt Moffett and Steve Frazier, "A World Apart: Area along Border of Mexico, U. S. Has a Culture All Its Own," May 3, 1985; Thomas Petzinger, Jr., Mark Zieman, Brian Burrough, and Dianna Solis, "Vital Resources: Illegal Immigrants Are Backbone of Economy in States of Southwest," May 7, 1985; Matt Moffett, "The Gatekeepers: Immigration Service Has Mammoth Task, Minimal Resources," May 9, 1985; Dianna Solis, "On the Move: From Farm to Farm, Migrant Workers Struggle to Survive," May 15, 1985; George Getschow, Thomas Petzinger, Jr., Matt Moffett, and Dianna Solis, "Illegal Immigrants in U. S. Are Problem Defying Easy Solution," May 30, 1985. See also "Business Becomes an Enforcer," *Business Week*, May 16, 1988, pp. 36–37.

2. Milton Friedman, "The Social Responsibility of Business Is to Increase Its Profits," *New York Times Magazine,* September 13, 1970, p. 126.

3. For example, Milton Friedman, *Capitalism and Freedom* (Chicago: University of Chicago Press, 1962), p. 21.

4. Kenneth D. Walters, "Corporate Social Responsibility and Political Ideology," *California Management Review,* 19 (Spring 1977), 40–51.

5. Ibid., p. 46.

6. Ibid., p. 42.

7. Ibid., p. 49.

8. A. L. Kroeber and Clyde Kluckhohn, *Culture* (Cambridge, MA: Harvard University Press, 1952).

9. This definition has been significantly modified from a definition offered by Morton H. Fried, *The Evolution of Political Society* (New York: Random House, 1967), p. 7.

10. Clyde Kluckhohn, et al., "Values and Value-Orientations in the Theory of Action," *Toward a General Theory of Action,* eds. Talcott Parsons and Edward A. Shils (New York: Harper & Row, Torchbooks, 1951), p. 395.

11. John Dewey, *Theory of Valuation* (Chicago: University of Chicago Press—a reprint from the International Encyclopedia of Unified Science, 1939), p. 2.

12. These issues are discussed in more detail in William G. Scott and David K. Hart, *Organizational America* (Boston: Houghton Mifflin, 1979).

13. James Madison, "The Federalist No. 10," *The Federalist,* ed. J. E. Cooke (Middletown, CT: Wesleyan University Press, 1961), p. 59.

14. Ibid., p. 58. Emphasis added.

15. James Willard Hurst, *The Legitimacy of the Business Corporation in the Law of the United States: 1780–1970* (Charlottesville: University Press of Virginia, 1970), pp. 8–9.

16. See the excellent book by Christopher D. Stone, *Where the Law Ends: The Social Control of Corporate Behavior* (New York: Harper & Row, 1975).

17. Stewart Powell, "Lloyd's of London: Modern Risks the Old-Fashioned Way," *U. S. News & World Report,* December 3, 1984, p. 47.

18. From Baumol and Blinder, pp. 667–68.

19. Stefan H. Robock and Kenneth Simmonds, *International Business and Multinational Enterprises* (Homewood, IL: Richard D. Irwin, Inc., 1983), pp. 16–21.

20. Kathleen K. Reardon, "It's the Thought That Counts," *Harvard Business Review,* September–October, 1984, pp.136–41.

21. Adapted from Richard D. Robinson, *International Management,* 2nd ed., (Hinsdale, IL: Dryden Press, 1978), pp. 651–55.

22. Adapted from Maria Recio and Brenton Welling, "The NFL Tries to Recruit Congress," *Business Week,* April 29, 1985, p. 60.

23. "In Ten Years, You'll See Nothing," *Fortune,* May 8, 1989, pp. 50–54.

CHAPTER 4

THE ETHICS OF FREE ENTERPRISE

CHAPTER OUTLINE

LEARNING OBJECTIVES

■ Understand the fundamental moral values underpinning both democracy and capitalism.

■ Explain Adam Smith's basic arguments regarding individual virtue and its central role in capitalism.

■ Understand the connection between a free government and capitalism as both being necessary for individual happiness.

■ Identify the obligations of individuals in a free society to assure that government and the economy function well.

■ Describe the moral system proposed by Adam Smith, and the ways in which his economic system is built upon his moral system.

■ Discuss the relationship between private and public spheres.

■ Understand what is gained by expressing capitalism as the enterprise of free individuals instead of free enterprise.

■ Define the basic moral obligations of capitalism, as conceived by Adam Smith. Describe how capitalism encourages and develops these virtues.

It was Dave White's first big social gathering since being transferred to London with Citibank. The cocktails had been flowing for several hours when he was introduced to John Montague, a guest who did not exactly mix with the crowd of merchant bankers, stock analysts, bankers, and large real estate developers. John, a friend of the host, was from a wealthy background and had graduated from the London School of Economics in 1980. After talking with John a few minutes, Dave could not help but think that John was quite unusual for the British aristocracy. John was a committed socialist and a protégé of the great socialist theoretician, Harold Laskey, who had influenced such luminaries as John F. Kennedy, Pierre Trudeau, and Jamaican Prime Minister, Michael Manley.

Both John and Dave were beginning to feel the effects of the champagne when John casually asked Dave what it was like to uphold the interests of the exploiters of the working class.

"You really must admit that capitalism doesn't have a moral leg to stand on," teased John.

"And you must admit that socialism is nothing more than a formula for shared poverty," retorted Dave.

"Just so much propaganda," rejoined John. "If the capitalists had any loyalty to their countries or, conversely, if they had no havens for their illicit wealth, socialist economies would likely outperform the leading capitalist economies. Every time a socialist government takes power, though, leading businessmen take flight to the U. S. or some other capitalist haven. That's going to change you know," John asserted. "The fundamental issue is fairness, and capitalists just don't care much about that. The people of the world are wising up to the game. The fatal mistake of the Wall Street types is their mass firing of middle managers and the destruction of the middle class as the result of their ever-greedy mergers and acquisitions."

Dave tried to retort, but he realized that John's arguments had a kernel of truth. Dave had read an article in *Fortune* just the previous week detailing the woes of middle managers fired when their companies had been taken over by other firms. In fact, he knew of several competent managers who had been sacked in just such cir-cumstances and realized with regret that one of his former business school classmates had turned to alcohol and then cocaine, nearly destroying his health and family in the process.

Dave had just read Milton Friedman's *Capitalism and Freedom,* however, and replied to John as follows: "Without the freedom to buy and sell freely, political freedom could not exist. Morally, corporations have a duty to make a profit for their shareholders. The duty that you suggest is owed to workers is nice in theory, but doesn't work in practice. By promoting inefficiency, the corporation that holds on to unneeded workers is hastening its own demise and returns nothing to the share-holders or workers when it is placed in bankruptcy. Individual short-term discomfort is a small price to pay for economic efficiency. In the long-run the market will adjust and everyone will be better off."

John just smiled. "How long do you think the middle class is going to be content with your answer, Dave. I mean, even if I agreed that capitalism creates more wealth than socialism, a proposition I reject, isn't it obvious that when enough people become dispossessed, the fact that others are wealthy will only make them angry. When people think the dream is out of reach, they won't be willing to wait for things to get better in the long-run. In the long-run, we're all dead, you know."

While Dave was not convinced, he knew that John would only be convinced by something more than clichés. Dave had seen the misery created by socialist policies in a number of countries, yet he did not have the theoretical background that John possessed and knew that further argument would shed much heat but little light. He determined to research the moral underpinnings of capitalism and to renew this discussion at some later date. ▼

INTRODUCTION

Dave's problem is typical of American businessmen confronted by highly educated socialist thinkers. Most businessmen feel a little guilty and woefully inadequate when confronted with statements such as those made by John. When they come face to face with the inadequacy of their knowledge, they resort to clichés and to what even they realize must sound like self-serving substitutes for analytic thinking. Businesspeople, while essential to our capitalist way of life, do not really understand the system they serve, nor do they understand why they do not get any respect in terms of the social worth of their work.

As many polls indicate, the most serious problem confronting American business is the pervasive low regard in which it is held. In universities, schools of business administration are dismissed as "trade schools," and "business scholarship" is taken as a contradiction in terms. Students majoring in business tend to be apologetic about their choice of a career: They are confident they will earn lots of money, but they seldom view business as an ennobling profession, such as medicine, law, or teaching. Finally, in fiction, drama, films, and television, the qualities of character assumed to be required and produced by business are scorned. One of John Steinbeck's protagonists caught this assumption quite well:

> "It has always seemed strange to me," said Doc. "The things we admire in men, kindness and generosity, openness, honesty, understanding and feeling are the concomitants of failure in our system. And those traits we detest, sharpness, greed, acquisitiveness, meanness, egotism and self-interest are the traits of success. And while men admire the quality of the first they love the produce of the second."[1]

It is not a healthy situation for any society when the major area of employment is believed to corrupt good character. Such egoistic, hedonistic, and "survival-of-the-fittest" attitudes are believed to be essential—even natural—to capitalism. But is that opinion correct? Not really. Americans have focused too much of their attention upon the technical and psychological problems of capitalism. What has been almost totally ignored is that, in the original conception, a necessary moral philosophy had to instruct all economic relations in a true capitalist system.

One of the greatest mistakes made by those who profess a belief in free enterprise is their failure to understand the importance of their philosophical foundations. In the impatience to get at the job at hand, Americans give short shrift to the moral philosophy that instructs the task. It is just assumed that everyone *knows* right from wrong and no efforts need to be made to develop that understanding. Nothing could be further from the truth.

It is commonplace in surveys to ask Americans if they believe in the Bill of Rights (they do) and then to ask them specific questions involving the application of those rights. Almost invariably the second answers contradict the first. For instance, the vast majority of Americans profess a belief in freedom of speech. Yet when asked if a communist should be allowed to speak at the local high school, many would refuse to allow the person to speak, indicating a lack of clarity about basic democratic values and the values behind our economic system.

The practical person might argue that businesspeople do not need to concern themselves with moral philosophy, since it is not of the "real world." The important thing is to get the job done. But looking at the power added to the numerous Marxist movements throughout the world, the perils of ignoring the moral foundations of capitalism are apparent. The irony of it is that the moral justification for capitalism is both thoroughly developed and morally acceptable within the framework of the fundamental values of this nation. The great spokesman for capitalism, Adam Smith, provided a powerful moral and economic philosophy, one which has been sadly misinterpreted in contemporary times.

How does this relate to business ethics? Another major mistake is the tendency to believe that business ethics involve only a set of rules to guide managers through the shoals of regulation without breaking the law. Some firms flaunt their ethical codes as a visible manifestation of an inward state of grace. But **ethics** are neither rules to stay out of jail by, nor a public relations patina: ethics involve the fundamental values that should instruct the lives of individuals in a democratic society with a free enterprise system. To understand those ethical premises requires the understanding of some moral philosophy.

Furthermore, it was also evident that capitalism (correctly understood) and democracy, as conceived by the Founding Fathers, were both rooted in a similar set of moral assumptions: that the justification and success of each system was dependent upon the individual virtue of all members of the society. The real strength, indeed the purpose, of society was to be found in the pervasiveness of virtue in the rank and file, much more than in the leaders. James Madison, in 1788, expressed the belief quite well:

> I go on this great republican principle, that the people will have virtue and intelligence to select men of virtue and wisdom. Is there no virtue among us? If there be

not, we are in a wretched situation. No theoretical checks—no form of government can render us secure. To suppose that any form of government will secure liberty or happiness without any virtue in the people, is a chimerical idea. If there be sufficient virtue and intelligence in the community, it will be exercised in the selection of these men. So that we do not depend on their virtue, or put confidence in our rulers, but in the people who are to choose them.[2]

The same condition is also true for a capitalist system and, in both cases, such citizen virtue had to be freely attained. They understood that virtue is not achieved through compulsion.

THE SIGNIFICANCE OF ADAM SMITH

The seminal philosopher of capitalism is, of course, Adam Smith (1723–1790), a professor of moral philosophy at the University of Glasgow, and later a commissioner of customs in Edinburgh. The foundations of capitalism are assumed to have been stated in his book *The Wealth of Nations* (1776),[3] but this is a misperception. Smith wrote an earlier book, *The Theory of Moral Sentiments* (1759),[4] wherein he laid out the necessary moral philosophy by which his later economic work was to be understood. By paying attention only to *The Wealth of Nations,* the most essential element of the free enterprise system he proposed is missed: that in order to work correctly, all economic relations had to be based upon intentional individual virtue.[5]

Adam Smith did not complete his philosophic system. However, he believed that his work would be interpreted within its intellectual context and then extended along the lines of its own moral logic. Thus, an understanding of the Scottish Enlightenment of the eighteenth century is the beginning of an understanding of the moral foundations of capitalism.[6] Perversely, the tendency has been to misinterpret Adam Smith as a utilitarian, through the philosophy of Jeremy Bentham and the Philosophic Radicals—a position he had emphatically rejected. As a result, the contemporary theory of capitalism has a decidedly utilitarian orientation, ironically based upon the egoism and hedonism Smith had gone to such lengths to reject. As such, contemporary capitalism has made a critical deviation from the original intention.

Utilitarianism[7] has led to some gross distortions of Adam Smith's original intentions, perhaps best summarized in the loathsome phrase "Well, business is business!" It expresses the assumption that an individual or firm may use just about any tactics, fair or foul, to gain economic advantage over another, and that it is all justified in the name of "the bottom line." Nothing could be further from the intention of Adam Smith, or from our Founding Fathers. It is this disparity between the Smithian ideal of capitalism, and the "calculus of self-interest" theories of contemporary capitalism that is at the root of the public disaffection with business. Confidence will not be restored until both the theory and practice of capitalism have been restructured to be congruent with the intent of both our country's founders and Adam Smith.

The eighteenth-century thinker Adam Smith, often misperceived as the originator of utilitarian economic theory, advocated a moral philosophy of capitalism based on individual virtue.

The central premise of this chapter is that the moral philosophy expounded by Adam Smith should serve as the ethical basis for contemporary American capitalism. Furthermore, those values must govern all managerial actions and prescriptions in business firms. Three reasons are advanced in support of this statement: (1) the values that form the basis of Smith's moral philosophy are morally correct; (2) the free enterprise system, as conceived by Adam Smith, will not function well unless those values are used as its necessary a priori;[8] (3) Smith's values are congruent with the values of the founders of this nation, as embodied in the enabling documents of our Republic. For that reason, capitalism (correctly conceived) is essential for American democracy (correctly conceived).

A NATION OF INDIVIDUALS

That reluctant democrat, Alexis de Tocqueville, lamented the fact that the inexorable movement toward democracy would spell the demise of national glory and individual nobility. In a famous passage, he paid homage to all of the noble characteristics that would fade away with the onset of democratic governments. Replacing them would be the mundane virtues of the middle class.

> But if you hold it expedient to divert the moral and intellectual activity of man to the production of comfort and the promotion of general well-being; if a clear understanding be more profitable to man than genius; if your object is not to stimulate the virtues of heroism, but the habits of peace; if you had rather witness vices than crimes, and are content to meet with fewer noble deeds, provided offenses be diminished in the same proportion; if, instead of living in the midst of a brilliant society, you are contented to have prosperity around you; if, in short, you are of the opinion that the principal object of a government is not to confer the greatest possible power and glory upon the body of the nation, but to ensure the greatest enjoyment and to avoid the most misery to each of the individuals who compose it—if such be your desire, then equalize the conditions of men and establish democratic institutions.[9]

That diminished notion of what democracy would engender has been, surprisingly, rather enduring. However, it is essentially incorrect. Our Founding Fathers had a somewhat larger conception of the possibilities of democracy. In spite of many fundamental disagreements, they believed in, and worked to achieve, a nation based upon individuals.

A Government to Serve Individuals

The early American thinkers were quite concerned about the moral character of the citizens of the nation, but they emphatically rejected the classical notion that the purpose of the state was to produce the highest character among those fit to be called citizens. Instead, they took a much bolder path. In spite of some profound differences, they understood that the virtue of individual citizens was the essential condition for a stable democracy, and that such virtue was only reliable when it was achieved without compulsion by individuals acting of their own volition.

The founders of our country understood that a nation could single out a special class or special people and, by subsidizing them and their talents, could produce exceptional people. But such a privileged class would require diminishing the lives of the majority. Even though the masses could bask in the luster of the achievement of the special few, that would not be sufficient recompense for their blighted life possibilities. Such a condition would lay the seeds of revolution and would guarantee political instability. But more than that, the Founding Fathers believed that individuals, by their nature, deserved those conditions that would allow them to achieve the potentials for their lives. It was for that reason they agreed with Jefferson's elegant summation of "Life, Liberty and the pursuit of Happiness."

To achieve the end of the fulfillment of individual lives, our Revolutionary leaders set about designing a new form of government that would provide order and stability, yet at the same time give ample opportunity for the development of individual talents. Central to their ideal was the role of the business system. Implicit in all that they did was a set of assumptions about the obligations of the individuals who would be the citizens of the new Republic. In order for the new forms to work and for the ideal to be achieved, each citizen incurred a series of obligations. Two of the most basic of those obligations were as follows.

The Obligations of Individuals in a Free Society

MORAL RESPONSIBILITY   First, each individual had the obligation to assume individual moral responsibility. Where injustice was encountered, it could not be passed off as the responsibility of institutions or other individuals. Individuals had the obligation to rectify unjust situations whenever they encountered them. If injustice was not seen as an individual challenge, then people would surrender the obligation to do something about it and would await a powerful leader to do it for them. The founders of our nation understood that the willingness to evade individual moral responsibility was the surest way to bring about a dictatorial form of government.

INDIVIDUAL INITIATIVE   Second, individuals had the obligation to develop their talents as far as they could. The Founding Fathers had a Puritan abhorrence of sloth, but even more they understood that democracy would perish and the economic system would not function properly if the people were not energetic in their pursuit of individual excellence and talent. The capitalist system they chose was first and foremost an economic system that provided the maximum advantage to all of the individuals in the society. It was the perfect, even necessary, counterpart of the democratic political system. It was chosen, however, for much better reasons than simple economic efficiency.

The Enterprise System Required by a Free People

It was Adam Smith's intention to outline that form of an enterprise system necessary for a free people, one which would conform to the innate moral needs of all individuals. Because all individuals are free, by nature, a successful economic system must reflect and enhance that condition of freedom. Smith's economic philosophy is quite complex, but it is necessary to consider five areas if we are to reorient our thinking about contemporary capitalism.

TRUTH VERSUS RELATIVISM   One of the most pervasive and destructive characteristics of American business theorists and practitioners is their refusal to consider the truth about the moral nature of the individual. They define truth as relative, something that changes with circumstances. All of the various theories of human nature are treated as offerings in an ethical cafeteria, with individuals free to choose any conception that fits their fancy because all are equally true. But even that is a bit of a charade, for most business theorists postulate a theory of innate human malleability as the truth—a theory congruent to the needs of modern organizations.[10]

Yet both Adam Smith and our Founding Fathers believed that they had discovered the basic truth about the moral nature of the individual. For them, all individuals were born with an innate need for, and ability to comprehend, that form of true happiness that was the result of a life of virtue. The founders of our country embodied these concepts in the enabling documents of our nation, which means that the political, legal, and social systems of the U. S. are predicated upon the assumption of their truth. That dependence is acknowledged in American oaths of office, demands for rights, and legal precedents.

Our early American leaders also believed that the economic system must be rooted in human virtue, and thus their thinking was compatible with that of Adam Smith and his Scottish colleagues. Democracy and capitalism were to be mutually reinforcing systems. Thus, it is necessary that the ethical assumptions underlying our economic system be congruent with those underlying the political system.

SYMPATHY   Central to an understanding of the economic philosophy of Adam Smith is the absolute importance of the concept of **sympathy**. He begins his first book with the bold assertion that men desire the happiness of others:

> How selfish soever man may be supposed, there are evidently some principles in his nature, which interest him in the fortune of others, and render their happiness necessary to him, though he derives nothing from it, except the pleasure of seeing it.[11]

This innate desire for the happiness of others is rooted in the natural need of individuals to sympathize (or empathize) with others.

Thus, all human relationships must be based upon a mutual sympathy of one for another, or else society will degenerate to the level of the Hobbesean war of "all against all." It is thus the primary moral obligation of each individual to develop consciously a feeling of love for all other individuals. To put it another way, each individual has the moral obligation to develop a sense of "brotherhood" and "sisterhood" with all other individuals—using those terms in their secular sense. As a final note, while people sympathize with both the sorrow and the joy of others, in fact they appreciate the joy of others more than their sorrow. Sympathy, in Smith's terms, was a very positive emotion.

Smith makes the obvious observation that people sympathize most adequately with those closest to them, and that the love of mankind is a form of moral **supererogation** (something above and beyond what is expected in human behavior). In other words, sympathy is not an easy task, but it is essential. It is a little less clear why people need to love others. Implicit in his writing is the assumption that human beings are, by nature, designed to view others as brothers or sisters, and to desire to be considered in the same manner by them. Humans not only need to love others, but to be loved by them. To put it another way, the highest relationship is to be loved by those whom we love.

Thus, all relationships in society—including economic relationships—must be guided by the sense of sympathy. This means that an individual must never take advan-

Displaying a sense of moral responsibility and sympathy for employee welfare, management at the Lowell mills in the 1830s
originally provided young women workers with comfortable
housing, recreational facilities, and instructional classes.

tage of others to advance his or her own cause. Smith is adamant about this, referring
to it as "... one of those sacred rules, upon which the tolerable observation of which
depends the whole security and peace of human society." He goes on to write:

> One individual must never prefer himself so much even to any other individual as to
> hurt or injure that other in order to benefit himself, though the benefit to the one
> should be much greater than the hurt or injury to the other. . . . [F]or one man to
> deprive another unjustly of any thing, or unjustly to promote his own advantage to
> the loss or disadvantage of another, is more contrary to nature than death, than pov-
> erty, than pain, than all the misfortunes which can affect him, either in his body, or in
> his external circumstances.[12]

One of the seamiest, most destructive aspects of the conventional wisdom about contemporary capitalism is that one is justified in taking advantage of others in order to increase profits. That is anathema to the correct theory of capitalism, whether it occurs in the impossible glorification of a product, the deliberate concealing of necessary information, or downright cheating. The justificatory phrase of "business is business" should be indicted for what it is: a contradiction of the most fundamental premise of capitalism, the sense of sympathy.

THE INNATE NEED FOR VIRTUE   Smith's view of the infinite moral worth of the individual permeates his work, and is reflected most clearly in his belief in the innate and imperative need of each individual for a life of virtue. The **virtuous qualities**—honor, justice, courage, magnanimity, benevolence, etc.—are the necessary conditions for true happiness. As John Locke said:

> For, God having, by an inseparable connexion, joined virtue and public happiness together, and made the practice thereof necessary to the preservation of society, and visibly beneficial to all with whom the virtuous man has to do; it is no wonder that every one should not only allow, but recommend and magnify those rules to others, from whose observance of them he is sure to reap advantage to himself.[13]

Praise versus Praiseworthiness   The necessity of virtue is well illustrated by Smith's distinction between "praise" and "praiseworthiness." Obviously, all people seek praise and go to great—even fraudulent—means to obtain it. But of more interest is the fact that true happiness comes not from the praise, but the awareness of one's praiseworthiness. Smith argues that true **praise** is evoked only by virtue made manifest in both intention and action. Thus, true praise acknowledges the moral worth of the individual in the esteem of loved others. But the happiness to the recipient comes only from the knowledge that the praise is both earned and deserved—being **praiseworthy**. Anything that denies or inhibits the possibilities of praiseworthiness (found only in the life of virtue), either internal (lack of education) or external (unjust institutions), denies the natural rights of the individual. The implications for the economic system are extraordinary, for it means that every economic relationship must be intentionally conducted with virtue.

Smith looked upon virtue a bit differently. For him, virtue was not fully realized by simply doing what is necessary. For instance, if a person falls to the ground with a stroke, and another goes to his aid, the act is of minimal virtue—the other is obligated (through sympathy) to help. Virtue is realized in carrying the ordinary obligations further than is required, and seeking excellence in them. Thus, to assist the stroke victim is but an obligation, while going the extra mile (perhaps by paying his medical bill if he is indigent) is a manifestation of virtue—an attempt to love another member of the human race.

Prudence   Adam Smith argues for the necessity of moral progress. This means that virtue—and the conditions of virtue—must constantly improve, or happiness will stagnate and disappear. Those who misinterpret Smith believe that his was a moral philosophy "fit only for shopkeepers," but they fail to understand his conception of a higher virtue realized through moral progress. To illustrate, he contrasts simple prudence (a "cold" passion) with the **superior prudence** that was his ideal:

> Wise and judicious conduct, when directed to greater and nobler purposes than the care of health, the fortune, the rank, and reputation, of the individual, is frequently and very properly called Prudence. We talk of the prudence of the great general, of the great statesman, of the great legislator. Prudence is, in all these cases, combined with many greater and more splendid virtues; with valour, with extensive and strong benevolence, with a sacred regard to the rules of justice, and all these supported by a proper degree of self-command. This superior prudence, when carried to the highest degree of perfection, necessarily supposes the art, the talent, and the habit or disposition of acting with the most perfect propriety in every possible circumstance and situation. It necessarily supposes the utmost perfection of all the intellectual and of all the moral virtues. It is the best head joined to the best heart. It is the most perfect wisdom combined with the most perfect virtue.[14]

Smith treats superior prudence with such approbation that it quickly becomes clear that it is his ideal for all people, even though most will not achieve it because of the injustices of the conditions of their lives.

The great enemy of the life of virtue was not so much sin as it was **sloth**: the tendency toward inertia in all human beings. True virtue requires enormous and continuous effort, in many areas. The main reason societies lose the ideal social, economic, and political arrangements is that they rest on their oars, after the great effort of achieving the ideal. It is sloth that defeats man. The life of virtue allows for no rest.

INTENTIONAL VIRTUE   For the most part, contemporary theories of capitalism ignore morality in the processes discussing production and consumption. They fall back upon a notion that an unfettered economic system based upon insatiable human greed will result in an overall public good—"private vices, public interest." The arbiter is to be the "market," guided by an "invisible hand." This viewpoint is a flagrant misinterpretation of the Smithian "invisible hand." The concept is most clearly developed in *The Theory of Moral Sentiments,* and the adequate operation of the invisible hand is dependent upon the intentional grounding of all economic relationships in virtue. When that happens, one can then trust that the randomness of the market in the selection of goods and services will be just and equitable.

SMITH'S IDEAL SOCIETY   Smith uses, throughout his work, a dual standard: the ideal society and the minimal society. He wrote:

> It is thus that man, who can subsist only in society, was fitted by nature to that situation for which he was made. All members of human society stand in need of each other's assistance, and are likewise exposed to mutual injuries. Where the necessary assistance is reciprocally afforded from love, from gratitude, from friendship, and esteem, the society flourishes and is happy. All the different members of it are bound together by the agreeable bands of love and affection, and are, as it were, drawn to one common centre of mutual good offices.[15]

This was the **ideal society** and, contradicting those who condemn Smith for a want of idealism, he believed such a society was not only obtainable, but had historic precedents.

THE MINIMALIST SOCIETY   However, Smith followed his description of the ideal with a description of the **minimal society**:

■ But though the necessary assistance should not be afforded from such generous and disinterested motives, though among the different members of the society there should be no mutual love and affection, the society, though less happy and agreeable, will not necessarily be dissolved. Society may subsist among different men, as among different merchants, from a sense of utility, without any mutual love or affection; and though no man in it should owe any obligation, or be bound in gratitude to any other, it may still be upheld by a mercenary exchange of good offices according to an agreed valuation.[16]

Interestingly, this statement is descriptive of contemporary America, a minimal society run by utilitarian rules. Utilitarianism has been adopted because Americans have largely abandoned the primacy of virtue in human affairs. This situation would have been soundly denounced by Adam Smith, as it was by Montesquieu:

■ But if the spirit of commerce unites nations, it does not in the same manner unite individuals. We see in countries where the people move only by the spirit of commerce, they make a traffic of all the humane, all the moral virtues; the most trifling things, those which humanity would demand, are there done, or there given, only for money.[17]

The major reason Americans have abandoned this ideal is that they lack courage. Virtue does not come for free. It requires moral risk taking, a willingness to base all actions upon your own sense of virtue, and, even more difficult, upon the sense of virtue of others. In this sense, the term "entrepreneur" applies not only to those individuals who are willing to risk money, but, more importantly, to those who are willing to risk all based upon their willingness to trust others. Thus, it becomes **moral entrepreneurism**, which is the heart and soul of capitalism.

This brings us to the crux of the contemporary misinterpretation of capitalism. The prior intention to bring virtue into every economic exchange was taken for granted. Once you were virtuous, then you could produce and sell in the market without trying to prejudge what is best for people. You could make a guess and submit that product to the test of the market, expecting a decent profit for your honorable endeavors. When it is put in this context, Smith's seemingly cynical observation about why the butcher sells you meat does not seem so cynical after all. An honorable butcher sells meat to people because it is his business, and he wants to make a decent profit. That is a completely admirable intention, provided that it is preceded by a prior imposition of virtue into all of his business behaviors.

In such a conception, then, the market emerges as the greatest arena for the resolution of problems that the world could imagine. Its participants were to be virtuous people, committed to excellence, who then offered imaginative goods and services to others in a great plurality. It was then that the "invisible hand" would operate as it was intended.

The Job as a Medium

Because of the essential nature of the economic process, it is often overlooked that Smith viewed working in larger terms. To put it simply, he viewed the job as a medium, wherein an individual could express himself or herself. In the terms of this essay, however, it was a medium wherein virtue could be developed and experienced. It is commonplace to observe that each economic transaction is also an education in economics: We learn how to be proficient buyers and sellers. For this reason, classical economic theory can assume that each adult will be instructed in economics. This is an acceptable proposition.

However, for Adam Smith, even more was involved. Each economic transaction was also to be an exercise in virtue. The assumption was that when one had preceded the exchange with intentional virtue, the exchange itself would be both an education in, and an experience of, virtue. This is best caught in the splendid phrase, "my handshake is my bond." Furthermore, since the attainment of virtue required no special talents, it was a condition that could be achieved by all. It was in the virtuous action that true equality was to be experienced. Thus, for Adam Smith, honor was to be found in endeavor and not in position. No reasonable task should ever be viewed as trivial.

To summarize, Smith viewed the processes of economic exchange, of production and consumption, not merely as necessary actions to ensure the continuance of life. Correctly understood, they were the means to human happiness, for nations as well as for individuals:

> By such maxims as these, however, nations have been taught that their interest consisted in beggaring all their neighbours. Each nation has been made to look with an invidious eye upon the prosperity of all nations with which it trades, and to consider their gain as its own loss. Commerce, which ought naturally to be, among nations, as among individuals, a bond of union and friendship, has become the most fertile source of discord and animosity.[18]

The economic system was to reinforce, and even to become the arena for the attainment and experience of virtue, which was the primary instrument of human happiness.

The Public Realm and the Private Realm

People today engage in a great deal of discussion about the difference between the conception of the public realm and the private realm. In particular, business leaders decry the intrusion of the public power into the private realm, arguing that public values are inimical to the conduct of business in a free society. These leaders are correct, even if they do not really understand why this is true. When queried, they invariably contend that the private realm is more efficient than the public realm. This may be correct some of the time, but is not an invariable condition. When asked to provide reasons beyond the "frail reed" of efficiency, they mutter something about "free enterprise" and that is supposed to end it. Unfortunately, although the distinction between the two realms is very important, it is not understood well at all.

PRIVATE VALUES AND THE PUBLIC REALM   While all of the attention has been given to the public intrusion into the private realm, the more prevalent trend has been the intrusion of private values into the public realm. This has occurred in a very subtle manner, scarcely noticed by scholars and practitioners alike.

The major advances in the administration of organizational personnel have taken place in business, and public administration scholars and practitioners have flocked like lemmings to the private sector for the administrative techniques, procedures, and criteria. But they have not come for free, for along with them come the values upon which they are based. Thus, the values of the private realm have been smuggled into the public realm to such an extent that any realistic conception of the distinctive characteristics of public service has been nearly lost. Public administration is moribund, a sickly cousin of business administration.

The founders of our nation were most emphatic about the importance of distinguishing between the two realms and maintaining that distinction in practice. They did not question that the activities appropriate to the private realm were superior to the activities appropriate to the public realm. For them, the major ambitions and desires of individuals were to be realized in the private realm. Contrary to our time, service in a public office was viewed as a duty—something to be performed well, but also to be escaped from as soon as possible. The classic example is Thomas Jefferson, who so detested the Presidency that he could hardly wait to return to civilian life.

Be that as it may, the main reason that the private realm was seen as superior to the public realm had to do with the quality of individual lives. Today, the argument is most often couched in terms of comparative economic efficiency, but that was not the most important distinction.

THE NATURE OF THE PUBLIC   What is most important can be seen by looking at the nature of the public. The notion of the public pertains to that which is common to everyone, and thus the public rules, or laws, are equally binding upon all. That being the case, to increase the scope of public influence through laws is to promote homogeneity because it brings more people under rules that do not allow for uniqueness among individuals. This is the fatal contradiction in the arguments of Milton Friedman about the social responsibilities of business. For this reason, then, our early American leaders advocated, in fact demanded, minimal state intrusion into the lives of individuals—that government is best which governs least. Finally, in line with their ideas about the individual and the attainment of virtue they wanted those good attributes to come about voluntarily, not by compulsion. Voluntarism is too important to be superseded by public rules. This meant that the numbers of people who serve in the public sector should be few. Furthermore, it meant that the rewards of public service were to be unique and not really commensurate with the rewards in the private sector.

The Sanctity of Private Property

The great virtue of the private realm was to be the freedom from compulsion. Because of that freedom, individuals were to have the opportunity to develop that which was unique to themselves, without either compulsion or constraint. Thus, the real importance of the private realm was that it was to be the place where the essential development of individuals took place. The undeniable economic advantages were an inevitable by-product. The very soul of American pluralism was to be nurtured in the freedoms of the private sector.

Given this heightened purpose for the private realm, the phrase "**right to privacy**" takes on a much enlarged meaning. Today, it is taken to mean simply that the government should not snoop in our personal affairs. But in the true sense of the term, the right to privacy refers to all of the conditions necessary for the achievement of personal individuality.

The true scope of the right to privacy, however, includes only those things which are (or should be) under the control of individuals—their "private property," whether home, possessions, or business. Furthermore, the characteristics of selfhood can also be encompassed within the phrase. At the basic level, the importance of private property stems from the fact that it is a place where public authority cannot enter—which is to say that both the political authorities and the public homogenizing rules cannot enter. Another advantage is that the possession of material things gives individuals a vested interest in the society, which tends to promote the stability of the social system.

But the more important argument for the sanctity of private property lies in the fact that it is the place for the embodiment of that which is unique about self. The most obvious example is, of course, one's own home. It is there that one can, without fear of others, imprint himself or herself most effectively. But it was also intended that one should be able to accomplish that in one's work. In fact, that was to be the main area for the expression of individual uniqueness. The dream of course, was of a widely various and multifaceted society, which is the essence of pluralism, that would be the inevitable product of a society of self-actualizing individuals. Again, the economic benefits were important, but secondary. However, the economic efficiencies resulting from such a system would be extraordinary.

This sanctity of private property entails a major obligation for individuals. While no one is, of course, compelled to develop self, nonetheless, if the system is to work as it should, individuals are required, of their own volition, to assume the obligation to understand, develop, and embody that which is unique about self. Unless this obligation is taken seriously, two major problems arise. First, individuals fail to realize their potentials, and thus fail to achieve happiness. As a result, they betray the society by failing to pursue happiness. Second, if they do not seek that uniqueness the very essential creativity in the society dwindles away. The assumption was that such a free system would promote such a multitude of ideas that creative solutions would be found for every problem. Not to pursue uniqueness is to betray the society.

The Enterprise of Free Individuals

In contemporary America, whenever the phrase "free enterprise" is used, it is used in reference to the entire system, and demands that the "enterprises" to be left free refer to specific organizations. One has the feeling that the corporate chieftain, like Moses, is calling out "let my corporation go!" CEOs want their companies to be left alone by the government (unless they want a bailout), but that infers nothing at all about the freedom, or lack of the same, for the individuals employed by those companies. Such an oversight is not only foolish, it misses the whole purpose for making enterprise free. If the phrase "free enterprise system" is reworded to "the system of enterprise of free individuals," the correct (and functional) meaning becomes clearer.

The key element in that economic system—that which justifies and defines it—must be the degree of freedom enjoyed by the individuals within that economic system. The irony of the contemporary use of the term "free enterprise" is that it refers to an organizational freedom, but it says nothing about the freedom of the individuals within those organizations. It is fair to say that the average business firm is rather authoritarian—as far as affairs are conducted within it. Thus, the argument that the U.S. has a free economic system has some significant weaknesses.

The rewording of "free enterprise" to "the enterprise of free individuals" focuses attention on the true problem: What organizational forms should the enterprise of free individuals take on? A system of free enterprise, then, means much more than just the production and distribution of goods and services. It must be a system that maximizes individual freedom. To do that, two issues are particularly important: contract and work.

CONTRACT   Freedom is not too great a problem for owners, professionals, and other independents. Their biggest problem is to understand the nature of freedom in the economic arena, to believe in that freedom, and then to convert those beliefs into practical action. The larger problem is with the vast majority of people employed within large organizations. What does freedom mean to their employers and what does it mean to them?

One of the most dismaying assumptions is the belief that those who pay the salaries can do almost anything they wish to do, and if employees do not like it, then they can go someplace else (expressed well in the phrase "it's my way or the highway"). The other, more critical point, is the assumption that those who pay the salaries have the right to suspend those political rights guaranteed by the Constitution. In other words, we have in fact granted employers the right to ignore certain basic political rights simply because of their control over money.

Aside from this being morally wrong, another consideration is that the free enterprise system does not work as well as it should when the importance of individual freedom is not recognized and embodied within the economic system. The system was designed to capitalize upon, and promote, those energies and talents that are released when free individuals are engaged in economic endeavor. If organizations

With the militia maintaining order during the 1912 strike in Lawrence, Massachusetts, textile workers eventually won the right to unionize and bargain collectively for work contracts.

are too authoritarian, few of the advantages that come from free individuals will accrue to them and the phrase "free enterprise" becomes a mockery. The primary justification of the system is the degree of freedom of the citizens within the system.

Managers may ask if the above advocates anarchy within their organizations, with visions of hippies doing their own thing on company time. Not at all. More to the point, however, is the real sadness in such a question, for it is just another indication of how far Americans have drifted from any knowledge of what freedom means. The disparity is evident in the desire of business leaders for a free economic system, but who cannot comprehend management within such a system without command.

The answer to this problem lies in rediscovering and applying the true meaning of the concept of contract. In the U. S., lawyers have claimed the concept—making it over into a legal problem that requires their professional services. The essence of its correct meaning, in the sense it is used here, is contained in the phrase: "my handshake is my bond," which imposes a moral obligation over the legal obligations. A contract is a bargain struck between honorable individuals, wherein the conditions for work are laid down. In terms of employment, at the minimum it means the employer agrees to pay a specific wage, and the employee agrees to produce a specific product. But more is involved. An employer, as an honorable person, cannot ask more of the employee than a free individual can give up (for example, the right to dignity, to privacy, etc.). Conversely, the employee, as an honorable person, can never surrender the nonnegotiable rights, or both free enterprise and democracy will be ruined. Some things are completely beyond negotiation and compromise such as racism, sexism, etc. Therefore, correctly understood, a contract is an association that only free and honorable individuals can enter into.

WORK   The next important distinction lies in the nature of work. It can only be understood by contrasting it with labor. This was a distinction many of the ancients understood quite well, and it was central to their moral philosophies.

Labor is what all animals must do to stay alive, to satisfy their animal nature. To the extent that humans have an animal nature, they must labor. If they, however, are never able to transcend labor, then they are forevermore the captive of that animal nature. It was not only in religion that they were to transcend the animal within, they were also to do it within the political and the economic spheres. In economics, this was achieved through the medium of work. Correctly understood, work was and is a purely human endeavor: Work is achieved when we can embody that which is unique about self upon something in the outside world. It requires, at the fundamental level, that individuals are able to comprehend their own uniqueness. Then it requires a medium for expression, a medium within which to make such an embodiment, and the freedom to express oneself upon the chosen medium.

The great moral obligation of business leadership thus is that *business leaders must be the guardians and guarantors of the possibilities of work for all people.* Thus the problems of individual freedom within the organization are met through the medium of the contract among honorable individuals. Such freedom is expressed in the possibilities of work. Since this motivation to work stems from one of our most powerful innate drives, its satisfaction leads to excellence and harmony. Economic excellence and harmony for the entire economy are possible if top management is just smart enough and brave enough to risk it.

Some very formidable moral obligations emerge from this conception of free enterprise. Managers have the moral obligation not only to provide work, but also to work. This presupposes that all parties are knowledgeable about the nature of work. As in all worthwhile activities in human life, philosophical understanding necessarily precedes practical application if full meaning is to be derived from the action. Further obligations include industriousness and continual creativity.

The rationale for such an economic system was the belief that this should be a nation of variety, not of homogeneity. The free enterprise system should be the primary instrument of that variety, the institutional and philosophical enemy of conformity. The result is a moral duty to oppose all homogeneity and mediocrity. An even broader meaning is apparent. All of that free-flowing creativity would ultimately result in the solution of all of the material problems of our society. Thus, the primary justification of the market is that it is the arena for releasing human creativity.

Further Obligations of Free Enterprise

One of the most venerable subjects in political philosophy is the concept of virtue: the qualities of excellent character necessary for the good life. Both the moral philosophers of the Enlightenment and the founders of our country believed that democracy could not be achieved unless all citizens were virtuous. The same is true for a free enterprise system, although traditionally the matter of virtue has not been central to economic thought. Regardless, certain qualities of character are required of citizens and are necessary to make both the political and economic systems function well. A few are listed below.

THE OBLIGATION TO ACT HONORABLY   The importance of rationality to the economic system is accepted without discussion; the consensus being that without rationality the system will not work. While rationality is important, it is even more important to act with honor. The ideal of capitalism is dependent upon honoring one's work (or contract), not engaging in deceptive practices, and not denying others their rights. In the original conception, the entrepreneurial behavior was defined as risk taking, not so much with money, but with people. The true entrepreneur is one who is willing to trust others, upon the exchange of their "handshakes." Granted, some will cheat, but they will be in the minority and their actions must not be allowed to undermine the importance of moral entrepreneurism.

Honor requires the constant improvement of conditions, as well as constant honorable conduct from business leaders. In this sense, it means that the most important characteristic of business leadership is **noblesse oblige**, which is the obligation of the leaders to treat others as honorable men and women. The Founders disagreed about many things, but not about this. The political and economic systems work best when all participants act honorably.

In this sense, the market becomes the school for honor. One of the articles of faith of capitalism is that in the market each economic exchange serves as an economic education for the participants. In this way, the market is the primary educator of people as to the requirements for economic behavior. In the same way, the market should act as the great educator of people into the concept of honor. Each economic exchange should also be evaluated as to the degree of honor involved. The market should become the arena for, and guarantor of, honor in the society.

THE OBLIGATION TO CIVILITY   The *Oxford English Dictionary* defines **civility** as that conduct necessary for "civilized intercourse among people." It is a concept much discussed by political philosophers as an essential characteristic of any stable humane society. What is not so well understood is the relationship of civility to capitalism.

First, all of the virtues that make one an effective democrat are also necessary for capitalism and are, in fact, enlarged by it. But a more particular meaning for civility is required. John Rawls developed the idea well when he wrote about the natural duty of civility. He began by arguing that individuals must never acquiesce in the denial of their basic liberties. Beyond that, however, they must not expect too much from human institutions.

> Instead, we submit our conduct to democratic authority only to the extent necessary to share equitably in the inevitable imperfections of a constitutional system. Accepting these hardships is simply recognizing and being willing to work within the limits imposed by the circumstances of human life. In view of this, we have a natural duty of civility not to invoke the faults of social arrangements as a too ready excuse for not complying with them, nor to exploit inevitable loopholes in the rules to advance our interests. The duty of civility imposes a due acceptance of the defects of institutions and a certain restraint in taking advantage of them. Without some recognition of this duty, mutual trust and confidence are liable to break down.[19]

He might have added that such a breakdown leads inexorably to increased rules and regulations.

THE OBLIGATION TO PRODUCE SURPLUSES   It is axiomatic that profitability is essential to capitalism and the primary justification for the production of surpluses is freedom: Surpluses free people from the slavery of necessity. Without surpluses, division of labor, research and development, finance capital, and leisure time do not exist. Surpluses are essential to democracy.

THE OBLIGATION TO PURSUE HAPPINESS   Jefferson was quite serious when he chose the phrase "the pursuit of happiness" for the Declaration of Independence. His definition of the term "happiness" was similar to the Stoic definition, and it was nearly synonymous with the conception of virtue. Happiness could only be achieved through right conduct. It was not the gratification of immediate desires, as the utilitarians would have it. (For instance, contrast Jefferson's meaning of happiness with the writings of Bentham, who conceived of happiness as the maximization of pleasure and the minimization of pain). The achievement of happiness in capitalism is more important than achieving efficiency. The system breaks down if all do not pursue happiness, in the sense of happiness coming from virtue.

COMPARATIVE STUDY: CAPITALISM AND COMMUNISM

The moral principles that underlie the free enterprise system have been reviewed at length. Without attempting to present an in-depth view of capitalism's major competitor in the marketplace of ideas, communism, a number of contrasts can be made. (See Box 4-1 for a comparison of the ethical and moral assumptions underlying both systems.) It is important to realize that communism in its true form does not exist anywhere in the world today; the system actually in place is socialism.

   Socialism is the last stage of the dialectic leading to the establishment of communism. Deviations from pure equality are justified in this intermediate stage because

Box 4-1
Capitalism versus Communism

ISSUE	CAPITALISM	COMMUNISM
View of Man	Man's highest achievements result when he is left free to develop his own potential as he sees fit. Man is capable of attaining a high moral life if left free.	A new man, free from corrupting influences (greed, exploitativeness) will emerge as capitalism and its perpetrators are suppressed and "made impossible."
Control of Property	Control of property is necessary for economic efficiency and political freedom. Abuse of property rights can be controlled by the state.	Property belongs to society as a whole and private ownership is not appropriate. State control is necessary until new man emerges and all ownership is abolished.
Profits	Profits are a necessary payment to those who supply capital. Profits honestly achieved are moral and ultimately benefit society.	All value is represented by the labor embodied in a product. Profit is the theft of this labor value from workers.
Role of the State	Government's purpose is to protect the freedom of individuals in the enjoyment of their inalienable rights, including the right to own and use property.	Promote the general welfare as exclusively determined by the communist party. Individual rights only exist to the extent that they further this end.
History	History reflects an evolution from rights based on status to rights based on contract. History is not inevitably moving in any direction and can be influenced by individuals.	History is the result of a dialectic process that will inevitably lead to communism. Capitalism is but one of the necessary stages of economic evolution.
Role of the Individual	The state exists to serve the individual who is free to pursue his/her own wishes within certain bounds and is morally obligated to seek a life of virtue.	Individualism is antithetical to the needs of society and must be suppressed. The individual is entitled to a standard of living as determined by the state.
Religion	The state is indifferent to the beliefs of individuals; only acts count. Religion may be helpful in restraining bad acts.	Religion is the "opiate of the people" and unscientific. Hostile to religion, but sometimes tolerant of believers.

the evolution of man is not yet complete; men are not yet prepared to give "each according to his ability" and to receive "each according to his need." This latter attitude is required for the establishment of the "classless society," which is communism's utopia.

Note in Box 4-1 that the two systems focus on very different means for addressing the ills of the world. Capitalism proposes that men and women of virtue, freed to follow their individual genius, will create and preserve a virtuous, and not so incidentally, prosperous society. Communism, on the other hand, suggests an inevitable progression toward a communist economy, a progression in which individual courage and virtue are irrelevant. Capitalism emphasizes individual importance, while communism teaches that history and the state predominate.

ENDING CASE
Just How Corrupt Is Wall Street?[20]

 Just a few rotten apples? Or the whole barrel? Clearly, something is rotten on Wall Street. The prominent investment firm Drexel Burnham Lambert pleaded guilty on December 21, 1988 to six counts of criminal fraud, a move which cost the company $650 million in fines. During the same week, Paul A. Bilzerian, chairman of Singer Co., was indicted for numerous fraudulent practices, and GAF Corp. went on trial for stock manipulation. An indictment of Michael R. Milken, Drexel's Beverly Hills junk-bond chief, was said to be imminent.

In addition to widely publicized cases relating to insider trading, the practice where an individual with access to confidential company information exploits that information in trading securities, illegal stock "parking" schemes were widespread. In a parking arrangement, an individual disguises ownership of a stock, usually by arranging for another firm or individual to hold or trade them on his behalf. Parking schemes can be used to create sham losses to avoid taxes, to evade laws requiring disclosure of stock ownership, and in some cases, to manipulate stock prices. Although Wall Streeters and the Securities and Exchange Commission long regarded parking as a relatively benign offense, like minor cheating on income taxes, the government is beginning to take a much harder line, perhaps taking action to elevate parking from a civil misdemeanor to a criminal felony.

Yet there is also a good deal of evidence that illegal and unethical practices are isolated cases on Wall Street, that "the great bulk of the [Wall Street] community does not condone [these practices] as a matter of policy," to quote Samuel L. Hayes III, professor of investment banking at Harvard Business School. Securities law expert Alan R. Bromberg of Southern Methodist University says "I don't think that the abuses go to the integrity of the market. And I don't think they are inherent in the takeover process to the extent that it couldn't go on as well without them. The process functions pretty effectively." For all their notoriety, the abuses seem to be the exception, not the rule.

Even Drexel Burnham Lambert's admission of guilt may not be as damning as it might seem. There is evidence that Drexel felt they had a very defensible case, but pleaded guilty to avoid a long and costly legal process, during which substantial portions of the firm's assets would have been frozen. This could have impaired access to credit markets and jeopardized the firm's survival. One attorney close to the case stated that "the government is forcing them to acknowledge wrongs they don't believe they committed." In any case, the violations took place at Drexel's Beverly Hills operation, which operated almost autonomously from the firm's senior executives in New York. There is no evidence that senior executives approved, or even knew of the violations.

There are some interesting lessons to be learned from these stories. First, the integrity of the system depends on the integrity of the individuals in the system. Laws, no matter how carefully defined and rigidly enforced, will not in and of themselves prevent abuses. Playing by the rules of the game requires that individuals and businesses take ethics seriously. Second, despite the notable exceptions which make headlines, ethics appear to be alive and in place at the vast majority of business concerns. Although some executives can be criticized for supervisory lapses, few can be accused of overt wrongdoing. ⊻

SUMMARY

Adam Smith wrote a philosophy of free enterprise that contains a moral philosophy of extraordinary beauty. If the philosophy is honored within the system, capitalism becomes—in conjunction with democracy—the best hope for all to obtain the good life. The great successes in the world have come about because of people committed to ideals. Americans have largely abandoned the ideals expressed in the enabling documents of our nation and in the works of Adam Smith, and, as a result, are alienated from the systems that should be, next to the family, of greatest importance to them. The solution is to return to these ideals.

Furthermore, capitalism is a system based upon that which is best in human beings. Writing about good actions, Smith observed:

> It is not the love of our neighbour, it is not the love of mankind, which upon many occasions prompts us to the practice of those divine virtues. It is a stronger love, a more powerful affection, which generally takes place upon such occasions; the love of what is honourable and noble, of the grandeur, and dignity, and superiority of our own characters.[21]

In the original, then, lies a moral philosophy that encourages a system of loveliness, virtue, and dignity. It is a philosophy that can win the hearts and minds of individuals.

Communism is the major competing moral and economic philosophy in the world today and has radically different premises than those of capitalism. Communism is the professed goal of roughly one-third of humanity and it is essential to understand its core premises. Some of communism's major premises were reviewed and compared with those of capitalism.

LIST OF KEY TERMS

Ethics
Utilitarianism
Moral responsibility
Individual initiative
Sympathy
Supererogation
Virtuous qualities
Praise
Praiseworthy
Superior prudence
Sloth
Smith's ideal society

Smith's minimal society
Moral entrepreneurism
Right to privacy
System of enterprise of free
    individuals
Contract
Work
Noblesse Oblige
Civility
Capitalism
Communism

REVIEW QUESTIONS

1. What power is added to Marxism by its method of expression?

2. Who is the great spokesperson for capitalism? In what book did he expound capitalist economic theory? Its moral foundation?

3. Of what value is *The Theory of Moral Sentiments* in explaining Smith's *Wealth of Nations*?

4. According to James Madison, what would happen if the people of the United States came to lack virtue and wisdom?

5. What phrase sums up one of the grossest distortions of Adam Smith's original intentions? Why is this phrase described as loathsome in this regard?

6. What events did Tocqueville say would accompany the establishment of democratic institutions?

7. Why did the Founding Fathers reject the classical notion that the purpose of the state is to produce the highest character among those fit to be called citizens?

8. What obligations did our early leaders place upon individual citizens?

9. What did our Founding Fathers and Adam Smith assume that individuals were capable of comprehending?

10. What is sympathy? What does it imply about our economic relationships with others?

11. How did Smith define virtue and how does his concept of superior prudence relate to it?

12. How do most contemporary theories of capitalism treat the matter of morality in business?

13. Compare and contrast Smith's ideal society with his minimalist society.

14. What prerequisite did Smoth postulate for the viability of markets in a free economy?

15. In what ways has the private realm intruded on the public realm?

16. Did the early shapers of our government foresee a large public sector? Support your answer.

17. What is the most important argument favoring the sanctity of private property?

18. What key element justifies and defines an economic system?

19. What is the true meaning of contract? What is the true nature of work?

20. What are four obligations incurred by citizens that will enable the economic and political systems to function well?

CHALLENGE QUESTIONS

1. Of what value is an insight into the moral nature of the capitalist economic system to a practical person?

2. Why can't virtue be obtained through compulsion? How do communism and capitalism differ in this regard?

3. How did Tocqueville's view of what would occur if democracy was implemented indicate that he fundamentally misunderstood the teachings of Adam Smith?

4. How is the philosophy that truth is relative to the situation at odds with the teachings of Adam Smith?

5. How is happiness different from economic well-being? Did not Adam Smith suggest that happiness was a prerequisite to true economic progress?

6. Compare and contrast the United States as you see it today with Smith's minimalist society. With his ideal society.

7. What is the purpose of a job according to Smith? How does this contrast with contemporary views of which you are aware?

8. What implications do Smith's concepts of work and contract have for American management and workers?

9. Why do the authors state that Milton Friedman's concept of corporate social responsibility (discussed in Chapter 20) is at odds with how the Founding Fathers conceived of the nature and scope of government?

10. How is personal freedom often not served by corporate policies?

11. What limits should exist on the right of employers to contract with employees?

12. Why is virtue necessary in economic life? How does virtue or its lack impact the market?

CASE AND RELATED QUESTIONS

1. Should efficiency be the only goal of an economic system? If not, what other values should it embody and why?

2. How do you think Adam Smith would have answered John's contention that the firing of large numbers of middle managers by businesses in the free world would lead to their acceptance of socialism?

3. Many mergers and acquisitions have as one of their goals the elimination of union contracts and the lowering of labor costs. How would Adam Smith view this practice in your estimation? What role would his concepts of sympathy, virtue, and contract play?

4. What assumption does John make about the motivation of individuals in an economic system? Is it in harmony with the perceptions of Adam Smith and the Founding Fathers?

ENDNOTES

1. John Steinbeck, *Cannery Row* (New York: Bantam, 1945), p. 89.

2. James Madison, "Virginia Convention, 20 June 1788," *The Complete Madison,* ed. Saul Padover (New York: Harper & Brothers, 1953), pp. 48–49.

3. The new Oxford edition is best: Adam Smith, *An Inquiry into the Nature and Causes of the Wealth of Nations,* ed. R. H. Campbell and A. S. Skinner (1776; Indianapolis: Liberty Classics, 1981), in two volumes.

4. The Oxford edition is best: Adam Smith, *The Theory of Moral Sentiments,* ed. D. D. Raphael and A. L. Macfie (1759; Indianapolis: Liberty Classics, 1982).

5. This has been well discussed by A. L. Macfie, "Adam Smith's *Moral Sentiments* as foundation for his *Wealth of Nations,*" *The Individual in Society* (London: George Allen & Unwin, 1967), pp. 59–81. There has been a long-standing concern about the apparent contradiction between the morality of Adam Smith's first book, and the self-interest of his second ("Das Adam Smith problem"). However,

the matter has been effectively resolved in favor of Smith's moral philosophy. See Glenn R. Morrow, *The Ethical and Economic Theories of Adam Smith* (1923; Clifton, NJ: Augustus M. Kelley, 1969).

6. Gladys Bryson, *Man and Society: The Scottish Inquiry of the Eighteenth Century* (1945; New York: Augustus M. Kelley, 1968).

7. Utilitarianism, as defined by Jeremy Bentham, is most closely associated with the pleasure–pain principle, that is, that the goal of human activity is the maximization of pleasure and the avoidance of pain.

8. This position has been well defended by Glenn R. Morrow, *The Ethical and Economic Theories of Adam Smith* (1923; Clifton, NJ: Augustus M. Kelly, 1969) and A. L. Macfie, *The Individual in Society: Papers on Adam Smith* (London: George Allen & Unwin, 1967).

9. Alexis de Tocqueville, *Democracy in America,* ed. P. Bradley (New York: Vintage, 1945), vol. I, 262–63.

10. William G. Scott and David K. Hart, *Organizational America* (Boston: Houghton Mifflin, 1979).

11. Adam Smith, *The Theory of Moral Sentiments* (1759; Indianapolis: Liberty Classics, 1976), p. 47.

12. Smith, *Moral Sentiments,* p. 236.

13. John Locke, *An Essay Concerning Human Understanding* (1690; New York: Dover, 1959), Bk. I, p. 70.

14. Smith, *Moral Sentiments,* pp. 353–54.

15. Ibid., p. 166.

16. Ibid.

17. Baron de Montesquieu, *The Spirit of the Laws,* trans. T. Nugent (1748; New York: Hafner, 1949), Vol. I, Bk. XX, pp.316–17.

18. Adam Smith, *The Wealth of Nations* (1776), Bk. IV, p. 519.

19. John Rawls, *A Theory of Justice* (Cambridge, MA: Harvard University Press, 1971), p. 355.

20. Chris Welles, "Just How Corrupt Is Wall Street?" and "And the Next Test Will Be Giuliani vs. Milken," *Business Week,* January 9, 1989, p. 34–37.

21. Smith, *Moral Sentiments,* p. 235.

PART II

THE CHALLENGE OF PLANNING

CHAPTER 5

PLANNING

LEARNING OBJECTIVES

■ Develop a broad understanding of the organizational need for planning and the benefits which result from it.

■ Understand planning as a manager's decision-making activity that leads to increased organization, leadership, and sense of direction.

■ Identify the four dimensions of organizational planning.

■ Describe long-range, intermediate, and short-term planning and their various roles in management.

■ Explain the difference between strategic and operational plans.

■ Give examples of some single-use and standing plans.

■ Describe the planning roles played by the various levels of management as described in the planning pyramid.

■ Discuss the advantages and disadvantages of top-down and bottom-up planning.

■ Understand the five steps in the planning process.

■ Diagnose the organizational barriers to effective planning and discuss ways to overcome them.

■ Understand management by objective, its four phases, and its strengths and limitations.

John Smith is the type of patient no hospital really wants—terminally ill, poor, and without insurance. His illness, however, does not take note of his inability to pay, and the chemotherapy he requires is expensive. Wealthier patients can afford profit-making hospitals that offer better care, but John's needs are such that these hospitals cannot service him profitably, so they do not service him at all. Nonprofit hospitals also find him a burden; rising costs have come at the same time as stricter government rules, creating a real squeeze on funds.

Nonprofit hospitals have hundreds of thousands of patients such as John that make up a major portion of their constituency. The problem is how to service them in an era of tight money.

Intermountain Health Care has become one of the most watched nonprofit hospital chains in the country by developing an innovative approach to the problem of serving patients such as John. The result is a strong cash position and a reputation for strong management. President Scott S. Parker and his management team have developed the following plan:

1. Restructure the company into a holding company with nonprofit hospital subsidiaries as well as profit-making subsidiaries. Use the profit centers to subsidize hospital operations.

2. Develop profit centers that are targeted at specific segments of the health-care market with high potential. These include:

   A. Satellite and freestanding clinics.

   B. Birthing clinics.

   C. "Doc-in-the-box" clinics which are cash clinics in high-density areas such as shopping malls.

   D. Occupational health centers which provide medical services to employers (such as physical exams) and are located in industrial parks.

   E. Purchasing and data processing services for other hospitals.

   F. An insurance company to serve hospitals. IHC has managed to cut its own costs by 10 to 20 percent and believes that it can help other hospitals do the same by providing a lower-cost insurance coverage to those hospitals that adopt its methods.

This plan is designed to create significant additional revenues to be used in IHC's hospital operations, allowing IHC to offer the same high-cost care to the poor that is now reserved for the rich.

Planning is critical if nonprofit hospitals are to provide quality health care in an era of increasing governmental regulations and rising costs.

INTRODUCTION

Henri Fayol, an early management theoretician introduced in Chapter 2, considered planning to be the most important function that managers perform. At IHC, Scott Parker and his staff saw that the nature of the health-care industry was changing. In response they planned an ideal structure to work for over the coming decades, then began to implement the plan by forming a holding company, building new types of facilities, and changing internal procedures. All organizations, from hospitals to businesses of all sizes to public agencies, change as they move into the future. Change is required by the fluid economic, political, technological, and competitive environment discussed in Chapter 3.

Planning is an activity which focuses on the future. Specifically, it is the process of setting objectives and determining what needs to be done to accomplish these goals. As one writer describes planning, managers decide "What is to be done, when it is to be done, how it is to be done, and who is to do it."[2]

Thus the challenge of planning is to make decisions that will ensure the future success of the organization. It is a process that does not end with the development of a plan; the plan must be successfully implemented. At anytime during the implementation and control process, plans may require modification or change to maximize their effectiveness. Thus planning is a decision-making activity that is the foundation of the

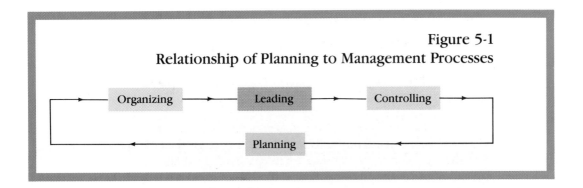

Figure 5-1
Relationship of Planning to Management Processes

management process. Planning helps managers in organizing, leading, and controlling by giving purpose and a sense of direction to the organization. Figure 5-1 suggests the relationship of planning to the other management functions.

The focus in this chapter is on ways of ensuring effective planning. The reasons why managers need to plan effectively will be discussed first. The types of plans used in organizations, their dimensions, and the steps in the planning process will then be reviewed. Finally, the barriers to effective planning, how to overcome them, and a review of one of the most frequently used planning systems, management by objectives (MBO) will be presented.

Because of their importance, strategic planning—determining strategies to accomplish objectives—and decision making—the process of choosing between alternative problem solutions—will be discussed more fully in Chapters 6 and 7.

THE IMPORTANCE OF EFFECTIVE PLANNING

Planning should occur at all levels in the organization. From production managers who establish proper work flow to marketing managers who establish channels of distribution and administrative managers who establish paper and information flows, effective planning is critical to success. Each manager establishes objectives and determines what needs to be done to achieve them. The degree to which a manager is responsible for planning depends on his or her specific function and the organization's size and purpose. A multinational company is more interested in long-range planning than a local grocery store. An automobile manufacturer makes investment commitments extending two or three years into the future, while a bookstore is more concerned with seasonal or annual goals. Regardless of the size or purpose of the organization, however, planning results in some specific benefits for all organizations. Among the benefits of planning are: (1) developing managerial skills, (2) increasing the likelihood of success, (3) coordinating interdepartmental efforts, and (4) preparing for change.

Developing Managers

Intermountain Health Care's (IHC) planners had to think systematically about the present and the future. They recognized that nonprofit hospitals no longer attracted wealthier patients, and that this affected the care they could give to indigent patients. They devised a plan to replace the lost revenues. IHC actually went a step further in that Parker and his staff devised a plan to enhance revenues beyond their previous levels and enable IHC's hospitals to provide "high cost" health care to the poor.

    The very nature of planning trains managers to think about the future of the organization, how to improve it, and their role in managing this change. Planning implies that managers need to be proactive—people who make things happen. Thus, the process of planning teaches managers to analyze and think about the future rigorously and to understand more fully their crucial role in effecting necessary change.

Improving Chances for Success

The chances that IHC will be successful in enhancing revenues are improved because of its planning activities. Research strongly supports the proposition that planning is linked to organization success.[3] Organizations with planning systems have significantly better financial success—return of investment, return on equity, and earnings-per-share growth.[4]

    Plans help define performance standards because objectives and assignments—who is to do what and when they are to do it—are clearer. These standards are then used to assess actual performance. Without the planning process, performance standards are likely to be subjective and less rational.

    A successful football team constantly talks about its "game plan" and the importance of preparation for the next game. Assume that two teams of equal ability are scheduled to play each other. One team spends significant effort in scouting the other to determine its strengths and weaknesses and designs its offense and defense to exploit the weaknesses and neutralize the strengths it finds. The other team makes no special preparation. Which team would you think has the better chance of victory?

Coordinating Efforts

If an organization does not have plans, it is forced to react to day-to-day events as they occur. On the other hand, with plans, managers are able to focus on desired objectives and the necessary action required to reach those objectives. Thus by working toward planned objectives the work of individuals and groups within an organization are more effectively coordinated.

Preparing for Change

Rapid change is a part of our society. Change is accelerating, too, especially technological change. Computers and robotics are revolutionizing manufacturing methods in today's industry. Changes are also being felt in the economy, government policies, and social norms and expectations. Coping with these changes is one of the great challenges facing managers; planning is the critical tool that enables managers to cope with change.

The manager who plans effectively and anticipates change will have more control than the manager who does not anticipate future events. History provides some clear examples of what happens to companies that are not prepared for change. The collapse of the Penn Central Railroad and the near bankruptcy of the A&P grocery chain were due in part to management's failure to anticipate and adapt to a changed environment. A&P turned its operation around when it adopted a more up-to-date plan.[5]

DIMENSIONS OF PLANNING WITHIN ORGANIZATIONS

With the increasing emphasis on planning in organizations, a large number of different types of plans, with varying degrees of emphasis and detail, have evolved. Figure 5-2 identifies four dimensions of the plans that managers use. These dimensions are time, scope, repetitiveness, and managerial level.

Time

The time horizon with which a plan is concerned is important. Generally, long-range plans cover five years or more and short-range plans cover a year or less.

LONG-RANGE PLANNING **Long-range plans** are those that deal with the broad competitive, technological, and strategic aspects of managing an organization, including the necessary allocation of resources. Long-range planning usually encompasses research and development, capital expansion, organization and management development, and meeting organizational financial requirements.

The activities of IBM and General Motors provide good examples of long-range planning. IBM's long-term manpower planning enables it to practice a policy of no layoffs.[6] General Motors' approach to its new Saturn automobile project is based on a long-range plan that calls for the use of the latest technologies, a restructuring of labor-management relations, and the formation of a new corporation to handle the project.[7]

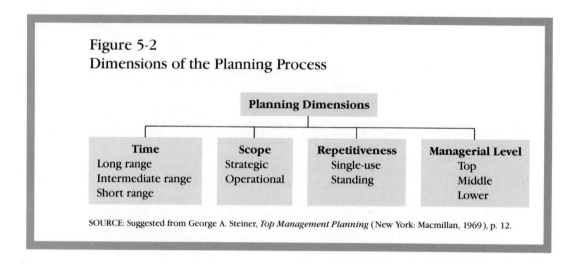

Figure 5-2
Dimensions of the Planning Process

Planning Dimensions

Time	**Scope**	**Repetitiveness**	**Managerial Level**
Long range	Strategic	Single-use	Top
Intermediate range	Operational	Standing	Middle
Short range			Lower

SOURCE: Suggested from George A. Steiner, *Top Management Planning* (New York: Macmillan, 1969), p. 12.

INTERMEDIATE PLANNING   **Intermediate plans** generally have a planning horizon of from one to three years. Whereas long-range plans serve more as general guidelines derived from the strategic planning process, intermediate plans are usually more detailed and relevant for middle and first-line management.

Intermediate plans frequently deal with the organic functions of the firm, such as finance, marketing, and production. For example, a long-range plan may call for market dominance in a particular industry in the next ten years, while the supporting intermediate plan calls for sales increases of seven percent in each of the next three years.

Because long-range planning is faced with so many uncertainties, intermediate planning receives the primary emphasis in many organizations.

The distinction between long-range and intermediate planning can be seen in the case of Walt Disney Productions. Twenty years ago, Walt Disney spoke of building a leisure-oriented complex covering some 28,000 acres of land near Orlando, Florida. Disney's vision was, in essence, a long-term plan. The building of Walt Disney World, Epcot Center, and, more recently, Disney-MGM Studios Theme Park constitute intermediate plans.[8]

SHORT-TERM PLANNING   **Short-term plans**, like intermediate plans, are derived from the long-range plans. These plans have a time horizon of a year or less and obviously have more impact on a manager's day-to-day activities than do either long-range or intermediate plans. They involve specific plans for meeting financial objectives (budgeting), inventory, advertising, employee training, etc.

Short-term plans at Walt Disney Productions include special promotions for theme parks and television (such as the celebration of Donald Duck's 50th birthday), recruitment of summer employees, scheduling premieres for new movies, and the setting of work schedules to accomplish these objectives.

Scope

Another dimension of planning is the **scope** or breadth and depth of activities that plans represent.

STRATEGIC PLANS   **Strategic plans** affect the entire organization, are generally developed by top-level managers, and are long-term in nature. Strategic plans address the mission and purpose of the organization and decide what the objectives of the organization should be.

The planning process starts with a formal mission statement which sets the overall direction and planning premises for the firm. Then company-wide strategic goals are determined and form the basis for the organization's operational plans. Thus, establishing the mission statement and the strategic plans to accomplish the firm's mission is the starting point for the planning process for the entire organization. These topics will be explored in depth in Chapter 6.

OPERATIONAL PLANS   Whereas strategic planning establishes the broad, general framework for an organization, **operational plans** are more limited in their scope. They focus on the day-to-day or month-to-month activities needed to execute strategic plans and achieve strategic goals. Operational plans are sometimes referred to as tactical plans and generally deal more with the allocation of resources and the scheduling of actual work activities. (See Figure 5-3 on page 124.)

Operational plans found in business firms include the following:

■ Marketing plans which focus on the sales and distribution of a company's product or services.

■ Production plans which focus on facilities, layouts, methods, and equipment needed to produce the product to be sold.

■ Financial plans which focus on managing the funds available to a firm and the acquisition of funds required to implement strategic plans.

■ Personnel plans which focus on the recruitment, selection, placement, and training of the human resources needed within the organization.

Recall the case of Intermountain Health Care. Parker formed a strategic plan that involved the use of a holding company with both profit-making and nonprofit subsidiaries. A number of niches in the health-care market were selected for their profit potential. IHC's tactical plan would involve such things as site selection for the new facilities, staffing, and budgeting.

More than other plans, operational or tactical plans involve the coordination and control of the flow of critical internal resources. Many of the topics covered later in this book relate to challenges and means available to managers to ensure coordination between strategic plans, operational plans, and the work effort of individuals and groups.

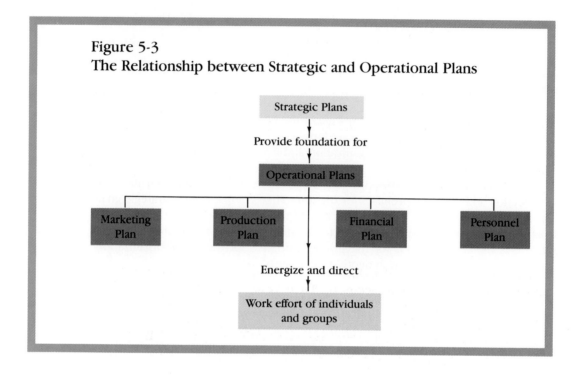

Figure 5-3
The Relationship between Strategic and Operational Plans

Repetitiveness

One of the important dimensions of plans is their frequency of use or repetitiveness. Two distinctions are generally made: single-use plans and standing plans.[9]

SINGLE-USE PLANS   **Single-use plans** are developed to carry out a course of action that is not likely to be repeated in the future. For example, when a hospital plans for expansion by building a new wing, it will be unable to use the original building plans because of the uniqueness of the addition, special needs that have arisen since the original building was constructed, labor availability, construction costs, etc. The major types of single-use plans are programs, projects, and budgets.

Programs   A **program** is a single-use plan used for broad activities that include many different functions and interactions. New incentive programs and a plan for introducing a new product line are examples. Guidelines for effective programs include the following:

1.   Divide the total set of activities into meaningful steps.
2.   Study the relationship between steps, noting any required sequence of steps.
3.   Assign responsibility for each step to appropriate managers and/or units.

4. Determine and allocate the resources needed for each step.

5. Estimate the starting and completion dates for each step.

6. Assign target dates for completion of each step.

A good example of a well-executed program is documented in the following case study of the 1982 attempt by Johnson & Johnson to save its market-leading Tylenol brand from extinction following product tampering, which resulted in the deaths of seven Chicago area residents from cyanide poisoning.

CASE

The Program to Save Tylenol[10]

In October of 1982 James Burke, chairman of Johnson & Johnson, made a decision to recall 31 million packages of Tylenol capsules. A killer had laced a number of Tylenol capsules in the Chicago area with cyanide, killing seven people. The Food and Drug Administration feared that such a recall might increase the panic already caused by the Chicago deaths. The FBI was concerned that such a move might demonstrate to potential terrorists that they could bring a giant corporation to its knees.

The panic following the poisonings had caused Tylenol's market share to fall from 35 percent to 7 percent in the $1.2 billion painkiller market. Most advertising executives viewed the product as dead. Burke's recall, however, was part of a carefully constructed program to save the product from extinction.

1. A redesigned triple-sealed package was introduced to make the product tamperproof once it left production.

2. The company distributed 80 million $2.50 coupons redeemable toward any Tylenol product to consumers.

3. A pep rally for sales representatives was held with the theme "We're Coming Back." Over one million sales calls were made on doctors and pharmacists between October and the end of 1982.

4. Testimonial-style television ads were aired.

5. Burke went the extra mile in seeing to it that his firm cooperated with the police investigation in every way, even offering a $100,000 reward for information leading to the arrest and conviction of the killer.

6. Burke appeared on television shows such as *Donahue* and *60 Minutes*.

In short, everything that could be done to win consumers' support was done and it was done within a three-month period. As one Wall Street observer put it: "Johnson & Johnson management were quick to cast themselves in the role of self-sacrificing servants of the people. They generated enormous public sympathy and managed to convince consumers that (the consumers) owed the company cooperation in saving the product."

The results were rather dramatic. By October of 1983 Tylenol's market share had climbed back to 29 percent, a clear sign of growing consumer confidence. The $50 million after-tax cost of the recall was clearly vindicated.

A similar episode in 1985 resulted in the withdrawal of Tylenol capsules from the market and their replacement with caplets (coated, oval-shaped tablets) which are much harder to tamper with. The company's prompt response to both episodes is generally credited with Tylenol's continued domination of the nonaspirin pain reliever market. ▨

Projects   A **project** is a single-use plan that is much narrower in its focus than a program, but more complex. In the hospital expansion illustration, typical projects are the preparation of construction plans, a report on labor availability, and recommendations for raising the needed capital to finance the expansion. Each project is the responsibility of assigned individuals who are given specific resources in the form of a budget and a deadline for completion.

Budget   Most programs and projects are developed and controlled with a budget. **Budgets** are plans for allocating specific financial resources to organizational units or activities. Budgets itemize income as well as expenditures and thus provide targets for the purpose of controlling activities and/or units.

STANDING PLANS   Whereas single-use plans are for nonrecurring situations, **standing plans** are developed to direct activities that occur regularly. Because similar situations are handled in a predetermined and consistent manner, managers save time and energy in the decision-making process. For instance, a university can more easily make decisions over student admissions if criteria are set in advance to evaluate academic potential. The major kinds of standing plans are policies, standard operating procedures, and rules.

Policies   **Policies** are guidelines for decision making. They set up boundaries around which decisions are made and generally flow from the organizations' goals and strategies.

Policies are frequently formed and developed by top managers who set them for various reasons: (1) to clear up confusion or misunderstanding at lower levels of the organization; (2) to improve effectiveness in achieving goals; (3) to have the organization reflect a certain value system (for example, a dress code); or (4) to allow managers to experience responsibility and make decisions within the framework of the established policies.

Going back to the university illustration, policies might be established concerning minimum acceptable test scores or high school grades or class standing. When those criteria have been met by applicants, they are admitted. Other policies might be established to evaluate special considerations involving students who do not meet admittance criteria.

In summary, policies guide decisions of managers and help implement strategic plans. A good policy is:

1. **Communicated**   All interested parties are advised. Unless a policy is known, it cannot effectively guide the decisions of managers.
2. **Understandable**   Managers need to know and understand a policy's purpose if it is to influence their behavior.
3. **Constant but not inflexible**   The risk is that managers may be less flexible or creative than they should be and tied to past practices. Thus, while it is important that policies not change so frequently so as to cause confusion, they do need to be administered flexibly and change over time as circumstances change.

Standard Procedures   A **standard procedure** is another form of standing plan. A procedure precisely describes what actions are to be taken in specific situations and are the means by which policies are frequently implemented. The admissions secretary at a university will have a set of procedures to follow in processing an application. These procedures include such activities as setting up a file, adding grades and test scores to the file, following through on letters of reference, and submitting the file to the appropriate individuals when the file is completed. Such detailed instructions guide the employee who performs these tasks and assure the organization that consistent approaches are applied to recurring situations.

Rules   A **rule** is the specific form of all standing plans. A rule is not a guide to decision making, but a substitute for it. Rules guide the actions of employees who are assigned to specific tasks—the only choice to be made is whether or not to apply them. In the university admissions task, examples of rules are deadlines for application, submission of test scores, and payment of the application fee. Rules and regulations can, of course, become a problem if they are excessive or enforced too rigidly.

Managerial Level

An important question in all organizations is: Who is responsible for planning? While top management is responsible to see to it that the planning function is carried out, all levels of management have important roles to play. Lower-level managers are highly involved in everyday operations and spend less time in planning than do middle- and upper-level managers. This focus on operating problems leads to a short-run planning horizon. Middle-level managers generally spend more of their time in planning than lower levels of management but less than top level. Their planning tends to focus on the intermediate future (from six months to a year) and frequently deals with what contributions subordinates can make to overall organizational objectives. Middle-level managers frequently play the major role in establishing policies, procedures, and budgets. Top-level management is generally felt to have major responsibility for the long-range or strategic planning of an organization.

TOP-DOWN VERSUS BOTTOM-UP PLANNING   **Top-down planning** occurs when upper-level management controls most of the planning for all levels of an organization. Because of fast-changing strategic and operating conditions, it is increasingly difficult for senior executives to keep abreast of developments. Thus, even seemingly brilliant strategies by top-level managers may not be successful because they miss the reach of people and/or units lower down in the organization.

To avoid some of these problems, experts have recommended a **bottom-up** rather than top-down planning process.[11] In this view, top management articulates what kinds of ideas it is interested in and middle managers and those who are closer to the operational problems formulate the actual plans.

A good example of bottom-up planning is found in the Malouf Company. Ron Malouf, the company's CEO, holds monthly meetings with his plant managers. These managers bring their problems and suggestions to the meeting for open discussion. The meetings are cordial but forthright and Malouf regularly reports back on what he had done about each suggestion. These suggestions from middle management clearly influence planning at the Malouf Company.

A major advantage of bottom-up planning is an increased sense of commitment and ownership by those involved in planning; however, when carried to extremes, it may result in a fragmented sense of direction and a loss of the vision in the organization. On the other hand, top-down planning creates unity and communicates the vision of top management, but often falls short in obtaining the commitment of those who need to implement and manage the plan. Involvement in the planning process is usually needed for subordinates to feel a sense of ownership in the plan.

THE PLANNING PYRAMID   Planning is considered by many to be the very foundation of management. To be most effective it must be carried out at all levels of management even though the type of planning at each level is substantially different (see Figure 5-4). Top management engages in strategic planning, middle management determines unit or group objectives in intermediate planning, and lower management performs the operational planning. Strategic planning, which will be discussed more fully in the next chapter, is the process of establishing the organization's long-term goals and determining how to accomplish them. Intermediate planning is the process of determining what the individual units can accomplish with their allocated resources. Operational planning focuses on the day-to-day and month-to-month activities needed to execute strategic and operational plans. Each level of planning is important and cannot stand alone without support of the other levels.

THE PLANNING PROCESS   Action plans are the result of a decision-making process. Planning involves decisions regarding the following questions:

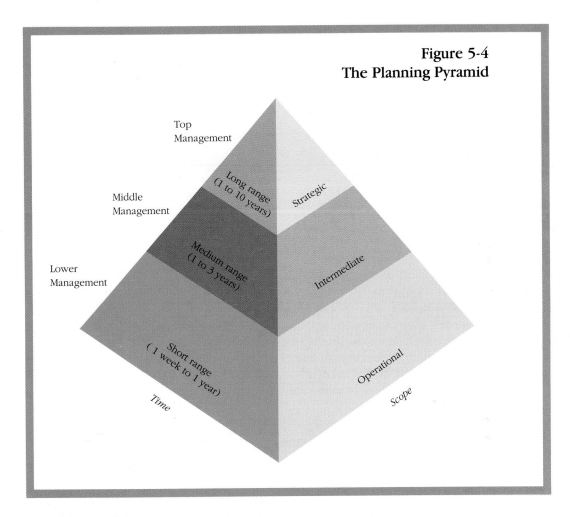

Figure 5-4
The Planning Pyramid

- What is to be done?
- When is it to be done?
- Where is it to be done?
- By whom is it to be done?
- How is it to be done?

In today's competitive and rapidly changing environment, an organization will not succeed unless its managers at all levels know how to ask and answer these questions as they plan. Every person in the organization should know what he or she is to accomplish and how, when, and with whose help it is to be done.

Like problem solving, planning can be thought of as a number of steps which can be adapted to all planning activities, at all organizational levels. Figure 5-5 illustrates these steps as follows:

Figure 5-5
Steps in the Planning Process

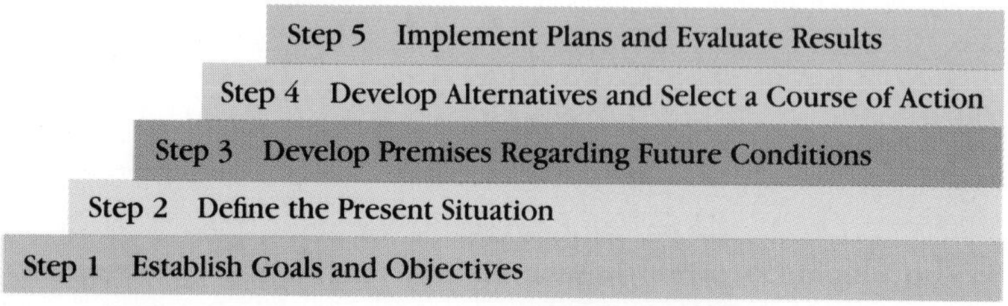

Step 5	Implement Plans and Evaluate Results
Step 4	Develop Alternatives and Select a Course of Action
Step 3	Develop Premises Regarding Future Conditions
Step 2	Define the Present Situation
Step 1	Establish Goals and Objectives

Step 1: Establishing Goals and Objectives The planning function begins with the establishment of goals and objectives. Without a clear statement of goals and objectives, organizations fail to focus on their priorities as they allocate resources.

Numerous attempts have been made over the years to identify the key result areas for which organizations should establish objectives. The most widely accepted list has been that developed by Peter Drucker.[12] Drucker holds that an organizaton needs to establish goals in areas vital to its continued existence. The eight "key result areas" Drucker identified are:

1. **Market standing**   Objectives should be established that measure results relative to competition. An example is a goal to increase market share by 12 percent within two years.

2. **Innovation**   Quality is a key to success and objectives need to be set for improving present products and services and the development of new products. Examples are the achievement of technological leadership in the medical equipment industry and creation of maintenance-free automobiles.

3. **Productivity**   Standards of production should be determined for all operational areas. An example is a goal to increase output per hour by 5 percent without increasing cost.

4. **Physical and financial resources**   Specific objectives need to be established for the utilization of physical and material resources and the supply of capital. Examples include goals to spend $10 million over the next two years to provide adequate warehouse facilities, to reduce long-term debt by 25 percent over the next three years, or to secure more favorable sources of raw materials.

5. **Profitability**   Minimum acceptable levels of financial performance need to be established. Examples include goals to increase return on investment by 10 percent in the next two years or to increase net profits by $3 million next year.

6. **Management performance and development**   Objectives for development of managerial talent, present and future, need to be established. Examples are the establishment of performance appraisal systems and plans to conduct in-house training programs or to pay tuition for university-level educational programs.

7. **Worker performance and attitude**   Objectives dealing with the performance and attitude of nonmanagerial employees need to be set. Examples are objectives dealing with absenteeism or turnover.

8. **Public (Social) responsibility**   Organizations need to determine how much they want to become involved in public service activities. These might include the support of community programs or the establishment of goals for minority hiring.

Step 2: Defining the Present Situation   Only after management has assessed the firm's competitive position vis-a-vis its competitors can plans be drawn up to chart future courses of action. In this analysis it is important to look carefully at the organization's strengths and weaknesses and the resources available for reaching established goals. This competitive analysis is crucial to the topic of strategic planning and will be discussed in Chapter 6.

Step 3: Developing Premises Regarding Future Conditions   During this step managers assess the internal and external environments for factors that may create problems in accomplishing objectives. Managers then forecast trends as they relate to these factors. Although difficult, anticipating problems and opportunities is an essential part of the planning process. The crucial role of forecasting will be discussed in greater detail in Chapter 7.

Each alternative for action needs to be evaluated carefully in terms of the assumptions that are necessary for that alternative to be effective. For example, two alternatives for increasing the return on investment might involve action to increase revenues. One alternative might be to increase sales of the present product, and the second might be to provide a new product. The first alternative assumes that the firm can increase its share of the market. The second alternative assumes that the firm would be able to capture the necessary portion of a new market. Again, competitive analysis and the ability to forecast future conditions accurately are important considerations in this step.

Step 4: Developing Alternatives and Selecting a Course of Action   During this step managers develop alternatives and choose that alternative which appears to be most appropriate. The evaluation includes a critique of the premises or assumptions upon which the alternative is based. If alternatives are based on unreasonable assumptions, managers can eliminate them from further consideration. Decisions are made about future action and the principles of effective decision making are most relevant.

Step 5: Implementing Plans and Evaluating Results   As discussed earlier in this chapter, planning is the first of the basic management functions and provides the foundation for the others. This step in the planning process highlights the relationship between planning and controlling and is illustrated in Figure 5-6.

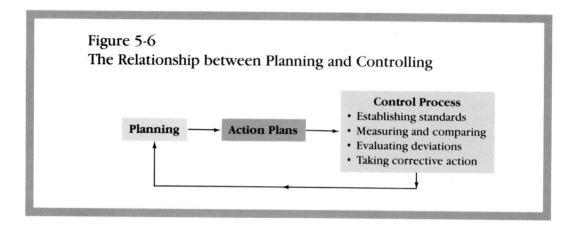

Figure 5-6
The Relationship between Planning and Controlling

As Figure 5-6 illustrates, action plans are the basis for the control process. **Action plans** identify the specific steps that are to be taken to reach the goals and objectives established in the planning process. In addition, for each goal and objective established, standards are set. The establishment of standards is the first step in the control process. The second step in the control process is to measure actual results and compare them with planned results. The third step is to evaluate the causes for any deviation between planned and actual results. This evaluation data is then sent back to the individual responsible for accomplishing the task. (These deviations can be positive as well as negative, and both types need to be part of the feedback process.) The final step is to take corrective action by altering objectives or changing plans which brings the manager back to the beginning or first step of the planning process.

Many reasons may explain deviations from planned results: erroneous assumptions about economic factors, setting unrealistically high goals, or inadequate **implementation** (putting the plan into action). The emphasis in the control function should be on evaluating the cause of deviations, feeding the information back to the people responsible for fixing them, and correcting the problems rather than trying to find someone to blame.

Planning and controlling are constantly interrelated in the process of management. Without control, planning would not be successfully implemented. Without planning, the control activities would lack direction. Hence, as shown in Figure 5-6, controls provide information about the effectiveness of action plans as well as input to the planning process. For example, market share data could have been used by Burke to determine the effectiveness of the plan to save Tylenol. If results did not occur as planned, Johnson & Johnson might have withdrawn capsules or introduced a new product such as caplets in 1982 instead of 1985.

Considering all that has been written and discussed about the importance of good planning, managerial resistance to the planning effort is surprisingly high.[13] This resistance may arise for several reasons. One of these concerns has to do with managers' reluctance to forecast events since uncertainty about the future makes planning less valuable. Other managers are concerned about a possible loss of creativity in their managerial style due to strict adherence to plans. One researcher found that 85 of the 350 European and American firms that he surveyed listed either resistance or lack of commitment/confidence in planning as their major problem.

BARRIERS TO EFFECTIVE PLANNING

A number of barriers exist in organizations that interfere with effective planning. When these barriers are overcome, planning can be of great benefit to managers. On the other hand, poor planning can have just as dramatic, but negative, effects on productivity. It is important to look at some of the commonly found barriers to planning and some guidelines to overcome them. Before reviewing these problems consider the case of Dome Petroleum and the results of poor planning.

CASE
The Bungled Takeover[14]

Dome Petroleum (Dome) first became interested in Hudson's Bay Oil & Gas (HBOG) in early 1981, shortly after the Canadian government announced that it would help Canadian corporations purchase foreign-owned oil companies.

HBOG seemed a perfect fit for Dome in that many of its properties were next to properties owned by Dome. The plan was simple. Dome would buy a block of Conoco stock (HBOG's U.S. parent corporation) and then trade the stock back to Conoco for its 53 percent share of HBOG. Dome would then sell some of the HBOG properties to companies that it controlled to reduce its indebtedness.

Conoco, however, did not sell as cheaply as expected. Dome was forced to pay $1.7 billion for Conoco's 53 percent of HBOG, a price far higher than planned.

Despite Dome's small size in relation to the acquisition, four Canadian banks loaned Dome the entire amount needed to buy HBOG.

Dome needed full ownership of HBOG in order to use HBOG's cash flow to pay the $30 million per month in interest it owed on the bank loan. Dome's finance department recommended a new stock issue to finance the purchase of the remaining 47 percent of HBOG because Dome stock was at an all-time high of $21 per share. Dome's charismatic founder-chairman, Jack Gallagher, did not want to dilute stockholders' equity and had not issued stock in over 20 years. He delayed by insisting that the results from some test wells in the Beaufort Sea would drive Dome's stock even higher.

Failure to plan effectively resulted in Dome Petroleum's disastrous takeover of Hudson Bay Oil & Gas.

The Beaufort results were disappointing and a worldwide recession had begun to set in. Dome's stock fell to $15. Meanwhile, the remaining HBOG stockholders demanded $1.8 billion in cash (making the total price of HBOG $3.5 billion). All funds would have to be borrowed.

The Canadian banks began to get cold feet as they belatedly recognized Dome's deteriorating position. Dome obtained some money from a syndicate of U.S. banks, but the Canadian banks were then able to stiffen their terms and demanded every unpledged Dome asset as security and insisted that Dome sell some of its assets to help repay their loan.

The Canadian banks then threatened to block the purchase of the remainder of HBOG unless Dome repaid the $1.7 billion by September of 1982 instead of within 10 years as originally planned. Bill Richards, Dome's president, accepted the acceleration without telling Gallagher.

By March of 1982, Dome needed $80 million more just to pay its bills. Richards convinced the Canadian government that Dome's failure could cause the collapse of the Canadian banking system, cost the country 30,000 jobs, and could destroy the government's energy policy. The government persuaded the banks to make the new loan.

By September, the government and the banks were forced to bail Dome out. Under the bailout plan, the banks and the government approved capital expenditures, appointed a majority of new directors to the Dome board, and took stock options that could triple Dome's equity shares if exercised.

In short, Dome's failure to properly plan and execute the takeover of HBOG resulted in the loss of the company's independence. Its stock ultimately fell to around $1.50 (Canadian) per share. Jack Gallagher and Bill Richards lost their jobs. Dome was bought by Amoco in 1988 for $4.18 billion.

What went wrong at Dome? The answer to this question cannot be limited to a simple generalization because many things went wrong. Dome's disastrous takeover of HBOG can best be understood when considered within the context of planning failures in general. ☒

Why Plans Fail

Kjell Ringbakk has identified ten major reasons why organizations can fail in their planning efforts.[15] In this particular study, Ringbakk surveyed 286 American and European companies by means of a detailed questionnaire that covered the most important aspects of planning practices. An additional 65 companies participated in in-depth interviews on the same topic. The findings suggest that planning failures often result from errors in perception and/or communication regarding the purposes of planning and from problems in implementation. More specifically, Ringbakk found the factors listed in Box 5-1 inhibit effective planning.

In a separate study, Steiner and Schollhammer found that of 50 planning pitfalls the two that most reduced the effectiveness of the planning process are: (1) top management's lack of awareness of the importance of the planning system, and (2) the failure to state corporate goals in clear and operational terms.[16]

Overcoming Barriers to Planning

Planning involves change and implementing and managing change are important dimensions of a manager's job. Managing change will be discussed in Chapter 12 and many of the principles suggested there are applicable to the problem of overcoming the barriers to change. For many of the problems identified by Ringbakk, some of the answers are implied by the problems themselves. Some suggestions to overcome those barriers are:

■ Emphasize and articulate the vision of planning. A results-oriented atmosphere and open communication are particularly helpful.

Box 5-1
Factors Inhibiting Effective Planning

1. Corporate planning is not integrated into the total management system. At Dome, planning was not fully integrated into financial decisions; as a result, Gallagher and Richards were forced to react to events.

2. Some aspects of the formal planning process are not fully understood by managers. Dome's managers totally failed to make contingency plans to deal with the unexpected moves by Conoco and the minority shareholders.

3. Management at all levels of the organization have not been properly involved in the planning activities. Gallagher and Richards seldom involved others in the planning process and even failed to keep each other informed.

4. Primary responsibility for planning has been given over solely to a planning department.

5. Long-range plans are considered unchangeable. Gallagher had two such plans: do not issue new equity and continued expansion, which made it virtually impossible for Gallagher to consider selling any assets.

6. In starting formal planning processes, more expensive or complex systems than are necessary are chosen.

7. Management fails to operate by the plan. When the price for HBOG exceeded expectations, Dome's answer was to pay whatever price it took to acquire HBOG.

8. Forecasting and budgeting projections are confused with planning. Dome confused its forecast scenario with a takeover plan; the plan lacked needed detail.

9. Inadequate inputs are used in planning. Dome failed to consider alternatives and to make contingency plans. The reactions of Conoco and the minority stockholders caught it entirely by surprise.

10. Managers fail to see the overall planning process and get bogged down in detail. Gallagher and Richards became so engrossed in the pursuit of HBOG, in reacting to the moves of the other players, that they failed to realize that the purpose of the HBOG purchase was to improve Dome's position.

SOURCE: Kjell Ringbakk, "Why Planning Fails," *European Business*, Spring 1971, pp. 15–27.

- The importance of planning and planning methods needs to be taught continually in the organization. This can be done formally in training programs or informally as managers review the plans of their subordinates.

- Adjust the organizational planning processes to fit the needs for implementation.

Be sure to involve managers in the planning process who will have key roles in the implementation and control stages.

- Involve key managers and their subordinates in the planning process rather than assigning that responsibility to a "specialist." Plans can be best developed by those who are directly involved with the problems.

- Schedule periodic reviews of plans. This evaluation and revision should be done at least once a year and should be an integral part of the planning-control cycle.

- Start with simple planning processes. It is easier to add new information and processes than to remove them.

- Communicate the plans of the organization to all key managers. Put them in writing and review them periodically in meetings.

- During the planning process, continually make clear that forecasting and budgeting are tools in the planning process. Forecasting helps to establish the premises upon which plans are made and budgets are essential for the implementation and control phase.

- Determine what information is necessary for effective planning and delegate to individuals or units the responsibility of gathering it.

- Always keep in mind the goals of planning so that you do not get bogged down in detail.

It should be clear from this discussion that planning is one of the key management functions and that some potential problems could cause it to be less effective unless management takes the necessary steps to maximize its usefulness. Dome Petroleum, while faced with the recession and oil glut facing other oil producers in the 1980s, would very likely be far more valuable to its shareholders had it effectively used the planning process in its takeover of Hudson's Bay Oil & Gas.

MANAGEMENT BY OBJECTIVES

The basic premise of this chapter is that planning provides the foundation for the other management functions, particularly for the decision-making activities highlighted in this text. In the previous section, the importance of good planning and the unfortunate decisions resulting from poor planning were emphasized. Some of the means of overcoming barriers to planning were also summarized—most of which involved participation and education. Perhaps the most extensively used planning, decision-making, and control system is management by objectives (**MBO**). The term "management by objectives" was popularized by Peter Drucker in 1954.[17] It has also been called "management by results," "goals management," "work planning and review," as well as other program names.

What is MBO?

Management by objectives programs come in many forms. The essence of all MBO programs, however, is a set of procedures that begins with goal setting and continues into a planning phase, a control process, and a system of periodic review, followed by a performance appraisal. This process is illustrated in Figure 5-7.

The key to a successful MBO program is a high degree of participation, involving managers and subordinates at every level of the organization. MBO is concerned with goal setting for individual managers and their units as opposed to overall organizational goals. As discussed later, goal setting needs to start at the top of the organization, and the goals of individual managers need to be consistent with the goals of the organization.

The purpose of MBO is to give subordinates a voice in the goal-setting process and to make it clear what they are to accomplish in a given time period. By doing this, it is expected that strong linkages will develop between the planning and controlling functions and that many of the barriers to effective planning will be overcome.

Goal Setting

For the MBO process to be effective, goals have to be identified at three levels within the organization. At the highest level, long-range goals and strategic plans are developed. It is at this level that the firms must answer such questions as: "What kind of company are we?" "What kind of company do we want to be?" and "Who are our customers?" When these questions have been answered, an overall direction for the firm will have been established, providing the basis for the goals and objectives at the second (operational) level. The third step in the goal-setting process is the establishment of individual goals and objectives necessary to achieve the operational objectives. It is at this stage that the collaborative goal setting which is the essence of MBO programs needs to occur.

DEFINITION OF JOB   The establishment of individual objectives is generally discussed as a series of tasks. The first task is **job definition**. At this point the subordinate discusses the job with his or her superior and they agree on the content and relative importance of its major duties. Some managers think that this step is unnecessary, but numerous studies show a lack of agreement between superior and subordinate regarding job responsibilities. Communication about important values and priorities is essential to reaching such agreement.

PERFORMANCE TARGETS   The next step is the establishment of the objectives or performance targets themselves. The key to this stage is collaboration. Experience has shown that objectives prepared solely by the manager are not accepted by the

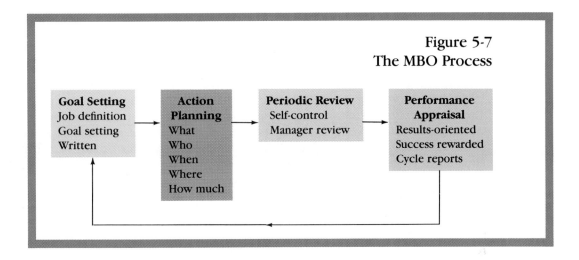

Figure 5-7
The MBO Process

subordinate and vice versa. The purpose is to agree on a set of objectives that satisfies both parties and to which each is committed. The best way to achieve this is to have both manager and subordinate involved in setting objectives.

The manager is responsible to make sure that the goals are consistent with operational plans and organizational goals. Additionally, the manager must make sure that the goals and performance targets are sufficiently high to cause the subordinate to expend a reasonable amount of effort to achieve them. On the other hand, the goals need to be such that the subordinate will not consider them unrealistic and attempts to reach them futile.

PUT OBJECTIVES IN WRITING   The third step is to write the objectives down so that they are verifiable. The goals should be written so that at the end of a specified period of time the manager and subordinate have no question as to whether the desired results have or have not been achieved. Over the years, practitioners have developed the following set of rules for writing objectives.

1. Make the objectives specific and measurable.
2. Include a time element in the objective statement.
3. Make the objective clear and unambiguous so that there is no question what the objective means and when it will have been accomplished.
4. Make the objective challenging but within the employee's capability. It should be one that a competent, diligent employee could reach most of the time; slightly out of reach, not out of sight.
5. Make the objective results-oriented.
6. Be sure the objective is consistent with organizational objectives and policies.
7. Limit the number of objectives to five or less, and list them in order of priority.

Action Planning

After the collaboration between manager and subordinate establishes what the objectives are, the next step is planning how these objectives are to be accomplished. The means for achieving a given objective are decided during the **action planning** phase. During this phase the manager determines what, who, when, where, and how much is needed to achieve a given goal. Managers at each level develop plans that incorporate the established goals. Higher-level managers are responsible for making sure that their direct subordinates' plans complement one another.

In his book on managing by objectives, Raio suggests that a good action plan can be developed by following seven basic steps.[18] These steps are listed in Box 5-2.

Periodic Reviews

One of the important features of an MBO system is the review process and emphasis on self-control. MBO recognizes the importance of controls and places the responsibility for control largely on the shoulders of the individual charged with carrying out the plan. All involved can control their own performance by constantly monitoring their progress toward the stated objective and taking corrective action when needed.

In addition to the emphasis on self-control, MBO programs call for periodic reviews of performance. MBO practitioners usually recommend one-on-one meetings between managers and subordinates at three-, six-, and nine-month intervals. These reviews also provide the manager with the opportunity to give subordinates needed feedback.

Performance Appraisal

At the end of the predetermined performance period, usually a year, the manager and subordinate meet to discuss results of the subordinate's efforts to meet the performance targets jointly established in a **performance appraisal** interview. The focus of this meeting should be on results[19] and actual performance rather than on personalities or excuses. The tone of this appraisal should be constructive and not fault-finding or critical. The control phase of the MBO cycle is completed when success is rewarded with promotion, merit pay, or other agreed-upon benefits and corrective action has been initiated to improve future performance.

After one round of MBO, the cycle repeats itself. Because of the significant time it takes to go through several cycles and learn from each experience, it takes five or more years for a fully developed MBO program to be installed in a moderate-size firm.

Box 5-2
Raio's Seven Steps to a Good Action Plan

1. Specify what is to be accomplished. An example would be a plan to increase the market share of a breakfast cereal by 10 percent.

2. Define the major activities required to support the objective. These would include the development of special advertising and promotional programs, packaging changes, deciding on the distribution channels to be used, and the sales effort required.

3. Establish the critical relationships between the major activities. Decide on advertising and sales promotions before designing special packaging. Estimate the number of sales calls required before making sales assignments.

4. Clarify roles and relationships and designate primary responsibility for each activity. For example, Marketing will be responsible for design of the promotion. Advertising will purchase media time. Art will design new packaging. Sales will hire new sales staff and promote the plan to customers.

5. Estimate time tables for completion of each major activity and its subactivities. All activities are coordinated so that the plan can be implemented in an effective way. Allow a margin for error.

6. Identify additional resources required for each activity. Prepare a budget showing the cost of advertising, sales promotion, and selling expenses. Include all incremental costs.

7. Verify deadline and modify the action plan. Leave enough flexibility that adjustments can be made without great expense. For example, do not commit to specific advertising schedules until you can be certain that all necessary prerequisites will be completed on schedule.

SOURCE: Anthony P. Raio, *Managing By Objectives* (Glenview, IL: Scott, Foresman, 1974).

The system ties planning, control, performance appraisal, and the reward system together. The preferred approach is to introduce the program at the top of the organization and add one additional organizational level with each cycle.

Research on MBO Effectiveness

Does MBO work in improving performance? Jack N. Kondrasuk summarized the research in this area and found overwhelming support for MBO's effectiveness.[20] For example, Kondrasuk found that out of 141 case studies, 123 had positive results, 8 had mixed results, and only 10 had negative results. Most of the research has been focused primarily on three aspects of MBO: the setting of goals, feedback of results, and subordinate participation in decision making.

Generally, goal setting results in improved performance. Individuals who set their own goals tend to desire improved performance. If they achieve their initial goals, they will generally set higher goals in the future. On the other hand, if they fail to meet their goals, they tend to be more conservative in the establishment of new goals. In addition, research evidence supports the suggestions that goals need to be specific, reasonable, and acceptable to the subordinate. If these conditions are not met, the practice of goal setting may result in decreased performance levels.

Feedback about performance levels generally results in improved performance. In addition, if the periodic review process *is* conducted in a tactful manner it *has* a positive impact on the way employees feel about their work. For feedback to have a positive impact, it needs to be timely, specific, and relevant to the task or the goals being accomplished.

The majority of studies indicate that subordinates who participate in setting their own goals attain higher performance levels than those who have their goals established for them.[21] The key variable seems to be whether or not the individual perceives the participation to be legitimate. If the subordinate feels that the superior only allows him to speak out but does not actually involve him in the process of establishing goals and action plans, productivity will probably fall.

Active employee participation in the goal-setting process improves productivity for two reasons. First, active involvement in goal setting is much more likely to result in goals that are accepted by subordinates and accepted goals are more likely to be realized. Second, employee participation leads to higher goals, which lead to better performance.

Limitations of MBO

Although the research data give general support to MBO programs, some limitations clearly exist. Present and future managers should be clear about the relative strengths and weaknesses of this management technique so that their expectations are realistic.

MBO can take too much time and effort and generate excessive paper work. In a study by Carroll and Tosi,[22] the major problem that emerged was the excessive requirement of completing forms, updating changes, and providing the required information for monitoring performance.

MBO is too often sold as a panacea for increasing productivity. MBO, of course, does not solve all of an organization's problems. The appraisal of performance is particularly difficult since it involves salaries and promotions. If conducted improperly it might cause tension and conflict between managers and subordinates. In addition, not all accomplishments can be quantified or measured. For instance, how do you measure the contribution and effectiveness of teachers or managers as developers of individuals? Even when results are measurable, the subordinates may not be responsible for them. For instance, a drop in sales for a unit may be caused by a competitor's actions and/or economic events beyond the control of the manager.

MBO is hindered by managers with an autocratic style and inflexible policies and rules. When managers and subordinates are not able to establish a relationship of trust, they are not likely to feel like peers of the managers. This atmosphere makes truly participative goal setting highly unlikely. In many hierarchical and autocratically managed firms, the perceived gap between the managers and their subordinates may be too wide to bridge. It is just too difficult for the managers to go from a "boss-judge" to a "helper-friend" and back again.

MBO's emphasis on measurable objectives may be used as a club by overaggressive managers. If the MBO system is used to establish unrealistic goals and punishment follows the failure to reach these goals, the employees will become wise to the misuse of MBO and it will lose its possible impact.

Strengths of MBO

As has been suggested, MBO has been both praised and criticized. Tosi and Carroll have identified six major advantages of MBO programs after surveying managers.[23]

1. It lets individuals know what is expected of them and clarifies their roles.
2. It aids in planning by improving problem identification and encouraging managers to establish action plans and target dates to solve problems.
3. It improves communication and motivation among managers.
4. It makes individuals more aware of organizational goals and directs their work activity toward the accomplishment of those goals.
5. It provides more objective appraisal criteria and makes the evaluation process more equitable.
6. It improves personnel development by letting subordinates know how well they are doing in relation to their goals.

From this analysis, it seems clear that MBO systems have major advantages to the individual as well as the organization. By clarifying exactly what is expected, by allowing employees a voice in establishing objectives, and by basing rewards on how well they accomplish their objectives rather than on personal traits or a superior's biases, organizations can create a powerful motivation system for their employees.

In addition, since all levels of the organization assist in the goal-setting process, the goals have a tendency to be more realistic and accepted by the employees. With this enhanced commitment and open communications, the organization will realize its goals more easily with an increased sense of unity.

In short, experience does suggest that proper use of MBO is related to positive changes in attitude, behavior, and performance. However, proper implementation of this tool is crucial if it is to be successful.

The Challenge of Implementation

Because of the widespread use of MBO, managers have learned a number of important lessons about how to make MBO work. First, top-level managers must demonstrate their continuing support. Unless they are willing to set and review objectives themselves, support for MBO programs among the employees will largely disappear. This continuing involvement is also essential because goal setting starts at the top and filters down into the organization.

Second, it is essential to educate and train managers adequately about the principles and processes of MBO as well as the skills necessary for successful implementation. If those involved do not understand MBO and the reasons for its use, the chances for success are small.

Third, objectives must be clear and precise. MBO works best when realistic, important, and measurable goals are agreed upon by both managers and subordinates and used to evaluate performance. It does not work when goals are too narrow, short-term, unimportant, or hard to measure.

Fourth, successful MBO programs need reinforcement and individuals need regular feedback. MBO works best when participants know where they stand relative to their goals. Regular performance reviews and objective feedback are essential to sustain commitment to these programs.

Finally, real participation must be encouraged. For MBO to work, employees must be actively involved in the goal-setting and action-planning phases. This implies some reallocation of power within the organization. MBO will not work if managers simply go through the motion of soliciting employee involvement. Employees will resent attempts to "play games" if their involvement is not perceived as important. The discomfort some managers feel in sharing power is a price that must be paid for MBO to be successful.

It can be seen by experience that MBO programs can be successful if these conditions are met by top-level management. Admittedly, organizations will need to alter MBO programs to fit the specific needs and problems they face. As a result, different MBO systems can be expected to develop. However, the basic principles of MBO described in this chapter are likely to be used with increasing frequency in both the private and public sectors in future years. The power of planning and the use of MBO systems are illustrated in the ending case.

ENDING CASE
Strategic or Tactical? What Decisions Should the CEO Need to Make?

Thirty percent growth per year and maintaining an after-tax profit of ten percent once the enterprise is up and going might be the only criteria Pat McGovern would give to a manager contemplating a new venture at his International Data Group (IDG).

IDG consists of 65 quasi-autonomous units of a publishing empire with sales of over $300 million in 36 countries. All of the publications deal with technology—some in specific product lines (*PC World, Macworld, CD-ROM Review*) and others focus on technology businesses.

Looking at the corporate staff of only fifteen, you would not think that this is a global company with sales in the hundreds of millions. Looks can be deceiving because of the unique style of management that McGovern uses in his company.

A broad objective of growth and profitability is given to the managers of each company in IDG and detailed plans are required for new ventures, but CEO McGovern does not make operational decisions anymore. At one time he did, as he relates, "My thinking probably went something like this in those days: 'Gee, my input is essential here. I've been at it longer and have more contacts, so my wisdom is obviously crucial to our success.' But then I thought: 'Now isn't this strange. There are probably, in the information business alone, thousands of very successful companies that seem to develop and prosper without a single word of advice or help from me. Perhaps I should go ahead and trust people, and if I've made the right initial decision about them, and if I've had the right concept about the market, then everything should go well.'" And well it has gone, from $15 million in sales when this approach was taken to over $300 million in sales 14 years later.

Though not articulated as such, this type of management is really the application of management by objective (MBO). The objectives of any new venture are set out from the beginning relating to growth and profitability. Managers are expected to know their market and prepare a comprehensive plan to make the venture a success. At IDG, the executives of each unit are compensated on the performance of the unit. This gives managers a performance incentive and the entrepreneurial drive that has made IDG a success. Only four publications out of over one hundred have failed.

Every employee at every unit fills out an evaluation card each year on the manager. These are used to evaluate and monitor the progress. Any major problems are brought up in periodic reviews as McGovern travels around the company. Reader surveys of the publications are also used to monitor performance, as these tend to be the precursor to next year's performance.

Enthusiasm radiates from McGovern as he visits the various units. He tries to see every U.S. employee who earned a bonus. Around Christmas he delivers the bonus and a card personally. This both improves morale and gives him a feel for the different units. At least once a year Pat visits the non-U.S. operations.

Responding to the customer needs quickly is an important objective also. The entrepreneurial style facilitates this objective. *Computerworld* was launched in three weeks. Another publication in Europe was launched in three days. Failures have occurred when publications are launched in response to competitor actions and not customer needs as happened with the *PC jr* magazine.

Pat McGovern has proven that the right people given well-defined objectives, with compensation incentives on the line can be a powerful resource for growth and profitability. Recognizing this fact has prompted him to establish an ESOP that currently owns 20 percent of the company and eventually will own over 50 percent by the early 1990s. ▨

Sound business planning is the blueprint of the managerial process to meet organizational goals.

SUMMARY

Planning is the process by which organizations attempt to anticipate change and effectively adapt so to meet organizational goals and objectives. Many management theorists regard planning as the most important task undertaken by managers.

Long-range planning deals with the broad competitive, technological, and strategic aspects of managing an organization and generally involves a planning horizon of more than five years. Strategic planning is a specialized type of long-range planning which deals with such topics as the mission of the organization and setting of ultimate objectives. Long-range and strategic plans are made by the top managers in an organization and they are usually judged on their success in carrying these plans out. All other plans flow from the strategic plan.

Intermediate planning usually deals with the functional areas of management (finance, marketing, and production) and has a planning horizon of one to five years. Intermediate plans attempt to translate long-range and strategic plans into concrete steps or goals. Intermediate plans are made by middle managers who also carry the major responsibility for their execution.

Short-term planning involves taking steps to ensure that an organization meets its objectives on a day-to-day basis. Short-term plans are generally made and carried out by lower-level managers and supervisors.

Management by objectives (MBO) is one of the most widely used planning and control systems used in organizations. MBO consists of goal setting, planning to meet the goals set, a self-control process and a system of periodic review, followed by a performance appraisal. When employees are actively involved in the setting of goals and a system of feedback is part of the MBO process, performance measurably improves.

LIST OF KEY TERMS

Planning

Long-range plans

Intermediate plans

Short-term plans

Scope

Strategic plans

Operational plans

Single-use plans

Programs

Projects

Budget

Standing plans

Policies

Standard procedures

Rules

Top-down planning

Bottom-up planning

Action plans

Implementation

MBO

Job definition

Action planning

Performance appraisal

REVIEW QUESTIONS

1. Why do organizations need to plan?

2. What is meant by "the challenge of planning?"

3. Who should an organization make responsible for its planning efforts?

4. What is the difference between operational and strategic plans?

5. Name the six types of plans discussed in the chapter that vary according to repetitiveness.

6. List the eight key result areas that Drucker identified for which organizations should establish goals and objectives.

7. List the five steps in the planning process as described in the chapter.

8. Give a brief definition of "management by objectives."

9. Why should employee performance targets be put in writing?

10. What are Raio's seven steps in developing a good action plan?

11. Does MBO work? Support your answer.

CHALLENGE QUESTIONS

1. Why are organizational objectives important to the planning process?

2. Some students of management believe that the process of planning is as important as the result. Why might this be true?

3. Describe an effective planning process as best you can.

4. How does the concept of level relate to horizon (time) in the planning process?

5. What are the advantages and pitfalls of top-down versus bottom-up planning? Which type do you recommend and why?

6. Describe the planning process suggested by the authors.

7. Explain the interaction between the planning and control processes.

8. In your experience, which of Ringbakk's ten reasons that plans fail best explain the planning failures that you have observed?

9. Why do you think employee participation in goal setting is easier to state as a principle than it is to put into practice?

10. Why do you think that companies experience such a difficult time in getting managers to use performance appraisal forms designed to help managers pinpoint employees' shortcomings when it seems obvious that both would benefit? Could the focus of such forms be wrong?

11. What conditions are necessary to make MBO work? Given the fact that some of these conditions are usually absent within a given organization, how do you explain the overwhelming evidence that MBO works?

12. What should the focus of planning efforts be?

CASE AND RELATED QUESTIONS

1. What are some of Intermountain Health Care's alternatives? How do the stated plans of IHC tie into the company's objectives?

2. Make a list of IHC's long-range, intermediate, and short-term plans from material provided or inferred from the case.

3. What actions should James Burke take if the Tylenol killer strikes again? Outline a program in some detail or defend your decision to withdraw the brand from the market.

4. What actions of Gallagher and Richards showed that they did not understand the planning process?

5. You have just been named to succeed Jack Gallagher as chairman of Dome. The Canadian government and the banks have asked Bill Richards to stay. You have a meeting with Richards tomorrow. The purpose of the meeting is to begin work on a new five-year plan for the company. Outline an agenda for the meeting and make a list of who you would invite. Be prepared to defend your agenda and invitation list in class.

ENDNOTES

1. Adapted from "Intermountain Health Care: Financing Hospital Treatment for the Poor," *Business Week,* May 16, 1983, p. 51.

2. George A. Steiner, *Top Management Planning* (New York: MacMillan, 1969), p. 7.

3. For a review of the literature in this area see Robin M. Hogarth and Spyros Makridakis, "Forecasting & Planning: An Evaluation," *Management Science,* February 1981, pp. 115–38. Also see Michel H. Montebello, "Long-range Planning and Managerial Perceptions of Corporate Effectiveness," *Management Science,* Summer 1981, pp. 48–58.

4. See Donald W. Beard and Gregory G. Dess, "Corporate-level Strategy, Business-level Strategy, and Firm Performance," *Academy of Management Journal,* December 1981, pp. 663–88, showing a positive correlation between profitability and the practice of actively using the planning process to determine what industries a firm should participate in (corporate-level strategy) and what stance the firm should take within that industry (business-level strategy). Another study demonstrated that the quality of planning is the key determinant in financial performance. See "The Effects of Long-range Planning on Small Business Performance," *Journal of Small Business Management,* January 1985, pp. 16–23.

5. A&P Chairman James Wood faced strong resistance to his plan to turn A&P around. See Gwen Kinkead, "The Executive-Suite Struggle behind A&P's Profits," *Fortune,* November 1, 1982, p. 92. He persevered and succeeded. See "A&P: Story of a Turnaround," *Chain Store Age Executive,* September 1983, p. 49.

6. Hastings H. Huggins, Jr., "IBM's Retraining Success Based on Long-term Manpower Planning," *Management Review,* August, 1983, p. 29.

7. Ronald Henkoff and Madlyn Resener, "GM's 'Saturn' Satellite," *Newsweek,* January 21, 1985, p. 56.

8. Michael Cieply, "Disney's Plan to Build Cities on Florida Tract Could Shape Its Future," *Wall Street Journal,* July 9, 1985, p. 1, col. 6.

9. F. Kast and S. E. Rosenzweig, *Organization and Management* (New York: McGraw-Hill, 1974), p. 44.

10. Adapted from "Tylenol's Miracle Comeback," *Time,* October 17, 1983, p. 67.

11. For a description of the work of L. Jay Bourgeois and David R. Brodwin, see Herbert Blanchett, "The Best Corporate Strategy May Be None at All," *Stanford Business School Magazine,* Spring 1985, pp. 8–9. Tom Peters of *In Search of Excellence* fame is reported to recommend planning that is "radically bottom-up." See James F. Kingsley, "Enfranchising *All* Managers to Plan: The Giant First Step to Superperformance," *Management Review,* March 1984, p. 8.

12. Peter F. Drucker, *The Practice of Management* (New York: Harper & Brothers, 1954), pp. 62–87.

13. Kjell Ringbakk, "Why Planning Fails," *European Business,* Spring 1971, p. 19. For a more recent study with similar results, see David Wright, "New Zealand: A Newcomer to Planning," *Long-Range Planning,* June 1982, p. 122.

14. Adapted from Shawn Tully, "How Dome Petroleum Got Crunched," *Fortune,* January 10, 1983, p. 84.

15. Ringbakk, pp. 15–27.

16. For a review of the Steiner and Schollhammer findings, see Peter Lorange, "Formal Planning Systems: Their Role in Strategy Formulation and Implementation," Dan E. Schendel and Charles W. Hofer, eds., *Strategic Management: A New View Of Business Policy And Planning,* (Boston: Little, Brown and Company, 1979), pp.233–34.

17. Peter F. Drucker, *The Practice of Management* (New York: Harper & Brothers, 1954).

18. Anthony P. Raio, *Managing By Objectives* (Glenview, IL: Scott, Foresman, 1974).

19. George S. Odiorne, *MBO II: A System Of Managerial Leadership* (Belmont, CA: Fearon Pitman, 1979), p. 47.

20. Jack N. Kondrasuk, "Studies in MBO Effectiveness," *Academy of Management Review,* July 1981, pp. 419–30. Also see Stephen S. Carroll, Jr. and Harry L. Tosi, *Management By Objectives: Applications and Research* (New York: MacMillan, 1973) for the results of an earlier study.

21. For example, see Miriam Erez, P. Christopher Earley, and Charles L. Hulin, "The Impact of Participation on Goal Acceptance and Performance: A Two-step Model," *Academy of Management Journal,* March 1985, pp. 50–65.

22. Stephen S. Carroll, Jr. and Harry L. Tosi, *Management by Objectives: Applications and Research* (New York: MacMillan, 1973).

23. Ibid., p. 23.

CHAPTER 6

STRATEGIC PLANNING

CHAPTER OUTLINE

LEARNING OBJECTIVES

■ Define strategic planning and its role in organizational success.

■ Understand the relationship between strategic plans and operational plans.

■ Describe the historical changes which led to the increased use of strategic planning.

■ Identify the three essential elements of the strategic planning process.

■ Indicate the major characteristics of a mission statement and its role in strategic planning.

■ Understand the role of industry and competitor analysis, the analysis of internal resources, and matching analysis.

■ Understand the tools for setting corporate strategy.

■ Discuss the business strategy tools described by Michael Porter and the product life cycle model.

■ Define the role of functional strategic planning.

■ Describe the importance of having control systems congruent to the objectives of the strategic plan.

The personal computer market represents the classic case of the tech- nology-based business. Entry into technology-based industries is usually achieved through some dazzling innovation that gives the new company a temporary monopoly while its competitors scramble to catch up. Compaq Computer Corporation, the most successful start-up company in terms of sales volume ($111 million) in U.S. corporate history, achieved its success by holding innovation in check. In contrast to other computer makers such as Apple and DEC, Compaq decided that the road to success was paved by industry giant IBM and that it need only hitch a ride on the Big Blue juggernaut.

The key to Compaq's strategy was simple: President Rod Canion reasoned that software manufacturers would cater to the IBM PC; his company's computers would have to be able to run the IBM software while creating a market niche of their own. The solution: a portable computer weighing 28 pounds that mimics the IBM operating system as closely as the law will allow and runs virtually all software written for the IBM PC. Combined with a distribution plan that allows dealers a higher markup than IBM (36 percent versus 33 percent) and a policy of noncompetition with dealers (most computer manufacturers, including IBM, employ a sales force to sell directly to large corporations), the Compaq portable found quick acceptance among dealers and the public alike.

The small size of the Compaq means that it uses less office space and, just as importantly, less retail floor space. To ensure continued good relations with retailers, Canion hired away the man who developed IBM's retail network, H. L. "Sparky" Sparks.

Compaq uses its strong position with retailers to do market research. The company brings key retailers to its headquarters several times a year to quiz them on consumer preferences. As Warren Winger, chairman of Dallas-based CompuShop observes: "Compaq's success isn't from the latest technology or a lot of razzle-dazzle, but from coming out with what dealers want."

Compaq's strategy is not without its risks. IBM has been known to make unexpected moves that have left other emulators unable to make respectable profits in the long run. Should IBM make major changes in its operating system and keep the information proprietary as some observers think the company will do as a prelude to a major entry into the software market, Compaq's strategy would be left in the lurch.

Canion is betting that IBM will not abandon the 2 million owners of its PC as it rolls out its future product line. In the meantime, Compaq's first major mistake (analysts agree that the company has executed the correct strategy flawlessly thus far) could turn out to be its last in the high stakes world of high tech.

INTRODUCTION

Compaq, like a number of companies in the computer industry, was started by a couple of engineers who saw a market need their old company was unwilling or unable to fill. Canion's industry background helped him do what many beginners fail to do: take a hard look at the competitive environment in which the company would operate. This analysis led him to several conclusions: (1) IBM was the dominant fact of life in the market for personal computers and Compaq could not hope to compete head-to-head; (2) while a portable desk-top computer was a market innovation, it could be (and was) easily copied by IBM and other companies; and (3) the computer business is notoriously volatile with rapidly changing technology; today's hot product and company could well be forgotten tomorrow. It was not enough to make a good, reliable computer to survive; a strategy that would overcome the above problems was necessary.

The strategy selected by Compaq was based on three principles: (1) IBM compatibility. By piggy-backing on IBM's success, the company assured itself of a vast array of software for its computer line. (2) A strong dealer network. This strategy included noncompetition with dealers, higher than average dealer margins, dealer input into marketing decisions, and a strong advertising program. (3) Offering features unavailable to IBM's customers. The portable nature of Compaq's computer and its use of a faster processing chip were part of its product differentiation strategy. With its identity (an IBM look-alike with enhanced features and dependent on its strong dealer network) established in the minds of the founders, it was a relatively easy step for Compaq to design its marketing, advertising, financial, and product development strategies to make this identity a reality. In other words, Compaq's operational plans were easily conceived once its strategic plan was in place.

This chapter will consist of a discussion of three major areas. First, the definition and meaning of strategic planning—what it is and why it is important—will be discussed. Second, the evolution of strategic planning in business organizations, its fundamental differences from operational planning, and the process of strategic planning will be examined. Finally, some generic strategies and contemporary strategic planning frameworks will be analyzed.

THE ROLE AND DEFINITION OF STRATEGIC PLANNING

Many companies face the future, and its accelerating change, unprepared. Though the planning process described in Chapter 4 has been incorporated in one form or another by many organizations, its use does not ensure success. In the constantly changing economic and competitive environment, the key to success lies not so much in

As industry technology becomes more advanced, as in this automated assembly line, planning strategies must likewise become more sophisticated.

the rigor and quality of operational planning as it does in the clarity of a firm's strategic thinking. To flourish, it is essential that firms understand what business they want to be in and where they want to be at some future date—**strategic planning**—as well as how to get there. It is the "getting there" responsibility that is aided by operational planning and decision-making processes.

Strategy should provide a picture of the organization as it wants to look in the future. Thus, strategy is vision. It is directed at "what" the organization should be rather than "how" it will get there. "Strategy" has been used in the literature and in practice to mean different things. Many of its uses seem to confuse the "what" and "how" dimension.

Frequently managers talk about a "market strategy" or a "financial strategy" when they really mean a plan to position their products in a particular market or a plan to allocate financial resources. Such "strategies" are really operational plans to help accomplish an overarching corporate strategy.

Strategic planning, then, has a precise meaning apart from operational planning. Strategy is defined as a framework that guides those choices that determine the nature and direction of an organization.[2] Thus strategy helps to create a unified direction for the organization in terms of its many objectives and operational goals. It provides a basis to guide the allocation of resources used to move the organization toward the accomplishment of those objectives.

Strategic planning sets direction and establishes goals. Operational planning is the day-to-day decision making done at lower levels in the organization. Strategic planning focuses on doing the right things (**effectiveness**) while operational planning stresses doing things right (**efficiency**).

Figure 6-1 illustrates the relationship between the strategic plan and operational plans. The strategic plan is implemented through the development of operational plans consistent with the mission, objectives, and strategies of the organization.[3]

CASE
GM Buys Electronic Data Systems

 Several years ago, General Motors (GM) bought Electronic Data Systems. Why? GM found itself at a competitive disadvantage in the fight for market share with the Japanese as a result of a shift in consumer preferences to smaller cars (due to higher fuel costs) in which the Japanese enjoyed major cost advantages. GM could not realistically hope to compete on the basis of wages; technology was a different story. GM reasoned that a high degree of automation would enable it to avoid high labor cost while improving its quality standards.

EDS was a very profitable provider of software systems and support and had the capability of integrating automated manufacturing systems. The purchase of EDS would enable GM not only to automate more effectively, but to tie together its manufacturing, purchasing, and marketing functions, thus greatly reducing costs. GM could also obtain operating synergies by reassigning its own systems personnel to the acquired company and consolidating duplicative functions. GM's financial muscle would enable EDS to compete for much larger contracts.

The case above illustrates many of the major elements and characteristics of strategic planning:

1. It deals with matching resources and skills of the organization with opportunities and risks existent in the external environment. In doing so it provides answers to such questions as: "What businesses are we in and where should we be in the future?" and "Who are our customers and who should they be?"

2. It provides a basis for more detailed planning and day-to-day operational decisions. When faced with decisions, effective managers might ask: "Which alternative is more consistent with our strategy?"

3. It has a long time frame.

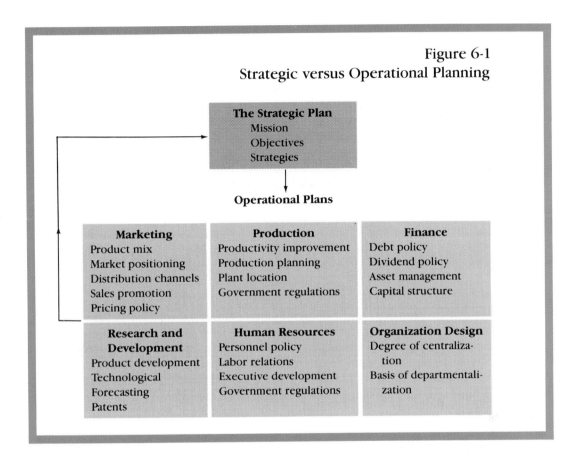

Figure 6-1
Strategic versus Operational Planning

The Strategic Plan
Mission
Objectives
Strategies

Operational Plans

Marketing	**Production**	**Finance**
Product mix	Productivity improvement	Debt policy
Market positioning	Production planning	Dividend policy
Distribution channels	Plant location	Asset management
Sales promotion	Government regulations	Capital structure
Pricing policy		
Research and Development	**Human Resources**	**Organization Design**
Product development	Personnel policy	Degree of centraliza-
Technological	Labor relations	tion
Forecasting	Executive development	Basis of departmentali-
Patents	Government regulations	zation

4. It is performed by top-level managers because they have the necessary information and because their commitment is necessary to obtain the level of commitment at lower levels necessary for successful implementation.

5. It is generally stated in relatively general and nonspecific terms.

DEVELOPMENT OF STRATEGIC PLANNING

In earlier, less dynamic periods of our society, the planning systems utilized by most organizations consisted primarily of preparing annual budgets and extrapolating current year sales and environmental trends for five and ten years. Based on these forecasts, managers decided resource allocation. In many instances these forecasts were fairly accurate because many environmental elements were stable.

Factors Leading to Development of Strategic Planning

In the years since World War II, however, significant changes in our society have occurred and the stability of many factors can no longer be counted upon. Several major developments have resulted in the increased importance of strategic planning.[4] Compaq Corporation provides an excellent example of the impact of these developments.

INCREASING RATE OF TECHNOLOGICAL CHANGE   With today's technological explosion whole new industries have developed. This rate of change has created a need for organizations to be proactive in seeking new opportunities rather than reacting to competitive forces. For example, the personal computer industry did not even exist until the late 1970s. This technology has forced even small businesses to grow increasingly sophisticated in the use of data and forecasting methods.

INCREASING COMPLEXITY OF THE MANAGER'S JOB   Managers today must deal with many more rapidly changing factors than did their predecessors. Inflation, demographic shifts, and matters relating to social responsibility all add to this increased complexity. Increased size due to internal growth and external acquisition have added to these complexities. Strategic planning allows managers to anticipate the problems and opportunities that result. Compaq's market for personal computers has greatly expanded as managers look for tools to help them cope with this complexity.

GROWING COMPLEXITY OF THE EXTERNAL ENVIRONMENT   Because of the increasing interdependencies in our environment, modern-day management cannot make decisions based solely on internal considerations. Management decisions must also take into account government regulations, stockholder expectations, legal decisions, public opinion, labor relations, and many other external elements. For example, some critics have raised health concerns on behalf of computer workers who must stare at their video display terminals all day. Compaq and other manufacturers must meet these concerns.

LONGER LEAD TIME BETWEEN DECISIONS AND RESULTS   The prospect for the economy and other important planning variables must be projected further ahead than ever before. The consequences of taking a short-term perspective can be severe as can be seen in the case of the steel and automobile industries. In steel, the failure to utilize the latest processes has resulted in the competitive disadvantage of U.S. steel makers to foreign competitors. The failure of the U.S. automobile industry to focus on the long-term need for fuel-efficient cars caused the industry to lose a large share of the market to imports, mainly from Japan. On the other hand, Compaq has taken a long-term view of IBM's market dominance and designed its operating system to be compatible with, but not infringing upon, IBM's system.

Massive closure of steel mills in the East demonstrates the consequences of an industry's failure to respond strategically to technological change.

These events have thus contributed to an evolution in the way an organization plans for its future. From a simple budget development process, organizations have progressed to the use of sophisticated planning tools, a greater concern for the external environment, and a new way of thinking strategically.

THE STRATEGIC PLANNING PROCESS

Strategic planning is a rational process that can and should be modified and used by managers in all types of organizations. While some disagreement among managers and academics may exist, the model in Figure 6-2 captures the key components of the

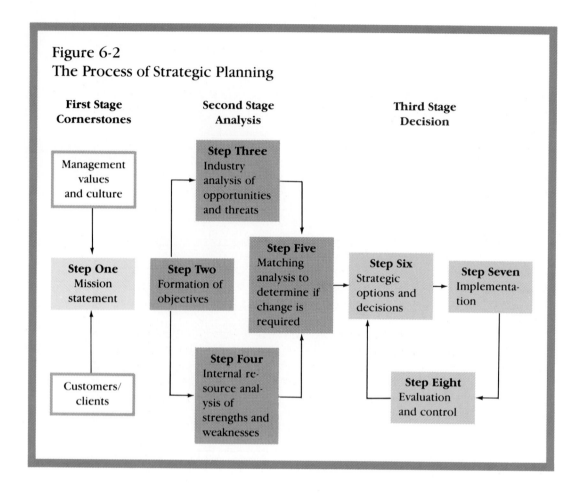

Figure 6-2
The Process of Strategic Planning

| First Stage | Second Stage | Third Stage |
| Cornerstones | Analysis | Decision |

Management values and culture

Step Three
Industry analysis of opportunities and threats

Step One
Mission statement

Step Two
Formation of objectives

Step Five
Matching analysis to determine if change is required

Step Six
Strategic options and decisions

Step Seven
Implementation

Customers/ clients

Step Four
Internal resource analysis of strengths and weaknesses

Step Eight
Evaluation and control

strategic planning process. The strategic planning process can be broken down into three general stages and eight major steps.

FIRST STAGE: CORNERSTONES

As management begins the strategic planning process, it is essential to establish cornerstones that will provide a solid foundation for the rest of the process. The major cornerstone is the establishment of a "vision" or direction for the company to pursue. This top organizational purpose or goal should be summed up clearly and specifically in a "mission statement." The mission statement should take into consideration the shared values of management as well as the needs of the customers or clients.

Step One: The Mission Statement

The first step in the strategic planning process is to identify and generate the organizational mission. "A corporation's identity is more fundamental than a strategic plan because effective strategy depends on committing to essential strengths which stem from identity."[5]

As businesses are started, the purpose or mission is usually known and well understood by the founders. However, as the organization expands, enters new markets, or merges, many firms shift from the original mission statement. "Recent mega-mergers suggest shifts in a number of basic industries: U.S. Steel and Marathon must grapple to determine what sort of corporation it is now. Du Pont and Conoco cannot escape the need to resolve the shape and thrust of this reconfigured company. Fluor and St. Joe Minerals must come to grips with how far they're going to integrate and what will emerge when they finally do."[6]

In addition, management may change or lose sight of the original mission as a result of "drifting" that occurs when the mission is not well defined or understood. A clear understanding of the company's mission is the first step in the strategic planning process.

The **mission statement**, like that of Merrill Lynch in Box 6-1, should be a long-term vision of what the organization is trying to become, what market it is trying to serve, and what needs are being met. It should describe the organization's products and markets in a way that reflects the values and priorities of the strategic decision makers. An effective mission statement is achievable, instructive, specific, reflective of management values and culture, and customer-oriented.

ACHIEVABLE   While a good mission statement will cause an organization to stretch its performance levels, it must also be possible to accomplish given the creative resources and unique competencies of the organization.

Box 6-1
Mission Statement of Merrill Lynch

Our mission is to be a client-focused, worldwide financial services organization, striving for excellence by serving the needs of individuals, corporations, governments, and institutions. Our objective is to be the acknowledged leader in the value we offer our clients, the returns we offer our shareholders and the rewards we offer our employees. This then will be our legacy of leadership.

SOURCE: *Merrill Lynch Annual Report,* 1985, cover.

INSTRUCTIVE   The mission statement provides a sense of shared purpose and values apart from the various functions and activities of the organization. It unites efforts and elicits a sense of commitment to shared values. Thus, such results as maximizing profits, increasing sales, or increasing number of patients cared for, can be seen as results of following a well-defined mission statement rather than the mission itself.

SPECIFIC   To be helpful to managers in establishing the strategic direction of an organization, the mission statement must clearly identify the key characteristics of the organization. Such statements as "maximizing the wealth of shareholders" or "producing the highest quality product at the lowest possible price" may sound good, but they do not provide specific enough direction to help managers make important decisions.

REFLECTIVE OF MANAGEMENT VALUES AND CULTURE   As important as the mission statement is, it must reflect the realities, as well as the ideals, of an organization. In setting goals, a manager must obviously understand competitive realities; however, managers must also recognize that they have personal values—important beliefs that they themselves hold. It is proper to recognize those values in strategy formulation, and to recognize corporate culture—the values shared by most company employees. As Figure 6-3 indicates, the values of top management and the organization's culture have a significant impact on the mission statement.[7] The mission statement then becomes a major driving force in the evolution of culture.

The influence of management values and organizational culture, which is largely influenced by the values of key executives, should not be underestimated. Examples of chief executives who had great influence shaping corporate culture are Alfred Sloan's desire for decentralization at General Motors, Bill Marriott's orientation to meeting customer needs, and Howard Head's entrepreneurial style at Head Ski Company. The values of top management are reflected in the strategic direction selected by organizations.

CUSTOMER-ORIENTED   The needs and desires of the customers or clients of any organization need to play a central role in the development of a mission statement. For many years, companies defined their business in terms of products rather than markets. With the rapid changes in the nature of products and services, it is necessary to write mission statements that are market-driven rather than product-driven. Peter Drucker states it well:

> A business is not defined by the company's name, statutes, or articles of incorporation. It is defined by the want the customer satisfies when he buys a product or service. To satisfy the customer is the mission and purpose of every business. The question "What is our business?" can, therefore, be answered only by looking at the business from the outside, from the point of view of customer and market.[8]

Compaq's entry into the personal computer market illustrates this point in several ways. Computer users wanted a machine that was portable, as well as smaller and

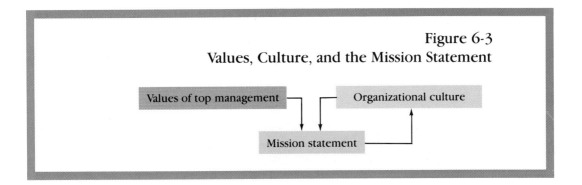

Figure 6-3
Values, Culture, and the Mission Statement

faster than other models on the market. Computer dealers wanted a machine that did not take too much valuable floor space and a supplier that would listen to them and not compete with them. Compaq's strategy indicates that the company defined itself in terms of these customer needs.

SECOND STAGE: ANALYSIS

After the establishment of cornerstones, the strategic planning process continues through an analysis stage. As a natural outgrowth of the organization's mission statement, objectives are first formulated. In deciding upon the strategic alternatives to accomplish these objectives, it is necessary to analyze the strengths and weaknesses of an organization's internal resources as well as the opportunities and threats from competitive forces in the industry. This analysis stage is necessary before strategic options can be considered.

Step Two: Formulation of Objectives

As Figure 6-1 indicates, organizational objectives are the natural outgrowth of an organization's mission statement. In the previous chapter, the critical role of objectives in enabling the organization to fulfill its mission was discussed, along with the performance areas in which objectives should be established. Establishing organizational objectives consistent with the mission statement is an important cornerstone in the development of corporate strategy.

Some key objectives in harmony with Compaq's mission are the development of strong dealer relationships, keeping the operating system as close to IBM as legally possible, and the introduction of unique features with high market appeal. The achievement of these objectives virtually ensures that the company's mission of bringing about a desktop computer that runs IBM software will be accomplished.

TYPES OF OBJECTIVES   As is evident from the discussion of Compaq, organizations establish objectives in many areas. These goals reflect the values of the organization's various constituencies.

Drucker, for instances, believes that organizations need to set objectives in all areas upon which the organization's survival depends.

> A business must first be able to create a customer. There is, therefore, need for a marketing objective. Businesses must be able to innovate or else their competitors will obsolesce them. There is need for an innovation objective. All businesses depend on the three factors of production of the economist, that is, on the human resource, the capital resource, and physical resources. There must be objectives for their supply, their employment, and their development. The resources must be employed productively and their productivity has to grow if the business is to survive. There is need, therefore, for productivity objectives. Business exists in society and community and, therefore, has to discharge social responsibilities, at least to the point where it takes responsibility for its impact upon the environment. Therefore, objectives in respect to the social dimensions of business are needed.
>
> Finally, there is need for profit—otherwise none of the objectives can be attained. They all require effort, that is, cost. And they can be financed only out of the profits of a business. They all entail risks; they all, therefore, require a profit to cover the risk of potential losses.[9]

Step Three: Industry Analysis

Once the mission statement has been formulated, the next step is to examine the firm's opportunities and threats as determined by its analysis of the external environment.[10]

OPPORTUNITIES   The external business environment is constantly changing. An **opportunity** becomes present when change creates a need or the ability to fulfill a long-felt need. An organization may not recognize an opportunity or be well-suited to take advantage of it, but the opportunity is present in the environment to help an organization achieve or exceed its strategic goals.

THREATS   Change can also produce **threats** to the organization. New products, changing consumer tastes, government regulations, court decisions, and economic conditions are just some of the factors that can create threats. Like opportunities, threats are not always recognized or coped with by organizations.

The fate of People's Express Airlines illustrates the importance of an accurate assessment of the competition and of the changing business environment.

CASE

People's Express: Strategic Blunders Lead to Bankruptcy[11]

People's Express Airlines was one of the boldest airlines ever to take to the skies. The company offered inexpensive fares and achieved low costs through very broad job classifications and salaries contingent in large part on profitability. Pilots, for example, were required to man a back-office computer, and employees were required to buy stock in the company (until the practice was declared illegal by a federal court).

People's believed in rapid expansion. The company bought Denver's Frontier Airlines and expanded its routes as rapidly as possible. In 1984 it began its most ambitious expansion by attempting to become the largest air carrier out of the New York market and began taking delivery of a new plane every 10 to 12 days.

The company's plan to take the New York market was based on several factors:

1. The largest competitors in New York, Pan American and Eastern, were among the industry's weakest companies financially.

2. People's had plenty of room to expand out of its Newark location while its competitors were restricted by the limited capability of LaGuardia and Kennedy airports to handle much more traffic.

3. People's toughest competitors, United and American, were concentrating their efforts on hubs elsewhere.

People's perceived a window of opportunity in the New York market that it felt well-suited to exploit.

The real test of People's strategy came when the airline reached its planned ten flights a day into Chicago and had to go head to head with United and American. The traffic that it projected did not materialize and the company was faced with long-term debt of $250 million and interest expense of $40 million. The 77 planes that People's had on hand by mid-1985 were rather hard to keep busy. People's reliance on its presence to increase the size of the market and avoid fare wars proved unfounded. In August 1986 People's Express was forced into bankruptcy as it could not generate the revenues to keep up with its expansion.

Many analysts ascribe the failure of People's to the fact that its management system was adapted well to a small maverick airline, but that this strength became a weakness when it sought to run a large, sophisticated business in the same way. Others claim that in its exuberance to expand, it overestimated its opportunities and strengths while underestimating its weaknesses and the threats of fare wars with competitors. While the major airlines could afford to ignore People's when it was a maverick, they could not do so when the upstart challenged their most profitable markets. Thus, People's illustrates the importance of a careful and accurate assessment of the opportunities and threats created by changing industry and competitor environment. ▼

FORCES DRIVING INDUSTRY COMPETITION   An industry analysis is fundamental in that it enables managers to identify opportunities available as well as threats in the environment. Sustained profitability or the continued functioning of any organization is strongly affected by the degree of competition in that industry. Accordingly, the thrust of strategic management must be to cope with competition and the forces which generate it in any given industry. While each industry has its unique mixture of competitive forces, enough similarities exist between industries to allow some generalizations about the major forces that appear to drive competition in any industry. The major competitive forces at work in any industry are discussed in Box 6-2 and illustrated in Figure 6-4.

Strength of Rivalry among Competitors   Rivalry in any industry occurs when one of the competitor firms makes a strategic move (pricing, advertising, a campaign, etc.) that, if successful, results in increased profits. If this competitive move, however, results in the reduction of a market share or profits of competitors, they are likely to respond. Factors affecting the strength of these competitive reactions are:

Box 6-2
Competitive Forces in Industry

1. Competition among firms in the industry, usually manifested in terms of price, quality, or service.

2. Competition with substitute products. The availability of substitute products effectively places limits on the prices, profits, and competitive forces in any industry.

3. Bargaining power with buyers and suppliers. Large buyers have potential bargaining power to drive down prices while significant suppliers have the potential power to increase costs or reduce quality of required inputs. In retailing, Sears and K-Mart can demand lower prices because of the volumes they can generate.

4. Entry of new competitors. The entry of new competitors reduces the sales of existing firms, tends to drive down prices, and/or increase costs, reducing profitability. Because individual firms in a given industry employ different strategies and position themselves accordingly, these competitive forces will impact on them differently.

---

1. Competition increases with the number, size, and capability of rival firms.

2. Competition is stronger when demand is growing slowly.

3. Competition increases when fixed costs are high, the product is perishable, or other factors exist to create a temptation to cut prices.

4. Competition increases when the product/services of an industry becomes less differentiated from the buyer's point of view.

Product Substitutes   Firms are not only in competition with other firms in the same industry, but with related industries producing products that their customers can substitute for their own. The producers of sliderules discovered this fact of life when calculator companies and personal computer manufacturers took most of their market.

The impact of the competitive forces created by product and service substitutes is felt in several ways.[12] First, product and service substitutes place a ceiling on the prices that can be charged and thereby reduce the profit potential of an industry. For example, the price of aluminum constrains the price that steel manufacturers can charge. Second, with the availability of product substitutes, sellers must upgrade quality or reduce prices to differentiate their product from their substitutes. In so doing they risk reduction of profit potential. Failure to do so risks lower growth rates, sales, and profits.

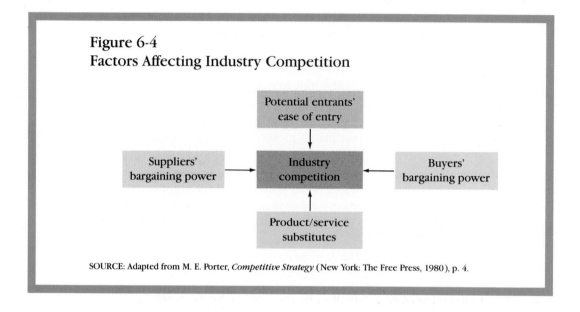

Figure 6-4
Factors Affecting Industry Competition

SOURCE: Adapted from M. E. Porter, *Competitive Strategy* (New York: The Free Press, 1980), p. 4.

Relative Bargaining Power of Suppliers   The impact that suppliers can have on the competitive forces in an industry is a function of the importance of their product in that industry's production process.[13] When the product of a particular supplier makes up a significant part of the industry's total costs or when it can significantly impact the quality of the final product, the potential bargaining power of the supplier is enhanced. A supplier of a patented high-speed microchip would thus be in a strong bargaining position relative to a computer start-up like Compaq.

The extent to which this potential is realized depends on several factors related to the structure of the industries in which these suppliers compete. In general, a group of supplier firms is more powerful when:[14]

- The supplier industry is dominated by a few companies and is more concentrated than the industry it sells to.

- Its product is differentiated so that it is costly or difficult for the buyer to switch from one supplier to another.

- The supplier does not have to compete with the product substitutes of suppliers in other industries.

- The buyers are not important customers of the supplier.

- The supplier's product is an important input to the buyers' businesses.

Relative Bargaining Power of Buyers   Just as powerful suppliers can influence the market they serve and are restrained by competitive pressures, powerful buyers can also influence suppliers and also face some restraints.[15] The power of buyers tends to be greater when:[16]

- Buyers are large, relatively few in number, and purchase in large quantities. With large quantities to be purchased, buyers may obtain concessions on price or terms of sales.
- The buyer purchases a significant portion of the selling industry's sales.
- The product is relatively standardized so that buyers can easily find new suppliers without incurring significant costs in searching for alternate suppliers.
- When the selling industry consists of a large number of relatively small sellers, or when it is feasible to purchase the input from several suppliers rather than one.

Consequently, the seller of the patented high-speed microchip in the example above must be careful in its treatment of a company like Compaq because new substitutes may be available tomorrow, and Compaq is one of the larger purchasers in this market. Therefore, the relative power of Compaq versus such a microchip supplier is much more balanced than the supplier's patent would initially suggest.

Potential for New Entrants   One of the major concerns in strategic management is the threat to the established competitive position caused by the possibility of new entrants into an industry. New entrants can bring new capacity and often significant resources to aid their desire to gain market share.

The seriousness of the threat of increased competition depends on two factors: barriers to entry and the expected reaction of existing firms to new entrants. Major barriers to entry are economies of scale, major capital requirements, access to distribution channels, and differentiated products. Note that Compaq's strategy was designed to overcome some of these barriers. The use of an operating system lowered capital requirements and economies of scale in three ways: (1) Compaq would not need to develop an operating system of its own; (2) it would not need to develop its own software; and (3) it could use parts standardized for IBM equipment. Compaq's distribution strategy, of course, was designed to make its product attractive to distributors and retailers.

Step Four: Internal Resource Analysis

Environmental analysis enables managers to identify opportunities and threats. After these have been assessed, managers must then focus on what their organizations can do. This analysis of internal resources helps to identify an organization's competitive advantages and disadvantages, its strengths and weaknesses relative to its main competitors.

STRENGTHS   A firm's **strengths** are its distinctive competencies in terms of products, services, management talent, financial resources, etc. Strengths allow a firm to

Table 6-1
Internal Resource Analysis

FACTOR	STRENGTH RELATIVE TO COMPETITORS				
	WEAK				STRONG
Personnel					
Managerial support	1	2	3	4	5
Marketing support	1	2	3	4	5
Technical/Operational support	1	2	3	4	5
Product Mix					
Differentiation	1	2	3	4	5
Pricing	1	2	3	4	5
Quality	1	2	3	4	5
Distribution	1	2	3	4	5
Operations					
Size	1	2	3	4	5
Efficiency	1	2	3	4	5
Age of plant and equipment	1	2	3	4	5
Financial					
Liquidity	1	2	3	4	5
Debt coverage	1	2	3	4	5
Capital structure	1	2	3	4	5
Asset base	1	2	3	4	5
Access to capital	1	2	3	4	5
Cost of inputs	1	2	3	4	5
Intangibles					
Reputation	1	2	3	4	5
Corporate responsibility	1	2	3	4	5
Vulnerability to suit	1	2	3	4	5
Patent protection	1	2	3	4	5
Research and development	1	2	3	4	5

take advantage of favorable environmental conditions and avoid the effects of unfavorable conditions.

WEAKNESSES   **Weaknesses** represent the organization's inability to bring sufficient resources to bear to take advantage of opportunities and to avoid threats. A realistic assessment of weaknesses allows a firm to avoid strategic blunders. One tool used by managers to assess strengths and weaknesses is an **internal resource analysis**. The kinds of internal resource factors that are considered are illustrated in Table 6-1. A great many factors are reviewed in assessing an organization's strengths and weaknesses. Any of the major categories can be a source of either competitive strength or weakness.

Internal resource analysis enables management to decide which strategies are consistent with available or readily obtainable resources. For example, a company such as Procter & Gamble, with great strengths in marketing, research and development, and a strong balance sheet may choose to roll out a new product offering on a national basis to establish a brand quickly as a leader. Smaller firms, with less expertise and financial capability, might have to restrict themselves to metropolitan or regional product rollouts, even if they have a competing brand that is clearly superior to the P&G offering.

Another contrasting example is Delta and Eastern Airlines different financial situations due to their internal resources. Delta has been able to grow rapidly because of its financial strength. It has a strong financial base, enjoys an excellent reputation with creditors, and has always been able to find the financing needed to support its strategy of acquiring new and more efficient aircraft. Eastern, on the other hand, has found itself heavily in debt from past purchases of aircraft and its profit performance has been insufficient to lessen its debt load.

In the analysis of internal resources, Hofer & Schendel suggest four steps:

1. Develop a profile of the organization's principal resources and skills in these broad areas: financial, physical, organizational and human, and technological.

2. Determine the key success requirement of the product/market segments in which the organization competes or might compete.

3. Compare the resource profile to the key success requirements to determine the major strengths on which an effective strategy can be based and the major weaknesses which must be overcome.

4. Compare the organization's strengths and weaknesses with those of its major competitors to identify which of its resources and skills are sufficient to yield meaningful competitive advantages in the marketplace.[17]

Step Five: Matching Analysis

After the external environment and internal resource analysis has been completed it is possible to identify the match, or gap, between opportunities/threats and the strengths/weaknesses stemming from internal resources. This integration of external and internal analysis (**matching analysis**) allows managers to forecast the results of existing or contemplated strategies. If gaps appear between anticipated performance and the goals of the organization, management will understand more completely the extent of the strategic change needed. The analysis of strengths, weaknesses, opportunities, and threats is frequently referred to as **SWOT analysis**.

In this matching analysis, there are four concepts that are important for managers to understand if they are to make good strategic decisions: leverage, constraints, vulnerabilities, and problems.[18]

LEVERAGE   **Leverage** comes into play when the internal strengths match or are consistent with opportunities found in the environmental analysis. The existence of this match would then support a strategy to take advantage of this opportunity. For example, Merrill Lynch could take advantage of a government policy change allowing more takeovers by devoting resources to the development of its merger and acquisition capabilities.

CONSTRAINTS   **Constraints** exist when opportunities available in the environment do not match up with the resource strengths of the organization. Additional resources will be required before opportunities can be taken advantage of. Compaq recognized the constraints that it faced in trying to gain retail distribution and consumer acceptance if software for its portable computer was limited to programs written for Compaq alone. Compaq, by becoming IBM compatible, could tap into the software reservoir created by its largest rival, making the cost of the additional resources minimal.

VULNERABILITIES   **Vulnerabilities** occur when an environmental condition poses a threat to an asset or strength of a firm. Even though an organization is doing something well, that strength may be threatened by events outside of the firm. IBM, while threatened by smaller rivals such as Compaq and Apple, faces a major threat in that AT&T has developed a unique operating system, Unix, to challenge IBM's industry standard, DOS (actually supplied by MicroSoft). The AT&T technology is particularly strong in the multi-user market, the highest growth market for personal computers.

PROBLEMS   In matching analysis a **problem** exists when one of the organization's weak points is in the same area as a threat being generated from the environmental analysis. This problem may be sufficiently large to endanger the existence of the organization, or it may alter the strategies available for use until the problem is resolved. General Motors, Ford, and Chrysler were weak in the small car market just at a time when consumer preferences changed to small cars because of higher oil prices. The Japanese manufacturers moved aggressively to exploit this weakness and captured 25 percent of the market before the Big Three had a chance to respond. Industry losses amounted to billions of dollars per year in 1981 and 1982. Chrysler required federal loans and loan guarantees to stave off bankruptcy.

THIRD STAGE: THE DECISION

After completing the first two important stages of the strategic planning process (developing cornerstones and conducting the analysis of strategic variables), the next step is to pull it all together and make important strategic decisions. If a change in strategy seems appropriate to close the **performance gap** (the gap between planned and actual performance), it then becomes appropriate to identify, evaluate, and select alternative strategic approaches. The large organization will typically develop strategy at three levels: (1) corporate, (2) business, and (3) functional. The selected alternative at each level must then be implemented. Finally, the results of the selected strategy must be evaluated and any needed changes made. This process requires a control system.

Step Six: Strategic Options and Tools—Corporate-level Strategy

Corporate-level strategy typically explores the ways a firm can develop a favorable "portfolio strategy." It includes such factors as decisions about the type of businesses a firm should be in and the flow of financial and other resources to and from its divisions called **strategic business units** (SBU). SBUs have a unique mission, product line, competitors, and markets relative to other SBUs in the corporation. Executives directing the entire corporation need to define an overall strategic direction—called a grand strategy—and then bring together a portfolio of strategic business units to carry it out.

GRAND STRATEGY Grand strategy is the general plan of major action by which a firm intends to achieve its long-term objectives. In developing the grand strategy, there have been important developments in recent years in ways of thinking about the types of businesses that firms should be engaged in. These developments center around the notion of a portfolio strategy.

PORTFOLIO STRATEGY Portfolio strategy pertains to the mix of business units that fit together to provide competitive advantage for the corporation. For example, an individual investor may wish to diversify his investment portfolio by investing in some growth stocks, income-producing stocks, bonds, and perhaps cash. Likewise, a corporation may want to have a balanced mix of SBUs.

MATRIX MODELS The first matrix model was proposed by the Boston Consulting Group.[19] This model examined the positioning of the product based on the internal potential of the product and the external market potential. The internal potential was defined as a competitive strength and it was measured by the product's market share. The external market potential was similar to the product life cycle model in that it addressed the growth of the demand of market for the product. Using a high and low classification for each of the dimensions resulted in a four-cell matrix. In Figure 6-5, which illustrates this matrix, each cell is given a title to describe the nature of the products that fall within it:

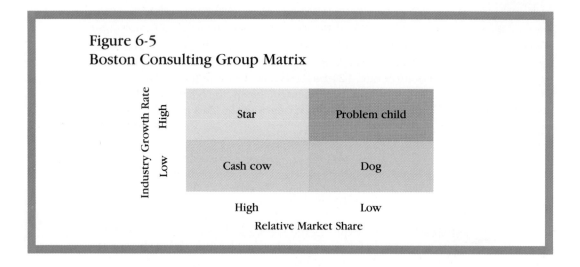

Figure 6-5
Boston Consulting Group Matrix

1. **Star** Large market share in a high-growth market. Great potential growth; however, may require infusions of cash to finance that growth. Examples: Diet Coke, Liquid Tide.

2. **Problem Child** Weak competitive position in high-growth markets. Require financing to improve competitive position, increase market share, and achieve "star" status. Without strength in competitive position, may lose position in market. Example: Pringles Potato Chips.

3. **Cash Cow** Commanding market share in low-growth markets. Require limited investment to maintain competitive position and provide internal cash that can be invested in strengthening "problem children" and "stars." In the long-term, the high-market growth of "stars" will decline, and these products will become "cash cows." Examples: Coke, Pepsi, Tide, Cheerios, and Monopoly.

4. **Dog** With weak competitive position and low-growth markets, products have limited potential. Lucky to break even on a cash basis. It is pointless to strengthen competitive position since market growth is very low and no potential for improvement is apparent. Examples: Ford Edsel and most American-made television sets.

Other matrix models have been developed using different measures of market potential and competitive strength. For example, Arthur D. Little Company uses a 20-cell matrix.[20] Each of the models attempts to determine the competitive positioning of the products that are being evaluated. After the evaluation, a strategy is developed to specify the route from one cell to another.

SELECTION OF STRATEGIES   Several different types of general purpose strategies have been proposed for individual products, product lines, divisions, or departments within an organization. After classifying each strategic business unit according to the business portfolio matrix just described, management must then decide which of four alternative brand strategies should be pursued by each unit. These strategies are:

1. **Build**   Appropriate for units believed to have star potential (probably a question mark at the present time). Short-term profits are sacrificed in order to provide the necessary financial resources to achieve this objective. The promotion that Ford put into the new Ford Taurus and Mercury Sable automobiles indicated that it felt these products were capable of star status.

2. **Hold**   Appropriate for cash cows. Allows organization to take advantage of a very positive cash flow. Procter & Gamble, for example, still promotes its Tide laundry detergent for this reason.

3. **Harvest**   Appropriate for all products or units except those classified as stars. The basic objective is to increase the short-term cash return without too much concern for the long-run impact. It is especially worthwhile when a firm has cash cows whose long-run prospects are not good because of a low market growth rate. Computer firms typically employ this strategy as their cash cows approach technical obsolescence.

4. **Divest**   Getting rid of products or divisions with low shares of low-growth markets is often appropriate. Problem Children and Dogs are particularly suited for this objective. IBM employed this strategy in its decision to discontinue the PC jr. personal computer.

G. E. Business Screen   The General Electric Company pioneered the development of a more sophisticated portfolio matrix which can be used to allocate resources among SBUs. It can also be used to reevaluate potential business acquisitions. The matrix is illustrated in Figure 6-6.

This business screen has nine categories based on two dimensions: industry attractiveness and business strength to compete in that industry. This matrix also provides a list of criteria for evaluating both. Industry attractiveness includes such considerations as market size and growth rate, economies of scale, profit margins and seasonality. Business strength is measured by such factors as relative market share, competitive strengths and weaknesses, and the quality of management.

Individual business units are represented in Figure 6-6 by the various-sized circles, with the area of the circle being proportional to the size of the industry. The black pie slice in each circle represents the market share the business maintains in that industry.

By evaluating each business unit in terms of scores on the two lists of criteria, strategic corporate-level decisions can be made. Business units that fall in the lower right-hand corner (shaded purple) are considered candidates for divestment because they rank low in both business strength and industry attractiveness. On the other hand, those SBUs in the upper left-hand corner (shaded turquoise) are just the opposite—strong businesses in attractive industries. The company should invest in and

Figure 6-6
General Electric's Nine-cell Portfolio Matrix

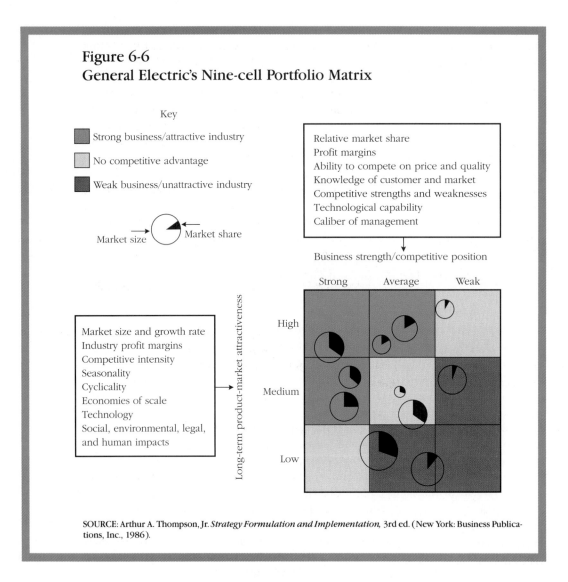

SOURCE: Arthur A. Thompson, Jr. *Strategy Formulation and Implementation,* 3rd ed. (New York: Business Publications, Inc., 1986).

develop these areas of their business. The businesses along the diagonal (shaded tan) should be handled selectively. While they do not appear to have significant competitive advantages, they are generally kept within the portfolio in expectation of improved performance.

BUSINESS-LEVEL STRATEGY AND GENERIC STRATEGIES   In contrast to the corporate-level strategy, business-level strategy usually occurs at the SBU or divisional level with emphasis on improving the competitive position of a corporation's products or services. Top management usually treats an SBU as an autonomous unit with the ability to develop its own strategy within the wider corporate objectives and grand strategy. In the development of business-level strategies, important frameworks to understand are the competitive strategies developed by Michael Porter, a professor at the Harvard Business School. Porter suggested that competitive business or **generic strategies** fall into three categories: (1) overall cost leadership, (2) differentiation, and (3) focus.[21] This identification of generic strategies is widely accepted among strategic management experts and deserves a closer look.

Overall Cost Leadership Strategy   Managers pursuing this strategy have as their major concern keeping costs, and therefore prices, lower than those of competitors. This leads to a plan that calls for the building of efficient facilities; light cost and overhead control, the achievement of cost reductions; the avoidance of marginal customer accounts, and minimal costs in research and development, service, sales and advertising. By maintaining a low-cost operation, lower prices, management will make it very difficult for competitors to match the price of their product or service.

The ability to make this strategy successful often requires a high market share, economies of scale, favorable access to labor and/or raw materials and a wide product line so that sales volume can be developed.

Differentiation Strategy   The focus of this strategy is on creating a uniqueness about a firm's product in comparison to other products produced in the industry. While management cannot ignore costs in the development of this strategy, minimizing costs is a secondary rather than a primary objective of the organization. Often the ability of an organization following a differentiation strategy to achieve a high market share would need to be sacrificed. Prices can be increased because of the perceived additional value, thus increasing profit margins. Some customers, however, may not be willing to pay the high price even though they perceive the product to be of superior quality.

Differentiation may be achieved by creative product engineering (Mercedes), strong marketing abilities (Crest Toothpaste), strong commitment to customer service (Nordstrom's Department Stores), or leading edge technology (Intel Corp).

Focus Strategy   Organizations pursuing a focus strategy attempt to gain a competitive edge by some combination of cost leadership or differentiation focusing on a narrow customer group, productions, or geographic market. The focus strategy thus provides products or services to a narrow segment, or niche, in the market. The reason for this is that a narrow segment can be served more effectively and efficiently than competing across the board. Examples of successful focus strategies would be Gray Computers which manufacture highly sophisticated computers for the government, and Fort Howard Paper which focuses on a narrow range of industrial grade papers and avoids consumer products more vulnerable to advertising and price battles.

PRODUCT LIFE CYCLE   Another important aspect in developing business-level strategies is the use of product life cycle models. Every business knows that products

Figure 6-7
The Product Life Cycle

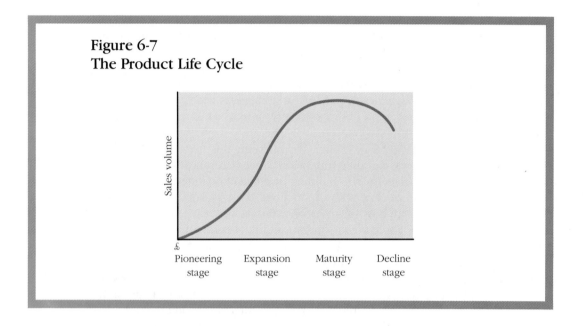

have a limited life. Understanding the various stages a product goes through is crucial in choosing the right competitive strategy. The product life cycle is illustrated in Figure 6-7. There are four typical stages in the demand of a product:

Pioneering Stage   The **pioneering stage** is the early stage of the development and introduction of a product. The new product is probably unique or unusual and has few competitors. The company must usually make significant investments in manufacturing, research and development, and marketing resulting in both negative cash flows and net losses during this stage of development.

Expansion Stage   In the **expansion stage**, the product has proven to be successful, and other companies have introduced competitive products. The market continues to expand but because of the increased competition, prices begin to fall. Nevertheless, the surviving companies begin to show a profit as they achieve economies of scale. Sales of the product continue to grow but at a decreasing rate. Development costs are reduced so that net income turns positive, but cash for investment in marketing and production facilities continues to be required. The financial needs are, however, less than in the pioneering stage.

Maturity Stage   As the market matures, the product enters the **maturity stage** where sales growth slows and marginal competitors in the product market are forced out. Price competition increases, and as a result, net income begins to decrease. However, cash requirements also decrease so the product begins to generate excess cash—cash that is not required for investment in marketing or production facilities—in sufficient amounts.

Decline Stage   In the **decline stage**, sales begin to decline. Net income continues to fall and may even become negative. Cash requirements level off, but may not decline since the company is making new investments in the product.

The duration of the various stages in the product life cycle differs between products. For instance, IBM's highly successful 360 series of computers had a growth period of several years following a relatively short production period. Fad items like hula hoops and pet rocks, on the other hand, may complete a full life cycle in several months.

Product life cycles reflect the unique nature and market potential of given products and services. Product life cycles in the future will probably be shorter—with movement through each stage at a much faster rate. Many experts believe that the trends in technology will contribute significantly to this development.

Strategy During the Product Life Cycle   Each stage of the product life cycle presents unique and significant strategic challenges. The pioneering stage is particularly risky because of the large cash outlays for supplies, facilities, and wages that are not offset by cash receipts. Compounding the negative cash flow problem during the pioneering stage is the threat of failure. The rejection of a new product in the marketplace can be very costly. Classic examples are the Ford Edsel, the Texas Instruments home computer, the IBM PC jr., and the movie disasters *Cleopatra* and *Heaven's Gate*. Each of these failures carried price tags of millions of dollars, and some cost hundreds of millions.

A recent study of 148 medium- and large-sized manufacturers revealed that roughly one out of every three products introduced during the late 1970s failed.[22] With a 33 percent failure rate, it becomes obvious that the need is great for intelligent product introduction strategies. Among the major strategic concerns during this stage are the following: (1) building relationships with reliable suppliers, (2) planning financing for negative cash flow during the pioneering stage, (3) developing production and marketing operations, and (4) anticipating and planning for competition.

In the expansion stage, industry faces an interesting challenge. Large profit margins and limited competition can easily persuade management into believing that things will remain the same for a long period of time. It is during this profitable stage that the seeds of destruction of a product are often sown in the absence of adequate strategic planning. For example, Apple Computer expanded very quickly during this stage of its development by adding plant, equipment, and staff, only to face the need to close a number of production facilities during a downturn in the personal computer market. The significant strategic concerns during this stage are:

1. Developing research and competitive innovations for the present products.

2. Keeping economies of scale and production.

3. Building brand preferences and product loyalties.

4. Studying competitors to be aware of the nature of future competition.

Strategy for the maturity stage necessarily focuses on trimming costs and promoting efficiencies because of the erosion of profit margins due to competition. As both sales and profits fall during the maturity stage, management often attempts to extend the product life cycle and the period of profitable operations by offering new features and by emphasizing customer service. For example, when the Frisbee craze reached maturity, new Frisbees that glowed in the dark, made whirring sounds, etc., were offered.

As both sales and profits fall rapidly during the decline stage, withdrawal plans should ensure that the organization is not burdened with excessive raw materials, supplies, facilities, idle labor, or a large inventory of unmarketable finished goods. Operations are scaled down during the decline stage, making way for new products and industries.

FUNCTIONAL-LEVEL STRATEGY   The principal focus of functional strategy is on maximizing resource productivity given the constraints of corporate and business strategies; functional departments—marketing, production, finance, and personnel—develop strategies to manage their resources and improve performance. These strategies are coordinated with the business-level strategy to achieve the organization's strategic goals.

For example, if a company were to introduce new products in the early stages of their life cycle consistent with its strategy of growth, the functional departments would need to develop strategies which were supportive of the corporate and business-level strategies. The personnel department would need to recruit new personnel as well as train present managers to move into new positions. The marketing department would need to conduct some test marketing or market research along with new promotional campaigns. The finance department would need to provide the necessary financing for increased working capital and physical plant required to support a higher level of sales. Production would have to plan to be sure to provide the necessary levels of product.

Step Seven: Strategy Implementation

Once strategic plans have been developed, it is necessary that they be incorporated into the operations of the organization, if any benefit is to result from them. Whether formalized or not, strategic decisions must be reflected in the appropriate operational plans, programs, and budgets. For example, People's Express has been criticized because it failed to change its personnel practices and corporate culture when it tried to become a major airline. The company's structure, culture, and control mechanisms may have been appropriate for a small, "rebel" airline, but not for the large, complex, unwieldy organization resulting from its growth.

As managers work to ensure that their strategic planning efforts are implemented, at least four issues tied to organizational factors, discussed more fully in Chapters 9, 10, 11, and 12, ought to be considered.

PEOPLE   In the implementation of strategy it is essential to have appropriate staffing. People with the right skills and abilities must be available for key assignments, and attention needs to be given to recruiting or developing managers that have the proper skills.

CULTURE   The predominant culture must be supportive of successfully implementing the corporate strategy. Is the "right way to do things around here" compatible with the new strategy?

ORGANIZATIONAL STRUCTURE   In this area top managers need to be sure that the organization structure is compatible with the planning process, with the managerial style, and with the strategy itself. Issues of centralization versus decentralization become crucial in the implementation of strategic plans. For example, Compaq would want to be sure that its structure allowed for top management to be directly involved with its distribution network and product design decisions.

CONTROL SYSTEMS   Control systems need to be in place in order to implement a strategy successfully. **Control systems** permit top management to assess the organization's performance in meeting strategic objectives. People's Express, for example, was heavily criticized for its failure to control overbookings. While overbooking may have been somewhat acceptable in its early days, this failure was totally incompatible with its attempts to attract business travellers on the New York to Chicago run.

Strategies that are supported in each of these four areas stand a much greater chance of achieving their intended purposes.

Step Eight: Strategic Control and Evaluation

After strategies are determined and plans are made, management's primary task is to take steps to ensure that these plans are carried out or modified as required. This is the critical control function of management. Since management involves directing the activities of others, a major part of the control function is to make sure that other people do what should be done to accomplish the successful implementation of plans.

Management literature is full of advice on how to achieve better control. This advice usually describes some type of measurement and feedback process.

> The basic control process, wherever it is found and whatever it controls, involves three steps: (1) establishing standards, (2) measuring performance against these standards, and (3) correcting deviations from standards and plans.[23]

> A good management control system stimulates action by spotting the significant variations from the original plan and highlighting them for the people who can set things right.[24]

> Controls need to focus on results.[25]

Thus, organizations conduct strategic control—the actual monitoring of results in a variety of ways. The types of systems utilized and further discussion of the important topic of control is contained in Chapter 18. The following case study illustrates what can happen when controls are inconsistent with strategic plans.

CASE
Moving Too Quickly[26]

 Two Silicon Valley computer start-ups, Cosmos Computer Corporation (later renamed Gavilan Computer Corporation) and a spinoff from Convergent Technologies (Workslate), present classic examples of failing to implement a control process to ensure that operational plans dovetail with strategic objectives.

In the rush to market their portable, notebook-size computers and thus establish themselves in this small but growing market, these firms made large shipping commitments before manufacturing problems had been solved. Designs were hastily conceived and production debugging was skipped by both firms in an attempt to meet deadlines. Consumers, however, use computers for their accuracy and for the increased ease of performing various tasks. Quality control, then, is essential to any successful product introduction strategy in this industry.

The results of a lack of quality control were dissatisfied customers, cancelled orders, and the withdrawal of Convergent Technologies from this market while Gavilan struggled for survival. Regarding the cancellation of Workslate after losses estimated between $15 and $30 million, Convergent Technologies' President Allen H. Michels said, "I was unwilling to invest resources in a crapshoot."

In the evaluation of a strategy—that is the process of determining whether or not a strategic choice is meeting the goals of an organization—a number of criteria should be applied. According to Tilles and Rumult,[27] some of the criteria to consider are the following:

Internal Consistency   Is the strategy consistent with the stated mission, goals, and internal resources of the organization? What an organization wants to do and has the resources to accomplish must be consistent with what they plan to do. In the case of Convergent Technologies' Workslate and Gavilan Computer, the shipping commitments were incompatible with the production of a computer of acceptable quality.

External Consistency   Is the current strategy consistent with the demands of the external environment? Workslate and Gavilan seemed to forget that being first on the market is an advantage only when consumers are happy with the product. While the rewards for success in this area are large, the penalties for failure to meet the demands of consumers can lead to major competitive disadvantages.

Competitive Advantage   Does the strategy lead to the development or maintenance of a competitive advantage in an area or product market? A **competitive advantage** exists when an organization can do something better than its competitors. Examples are Honda (cost leadership), IBM (service), Hewlett-Packard (quality), Procter & Gamble (marketing), and Bechtel (doing the impossible).

Acceptable Degree of Risk   Is the strategy consistent with the risk preference of the organization? Is the strategy a high risk given the level of risk selected by the organization in the past? The development of its own operating system requiring totally new approaches to software development would thus appear to be incompatible with Compaq's risk strategy.

Contribution to Society   Is the strategy consistent with the organization's desired contribution to society? An organization's social goals are very important to consider. Apple Computer, for example, has on numerous occasions stated its commitment to provide computer users with the benefits of its alternate technology (said to allow applications that would be impossible with other operating systems). A strategy that committed Apple to 100 percent IBM compatibility, such as practiced by Compaq, would be inconsistent with its desired contribution.

The ending case illustrates the strategic plan of the Marriott Corporation and many of the concepts discussed in this chapter.

ENDING CASE
Making an Elephant Jump[28]

Making a $3 billion business grow by 20 percent per year is not an easy task. The Marriott Corporation is a $3 billion hotel, restaurant, and theme park company with the following goals:

1. Increase revenues and profits by 20 percent per year.
2. Earn a 20 percent return on equity every year.
3. Increase revenues to $9 billion per year by the mid 1990s.

Marriott's foray into new market areas is part of the corporate strategic plan to grow by 20 percent per year.

Prime hotel sites are becoming harder for Marriott to find, prompting Daniel R. Lee, a hotel industry analyst for Drexel, Burnham, Lambert, Inc., to say of Marriott, "Elephants don't jump."

Bill Marriott, CEO of the giant chain, disagrees with Mr. Lee and has developed a strategic plan to reach his firm's goals while maintaining the company's emphasis on the leisure-guest market. The strategic plan calls for Marriott to move into four new segments:

1. Courtyard Hotels will cater to the $35 to $60 segment. Though competing with the likes of Holiday Inns, Marriott research shows that consumers in this segment would be attracted to newer hotels with larger rooms.
2. "All suite" hotels are smaller versions of the traditional Marriott Hotels with an average size of 250 instead of 350 rooms.
3. Life-care communities for senior citizens are apartments with on-site medical staff. Explosive growth as the baby boom reaches its retirement years is expected.
4. Time-share condominiums in conjunction with resorts to take advantage of the growing leisure market and Marriott's excellent reputation.

The company plans to spend in excess of $1 billion on the Courtyard Hotel concept alone. The concept requires a change of corporate culture to prevent the quality at its upscale hotels from declining while services and costs at Courtyards increase. To achieve this change the management of Courtyards has been transferred to the food-service division. The company believes that its competitors in this market, Holiday Inns and Ramada, among others, will not lose sufficient business to make substantial overhaul of their own facilities worthwhile.

The "all suites" concept will allow Marriott to invade many suburban markets that cannot support a full-size Marriott hotel. The concept offers higher overall margins as 80 percent of revenues come from room rentals (a higher margin business than food sales) versus 60 percent room rental revenue for typical hotels.

Marriott is counting on its name to lend credibility to time-sharing, which it sees as a hedge against the general erosion of leisure-guest attendance at hotels. Most hoteliers are avoiding this market as one involving too much risk. Marriott's approach involves time-sharing in conjunction with resorts (Marriott's resort in Orlando, Florida is expected to see the first time-share); time-share customers would patronize resort restaurants and provide a network for time-share and resort properties. Prospective time-share buyers would also be attracted from the resorts. The risk involves less than 1 percent of corporate assets.

Marriott plans to build three prototype communities to test its life-care concept. While most of the industry is nonprofit, Marriott believes that its experience in management and finance will enable it to do the job better.

While analysts do not all agree, Marriott points to the fact that the company met similar goals despite the analysts' predictions and the worst recession in post-war history during the 1979–1983 period. Several billion Marriott dollars say, "Elephants do jump."

SUMMARY

Strategy is a framework that guides those choices that determine the nature and direction of an organization; it is a vision of how the organization will look in the future. Operational planning, on the other hand, provides a structure for the day-to-day decision making at the lower levels of an organization.

The mission statement is the most fundamental part of the strategic planning process; effective strategy depends on committing to essential strengths which flow from identity. An effective mission statement is achievable, instructive, specific, and reflective of organizational values.

With the mission statement in place, the organization turns its attention to formulating objectives and analyzing its industry, its competitors, and its internal resources. Strengths are then matched with available opportunities and strategic decisions are made. Strategy is then implemented. Performance is assessed through the control process and necessary adjustments are made.

KEY TERMS

Strategic planning	Vulnerability
Strategy	Problems
Effectiveness	Performance Gap
Efficiency	Strategic business units
Mission statement	Cash cow
Industry analysis	Star
Competitor analysis	Problem child
Opportunity	Dog
Threats	Generic strategies
Product substitutes	Product life cycle
Internal resource analysis	Pioneer stage
Strengths	Expansion stage
Weaknesses	Maturity stage
Matching analysis	Decline stage
SWOT Analysis	Control system
Leverage	Competitive advantage
Constraint	

REVIEW QUESTIONS

1. What types of choices are guided by the strategic plan?
2. What are five major elements of strategic planning?
3. What is the difference between strategic and operational planning?
4. What inputs should most managers have in the strategic planning process?
5. What forces led to the increased importance of strategic planning?
6. How does the mission statement aid in establishing organizational identity?
7. Why is corporate identity more fundamental than strategic planning?
8. What three company characteristics does the mission statement describe?
9. What three characteristics does an effective mission statement display?
10. How does Drucker define a business?

11. What are four competitive factors that a firm should take into account in formulating its strategic plan?

12. What factors tend to increase the bargaining power of suppliers? Of buyers?

13. What are five categories of internal resources that are important to analyze in relationship to competitors?

14. What is the purpose of matching analysis?

15. Of what significance is the product life cycle stage in strategic planning?

16. What two factors are considered in the Boston Consulting Group Matrix model?

17. Name four generic strategies and how they are used.

18. What four organizational factors should be assessed in the implementation phase of strategic planning?

19. What are the three steps of the control process?

20. What are some of the criteria that Tilles & Rumult say should be considered in the evaluation of strategic choices?

CHALLENGE QUESTIONS

1. Answer the contention of some that in a rapidly changing world strategic plans are simply irrelevant in that no one can adequately plan for a future that is so uncertain.

2. How does the mission statement impact on strategic plans and why?

3. Analyze the Merrill Lynch mission statement in terms of the following:
   A. Long-term vision
   B. Description of the firm's service and market
   C. Values and priorities

4. Is the Merrill Lynch mission statement achievable? Instructive? Specific? How?

5. Given the values and culture of General Motors and Electronic Data Systems as you perceive them, what potential problems do you see in the acquisition of EDS by GM? Are the firms compatible?

6. Analyze the U.S. auto industry in terms of the four competitive forces that shape strategy in this industry. Which of these factors would bear most heavily on a local plant manager?

7. Rate a business that you are familiar with in terms of its strengths and weaknesses versus that of its competitors in terms of personnel, product mix, operations, finances, and intangible factors listed in Box 6-2.

8. Continuing with the same business that you analyzed in Question 7, determine the key success requirements for the company in at least one market segment. Compare the firm's strengths with those required in this market. Then compare

this organization with its competitors. Can you discern the elements of a strategy that might be employed by this firm to capitalize on this market?

9. How does knowledge of the product life cycle help a manager to analyze competitive situations? Can you think of any products for which the product life cycle is particularly useful? Not very helpful?

10. Into what segments of the Boston Consulting Group Matrix would you put the following products and why? Where are these products in terms of the product life cycle?
A. Campbell's tomato soup
B. MacIntosh personal computer
C. Barbie dolls
D. Orange Crush pop
E. Visa charge cards
F. Sony big-screen television sets

11. What generic strategy would you apply to each of the products in Question 10?

12. What type of control procedures would be appropriate to measure the effectiveness of the implementation of strategic plans for each of the following goals:
A. High-quality image
B. Best labor relations
C. Best-trained sales force

CASE AND RELATED QUESTIONS

1. Why is Compaq's strategy seen as counterintuitive for a firm in the business of selling high technology?

2. How is Compaq's strategy tailored to meet Rod Canion's perceptions of the personal computer market?

3. What are Compaq's strengths? Weaknesses?

4. Does General Motors' acquisition of Electronic Data Systems make sense in terms of meeting key strategic objectives?

5. What competitive weaknesses did People's Express Airlines hope to exploit in its attempt to become the largest air carrier out of New York? What strengths did People's have that could have helped it? What threats did it face?

6. How would the product life cycle concept and the Boston Consulting Group Matrix be useful in conducting Drucker's audit procedure? Which types of products would he recommend for abandonment?

7. How would better control procedures have helped Gavilan and Workslate? What major flaw does their mistake indicate was present in their strategic thinking?

8. Why do you think that achievement of 20 percent compound annual growth at Marriott Corporation has been compared to making an elephant jump? What factors do you think make 20 percent growth difficult in the hotel industry?

9. Analyze the four prongs of Marriott's strategy. Are they sufficiently related for Marriott to achieve operating synergies? What is the competitive environment in each segment? What strengths does Marriott bring to bear in each area? What weaknesses does the company have that could affect it in each market? What data would you want to have to assist your analysis?

ENDNOTES

1. Adapted from Brian O'Reilly, "Compaq's Grip on IBM's Slippery Tail," *Fortune,* February 18, 1985, pp. 74–83.

2. This definition borrows from that given by Benjamin B. Tregoe and John W. Zimmerman, "Strategic Thinking: Key to Corporate Survival," *Management Review,* February 1979, p. 8.

3. For related discussions, see E. Gummesson, "Organizing for Strategic Management—A Conceptual Model," *Long-range Planning,* April 1974, pp.13–18.

4. George A. Steiner, *Strategic Planning: What Every Manager Must Know* (New York, The Free Press, 1979).

5. Laurence D. Ackerman, "The Psychology of Corporation: How Identity Influences Business," *The Journal of Business Strategy,* Summer 1984, p. 57.

6. Ibid., p. 58.

7. For more of this issue see Andrews, *The Concept of Corporate Strategy,* and T. E. Deal & A. A. Kennedy, *Corporate Cultures* (Reading, MA; Addison & Wesley, 1982).

8. Peter F. Drucker, *Management: Tasks, Responsibilities, Practices* (New York: Harper & Row, 1974), pp. 77–89.

9. Ibid.

10. This material is drawn from the work of Michael Porter. See, Michael Porter, "How Competitive Forces Shape Strategy," *Harvard Business Review 57 No. 2,* March–April 1979, pp. 137–45; and, see also, Michael Porter, *Competitive Strategy* (New York: The Free Press, 1980).

11. David Pauly, and Doug Tsuruoka with William J. Cook and Daniel Shapiro, "Peoples Takes on the Big Boys," *Newsweek,* August 27, 1984, p. 52.

12. Porter, "How Competitive Forces Shape Strategy," p. 142.

13. Porter, *Competitive Strategy,* p. 40.

14. Ibid., pp. 27–28.

15. Porter, "How Competitive Forces Shape Strategy," pp. 140–41.

16. Porter, *Competitive Strategy,* pp.24–26.

17. C. W. Hofer and D. Schendel, *Strategy Formulation: Analytical Concepts* (St. Paul, MN: West, 1978), pp. 144–53.

18. Ibid.

19. Bruce D. Henderson, *Henderson on Corporate Strategy* (Cambridge, MA: Abbott Books, 1979).

20. Thomas H. Naylor, "Strategic Planning Models," *Managerial Planning,* July–August 1981.

21. Porter, *Competitive Strategy,* p. 35.

22. "New Product Success Rate—One Out of Three," *Research Management* 23, March 1980.

23. H. Koontz, C. O'Donnell, and H. Weihrich, *Management,* 7th ed. (New York: McGraw-Hill, 1980), p. 722.

24. W. D. Brinckloe and M. T. Goughlin, *Managing Organizations* (Encino, CA: Glencoe Press, 1977), p. 497.

25. Peter F. Drucker, *Management: Tasks, Responsibilities, Practices* (New York: Harper & Row, 1974), p. 497.

26. "Two Lessons in Failure from Silicon Valley," *Business Week,* September 10, 1984, p. 78.

27. R. Rumult, "The Evaluation of Business Strategy" in W. F. Gluck, *Strategic Management & Business Policy,* (New York: McGraw-Hill, 1980), pp. 359–67 and S. Tilles, "How to Evaluate Corporate Strategy," *Harvard Business Review,* (July–August 1963), pp. 111–21.

28. Adapted from, "Bill Marriott's Grand Design for Growth: Upscale and Down in the Lodging Market," *Business Week,* October 1, 1984, pp. 60–62.

CHAPTER 7

MANAGERIAL DECISION MAKING

LEARNING OBJECTIVES

■ Understand the importance of decision making as the central activity of management.

■ Identify the types of decisions managers must make and give some examples of each.

■ Describe the prerequisites for decision making.

■ Discuss the types of conditions under which managers must make decisions.

■ Understand the manager's role in decision making—in choosing when to become personally involved, in establishing goals, their values, and the external and internal environment of the company.

■ Understand the steps of the rational decision-making process and how this is used by effective managers.

■ Discuss methods for improving the effectiveness of managerial decisions by improving the quality of the decision and the commitment of those who must implement it.

■ Describe some pros and cons of group decision-making techniques.

Roberto C. Goizueta, chairman of Coca-Cola Co., faced the biggest decision in the history of the 99-year-old firm. While doing research to find a suitable formula for diet Coke®, company chemists stumbled upon a formula that tasted smoother than regular Coke. Blind taste tests with 190,000 consumers were conducted and a clear majority liked the new product better. Should Goizueta introduce the new product or put it back on the laboratory shelf?

Each alternative presented unique risks. The company's product had been losing market share to Pepsi® for several years. Consumer tastes had been shifting to a smoother, sweeter taste, reflecting the preferences of younger drinkers. Image was also important and Pepsi had been very successful in positioning itself to the youth market (beginning the "Pepsi Generation" campaign).

Failure to make the change could lead to continuing losses in market share in the nondiet cola market. On the other hand, why tamper with success? Regular Coke still commanded 21.7 percent of the U.S. market as opposed to 18.8 percent for Pepsi. And while 55 percent of consumers in all 25 test markets had preferred the new product, 45 percent preferred the older formulation. Changing Coke could alienate a large share of current Coke drinkers and fail to win over sufficient new customers.

The stakes were large. Coke was the undisputed leader in the $25 billion soft drink market. A massive commitment of resources would be required to sell the change. Goizueta was confident that his company was equal to any challenge.

The decision was made to change the venerable Coke formula. Reaction was almost instantaneous. Pepsi ran advertisements claiming victory with statements like the following: "We've gone eyeball to eyeball for 87 years and the other guy just blinked." Consumer groups around the country rallied to save "old Coke." Within three months of the announcement, the old Coke was back on the shelves in the supermarkets under the name "Coca-Cola Classic." What happened in the original decision-making process to lead to this failure? Follow-up research revealed that brand loyalty is an elusive quality that is difficult to measure. People had an emotional attachment to the original Coca-Cola, and the heavy advertising campaign could not swing enough people to the new Coke flavor.

INTRODUCTION

Decision making is the central activity of management. All other management activities are designed to ensure either that correct decisions will be made or that decisions, once made, will be implemented and their effectiveness monitored.

In the introductory case, Coca-Cola Chairman Goizueta had a decision to make about the future of his company. Decision making lies at the heart of the planning process and is the most characteristic responsibility of the manager. Effective managers are confronted with decisions constantly; indeed, they actively try to locate problems that need to be solved. Managers make decisions about appropriate solutions and take action to implement their decisions.

Goizueta's decision illustrates the uncertainty that managers face. Seldom are major decisions clear cut; risks and tradeoffs are almost always present. Did Goizueta make the correct decision? How could his decision-making process have been improved? At what point should his decision be changed and what kind of information should he rely on in doing so? These are some of the questions that this chapter will attempt to answer.

The last two chapters have dealt with the issues of strategic planning in light of an organization's goals and objectives, and the development and implementation of plans to achieve this strategic direction. Decision making is implicit in the planning process. To determine which product markets to enter involves a decision. Selecting a goal of 14 percent return on equity instead of 12 or 16 percent, and selecting from among alternative plans to accomplish that goal are all managerial decisions.

This chapter examines the decision-making process, looking first at the conditions required for effective decision making, the types of decisions managers make, and the decision-making environment. Next, decision making in organizations, including the rational decision-making process, is discussed. Finally, ways to improve decision-making effectiveness, including the appropriate use of group decision-making methods, are examined.

DECISION MAKING: TYPES, PREREQUISITES, AND ENVIRONMENT

Though decision making has never been easy, in today's fast changing and complex world it has become increasingly challenging to managers. Decision makers are constrained by the environments in which they operate. While decision making is a dynamic, ongoing process, all decisions have some elements in common. Each decision is made in the context of its surrounding environments and the forces acting upon the organization and each involves certain basic steps. This section will explore the types of decisions managers make, the conditions in the environment that make decisions necessary, and the conditions in the environment that affect how decisions are made.

Types of Decisions

Managers make decisions under many different circumstances. The types of decisions made vary with the manager's level in the organization as well as the specific nature of his or her assignment.

Table 7-1
Programmed versus Nonprogrammed Decisions

TYPE OF DECISION	NATURE OF PROBLEM	EXAMPLES
Programmed	Repetitive Routine	Sales returns Routine hiring Purchase quantities
Nonprogrammed	Complex New	New products Acquisitions Reorganization

In identifying the types of decisions made in organizations and who makes them, Herbert Simon made a useful distinction.[2] Simon identified two broad classes of decisions—programmed decisions and nonprogrammed decisions (see Table 7-1).

PROGRAMMED DECISIONS **Programmed decisions** are repetitive and routine. If a particular situation occurs frequently, managers develop a habit, rule, or procedure for dealing with it. Every organization has written and unwritten policies that simplify decision making, save managers valuable time, and assist organizations in coordinating and controlling their activities. Hiring and salary decisions in a personnel office, reordering supplies in a purchasing department, admitting procedures in a hospital, and registration policies and procedures for a university are all examples of programmed decisions.

Programmed decisions are obviously the easiest for managers to make. It is quicker and much easier to refer to a policy than to think a problem through considering its alternative solutions. While managers should treat these decisions quickly, they must also remember that these decision rules were based on certain assumptions and conditions. If these conditions change then the rules or standard operating procedures may need to be altered.

Routine, or programmed decisions are not necessarily simple or unimportant to organizations. If a problem continually recurs and if its elements can be defined, predicted, and analyzed then it may be possible to develop a programmed decision for that problem. Many complex business decisions have been reduced to programmed decisions by the use of mathematical formulas, statistics, and research. These tools will be discussed in the next chapter.

NONPROGRAMMED DECISIONS **Nonprogrammed decisions** are those made for unstructured or unique situations. Established procedures have not been created for solving such problems either because they have not occurred before or because they are extremely complex and important. Examples of nonprogrammed decisions are the decision to enter a new product line, decisions affecting resource allocation, the selection of a new marketing vice-president, and the decision of whether or not to go to graduate school. In fact, most of the significant decisions a manager will face are of the unprogrammed nature.

As a manager moves up in the organization, the ability to make nonprogrammed decisions becomes more important. Ideally the focus of top management should be on nonprogrammed issues while first-level supervisors are generally concerned with programmed decisions. Unfortunately, many top-level managers spend inappropriate amounts of time on programmed decisions that could be spent on higher priority matters and nonprogrammed decisions.

Herbert Simon referred to an important principle of decision making within an organization called "Gresham's Law of Planning." This law suggests that programmed activity tends to replace nonprogrammed activity. If a manager's job involves both kinds of decisions, the tendency is to emphasize programmed decisions at the expense of nonprogrammed decisions. A possible reason for the phenomenon, according to Peter Drucker,[3] is the manager's difficulty in identifying whether a particular situation is generic (requiring a programmed decision in Simon's terminology) or represents an exception (requiring a nonprogrammed decision or development of a new policy or procedure). The tendency is to treat the generic as an exception, thus giving the executive the illusion of deciding the important when, in fact, his time has been wasted on issues that have already been decided. For this reason, managers need to constantly prioritize their efforts and identify those decisions that can be treated quickly and effectively as programmed decisions.

Most management development programs focus on improving the ability of managers to make nonprogrammed decisions. The decision-making process described later in this chapter is used mainly for nonprogrammed decisions.

Conditions Required for Decision Making

As Roberto Goizueta (Coca-Cola case) proceeded with the challenge of deciding whether to tamper with Coke's formula, four conditions existed that created the need for important decisions to be made. These conditions were indicated by the answers to the following questions. Goizueta should only engage in decision making if the answers to the following four questions are yes.[4]

1. Is there a gap between some desired result and the present situation? Yes. The market had been moving toward a sweeter, smoother taste than was present in the old Coke; Coke had been losing market share to Pepsi.

2. Is the decision maker aware of the gap? Yes. Goizueta was painfully aware of the gap. The loss of market share was especially noticeable at the retail grocery level and in international sales.

3. Is the decision maker motivated to reduce the gap? Yes. The stakes in the soft drink market amount to billions of dollars with each market share point worth hundreds of millions of dollars in sales.

4. Does the decision maker have the resources available that are necessary to reduce the gap? Yes. Coca-Cola Company possesses the needed resources to proceed with any decision that Goizueta might make. Within 24 hours of the announcement of his decision 85 percent of those polled were aware of the change.

These conditions are universal and while the decision to be made may not be as monumental as the one made by Goizueta, when they exist in any managerial situation a change is called for. To effect a needed change, a manager must first make a decision as to what the change will be.

Decision-Making Conditions

One of the major forces influencing managers in the decision-making process is the degree of **uncertainty** (unpredictability of the outcome) surrounding the possible outcomes of each alternative. In organizations, managers make decisions under conditions of certainty or risk.

DECISION MAKING UNDER CERTAINTY   When managers know with full confidence what their alternatives are and what outcome is associated with each alternative, a condition of certainty exists. Some investment decisions such as selecting from a range of high-grade government securities would be an example of decisions made under conditions of relative certainty. Outcomes are known and backed by the general credit of the U.S. government.

In organizational settings, however, few decisions are made under conditions of certainty. The complexity and changing nature of society make such situations rare. Somewhat like the concept of pure competition, however, the concept of certainty provides a conceptual anchor point for a framework of looking at the issue of risk and decision making.

The level of confidence that a manager has in a particular decision is a function of the degree of uncertainty surrounding that decision. In other words, the more certain a manager is about the possible outcomes of a decision the more confidence he or she will have in making the decision.

DECISION MAKING UNDER RISK   A more common decision-making environment for managers is a state of risk. A condition of **risk** exists when decisions must be made on the basis of incomplete but factual information. Although the information is incomplete, it is possible for managers to calculate **probabilities** (likelihoods) of events and their likely payoffs and costs, and then select the decision alternative with the most favorable odds. These probabilities may be determined objectively from historical data, or subjectively on the basis of past experience or **intuition** (hunch).

Decision making on the basis of probabilities is common in management today.[5] Marketing managers would not think of introducing a new product without first estimating its probability of success. Finance managers would not commit large resources

An American manufacturer would not consider entering the Japanese-dominated television market without first evaluating the risk involved.

without an analysis of probable outcomes. Illustrative of this is the analysis of a sporting goods manufacturer considering the acquisition of another firm to strengthen sales during the off-season. Several candidates with varying potentials are identified, each having a different pattern of sales and profits. Candidate A has a pattern of steady and constant sales and profits. Candidate B, on the other hand, has greater potential for growth but has a more erratic pattern of sales and profits. After careful analysis, management might determine that Candidate B has a 15 percent probability of going broke, a 35 percent chance of doing as well as the first candidate, and a 50 percent probability of performing substantially better. On the basis of these estimates, it is possible for management to make improved decisions and to determine rationally how much risk they are willing to assume. A more complete discussion of the use of probabilities as a decision tool is in Chapter 8.

Examples of both bad and good decisions under conditions of risk abound in the business world. Texas Instruments both overestimated the personal computer market and its share of that market with a resulting $300 million loss. Mattel made a number of attempts to diversify before being forced by a negative net worth of $120 million to retrench to its original business, toys. On the other hand, IBM was a latecomer to the personal computer market in 1981, but had passed both Apple and Tandy by 1983.[6]

DECISION MAKING UNDER UNCERTAINTY   In many situations the manager lacks factual information, and it becomes difficult to assign objective probabilities to possible outcomes. Because of the complexity of today's world, managers will frequently find themselves in this environment. In these situations, intuition and "feel" for the decision environments are relied heavily upon by effective managers.[7] Decision confidence is lowest under these conditions because of the absence of historical data. Classic examples of these types of decisions would be the decisions concerning investment in research and development, investment in capital equipment that is subject to technological obsolescence in the near to intermediate future, and inventory decisions based on economic forecasts.

DECISIONAL QUICKSAND   As we have seen in the Coca-Cola case, top management reversed its original decision to replace the old formula within three months. Coca-Cola Chairman Goizueta commented, "Had I known in April what I know today, I definitely would have introduced the new Coke. Then I would have said I planned the whole thing."

Coca-Cola's decision to introduce a new flavor ultimately ended in success. Strategic decisions, however, are made under conditions of risk, and an important issue facing strategic decision makers is when to terminate a decision that is not working out well. For example, a manager authorizes the expenditure of $750,000 for what is thought to be a promising new project, but the results are disappointing. The project's sponsors argue that with an additional $400,000 they can turn things around. Without the extra funding there is little hope. Does the manager spend the extra money, or does he cut off the project and accept the $750,000 write-off?

Managers face such situations regularly. In many situations a decision to persevere only escalates the risks. Good management is knowing when to pull the plug. In an important *Harvard Business Review* article, Staw and Ross identified four major reasons for projects going out of control:[8]

1. **The project itself**   This set of factors have to do with the project itself. Are the problems temporary (bad weather or soon to be settled strike) or more permanent (a downturn in demand). Expected or short-term problems may cause a manager to continue a project.

2. **Managers' intuitions**   Perhaps a manager has perceptions that sticking it out through tough times will be rewarded in the organization. Alternatively, some managers have a tendency to see only what is consistent with their perceptions or beliefs. Other managers may look at bad news about a new project as a personnel or personal failure. These managers may hang on or even invest further resources to "prove" the project a success.

3. **Social pressures**   Managers may persist in a project not only because they do not want to admit error to themselves, but also do not want to expose their mistakes to others. No one wants to appear incompetent.

4. **Organizational inertia**   Perhaps the simplest factor impeding withdrawal from losing projects is organizational inertia. All of the procedures and routines

involved in a change of a strategic decision cause administrative inertia. Dropping a line of business may mean changing corporate layoff policies or moving people to other projects at different locations. Sometimes it is easier not to rock the boat.

Knowing when to "pull the plug" on a poor strategic decision is one of the important characteristics of effective managers, and we saw in the Coca-Cola example an illustration of an executive who met his challenge effectively.

DECISION MAKING IN ORGANIZATIONS

Managers have many pressures placed upon them and they cannot respond personally to all problem situations. The effective manager will know when to get others involved in the decision, when to delegate it, and when not to act at all. Managers should therefore ask themselves the following questions:[9]

Is the problem easy to deal with?   Some problems are complex and difficult and require more systematic and careful attention. Many problems, however, are small and less significant. Effective managers avoid getting involved in these problems and assign them to others. It is important that managers have a sense of priorities about which decisions they will become involved in and how long they will take to make less significant decisions.

Might the decision resolve itself?   When managers rank the importance of problems and demands on their time, the less significant ones are left until last. With the passage of time, these matters frequently take care of themselves or will be solved by others. If one of the problems gets more serious it will be reassessed and given a higher priority.

Is this my decision to make?   When faced with a decision, the effective manager needs to determine if he or she is responsible for making the decision. Generally, decisions should be moved as close to the origin of the problem as possible, usually requiring delegation to individuals lower in the organization since those closest to the problems are generally able to make better decisions. Those decisions that affect the larger organization or are of key strategic importance should be made by those at higher levels.

Should I make the decision myself or involve others?   Several important issues should be considered in answering this question. First, does the manager have all the information needed to make the decision and is the quality of the decision important? Next, how crucial is commitment to the effectiveness of the decision? If commitment to the solution is crucial for implementation then the key people need to be involved in the decision-making process. Finally, the concerns of time pressure and the need for development of managers need to be considered.

Organizational Limits

Managers generally establish several goals that they desire their organizations attain. The organization then develops action plans and policies to accomplish these goals. While this process may be well understood, several related factors in the goal-setting process impose organizational limits on the kinds of decisions that managers can make.

LACK OF COMMITMENT TO GOALS   An individual manager fills many roles—manager, subordinate, parent, spouse, community and church member—and has goals with regard to each. One type of **goal conflict** occurs when organizational and individual goals are not in harmony, resulting in trade-offs between the two and reduced commitment to at least one of them. For example, if the accomplishment of organizational goals continually requires 60 to 65 hours a week or more of a manager's time with negative consequences to his or her family life, a reduction of commitment to either family or organizational goals is likely to occur.

In addition to these pressures, the very process of goal selection affects the commitment of the individual manager. If a manager is involved in goal selection in legitimate ways and feels that his or her input is listened to, a greater degree of commitment will occur.[10] In short, in almost any organization, some members will disagree with or be less committed to some of the organizational goals.[11]

CONFLICTS IN GOALS   Another type of goal conflict occurs between the goals of separate organizational units. The marketing department, for example, will want to increase sales. That goal may conflict with the finance manager's desire to produce the product at the lowest cost per unit. The production department may desire standardized outputs and long production runs. These goals may conflict with the marketing department's goal of a greater variety of products and timely delivery.

CHANGING GOALS   The types and levels of organizational goals present continuing challenges to individual managers. For instance, while an organization's major goals of growth and profitability may remain stable, its **subgoals**, such as types of services rendered and marketing strategy, frequently change over time. An example of an organization changing its subgoals is K-Mart's decision in 1984 to upscale its retailing operations by stressing national brands and higher-quality private labels as well as installing snappier displays and modern fixtures.[12]

VALUES   Personal values also affect a manager's decision-making process.[13] Generally defined, **values** are abstract ideals that shape an individual's thinking and behavior.[14] Contemporary observers note that well-managed firms also have strong and clearly articulated value systems.[15] Individual managers operating within these corporate systems need to share these values in order to succeed. A good example of a company's stated values are those of AT&T. The following statement of values was written in 1910 and served the company for over seventy years:

> It is believed that the telephone system should be universal, interdependent and intercommunicating, affording opportunity for any subscriber of any exchange to communicate with any other subscriber of any other exchange. . . . It is believed that some sort of a connection with the telephone system should be within the reach of all . . .
>
> It is believed that all this can be accomplished to the reasonable satisfaction of the public with its acquiescence, under such control and regulation as will afford the public much better service at less cost than any competition or government-owned monopoly could permanently afford and at the same time be self-sustaining. . . .[16]

The above statement was written by Theodore Vail, the early AT&T chairman commonly credited as the organizing genius behind the Bell System. In the era following its well-publicized divestiture, the company's guiding principles needed revision to reflect the new reality of the competitive marketplace. The new "Statement of Policy," set forth by Chairman Charles L. Brown in 1981, emphasized the fact that AT&T was no longer just a telephone company:

> Today we're not just in the telephone business. We're not just in the telecommunications business. Ours is the business of moving information—voice, video, data, graphics, etc.—from just about any place in the United States to just about any other place in the United States—or, for that matter, the world.
>
> However, as we seek to enlarge the scope of our business, we must carefully define its limits, too. There is just so much we can manage and manage well. Accordingly, it is our policy to undertake only those activities which support and enhance our business' service objective and none that compromises or impairs it.
>
> It would be a mistake to assume that any aspect of our business, regulated or otherwise, will be exempt from competition. That means that in every aspect of our business we must act—as indeed our responsibility to the public requires us to act—competitively.[17]

The 1981 statement goes on to outline AT&T's commitment to its customers, shareholders, employees, the community and the nation, as well as its commitment to innovation and service. The statement of policy outlines the need to restructure the company to meet new environmental challenges, it talks of changes in pricing policy, and sets forth the company's goals for the 1980s. In short, the new statement of policy is designed to set forth the company's altered mission.

Behavioral scientists have identified two basic sets of values. One set of values defines a certain behavior as appropriate in all situations. These values are known as **instrumental values** and are represented by such beliefs as honesty, love, and obedience. On the other hand, **terminal values** are those beliefs that a certain condition or state is worth striving for. For example, one manager may strive for financial independence while another desires family togetherness. Individual managers hold different instrumental and terminal values which affect the decisions they make.

Unfortunately, many managers do not systematically identify and prioritize the basic values they hold. **Value prioritization** reveals the conflict among the values that managers hold. For instance, some people may experience a serious conflict between the drive for success and honesty. This conflict is manifested frequently in both the public and the private sectors and seems to have been present in the Watergate affair as young and aggressive men engaged in practices that are commonly held to be dishonest. Conflicts also arise between the values of achievement and family togetherness. Trade-offs made to resolve these conflicts are never very clear because the decisions are always made incrementally or one at a time. The decision is never "should I neglect my family" but is frequently put in such terms as "should I work on more weekends."

The increasing frequency of white-collar crime,[18] such as insider stock trading, combined with age and sex discrimination, sale of defective products, and deceptive advertising suggests a serious erosion of values held by some managers.[19] These trends are alarming and a reversal of them is made more difficult by the notion that "everyone does it."[20] Unless managers respond more positively to the values of honesty and integrity in the decision-making process, the quality of organizational life and the decisions that impact upon it can only worsen.

A good starting point in the development of a strong value-oriented culture may be a written statement of ethics that covers many of the broad issues that managers face. While a flurry of activity in developing such codes after Watergate and the Lockheed scandal occurred, research has shown that most such activity has stopped and that most corporate codes of ethics limit themselves to conflict of interest situations,[21] a fact that critics point to as evidence that business is only concerned with those values that protect its own interests.

CULTURE   Chapter 3 discussed the importance of culture in the management of an organization. It is in the area of decision making, however, that cultural differences may be most pronounced.

Several authors[22] have identified a style of decision making in Japan that is much different than the typical style used in the United States. The Japanese place much more emphasis on participative or consultative decision making while Americans traditionally stress individual responsibility and accountability. For example, in labor relations, Japanese firms actively seek the ideas of workers and pay attention to their concerns while American companies generally assume that the goals of management and labor are inherently incompatible.

The Japanese typically push the decision-making process much lower into the organization. Lower-level managers, as a group, will analyze problem situations and recommend preferred solutions to high-level managers who retain the authority to make decisions. While the advantages and disadvantages of this decision-making style will be looked at later in this chapter, the culture of Japanese managers clearly facilitates it.

Because of Japan's small size, its culture has emphasized the interdependency of all elements of society—the family, individual, business, and government. These

The Japanese decision-making style emphasizes group participation and respects the
ideas and concerns of workers.

cultural values influence Japanese managers, not only in their decision-making processes but also in such policies as job tenure and the obligation that they hold to all
elements of society.

Internal and External Environment

Apart from uncertainty, goals, values, and culture, a number of other environmental
factors influence managerial decision making. Studies have been conducted to identify these factors. In one such study,[23] Duncan identified these factors and grouped
them into the internal and external environment. Factors in the internal environment
include organizational goals and objectives, resources available to the decision maker,
skill levels of personnel, and the degree of unity or conflict and pressures exerted by
superiors, peers, and subordinates. External environment factors are such things as
governmental policies, strategies of competitors, suppliers and customer needs, and
technological developments. Box 7-1 summarizes these factors that influence managerial decisions.

Box 7-1
Environment and Perceived Uncertainty

INTERNAL ENVIRONMENT

1. Organizational personnel component
   A. Educational and technological background and skills
   B. Previous technological and managerial skill
   C. Individual member's involvement and commitment to attaining system's goals
   D. Interpersonal behavior styles
   E. Availability of manpower for utilization within the system

2. Organizational functional and staff units component
   A. Technological characteristics of organizational units
   B. Interdependence of organizational units in carrying out their objectives
   C. Intraunit conflict among organizational functional and staff units
   D. Interunit conflict among organizational functional and staff units

3. Organizational-level component
   A. Organizational objectives and goals
   B. Integrative process integrating individuals and groups into contributing maximally to attaining organizational goals
   C. Nature of the organization's product or service

EXTERNAL ENVIRONMENT

4. Customer component
   A. Distributors of product or service
   B. Actual users of product or service

5. Supplier component
   A. New materials suppliers
   B. Equipment suppliers
   C. Product parts suppliers
   D. Labor supply

6. Competitor component
   A. Competitors for suppliers
   B. Competitors for customers

7. Sociopolitical component
   A. Government regulatory control over the industry
   B. Public political attitude towards industry and its particular product
   C. Relationship with trade unions with jurisdiction in the organization

8. Technological component
   A. Meeting new technological requirements of own industry and related industries in production of product or service
   B. Improving and developing new products by implementing new technological advances in the industry

SOURCE: Robert B. Duncan, "Characteristics of Organizational Environments and Perceived Environmental Uncertainty," *Administrative Science Quarterly 17, no. 3* (September 1972), p. 315.

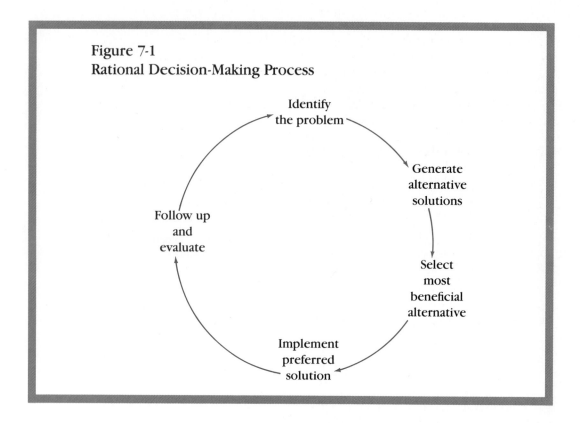

Figure 7-1
Rational Decision-Making Process

In summary, several major factors influence a manager's decision-making processes. These factors are the element of uncertainty concerning possible outcomes, the goals of the organization and individual, the values of the decision maker and the culture, along with a wide range of internal and external considerations.

Rational Decision-Making Process

The idea that managers are decision makers creates the image of effective managers solving all problems that come to them in a precise and successful manner. In reality, effective managers do not attempt to solve all problems that are brought to them—rather they delegate this decision-making responsibility to others and spend their efforts on issues that make a real difference in the accomplishment of their goals. In addition, while all managerial decisions have common ingredients, many are made in an intuitive, and at times, haphazard manner. Difficulties arise and managers quickly look for an answer to solve the problem. A more systematic decision-making process is necessary, however, for solving more difficult and complex nonprogrammed problem situations.

Although the environment and conditions surrounding each decision vary considerably, common ingredients are present in all managerial decisions. A decision is choosing one alternative from a set of possible alternatives. The rational decision-making process consists of the steps that effective managers take, either formally or intuitively, to choose the alternative.

A model of this process is presented in Figure 7-1 and consists of five steps. This five-step sequence is: (1) identifying the problem, (2) generating alternative solutions, (3) selecting the most beneficial alternative, (4) implementing the selected alternative, and (5) gathering feedback to see if the problem is being resolved.

STEP ONE: IDENTIFYING THE PROBLEM   One of the most common of all problem-solving difficulties is the adequate identification of the problem. Managers all too frequently rush into selection of alternatives before the fundamental problem has been identified. Peter Drucker has indicated that "the most common source of mistakes in management decisions is emphasis on finding the right answers rather than the right questions."[24]

CASE
AT&T Decides to Get on with the Future[25]

The decision that Charles Lee "Charlie" Brown, Chairman of American Telephone & Telegraph, faced was the most difficult in his 37 years with the company. AT&T had lost its historic antitrust suit to MCI Communications, and the Justice Department had just issued its plan to break up the giant company. The reorganization ordered by the Justice Department would be the most extensive in U.S. history. Should the company fight the details of the reorganization in an attempt to get a better deal for its stockholders? If the company fought, the battle could take years and the company would be unable to plan effectively during the interim.

Brown decided not to fight the order: "Time was not on our side. The government's determination to restructure the Bell System would have gone on for years, draining our energy and preventing us from planning our own future." Rather than cling to the past, Brown decided that it was time to get on with the exciting business of building the new AT&T. After spending nearly four decades in a company shackled with government regulation, he was eager to show what the new AT&T could do in a competitive environment. As *Time* put it: "He is sure that the competition will soon be saying in awe, 'Good grief, Charlie Brown.'"

Brown was faced with a number of possible alternatives in addition to his final decision not to fight the divestiture order. The company could have elected to fight the Justice Department order in full or in part. The company could also have embarked on a delaying strategy in which it milked the subsidiary corporations' as the case made its way through the courts.

The true problem faced by AT&T, however, was not the government order to divest itself of certain of its subsidiary companies. The solution in that case would have involved following one of the alternative strategies outlined above. Brown might very well have secured some advantages for his company had he seen the problem in this light and followed the logical course that such a problem definition dictated.

The problem as defined by Brown was that of uncertainty. A company as large as AT&T (the largest corporation in the world before the divestiture) needs to know what its competitive environment will be in order that it can make the massive investment decisions that are a necessary part of its operation. The company's entire competitive strategy would have remained in a state of suspended animation while the court case dragged on. Opportunities would have come and gone without AT&T being in a position to capitalize on them. Even a knowledgeable critic of the Bell System called Brown's decision a "brilliant move," and was led to say, "They've traded the past for the future."[26]

Barriers to Correct Problem Definition   Problems are often disguised. Many barriers exist to the correct identification of business problems. It is the mark of the effective executive to be able to identify and solve the real problem in such a situation. Common among these barriers would be the following:

Focusing on symptoms instead of causes   All too frequently managers define problems in terms of symptoms rather than causes. For a rapidly growing electronics firm, having difficulty paying its bills, the shortage of cash would generally be a symptom and the problem might not be solved simply by borrowing funds to meet current obligations. Rather the problem might lie in the marketing effort or inventory policies. Effective managers know what symptoms to look for in work situations and how to understand what they find.

If managers, like physicians, were only to treat symptoms, in the long run the symptoms would reappear and the causes would only get worse. Thus, the effective manager is able to look past the problem indicators such as liquidity, employee turnover, poor quality work, declining profitability, and negative attitudes to find the underlying cause. Just as physicians are schooled in this diagnostic process, so too must effective managers be schooled in problem finding and diagnostic skills.

Selective perception   Each of us has a set of perceptions determined by our own experience. As a result, managers often have a tendency to define problems in terms of their own background and training (**selective perception**). Managers trained in marketing might look at a problem and define it in completely different ways than would a financially oriented manager. The danger with this selective perception is that it might lead to biased problem definitions. One way to avoid this risk is to make sure that different points of view are obtained before finalizing the problem definition stage.

Defining the problem by the solution   Another obstacle to adequate problem definition is diagnosing problems in terms of solutions. Examples of this
dilemma are, "Our performance appraisal isn't working very well because our
supervisors are not well trained," or that, "Our sales have declined because we
haven't spent enough money on advertising." Defining problems in this manner
may prevent managers from discovering that sales are declining because of poor
product quality rather than insufficient advertising. Providing additional training
and spending more money may be appropriate solutions to some problems but
performance appraisal difficulties and declining sales can be caused by many
variables which should be carefully analyzed before decisions are made.

What Is a Problem?   The process of identifying problems is crucial to the selection
of the best alternative. Effective managers continually search the environment for
opportunities and problems to be solved. Four approaches that assist managers in this
stage of the decision-making process are:[27]

1. **Deviations from past performance**   If an established, satisfactory pattern of
    performance is altered, managers are alerted to the existence of a problem. A
    sales decline, an increase in operating expenses, or an increase in employee turn-
    over each generally indicate the existence of a problem.
2. **Deviation from the plan**   A gap between performance and projections indi-
    cates that one or more problems may exist. For example, a new product does not
    meet its sales forecast, the construction of a new plant is over budget, or profit
    levels are lower than expected signal that plans are off course and potential prob-
    lems exist.
3. **Feedback from others**   Speaking with suppliers, customers, subordinates, or
    supervisors can provide managers with evidence that problems exist. Increasing
    customer complaints, a list of grievances from workers, and concerns expressed
    by a manager's boss are examples of problems identified by feedback.
4. **Competition**   The relative performance of a manager's organization with its
    competitors can be a good indicator of existing or potential problems. The com-
    petitor who introduces a successful new product creates decision situations. Like-
    wise, relative performance of subunits within an organization can provide insight
    to a manager about potential problems.

STEP TWO: GENERATING ALTERNATIVE SOLUTIONS   Once the problem has
been recognized and appropriately defined, the second step in the process of making
rational decisions is generating alternative solutions. Richard M. Cyert and James G.
March theorize that managers begin the search for alternatives by identifying alternative approaches that had been used in previous situations. If these alternatives seem
inappropriate then less familiar possibilities are explored.[28] Thus, creativity is very
important at this stage of the process.

A useful approach to stimulate creativity in the alternative generation phase of
the process is called brainstorming. In a **brainstorming** session, key individuals are

gathered together with the objective of generating alternative approaches to solving a given problem, regardless of how novel or unfamiliar they might be. One of the rules of a brainstorming session is that evaluation or criticism of suggestions is withheld so that participants might feel free to offer their suggestions. Ideas generated in brain storming sessions often provide important alternatives to be considered in the decision-making process.

In searching for alternatives, decision makers face **constraints** that limit the set of feasible alternatives. These constraints may be caused by limited financial resources, human factors within an organization that may limit implementation of certain alternatives, technological considerations, or inappropriate physical facilities.[29] It is important for decision makers to have a clear understanding of these constraints so that valuable time will not be spent considering alternatives that are precluded by one or more of these barriers. Likewise, significant alternatives could be eliminated from serious consideration if managers do not have a realistic view of the existing constraints. For example, a new manufacturing process may be more efficient, but the equipment cost exceeds the firm's ability to implement the decision.

STEP THREE: SELECTING THE MOST BENEFICIAL ALTERNATIVE   After the alternative solutions have been identified, they must be evaluated and compared in terms of their feasibility and consequences. The "best" decision is then selected where "best" is defined in terms of the goals and objectives of the organization. Quantitative techniques have been developed to assist the manager in this evaluation and will be discussed in Chapter 8.

The selection of the most beneficial alternative may look to be a straightforward process of identifying the advantages and disadvantages of each of the alternatives and choosing the preferred or "best" alternative. Unfortunately the choice is difficult when the decision is complex and involves high degrees of uncertainty or risk. Several of these difficulties are identified below:[30]

1. Two or more alternative courses of action could appear to be equally attractive. Under these conditions more analysis and evaluation might be called for to assist the decision maker.

2. Perhaps no single alternative would accomplish the desired objective. Under these conditions, it might be desirable to implement two or three alternatives. The goal of increasing profitability may be accomplished, for example, by action to increase profit margins as well as by alternatives to increase asset turnover.

3. There may be no alternative that will accomplish the desired objective. When this occurs, a further search for alternatives would be in order.

4. The decision maker may be confused because there are so many attractive alternatives. This would also require further effort to compare and evaluate alternatives.

Because managers have only partial knowledge about the available alternatives and their consequences, they may choose the first alternative available to them that

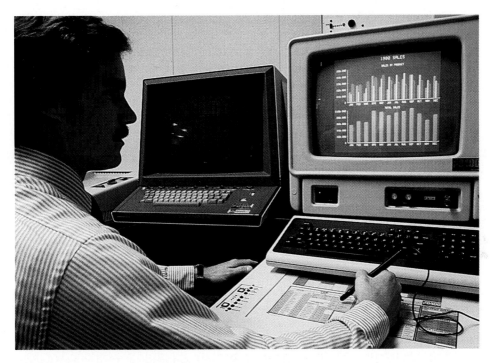

Quantitative techniques of analysis assist managers in evaluating the risks of alternative solutions to problems.

appears to resolve the problem satisfactorily. In Nobel-prize-winning research, Herbert A. Simon drew a distinction between "economic man and real life administrative man."[31] Simon suggested that once managers had identified a limited set of alternatives, they deviated from totally rational behavior by selecting the first course of action deemed "satisfactory" or "good enough" rather than order them all by a set of well-organized preferences. Simon used the word "**satisficing**" to describe this behavior.

An example of such behavior may be illustrated by the job search of university graduates. In order to make a completely rational choice, a student would have to investigate all the available jobs in the world to find the best one. Most likely, however, the student will select the first job that comes along that meets his or her minimal criteria (good chance for growth and advancement, acceptable pay, desired location, etc.)

STEP FOUR: IMPLEMENTING THE PREFERRED SOLUTION   Once an alternative has been selected, appropriate actions must be taken to see that it is implemented. The best decisions possible are worthless if not put into operation effectively.

The key to effective implementation is good communication and action planning. The individuals affected by the decision need to be properly informed and support gathered for the implementation plan. Resources must be acquired and **allo-cated** (divided between departments and projects to achieve organizational goals). Managers set up budgets and detailed operational plans for the actions they have decided upon, allowing progress to be monitored. Next, managers are assigned responsibility for the specific tasks that need to be accomplished. For example, management may have determined that a decline in overall profitability may have been caused by failure to penetrate a particular geographical market. The solution might be to withdraw from that market with lower-level managers being given the assignment of developing a plan to close down plants, move employees, and service some accounts, etc.

Although implementation has been identified as the fourth stage in the decision-making process, it is a basic part of the entire management process. Implementation is bound to each of the management functions and will be discussed throughout this book. It is often the most difficult phase of the decision-making process, "the acid test of a leader's skills."[32]

STEP FIVE: FOLLOW-UP AND EVALUATION   Evaluation is frequently the neglected stage in the decision-making process; nevertheless, it is an essential element. Effective managers will always want to compare actual results with the expected outcome to see if the problems have really been solved. It is surprising how often managers neglect to do this.

When the chosen decision alternative does not appear to be working, the manager may respond in different ways. One of the alternatives that was identified earlier may be adopted and implemented. Perhaps the manager feels that not enough time has been given for the implementation plan to work and thus chooses to wait. Finally, the manager may decide that the original problem was not properly identified and that the entire decision-making process needs to be started all over again. As might be clear, evaluation and the managerial control function are intertwined. Control will receive detailed treatment in Chapter 18.

Evaluation allows managers to learn from their experience and thereby increase their capacity for making and implementing effective decisions. Thus proper attention to evaluation ensures that problem solving becomes a dynamic and ongoing activity for effective managers.

IMPROVING THE EFFECTIVENESS OF MANAGERIAL DECISION MAKING

Experienced managers realize that a decision's effectiveness is determined by two criteria: (1) the quality of the decision and (2) the commitment of those who must implement it. The quality of the decision is determined by how well the decision-making process is carried out. A high-quality decision that is not implemented properly, however, is ineffective. Implementation is determined by commitment; consequently, affirming a high level of commitment of those who will implement the decision is necessary to the decision-making process.

Most managers are aware that decisions are made with imperfect information about future events. Unforeseen occurrences can and often do affect the outcome of even the most carefully thought out decisions. In addition, managers realize that they will be evaluated by their superiors, peers, and subordinates as part of the effectiveness of their decision. For these reasons, most managers experience some tension in deciding how to go about solving a problem and effectively implementing a solution. It is not unusual for managers feeling this tension to set up "barriers to decision making" or justifications for avoiding difficult problems that face them. To make effective decisions, managers must overcome barriers which discourage them from addressing problems and challenges they face in their organizations.

Barriers to Decision Making

Irving L. Janis and Leon Mann identified four defective problem-recognition and problem-solving approaches.[33] Each of these approaches is likely to lead to ineffective decisions.

UNCONFLICTED INERTIA   **Unconflicted inertia** occurs when the manager believes the consequences of the failure to act or decide are not very great. An operations manager may decide, for example, that a complaining customer is not in a position to complain much about inferior service. Actions that could be taken to satisfy the customer are ignored. Poor customer service eventually comes back to haunt the firm. Although this model contemplates the acts of individual managers, entire industries can be guilty of relaxed avoidance. The U.S. automobile industry appears to have taken this approach, and for years the industry got away with it. Today, however, Japanese manufacturers have made major gains in this market, largely as a result of perceived differences in quality and service.

UNCONFLICTED CHANGE   With **unconflicted change** the manager decides to take action because the failure to do so will have serious repercussions; however, analysis gives way as the first feasible alternative appearing to involve low risk is taken. Perhaps inventory is high so the manager cuts purchases. What he failed to realize, however, was that workers were hoarding critical parts so as to be able to meet special orders. Upon hearing that parts will be scarce in the future, hoarding increases and work-in-process inventory swells even further.

DEFENSIVE AVOIDANCE   When a problem is not quickly solved and the manager tries to avoid the consequences of failure by "passing the buck" or avoiding the situation, this is called **defensive avoidance**. Perhaps a customer has been waiting weeks for delivery and, despite the manager's best efforts, delivery is no more certain now than it was a month ago. When the customer calls, the manager tells the secretary to say that he is out of the office. When the customer finally gets through, the manager blames the post office, the factory, or even the customer for the poor service. The customer, however, might be satisfied by an item that is in stock. This manager never takes the time to find out because he is too busy defending himself to solve the problem.

HYPERVIGILANCE   When the inability to find a solution is coupled with a time deadline the manager experiences a tremendous amount of stress. Sleep is difficult and the manager is irritable. Alcohol often becomes an outlet to relieve the anxiety. Perhaps a major customer has threatened to withdraw its account if the company fails to make delivery by a given date. As the date approaches, the manager realizes that his company is dreadfully behind schedule. The manager enters a state of **hyper-vigilance**, and, as panic sets in, other orders are bumped and top priority is given to the major account. Now other customers are angry. Perhaps the major account really just wanted the manager to come out and discuss a series of minor irritants or would be satisfied by a partial delivery. The manager in a panic is not likely to discover the customer's true interests.

Managers who feel tension in decision making often opt for a safe and relatively simple approach to decision making. Such an approach might be to make only marginal changes in existing conditions. At times this approach is most appropriate because it saves time and money and the results are relatively predictable. However, such an approach frequently results in ineffective decisions because little innovative thinking is applied to the problem and new ideas are not considered. In addition, it is quite likely that long-run advantages will be sacrificed for short-term results.

Overcoming Barriers to Effective Problem Solving

In addition to effectively utilizing the rational problem-solving approach, several other methods are available to enable managers to overcome barriers to effective problem solving.

SET PRIORITIES   Managers are faced with many tasks and responsibilities and frequently are not able to complete them all. The feeling of being overwhelmed can be minimized by placing higher priority on those tasks that are really important as opposed to those that are urgent, but less important. The process of setting priorities is central to time management and it may well be the single most important way managers can improve their overall efficiency.[34]

PROCEED WITH CARE   The rational decision-making approach works when it is used carefully. Some common mistakes made in its application need to be avoided.

For example, during the first step of the process some managers tend to define problems in terms of symptoms rather than the underlying causes. Other managers focus on lower priority goals in establishing problems to be addressed. During the second step, the tendency is to generate too few alternatives, preventing the manager from making full use of the decision-making process. In the evaluation step, managers often proceed in a hit-or-miss fashion, not carefully considering the strengths and weaknesses of each alternative. Finally, difficulties are often encountered in the implementation stage. Managers may not communicate with or interest those who will be involved in the implementation of the decision. Full acceptance of and commitment to the decision, critical to its effectiveness, may thus be lacking. The following section on group decision making will demonstrate how this commitment can be obtained.

Gaining Commitment: Group Decision Making

This chapter has focused on the importance and process of decision making for the individual manager. Managerial decision making, however, need not be a solitary process. Because effective managers are aware of the importance of implementation, they know that it is important not only to make good quality decisions, but also to gather the commitment of subordinates for its implementation.

QUALITY AND COMMITMENT   Both quality and "commitment" become the important criteria for effective decisions, and managers take this into consideration as they develop their decision-making procedures. In some situations quality is very important but commitment is not. These situations generally involve the more technical areas—engineering, finance, purchasing—where the individual manager either has the necessary knowledge or access to it to make decisions working alone.

With other problems, however, high commitment is essential and quality is less important. Involving the interested parties in the decision-making process in these situations is more likely to elicit this high-level acceptance of the decision. A problem concerning the work environment of the employees such as whether to adopt flexible hours would be an example of this kind of decision.

Finally, for a large number of decisions, both high quality and high commitment are desirable. For these decisions, the group process is frequently the most effective. While common in the Japanese culture, group decision making has been less utilized in American management. Indeed there has been considerable debate over the advantages and disadvantages of group decisions.

ADVANTAGES AND DISADVANTAGES OF GROUP DECISION MAKING   The advantages and disadvantages of group decision making are summarized in Table 7-2. Essentially the advantages can be summarized by the old axiom "two heads are better than one." With increased participation, it is likely that better decisions will result because of the added perspective that comes through groups. In addition, group

Table 7-2
Advantages and Disadvantages of Group Decision Making

ADVANTAGES	DISADVANTAGES
1. More information and knowledge are brought to the decision making process.	1. The group decision-making process takes more time hence it is more costly.
2. More alternatives will be generated with more managers involved.	2. Since groups cannot be held responsible for successful implementation, this approach may result in a situation where no one is responsible.
3. The commitment to the final decision will be increased by the managers involved.	3. Members of the group may feel pressure to accept the decision favored by the majority. One or more members may also dominate the group, reducing its effectiveness.
4. Improved communication may result. Managers involved in making the decision can inform their units of the reasons for it.	4. Group decisions may, in some situations, be the result of compromise or indecision on the part of the group.
5. In selecting from among the alternatives, groups are likely to accept more risk than an individual decision maker.	5. Individuals may begin to think that they should be involved in all decisions, including those that are appropriately made unilaterally and handed down by superiors.
6. Increased creativity generally results as different approaches and viewpoints are brought to the problem.	6. Group think may occur.
7. Subordinates increase their capacity to make decisions.	

members are likely to feel increased commitment to successful implementation because the group members feel some "ownership" in the decision.

Cost is probably the biggest drawback of the group decision-making process. Group decision-making processes are not efficient and require much more time than do individual decisions. If a manager's time is worth $40 per hour and it takes 2 hours to make a decision working alone, the labor cost of making that decision is $80. If a group of six managers takes 4 hours to make the same decision, the cost to the company would be $960. Thus, group decisions should be used only when the importance of the decision justifies the added cost.

President Kennedy and his cabinet might have been victims of "group think" during the planning of the Bay of Pigs invasion.

GROUP THINK Irving Janis[35] analyzed the phenomenon of group think in organizations. **Group think** occurs when the group has a stronger desire for consensus and cohesiveness than for arriving at the best possible solution. Some causes of group think are: (1) the group is insulated from external pressures and information; (2) the group is led by a very forceful and dominant leader; and (3) the group lacks procedures for adequately searching for alternatives and ensuring that all points of view are considered.

Janis focused his work on some well-known fiascos including the Bay of Pigs decision and the buildup of American military forces in Vietnam during the early 1960s. President John F. Kennedy, and his advisors, came to the decision to support the Bay of Pigs invasion in the early 1960s fully confident that it would help to undermine the government of Fidel Castro in Cuba. They made assumptions concerning the secret participation of the U.S. government and the effectiveness of the Cuban military that proved to be false. The tragedy that followed was inevitable.

Fortunately, however, a manager can take steps to ensure that a group avoids the problems of group think. It is necessary for each member of the group to evaluate all of the alternatives critically, and the manager must be very skillful in making sure that both advantages and disadvantages of each alternative are carefully considered.

Peter Drucker tells an interesting story of an experience he had with Alfred Sloan, the managerial genius behind the establishment of General Motors. Sloan brought a proposal to the board of directors of General Motors for consideration. Everyone in the group favored the alternative, including Sloan. When Sloan asked for

Box 7-2
Decision-Making Styles

A_1 You solve the problem or make the decision yourself, using information available to you at that time.

A_{11} You obtain the necessary information from your subordinate(s), then decide on the solution to the problem yourself. You may not tell your subordinates what the problem is in getting the information from them. The role played by subordinates in making the decision is clearly one of providing the necessary information to you, rather than generating or evaluating alternative solutions.

C_1 You share the problem with relevant subordinates individually, getting their ideas and suggestions without bringing them together as a group. Then you make a decision that may or may not reflect your subordinates' influence.

C_{11} You share the problem with your subordinates as a group, collectively obtaining their ideas and suggestions. Then you make the decision that may or may not reflect your subordinates' influence.

G_{11} You share a problem with your subordinates as a group. Together you generate and evaluate alternatives and attempt to reach agreement (consensus) on a solution. Your role is much like that of a chairman. You do not try to influence the group to adopt "your" solution and you are willing to accept and implement any solution that has the support of the entire group.

SOURCE: Reprinted from *Leadership and Decision-Making*, by Victor H. Vroom and Philip W. Yetton, by permission of the University of Pittsburgh Press, p. 13. © 1973 by University of Pittsburgh Press.

the disadvantages of the alternative there was no response and so Sloan postponed discussion of the proposal until the next meeting so that more careful consideration could be given to the proposal. When the board of directors reconvened the proposal was rejected.[36] The key principle involved was that without a full and open consideration of all the advantages and disadvantages of a given alternative, the group decision-making process loses its effectiveness and runs the risk of "group think."

WHEN TO INVOLVE SUBORDINATES   While much had been written about the advantages of the group decision-making process, it was not until the work of Victor Vroom and Phillip Yetton that operating managers had some guidelines for deciding under what conditions it would be appropriate to involve subordinates in the decision process.[37]

The **Vroom-Yetton model** identifies five basic decision-making styles (see Box 7-2) each involving a different level of subordinate participation. The letters A, C, and G represent a continuum from authoritarian (A), to consultative (C), to fully participative, or group decisions (G).

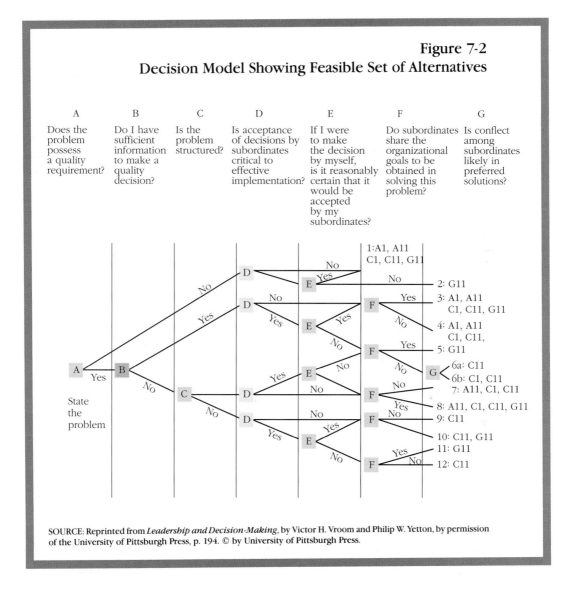

Figure 7-2
Decision Model Showing Feasible Set of Alternatives

A	B	C	D	E	F	G
Does the problem possess a quality requirement?	Do I have sufficient information to make a quality decision?	Is the problem structured?	Is acceptance of decisions by subordinates critical to effective implementation?	If I were to make the decision by myself, is it reasonably certain that it would be accepted by my subordinates?	Do subordinates share the organizational goals to be obtained in solving this problem?	Is conflict among subordinates likely in preferred solutions?

SOURCE: Reprinted from *Leadership and Decision-Making*, by Victor H. Vroom and Philip W. Yetton, by permission of the University of Pittsburgh Press, p. 194. © by University of Pittsburgh Press.

In selecting from among decision-making styles, Vroom and Yetton identified three criteria for evaluating the success of a decision: (1) the quality of the decision; (2) the commitment of subordinates to implement the decision; and (3) the time required to make a decision. A final requirement they identified was the need for developing decision-making skills in subordinates.

These criteria have been combined into a series of seven questions that managers should ask themselves before deciding upon a decision-making style. When these questions have been answered, the model indicates the preferred set of decision processes to be used. The questions were arranged in sequential fashion and a decision tree was designed (see Figure 7-2).

A manager using this model would first state and identify the decision to be made. When contemplating exactly how subordinates should be involved, the manager analyzes the situation by answering questions A through G. A preferred set of decision approaches is identified for each of the situations often encountered. For example, a "no" answer to Question A, a "yes" answer to Question D, a "no" answer to Question E would suggest a G_{11} decision approach. Alternatively, a "yes" answer to A, a "yes" answer to B, a "no" answer to D, a "no" answer to F would suggest a preferred style of A_1. In choosing from among the set, Vroom and Yetton suggest that the criteria of time and employee development be the differentiating issues. When decisions must be made quickly then managers should choose authoritarian styles. When managers wish to emphasize subordinate development then it would be appropriate to use more participative styles.

The Vroom model has made an important contribution to management practice. It can help to improve the quality of decisions and increase the commitment of subordinates to implement them. The guidelines provided by the model give specific assistance to managers in helping them decide when it is appropriate to involve subordinates in the important managerial role of decision making. That decision, by itself, is one of the more important issues facing managers today.

GROUP DECISION TECHNIQUES   When the decision has been made to involve others in the decision-making process, there are several techniques that can be used in group decision making. These techniques are the interactive group, the Delphi group, and the nominal group. While each technique is similar, each has different characteristics which make it more suitable for certain situations. The Delphi and nominal approaches are useful, for instance, when increased creativity is required. The interactive technique is found in most committees and work groups.

Interactive Groups   An interactive group simply means that members of the group are brought together with an agenda and a problem to solve. These groups generally start with the group leader stating the problem and asking for inputs. Discussion is unstructured and frequently even unorganized. Alternatives are generated and evaluated. The group leader's task is summarizing at appropriate times, making sure that all group members are participating, and contributing her or his ideas. At an appropriate time a vote will take place or a consensus might be reached. A staff meeting to decide on next year's goals would be a legitimate use of the interactive group process.

Delphi Groups   The Delphi technique is a method for developing a consensus of expert opinion. Developed by the Rand Corporation, the Delphi technique solicits written input from a panel of experts who contribute individually. After the initial written responses are gathered on the topic being discussed, a summary of the opinions is developed and distributed to the participants. A new questionnaire on the new topic is then distributed. In the second round, participants have the advantage of knowing the other experts' opinions and can modify their initial responses to reflect this new information. This process of summarizing results and sending out new questionnaires can continue for as long as desired or until a consensus is reached. The "average" prediction can then be taken to represent the decision of the "group" of experts.

The time, expense, and logistics of the Delphi method rule out use in routine or everyday decisions. It has been successfully used, however, to determine the range of possible alternatives, forecasting future economic conditions, forecasting market potential for new products, and uncovering information that will lead to consensus among group members.[38]

Nominal Groups   The nominal group technique was developed to ensure that every participant in the group had equal input in the decision-making process. Because some participants may be more verbal and dominate group decisions in interactive groups, the nominal group is structured so that equal participation is assured.

To begin, the manager gathers a group of knowledgeable people and outlines the problem for them. The individual members are then asked to write down individually as many alternatives as they can think of. The members then take turns stating their ideas which are recorded on a flip chart or blackboard for all members to see. Discussion is limited to simple clarification. After all alternatives have been listed, more open discussion takes place. Group members then vote, ranking the alternatives. The highest-ranking alternative is the decision of the group.[39]

The challenge of making effective decisions in complex and rapidly-changing environments while maintaining a long-term perspective is reflected in the following case in the decision facing Henry Schact, CEO of Cummins Engine Company.

ENDING CASE
A Preemptive Action or Wait?

Your customers call to say they are testing a competitor's product that is priced 25 percent lower than yours. Do you make a decision quickly or wait to see if your market share falls?

That is the predicament that Henry Schacht found himself in during 1984. As CEO of Cummins Engine Company, a $2.8 billion-a-year industrial company with 50 percent of the North American diesel engine market, Schacht was looking at the initial assault on the U.S. market by some Japanese heavyweights like Komatsu and Nissan. Schacht could move quickly to lower prices or wait to see the response of his customers.

The decisive Schacht was quick to react to the Japanese threat. The consensus of management was a potential sales drop of 20 percent or more if no action was taken. With the full backing of the board, Cummins reduced the prices on many of their engines by 20 to 40 percent nearly overnight. This action has hurt profits and forced the company to lower costs as well.

The track record of Henry Schacht was impressive. During his tenure at Cummins he had always stayed on top in innovation and planning for the long term. This long-term approach had taken a lot of courage as many investors wanted immediate profits and not promises of the future. He had spent more than $1 billion on a new plant and equipment in the last six years. He also eliminated 3,400 of 13,000 engine jobs. Flexible work rules have been instituted in many plants, and maintaining market share at the expense of profit has sometimes occurred.

Was it the right decision? Not a single Japanese engine can be found in U.S. built tractor-trailers today. Cummins maintains over a 50 percent market share in the U.S. The profit in this strategy may still be some years away as Cummins is projected to earn only about $32 million this year on sales of $3.2 billion. Many managers think that in the next few years the profits will explode. Others compare this kind of long-term decision making with the Japanese style of management that has been so successful.

Henry Schacht has so far withstood the critics of his short-term performance, even though he does brief security analysts on the company outlook frequently. The stock is trading at about where it was six years ago. The current expansion has been a period of erratic earnings for Cummins—from a high of $188 million in profits in 1984 to a loss of $107 million two years later after the price cuts. Reducing costs and restoring margins are the focus of Cummins these days.

The Japanese assault has been repelled for now. The real war may only be beginning for Cummins. Long-term profitability is the goal, and Schacht is making decisions for that time frame. In today's environment of corporate restructuring, hostile takeovers, and LBOs to maximize share price, Cummins may face a tough battle if profits are not forthcoming. Then again Cummins may be one of the few global competitors that survive in the 1990s.

SUMMARY

Effective managers must solve problems and make solid decisions. Indeed, they actively try to find emerging problems to solve. In the modern organization, four conditions exist which create the need for important decisions to be made. Those conditions are: (1) a gap between the present situation and a desired goal; (2) an awareness of this gap; (3) incentive to reduce the gap; and (4) resources that can be applied to reducing the gap.

Programmed decisions are those that are repetitive or routine and are made by habit or policy. Nonprogrammed decisions, however, are unstructured or unique. This chapter deals primarily with the issue of making nonprogrammed decisions in effective ways.

Managers make decisions in complex and rapidly changing environments which significantly influence the decisions that managers make. Some of the key environmental influences are the amount of information known by the manager and the resulting degree of certainty, risk, or uncertainty; the personal and organizational goals facing the manager; the personal value systems of managers and the culture of the organization along with a host of other internal and external environmental considerations.

In making nonprogrammed decisions, effective managers need to determine which problems they will spend their time on. Some decisions need to be delegated so they spend their energies on problems that make a real difference in the accomplishment of their goals. Once managers decide what problems they will devote their attention to, it is useful for them to follow a rational procedure for decision making.

Finally, another key decision that managers must make is when and how to involve the subordinates. This is especially important if the quality of the decision and the commitment to its effective implementation is to be maximized. Since making group decisions is costly, the extent to which subordinates should become involved depends on the type of problem and the conditions under which the decisions are being made. Helpful guidelines as to when to involve subordinates are provided by the Vroom-Yetton model.

KEY TERMS

Programmed decisions
Nonprogrammed decisions
Gresham's Law of Planning
Uncertainty
Risk
Probabilities
Intuition
Goal conflict
Subgoals
Values
Instrumental values
Terminal values
Value prioritization

Rational decision-making process
Selective perception
Brainstorming
Constraints
Satisficing
Allocate
Unconflicted inertia
Unconflicted change
Defensive avoidance
Hypervigilance
Group think
Vroom-Yetton model

REVIEW QUESTIONS

1. What are the four conditions that create the need for managerial decisions?
2. What is the difference between programmed and nonprogrammed decisions?
3. How do instrumental values differ from terminal values?

4. What are some of the benefits to be gained by a manager who identifies and prioritizes his or her basic values?

5. What is meant by the rational decision-making process?

6. What are the four questions that managers should ask themselves when faced with a problem or question that requires a decision?

7. What are the five steps in the decision-making process?

8. What are some of the approaches that managers use to identify problems and opportunities?

9. Define and describe the term "satisficing" as used by Simon.

10. Explain unconflicted avoidance and why it leads to poor decisions.

11. What factors lead to hypervigilance and why does a state of panic often characterize a manager in this state?

12. For what type of decision is the group process frequently most effective?

13. What are some of the most common pitfalls in using group decision-making processes?

14. Discuss the relationship between quality and commitment in decision making.

CHALLENGE QUESTIONS

1. Why is it helpful to quantify the degree of risk or uncertainty in a decision? How might this be done?

2. What kinds of decisions lend themselves to objective analysis such as the use of probabilities? What kinds of decisions lend themselves to subjective or intuitive solutions?

3. What implications do goal conflicts have for today's managers?

4. What are some elements of American culture that impact the decision-making process of corporate managers? Are they different from those cultural elements that would impact on managers in nonprofit or governmental organizatons?

5. What are some ways that managers can ensure that they maintain a strong awareness of internal and external environmental changes? Which of these environments is more important in terms of future problems and opportunities?

6. Use the Vroom-Yetton model to decide what parties to involve in the following decision:

    You are the personnel manager for a large division of a Fortune 500 manufacturing corporation. The division is partially unionized. A high seniority worker with an excellent record in a nonunion plant has assaulted a foreman who made a pass at a female employee. The supervisor fired the man on the spot. The plant superintendent upheld the supervisor because the foreman had a reputation for good-natured teasing and there was no indication that this incident was any different.

The union has been active at this plant and you would like to keep it out for competitive reasons. The worker has appealed to you to reinstate him and has threatened to take his case to the union if you do not.

CASE AND RELATED QUESTIONS

1. What kind of risks were inherent in the decision facing Goizueta of Coca-Cola? What kind of information is missing in the type of data that he relied on in making his decision?

2. What are some of the ways that selective perception might influence the way in which the managers from the following areas of specialization might define the problem in the Coca-Cola case?

   A. Advertising
   B. Marketing
   C. Special promotions
   D. Institutional and restaurant sales
   E. Grocery sales

3. Organizations spend a great deal of money to have effective decision-making processes. Why do you think so many major decisions turn out so poorly? Should managers of businesses who make a mistake be forced out when they just guessed wrong and events could just as well have turned out the way they predicted?

4. Given that managers often do lose their jobs for making wrong decisions, what effect is this likely to have on the decision-making process? Does this explain some of the conservative bias in business decisions? How can companies overcome this bias?

5. What assumptions are implicit in K-Mart's decision to upgrade the quality of merchandise in its stores? What risks is K-Mart taking in implementing this strategy?

6. Brown decided that it was more important to know the rules of the game that AT&T would be playing in than to take extra years trying to influence the rules to be more in AT&T's favor. Do you agree with his decision?

7. Using the AT&T example, identify the five steps in the decision-making process discussed in the chapter with the steps taken by Brown. As the alternatives that Brown used are not listed, develop some alternatives of your own. What would the implementation step consist of in this case?

ENDNOTES

1. "Coke Tampers with Success," *Newsweek*, May 6, 1985, p. 50.
2. Herbert Simon, *The New Science of Management Decision* (New York: Harper Row, 1960).

3. Peter F. Drucker, *The Effective Executive* (New York: Harper & Row, 1967), pp. 123–30.

4. K. MacCremman and R. Taylor, "Decision Making & Problem Solving," in *Handbook of Industrial and Organizational Psychology*, ed. M. Dunnette (Chicago: Rand McNally, 1976), pp. 1397–453.

5. "Decision-Making: A Systematic Procedure," *Small Business Report*, August, 1982, pp. 11–15.

6. Michael A. McGinnis, "The Key to Strategic Planning: Integrating Analysis and Intuition," *Sloan Management Review*, Fall 1984, pp. 45–52.

7. McGinnis, pp. 45–52.

8. Barry M. Staw and Jerry Ross, "Knowing When to Pull the Plug," *Harvard Business Review*, March–April 1987, pp. 68–74.

9. James A. F. Stoner, *Management*, 2nd ed. (Englewood Cliffs, NJ: Prentice Hall, 1982), pp. 167–68.

10. Stanley R. Hinckley, Jr., "A Closer Look at Participation," *Organizational Dynamics*, Winter 1985, pp. 57–67. Some writers see participation in management decisions as required by ethical considerations. For such a discussion see Marshall Sashkin, "Participative Management is an Ethical Imperative," *Organizational Dynamics*, Spring 1984, pp. 5–21.

11. M. Kelley, "Organizational Analogy: A Comparison of Organismic and Social Contract Models," *Administrative Science Quarterly*, 25, 1980, pp..337–62.

12. "K Mart: The No. 2 Retailer Starts to Make an Upscale Move—At Last," *Business Week*, June 4, 1984, p. 50.

13. For a discussion of management-oriented values, see Barry Z. Posner and J. Michael Munson, "The Importance of Values in Understanding Organizational Behavior," *Human Resource Management* 18 (Fall 1979), pp. 9–14.

14. Milton Rokeach, *Beliefs, Attitudes, and Values* (San Francisco: Jossey-Bass, 1968), p. 124.

15. Thomas H. Peters and Robert H. Waterman, *In Search of Excellence* (New York: Harper & Row, 1982).

16. AT&T Annual Report, 1910, pp. 22–25, as quoted in Alvin von Auw, *Heritage and Destiny: Reflections on the Bell System in Transition* (New York: Praeger Publishers, 1983), p. 5.

17. "A Statement of Policy," *American Telephone and Telegraph Company and Associated Companies, 1981*, as quoted in von Auw, p. 439.

18. $30 million in fines and damages were collected by the white-collar crime division of the U.S. Department of Justice in 1979, ten times the amount collected in 1977. See Bruce Horovitz, "Executive Crime," *Industry Week*, February 18, 1980, p. 49.

19. For an extended discussion of both the statistical evidence of the increase in white-collar crime and the value system and circumstances leading to it read the complete Horovitz article cited above. A more recent examination of the evidence and the increasing crackdown on the part of government agencies can be found in Carol J. Loomis, "The Limited War on White-Collar Crime," *Fortune*, July 22, 1985, p. 90.

20. How pervasive is the problem? See some of the following articles from *Business Week*: "We've Got Some of These Guys Dead to Rights," July 4, 1988; "General Dynamics under Fire," March 25, 1985; "Why the E. F. Hutton Scandal May Be Far from Over," February 24, 1986; "Money Laundering: Who's Involved, How It Works and Where It's Spreading," March 18, 1985, "The $7 Billion Grey Market: Where It Stops, Nobody Knows," April 15, 1985; "The Rise and Fall of Marvin Warner," May 6, 1985 (This is the one linking the Ohio Savings & Loan crisis to a securities fraud.); and "The Epidemic of Insider Trading," April 29, 1985 (stock market abuses).

21. Robert Chatov, "What Corporate Ethics Statements Say," *California Management Review*, Summer 1980, pp. 20–29; and Bernard J. White and B. Ruth Montgomery, "Corporate Codes of Conduct," *California Management Review*, Winter 1980, pp. 80–86.

22. William G. Ouchi, *Theory Z: How American Business Can Meet the Japanese Challenge* (Reading, MA: Addison-Wesley, 1981); and Richard T. Pascale and Anthony G. Athos, *The Art of Japanese Management: Applications for American Executives* (New York: Simon and Schuster, 1981).

23. Robert B. Duncan, "Characteristics of Organizational Environments and Perceived Environmental Uncertainty," *Administrative Science Quarterly* 17, no. 3 (September 1972), pp. 313–27.

24. Peter F. Drucker, *The Practice of Management* (New York: Harper Row, 1954), p. 531.

25. "Hi, I'm Charlie Brown," *Time*, November 21, 1983, p. 64.

26. Irwin Manley, professor of economics at the University of New Hampshire and long-time consultant to the staff of the FCC, as quoted by the Associated Press, January 11, 1982 and reproduced by von Auw, p. 5.

27. William F. Pounds, "The Precise of Problem Finding," *Industrial Management Review* 11 (Fall 1969), pp. 1–19.

28. R. M. Cyert and J. G. March, *A Behavioral Theory of the Firm* (Englewood Cliffs, NJ: Prentice-Hall, 1963), pp. 120–22.

29. For a more thorough discussion see Robert Tanner Baum, Irving R. Weschler, and Fred Massarik, *Leadership and Organization: A Behavioral Science Approach* (New York: McGraw Hill, 1961), pp. 277–278.

30. M. Holmes, *Executive Decision Making* (Homewood, IL: Richard D. Irwin, 1962), pp. 90–92.

31. Herbert A. Simon, *Administrative Behavior: A Study of Decision-Making Processes in Administrative Organization*, 3rd ed. (New York: Free Press, 1976). For a review of research building on Simon's work, see Noreen M. Klein, "Utility and Decisions Strategies: A Second Look at the Rational Decision Maker," *Organizational Behavior and Human Performance* 31 (1983), pp. 1–25.

32. Yvan Allaire and Mihaela Firsirotu, "How to Implement Radical Strategies in Large Organizations," *Sloan Management Review*, Spring 1985, pp. 19–34.

33. Irving L. Janis and Leon Mann, *Decision Making: A Psychological Analysis of Conflict, Choice, and Commitment* (New York: The Free Press, 1977).

34. Some useful books in the area of time management are: R. MacKenzie, *The Time Trap* (New York: AMACOM, 1972); and Ross A. Webber, *Time is Money* (New York: The Free Press, 1980).

35. See Irving L. Janis, *Group Think*, 2nd ed. (Boston: Houghton Mifflin, 1982).

36. Peter F. Drucker, *The Effective Executive* (New York: Harper & Row, 1967), p. 148.

37. Victor H. Vroom & Philip W. Yetton, *Leadership and Decision-Making* (Pittsburgh: University of Pittsburgh Press, 1973).

38. John F. Preble, "The Selection of Delphi Panels for Strategic Planning Purposes," *Strategic Management Journal*, 5, 1984, pp. 157–70; and N. Delkey, "The Delphi Method: An Experimental Study of Group Opinion" (Santa Monica, CA: Rand Corporation, 1969).

39. Richard Woodman, "Use of the Nominal Group Technique for Idea Generation and Decision Making," *The Texas Business Executive*, Spring 1981, pp. 50–53.

CHAPTER 8

PLANNING AND
DECISION-MAKING TOOLS

CHAPTER OUTLINE

LEARNING OBJECTIVES

■ Develop an appreciation for the practical benefits of planning and decision-making tools.

■ Understand the application of linear programming—its uses and limitations.

■ Obtain a familiarity with Program Evaluation and Review Technique (PERT) as a scheduling tool.

■ Understand the uses of quantitative and qualitative methods as forecasting aids.

■ Describe how to apply decision analysis and decision trees.

■ Understand the logic behind the use of mathematical models to simulate management situations.

Simulation Modeling Improves Operations, Planning, and
Productivity at Burger King[1]

In 1977 and early 1978, beef prices, the primary component of Burger
King's hamburgers, began to fluctuate widely. The Operations Research
department developed a computer model to determine what kind of
meat to buy from which supplier so as to have the correct hamburger
formulation at minimum cost. The resulting savings of ¾ cents per pound may not
seem like much, but when you use 3 million pounds of hamburger a week the savings
is $22,000 per week or over $1 million per year. This and other experiences led the
management of Burger King to seek a method of testing all proposed changes in
operations before they were implemented in the 400 company-owned outlets or
recommended to franchisees.

Operations Research set out to develop a model that would allow it to simulate
actual store conditions. It was decided to view each restaurant as three interrelated
subsystems: the Customer System, the Production System, and the Delivery System.
The Customer System consists of the in-store and drive-thru areas where customers
place their orders, and orders are transmitted to the kitchen. The Production System
consists of the kitchen and inventory system. The Delivery System makes change for
the customer and assembles the order.

Sales volumes in a typical Burger King restaurant can vary by as much as 1000
percent within a 30-minute interval. The peak service hour is the noon luncheon
business. Luncheon business can be increased by increasing the speed with which
customers are served. For a Burger King to increase its sales, it must either raise prices
(which is difficult because of competition) or it must increase the number of customers served. The solution is simple: increase the speed of service to increase sales
and profit.

A simulation approach was selected because of the dynamic aspects of the operation and the multiple interrelated queuing problems in the customer, production, and
delivery areas. To gain support for the simulation approach, the Operations Research
group invited management and franchisees to a live demonstration of the model in
action. They reproduced the manufacturing and service systems of a typical restaurant in a warehouse, staffed it with actual crew members from nearby units, and
subjected the "restaurant" to a variety of customer arrival patterns at varying staff
levels. They videotaped these computer predicted results for comparison with actual
restaurant conditions. Credibility was established beyond any doubt.

The simulation model provided a method to evaluate suggestions for productivity improvement. The result was the introduction of a Productivity Planning for
Profit Kit (PPP). The Kit serves three functions by: (1) allowing restaurant operators
to project achievable sales growth, (2) determining what changes must be made to
achieve these goals, and (3) allowing the restaurant operator to determine the return

Burger King simulated a restaurant environment to test the validity of its computer-based findings on customer-arrival patterns.

on investment and payback period of each productivity improvement. At the conclusion of the PPP process the operator has a five-year productivity improvement plan for his or her restaurant.

A restaurant operator begins by analyzing any bottlenecks. The 100 Improvement Resource Cards contained in the kit enable the operator to determine the sales potential available through elimination of the bottleneck. The operator can predict the return on investment for each productivity upgrade.

What results has Burger King attained with its simulation system? The following is a partial list:

1. The company can serve 13 extra customers per hour for an additional $30 per hour in sales per restaurant, worth $15 million in system-wide sales per year.

2. An analysis of a second drive-thru window indicated that an additional $13,000 per restaurant could be realized.

3. The company avoided adding small specialty sandwiches to the menu and an increase in wait time by an average of 8 seconds, a $13,000 loss per restaurant or $39 million for the entire system.

4. New restaurant locations are analyzed with the simulation to determine the ideal size of restaurant to be built.

5. The model accurately determined the size of crew needed and its placement within the restaurant. Projected savings were 1.5 percent of sales, $11,250 per restaurant or $33 million per year. Actual savings were 2 percent of sales.

6. An increase in market share of almost 1 percent per year—each percentage point representing $200 million in sales.

7. Kitchens designed with the aid of the simulation model save an additional 1.5 percent of sales in labor costs, an increase in profit of almost $33 million annually for the system as a whole.

As Wally Crawford, who operates a group of highly successful Burger King restaurants in Omaha, Nebraska, says of the program: "Seat-of-the-pants judgment is hardly the best means of managing a $1 million plus investment . . . even if one has worked in fast-food restaurants most of one's life. Yet, until the introduction of the Productivity Improvement Program . . . sophisticated guesswork was the only tool we had available . . . No other tool yet developed in the fast-food industry . . . contributes so much to assuring a franchisee's peace of mind as he contemplates additional investments in existing or new restaurants."

INTRODUCTION

Burger King used a simulation model in analyzing its operations. This chapter discusses five formal tools which managers have found to be helpful in decision making. Two of them, linear programming and scheduling, are used primarily where uncertainty about a given situation is not a major factor. The other three, forecasting, decision analysis, and simulation, are designed specifically to deal with planning under uncertainty. Only one of these tools is mentioned in the Burger King case, but all have found wide application in practice. The chapter ends with a discussion of how to use formal decision-making techniques intelligently.

CASE
Production Scheduling in the Housewares Division

Diane Furuhashi thoroughly enjoyed her job as production scheduler for the Housewares Division, although she had to admit that life had become more hectic the last few years. As production scheduler, one of Diane's major jobs was to generate regular quarterly production plans, showing

Production scheduling is the process of determining how many units factory workers will assemble over a given period.

the number of each product to be made each month. An important headache has been determining how many of each of the two different kinds of washing machines to produce.

Three years ago the Housewares Division introduced a new heavy-duty washer, and demand for both the regular and heavy-duty models was strong. Diane knew that the division could sell as much of either model as desired; her job was to schedule production so the division would realize as much profit as possible.

Heavy-duty washers are the more attractive product—the profit per unit is $60 versus $40 for the regular machines. However, heavy-duty machines require time on Houseware's only large forming press and extra time on the assembly line. Diane needs to balance these and other factors to find the best production schedule. She can use common sense and her experience to find a production plan that meets all the requirements and gives a reasonably good profit. However, she can save herself some effort and find a guaranteed best solution through a tool called **linear programming** (LP).[2]

	REGULAR MACHINE (R)	HEAVY-DUTY MACHINE (H)	TOTAL AVAILABLE
			Table 8-1
			Washing Machine Data
Profit per unit	$ 40	$ 60	
Production limits			
Medium press (minutes/unit)	12	4	7,200 minutes
Large press (minutes/unit)	0	5	3,000 minutes
Relative time for assembly	1	2	1,400 units
Relative time for painting	1	1	900 units
Minimum production requirements per week (units)	100	200	

LINEAR PROGRAMMING

To illustrate linear programming and how Diane can use it to help her, we will view her scheduling problem from an LP approach. Table 8-1 summarizes the major considerations for this problem. Let R and H stand for the number of regular and heavy-duty models that Diane decides to produce per week. Notice that the total profit per week would be:

$$\text{Total Profit} = 60R + 40H$$

To find the best solution, Diane needs to **maximize** this number (realizing the greatest profit).

Both washers require time on the medium forming press. One press is assigned full-time to washer production, and has 7,200 minutes per week available (24 hours per day times 5 days per week times 60 minutes per hour). With each regular machine requiring 12 minutes on the medium forming press and each heavy-duty machine requiring 4 minutes, the following must be true:

$$12R + 4H \leq 7,200$$

A chart showing this inequality can be drawn as a straight line. Everything to the left of and below the line on Figure 8-1 satisfies the inequality, and is said to be **feasible**. This area is shaded in the figure.

For the heavy-duty press Diane can write a similar expression. The regular washers do not require time on this press, but the heavy-duty washers require 5 minutes each. Because of commitments to other products, only 3,000 minutes per

Figure 8-1
Production Limit on Medium Forming Presses

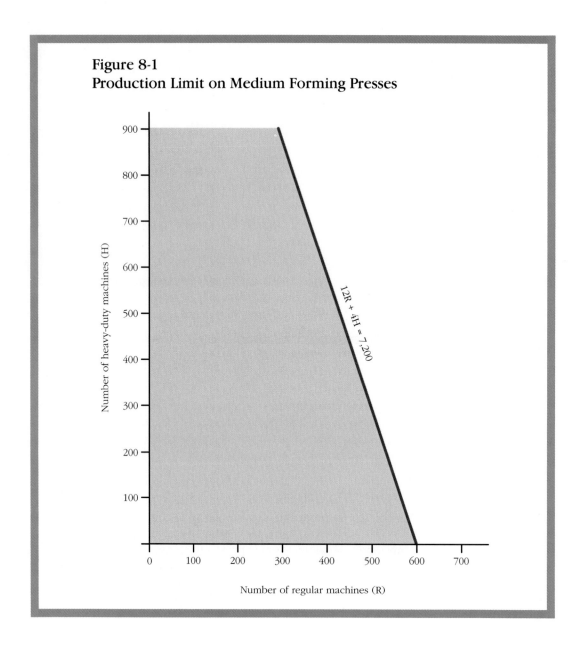

week are available on the heavy-duty press. The following equation expresses this limitation:

$$OR + 5H \leq 3,000$$

Figure 8-2 shows the corresponding line and **feasible region**—the area within which Diane can operate given the **constraints**.

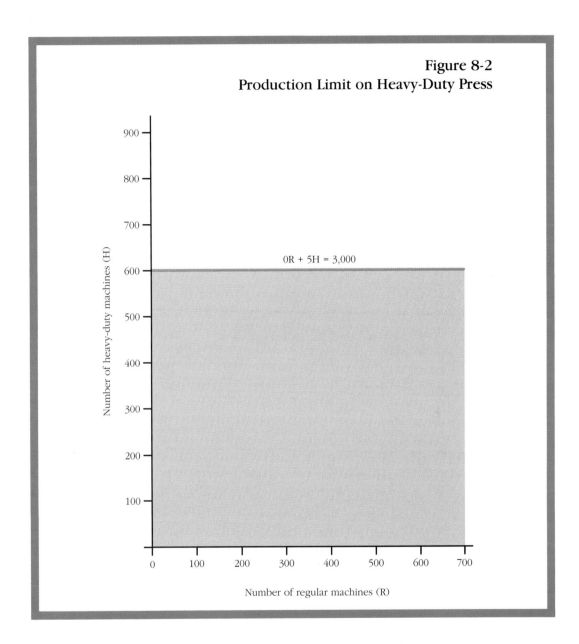

Figure 8-2
Production Limit on Heavy-Duty Press

The next problem concerns the assembly area. When assembling only regular washers, 1,400 machines per week can be built. Heavy-duty washers, however, take twice as long to assemble. Any combination of regular and heavy-duty machines can be built during any given day within these limits. The contraint is illustrated in Figure 8-3 and can be written:

$$1R + 2H \leq 1,400$$

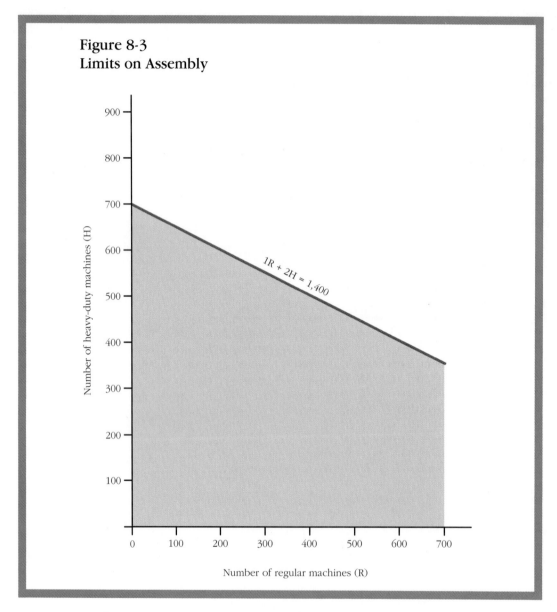

Figure 8-3
Limits on Assembly

Finally, the painting area can process only 900 units (both regular and heavy-duty machines require the same amount of time) per week. Also, the marketing department insists that at least 100 regular machines and 200 heavy-duty machines are made per week. These limits can be written as:

$$1R + 1H \leq 900$$
$$1R \geq 100$$
$$1H \geq 200$$

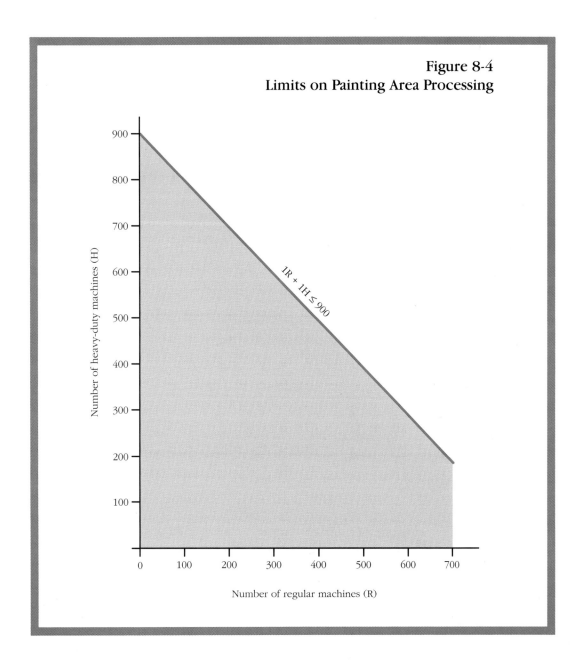

Figure 8-4
Limits on Painting Area Processing

Figures 8-4 and 8-5 illustrate these final constraints on production.

When all of the contraints are combined and plotted on the same graph (Figure 8-6) notice that the feasible region consists of that area which satisfies all of the contraints.

Each of these expressions looks much the same:

Figure 8-5
Marketing Requirements

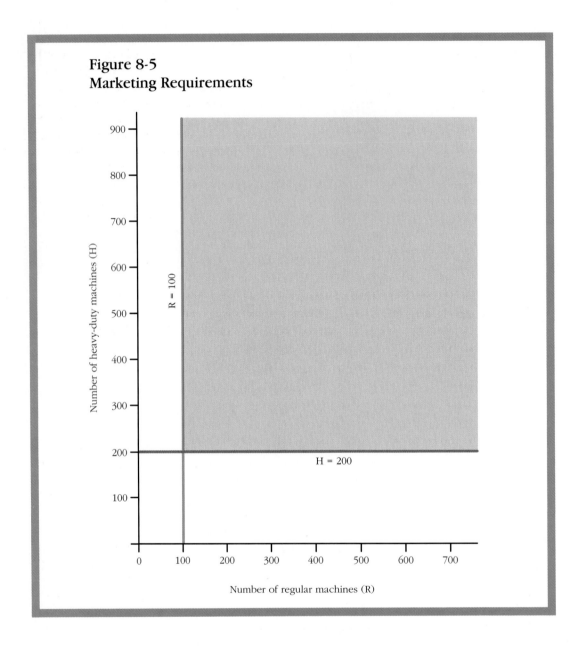

	a number	plus	a number	≤ or ≥	
	times R	(or minus)	times H	(or =)	a number.

If a problem consists of expressions like these, it is an **LP problem**. The term "linear" refers to the fact that each of the constraints can be plotted as a straight line. In contrast, if a problem includes expressions like:

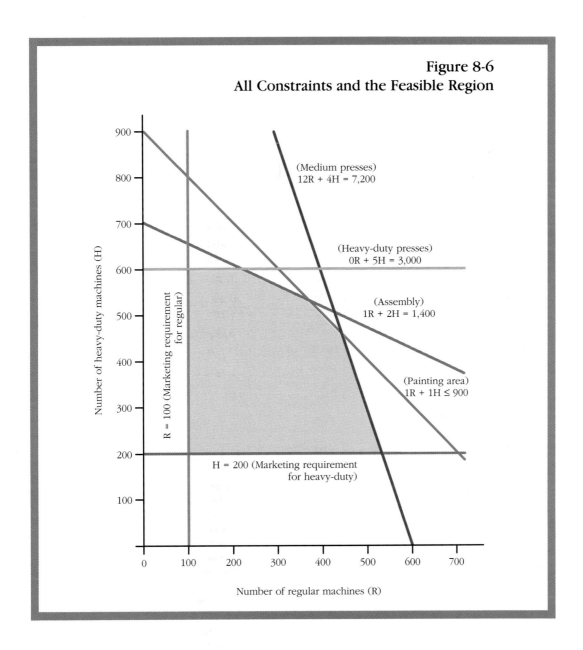

Figure 8-6
All Constraints and the Feasible Region

$$R \times H \geq 42$$

or

$$15R^2 - 2H = 23$$

then the lines would be curved lines, and it is *not* an LP problem. Multiplication, division, and exponents other than unity are not allowed in LP problems.

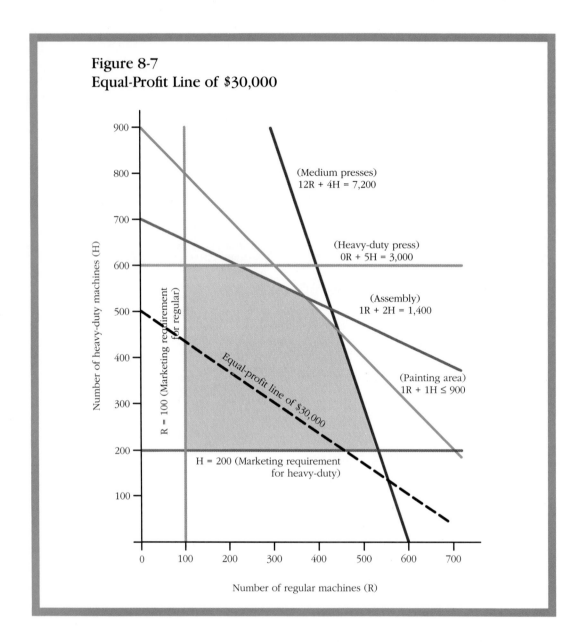

Figure 8-7
Equal-Profit Line of $30,000

Solving Linear Programming Problems

Figure 8-7 shows the same feasible region of Figure 8-6, and adds an **equal-profit line** showing all production schedules yielding a profit of $30,000. Notice that not all of this line falls in the feasible region, but a portion of it does. Diane can choose any

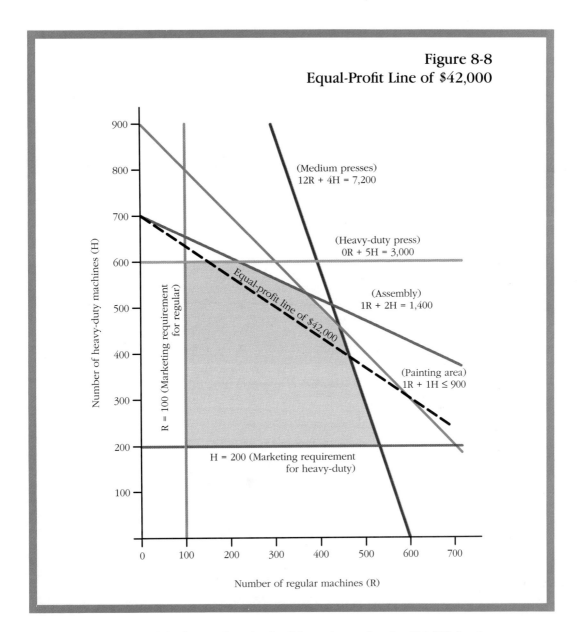

**Figure 8-8
Equal-Profit Line of $42,000**

(Medium presses)
12R + 4H = 7,200

(Heavy-duty press)
0R + 5H = 3,000

(Assembly)
1R + 2H = 1,400

(Painting area)
1R + 1H ≤ 900

Equal-profit line of $42,000

R = 100 (Marketing requirement for regular)

H = 200 (Marketing requirement for heavy-duty)

Number of heavy-duty machines (H)

Number of regular machines (R)

schedule on the part of the line within the feasible region and make $30,000 for the company.

Figure 8-8 shows a different equal-profit line, this time with a profit of $42,000. Since a $42,000 profit is better than $30,000, the new line is preferred to the old. Note that a good part of the higher line still falls in the feasible region, so many realistic production schedules giving profits of $42,000 could be constructed. Can Diane do even better?

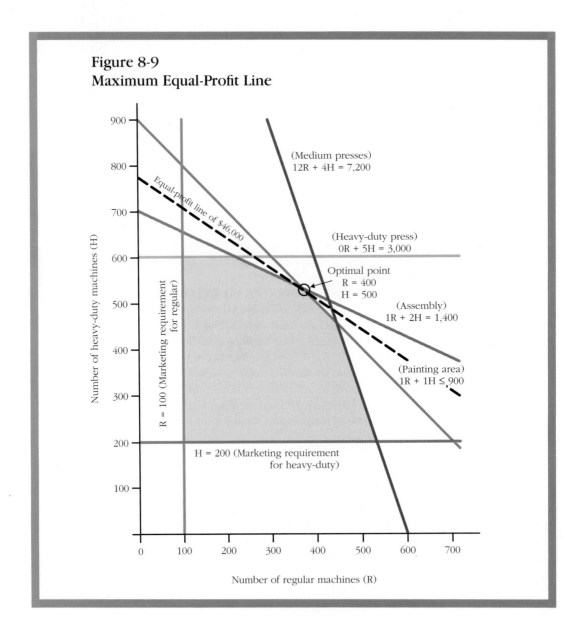

Figure 8-9
Maximum Equal-Profit Line

(Medium presses)
12R + 4H = 7,200

(Heavy-duty press)
0R + 5H = 3,000

Equal-profit line of $46,000

Optimal point
R = 400
H = 500

(Assembly)
1R + 2H = 1,400

(Painting area)
1R + 1H ≤ 900

R = 100 (Marketing requirement for regular)

H = 200 (Marketing requirement for heavy-duty)

Number of heavy-duty machines (H)

Number of regular machines (R)

In comparing Figures 8-7 and 8-8, notice that raising profits moves the line upward parallel to itself. Some room in the feasible region above the $42,000 line still exists, so more profit is possible. When the line is raised as far as possible without leaving the feasible region entirely, the profit is $46,000 and the corresponding equal-profit line is as shown in Figure 8-9. The equal-profit line touches the feasible region at just one point, corresponding to producing 400 regular and 500 heavy-duty washers. The profit at this point is $46,000, as can be seen by multiplying 400 regular washers times $40 per unit profit and adding to the product of 500 heavy-duty washers times $60 per unit profit. The equal-profit line cannot be moved further without leaving the feasible region, indicating that the best schedule has been found.

Advantages of Linear Programming

Once a management problem has been recognized as a linear programming problem, it can be solved easily and quickly. Useful as this information is, it is also useful to know how the solution changes when some of the data changes. For example, how would the solution change if capacity was added in the painting area? What if more time could be made available on the heavy-duty press? If extra time could only be purchased at a premium, what is the most one should be willing to pay? Information such as this is generated automatically in linear programming.

One final advantage is that many different types of problems can be formulated as linear programming problems. Diane's situation exemplifies a resource allocation problem, a classic type of LP problem. Burger King's optimal hamburger formulation might well have been developed using LP. Similar applications are finding optimal feedstocks in refineries and blast furnaces. LP has also been used to construct schedules, design shipping routes, find the best way to trim rolls of paper, and determine the cheapest feeds for livestock.

SCHEDULING

Suppose that you and your staff are preparing to make an important presentation to all divisional and executive vice-presidents, and want to do an exceptionally good job. In thinking about what must be done, you can identify many steps that you should perform. Some steps will obviously have to be done before others, and some will take longer than others. You can also see lots of things you could get started on right away, but you are a lot less sure about the priorities. Your boss wants you to **schedule** the presentation as soon as possible, and has asked you to give a firm estimate of when that will be. At the moment, you haven't the foggiest idea how long to allow.

Program Evaluation and Review Technique (PERT)

Fortunately, a tool, called PERT charting, can help you in the example given above. **PERT** (Program Evaluation and Review Technique),[3] also known as **Critical Path Method** (CPM),[4] was developed in the early 1960s as a method of managing complex projects. In recent years PERT has been used to control projects as complex as

Table 8-2
Tasks for Presentation Project

	TASK	TIME NEEDED
A	Check audio-visual equipment availability	4 hours
B	Requisition and pick up equipment	7
C	Set up room	8
D	Negotiate with graphics design department	12
E	Organize material into logical sequence	13
F	Note visual aid needs	2
G	Design handouts	5
H	Produce handouts	10
I	Lay out and produce graphics	6
J	Rehearse presentation	9

launching the space shuttle, and as simple as planning a wedding—or a management presentation.

The first step is to break the overall job down into manageable pieces, then estimate how long each piece will take and how the pieces interrelate. In scheduling the presentation, this might occur as follows. First, you must find out about the audio-visual equipment available. This will take 4 hours. Then someone must requisition the equipment (7 hours), and then set up the room (8 hours). When you know what equipment is available, you must also begin negotiating with the graphics design department for artwork. Relations with this group have been extremely touchy in the past, and you will need to devote a good deal of time—12 hours total—to smooth over all the past rough spots.

Simultaneously, your group can digest and organize the material into logical sequence. This will take 13 hours. Once the material is organized, the staff can work on two separate tasks: note where visual aids are needed (2 hours), and design a packet of handouts to be given to each attendee at the conclusion of the presentation. Handout design will take 5 hours, then you will need 10 hours to produce the handouts.

When you have completed smoothing over the ruffled feelings in the graphics design department and also identified where visual aids are needed, 6 hours are needed with graphics design to lay out and produce the graphics. When this task is completed and the room is set up, you can rehearse the presentation, which will take 9 hours.

The tasks and time estimates are summarized in Table 8-2. For convenience in subsequent discussions, each task is labelled A, B, C, and so forth. Notice how the tasks interrelate. For example, task B (requisition equipment) cannot take place until task A (check the availability of equipment) is completed. Likewise, task C (set up the

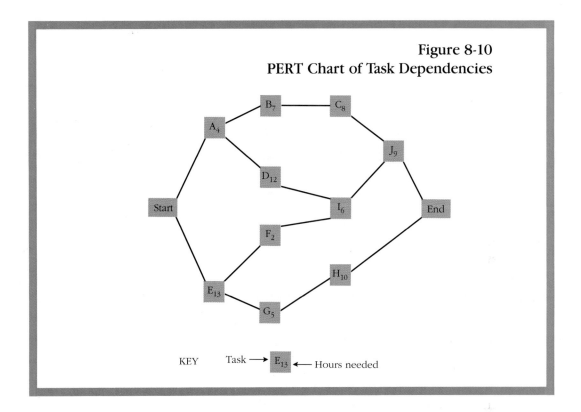

Figure 8-10
PERT Chart of Task Dependencies

KEY   Task ⟶ E₁₃ ⟵ Hours needed

room) cannot occur until you complete task B. Figure 8-10 illustrates this **task dependence**.

Notice how much easier it is to understand the chart than the original description. Even if PERT charts did no more than show which tasks come first and how they depend on each other, they would be useful. However, the information can also be used to put priorities on tasks and to estimate how long the entire project will take.

Notice that task A will take 4 hours, as noted inside the box for task A on Figure 8-10. Thus, if task A is started as soon as possible, it will start now (time 0) and end in 4 hours. If task B, in turn, is started as soon as possible, it will start at hour 4 and end at hour 11, since it takes 7 hours to complete. Likewise, task C (which takes 8 hours) at the earliest can start at hour 11 and finish at hour 19. Figure 8-11 shows the **early start** and **early finish** times for each activity.

Two additional facts are worth noting. Activity I depends on two preceding activities, D and F (exhibiting **task dependence** on D and F). Notice that you cannot start until *both* D and F are completed. Thus the early start time for I is 16—the later of the preceding completion times. A similar statement could be made for activity J. Likewise, notice that the end of the project is not reached until *all* preceding activities have been completed. Thus, the project will take 31 hours total.

Second, some activities are more crucial to completing the project on time than others. Activity A, for example, must be started immediately if the project is not to be

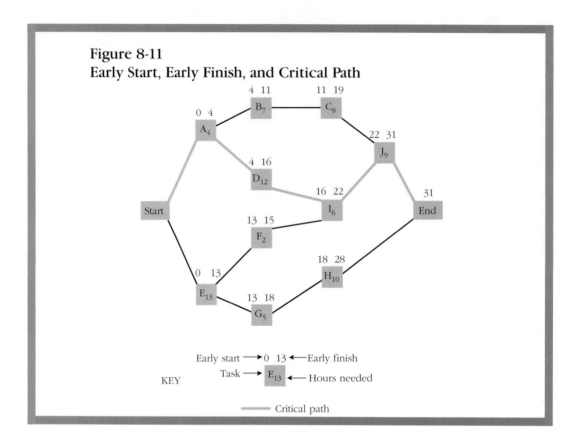

Figure 8-11
Early Start, Early Finish, and Critical Path

KEY

Early start ⟶ 0 13 ⟵ Early finish
Task ⟶ E_{13} ⟵ Hours needed

───── Critical path

delayed, while activity E can be put off somewhat without affecting completion. The colored line shows the activities which must be completed on schedule in order to finish in 31 hours. This is called the **critical path**. The activities along the critical path are called **critical tasks**.

A feeling for the urgency of each task can be obtained by starting at the end of the project and working backwards. For example, tasks J and H would both have to be done by hour 31 in order to complete the project in 31 hours. This means that, at the latest, task J would have to start by hour 22 and task H would have to start by hour 21. The **late finish** and **late start** times for each activity can be found in this manner. These numbers are shown on Figure 8-12. Also shown are the **slack times**, which are found by taking the difference between either the early start and early finish times, or the late start and finish times. Activity H, for example can start as early as hour 18 or as late as hour 21, giving a slack time of 3 hours. Note that the difference between the early and late finish times, 28 and 31 hours respectively, is also 3 hours. The slack time tells you how much an activity can be delayed without jeopardizing timely project completion.

In conclusion, you now can make a very good estimate of the total amount of time it will take to prepare. Furthermore, you know which tasks you must start on

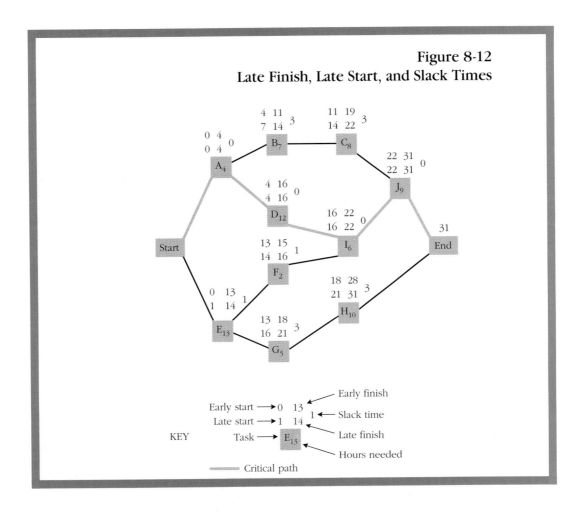

Figure 8-12
Late Finish, Late Start, and Slack Times

immediately, and which can be delayed slightly if necessary. You can also see in advance which tasks are coming next, in order to do some advanced planning.

As discussed here, PERT charts are useful when time estimates for each activity can be estimated with relatively little uncertainty. Some versions of PERT allow you to incorporate uncertainty by estimating a range of times for each task. The bibliographic references discuss this issue in more depth.

FORECASTING

Everyone looks into the future to some extent to plan their activities. Businesses must do the same, and the stakes involved are often substantial. Thus, it is worth some effort to make forecasts accurate. In this section four major topics—organizing for forecasting, deciding what to forecast, data issues, and mathematical tools for forecasting—are discussed.

Organizing for Forecasting

Forecasts are extremely important to all businesses.[5] Forecasts determine how many nurses, tons of sheet steel, or grocery bags will be needed tomorrow. Longer-range forecasts indicate the number of hospitals, auto assembly lines, and grocery stores that will be needed in ten years. The simulation model used by Burger King enabled the company to forecast manpower requirements and the flow of customers at possible restaurant sites. This information allowed the company to minimize payroll expenses and build the optimal size restaurant at each new location, saving millions of dollars.

It is not clear who in the company should actually make corporate forecasts, since all parts of the organization should be involved. Marketing, production, finance, personnel, top management—all are interested in forecasts, and have valuable information to feed into the forecasting process. But which of these should be in charge of forecasting?

Forecasting is an imprecise art and forecasters need judgment as well as technical skill. Certain parts of the marketing group, for example, would like to see forecasts shaded towards the optimistic side. This would force operations to make plenty of product or provide ample capacity. If sales do live up to the high expectations, fine. If sales fall short, however, excess inventory or capacity are the result. If operations managers are rewarded for keeping inventories low and excess capacity to a minimum, as they often are, these managers want to keep forecasts on the pessimistic side.

Some companies make one organization (often marketing) responsible for forecasting. Others form an independent staff group for this purpose. Sometimes a group is formed of representatives of each interested department. Often each organization is responsible for developing their own forecasts for figures that interest them. Each approach has advantages and disadvantages, and each is found in practice.

Deciding What to Forecast

Suppose you are in charge of forecasting for Chrysler Motor Corporation. Should you forecast the demand for the number of white Dodge Aries 4-door sedans with the red interior, equipped with power steering and brakes, air conditioning, automatic transmissions, and the AM/FM radio? Should you then repeat that forecast for every possible model and color of car with every conceivable mixture of options?

Most managers do not need this amount of detail. When planning the production of automatic transmissions, for example, the model and color of car they will go in does not matter. Likewise, managers can plan the production of fenders, radios, and other components with no concern about the combinations they will eventually come together in. If a company is forecasting demand ten years into the future so it can see if the company will have enough assembly capacity, it can simply forecast total auto sales. As forecasts look a shorter time into the future they will need to become more detailed. However, it is easier to forecast a short time ahead than a long time ahead. Eventually, the white Dodge Aries with the red interior will be built, but the time horizon for this decision is short enough that an order might well be in hand for that specific car.

This example illustrates two important rules of forecasting:

1. Always forecast the broadest, most inclusive categories possible. This not only makes your job easier, but gives more accurate forecasts.

2. Always forecast ahead as short a time as possible, given the purpose for which the forecast is made.

Consequently, long-range forecasts should generally be very broad and deal primarily with broad totals. Periodically the forecast is revised as new information becomes available, and forecasts should simultaneously take on more and more detail as the time horizon shortens.

Data Issues

Most forecasting methods rely on past data. If the data do not accurately represent current conditions, then the best methods in the world will give misleading results. Thus, those responsible for forecasting must ensure that all significant changes in markets, products, and data collection methods are corrected.

Unfortunately all these factors change with discouraging regularity in any dynamic, growing, changing company. Three months ago a major product line was switched from Division A to Division B, distorting sales histories for both groups. Two improved models were introduced two months ago, and prices were changed on seven others. Last month the competition announced a major design change, and your sales force changed the method they use for counting when a sale is made. Your forecasting group can never hope to correct for all such incidents, but the major changes must be flagged or else you run the risk of using sales of apples to project sales of oranges. Gathering and verifying data is generally the most difficult, time consuming, and costly activity in forecasting.

As illustrated in Figure 8-13, companies can use qualitative tools, quantitative tools, or combinations of both to derive forecasts. **Qualitative tools** rely on expert judgment or experimental data to project the future. Forecasts derived in this way

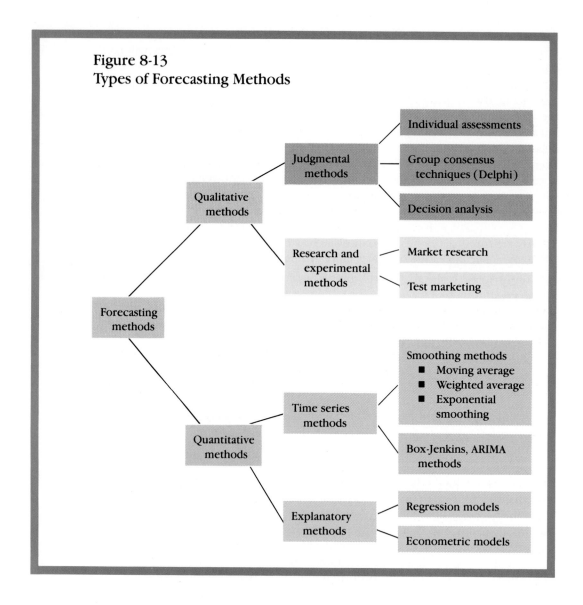

Figure 8-13
Types of Forecasting Methods

usually are costly, and are subject to the errors and biases common to human judgment and experimental conditions. They are especially useful when past data is lacking, or when future conditions are changed to the point that past results would be misleading. **Quantitative tools** identify patterns in past data, and project the patterns into the future to derive the forecast. Forecasts based on quantitative methods are relatively inexpensive, and if past data truly represent the future, can be quite accurate. Two common quantitative tools are exponential smoothing and regression analysis.

Mathematical Tools for Forecasting

EXPONENTIAL SMOOTHING   In its simplest form, exponential smoothing uses the formula

$$\text{forecast} = \text{past forecast} + (\bar{a})(\text{error})$$

where $\bar{a}$ is a number (called the **smoothing constant**) between zero and one, and the **forecast error** is the actual result for the previous period minus the forecast for that period (see Example 8-1).

Exponential smoothing relies on the idea that data fluctuates randomly around some average figure, and that the best way to forecast is to find the average and not try to anticipate the **random fluctuations**. Exponential smoothing essentially averages all past data, giving increasingly greater emphasis to more recent data. The value of $\bar{a}$ determines how the averaging is done. Small values give **stable**, smooth forecasts, while larger values give more **nervous** results in which forecasts more closely follow the random fluctuations. However, if a systematic change is present in the data (for example, if sales rise to a higher level and stabilize), the forecasts using small values for $\bar{a}$ react more slowly than forecasts with larger $\bar{a}$. Table 8-3 illustrates these points and Figure 8-14 presents the results graphically. (See pages 254–55.)

In the simple form discussed here, exponential smoothing is not particularly useful for real problems. For example, sales for many products have annual **cycles** (predictable fluctuations) and exhibit long-term growth **trends** (movement in a definite direction). Simple exponential smoothing forecasts always **lag** behind cycles and trends. As discussed in the bibliographic references, however, more sophisticated versions of this technique overcome these shortcomings.

REGRESSION ANALYSIS   The second technique is called **regression analysis**.[6] The main idea in regression analysis is to draw a straight line (or a curved line in more sophisticated applications) in such a manner that the line goes through past data points as closely as possible (where "closely" is defined in a particular, precise manner). Forecasts are determined by noting where the line falls in future time periods (see Example 8-2 on page 256).

Example 8-1

Suppose that a service station had forecast that 23 customers would arrive at an auto tune-up shop on May 29, and that 27 customers actually arrived. If you were using an exponential smoothing method with $\bar{a} = .2$, then your forecast for May 30 would be:

$$\text{Forecast} = 23 + (.2)(27 - 23) = 23.8$$

Table 8-3
Exponential Smoothing Example Forecasts
Using Two Different Constants

DAY	CUSTOMER ARRIVALS	SMOOTHING CONSTANT $\tilde{a} = .1$	SMOOTHING CONSTANT $\tilde{a} = .3$
1	98	100.00	100.00
2	98	98.80	99.40
3	106	99.62	98.98
4	97	100.26	101.09
5	102	99.93	99.86
6	103	100.14	100.50
7	114	100.43	100.25
8	102	101.78	105.08
9	98	101.80	102.31
10	107	101.42	102.31
11	146	101.98	103.72
12	154	106.38	116.40
13	140	111.15	127.68
14	156	114.03	131.38
15	146	118.23	138.76
16	147	121.00	140.93
17	152	123.60	142.75
18	144	126.44	145.53
19	161	128.20	145.07
20	146	131.48	149.85

Regression analysis can be made even more useful by including additional data for past years. For example, data on past prices and advertising budgets can be included. The resulting regression constants then indicate how strongly sales respond to changes in prices and advertising.

CASE
Product Marketing Decision

Frank James, Manager of Industrial Marketing for a major industrial products company, was concerned about which of two products to emphasize in this year's research budget. Both products involved developing flat panel video displays. Frank felt that some day flat panel displays would become an extremely important product, taking the place of cathode ray pic-

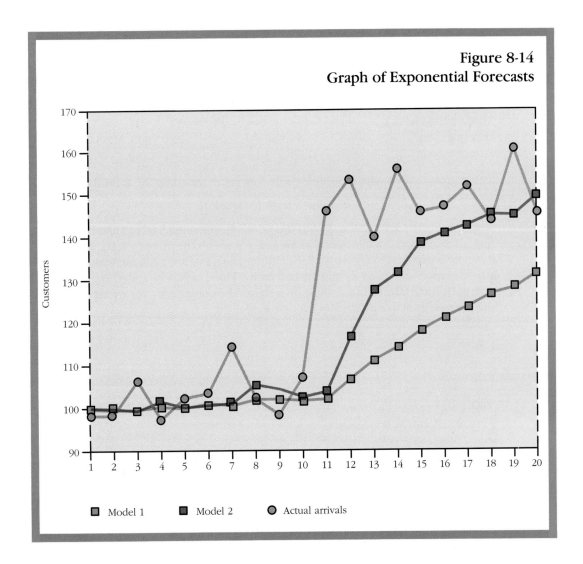

Figure 8-14
Graph of Exponential Forecasts

ture tubes (so that future television sets might be only a few inches thick), and also having important applications in instrument readouts, radar sets, and similar uses.

Frank's lab had been working on two different technical approaches, and he felt that the increasingly expensive work along two lines could no longer be justified. Thus, he wanted to select the more promising product for funding. The main characteristics of both products are summarized in Table 8-4. Product A had fewer development risks but was less exciting. Product B would be assured market success if two technical problems could be overcome.

In making his choice between Product A and Product B, Frank can turn to another formal decision-making tool called **decision analysis**. ⚘

Example 8-2

Over the past several years sales have been:

YEAR:	1980	1981	1982	1983	1984	1985	1986	1987
Sales ($ thousands):	14	16	24	24	27	31	32	36
Forecast	14.7	17.8	20.9	24	27	30.1	33.2	36.2
Forecast error	−.7	−1.8	3.1	0	0	.9	−.2	−.2

The regression line which best fits these data is described by the formula:

$$\text{Sales} = b_0 + (b_1)(\text{year})$$

where b_0 and b_1 are constants with the values b_0 equalling 3.07143 and b_1 equalling −6,069.74857, while "year" is the year for which the forecast is wanted. This example is graphed in Figure 8-15. Computer programs are available which calculate the values of b_0 and b_1 quickly and easily. These numbers, called **regression constants**, are interesting in their own right. The constant b_1, for example, gives the average growth rate in sales each year.

Table 8-4
Product Characteristics

	PRODUCT A	PRODUCT B
Cost	Medium	Very high, but might become lower
Power needs	Medium	Low
Compatibility	Excellent	Poor, but excellent if one problem could be overcome
Ruggedness	Good	Excellent

DECISION ANALYSIS

Four steps are involved in applying decision analysis: structuring the problem, assigning probabilities, measuring outcomes, and problem analysis.[7] We will illustrate these four steps in turn by showing how they would apply to Frank's decision in the case above.

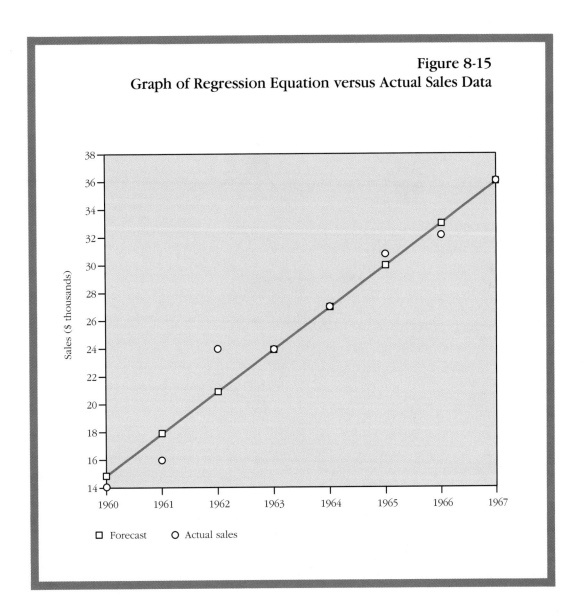

Figure 8-15
Graph of Regression Equation versus Actual Sales Data

Structuring the Problem

Frank's decision now will lead to various outcomes in the future. Some of these outcomes are uncertain. Figure 8-16 shows how this problem can be structured in a **decision tree**. The decision tree starts with a square box, which represents a decision. Two branches lead from the decision box, indicating that Frank can choose to fund either Product A or Product B.

Figure 8-16
Decision Tree Analysis of Product Marketing Decision

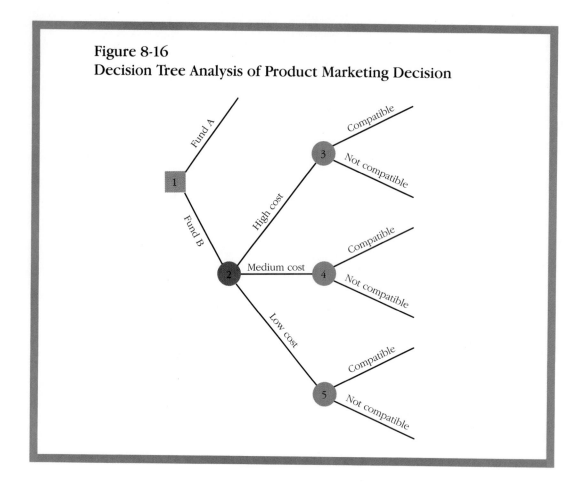

If Frank chooses Product A, he feels quite certain that the product would be moderately successful in a few years. No major decisions or uncertainties are left, so this branch of the decision tree ends.

If Frank decides to fund Product B, it is not clear what the eventual manufacturing cost will be. Frank decides to look at three possible cost ranges. Also, the solution to the compatibility problem is not guaranteed. The decision tree shows all possible outcomes of these two uncertainties.

Assigning Probabilities

Frank has no way of predicting whether the cost of Product B will come down, or how far it might come down. However, he and others in the company have a good deal of experience in the industry, and can, with the help of other experts, estimate the

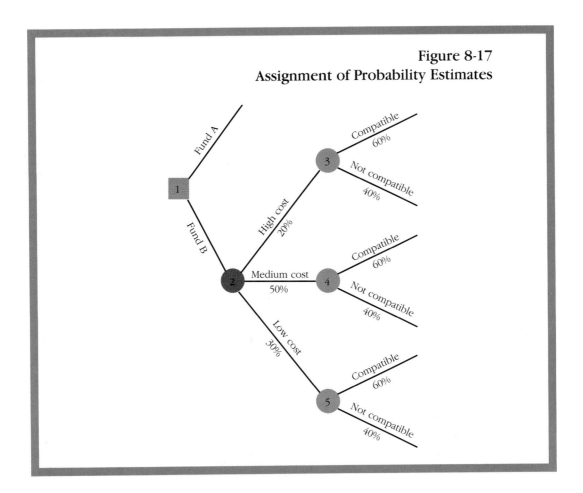

Figure 8-17
Assignment of Probability Estimates

chances of each price level. Likewise, he can estimate the probability of solving the compatibility problem. Figure 8-17 shows his assessments. In some problems, it is possible to use formal analysis to find probabilities. If the new product is similar to some already on the market, for example, the forecasting tools discussed earlier might be used to predict costs. Often, however, especially when new ideas or products are involved, personal estimates represent the best information obtainable.

Measuring Outcomes

Frank views Product A as unexciting but safe, while Product B is potentially very profitable, though risky. But he must now become more specific about what terms like "unexciting" and "very profitable" mean in dollars and cents. Frank chooses to

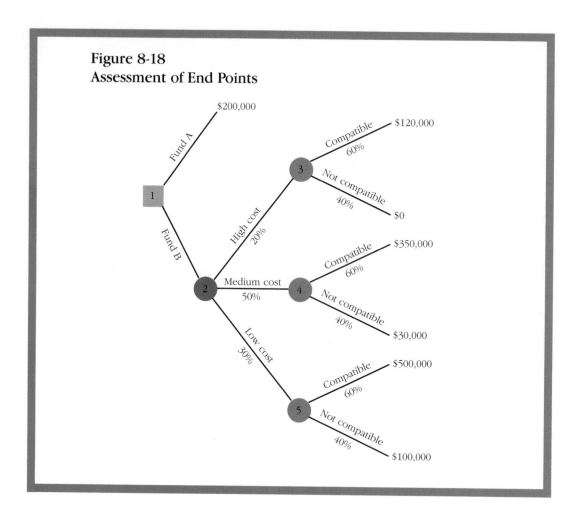

Figure 8-18
Assessment of End Points

estimate the annual profits at each possible end point. Thus, he estimates that Product A would yield annual profits of about $200,000. If he chooses Product B, and then he finds that the cost remains high but the compatibility problem is solved, he would expect to make about $120,000 per year. If the price remains high and the compatibility problem is not solved, then no profits will be realized. Other end points shown in Figure 8-18 are assessed similarly.

Frank could have chosen other measures. For example, he ignores the fact that Product B, if successful, might be a major seller for the division years longer than Product A would. He also ignores such nondollar considerations as the effect on the morale of lab personnel, and possible cross-fertilization with other research work. Sometimes such factors cannot be ignored, and techniques are available for dealing with them should it be necessary. The references cited in the chapter endnotes go into these issues.

Problem Analysis

Before completing the discussion of Frank's problem, it is necessary to digress for a moment to discuss how outcomes are valued. Suppose that you hold a lottery ticket and you have a 50 percent chance of winning $5,000, and a 50 percent chance of winning nothing. In just a few moments, the lottery will be resolved, and you will find out whether you win or not. You are assured that the lottery is fair. Now, just moments before the lottery, someone offers you $x for your ticket. How large would $x have to be to induce you to sell?

Note that this is a personal decision. If you were poor you might sell at a lower price than if you were wealthy. Most of us would probably want more than a few dollars, and few people would demand more than $2,500, but beyond that it is hard to find much agreement among different people. **Utility theory** takes these individual feelings into account. For the sake of simplicity, however, we will ignore these issues here and assume that you would sell your ticket for $2,500 and would not sell for even a dollar less. As a result, the gamble is worth the average winnings, which is given by:

probability of "win"		probability of "loss"
times	plus	times
amount gained from "win"		amount gained from "loss"

Thus, if the lottery gave a 60 percent chance of winning $5,000 and a 40 percent chance of losing $1,000, for example, the average winnings would be:

$$(.6 \times \$5,000) + (.4 \times (-\$1,000)) = \$2,600$$

With these concepts, Frank's problem becomes easier to solve.

Suppose Frank decides to develop Product B, and the cost turns out to be high. He then ends up in the circle node marked "3" in Figure 8-18. At this point, he has a 60 percent chance of making $120,000 per year and a 40 percent chance of making no profits. By the same logic as above, his average profits (also called expected profits or more generally, the **expected outcome**) will be $72,000 per year [(60% × $120,000) + (40% × $0) = $72,000)]. Likewise, the expected profits if Frank ends up at nodes "4" or "5" will be $222,000 and $340,000, respectively.

Now consider node "2". If Frank is at this point, he does not know yet what the cost will be. The chance the cost will be high is 20 percent, in which case he would be at node "3" with expected profits of $72,000. Likewise, the chance of a medium cost giving expected profits of $222,000 is 50 percent, and the chance of getting profits of $340,000 is 30 percent. Expected profits at node "2" are:

$$(.2 \times \$72,000) + (.5 \times \$222,000) + (.3 \times \$340,000) = \$227,400.$$

At this point, Frank can move back to node "1". Note that this is a **square** node, indicating a decision. At the **round** nodes Frank did not know which path he would take. The probabilities controlled his path, so these are known as **chance** nodes. At **decision** nodes, however, Frank can choose the path he prefers. As shown on Figure

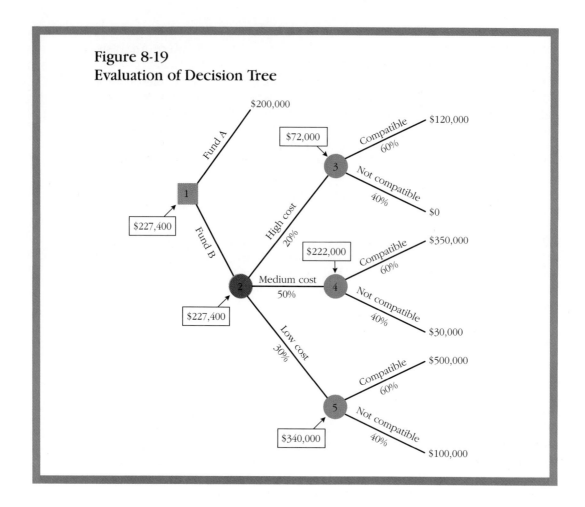

Figure 8-19
Evaluation of Decision Tree

8-19, he can choose Product A, with a known profit of $200,000, or Product B, with expected annual profits of $227,400. Obviously he would choose B if he wished to maximize expected profits.

Practical Issues

The decision analysis problem above is a simple one. The ideas explained, however, can be used to build much more complex trees, and the same methods still apply. For example, Frank might focus on either a retail market or on selling to other manufacturers, and he might want to see what the cost will be before making that decision. He can add decision nodes at the tips of the branches to represent future decisions.

Likewise, he can add chance nodes to represent uncertain events that affect the outcomes of future decisions.

No limit restricts how far Frank can push his tree—he can keep on adding nodes as long as he wants to. However, at some point decision trees turn into bushy messes. It is impossible to build a perfectly complete model of any real situation. Each decision has too many possible outcomes and uncertainties to capture completely. A more fruitful way of using decision analysis consists of:

1. Building a simple model, representing the major decisions and uncertainties.
2. Analyzing the simple tree to find the most promising actions.
3. **Pruning the tree** by trimming off the obviously bad actions, then expanding what is left into a more complete tree.

Thus, the analysis goes in circles. The tree is built, analyzed and simplified, the promising parts expanded, and the problem reanalyzed and resimplified. The process is repeated as often as needed.

SIMULATION

In the Burger King case that opened the chapter, simulation helped save a good deal of money. Similar stories from many different settings could be repeated. **Simulation** is a representation of reality.[8] Through repeated trials, management can mathematically measure the outcome of proposed actions. Simulation is very flexible, and quite easy to understand. With the development of powerful tools that allow managers to develop simulations quickly and easily, simulation has become one of the more commonly used tools in business.

To demonstrate how simulation works, suppose you work for a company like Burger King, and are wondering how many waiters should staff the front counter during midafternoon. On the average, one customer arrives each 35 seconds. Again on average, a waiter takes 60 seconds to serve each customer. Alas, both customer arrivals and service times vary. Customers sometimes arrive in bunches with slack periods in between. Some customers can be served quickly, while others take more time. Thus, even though two waiters should be enough, on average, random fluctuations might cause some customers to have to wait in line. You are interested in how long the wait might be.

To use simulation to solve this problem,[9] you must first describe the uncertainty in arrival rates and service times. Table 8-5 gives the data used in this example. Note that the average arrival rates and service times are given above.

We will simulate what would happen with two waiters. Assume that both waiters are idle and the simulation begins with the arrival of a customer.

Table 8-5
Probability of Arrival Rates and Service Times at Burger King

ARRIVAL RATES		
TIME BETWEEN CUSTOMERS (SECONDS)	PROBABILITY	RANDOM NUMBERS
15	25%	00–24
35	50	25–74
55	25	75–99

Average time between arrivals $= (15)(.25) + (35)(.50) + (55)(.25) = 35$ seconds

SERVICE TIMES		
SERVICE TIME (SECONDS)	PROBABILITY	RANDOM NUMBERS
40	10%	00–09
50	30	10–39
60	35	40–74
80	25	75–99

Average time to serve a customer $= (40)(.10) + (50)(.30) + (60)(.35) + (80)(.25) = 60$ seconds

A random choice of customer service times given in Table 8-5 is desired such that the chance that service will take 40 seconds is 10 percent, the chance it will take 50 seconds is 30 percent, and so forth. A convenient method for doing so is to pick a number between 00 and 99 at random, and then to use the "**Random Number**" column. For example, pick a random number from the table in Appendix I. The first two digits in the table are 53. The "Random Number" column for service times indicates that this corresponds to a service time of 60 seconds. Thus, the first waiter will be busy from time zero (now) to time 60.

The second customer arrival is now needed. Again, select a two-digit random number from the table. The next numbers in the table are 42. As Table 8-6 shows, the next customer will arrive 35 seconds from now. The situation so far is summarized in Table 8-6.

Now repeat the process for the second customer. The next two random numbers from the table are 51 and 73, indicating a service time of 60 seconds, and 35 seconds to the next customer arrival. These data are entered in Table 8-7. The table shows that although the first waiter is busy when the second customer arrives, the second waiter is free to serve the new customer.

When the third customer arrives at time 70, the first waiter will be free to serve her. The two random numbers for the third customer are 27 and 17, indicating a

Table 8-6
First Customer Arrival

CUSTOMER NUMBER	ARRIVAL TIME	RANDOM NUMBER	NEXT ARRIVAL	RANDOM NUMBER	SERVICE TIME	FIRST WAITER		SECOND WAITER	
						BEGIN	END	BEGIN	END
1	0	42	35	53	60	0	60	Idle	
2	35								

Table 8-7
Second Customer Arrival

CUSTOMER NUMBER	ARRIVAL TIME	RANDOM NUMBER	NEXT ARRIVAL	RANDOM NUMBER	SERVICE TIME	FIRST WAITER		SECOND WAITER	
						BEGIN	END	BEGIN	END
1	0	42	35	53	60	0	60	Idle	
2	35	73	35	51	60	Busy		35	85
3	70								

service time of 50 seconds and time to the next customer of 15 seconds. Table 8-8 shows these data. None of the first three customers have had to wait, but note that when the fourth customer arrives both waiters will be busy. The fourth customer will have to wait for 10 seconds, until the second waiter finishes with the second customer.

This process is continued as long as desired. Generally, thousands of customer arrivals are examined and statistics are gathered on how many customers have to wait, how long the average and maximum waits are, the percentage of time the waiters are idle, and other useful measures. Then, the process is repeated assuming three, or perhaps four waiters. Management can then choose the number of waiters with full knowledge of how service will be affected.

How reliable are simulation results? After all, service and arrival times were found by simply picking random numbers. If a different random number table was used, wouldn't the results be different? The answer is "Yes, the *details* would be different." However, long-run performance would be the same. Using thousands of customer arrivals, the law of averages prevails. The long-term average performance of the system can be successfully predicted no matter what random number table is used.

The logic behind simulation is quite simple. Pick a random number, find the corresponding service time or customer arrival time, then keep track of who is busy,

Table 8-8
Third Customer Arrival

CUSTOMER NUMBER	ARRIVAL TIME	RANDOM NUMBER	NEXT ARRIVAL	RANDOM NUMBER	SERVICE TIME	FIRST WAITER		SECOND WAITER	
						BEGIN	END	BEGIN	END
1	0	42	35	53	60	0	60	Idle	
2	35	73	35	51	60	Busy		35	95
3	70	17	15	27	50	70	120	Busy	
4	85								

who is free, and how long the customer has to wait. This simple logical structure applies even to complex simulations. One of the attractive features of simulation, in fact, is that complex interactions and relationships can easily be represented. For example, suppose waiters work faster when lines of customers form or customers go to another restaurant if lines are too long. These factors can readily be simulated.

Finally, several computer languages developed during the past decade are especially designed for simulation. Twenty years ago most simulations were written in high-level computer languages, such as FORTRAN; writing simulation programs was then a difficult and tedious task. In the 1960s a simulation language called **GPSS** came into use, making it much easier to design simulations. Currently, many powerful, well-designed simulation languages are available. These are now subdivided into general simulation languages, such as GPSS, **SLAM**, and **SIMSCRIPT**, and special-purpose simulation languages designed to model manufacturing systems, financial systems, or other problems of special interest. If you use a simulation language, it is easy to program and analyze the customer service example above in less than a half-hour.

PRACTICAL ISSUES

The concepts summarized in this chapter have proven to be powerful management tools. As the Burger King case illustrates, the potential for payoffs is enormous in many business situations. However, formal methods of decision making are no substitutes for intelligence. Rather, they are best used to develop insights into complex situations.

All real problems are much too complex to capture completely by any formal method. Linear programming, decision analysis—all such methods represent only a tiny portion of the real problem. Thus, judgment is required to decide just which portions of the real problem need to be modelled, to determine whether the model adequately captures the essence of the problem, and to make corrections for those factors which will inevitably be omitted. The following steps have proven useful in verifying and interpreting model results:

1. Either spend time yourself working on the real problem, or have someone involved with the modelling effort who has. Crucial details can otherwise be overlooked.

2. Compare model results with current decisions. Usually, the people making decisions do not make gross errors. If model results are radically different than current practice, the model probably is in error.

3. Feed the model data representing simple, easily understood situations, and see if the model comes up with sensible results.

4. Make the model available and transparent to field people. Let them see how inputs affect results. Allow them to compare the model's decisions with their own, and see which performs better in practice.

5. Keep the model as simple as possible. Rather than attempting to build a complex model incorporating every possible factor, it is far better to have a simple, easily understood model to develop preliminary recommendations, then allow field operators to adjust results as required.

If these simple steps are followed, the models developed with the tools discussed in this chapter will approximate reality well enough to greatly simplify the decision-making process.

ENDING CASE
Polishing the Big Apple[10]

In 1980, New York City—never known as a clean place—hit an all time high (or low) in dirtiness; one rating system showed that only 53 percent of the streets were acceptably clean. There were only 800 street cleaners on the force, while only five years previously there had been about 2,500. In 1980 the city council rejected a Department of Sanitation proposal to expand the force, citing lack of confidence in the department's ability to manage the additional resources and to get a sufficient payoff for the public. Understandably, morale was low. The work force was embittered by the constant abuse showered upon them by the public and media, while pushing brooms was perceived by many workers to be less manly than garbage collection.

In 1981 the department began to examine the street cleaning problem using analysis tools discussed in this chapter. The first step was to discover the relationship

New York City employed regression analysis and simulation as tools to attack the city's littered streets.

between additional workers and cleaner streets. Even experienced people in the department had no idea how much difference additional workers would make. Many people even thought that there was no relationship—that natural rainfall did most of the cleaning. The department first gathered data on the relationship between cleanliness and sweeping man-hours. Mark Twain is reported to have said that data is like garbage: you have to know what to do with it before you collect it. The department now reports they understand both sides of that statement. Regression analysis was then used to show a strong, clear, and unmistakable relationship. With these results, the department could now predict the effects of hiring more people, and those predictions could be used in both budget proposals and performance evaluations. Starting in fiscal year 1982, the city has added more cleaners each year, and each year cleanliness ratings have gone up almost exactly as predicted. With each success management credibility increased and budget discussions were given more respect.

Regression showed that there was a wide range in cleaner effectiveness from district to district. Some areas needed five times as many cleaners as others to improve ratings by one percentage point. Further, results indicated that additional cleaners were least effective in the most highly littered areas; this seemed counterintuitive. You would think that a sweeper in a dirty area would pick up more litter and affect cleanliness ratings more. However, notice that if you put a cleaner in a clean area (such as Staten Island) and he does a good job cleaning the street, that street will stay clean for several weeks. However, if that same cleaner worked in midtown Manhattan, a high litter area, then even if he does an excellent job, the street would remain clean for only a few hours. Thus, litter rate is the major factor in predicting cleaning effectiveness. This insight was also the result of regression analysis.

The final type of analysis was a simulation study on the effects of illegally parked cars on cleaning effectiveness. It was found that in some cases, even one less illegal car increased the chances of an acceptably clean street by 20 percent or more. Prior to this finding, no one had been able to prove that programs focusing on illegal parking made any difference, but now there was a fundamental change in the department's approach. Now up to 30 percent of the mobile ticketing officers are used in conjunction with the cleanliness program.

The models developed in this work have been useful in several other ways. The department has the ability to set meaningful standards and hold managers accountable for meeting those standards, something not always found in public administration. Models have showed how important new cleaning equipment can be, and have justified purchase of new brooms and small trucks. Management can now predict effects of changes or policies accurately. For example, they were able to analyze how a proposed bottle bill would affect street cleanliness. Finally, the program led to worker incentive programs.

Overall, the city is now approaching record cleanliness levels, rather than record filthiness levels. Further, they are doing so with 700 fewer workers than several years ago, before the deterioration in cleanliness levels began. Estimated savings amount to $12 million per year. ▨

SUMMARY

This chapter has introduced some of the formal decision-making tools that managers use.

Linear programming (LP) works best with resource allocation problems in which maximization of outputs or profits, or minimization of inputs or costs is desired. Because most problems of this type involve multiple constraints, computer solution of the LP model is often the only efficient alternative. LP is particularly helpful in analyzing changes in output or input as constraints are changed.

Program Evaluation and Review Technique (PERT) is a method used to find the most efficient way to schedule a job that consists of a number of steps. By analyzing all the tasks in a project, constructing a visual chart of how the tasks interrelate and the time that each task takes, it is possible to find the shortest possible time that it will take for the project to be completed.

Forecasting involves the prediction of future events. The first step is to decide what to forecast. In terms of accuracy, it is best to forecast the broadest, most inclusive categories possible and to do so over the shortest time period possible. Forecast tools can be either quantitative or qualitative.

Decision analysis uses the decision-tree technique to systematically assess the probabilities associated with possible outcomes. By explicitly taking into account such things as risk and risk preference, it is possible to quantify the key decision elements and mathematically rank the alternatives.

Simulation is the process of approximating real-life outcomes by entering known data into the model and observing the resulting outcomes. While simulation can be done by hand, computer simulation allows much more accurate results because it is possible to observe the outcomes of as many trials as is necessary to ensure accuracy. Simulation is especially useful in predicting long-term outcomes as it depends on the law of averages for its accuracy.

Finally, all formal techniques can only hope to capture a small portion of a real-life problem. Human judgment remains the key to effective modelling.

KEY TERMS

Linear programming	Exponential smoothing
Maximize	Smoothing constant
Feasible	Forecast error
Feasibility region	Random fluctuation
Constraint	Stable versus nervous
LP problem	Cycle
Equal-profit line	Trend
Schedule	Lag
PERT	Regression analysis
Critical path method	Regression constants
Early start	Decision analysis
Early finish	Probability
Task dependence	Decision tree
Critical path	Utility theory
Critical tasks	Expected outcome
Late start	Square versus round node
Late finish	Decision versus chance node
Slack time	Pruning the tree
Qualitative tools	Simulation
Quantitative tools	GPSS

REVIEW QUESTIONS

1. What types of problems are best suited to solution by means of linear programming?

2. What types of mathematical expressions are not allowed in linear programming models?

3. Of what significance is the feasible region in a linear programming problem?

4. What is the function of the equal-profit line in a linear programming problem?

5. Name two advantages of linear programming.

6. What are the steps in finding the best schedule using PERT?

7. What is the critical path and what is its function?

8. When are PERT charts most useful?

9. What are the two important rules of forecasting referred to in the chapter?

10. What is implicitly assumed when forecasts are made using past data?

11. What is the purpose of the smoothing constant in exponential forecasting? How does the value of this constant relate to the accuracy of the forecast?

12. Assuming a simple two dimensional graph with an X horizontal and a Y vertical axis, what do the regression constants b_0 and b_1 signify?

13. What is the purpose of a decision tree?

14. What is the difference between a square and a round node in a decision tree?

15. What are some practical rules to follow in making decision analysis more useful?

16. How are random numbers used to represent probabilities in simulation models?

17. What kind of results do simulation models give? How are these results helpful?

18. What are the five rules given in the chapter for verifying and interpreting model results (for any type of model)?

CHALLENGE QUESTIONS

1. Name three types of problems with which you are familiar that could be solved using linear programming.

2. Construct a PERT chart for preparing a steak barbecue for yourself and three friends. Assume that the meal consists of steak, baked potatoes, salad, and a vegetable. Assume your barbecue can handle all four steaks at once and that you have all the needed food on hand.

3. What is the significance of slack time and how is it calculated?

4. Assume that you are preparing forecasts for the following items. Which item would have the highest value smoothing constant? The lowest? Why?
   A. Price of an auto stock you hold
   B. Five-year forecast for auto sales
   C. Yearly forecast for Ford auto sales in the U.S.
   D. Yearly forecast for total domestic output of autos

5. How are individual preferences for risk taken into account in decision analysis?

6. Why does using a different random number table or generator change the details of a simulation but not the final result?

7. If you were designing a simulation model to determine at what times to allow cashiers in a grocery store to go to lunch, what factors would you include in your analysis and to whom would you talk before making your final recommendations?

CASE AND RELATED QUESTIONS

1. What factors would have restricted the usefulness of linear programming within the context of the problems faced by Burger King? What aspects of simulation solved these problems?

2. What is the difference between sophisticated guesswork and simulation?

3. How would you go about testing the effect of an increase in painting capacity in the Housewares problem faced by Diane Furuhashi?

4. How is a higher preference for risk likely to affect Frank James' decision? Would it ever be rational to accept an alternative with a lower expected value?

5. In the restaurant customer arrival rate example, what other decisions might be made easier by the information gained from the simulation?

ENDNOTES

1. Adapted from William Swart and Luca Donno, "Simulation Modeling Improves Operations, Planning, and Productivity of Fast-Food Restaurants," *Interfaces*, December 1981, pp. 35–47.

2. The theory and practice of linear programming is developed and explained in great depth in numerous books. For a concise, intuitive discussion, see Rick Hesse and Gene Woolsey, *Applied Management Science: A Quick and Dirty Approach* (Chicago: Science Research Associates, 1980), Chapter 6. A good, thorough discussion of basics and applications is contained in Stephen P. Bradley, Arnoldo C. Hax, and Thomas L. Magnanti, *Applied Mathematical Programming* (Reading, MA: Addison-Wesley, 1977).

3. Jerome D. Wiest and Ferdinand K. Levy, *A Management Guide to PERT/CMP* (Englewood Cliffs, NJ: Prentice-Hall, 1977).

4. PERT and CPM are, technically speaking, slightly different techniques developed independently. Over time, however, the terms have come to be used almost interchangeably.

5. For a general review of forecasting principles, see William J. Sawaya and William C. Giauque, *Production and Operations Management* (San Diego: Harcourt Brace Jovanovich, 1986), Chapter 5. A much more detailed and technical discussion is contained in Spyros Makridakis and Steven C. Wheelwright, *Forecasting: Methods and Applications* (New York: John Wiley & Sons, 1978).

6. In addition to the forecasting texts, regression analysis is treated in most books on statistics. See William Mendenhall et al. *Statistics for Management and Economics* (Boston: Duxbury Press, 1986), Chapters 11, 12, and 14.

7. A good general introduction to decision analysis is contained in Howard Raiffa, *Decision Analysis: Introductory Lectures in Choices under Uncertainty* (Reading, MA: Addison-Wesley, 1968).

8. Introductory chapters on simulation can be found in Sawaya and Giauque, Chapter 21, and in Harvey M. Wagner, *Principles of Operations Research With Applications to Managerial Decisions* (Englewood Cliffs, NJ: Prentice-Hall, Inc., 1969).

9. This particular problem can be easily solved without using simulation. However, the concepts used in simulation can be readily used in more complicated cases.

10. Lucius J. Riccio, Joseph Miller, and Ann Litke, "Polishing the Big Apple: How Management Science Has Helped Make New York Streets Cleaner," *Interfaces*, January–February 1986, pp. 83–88.

PART III

THE CHALLENGE OF
ORGANIZATION

CHAPTER 9

THE NATURE OF THE
ORGANIZATION

LEARNING OBJECTIVES

■ Develop a personal framework for understanding and analyzing organizations.

■ Define organizational concepts and terminology.

■ Understand the open systems model for looking at organizations.

■ Identify the elements of organizational culture.

■ Evaluate the eight characteristics of an effective organization according to the Peters and Waterman work on "excellent" companies.

■ Discuss how college students perceive organizations—their fears and desired organizational values.

■ Develop a basis for evaluating organizational effectiveness.

■ Illustrate some of the possible outcomes of implementing innovative organizational concepts in an actual factory setting.

■ Analyze the places in an organization where problems can occur.

■ Understand the strengths and weaknesses of organizations to which you now belong.

■ Know how to ask intelligent questions about the organization that you may join.

In 1968, General Foods was considering the construction of a plant in Topeka, Kansas, to manufacture pet foods. Because of continuing problems at their existing plants—product waste, sabotage, frequent shutdowns, and low morale—the management of General Foods wanted to try a set of innovative motivational techniques at this new plant. The basic design of the new plant was oriented around the principles of skills development, challenging jobs, and teamwork. The organization of the work environment included the following:

Autonomous work groups   The work force of seventy employees was divided into teams of seven to fourteen employees. Three types of teams were created: processing, packaging, and shipping. These teams were self-managed by the workers; they were involved in assigning work responsibilities, screening and selecting new members, and making decisions for large segments of the plant's operations.

Challenging jobs   The basic design of each job was developed to eliminate the boring and routine aspects as much as possible. Each job—whether on the manufacturing line or in the warehouse—was designed to include a high degree of variety, autonomy, planning, liaison work with other teams, and responsibility for diagnosing and correcting mechanical or process problems.

Job mobility and rewards for learning   Because each set of jobs was designed to be equally challenging, it was possible to have a single job classification for all operators. Employees could receive pay increases by developing new skills and mastering different jobs. Team members were, in essence, paid for learning more and more of the plant's operations.

Information availability   Unlike most manufacturing plants, the operations at this plant provided the necessary economic, quantity, and quality information normally reserved for managers.

Self-government   Rather than working with a set of predetermined rules and procedures, such policies were developed as the need arose. This resulted in fewer unnecessary rules to guide the work. Only critical guidelines or rules were developed, and generally these were based on the collective experience of the team.

Status symbols   The typical physical and social status symbols of assigned parking spaces, wide variations in the decor of offices and rooms, and separate entrance and eating facilities were eliminated. The plant had an open parking lot, a single entrance for both office and plant workers, and a common decor throughout the entire plant.

Learning and evaluation   The most basic feature of the plant was the commitment to evaluate continually both plant productivity and the state of employee morale. Before any change was made in the plant, an evaluation of its impact on productivity and worker morale was made.

As in any major redesign program, management at the new plant was faced with a number of implementation problems. First, tension among employees developed concerning pay rates. Four basic pay rates existed in the plant: (1) starting rate, (2) single rate (mastery of one job), (3) team rate (mastery of all jobs within the team), and (4) plant rate (mastery of all operator jobs within the plant). Because the decision on pay rates was primarily the responsibility of the team leader, certain questions about the judgment of job mastery and whether workers had an equal opportunity to learn jobs developed.

Second, because the management philosophy at this particular plant was quite different from that at the other plants, difficulties arose whenever employees of the new plant interacted with other General Foods personnel. Problems of resistance and a lack of acceptance and support developed.

Finally, the expectations of a small minority of workers did not coincide with the new teamwork concept of the plant. Certain employees resisted the movement toward greater responsibility. Again, individual differences among employees were shown to be important to the job redesign movement. ⬛

INTRODUCTION

Modern society is a complex of organizations. Almost every facet of man's existence is serviced, regulated, assisted, or facilitated by one organization or another. The waking hours of almost every modern person are expended within the structures and processes of some type of organization, whether it is a family, school, government, church, business, industry, or club.

Definition of Organization

An organization, simply defined, is the arrangement and utilization of resources—human, financial, and material—for the accomplishment of goals. All organizations include in some form a set of goals or objectives, the allocation of power or authority, expectations of duties or functions, channels of communication, and some method of assessing goal accomplishment. The universal nature of organizations has made it

An organization utilizes human, financial, and material resources to accomplish goals.

both the object of admiration and the butt of jokes, negative stories, and invective. On the one hand, one hears about a company that "runs a tight ship" or "operates like a well-oiled machine." But in the next breath, people will complain about "red tape," being treated like a number not a person, or getting lost in the big bureaucracy. An Air Force story recounts how an officer in Vietnam was in the front lines area and got word to report back to headquarters. He went to the makeshift airstrip and asked for a plane ride to the rear. The sergeant quickly arranged transportation and then said, "You're lucky, we aren't organized yet. Right now I can get you a ride easily but if we were organized, I would have to go through the formal channels and you would be lucky to get out of here in three days."

Even a simple organization like a committee—a temporary organization set up to solve a problem—comes in for some hard biting humor.

"A committee is a place where you take minutes and waste hours."

"A committee is a situation where the incompetent lead the uninformed about the unimportant."

"The best committees are made up of three people—one of whom is sick and another of whom is out of town."

"For God so loved the world that he didn't set up a committee."

Organizations Are Tools

The ambivalence about organizations represents a key issue for people in management; namely, is the organization the master or the slave? If one sees organization as the master, then one takes everything in the system as a given, and everyone must adapt to the structure, policies, goals, values, and demands already in place in the organization. The slogan of a manager with this idea of the "fixed" organization could easily be: "Yours is not to reason why, yours is but to do or die." The role of the manager is to hold the organization sacred and see that everyone complies with the givens in the system.

It is also possible to see the organization as the slave—or rather as a tool—that managers have available to help achieve goals. If a certain arrangement of resources is not getting people where they would like to go, then the wise action is to change something in the organization. The Volvo automobile company in Sweden was not satisfied with the quality of automobile the standard assembly line method was producing. Top management made a key decision to change the technical structure of the organization. They eliminated the assembly line and created work teams whose responsibility was to build the total automobile. The result of this change was a marked increase in the quality of the finished product, and an increase in the pride and satisfaction the employees felt in their work.

Organizations Must Change with Situational Demands

History is replete with examples of the failure of managers or administrators to modify the organization to meet the demands of existing situations. The British army, organized to meet the customs of European warfare where armies in solid ranks marched forth and fired at each other until one side capitulated, was ill-prepared in North America in the 1690s to meet the French and Indians who fought from ambush. It took a number of costly defeats to get the top brass to reorganize the army and its methods of warfare.

Athletic history is also filled with cases of new and outmoded organizations. In football, the T-formation and wish-bone offense made the old single and double wing formations obsolete. Coaches who were wedded to a single kind of organization were soon dominated by the new innovations, and they had to change or lose.

In business organizations, certain companies like Union Carbide, Procter and Gamble, and General Foods among others developed a new organizational form called the **matrix organization** that gave them an advantage over their competitors.[1] This new form created product or project teams that drew members from several existing departments. Each team member had two bosses—the product team leader and the old department leader. This new form allowed the team to have all the resources needed to produce and market a new product in a very short time. The old form required the cumbersome process of review by every department before a new product got to market.

Before its breakup into individual companies, AT&T was the largest company in the world with about one million employees. Just before divestiture of its regional operating companies (because of the court ruling declaring AT&T to be an unfair monopoly), the company went through a major reorganization. It was transformed from a company organized along functional lines—installation, service, customer complaints, yellow pages, local and long distance calls—to a new organization around market segments—commercial accounts, residence accounts, special customers. Competitive pressure from other telecommunications companies forced AT&T to focus on the market rather than the traditional functions.

The above are examples of managers thinking of the organization as a tool that can be changed and used in a variety of different ways to help accomplish the goals or mission of the organization.

AN OPEN SYSTEM THEORY OF ORGANIZATIONS

To get a clear picture of the function of an organization it is important to view the organization as an **open system**, which means the organization is continually interacting with its environment in a dynamic way.[2]

Most research and theory concerning organizations is based on a closed-system model. For purposes of analysis, the organization is presumed to be contained within the confines of its physical operating structures and the existing organization chart. An automobile assembly plant, for example, is seen as a set of workers in a particular location producing cars. If output is reduced or restricted, problem diagnosis and corrective action generally take place within the confines of the plant.

Almost all organization theorists, however, recognize that any organization exists within a wider environment and can be influenced considerably by conditions outside its walls. The automobile plant is affected by general economic conditions, government regulations on automobile safety and pollution-reducing equipment, demands of labor unions, availability and cost of raw materials, taxes, prices of competing products, and on and on. In this sense the organization is an "open system." Planning must accommodate the external environment, the components of which appear in Figure 9-1. The outside environment supplies **inputs** (raw materials, labor, etc.) that are processed or converted by the organization, via its work, or **throughput** activities, into outputs. **Outputs** (final products) go back into the environment and may subsequently alter or influence new inputs, which again are funneled into the system. This is an ongoing cycle for all organizations.[3]

The automobile plant takes in from the environment its supply of labor, raw materials, and equipment. In addition, if management is wise, it takes in all possible information regarding such external conditions as prices, markets, taxes, regulations, and the like. This data is used to formulate decisions on wages, prices, design, dividends paid to investors, public relations activities, markets, and expansion or reduction of facilities or the work force. The internal or "closed" part of the organization

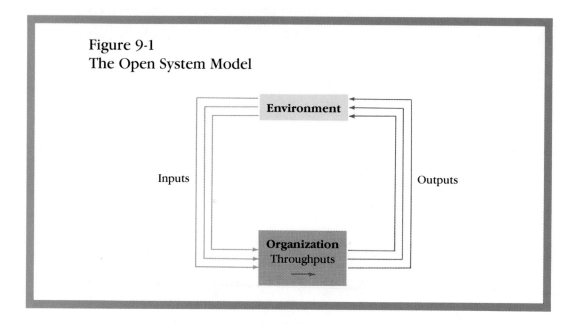

Figure 9-1
The Open System Model

processes the inputs through its production setup (assembly line, groups of crafts people, or service departments) and transforms the inputs into a product or service (output) that is returned to the outside environment.

A similar procedure recurs daily: Workers bring in with them from the environment attitudes, reactions, and feelings that may influence their work during the throughput activity. At the end of the day, they return to the community environment and discharge their feelings and reactions about the company. These feelings in turn influence how others respond to the worker and the company and the loop is complete: What goes out influences what comes in and what comes in influences what goes out.

Internal Systems

When an organization is viewed as a system, it is considered as a total functioning unit made up of necessary integrated parts that allow the unit to function or operate as it strives to accomplish its purposes or goals.[4] A common analogy is to see the organizational system as similar to the human body. The body is made up of a series of integrated parts or subsystems, all of which must function together to allow the person to function adequately. Thus, the human nervous, endocrine, respiratory, and cardiovascular systems combine to make up the total human system. Each subsystem can be examined individually or in concert with other subsystems. When a person becomes "sick" or disabled in some way, a diagnostic process is used to see which of the

This office that allows children to visit parents during the workday is a concrete demonstration of the organization as an open system, continually interacting with the outside environment.

various subsystems is malfunctioning so that a plan for improvement can be initiated. In an organization these subsystems include the **social system, technical or operating system**, and the **administrative system**. See Figure 9-2.

Almost all organizations have these three basic interlocking internal systems in some form.

THE SOCIAL SYSTEM   Every organization has its social world, which is that dynamic condition made up of people in different positions interacting with each other—talking, arguing, helping, deciding, solving problems, and working in some way with each other, trying to achieve some of the goals of the organization and to satisfy some of their own personal needs. Every **social system** has some basic components:

Climate   The prevailing emotional state shared by members in the system. The **climate** may be formal, relaxed, defensive, cautious, accepting, trusting, etc.

Figure 9-2
Internal Organization Systems

Social System	Technical System	Administrative System
Climate	Equipment	Policies
Decision Making	Material	Rules/regulation
Interaction/influence	Physical layout	Procedures
Leadership	Work arrangements	Wage/salary
Communications	Work flow	Promotions
Rewards/punishments	Location	Budgets
Individuals	Size/numbers	Audits
		Reports
		Structure

Communication network   Formal and informal patterns that determine who talks with whom, when, how often, and about what are called **communication networks**.

Status-role structure   Some division of labor always exists; different people perform different functions. Some people, because of their function or position, have higher **status** because of their **role** than others, hence more power and more influence.

Pattern of management   Some people in the organization have the responsibility to work in subordinate positions relative to others, with the assignment to help subordinated in their work. The particular **pattern of management** or style of handling this subordinate action (for example, authoritarian versus participative) that develops in the social system starts at the top in an organization and tends to be adopted throughout.

Decision-making method   Since the basic process in any organization is to solve problems and make decisions, a **decision-making method** for handling problem-solving and decision-making requirements gets established in the social system. It is closely linked to the pattern of management but also includes whether decisions are made by few or many, the use of all relevant resources in problem solving, the creativity of decisions, and the degree of commitment to implement the decisions.

Individuals   Many processes in the social system vary with the kinds of people who make up the system. For example, it might be expected that a group of older workers would behave differently than a group of people in their adolescent years.

THE TECHNICAL OR OPERATING SYSTEM   Every organization develops its method for getting work done. The **technical** or **operating system** is the unique arrangement of equipment, material, people, and processes used to accomplish work. A common industrial operation system is the assembly line, in which workers are arranged along a conveyor belt of some type with the product to be assembled moving along the belt and each worker doing a specific task. The operation system can be altered by changing equipment, using different basic or raw materials, arranging people differently, or changing work assignments.

It is immediately apparent that the social system is integrally connected with the technical system, for the arrangements of people will affect their ability to communicate with each other. Work assignments and work flow influence the patterns of management used and perhaps the way decisions are made. This interplay between the social system and the technical aspects of work is commonly referred to as the **socio-technical system**. (See Box 9-1 for a look at a socio-technical problem of the future.)

However, some elements in the technical system are distinct from the social system and can be altered separately (although some effects in the social system may be noticed). The technical/operating system can be changed in any organization. A common university operating system has a professor in a large lecture hall, standing at a podium in front and lecturing to a whole class. If the class is broken up into small student groups, arranged in a circle with the professor sitting in the circle, a different learning process is likely to occur. The professor, however, may continue to dominate the situation, to lecture, and to control the social system. For real change to take place, some modification is necessary in both the operational and social systems. The lecturing professor will probably find it almost impossible to change the basic nature of instruction unless some changes are made in the existing operating system.

THE ADMINISTRATIVE SYSTEM   Interlocking with the socio-technical system is a network of policy, procedure, auditing, reporting, and formal structure that represents the administrative system. Every organization has established certain formalized procedures for setting down the standards, rules, and regulations that influence what happens in the social and technical systems. Some important elements in the administrative system are as follows:

1. Wage and salary administration. Organizations establish procedures by which pay levels are established and outline the ways in which increases in salary are obtained or bonuses or special benefits are possible.

2. Hiring-firing-promotions. Each organization has prescribed methods for hiring and firing and for making promotions—all laid out by the administrative system.

3. Report-auditing. Many organizations collect data on such matters as use of materials, finances, work output, and quality control. It usually takes the form of report-making or auditing procedures to help determine what is happening to resources.

4. Fringe benefits. Organizations usually establish criteria and methods for allocating fringe benefits such as leave time, vacations, sick leave, retirement, and insurance.

Box 9-1
A Socio-Technical Problem of the Future

With the arrival of the 1980s, increased robotization of leading American industrial firms has led to much conjecture. Existing literature is dotted with dubious speculations about the transformation currently underway in our industries. For the enthusiasts, robotization constitutes a messianic advance that liberates mankind from the doldrums of ungratifying work and poverty. The same phenomenon is viewed by skeptics as an ominous contributor to widespread unemployment. These same individuals suggest that the implementation of robotics is likely to result in a greater class division between the haves and the have-nots.

The actual and anticipated human, organizational, and societal impacts of robotization on the major industrial giants have heretofore been predicated primarily upon supposition rather than empirical investigation. The prevailing state of affairs has been characterized in this way:

Little attention is being given to the anticipation and solution of problems on the human and organizational side of the robotics man-machine interface. Research and development interests appear to be concentrated overwhelmingly on the development of the hardware and software components of engineering systems. More than a dozen academic organizations are contributing to robotic technology. However, . . . only one is known to have sought data on the social impact of robotics. Discussions with robot manufacturers and robot users indicate high levels of interest in obtaining such information and a demonstrated willingness to participate in projects to generate it. The Robot Institute of America, the trade association which keeps abreast of the development of robotic technology, verifies this lack of information. The consensus is that, though the technical engineering aspects of robotics have been highly developed, the human and organizational components have been largely ignored.

The final transition is for public decision makers to view robotization as an integral component of modern industrial technology rather than as an isolated phenomenon. As one Fortune 500 robotic user suggested, "The impact of computer-based technology—computer-aided design, computer-aided manufacturing, flexible machine centers, automation in white collar areas, and so forth—will have a far greater effect than the introduction of robots."

SOURCE: Reprinted from *Robotics & Industrial Engineering: Selected Readings*, ed. Edward L. Fisher (Norcross GA: Institute of Industrial Engineers, 1983), chapter 12.

5. Budgets. The building of the budget is a critical issue in determining the priorities and activities of every unit in the organization.

Table 9-1 shows the factors in each of the three subsystems that may positively affect the achievement of organizational goals. It is the responsibility of managers to handle these factors to improve the goal achievement of the organization.

Table 9-1

System Conditions That Seem to Positively Affect Organization Goals

SOCIAL SYSTEM	OPERATING SYSTEM	ADMINISTRATIVE SYSTEM
Workers are involved in setting goals and making decisions.	Physical conditions are comfortable and do not require excess work; safety conditions prevail.	Rules and regulations are jointly established by management and workers when feasible.
Communications are open; people are kept informed as to what is happening in the system.	System allows workers time to interact with each other and build social support.	Policies and procedures do not restrict adequate development of the social system.
High level of trust and acceptance exists.	Workers are responsible for the quality of output of the operation system.	Formal rewards are given for appropriate management and worker behavior.
Management is highly person-centered as well as concerned about production.	Workers have some control over the operation system; they are not entirely controlled by it.	All benefits are distributed in an equitable fashion.
Workers feel needed, useful, doing something worthwhile.	Operation system requirements are matched to an adequate degree to the personal resources of the workers.	Procedures and rules are not inflexible and are amenable to modification.
Team spirit develops, and workers have pride in their work group.	Workers have an opportunity to use a variety of skills and abilities on the job, as desired.	Workers are involved in setting goals and doing work planning.
Workers feel support and recognition from supervisors and others.	Operation system does not require too many conflicting interfaces.	Restrictive reporting and auditing as control measures are not used.
Workers experience "coaching" or help when needed.		Authority and responsibility are appropriately delegated.
No undue pressure is exerted.		Advancements and promotions result from open review between superior and subordinate.

The model of an organization presented in Table 9-1 is one with both an open system and composed internally of three interlocking subsystems—social, operating, and administrative. The following case illustrates how this model might be used in analyzing the problems of a restaurant.

CASE
Breakdown in the Operating System

 William Foote Whyte was asked to consult with a restaurant experiencing the loss of waitress performance during rush times of the day.[5] The waitresses would leave the job and spend time in the restroom upset and crying. An examination of the situation led to the following analysis: Waitresses were caught between the customers and the chef. Upon receiving an order, the waitress handed the order slip directly to the chef, often with requests for immediate action or special service. The chef began to bristle with resentment as several waitresses gave him orders, and he would slow down the orders. The waitresses would then try to placate the customers and put more pressure on the chef to meet customer needs. The chef was the ultimate factor in the output of food, and he was able to withhold service from certain waitresses; some waitresses would become so frustrated and upset they would leave the job for a period of time.

Whyte's analysis of the situation is interesting. He saw this as a problem in the work flow or operating system, for in his view the "system" required lower-status personnel (waitresses) to initiate work for a higher-status person (the chef). Whyte concluded that any operating or technical system so designed would result in negative reactions from the higher-status person. Based on this analysis, Whyte created an intervention to alter the work flow system and to terminate the interface between waitresses and chef. He had a wall constructed blocking off direct contact between the waitresses and the chef. A rotating spindle was located in the wall so waitresses could clip their orders on the spindle, getting information to the chef without direct interaction. The chef could now organize his work without pressure from waitresses. Should waitresses have a complaint, they were now to go to the assistant manager, who would talk with the chef, thus preserving an appropriate line of authority. The line of authority is part of the administrative system. ◩

It is possible that this case could have had a different diagnosis and that other parts of the internal system could have been involved. The following are examples of other diagnoses:

Waitress-chef interaction   Some might see in this a classic case of people applying pressure to control the behavior of others, resulting in a hostile re-

A breakdown in the operating system of a restaurant can be attributable to a number of causes.

sponse. This would be a problem in the social system. If the waitresses and chef could meet together in a typical "team building" format, they could make agreements about pressure situations, unacceptable demands, and a priority system agreeable to all, resulting in a smoother flow of work, keeping the work flow system intact. This intervention would have required a great deal of time and skillful interpersonal problem solving to work through to a solution.

Distribution of rewards   Others might see this situation as one where the rewards of one party (tips to waitresses) are in jeopardy because of the control of another party (the chef). The problem of rewards is usually a policy matter and is handled in the administrative system. In situations like this a successful solution has been to work out a tip-sharing procedure approved by all parties so the chef feels a stake in cooperating with waitresses for direct financial benefit.

"Personality" conflict   A more simplistic analysis—with some concrete support from Whyte's data—is that some chefs are "ornery" and some waitresses "too sensitive," a classic problem in the social system. The result is a personality clash as ornery chefs are very disruptive to sensitive waitresses. Whyte found some chefs who were more belligerent, especially when working with females. He also saw that certain dependent, inexperienced waitresses had difficulty in dealing with aggressive chefs. Using this diagnosis, possible solutions are better selection of waitresses or replacement of the chef. If more experienced waitresses who can handle pressure and difficult chefs are hired, the situation might be stabilized. Replacing the chef is generally not preferred because turnover of personnel as a plan of action usually has some disruptive consequences. It is also possible to ask "ornery" chefs or "overly sensitive" waitresses to engage in some type of counseling, therapy, or individually focused workshop.

Inadequate resources   Still another diagnosis might be that the problem is one of inadequate resources—either not enough help for the chef or not enough equipment to handle the press of rush orders. This too would be an administrative issue. If this were in fact the case, the frustrated chef could be venting his frustration on the waitresses. The problem, then, is not the interface between these two parties—the points of conflict are only symptoms of a deficiency located elsewhere. Constructing a spindle would eliminate the open, observable conflict but not the frustration or the slow service, because the problem is located elsewhere.

Reducing waitress-customer pressure   Still another diagnosis-action sequence could be centered on the customer-waitress interface. This diagnosis looks at a mix of external factors (the customer) and the internal system—probably aspects of all three subsystems. It could be that customers are putting unreasonable pressure for rush service on the waitress, and her most obvious response is to pass the pressure on to the chef. In such a situation, it may be possible to reduce this pressure by:

1.   Having a set menu that eliminates special orders.

2.   Putting a notice by certain items that additional time is required.

3.   Having a salad bar to speed up direct service.

4.   Having only experienced waitresses work during rush hours or using only those waitresses who can cope with customer pressure.

It is an important function of management to have a way of thinking about organizations so when problems occur an appropriate organizational diagnosis can be made.

THE ORGANIZATION AS A CULTURE

The most recent way of viewing an organization is to view it as a culture or a cultural unit with its own cultural elements.

Early anthropologists quickly distinguished between material and nonmaterial culture—the physical artifacts and objects and the basic belief systems that were shared by and directed the thinking, feelings, perceptions, and behaviors of the peoples of that culture. Differing belief systems account for the fact that people in some cultures marry siblings while other cultures make any physical contact between relatives a strict taboo.

To determine why some people got into trouble—were rejected or punished—a look at the belief system and the attendant mores and norms that guided behavior was necessary. Flowing out of these early distinctions, the following four elements of an organization's culture have been identified: (1) artifacts, (2) perspectives, (3) values, and (4) assumptions.[6]

Artifacts   Artifacts are the more "tangible" aspects of an organization's culture. Artifacts can be physical (office layout, company logo, employee dress), behavioral (rituals, ceremonies), and verbal (language, stories, and myths shared by members of an organization). These artifacts are the surface manifestations or symbols of shared perspectives, values, and assumptions which form the belief system.

Perspectives   Perspectives are those shared ideas and actions that help people act "appropriately" in a given situation. For example, perspectives often develop around rules for "correctly" handling such structured situations as a performance review or a more ambiguous situation such as winning a promotion. In one organization, the common perspective was that people had to be "innovative" and "aggressive" by taking on as much responsibility as possible in order to get ahead. In another organization however, innovation was not as important as "conformity" to group norms to achieve success. Such differences in perspectives represent two very different organization cultures.

Values   Values are broad principles that transcend individual events. They denote the general ideals, standards, or "sins" of the organizations such as "career employment," "promote from within," "protect the environment," "be honest with customers," etc. Such values are often articulated in the formal statement of the organization's "management philosophy"

Basic Assumptions   Basic assumptions are at the core of culture. They are the taken-for-granted beliefs group members hold about themselves, others and the world in which they live. Since assumptions are considered a "given" they are rarely, if ever, called into question and the set of tacit assumptions form a pattern or paradigm that creates a unique culture. A study of one well-known computer company showed the following basic assumptions:

1. Truth and knowledge are discovered through conflict.

2. People are basically good and capable of governing themselves.

3. Relationships are collateral in nature—like a family.

Given this set of assumptions, the artifacts, perspectives, and values of this organization were reflected in a highly combative, independent work force that was also highly supportive of each member.

It is possible, using the above models, to think of an organization as either a system or a culture since all organizations have both systemic and cultural qualities.

Whether one looks at an organization as a system or a culture depends on the condition one is trying to understand or change.

If people are bored, unchallenged, and feel apathetic and unmotivated because of routine work, it would be well to look at the organization as a system, particularly the technical system. Changing the technical system through some form of job enrichment might improve the problem condition. On the other hand if the problem is one of employee theft or callous treatment of customers, it might be more useful to look at the organization's culture. Perhaps no clear ethical standards are in place in the organization or a norm that customers are not really important has developed. In the beginning case of this chapter, General Foods began a new plant with a great many innovations in the social, technical, and administrative systems. At first, the results seemed to be positive, but over time problems began to occur as this chapter's ending case will point out. Apparently the new systems were in violation of the older GF culture—the old ways of doing things. People began to be threatened by these new practices and resistance occurred.

Having looked at frameworks for understanding what constitutes an organization, it is important to consider what makes an organization effective or ineffective.

Maintaining a High-Performance Culture

A strong culture—a set of shared values, norms, and beliefs that unify a company and get everyone moving toward the same goal—is common to high-performance companies. The building of a strong culture involves the resolution of a dilemma: while a degree of uniformity enables the organization to function more effectively, the manipulation of individuals and the loss of individual identity runs counter to deeply held societal values. How then do companies with strong cultures pass on their values to new employees without alienating them?

Looking at the winners one by one, it is evident that these companies all put new employees through the seven steps of socialization:

Step One   The candidate for employment is subjected to a process that is so rigorous that it seems designed to discourage rather than encourage him to take the job. The object of this exercise is to get a job applicant to take himself out of contention if he thinks the organization will not fit his style and values. Morgan Stanley, for example, encourages recruits to discuss the demands of the job (new recruits sometimes work 100 hours a week) with their spouses, or others whose opinions could affect their performance.

Step Two   The company subjects new recruits to experiences designed to induce humility and to make them question prior behavior, beliefs, and values. By making recruits less comfortable with themselves, it is hoped that they will be more open to the company's norms and values. At IBM and Morgan Guaranty, to quote one participant, "You work every night until 2 A.M. on your own material, and then help others."

Step Three   Recruits are sent out into the trenches where, it is hoped, the orientation to problem solving and doing business learned in the training program is cemented. They are expected to master one of the disciplines at the core of the company's business, and promotions are tied to how well they do in that discipline. They are given lots of carefully monitored experience. At IBM virtually all recruits, regardless of advanced degrees or prior experience, start at the same level as college recruits and go through the same training programs.

Step Four   Operating results are measured at every step and rewards are given accordingly. Systems for measuring performance are comprehensive and consistent and focus on aspects of the business that make for competitive success and for the perpetuation of core values. Procter and Gamble, for example, measures performance on three factors deemed critical to the success of its brands: building volume, building profit, and conducting planned change (altering a product to make it perform more effectively in the marketplace).

Step Five   All along the way, the company promotes adherence to its transcendent or core values, those overarching purposes that are more important than the day-to-day pressure to make a buck. Adherence to such values makes it easier for recruits to accept the sacrifices asked of them during their careers. The old AT&T, for example, placed its greatest emphasis on guaranteeing phone service to customers through any emergency.

Step Six   The company harps on watershed events in the firm's history that reaffirm the importance and validity of the company culture. At AT&T this took the form of extolling the virtues of employees who made heroic sacrifices to keep the phones working. Bell folklore was so strong that the company was able to respond quickly, cutting red tape and pulling together in ways that would not normally be permitted, in order to restore phone service.

Step Seven   The company supplies promising individuals with role models. These role models each display the same characteristics. P&G's brand managers, for example, display remarkable consistency in several traits—they are analytical, energetic, and adept at motivating others.

    While most companies practice one or more of the steps leading to a strong, enduring culture, consistency across all seven steps sets the strong culture firms apart from their peers. When an organization can instill a strong set of commonly shared values, these values act as a sort of common law that helps in resolving the ambiguities in the formal system of rules, policies, and procedures, which allows management to get on with the job. A former IBMer says: "At IBM you spend 50 percent of your time managing the internal context. At most companies it's more like 75 percent."

    Lack of a strong culture can have the opposite effect. A marketing manager for Atari recalls the days before new management was installed: "You can't imagine how much time and energy around here went into politics. You had to determine who was on first base this month in order to figure out how to obtain what you needed to get the job done. There were no rules. There were no clear values . . . Without rules for working with one another, a lot of people got hurt, got burned out, and were never taught the 'Atari way' of doing things because there wasn't any Atari way." Atari managers spent most of their time managing relationships; they had less time for customers and market-related activities.

Some might worry that a strong culture leads to a lack of individuality and a loss of freedom. A P&G executive puts it this way: "There is a great deal of consistency around here in how certain things are done, and these are rather critical to our sustained success. Beyond that, there are very few hard and fast rules. People on the outside might portray our culture as imposing lock-step uniformity. It doesn't feel rigid when you're inside. It feels like it accommodates you. And best of all, you know the game you're in—you know whether you're playing soccer or football; you can find out very clearly what it takes to succeed and you can bank your career on that."

Most strong culture firms protect themselves from becoming incestuous or myopic—so concerned with what's happening inside the firm that they fail to adjust to changes in the outside environment—by focusing at least one part of their culture on the external context. This normally takes the form of an obsession with some aspect of market performance—for IBM it's customer service, for 3M it's innovation, and for McDonald's it's quality control. This trait keeps the organization in tune with its external environment, and although it results in many fire drills, the organization retains the ability to adjust quickly when a real emergency arises.

THE EFFECTIVE ORGANIZATION

In Search of Excellence, the 1982 best-seller about America's supposedly best-run and most innovative corporations, had a great impact on management in the 1980s. In this work, management consultants Thomas J. Peters and Robert H. Waterman identified eight characteristics common to forty-two highly successful American companies. The sample included such firms as Digital Equipment, Hewlett-Packard, Texas Instruments, Procter and Gamble, Johnson and Johnson, Exxon, 3M, Delta Airlines, General Electric, and TRW. As measures of success, Peters and Waterman used the following criteria:

1. Growth of assets from 1961 to 1980.
2. Equity growth from 1961 to 1980.
3. The average ratio of market value to book value. (Market value equaling the closing share price times common shares outstanding, divided by common book-value equity as of December 1, 1961 through 1980.)
4. Average return on capital from 1961 to 1980.
5. Average return on equity from 1961 to 1980.
6. Average return on sales from 1961 to 1980.

7. Measure of innovativeness—a rating of the innovativeness of the company over the 20-year period.[7]

One might feel these criteria of excellence are too narrow. Only those large companies that had been profitable and financially successful over a long period of time were selected. It could be argued that a company might be profitable due to the demand for its product and not necessarily because it is an effective organization. On the other hand, even if one has a good product, competition is such that without an effective organization the company would not be continually profitable for twenty years.

Peters and Waterman identified the following eight attributes as characteristic of "excellent" organizations.

1. **A bias for action**   These organizations were not paralyzed by indecision. They have an orientation toward action. "Do it, fix it, try it." This orientation moves the company to experiment, try out new ideas, and not analyze everything ad infinitum.

2. **Closeness with the customer**   This attribute reflects a high concern for customers and a practice of talking with and getting feedback from them. They get ideas for new products and services from listening to their customers.

3. **Autonomy and entrepreneurship**   These companies foster innovation, new ideas, and entrepreneurship *inside* the organization. They allow autonomy and encourage new ideas and risk taking and then try to champion and support the innovations to a successful conclusion.

4. **Productivity through people**   Excellent companies treat people as their most valuable resource. IBM head Thomas Watson, Jr., said that the company philosophy began with "our respect for the individual." The general feeling is that people are important as total persons and not just seen as a number or a pair of hands. The key elements are trust and treating people with dignity and respect.

5. **Hands-on and value-driven management**   This means that managers in the organization do not stay isolated from day-to-day activities. The philosophy called MBWA (management by wandering around) is often practiced. People in the organization see managers who hold high values interacting directly with them. Some of the values that drive these organizations are:
    A. A belief in being the "best."
    B. A belief in doing the job well, paying attention to details.
    C. A belief in the importance of people as individuals.
    D. A belief in superior quality and service.
    E. A belief in supporting innovation.
    F. A belief in the importance of communications.
    G. A belief in recognizing the importance of economic growth and profits.[8]

6. **Stick to the knitting**   These organizations know what their business is and they stay close to what they know. If an organization branches out, it stays in a field or

area that it understands. One chief executive put it this way, "Never acquire a business you don't know how to run!"

7.   **Simple form and lean staff**   Although large and profitable, the organization structure is simple and the number of people in the top-level staff is kept to a minimum. It is not uncommon to find a corporate staff of fewer than 100 people running a multi-billion-dollar enterprise. To be as flexible as companies need to be in a rapidly changing economic and technological world, a simple structure with smaller units in size makes it easier to change to meet new demands.

Given the orientation of keeping organizations simple and lean, Peters and Waterman have developed what they feel is the organizational structure of the 1980s. Figure 9-3, which is a model of Peters and Waterman's simplified organizational form, illustrates that the basic needs of organizations are: a need for efficiency, for regular innovation, and for flexibility. The stability pillar ensures efficiency; the entrepreneurial pillar responds to the need for innovation; and the flexibility pillar avoids rigidity and classification.

8.   **Simultaneous loose-tight properties**   Excellent companies are both centralized and decentralized. They try to give autonomy and shift authority down in terms of getting decision making close to the point where decisions are made and yet keep certain key functions centralized. Organizations that are both tight and loose are on the one hand rigidly controlled—particularly in the areas of core values—and at the same time allow autonomy, innovation and entrepreneurship.

The Peters and Waterman analysis has had a wide impact on the thinking of management in the 1980s. It is more remarkable when one looks at the analysis and notes that it is based on very flimsy research. Little systematic data were gathered—almost all data came from interviews with selected people—and the eight factors, while having a certain degree of face validity, are not clearly supported by sound research data. Still many companies have used these attributes to review the workings of their organizations to see what they would need to change to become more effective.

CASE
"Excellence" Revisited

 In Search of Excellence has made authors Peters and Waterman very rich men. Their lectures are among the hottest tickets on the lecture circuit, and they have sold over 2.8 million copies of the book so far. Their list of forty-two companies may have been flawed, according to studies by *Business Week*, management consultants McKinsey and Co. (where Peters is a director, and Waterman a former member), and Standard and Poor's Compustat Service,

Figure 9-3
Peters and Waterman's Organizational Structure of the 1980s

Basic Organizational Needs		
Stability	**Entrepreneurship**	**Flexibility**
■ Simple, basic underlying form ■ Dominating values (superordinate goals) ■ Minimizing/simplifying interfaces	■ Entrepreneurial, "small is beautiful," units ■ Cabals, other problem-solving implementation groups ■ Measurement systems based on amount of entrepreneurship, implementation	■ Regular reorganization ■ Major thrust outlays ■ Experimental units ■ Systems focusing on one dimension

SOURCE: Thomas J. Peters and Robert H. Waterman, Jr., *In Search of Excellence* (New York, Harper & Row, 1982), p. 316. Used with permission.

Inc. It now appears that at least fourteen of the "excellent" companies are experiencing hard times, including Delta Air Lines, Eastman Kodak, and Texas Instruments.

All have suffered from significant declines in earnings caused by serious business problems, management problems, or both, according to *Business Week*. These companies' current woes have led many to question whether the book's "eight attributes of excellence"—a bias for action; staying close to the customer; autonomy and entrepreneurship; productivity through people; hands-on, value-driven culture; "sticking to the knitting"; simple form and lean staff; and simultaneous loose-tight properties—are really the right ones, or only ones that matter. Management expert Peter F. Drucker calls *In Search of Excellence* "a book of juveniles," and others have been quick to label it a fad soon to die out.

Peters and Waterman counter these criticisms with the argument that no prescription for good management is all-inclusive or infallible; the fact that the book sold so well is an indication that American managers in the early 1980s needed and wanted a fresh look at how companies should be run. At that time, the Japanese were encroaching on U.S. markets and challenging American hegemony over technology, and corporations were too often bogged down in overanalysis, bureaucracy, and shortsighted planning.

The book's main argument was that U.S. companies could regain their lost competitive edge if they only paid more attention to their own employees and customers, and stuck to the skills and values they had already developed (sticking to the knitting).

So why are so many of these corporate stars in trouble? "There's no real reason to have ever expected that all of these companies would have done well forever and ever," Peters told *Business Week*. Waterman added, "If you're big, you've got the seeds of your own destruction in there." The forty-two companies, they contend, were just big corporations that were "losing less fast."

The lessons from all this? For one, that nothing lasts forever; even corporate excellence is an illusive and often fragile commodity. For another, that any theory of management should be used when and where it works, and abandoned where it does not. As Waterman points out, "The book has been so popular that people have taken it as a formula for success rather than what it was intended to be. We were writing about the art, not the science, of management." ☒

Other Measures of Organizational Effectiveness

Peters and Waterman present one way of looking at the effective organization and what constitutes effectiveness. Following are some other ways of thinking about effectiveness.

GOAL ATTAINMENT   One way to think about effectiveness in an organization is to determine whether or not the goals of the organization are being achieved.[9] The more goals that are accomplished, the higher the level of effectiveness. If an organization is able to quantify its goals in terms of profit, sales, or market share, and can show in hard numbers that these goals are being achieved, many observers would agree that the organization is effective.

However, goal attainment is a difficult process to use in assessing certain kinds of organizations. Some organizations have goals that are very difficult to quantify. The goal of a service organization may be to "provide service that will lead to the growth and betterment of the community." How are growth and betterment measured in this context? How can it be known if the service rendered actually helped in any way? Organizations may also have official goals that do not represent the informal or unofficial goals of the members. Which are the real goals of the organization—the official or the unofficial ones?

INDIVIDUAL OR GROUP PERFORMANCE   Another way to assess an organization's effectiveness is to think of the organization as the vehicle through which individual performance is achieved. The degree of effectiveness is determined by looking at all individuals and seeing if each is achieving personal goals and objectives. If a substantial number are not achieving goals, the organization may not be effective.

It is immediately apparent that this method also has flaws. Some organizations work mostly in teams or units and one can only measure success by looking at the unit, not the individual. If group performance is taken as the measure the same problem surfaces since some individuals are not really a part of a group, and some groups can only be considered in light of the group's contribution to that product or service.

SYSTEM EFFECTIVENESS   The organization as an open system has already been described. In a systems approach to effectiveness, effectiveness is determined by assessing how well the organization handles external demands and interfaces. If an organization is unable to deal with competitors, unions, or economic conditions, the organization may be viewed as ineffective as an open system.

In the internal aspects of the system, if an organization cannot get adequate inputs, or cannot process the inputs adequately so the outputs are not achieved, then the organization can be said to be ineffective. Since outputs are often stated as goals, elements of the goal attainment approach are present.

Since systems analysis identifies the areas either inside or outside the organization that impact the outputs, one major advantage to the systems approach is the ability to diagnose those factors causing outputs to diminish.

STRENGTH OF CULTURE   A fourth approach to looking at effectiveness is to assess the strength of the organization's culture. This means determining the extent that people in the organization understand and live by the norms, standards, and values of the organization. In a weak culture, people either do not understand the values or, understanding them, they do not comply with them. In a strong culture people accept and live by the cultural values that are clearly in evidence in the organization. The effective organization has a strong culture: norms and values are clear and widely shared, people at all levels understand and accept them, and people at all levels behave consistent with these values.

Measuring Effectiveness

Given any of the above approaches, the need remains to measure what is meant by effectiveness. The following are some of the measures commonly used in organizations:

Productivity   The ability of the organization to convert inputs into outputs in the desired quantity and quality. Measurements such as output per man-hour or output per machine-hour are common measures of productivity (see Box 9-2).

Member satisfaction   This measurement is concerned with how well the organization meets the needs of members and maintains morale. Employee turnover, grievances per worker, and percentage rate of absenteeism per day are commonly used measurements.

Box 9-2
A New Method of Measuring Productivity

Throughout the 1980s American managers have been chasing the grail of increased productivity, the economist's measure of output per worker-hour. Between 1947 and 1966, productivity rose nationwide at about 3.2 percent each year. The growth rate dropped to 2.1 percent between 1966 and 1973, then leveled out at 0.8 percent through 1979. Economists called the productivity growth falloff an even greater danger to the economy than the rapidly rising inflation rate. As the decade began, U.S. industry began to play an aggressive game of productivity catch-up.

A Massachusetts economist has designed an easy way for any business to keep track of its productivity. Take the firm's annual net sales, then subtract the cost of outside purchases. The result is the "Gross Corporate Product," or GCP. The GCP measures the business's contribution to the national economy.

Now divide the GCP by the number of employees. That figure, says Christos Athanasopoulos of Western New England University's Delphi Research Center, indicates the average employee's contribution to the company—his or her productivity. The percentage of change from year to year measures change in corporate productivity.

Imagine a company with 100 workers. If, in 1983, its GCP was $100 million, then each worker added a millon dollars to the company. If its 1984 GCP was $154 million, each worker added $1,540,000. Productivity went up 54 percent. (In Athanasopoulos's terms, the "human productivity index" was 154).

Cost   An organization that expends more resources than it takes in is not effective. Since some organizations are not-for-profit, it sometimes is more useful to think of them as cost centers rather than profit centers. Effectiveness in a profit center is measured by comparing income with expense. Effectiveness in a cost center is measured by performance against a budget. One measure of cost effectiveness is **efficiency**—the amount of out-put per unit of resource expended. It is possible for an organization to be efficient—get a lot of work done per man-hour of labor—and still be ineffective. If the people are working on wrong priorities they could be working very hard and being very efficient but not really achieving the goals that are most important.

Adaptiveness   This represents the interface with the external environment and looks at the degree to which the organization deals with those forces that place demands on the organization. If the organization cannot manage its external forces to the point it cannot get appropriate inputs, throughputs, or outputs, the organization is not effective.

CONCERNS ABOUT ORGANIZATIONS

Fears about Organizations

A survey of 1,082 college students in 1983 showed that they had some major concerns about the kind of future they would have when they went to work in an organization. Table 9-2 lists the 11 concerns identified by these students.

Interestingly, the major concern (highest percentage on "extreme or strong concern") for college students is that they will have to work under a superior they do not respect. Students have a rather clear image of the kind of leadership style they prefer; consequently, they have a real concern that they will find themselves working for a boss they do not feel good about.

The second highest ranked concern in terms of percentage of respondents who marked "extreme or strong concern" reflects anxiety about future income level. The basic fear is that the student may not be able to earn enough income to live at an adequate standard of living. This fear is closely associated with the fear of getting trapped in an organization that is not liked just to earn an adequate income. While students want to work in organizations that do something worthwhile, be competent, and have a chance to grow, the need for income may require them to forego working for the preferred type of organization.

The fears of working under a superior who is not respected or the dilemma about earning an adequate income are followed by another major concern—that they will get lost in the organization. This concern deals with the fear that they will get into an organization where they will not be able to do anything important and will get lost in the shuffle. Thus, they would be unable to display their true abilities or have an opportunity to learn and grow. Other research has shown that this latter fear is also a major concern of those already in organizations.

On the other side of the issue, students were least worried about giving up or being ignored. About one-third of the students indicated that they had relatively low concern about just giving up, going through their whole work life being ignored, or not doing anything worthwhile. But even in this area another third did indicate that this was a problem for them. Apparently, the majority of the students have fears about the impersonal, large organization, but one-third of the respondents do not see themselves just giving up and wasting their lives in organizations in which they see their efforts as fruitless.[10]

Desired Organizational Values

The same survey of students also indicated a preference for the following organizational values:

Table 9-2
Organizational Concerns of College Students

RANK	FEARS OR CONCERNS ABOUT ORGANIZATIONAL FUTURE	EXTREME	STRONG	LOW
1	I will find myself under superiors who I will not respect or be able to follow with real commitment.	19%	54%	15%
2	I will not be able to earn enough income to live at an appropriate standard of living.	22	45	27
3	I will have to work in an organization I do not really like just so I can make enough money to live adequately.	18	48	20
4	No one will recognize my real worth, and I will never be able to show my true abilities and be recognized or rewarded for what I am truly capable of doing.	19	42	28
5	I will give up and become a part of the system I do not really like.	16	41	35
6	I will live and die working in an organization, and my life will not have made any real contribution to anything.	16	40	33
7	I will get lost in the shuffle and become a nameless, faceless number.	16	39	32
8	The organization will not have any decent program or procedure for helping me grow, develop, and become a more useful, productive person.	14	41	28
9	I will get caught up in a "bad" organization and will be unable to get out or make any changes.	14	40	31
10	Only "wheeler-dealer" types get ahead and get the rewards.	14	38	29
11	I will try to do something significant but I will get rejected, put down, or ignored.	11	34	34

NOTE: Percentages for any one concern do not add up to 100 percent because not all respondents answered all questions.

SOURCE: William G. Dyer and Jeffrey H. Dyer, "The M*A*S*H* Generation: Implications for Future Organizational Values," *Organizational Dynamics*, Summer 1984, p. 72.

1. Everyone knows that others in the organization can be trusted to help, be loyal, and stick by them in times of crisis.

2. People work at jobs that are important, and they make contributions to something worthwhile.

3. Competence is recognized and rewarded. (The condition contrary to this desirable value is expressed by the frequently heard cynical statement "it isn't what you know but who you know that gets you ahead around here.")

4. Organizational superiors treat subordinates with concern, understanding, and respect.

5. Although people may be different in a variety of dimensions, the differences are overlooked and teamwork and loyalty occur because everyone is working for common important goals and they are generally competent.

6. People function in difficult situations with a saving sense of humor. Practical jokes, however, may be the subject of laughter but they are not seen as being part of desirable organizational behavior.

ENDING CASE
General Foods: The Result

Was the new General Foods plant discussed in the beginning case successful with its innovative work arrangements? A review after eighteen months of operation suggested positive results. For example, fixed overhead costs were 33 percent lower than in older plants, quality rejects were reduced by 92 percent, and the safety record was one of the best in the company. Focusing on the human resource side, morale was high, absenteeism was 9 percent below the industry norm, and turnover was far below normal.

The plant was widely heralded as a model for the future, and General Foods claims that it still is. In fact, GF has applied a similar system at a second dog food plant in Topeka and at a coffee plant in New Jersey. And it says it may eventually do the same at two plants in Mexico and among white-collar workers at its White Plains headquarters.

But management analysts and former employees tell a different story, and General Foods, which once encouraged publicity about the Topeka plant, now refuses to let reporters inside. Critics say that after the initial euphoria, the system, faced with indifference and outright hostility from some GF managers, has been eroding steadily.

"The system went to heck. It didn't work," says one former manager. Adds another ex-employee: "It was a mixed bag. Economically it was a success, but it became a power struggle. It was too threatening to too many people." He predicts that the plant will eventually switch to a traditional factory system. In fact, he says, the transition has already begun.

The problem has been not so much that workers could not manage their own affairs as that some management and staff personnel saw their own positions threatened because the workers performed almost too well. One former employee says the system—built around a team concept—came squarely up against the company's bureaucracy. Lawyers, fearing reaction from the National Labor Relations Board, opposed allowing team members to vote on pay raises; personnel managers objected to team members making hiring decisions; engineers resented workers doing engineering work.

Consequently, critics say, the Topeka system has stiffened: more job classifications, less participation, more supervision. GF has added seven management positions to the plant, including controller, plant engineering manager, and manufacturing services manager. GF says these were necessary because of a plant expansion. When GF geared up a plant adjacent to the first one to produce a new canned dog food, it introduced the Topeka process but deferred several elements of the system. ⊠

SUMMARY

This chapter identifies the significant role organizations play in our lives and introduces the student to some of the basic concepts regarding the "organization." The open system model was presented with a discussion of the three internal subsystems, social, technical, and administrative. The concept of organizational culture was developed as well as various elements of effective organizations. The case study of the General Foods plant illustrated some outcomes of an application of some of the presented concepts, and responses of college students to a research questionnaire offers some insight into organization concerns and desired organizational values.

KEY TERMS

Matrix organization	Status-role structure
Open system	Pattern of management
Input	Decision-making method
Throughput	Socio-technical system
Output	Artifacts
Subsystem	Perspectives
Social System	Values
Technical or operating system	Assumptions
Administrative system	Value-driven
Climate	Efficiency
Communication Network	Adaptiveness

REVIEW QUESTIONS

1. Explain the concept of an open system.
2. What are the three subsystems of an open system?
3. What is the relationship between the three subsystems?
4. How can an organization be efficient but not effective?
5. What does it mean to have "loose-tight" proportions?
6. Describe what is meant by an organization being "simple and lean."
7. How are individual goals used to measure organizational effectiveness? What is the inherent problem with this approach?
8. How can the systems model of organizations be applied as a measure of effectiveness? What is the most obvious advantage of this application?
9. What is a major weakness of the Peters and Waterman data on excellent companies?

CHALLENGE QUESTIONS

1. How would you go about assessing or determining the culture of an organization?
2. How do the concepts of culture relate to the right characteristics of excellent companies? How would you integrate these two general frameworks?
3. How might the official and unofficial goals of an organization be different? Cite an example.
4. How would a strong culture contribute to an organization's effectiveness?
5. Why is member satisfaction important for organizational effectiveness?
6. What do concepts like "culture," "systems," and "loose-tight proportions" have to do with productivity?
7. "Adaptiveness" was suggested as one criterion for evaluating organizational effectiveness. How does this concept relate to the notion of an open system?

CASE QUESTIONS

1. The General Foods Topeka plant involved a major change in the way in which employees were treated. Note that the Saturn plant discussed in Chapter 2 involved many of the same approaches to problems as GF tried. What differences may allow Saturn to succeed where the GF experiment failed?
2. Knowing what you do about organizational culture, what could General Foods learn about creating a strong culture from the likes of IBM, Morgan Stanley, and

Procter and Gamble? Would the seven steps of socialization work on the plant floor as easily as they would in a management-training program?

3. Are the lessons of strong culture firms applicable in an environment where workers are represented by a strong union? What problems are likely to arise?

4. What does the case of waitress and chef indicate about the difficulty in approaching problems that are essentially problems between people? How would you have analyzed the problem? Is Whyte's solution likely to work?

5. Does a strong culture company appeal to you? What are some of the advantages and disadvantages of working for a strong culture company?

6. Do strong culture companies answer the concerns that students have about working for organizations? Which concerns are answered best by this type of company? Which are not answered?

7. Does the fact that about 33 percent of Peters and Waterman's "excellent" companies ran into trouble indicate anything about the validity of their approach? Are the criticisms of academics overly technical?

8. If a firm's cost of outside purchases increases faster than the firm's ability to pass along the higher costs, should this be reflected in its measure of productivity as suggested by Athanasopoulos? Is his human productivity index more valid when used for the economy as a whole than when used by individual firms? In short, would his index supply management with useful information and, if so, what constraints would you put upon its use?

9. Assume that the General Foods Topeka plant is unionized (essentially the condition present at GM's Saturn plant discussed in Chapter 2). Certain court decisions require that employee organizations not be dominated by companies. If management employees are involved in the General Foods work teams, should such involvement indicate employer domination of a labor organization? What public policies are at stake?

ENDNOTES

1. Jay Galbraith, *Organization Design* (Reading, MA: Addison-Wesley, 1977), chapter on matrix organizations.

2. William Dyer, "Open System Analysis and Planning" in *Strategies for Managing Change* (Reading, MA: Addison-Wesley, 1984), Chapter 19.

3. Dyer, pp. 147–53.

4. See F. Baker, *Organizational Systems: General Systems Approach to Complex Organizations* (Homewood, IL: Irwin, 1973), and F. E. Kast and J. E. Rosenweig, *Organization and Management: A Systems Approach* (New York: McGraw-Hill, 1974).

5. W. F. Whyte, *Men at Work* (Homewood, IL: Dorsey Press, 1961), pp. 125–35.

6. W. Gibb Dyer, Jr. "Organization Culture: Analysis and Change" in *Strategies for Managing Change* (Reading, MA: Addison-Wesley, 1984), Chapter 20.

7. Thomas J. Peters and Robert H. Waterman, Jr., *In Search of Excellence: Lessons From America's Best-Run Companies* (New York: Harper & Row, 1982).

8. Ibid., p. 285.

9. K. S. Cameron and D. A. Whetten, "Perceptions of Organizational Effectiveness over Organizational Life Cycles," *Administrative Science Quarterly*, 26, 1981, pp. 524–44.

10. William G. Dyer and Jeffrey H. Dyer, "The M*A*S*H Generation: Implications for Future Organizational Values," *Organizational Dynamics*, Summer 1984, pp. 72–73.

CHAPTER 10

ORGANIZATION STRUCTURE

LEARNING OBJECTIVES

■ Discuss the roles of structure and function in determining how organizations function.

■ Illustrate the growth of a simple organization over time with the resulting decisions that must be faced because of that growth.

■ Describe the effect of centralization, decentralization, and diversification on the design of organizational structure.

■ Understand how a matrix organization is organized and functions.

■ Understand how span of control is exercised by individual managers within an organization.

■ Explain why individual tasks and departments are the basic in the design of an organization.

■ Discuss the differentiation-integration approach to organizations and the reasons separate functions need to be organized differently.

■ Discuss the roles and usefulness of temporary structures in organizational design.

■ Describe how job redesign can increase organizational effectiveness.

■ Describe how decentralization can achieve greater organizational effectiveness.

Rose Raku made pottery in her basement. That involved a number of distinct tasks—wedging clay, forming pots, tooling the pots when semi-dry, preparing and applying the glazes, and firing the pots in the kiln. But the coordination of all these tasks presented no problem: she did them all herself.

The problem was her ambition and the attractiveness of her pots: the orders exceeded her production capacity. So she hired Sandy Bisque, who was eager to learn pottery. But this meant Raku had to divide up the work. Since the craft shops wanted pottery made by Raku, it was decided that Bisque would wedge the clay and prepare the glazes, and Raku would do the rest. This required some coordination of the work, a small problem, in fact, with two people in a pottery studio: they simply communicated informally.

The arrangement worked well, so well that before long Raku was again swamped with orders. More assistants were needed, but this time, foreseeing the day when they would be forming pots themselves, Raku decided to hire them right out of the local pottery school. So while it had taken some time to train Bisque, the three new assistants knew exactly what to do at the outset and blended right in; even with five people, coordination presented no problem.

As two more assistants were added, however, coordination problems did arise. One day Bisque tripped over a pail of glaze and broke five pots; another day Raku opened the kiln to find that the hanging planters had all been glazed fuchsia by mistake. At this point, she realized that seven people in a small pottery studio could not coordinate all of their work through the simple mechanism of informal communication. (There were 21 possible channels by which two people could communicate.) Making matters worse was the fact that Raku, now calling herself president of Ceramics Limited, was forced to spend more and more time with customers; indeed, these days she was more likely found in a business suit than a pair of jeans. So she named Bisque studio manager and occupied herself full-time with supervising and coordinating the work of the five assistant potters.

The firm continued to grow. Major changes again took place when an analyst was hired to conduct a workstudy of the studio. He recommended that each individual perform only one task for one of the product lines (pots, ashtrays, hanging planters, and ceramic animals)—the first to wedge, the second to form, the third to tool, and so on. Thus, production took the form of four assembly lines. Each person followed a set of standard instructions, worked out in advance to ensure the coordination of all their work. Of course, Ceramics Limited no longer sold to craft shops; Raku would only accept orders by the gross, most of which came from chains of discount stores.

Raku's ambition was limitless, and when the chance came to diversify, she did—first ceramic tiles, then bathroom fixtures, finally clay bricks. The firm was subsequently partitioned into three divisions—consumer products, building products, and

A pottery business in which the owner does everything from forming to selling pots is an example of a simple structure.

industrial products. From her office on the fifty-fifth story of the Potter Tower, she coordinated the activities of the divisions by reviewing their performance each quarter of the year and taking personal action when their profit and growth figures dipped below their budget. It was while sitting at her desk one day going over these budgets that Raku gazed out at the surrounding skyscrapers and decided to rename her company "Ceramico."

INTRODUCTION

An organization is the arrangement and use of resources (human, material, financial) for the accomplishment of goals. Implicit in this definition is the proposition that if an organization is ineffectively or inappropriately set up in either its arrangements or structure, or in its uses or processes, it will not be effective in achieving its goals.

Managers, therefore, must be concerned about how the organization is designed or structured, and how well it operates or functions. This dual examination of organization and operation has been called the **structure-function approach** to organization analysis.

Structure versus Function

Theorists disagree about the linkage between structure and function. Some feel that one should first set up the organizational structure (**form**), and the structure will then determine how the organization will operate (**function**). Others take the position that *form follows function*—that is, the structure should be set up to help facilitate the function. In the discussion that follows we will look at the relationship between structure and function.

ORGANIZATION STRUCTURE

Most profit-making organizations begin when a person (the entrepreneur) has an idea for a product that it is hoped will be wanted in the marketplace. The fundamental tasks are then to get the needed capital to finance the enterprise, get the raw materials, develop or buy the equipment needed, hire the workers, manufacture the product, and then sell it to the public.

Simple Structure

All of the tasks in the incipient organization are at first under the direction of the founder, which leads to an organization form that Henry Mintzberg, one of the leading authorities on organization structure, calls a **simple structure**. Figure 10-1 shows the simple structure[2] of a new organization when its founder runs everything.

It is apparent in Figure 10-1 that the power of the organization is located almost entirely in one person. Decision making is easy and efficient—if not always effective. The CEO must be involved in all areas of the total organization, which means this person carries a heavy burden being responsible for all human and task conditions. The simple structure is the riskiest of all structures since it hangs on the wants and whim of one individual.

In the beginning case, Raku's organization starts out as a simple structure: she controls everything. But as her business grows, the owner must abandon the position of being responsible for everything. This leads to devising a more complex form of

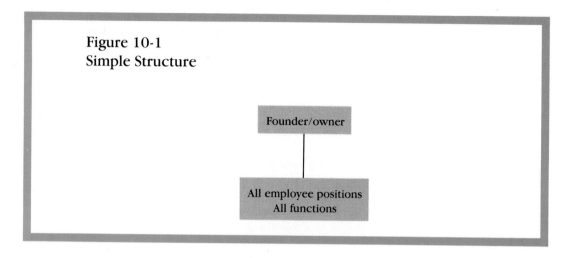

Figure 10-1
Simple Structure

organization—dividing work up in some fashion and then turning these work units over to others to manage (**division of labor**).

Organizational Groupings

How do you go about dividing up an organization into groups or work units? Bear in mind that you want to group people together in such a way that the grouping will increase communications, coordinations of work, cooperation between people, and a sharing of common goals and needed resources.

The literature in the field of organization structure[3] points out the following ways groupings are formed:

1. **Grouping by knowledge or skill**   Almost all universities are organized around knowledge or discipline areas. University functions are then differentiated by *level* of knowledge or skill—instructors up to full professors. Another organization that groups by this method is the hospital—departments of surgeons, internal medicine, psychiatry, etc.

2. **Grouping by work process and function**   Most business organizations involved in manufacturing divide along these lines. Some people are involved in the function of manufacturing, some in research and development, others in sales or marketing, and still others in finance and accounting, or personnel.

3. **Grouping by time**   Sometimes people are grouped together because of the time they work—day shift, swing shift, night shift. This grouping may be used in connection with work process or function. People may be first grouped by function and then later by time. A radio station will have a group of announcers but they may be divided into the time of the day they work.

4. **Grouping by product or output** In this method units are formed on the basis of the product or service rendered. General Foods, for example, is divided up according to product: fast foods, desserts, coffee, cereals, pet foods, etc.

5. **Grouping by client** Some organizations find it most useful to cluster around different clients. The telephone companies, particularly those units responsible for putting ads in the yellow pages, will divide up the world chart—industry, health, professions, retail business, etc.

6. **Grouping by place** This usually means that units are formed according to the geographical area they service or in which they are located. Sales organizations are usually divided up by area—some in the North, South, Midwest, East, and West. Many government organizations divide up the country into regions for purpose of administration.

In some cases there may be a number of different groupings occurring in the same organization. Figure 10-2 shows an organization chart that includes a variety of groupings.

It is anticipated that organizational groupings will lead to certain benefits—otherwise the groupings would not make much sense. Groupings should lead to greater interdependency in the work-flow process. This means that people can get work done faster and easier because they are grouped together. Sometimes groupings should lead to more social interaction and communication, particularly when people must work together. In the case of a football team, for some training purposes the squad is divided up by function—offensive linemen go for one kind of practice as do running backs, receivers, defensive linemen, defensive backs, and so on. However, they then must also come together in new groupings as the complete offensive or defensive team, and learn to coordinate all of their functions together.

Job Positions

Whatever the groupings in an organization, it is also important to establish the viability of each individual position with a job description. Job descriptions should also include how positions connect with other positions in the same grouping. When the positions are being established, it is important to determine whether the position should be kept simple (smallest task possible) or made more complex. The current trend in job design is to try to enlarge and enrich the job rather than to reduce it.[4]

Line and Staff Functions

Suppose in the pottery case discussed at the beginning, the company continues to grow. Every department may need to hire new people. Should every work area spend

Figure 10-2
Organization Chart

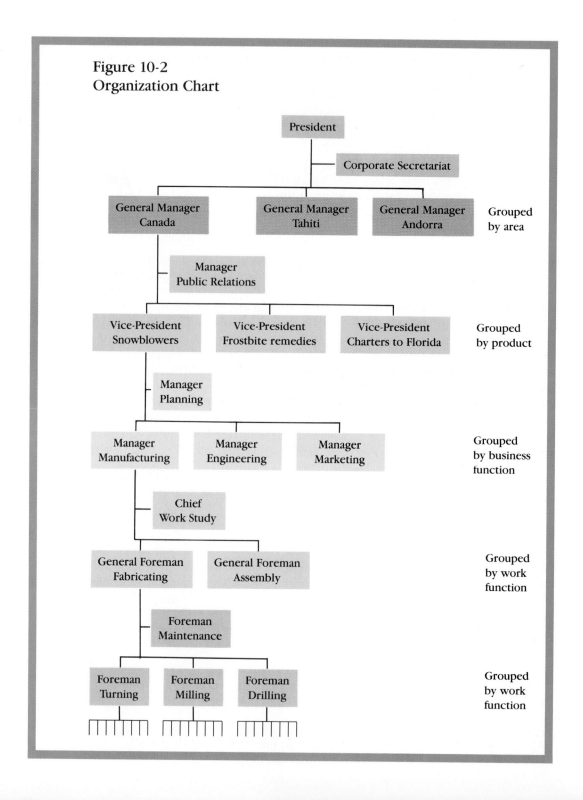

the time to find, interview, and hire new people, or would it be more efficient to have one person responsible for the hiring? If the decision is to consolidate the hiring of people into one position, where should that position be located? Since it is outside of the production areas, perhaps the business should form a separate, new area called "Personnel" to handle all the matters affecting people—hiring, wages, and standards of the organization. This new activity is outside the direct production of pottery, which is usually referred to as the **line** organization. This and other outside activities—purchasing, hiring, training, accounting—all support the line activities and keep the core work going. These activities are generally called **staff activities**.

Centralization and Decentralization

Now suppose Rose Raku wanted to open up a branch of the firm in another country. Who would make sure the new store would be up to standard? Should the original owner set up the store, make the product at the original site and deliver it to the branch, or should the branch make its own product? We now get to the issue of *centralization* versus *decentralization*. Is it more efficient and effective to perform all of the functions (production and administration) except sales at the original location (**centralization**) or should they let the branch run an autonomous operation (**decentralization**)? If she allows the new store to have autonomy, how can Raku ensure that she would get a reasonable profit for letting someone else open up a branch of the business? The best way might be to centralize all production, but perhaps it would even be better to centralize the setting of prices and the collection of sales. But this is somewhat inefficient since Raku would have to disburse funds back to the branch in order for it to buy supplies and pay wages. Perhaps it would be better to let the branch run its own operation. The branch could be a profit center, buy the pottery from headquarters, be responsible for all of its own expenses and personnel, and turn profits over to Raku. This would mean keeping track of all sales and employing honest people who would not lie about sales figures.

If the pottery company expanded into new products, how should the business reorganize if these new products are successful? It might be wise to organize the business around products, which is a model followed by many companies. General Motors, for example, organized into the Cadillac, Buick, Oldsmobile, and Chevrolet divisions until very recently. Each was run like a separate company, but with some centralized functions, like research and development (R&D) that does basic engineering research for all divisions.

Matrix Organization

Another way to reorganize a business around new products would be to combine the new products with the already established main functions in what we discussed in

Figure 10-3
Matrix Organization of Ceramico

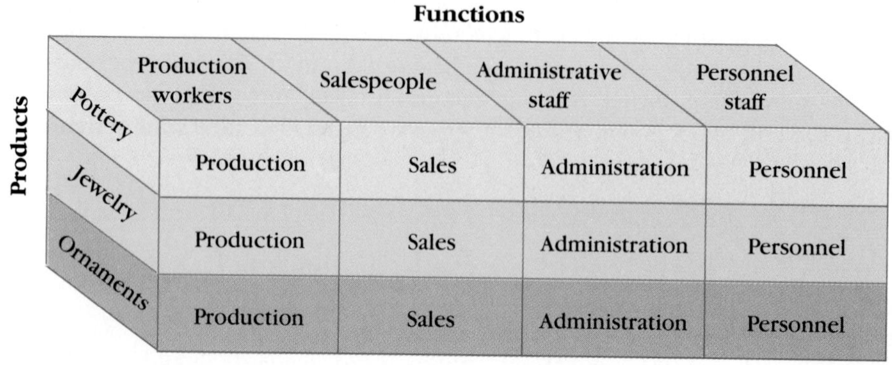

Chapter 9 as a matrix organization. Our new pottery company (Ceramico) would look like Figure 10-3. Every person who worked for a product group would also be connected to an original main function. Thus the pottery group would have some production people, and some from sales, administration, and personnel. Each person would have two bosses—a product boss and a functions boss. This dual loyalty often creates a problem in matrix organizations (in companies like Union Carbide and General Foods), for a person may not know to which boss he should give primary loyalty in the event of a disagreement between the two. To make this kind of organization work, both bosses must be seen as equal, must be consistent in their management policies and priorities, and must be fair in allocating rewards or punishments to employees.

ISSUES IN ORGANIZATIONAL PLANNING

Now that the basic frameworks of organizational structure have been presented, let us look at some of the major issues facing managers in setting up organizations.

Span of Control

The first issue in organizational planning is the matter of **span of control**, or the number of subordinates for whom a manager is directly responsible. The most desirable or effective span of control has long been a subject of disagreement. Some authorities have felt that the desirable span of control is six to eight people. They argue that if a manager is responsible for more than that number the span is too great for the manager to be able to work closely with each one. If the span is less than this number, the manager would have too few to manage and would begin to overmanage people. A major successful experiment by Sears (formerly Sears-Roebuck) department stores provided a new view of span of control.[5] In the 1950s, Sears noticed that regional managers had so few stores under their direction that they were overmanaging. Store managers complained that they needed more autonomy to run the business as they felt appropriate. Upper management decided to widen the span of control of the regional managers to twenty stores, forcing the regional managers to delegate and increasing the autonomy of the store managers.

How far can this practice be taken? The limits are unknown. A contingency orientation suggests that span of control, like many other conditions in management, depends on the situation. It may be that in some situations a very narrow span of control would be appropriate while in other situations a very wide span would be most effective. No longer can any management theorist say that the span of control must be six or eight subordinates.

In determining the span of control, some of the factors that must be taken into account are the following:

1. The complexity of the task. Some work activities may be very complex and require more direct involvement by the manager than simpler, more routine activities.

2. The experience and capabilities of those being managed. It could be that some people have limited experience or capabilities and would need more direct contact with a manager, at least until they gained experience or expanded their capabilities. This might mean a narrow span of control at first, but an expanded span later on.

3. The philosophy of management in the organization. This factor could vary in many directions. In the Sears case, the philosophy was to decentralize and give autonomy at the store level. Given this philosophy, a wide span of control was introduced. Other organizations may have a more centralist orientation and this would lead to a narrower span of control.

4. The capabilities and experience of the manager. Just as those managed may be inexperienced and need development, so it might be with the manager. Some managers may be lacking in experience and might be more effective with a limited span of control to start. This would suggest that span of control may at best be a variable condition—not something that can be put in place and kept as though fixed in concrete. Nothing dictates that all managers should have the same span of control even if they are in the same area.

5. The demand for product or services. Some areas will have a wider span of control because a greater demand for the product or service requires more people. For example, most universities are divided into colleges. The current strong demand for business and management education means that the dean of a school of busi-

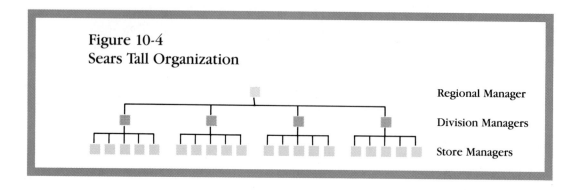

Figure 10-4
Sears Tall Organization

Regional Manager

Division Managers

Store Managers

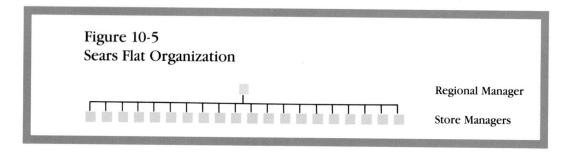

Figure 10-5
Sears Flat Organization

Regional Manager

Store Managers

ness and management may have as many as a dozen departments inside the college. In a smaller college with relatively few majors and only a few departments, the span of control of the dean will be small.

Hierarchy and Span of Control

Another organizational feature connected to span of control is the size of the **hierarchy** or the number of levels in the organization. Some organizations are relatively **flat**—that is, they have relatively few hierarchical levels. Other organizations have many levels (**tall organizations**). Generally, those organizations that have a large span of control would have fewer levels and would be considered "flat."

If the Sears organization were to be diagrammed before they went to a wide span of control, the organization would look like Figure 10-4, which shows three levels in the hierarchy. The regional manager is responsible for four division managers and each division has five stores. With a wider span of control, the organization was restructured into a flatter design illustrated in Figure 10-5. In the new organization, a whole level of the hierarchy has been eliminated by widening the span of control of the regional managers.

Some of the major differences between "tall" and "flat" organizations are shown in Box 10-1. Obviously, the lines of communication are lengthened and the possibil-

Box 10-1
Tall versus Flat Organizations

TALL	FLAT
1. Narrow span of control.	1. Wide span of control.
2. Increases the length of lines of communication.	2. Shorter lines of communication.
3. Can closely manage fewer people.	3. Cannot manage closely—too many subordinates.
4. Authority shared across several levels with many managers.	4. Authority located in fewer levels.
5. Delegation not as essential as direct supervision.	5. Delegation essential.

ity of distortion or blockage of information is magnified in a tall organization. Also, in flat organizations managers usually delegate more and give more autonomy to subordinates.

Recently many businesses have moved to flatter organizations in order to increase communications, make people more likely to delegate, and increase worker responsibility, while eliminating an expensive level of management. However, there have been some unanticipated negative consequences to these flatter organizations. Some lower-level managers who have seen levels of management reduced along with their opportunities for advancement have begun to look for other jobs. Also, since more power is controlled by fewer managers, an abuser of that power can affect far more people than in the small span-of-control situation. The wide span-of-control, flat organizations are highly dependent on truly effective managers functioning in the management positions.[6]

The ability of many Japanese organizations to function with far fewer supervisors and managers than American organizations is attributed in part to their willingness to function with fewer levels and a much wider span of control. These elements of organizations are also more consistent with their philosophy of management which emphasizes autonomy and a willingness and an expectation that people will carry out their duties without a high degree of supervision.

Organization Design

Let us now more systematically look at what goes into the design of any organization. Most of these design elements have been referred to in our earlier discussion of Rose Raku's pottery company.

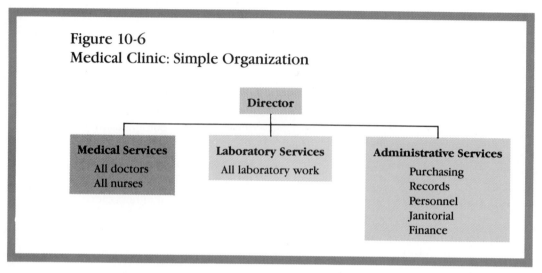

Figure 10-6
Medical Clinic: Simple Organization

INDIVIDUAL TASK   The basic unit of any organization is the individual **task** or assignment. These tasks are determined by first looking at the functions needed to run the business. Since it can be argued that form follows function, the building block of the organization's form can be seen as the task. A single task is most often thought of as being filled by one individual, but some organizations now are viewing the single job as a team effort and not just to be handled by one person. For example, Volvo shifted its basic concept of the organization from thinking of the basic unit as an individual doing one task to seeing the basic unit as the team working together.[7] Within the team are individuals, but since all individuals are capable of performing any task, it makes more sense to identify the tasks for the team than to think of the individual as the primary unit. This approach is also being implemented at GM's new Saturn Corporation.

In the more conventional organization, the individual tasks are filled by individuals and these people and their tasks are put together into a natural working unit variously called a work gang, crew, section, or department. In a doctor's office, this unit is called an office and has various individuals in different task positions—a receptionist, a bookkeeper or accountant, a registered nurse, a laboratory technician, a janitor, and then the doctor(s).

DEPARTMENTS   As the organization gets larger, the individual tasks get combined into some type of subunits, or **departments**. It is another major organizational decision to decide how many departments to have. If a group of doctors decide to practice together, they form a clinic. They feel this organization is better for them than their own private offices, for it provides the doctors with more services, more access to other professional help from other doctors, more available equipment, more possible relief from long hours and patient demands, all while cutting costs by sharing space, equipment, and personnel expenses. The clinic might at first have very few departments when the patient load is small. It might be divided into medical services, which includes all doctors and two support services groups as seen in Figure 10-6. However,

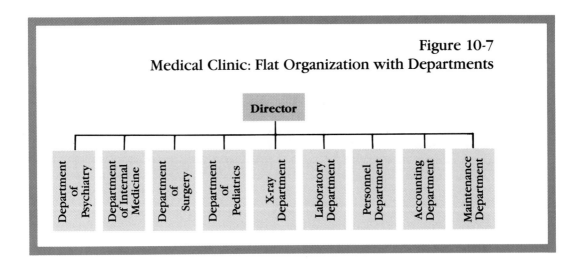

Figure 10-7
Medical Clinic: Flat Organization with Departments

as the clinic gets larger, each of these three basic units may find that there are just too many individual tasks that must be coordinated all together in one department. The medical services area may then be divided into several departments as well as the other two units. Its organization might look like Figure 10-7.

The medical services now have too many individual tasks to all function together, and the departments are formed around the area of medical specialty or functions. Likewise, the laboratory work is divided into X-ray and other laboratory work and administration is divided into three separate departments. You can see it is possible to have a flat organization and have every unit report to the director of the clinic, or you could add a level of management and have, under the director, a medical director, laboratory manager, and an administration manager. There are many ways to combine these subunits into other units. For example, the clinic could be organized as in Figure 10-8. This organization form puts a layer of management between the director and the departments. In this case the layer consists of two assistants to the director. It would also be possible to have three people in the level between departments and the director. One cluster (the medical section) would be composed of the several medical departments reporting to a medical head. There would be another cluster of laboratory departments reporting to a laboratory head, and a third cluster of administrative departments reporting to an administrative chief. These three section heads would then report to the medical director.

In some organizations the possibility of organizing departments around different common elements exists. The various individual tasks could be divided by function, by area or territory, by product, by customer, or perhaps by time period or even some other central dimension. It is also possible to form departments by one central dimension and then cluster departments around a different dimension. In the pottery example, departments could be organized around function—preparers, sales, and administration. It would then be possible to create other units around either product, area, or time period. For example, there could be regional units—North, South, East, and West that could handle all products for that region.

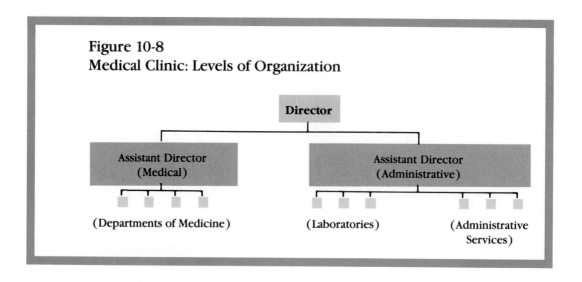

Figure 10-8
Medical Clinic: Levels of Organization

Product units could be also created—pots, jars, ornaments—with each product unit controlling all of its organizational functions. An organization could also be organized around time periods—summer products and winter products. In this case it might be desirable to organize around customers—kids toys, teenage items, and adult items. All of this indicates that an organization can be structured or designed in several ways. The idea is to create a structure that pulls together people and tasks in such a way that communications, cooperation, task accomplishment, distribution of resources, and decision making are all accomplished in the most efficient and effective manner possible.

Differentiation-Integration Model

As we look at different functions, even in the same organization, it is useful to examine the thinking of two organization theorists at Harvard University, Paul Lawrence and Jay Lorsch, who developed what has been called the differentiation-integration model of organizations.[8] Lawrence and Lorsch followed the lead of earlier British writers Woodward, and Burns and Stalker,[9] who first pointed out that companies producing different products were organized and managed differently. For example, continuous flow production, like an oil refinery or an assembly line making automobiles, is organized differently than a business composed of skilled craftsmen each making a piece of custom-made furniture. The British researchers correctly pointed out that the organization is strongly influenced by the task or product being produced.

Lawrence and Lorsch expanded this notion and found in their research that not only should companies producing different products be organized and managed differently, but separate subunits or departments *within* a company have different tasks, goals, people, and time demands and should also be different in the way they

An expanding medical clinic can be organized into either a flat or tall structure.

are organized and managed. Thus **differentiation** in an organization should be recognized and planned for. However, these different units (manufacturing, sales, maintenance, accounting, research and development), while having their unique characteristics, also should be **integrated** so they can cooperate in achieving common goals.

The challenge in organizations is to allow needed differentiation but to also provide for necessary integration. Certain integration devices are possible to tie together various organizational units. Many organizations will have an integrating council or committee—often called its executive committee or management council—where representatives of the various subunits (sections or departments) meet on a regular basis to coordinate activities, solve problems, and make decisions. Other organizations will have a coordinating person—one whose job it is to contact the different units and provide a liaison between them. There are some public organizations that have an ombudsman office—a place where people who have differences can go to get a hearing and a chance to be represented. Integration mechanisms are important in organizations that also allow units to develop differently.

Temporary Structures

Sometimes the existing organization design is not adequate to handle unanticipated problems that arise, and new, often temporary, units or mechanisms need to be created. The most common of these temporary units are the **task force** and **committee**—terms that are very similar and are sometimes used interchangeably. However, a task force is usually thought of as a group of people assigned to work together on a limited task for a limited time. A committee may be appointed for a longer period of time to deal with recurring matters. Some organizations have standing committees to handle regular activities that occur. Most academic departments in a university will have several standing committees, such as those for admissions, curriculum, research, and recruitment. The committees are constant, but their membership may change from year to year. The academic department may also form a task force to deal with a specific matter. For example, it could form a task force of faculty and students to investigate cheating and to give recommendations for handling such a matter.

Committees and task forces are often used as an integrating device. Businesses may form committees to oversee coordination of departments or projects. If two or more units are involved in a disagreement that is a one-time or unusual occurrence, it may be advisable to form a task force of members from all involved units to investigate the issue and to make recommendations to the total group. This saves time and energy, and solves the potentially impossible task of getting everyone together to try and work out differences.

A recent structural invention that falls somewhat in-between a committee and a task force is the **quality circle**. The quality circle (or quality control circle as it was originally called) was an organization invention, created by American advisors to Japan following World War II, and following its extraordinary success, was imported back to America. A quality circle is a group of people, often from different parts of the same organization, set up to examine and make recommendations for the improvement of work in the organization. Some quality circle groups meet for years and will look at a number of different problem areas. Other organizations have set up quality circles, used them for a period of time, and then disbanded them. A report on the use of quality circles in Japan by Robert Cole indicates that even the best operating quality circle programs in Japan have perhaps one-third of all circles working well, another one-third that are marginally effective, and one-third that do not contribute at all.[10]

Job Redesign

Once a manager becomes familiar with organization structure, it is apparent that some existing structures may not be the most effective ways to arrange the organization. To make activities more effective, sometimes it is essential to restructure or redesign the organization, or parts of it. The case at the beginning of this chapter is an example of one small pottery company that changed from essentially an assembly-line structure where each person did only one simple task, to an autonomous workteam design where the members of the team did everything and all team members learned every task.

JOB ENRICHMENT   One way to redesign an organization is to restructure the individual tasks so people are doing *total* jobs and not just a single piece of the job. This reshaping of job design has been called **job enrichment** and has been emphasized heavily by Frederick Herzberg, a well-known organization researcher and writer. Herzberg claims that people are demotivated when they feel their work gives them little self-growth, little recognition, and a feeling of making no real contribution. The key to increase motivation is to restructure the basic tasks.[11]

Increased motivation is accomplished when tasks are combined in such a way that people can see they are doing something that counts and contributes to the success of the organization. Workers take satisfaction in seeing the total job completed, and their expanded tasks help them feel they are learning new skills. This is what is meant by enriching the job—giving more autonomy, variety, and chance for more interpersonal contact.

CASE
The Volvo Innovation[12]

In an industry where the assembly line was almost a sacred practice, the Volvo Company of Sweden created a major change in organization design in their Kalmar plant. Under the leadership of President Pehr G. Gyllenhammar, the attempt was made to create an organizational production system that would reduce monotony and increase the feeling that each worker was building something in its totality. Gyllenhammar wanted every employee to see a Volvo driving down the street and be able to say, "I made that car."

Under the old assembly-line process, the turnover rate was 52 percent per year and absenteeism was a major problem. The new design was startling in its concept: Instead of the conventional assembly line that moved through the building, stationary work stations of about 20 people were created with all materials being brought to that station. A special carrier was devised to move around the entire automobile being assembled.

The groups of 20 people were organized to perform all the work on various automobile systems: electrical, instrumentation, steering and controls, and interiors. Each team had its own area on the shop floor and its own rest area. Each group was allowed to organize itself without interference from management. Teams could choose to organize themselves so that each member specialized in an individual job, or they could divide themselves into subteams to do parts of the job, or they could have a rotating procedure. The team essentially contracted with management to deliver a certain number of products a day, such as finished doors, brake systems, and interiors. The teams would conduct their own inspections, and a computer-based quality control system would flash the results directly back to the team via a television screen.

Job enrichment at Volvo provided workers with more autonomy, variety, and recognizable accomplishment.

This case shows the possibility of achieving the major elements of job enrichment. Two researchers, J. R. Hackman and G. R. Oldham, created a model that identified the major elements of job enrichment as being: increased skill variety, task identity (doing the whole job), task significance (doing something important that is recognized by others), autonomy, and feedback.[13]

JOB ENLARGEMENT   A close kin to job enrichment is **job enlargement**, which means making the work task broader in scope. It is, however, possible to enlarge a person's job without necessarily enriching it. A maintenance worker who has four offices to clean may be asked to now clean six offices. His job has been enlarged (expanded), but not necessarily enriched. By giving him more work, he may be forced to organize his time better and the company may be getting more done for the same pay, but the worker may experience no real growth or professional development. It sometimes occurs that people are bored and ineffective because they do not have enough to do. Job enlargement makes sense in such a case.

Decentralization

Another way to redesign an organization is to decentralize it by shifting authority and responsibility down the organization so that decisions and activities formerly handled at the upper levels are now close to the actual operating or work level.

As a company grows, certain tasks or functions could still be kept under the control of the top management group that founded the business. For example, the top management of an expanding lemonade-stand company could keep all accounting, hiring, firing, and purchasing of all products for all lemonade stands centralized. They could also centralize standards of product quality and cleanliness of facilities. However, it may make more sense to decentralize some functions, both to relieve top management of some of the work load, and to increase the involvement of lower-level people in the business. Each individual lemonade stand could be given control over watching its own income and expenses, hiring and firing its own people, and doing its own purchasing. Almost all companies, as they grow, must decide how many activities to keep centralized and how many to decentralize.

ENDING CASE
American Transtech[14]

Along with its breathtaking innovations in high technology, Silicon Valley is producing a new kind of management consultant—one whose mission it is to help create a entirely new kind of corporation. This new breed of consultant comes from an emerging discipline called **sociotechnology**. The consultant's task is to help people use their full creativity and thereby upgrade the quality of American work life.

Paul Gustavson of San Jose, California, is an expert in this developing field. With a degree in "Organizational Behavior" from Brigham Young University, Gustavson is essentially a psychologist for corporations and a creator of a new kind of management based on worker teams. He has been in charge of human resources at Standard Oil and Zilog, a subsidiary of Exxon. Most recently, he has taken on the challenge of redesigning American Transtech, a Jacksonville, Florida subsidiary of AT&T.

American Transtech is a small but growing data processing company originally formed to handle complex stock transfers during AT&T divestiture—the largest such transaction in history. Now with 1,500 employees, the company is providing high volume financial services to the new regional communications companies and other outside clients.

Their chief problem was motivating workers and making routine operations *interesting*. In short, American Transtech was looking for a way to give workers a new sense of mission and personal responsibility.

Gustavson felt the solution was to move away from traditional multilayers of management, and toward a new way of working based on shared *awareness*. Gustavson claims that the new American corporation lacks a hierarchy. Replacing hierarchies are three separate systems whose sole purpose is to ask important questions. The strategic system (formerly senior management) asks: "What is happening in the marketplace and how should we adapt?" The managing system asks: "How can we make this strategy work?" The operations system is composed of teams who ask: "How can production obtain the desired results in the best and most efficient way?"

The exciting thing is that by the end of this process, management is transformed. Quite simply, these systems give more leeway to employees and make administrative monitoring and managerial "rule-setting" obsolete.

The American Transtech Experiment

Just how did the American Transtech experiment begin? With a pilot program of 18 people, consisting of keypunch operators, information processors, and top management, the core group took end-to-end responsibility for all information services, from fulfilling the client's request to providing a final cost analysis and assessment of the quality of their work. The goal was to eliminate old pay scales and job categories and directly reward team performance with a share of corporate profits. The following are some of the key changes of Gustavson's program.

GET RID OF THE OLD CASTE SYSTEM   Before the reorganization, the console operators at American Transtech were the upper caste: they sat behind glass on raised platforms and watched everything that was going on. To get to see these operators, you had to penetrate the doors of their glassed-in inner sanctuary.

The lowest caste happened to be the tape hangers whose sole task was to clear and store 1,500 tapes every night. Tape hangers were all paid differently because management thought there were five different levels of work. As a result the workers were frustrated. Managers were upset because the quality of work was not as high as it should have been. When employees left their shifts, their replacements did not know what was going on. In short, the operation was organized around an old way of thinking based on economies of scale, fractioning the job into segments, and having people perform repetitive tasks.

The first thing Gustavson did was break down the information barriers that generally create these castes. Typical corporate hierarchies are closed systems, however. "Who knows what" is tightly controlled because people do not want anyone else to know what they do because someone might get ahead that way. Gustavson got rid of the old notion that "information is power" and designed a team system that cannot function unless team members share what they know.

ROTATE LEADERSHIP   The new system does not require fixed supervision. Instead team leadership rotates depending on the skills and expertise needed for each work situation. As leadership changes hands, more people rise up and ask questions. Ultimately, more leaders are developed.

REWARD TEAMWORK OVER COMPETITION   Effective teamwork requires a diversity of knowledge and skills and leaves no room for negative competition. To foster such teamwork, workers were asked to come up with different names based on the word "Transtech." One group came up with 46 different concepts, all based on different notions of the corporation. When workers offer diverse ideas and learn to build on these ideas, you create an exciting organization.

SHARE THE WEALTH   Gustavson believes that the new American company as represented by American Transtech should be designed into a completely different structure aimed at creating *wealth* rather than **entitlement**. The main difference is this: when the company makes money, it has to share that money with the people who helped make it. Most companies promise the worker rewards—but always at some future date. The goal at American Transtech is to make each team into a miniprofit center. Pay is not based on seniority or automatic merit raises but on a team's contribution to the corporate profit. Under this new system, there is no opportunity for situations where lower-level employees work late for six months while their boss gets a bonus and a free trip to Hawaii.

GIVE PEOPLE THE FREEDOM TO GET THE JOB DONE   In many organizations, being successful means keeping visible to top management, rather than having a clear vision of your job. But when people put their time and energy into covering for themselves, it is not very cost-efficient for the company. This attitude does not work in an organization where the individuals are responsible for their own work. At American Transtech before the reorganization the data processing department traditionally worked on three shifts based on morning, afternoon, and evening hours. Gustavson threw out the shift idea and asked, "When do we need to have these jobs done?" Now some workers come in at 4 A.M., others at 2 P.M., or whenever the team decides will be efficient. They structure their time around the product and cover the work 24 hours a day, 7 days a week.

CREATE A UNIFIED VISION   What is management's role in the new corporation? The American Transtech team shows how well a group works with *clarity of purpose*, by creating a managing system that does not aim to control but to provide a clear vision of the company's goals.

USE THE NEW TECHNOLOGY   The new managers at American Transtech must be adept information processors, using personal computers and the latest ways to analyze market data.

FOCUS ON THE FUTURE   Too often top management is turned the wrong way around, broadcasting to the outside world, rather than trying to understand and absorb it. The best thing management can do is interpret the needs and demands of the marketplace and then organize the company so it can meet those new demands. To do so, you have to have a vision of the future: people have to know where they are going.

THE CUSTOMER IS ALWAYS RIGHT   The first concern is *customer focus*. The second is *trust*. You have to reassess your customer's needs constantly, and then you have to trust your employees to work 24 hours a day, 7 days a week to fulfill them. ▼

SUMMARY

In this chapter we have seen that the structure or form of an organization is dependent on its function, or what needs to be done. As organizations evolve from small, single function units to large, complex units involved in many activities, it becomes advantageous, even necessary, to divide the tasks among members so that the work can be accomplished more efficiently. Furthermore, new tasks (staff functions) evolve that facilitate the main work of the organization. The need to coordinate the various activities gives rise to a hierarchy that is designed to help management control the organization, better meet the needs of its people, and make better decisions. We looked at various ways in which organizations seek to structure themselves to meet these goals and some of the issues management must concern itself with in doing so. We then discussed the need for organizations to take account of both the diversity of their activities and the need to integrate these activities in a way that will enable the organization to meet its objectives. Finally, we discussed ways in which organizations face the issues brought about by the constantly changing environment and some of the ways managers can restructure both the organization and the work assignments of members to better adapt to the new environment.

KEY TERMS

Structure-function approach	Span of control
Form	Hierarchy
Function	Flat organization
Simple structure	Tall organization
Division of labor	Organization design
Line activities	Task
Staff activities	Department
Centralization	Differentiation
Decentralization	Integration

Temporary structures   Job redesign
Task force   Job enrichment
Committee   Job enlargement
Quality circle   Sociotechnology

REVIEW QUESTIONS

1. What is the structure-function approach to organization analysis?

2. What do we mean when we say that form follows function?

3. What is meant by the location of a function?

4. What issues are we concerned with in decisions involving the degree of central-ization in an organization?

5. What is the chief characteristic of a matrix organization?

6. What is the purpose of a matrix organization?

7. What is the main problem that is encountered with the matrix form of organiza-tion? The main benefit?

8. How is span of control related to the issue of overmanagement?

9. What are some of the factors to be taken into account in determining the appro-priate span of control?

10. How is span of control related to the "tallness" or "flatness" of an organization?

11. What are the advantages and disadvantages of a tall organization?

12. What are the advantages and disadvantages of a flat organization?

13. What is basic building block of the organization's form?

14. What are the basic issues to be concerned with in the organization of de-partments?

15. What are some of the common elements around which departments can be organized?

16. Describe the differentiation-integration model of organizations.

17. Name the two basic ways in which jobs can be redesigned. In what kinds of situations would each be appropriate?

CHALLENGE QUESTIONS

1. How would the location of a function affect the effectiveness of the person per-forming that function?

2. What kinds of projects are suitable for using the matrix form of organization?

3. How would you relate span of control to the issue of centralization versus decentralization?

4. What span of control would you expect to find in a company such as Apple Computer as it went through its explosive growth stage and why?

5. What kinds of organizations would likely run better with a flat form of organization structure? A high form?

6. What types of companies would you expect to organize departments around product? Territory? Customer?

7. What type of temporary structure would you organize to deal with the following problems and why?
    A. To ensure compliance with government pollution standards.
    B. To formulate a takeover strategy.
    C. To review the competitiveness of employee compensation and benefits.
    D. To develop and launch a new product within 12 months.

8. What would be some indicators that might indicate a need for job redesign? What factors would help you determine whether the need was for job enrichment or job enlargement?

CASE AND RELATED QUESTIONS

1. Can you rationalize the viewpoint that meetings are lost productive time with Peters and Waterman's finding that excellent organizations have a bias for action?

2. What factors would you look at in determining an appropriate time frame for measuring productivity increases for teams?

3. What factors are relevant to determining the pay of team members? Design a matrix that you think the committee on compensation in the Sears company would have come up with. Be prepared to defend it in class.

4. What factors led Sears to move to a flat organization structure? What do you think the limiting factor as to how many stores each regional manager could handle would be?

5. What types of demands is the "information age" making on organizations?

6. What type of organization, flat or tall, seems best suited to the needs of information workers and why?

7. What are some of the problems that arise when a company shares its earnings "with the people who helped make it?" Should all employees share equally in company profits? If teams are the basic work unit, how do you differentiate between poor team performers and high performers?

8. What are some of the limits on organizing work times according to the preferences of team members?

9. What kind of manager would function most effectively at American Transtech? What type of manager is likely to fail?

ENDNOTES

1. Adapted from Henry Mintzberg, *The Structuring of Organizations* (Englewood Cliffs, NJ: Prentice-Hall, 1979) pp. 1–2.

2. Ibid., p. 307.

3. Ibid.

4. Daniel Robey, *Designing Organizations: A Macro Perspective* (Homewood, IL: Richard D. Irwin, 1982).

5. James Worthy, "Organizational Structure and Company Morale," *American Sociological Review* 15 (1950), pp. 169–70.

6. For a discussion of problems concerning a change in levels of hierarchy, see Edgar H. Schein, *Organizational Psychology*, 3rd ed. (Englewood Cliffs, NJ: Prentice-Hall, 1980), p. 219.

7. R. E. Walton, "From Hawthorne to Topeka to Kalmar," *Man and Work in Society*, eds. E. L. Cass and F. G. Zimmer (New York: Van Nostrand Reinhold, 1975).

8. P. R. Lawrence and J. W. Lorsch, *Organization and Environment: Managing Differentiation and Integration* (Boston: Graduate School of Business Administration, Harvard University, 1967).

9. Joan Woodward, *Industrial Organization: Theory and Practice* (London: Oxford University Press, 1965); and Tom Burns and G. M. Stalker, *The Management of Innovation* (London: Tavistock Publication, 1961).

10. Robert Cole, *Work, Mobility and Participation: A Corporation Study of American and Japanese Industry* (Berkeley: University of California Press, 1979).

11. Frederick Herzberg, *Work and the Nature of Man* (Cleveland, OH: World Publishing, 1966); and Frederick Herzberg, Bernard Mausner and Barbara Synderman, *The Motivation to Work* (New York: John Wiley and Sons, 1959).

12. Adapted from P. G. Gyllenhammar, *People at Work* (Reading, MA: Addison-Wesley, 1977).

13. J. R. Hackman and G. R. Oldham, *Work Redesign* (Reading, MA: Addison-Wesley, 1980).

14. Adapted from Sally VanWagenen Keil, "Designing America's New Corporate Culture," *The Tarrytown Letter* (Tarrytown, NY: The Tarrytown Group, April 1985), pp. 18–20.

CHAPTER 11

TEAM BUILDING AND GROUP DYNAMICS

LEARNING OBJECTIVES

■ Recognize the symptoms of ineffective teams, and how ineffectiveness can be overcome.

■ Describe the history and development of the team concept as applied to organizations.

■ Understand the ways in which a group can influence an individual.

■ Describe the type of climate that promotes a healthy team.

■ Evaluate the various methods of team building and indicate when each is used.

■ Explain why commitment is a major factor in the success or failure of team-building attempts.

■ Define the difference between the task and relationship functions of group action.

■ Identify the activities that facilitate both task and relationship functions in a group.

■ Understand why informal leaders emerge in a group, even when formal leaders have been established.

■ Discuss the importance of active participation in the decision-making process—why it is more desirable than acceptance of decisions through exhortation.

■ Understand why it is often essential for leaders to delegate responsibility to group members.

■ Explain the importance of feedback to the success of the group, and what is required to promote it.

Jim Thomas manages the Mountain Side plant of National Alloys Company. He has a tough production schedule that demands solid performance from all of his people, in all areas of the plant. Jim wants to do a
top-flight job and becomes concerned when production drops, when
problems go unsolved, or when morale sags.

After his job and family, Jim's greatest interest is pro football—particularly as
played by the Dallas Cowboys. Being a native Texan, Jim has followed the Dallas team
from its inception. He attends an occasional game and watches them regularly on
television or listens to them on the radio. When the game is over, Jim can give a clear,
detailed accounting for the team's success or failure.

What raises Jim's boiling point higher than anything is to watch his team fail to
play together. He can spot in an instant when someone misses a block, loafs on the
job, fails to pass on obvious information to the quarterback, or tries to "shine" at the
expense of the entire team. He can diagnose the Cowboys' areas of weakness, and, if
the coach could only hear him, he would tell him what to do to remedy the situation.
But with all of his insight about teamwork and football, Jim fails to see the parallels
between what is needed to improve the Dallas Cowboys and what is needed to
shape up the management team at National Alloys. Many of the problems are exactly
the same:

1. Some individuals have never really learned what their assignments are, particularly for certain plays or situations.

2. Some are afraid of their coach, so they pretend to know things that they should be
   asking questions about.

3. Some want to do things "the old way," while others feel that more modern
   methods are needed.

4. Factions and cliques quarrel and fight among one another.

5. The whole unit has not come together to develop common goals to which everyone is committed.

6. Decisions are made by someone, but some people either do not "get the word"
   or they disagree with the decision and drag their feet.

7. The units are jealous of each other and do not have fun together.

8. Even when people are aware of a problem, they do not know exactly what to do
   about it.

Teams are collections of people who must rely on group collaboration if each
member is to experience the optimum of success and goal achievement. It is obvious
that in order to score touchdowns (and prevent the opponent from scoring) a foot-

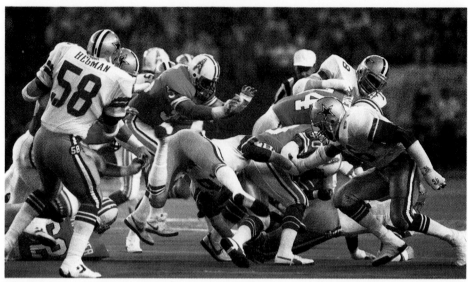

Like the Dallas Cowboys, organizations rely on effective teamwork in order to be successful.

ball team has to play together. It should be just as obvious that a work unit or management group must also work together to ensure success. A football team practices over and over again how it will execute its plays. The team has "skull" practice where they talk over plans and strategies. They review films of past games, identify mistakes, set up goals for the next week. Unfortunately, Jim Thomas' management group does not engage in any similar types of activities. They do not review their past actions, and they do not really plan new strategies. They do not come together to learn from their mistakes, nor do they practice or get coaching on new methods, set new goals, or build up their team "spirit." Jim Thomas can spot the absence of teamwork on the playing field, but cannot see similar symptoms in the work plant. He is aware that sometimes things are not running smoothly at work, but he is not sure just what is wrong and he does not know what he can do about it. 🔽

INTRODUCTION

If you were to look at most organization charts you would see a framework that shows a set of individuals all reporting to or working under other individuals. The chart would make it seem that the individual is the basic unit of the organization. Rensis Likert, an early writer about organizations, clearly demonstrated that almost every

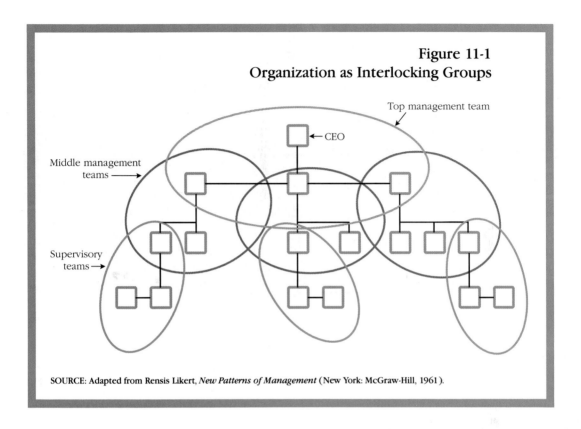

Figure 11-1
Organization as Interlocking Groups

Top management team

← CEO

Middle management
teams →

Supervisory
teams →

SOURCE: Adapted from Rensis Likert, *New Patterns of Management* (New York: McGraw-Hill, 1961).

individual in an organization is assigned to a work group (or team) and it is the group that is the basic work unit of the organization.[2] Organizations really look like the illustration in Figure 11-1.

Every manager is a member of two teams—one where she is a team member and the other when she is the team leader. In Figure 11-1, Manager X is a subordinate in Team I and the superior in Team II. People in teams must learn to work together within the team (intrateamwork) and between teams (interteamwork) if organizations are to function effectively.

In a recent analysis of America's 100 best companies, effective teamwork was cited as a characteristic of these companies.[3] In a separate survey taken at a management conference, all of the 300 managers present expressed a belief that teamwork was essential to the success of an organization.[4] Given the agreement regarding the need for teamwork, why would people in one organization, which is especially supportive of the concept of teamwork, give the following responses about their teams?

"It's no fun working with those people. They just seem to be so involved in their own work that they don't want to do anything for anyone else."

"Our meetings are chaos. When we get together and try to get work accomplished, nobody listens—we fight and argue and nobody supports anyone else."

"We never do anything that is teamlike. We don't set goals, we don't plan, we don't do work together. Everything is done in one-on-one meetings with the boss. When we have a staff meeting it is just one person at a time talking to the boss while the rest listen."

"I don't trust anyone in that bunch I work with. They would all knife you in the back if they thought it would help their cause. At times they can act so friendly but when the crunch comes it is each person for himself."

"People talk about teamwork around here but I don't know what that means. I go to work, I sit at my desk and take care of my assignments. From time to time I go to meetings that are usually a waste of time. I get a yearly performance review that hasn't changed much in years, and I draw my pay. I don't see what teamwork means in my job."

"There are some people I work with that I really like and enjoy working with, but there are others that bother me and we don't get along. I find it easier to avoid them or get things done with as little interaction as possible."

"My boss is so busy that he doesn't even talk about how our staff could become a team. He has his favorites that he talks to but the rest of us just do our work and hardly ever have any significant involvement with the boss."

It is obvious that despite the formal policy, the teams at the informal level are not functioning effectively.

DIAGNOSING TEAM EFFECTIVENESS

The case of Jim Thomas shows at least one of the dimensions that occurs and blocks a group of people from developing into an effective working unit or team. Jim Thomas does not think of a work group as a team. He sees his subordinates primarily as people who report to him and, as a result, he deals with his people one-on-one to solve most problems. His group has not learned to work together, to make common decisions, or to set goals that all support. Modern managers must be able to work with individuals, but they must also develop the ability to manage a team. What is a team in an organization like? Box 11-1 lists the major characteristics of a mature team.

Teamness

All work units do not require the same amount of teamwork or **collaboration**. Figure 11-2 shows the range of **teamness** in different types of organizations. The issue in teamwork is: How much collaboration is required? To what extent is a person able to accomplish goals without the collaborative efforts of others? A university department

Box 11-1
Characteristics of a Mature Team

1. Members understand and accept a common set of goals.
2. The team climate is one of trust and support.
3. People feel they can influence what happens.
4. Members communicate with each other and share all relevant data.
5. People accept and implement assignments and decisions.
6. Leadership is not restrictive, punitive, or highly authoritarian.
7. Members are able to disagree and work through the disagreements.

Figure 11-2
Degrees of Teamwork Required in Organization

Low Teamwork	**Normal Teamwork**	**High Teamwork**
Chess team	Baseball team	Football team
Association of doctors	Refinery management team	Spaceship crew
University department	Faculty committee	Faculty teaching team

ordinarily requires rather low teamwork. It is possible for an individual faculty member to do much of his or her work without collaborating with other faculty members. The professor can prepare and teach classes, counsel students, write, and conduct research quite independent from others. The departmental faculty must work to develop a moderate level of teamwork if members are to feel committed to some decisions. They must get together to make decisions about new faculty, who gets graduate student assistants, and who teaches what classes at what times. Two faculty members teaching a class together require a higher degree of teamwork if they are to be effective. Lessons must be coherent, focused, and nonrepetitive, and class goals are not achieved without a great deal of collaboration.

A spaceship crew has many tasks it has to do, many in concert with the ground control team, and fine-tuned collaboration is absolutely essential to be able to accomplish the mission and survive. In athletics, different sports require differing amounts of teamwork. On each play in football every offensive or defensive player has a specific assignment and is involved continually when on the field. Baseball requires a different amount of teamness. If the pitcher strikes out most of the opposition, the rest of the team (except the catcher) has very little to do. In the course of a game, the individual comes to bat only about four times. Only on occasions such as in a double play, hit-and-run, or squeeze play is teamwork required and then only for a few, but not all, of the players.

It is safe to say that almost everyone who works in an organization or who manages must at some time collaborate with others or try to manage situations in which people must work together. A core management value is that teamwork is essential to organizational effectiveness and a core management skill is the ability to build and manage a team.

Diagnosing the Need for Team Development

How does a manager know if the correct amount of time and energy is spent working on improving team work? Box 11-2 gives a check list that can help a person see if **team development** is needed. The check list points out some of the common problems that occur in work units. If these conditions persist to a destructive level, then it is important that the manager be aware of these conditions and be prepared to take some positive action.

Another example of a checklist that members of a work unit can fill out to discover the level of effectiveness at which the team is functioning is illustrated in Box 11-3. This type of instrument also helps identify the areas where the group may need to concentrate its efforts in order to improve.

Symptoms of Ineffective Teams

In trying to diagnose ineffective team functioning, the following are some key signs or indicators which give evidence that all is not well.

COMMUNICATING OUTSIDE, NOT INSIDE THE GROUP   One sign of ineffective teamwork is when little discussion of the issue at hand occurs during unit or staff meetings, but as soon as the meeting is over, people collect behind closed doors or in corners to review the issues and express their disagreements or concerns. When people, for any reason, are afraid or unwilling to get necessary information out in the open it usually means something is wrong in the functioning of the team.

OVERDEPENDENCY ON THE LEADER   In an effective team, members are able to take initiative and move ahead on their own to deal with matters or fill assignments. An ineffective team becomes immobilized when its leader is not present. A team that cannot have a meeting without the leader or cannot carry out action unless the leader is present has symptoms of possible **overdependency**. While the leader is important, members should have enough confidence to move ahead with action when it is clear that action is needed.

Box 11-2
Team Building Checklist

Problem identification (to what extent do you see evidence of the following problems in your work unit?)

	LOW EVIDENCE		SOME EVIDENCE		HIGH EVIDENCE
1. Loss of production or work unit output.	1	2	3	4	5
2. Grievances within the work unit.	1	2	3	4	5
3. Conflicts or hostility between unit members.	1	2	3	4	5
4. Confusion about assignments or unclear relationships between people.	1	2	3	4	5
5. Lack of clear goals, or low commitment to goals.	1	2	3	4	5
6. Apathy or general lack of interest or involvement of unit members.	1	2	3	4	5
7. Lack of innovation, risk taking, imagination, or initiative.	1	2	3	4	5
8. Ineffective staff meetings.	1	2	3	4	5
9. Problems in working with the boss.	1	2	3	4	5
10. Poor communications: people afraid to speak up, not listening to each other, or not talking together.	1	2	3	4	5
11. The lack of trust between boss and member or between members.	1	2	3	4	5
12. Decisions made that people do not understand or agree with.	1	2	3	4	5
13. People feel that good work is not recognized or rewarded.	1	2	3	4	5
14. People are not encouraged to work together for better team effort.	1	2	3	4	5

Scoring: Add up the score for the 14 items and interpret as follows:

14–28: Few indications of a need for teambuilding.
29–42: Some evidence of a need, but no immediate pressure unless two or three items are very high.
43–56: Seriously think about a team-building program.
57–70: Make team building a top priority.

Box 11-3
Team Development Scale

1. To what extent do I feel a real part of the team?

1	2	3	4	5
Completely all the time.	Most of the time.	On the edge, sometimes in, sometimes out.	Generally outside, except for one or two periods.	On the outside; not really a part of the team.

2. How safe is it in this team to be at ease, relaxed, and myself?

1	2	3	4	5
I feel perfectly safe being myself; they won't hold mistakes against me.	I feel most people accept me if I am completely myself, but I am not sure about some.	Generally you have to be careful what you say or do in this team.	I am quite fearful about being completely myself on this team.	A person would have to be a fool to be him/herself on this team.

3. To what extent do I feel "under wraps," that is, have private thoughts, unspoken reservations, or unexpressed feelings and opinions that I have not felt comfortable bringing out into the open?

1	2	3	4	5
Almost completely under wraps.	Under wraps many times.	Slightly more free and expressive than under wraps.	Quite free and expressive much of the time.	Almost completely free and expressive.

4. How effective are we, in our team, in getting out and using the ideas, opinions, and information of all team members in making decisions?

1	2	3	4	5
Not everyone encouraged to share their ideas, opinions, and information with the team in making decisions.	Only the ideas, opinions, and information of a few are really known and used in making decisions.	Sometimes we hear the views of most members before making decisions and sometimes we disregard most members.	A few are hesitant about sharing their opinions, but we generally have good participation in decision making.	Everyone feels their opinions, ideas, and information are given a fair hearing.

5. To what extent are the goals the team is working toward understood and have meaning to you?

1	2	3	4	5
I feel extremely good about goals of our team.	I feel fairly good, but some things are not too clear or meaningful.	A few things we are doing are clear and meaningful.	Much of the activity is not clear or meaningful to me.	I really do not understand or feel involved in the goals of the team.

6. How well does the team work at its tasks?

1	2	3	4	5
Coasts, loafs, and makes no progress.	Makes a little progress; most members loaf.	Progress is slow; spurts of effective work.	Above average progress and pace of work.	Works well; achieves definite progress.

7. Our planning and the way we operate as a team is largely influenced by:

1	2	3	4	5
One or two team members.	A clique.	Shifts from one person or clique to another.	Shared by the members; some left out.	Shared by all members of the team.

8. What is the level of responsibility for work in our team?

1	2	3	4	5
Each person assumes personal responsibility for getting work done.	A majority of the members assume responsibility for getting work done.	About half assume responsibility; about half do not.	Only a few assume responsibility for getting work done.	Nobody (except for perhaps one) really assumes responsibility for getting work done.

9. How are differences or conflicts handled in our team?

1	2	3	4	5
Differences or conflicts are denied, suppressed, or avoided at all costs.	Differences or conflicts are recognized but remain unresolved.	Differences or conflicts are recognized, and some attempts are made to work them through by some members, often outside the team meetings.	Differences or conflicts are recognized, and some attempts are made to resolve them within the team.	Differences or conflicts are recognized, and the team is usually successful in resolving them within team.

10. What suggestions do you have for improving our team functioning?

LOST DECISIONS   Other key symptoms of ineffectiveness are **lost decisions—** decisions that are made but are not carried out. In these situations nothing happens, and a few weeks later the same matter is raised again. At that point someone comments, "It seems to me we made a decision about that some time ago. Does anyone remember?" Lost decisions are evidence that people are working on matters of low concern, or that decisions are made to which people are not committed. One way of negating an unpopular decision is conveniently to forget that it was made.

CONFLICTS ARE HIDDEN OR SMOOTHED OVER   The effective team can tolerate disagreements and has enough strength to work them through. Teams with low strength or maturity are upset and worried about disagreements. If members take contrary positions the ineffective team finds ways to pretend that differences do not really exist or it ignores the point of conflict.

FIGHTING WITHOUT RESOLUTION IS THE NORM   The reverse of the previous symptom is the continual presence of open verbal fighting. Physical fighting may be more common among some teenage groups, but is not usually found in adult organizations. Verbally trying to put down, devastate, wound, or deject others is a symptom of a deep-rooted team problem.

SELF-INTEREST SUBGROUPS   In almost any group some people get together or associate more with a few members rather than the team as a whole. It may be they have common interests or a stronger work relationship. But when the team needs to deal with matters together, they come together and consider the good of the whole. The subgroups in ineffective teams hold to the subgroups rather than first considering the needs of the total unit.

In considering team effectiveness, note how potential conflicts are dealt with at Intel in the case that follows. Does Intel's approach suggest anything about how conflict can be used to generate new ideas and, ultimately, better decisions?

CASE
Constructive Confrontation at Intel[5]

 "I just don't understand how your new way of measuring things around here will help us at all," the plant manager said, grimacing. Others at the meeting looked puzzled. The vice-president of manufacturing, the plant manager's direct superior, had just finished a presentation in which he strongly urged the use of a statistical indicator to determine whether Intel's plants were delivering products on time. Now the vice-president had to redouble his efforts to convince the doubtful plant manager. Arguments were generated as others at the meeting began to make suggestions. Most of the new ideas were immediately rejected but eventually the arguments dissipated when the still-animated group of people realized that they had come up with the right indicator for the problem at hand.

The vice-president was not at all discouraged by the display of disagreement. In fact, he commented, "It's too bad that people are so reticent." As President Andrew S. Grove of Intel puts it: "As we struggled to establish Intel's place in the sun, people focused almost completely on the task at hand, with no one too concerned about protocol and formality in dealing with co-workers. We kept this style as the company grew." A consultant hired by the company noted the firm's unusual way of handling problems and came up with the term "constructive confrontation" to describe it.

Grove explains the philosophy behind constructive confrontation: "Dealing with conflicts lies at the heart of managing any business. As a result, confrontation—facing issues about which there is disagreement—can be avoided only at the manager's peril. . . . Conflicts must be resolved if the organization is to go forward." ◩

Group-Team Concepts in Management

The importance of teamwork and the synergistic effect of collaboration was recognized early in the development of management. We have already mentioned the Hawthorne studies, which demonstrated the powerful influence a group can have on behavior. Since the Hawthorne studies, a strong emphasis on groups or teams has developed in management research.

Douglas McGregor was another early management writer who emphasized the group-team concept as an important part of organization and management theory. He described a highly effective management team studied by researchers and noted the researchers' conclusion that **unity of purpose** was the main distinguishing characteristic of this successful unit.

> The significance of unity of purpose within a managerial team is given some lip service by most managers, but it is not always recognized that this objective can only be achieved by a closely knit group. Most so-called managerial teams are not teams at all, but collections of individual relationships with the boss in which each individual vies with every other for power, prestige, recognition, and personal autonomy. Under such conditions unit of purpose is a myth.[6]

Another research study of top management groups found that 85 percent of the communications within the group took place between individual subordinates and the superior (up and down), and only 15 percent laterally between the subordinates.[7] Many executives who talk about their "teams" of subordinates would be appalled to discover how low is the actual level of collaboration among them, and how high is the mutual suspicion and antagonism. Yet these same executives generally create the very conditions, which would appall them if recognized, by managing individuals rather than helping to create a genuine group.

At the time McGregor was writing, William W. Whyte had just written *The Orga-nization Man* in which he decried the use of groups in organizations, claiming that group activities had a depressing or leveling effect on individual performance and stultified creativity and individual expression.[8] McGregor commented:

> These views [of Whyte] deny the realities of organizational life. Many activities simply cannot be carried on and many problems cannot be solved on an individual basis or in two person relationships. . . .
>
> In general we are remarkably inept in accomplishing objectives through group effort. This is not inevitable. It is a result of inadequate understanding and skill with respect to the unique aspects of group operation. Whyte's thesis that we have given undue emphasis to group phenomena, and in the process lost track of individuals, misses the point altogether. The real problem is that we have given so little attention to group behavior that management does not know enough about how to create the conditions for individual growth and integrity in the group situation. The problem is one of ignorance based on under, not overemphasis.[9]

Robert Blake and Jane Mouton have widely used the team analogy in describing their **9,9 management** in their writings on organizations. They saw management as a grid along two dimensions—concerns for work results and concerns for the workers, (see Chapter 13). At the 9,9 level both concerns are handled by the team.

> Because the word team is likely to be used to refer to any set of individuals who cooperate in accomplishing a single overall result, the question can be asked whether team action of the kind being described leads to conformity pressures which dampen individuality and stifle independence of effort. The answer is that the opposite is true. True team action is more like a football situation where division of effort is meshed into a single coordinated result; where the whole is more, and different, than the sum of its individual parts. Here, there is a common set of signals, based on understanding, which dictate action—a division of closely knitted individual activity combined with interdependent effort is the 9,9 pattern of integrating individual with organizational effort.[10]

They point out that a good team has task specialization and division of labor.

> Each person shoulders a different part of the total job, with each having 100 percent responsibility for success of a whole . . . Furthermore, it has in common a set of strategies to fit a variety of situations and signals which are well understood . . . and includes:
>
> 1. Team action based on synchronized effort of all.
>
> 2. Pair action, i.e., based on meshing of effort between coach-quarterback, quarter-back-center, etc.
>
> 3. Solo effort, i.e., broken field running, pass interception, etc.[11]

How are managers trained to manage teams? Blake and Mouton state: "The ques-tion becomes, How do organizations which recognize the importance of team action go about training to get it?"[12] A simple answer can be given by analogy to a baseball or football team. Both of these are team organizations in a very real sense, and both are concerned with action. Ridiculous though it sounds, if the conventional approach of training individuals one-by-one were applied in developing a baseball or a football team, each team member would be trained by specialists, also one-by-one, away from the organizations and isolated from the other members of the team. Then all members would be returned to the organization and thrown together on the assumption that since all had learned individually, they automatically would be able to work together effectively. The team would have no need for practice, and no one would think to help the team develop a set of common signals, because each person should have learned all that was needed to become an effective team member in the specialized training program.

The players could also gain specialized training in schools, with one school concerned with training guards, another with centers, etc. After each group has been trained individually, they would be returned to the football club to play together. Both of these examples would lead to absurd results. Each points to the fallacy in logic of a conventional approach to training when the goal of organizational health is successful team action.

DYNAMICS OF GROUPS

Since managers must be able to handle groups of people, the dynamics of group behavior are important for the manager to understand and to manage.

The Decision-Making Dimension[13]

When a group of people works together well, decision-making improves. Research has shown that certain kinds of problem solving—particularly where every group member has a contribution to make—are consistently better, more accurate, and command a greater commitment from members than decisions made by individuals or by voting or averaging the group contributions.[14] But it is important that the group use a consensus process through which all members have an opportunity to express their ideas and opinions and all input is taken into account before reaching the final decision.

If the group is not working well together, the formal decision-making process may be strongly influenced by one dominant person or by a clique or subgroup. Under such conditions, decisions may not represent the best thinking of which the group is capable, and the group may not be strongly committed to implementing the decision. At times decisions should not be made by the total group because the problem is not amenable to group problem solving, or because other constraints make an individual decision more appropriate.[15] Part of the assessment of group process is to determine if the group is using its resources on appropriate decisions.

Sometimes people are intimidated by other group members and become quiet, nonparticipative, and unimaginative. However, if group members can learn such processes as sharing analogies or new ideas and brainstorming, the group can be a stimulus to creative thinking.

Decisions in groups are made at formal and informal levels. Formal decisions with which group members informally disagree are usually either not implemented or ineffective. Open discussion of formal decisions often avoids the problem of contrary informal decisions being made. Whether an open discussion of the formal decision occurs depends on certain other group dimensions already discussed, especially the influence of the authority figure and the prevailing climate.

Group Norms

Every group arrives at a set of formal and/or informal standards or norms that identify for the group member what kinds of behaviors are expected. Sometimes these standards are unrealistic and people work under constant pressure trying to meet the standards established. At the same time, the permissible degree of variance or deviance from the norm is also established.

It is interesting that in many groups the norms that define behavior have never been discussed, let alone written or voted on. Similarly, most families maintain a wide range of unwritten, undiscussed, but clearly understood standards. In some families the standard for the children is to be like the oldest boy or girl. Younger children sometimes go through life trying to measure up to an unfortunate standard. Consider what college students might do if they were taking five classes where each professor establishes a standard of two hours of homework for each hour in class, a physically unrealistic standard. They could defend themselves by copying each other's work, cheating on exams, sharing assignments, trading book reports, and so on.

If a person does not achieve the standards set by the group, self-esteem suffers. Real feelings of inadequacy or guilt may develop. New students in a classroom, or new members of a community often run into standards of work and excellence for which they are unprepared, and they suffer from their inadequacies. Groups need constantly to examine their standards to see if they are realistic in terms of the resources of group members.

Groups also have at their command a kind of awesome power to induce members to conform to their standards. Group members are rewarded by being accepted, included, and praised if they abide by the group norms, but are rejected, excluded, and ridiculed if they do not conform.

THE HAWTHORNE STUDIES   One of the early discoveries made by the Hawthorne studies was the power of group norms. In an effort to determine if worker performance could be enhanced by a monetary incentive, one group of workers was offered a bonus if they would increase their output. Nothing happened, production stayed at the same level whether incentives were added or taken away. When a researcher asked the workers why they did not respond to the incentive, he was told that the group had decided it was not to their advantage to increase production. If they produced more, they reasoned, one of two negative things would result: (1) management either would raise the required output or (2) management would find that the increased output decreased the number of workers needed. Hence, the group norm that evolved, stipulated that no one would produce more than the group standard. Informal group rewards and punishments were applied to ensure compliance.[16]

THE EXPERIMENTS OF SHERIF   The early work of the social psychologist Muzafer Sherif showed how a group can influence an individual's actions. Sherif used the autokinetic effect in some group experiments. He knew that all humans experience the same effect when they stare at a point of light in a dark field. After staring for a time, the dot of light *appears* to move (autokinetic effect). He tested individuals and found that some saw the light shifting 6 inches, others as much as 3 feet.

Each tested individual was then put into a dark room with five other people who were all confederates of the researcher. The researcher knew the naive subjects saw the dot only moving 6 inches. The confederates, who spoke first, were told to say they saw the light move somewhere between 1½ and 2 feet. As each confederate reported, the subject heard people say they saw the light move far greater than the subject did. When it came time for the naive subject to report, nearly half of the subjects would deny their own visual description and would say they saw the light move between 1½ and 2 feet. They did not want to be at variance with the group for one thing, and the report of others made them doubt the accuracy of their own position.[17]

GROUP NORMS AND ORGANIZATIONAL NEEDS   Some group standards may be regarded as contrary to the needs of the organization or management, while others contribute to the formal organization. In one manufacturing company, the norm allowed workers to take as long as they needed on their rest breaks. The occasional lengthy rest periods that resulted could be interpreted as contrary to the best interests of the company. According to another of the workers' norms, however, everyone would pitch in and work extra hard or long without extra compensation in times of emergency. The two conditions balanced out for the company, and management agreed to the work crews' norms. The point is that if an introduced change opposes group norms, resistance is predictable. Anyone planning change would be well advised to study the norms of the groups involved by observing group action or asking group members why certain behaviors or conditions exist.

Group Involvement

The essence of the involvement principle is that most people work most productively and happily when they are involved in establishing their own goals and procedures. When all of the group members work together with a high degree of involvement in setting up what they are to do and how they are to do it, they have a sense of commitment that is not present when the goals are imposed on them. The high degree of personal involvement among the managers at Intel, for instance, helps to ensure that the group is committed to the final decision.

Kurt Lewin found that in decision making, where the group as a whole made the decision to have the group members change their method of operation, the results were from two to ten times more effective than in situations where groups were asked to make changes as a result of lectures exhorting them to change.[18]

In industry the results are striking. When groups are given the responsibility for their own goals and procedures, productivity and morale are increased.

Groups are often caught in an interesting dilemma in setting their own goals. On one hand, people like to be involved and to participate in the planning for their own actions. On the other hand, when they are not used to doing this, or they run into conflict with people who have slightly different goals, or they cannot agree on procedures, it is often easier to rely on an authority to tell them what to do and how to do it. In this case it is the supervisor's job to keep after them to do the job, and it is her problem if the work does not get done. When a group constantly turns to authorities to do this work, dependency is reinforced. When people are not involved in the decision making, they can belong to a group for years and never really participate.

Feedback

Feedback is a term drawn from the field of engineering. In missile guidance systems feedback is the process whereby electronic computers detect the missile going off course and feedback data into the direction device allowing the missile to get back on the right track. Groups and individuals need to have a similar type of mechanism; that is, some way of finding out when they are behaving in ways that are seen as "off the track" so they can find out how they can get back on the right course.

It is not easy either to give or to receive feedback. People are reluctant to tell others their mistakes; as one well-known commercial for breath fresheners advertises, "even your best friends won't tell you." Also, people who are told they are "off the track" often react in very defensive ways to protect themselves. A common reaction when someone tells us our errors is to attack and point out the other person's faults.

Groups need to develop the kind of **climate** or atmosphere in which feedback can be expressed with the real understanding that it is given in a helpful way. More groups need to have some way of looking at what they are doing and getting some evaluation and feedback on how the group is working. Individuals and groups can err. If they are to improve, they need to recognize their errors in such a way that the persons involved are not damaged, but helped.

Group Climate

The emotional climate or atmosphere in a business setting is very real yet very difficult to measure. People are affected dramatically by the emotional milieu within

Groups need to maintain the kind of climate that fosters honest feedback.

which they must live and work. There is a great contrast between the permissive or accepting climate and the defensive or rejecting one. Everyone has been in work situations where the prevailing mood of the group was cold or formal or fun or sad. Most people have been involved with a group where everything seemed to go right; where the good feeling was so strong that people hated to see the meeting or activity come to a close.

What are some of the ingredients that go into creating the type of climate that produces this type of healthy well-being? Some factors have already been mentioned—involvement of the total group in the problem at hand, adequate and helpful group standards, leaders who work *with* not *over* their subordinates, and a healthy feedback system. The following factors should also be considered.

ACCEPTANCE OF THOSE DIFFERENT FROM OURSELVES   People are not all cut from the same cloth, and all have something to contribute. Acceptance does not require liking everyone on an intimate basis; individuals can learn to appreciate others despite major differences. In one study, a group of managers were asked first: "Who do you like best in the organization?" After they listed their choices, they were asked: "Who has the best ideas in the organization?" As might be expected, they listed the same choices.[19] The managers would probably admit that the people they liked were not all brilliant, creative, sensitive, and so on. But their answers indicate a need for all managers to beware of letting their personal feelings distort their perceptions of others.

REAL, NOT PRETENDED INTEREST   Some interesting studies have shown that people can readily detect persons who are sincerely interested in others in contrast to persons who are only pretending an interest. Most people shudder at the hearty, "Well, how are you today?" given by doctors, salesmen, and others who assume a professional but not a real interest. In a study of a hospital ward the patients were asked with whom they talked over their important problems. The professional staff were greatly surprised when patients listed such persons as the janitor, the elevator boy, their mothers, the patient in the next bed, etc. In the 75 interviews made, not a single mention was made of the professional people working with the patient.[20] Fortunately, research has also shown that people are capable of becoming more open and honestly concerned about others.[21]

HONEST APPROVAL AND DISAPPROVAL   People like to work and live in situations where they receive approval for work well done and are told honestly and fairly when their work is below par. Too often people assume that others they are close to—family, friends, colleagues—know that they approve of and like them and thus never share their approval.

In giving praise and criticism, managers should be careful about using the so-called sandwich technique—slipping a piece of criticism between two slices of praise. "John, you did a real fine job last week, *but* I want to talk to you about what you did yesterday. Aside from this problem you are doing a fine job." The sandwich technique robs the praise of any impact. Subordinates soon learn to brace themselves for criticism any time they hear a statement of praise.

LISTENING INSTEAD OF ALWAYS TELLING   Communication is part listening and part telling, but often listening skills are very low. The climate of a group is drastically different when people feel they are listened to rather than feeling that they have to fight to get a word in edgewise.

ALLOWING PEOPLE TO MAKE MISTAKES   In a defensive climate, people usually spend their time trying to defend themselves against those in authority. They do not have the time or emotional energy to be creative—to grow and mature—for their energies are dissipated in trying to protect themselves. The creation of an accepting group atmosphere fosters the emotional health and maturity of individual group members.

In summary, the impact of the group on individual behavior is great. A smooth-running group can enhance the contributions of individuals, while certain group behaviors may stifle these individual contributions and prevent the synergistic effect associated with the group decision-making process. Groups whose members are not understanding, involved, and open may face serious problems.

METHODS OF TEAM BUILDING

Managerial groups make mistakes because they cannot work effectively as a team. For the work unit that has decided that some problems are blocking their collaborative efforts or that the group dynamics are poor, several traditional ways to engage in team-building programs are available. The following are three of the most widely used team-building formats.

Problem-Solving Approach

This widely used method represents classic problem solving applied to team situations. Either by use of interviews, surveys, or direct input by workers, data are gathered to address the question: "What keeps this unit from being as effective as it could be?" When a list of problems or barriers is compiled, the next step is to engage in some type of action-taking or problem-solving behavior that removes the barriers. This is a rational approach to the matter, but unfortunately the problems often do not lend themselves to an easy rational solution. If the barriers to effective teamwork are (1) a lack of trust between members, (2) a failure to share sensitive information, (3) a feeling of competition for advancements, or (4) a supervisor's abrasive style—what set of actions can be devised to address these issues? Team building often bogs down in the problem-solving approach because the unit cannot just "do" what must be done to deal with the problems that have been identified.

Process Analysis Approach

It is possible to combine process analysis with the problem-solving approach, but basically this approach involves helping people look at the kinds of interactions the team is experiencing and the ways the team gets work done. Process analysis centers on watching the team work together, focusing on how the team works on problems. This approach comes out of the group dynamics movement, including its use of the T-group or encounter group. The advantage of process analysis over problem solving is the opportunity it provides to watch the team in action, confront members with their actual behaviors, and then look at changes or modifications that should be made.

The disadvantage of process analysis is that certain key team issues may not get translated directly into observable group process. Examples include a team member's lack of technical competence that reduces the willingness of others to use that person's expertise, a member's uneasiness with the ability of the manager to represent the team upward in the organization or to the external public, and the need for the redesign of work to improve the effectiveness of the team functioning.

Role and Expectation Clarification

A useful team-building approach—for certain kinds of team problems—has been to find out each team member's expectation of himself or herself—what his or her role is, and what, when, and how that person feels he or she is expected to perform. Others in the work group then give their understanding of what they expect of this team member. Differing expectations result in clarification and adjustment. Roles are defined and feedback is shared as people talk with each other about unmet expectations and their feelings about such matters. This model addresses most of the problems teams face, but does not handle process problems, unless process observation and consultation is included.

The Role of Commitment

A key ingredient that spells success or failure regardless of the team building approach used is the shared, verbal commitment of team managers or leaders and the level of commitment of unit members. Many who have conducted team-building sessions in organizations have observed that nothing really changes in the team's behavior. This has led to an in-depth review and analysis of activity to determine what went wrong. Was the manager using an inappropriate approach? Were they not spending enough time on team building? Were the skills of the manager inadequate? Were problems so deep or pervasive that nothing could surface and handle them?

The most critical factor in lack of team success appears to be the lack of commitment of the unit manager and/or unit members in truly wanting to build a better work team. The success of team-building programs is unlikely if the leader is suspicious, unconvinced, half-hearted, or engaging in the activity because of pressure from above. It is important to hear the manager as he or she talks to the subordinates say something like: "I want this work group to be as good as it can be. Some things keep us from being as effective as we could be. That disturbs me, and it disturbs me that I may be part of the problem. But I am willing to spend my time, energy, and resources to make this group as effective as possible, and I am willing to make needed changes. I need to know how you feel about building the team. What are your real feelings? I don't think we ought to start unless all of us are truly committed to the activity."

Group or Team Leadership

Although many leadership issues are handled in detail in the formal "leadership" chapter, it is valuable here to talk about leadership as it applies to group dynamics and teams. An old Chinese proverb from Lao-tzu describes what makes a good leader:

> A leader is best when people barely know he exists, not so good when they obey him, worse when they despise him. But of a good leader, who talks little, when his work is done and his aim fulfilled, they will say, "We did it ourselves."

With the emergence of teams as the primary vehicle through which work gets done in modern organizations, team leadership has become increasingly important. The team leader represents a different situational context for looking at the leader's role and actions. One who manages or leads these teams must be able to deal with the dynamics of a working group.

Box 11-4

Task and Relationship Functions in Teams

Task Functions

1. **Initiating** Getting actions started, suggesting goals, procedures, ways of working or handling issues.

2. **Opinion giving** Sharing your opinion or ideas about actions.

3. **Opinion seeking** Asking others for their ideas or opinions.

4. **Elaborating** Developing or expanding another's idea or suggestion.

5. **Coordinating** Pulling together and integrating the various contributions already made.

6. **Summarizing** Developing a conclusion that summarizes the work of the group.

7. **Decision testing** Seeing if people are ready to make a decision, and if so, arriving at a group decision.

Relationship Functions

1. **Encouraging** Asking for and stimulating others to make their contribution.

2. **Supporting** Giving recognition, praise, and understanding.

3. **Tension releasing** Providing humor and releasing built-up pressure or stress.

4. **Gate keeping** Facilitating the involvement and participation of others—calling on them or asking for their contribution. Literally opening the conversation so they can get in to the discussion.

---

1. **Process observation** Stopping and assessing what one sees happening in the group.

2. **Critiquing** At the end of a group session, getting people to critique the session—what went well, what needs to be improved.

3. **Feedback** Sharing data with others as to the impact others have in the group and recommendations for improvement.

THE TASK-FEELING LEVEL One of the most significant findings of research on groups has been the recognition of two levels of group action: actions to complete the task at hand and actions to maintain the ability of the team to function. (See Box 11-4.) People need maintenance; they get tired, angry, frustrated, apathetic, tense, and so forth while working together. Too often groups ignore these feelings and try to move all the more quickly to finish the task before the group blows up. Just getting the group to agree on the action to be taken is assumed to be all that is needed; however, if work is to be accomplished in teams, certain key functions at both the task and relationship levels, as listed in Box 11-4, must be accomplished.

Observing the range of functions that should be performed in a successful team, it is apparent that if the team leader performs all of these alone, the leader will be a very busy person indeed. One way for the team leader to handle these functions is to involve others and get greater contributions from everyone by adopting a shared leadership stance.

SHARED LEADERSHIP   Shared leadership means that the leader is willing to allow and even encourages others to perform some of the task or relationship functions. A leader must have enough confidence, however, not to feel threatened by sharing leadership with others. This can be done in several ways: (1) allow others to conduct the group meeting from time to time; (2) appoint different people to be responsible for a particular function during a group meeting. For example: "Mary, you are to be the group's gatekeeper this session. Tom, your responsibility will be to try and summarize our discussion and see if we have reached a decision."

It is not a waste of time for groups to take time to ensure that misunderstandings are cleared, to relieve tension, visit and relax, tell jokes, and exchange personal experiences. These are some of the maintenance functions that keep the group in a state of health so it can accomplish its task. While society is more and more task-oriented, groups that carry out those tasks ignore the feelings and emotions of people at their own peril.

ENDING CASE
The Trip to Abilene: A Modern Parable[22]

 A young man and his bride are visiting her folks in the town of Coleman, Texas. Coleman is in the middle of the plains; the wind blows, and it gets hot. It is the middle of the summer and the town of five thousand has little to do. The young man, his wife, and her parents are sitting around on a Sunday afternoon, drinking lemonade and playing dominoes. From all appearances, the family is having a good time. Suddenly and surprisingly the father-in-law says, "Why don't we all get dressed and drive to Abilene." Abilene is 53 miles away over a winding road. The son-in-law knows that their automobile does not have air conditioning, and in order to keep the wind from blowing the dust in, they would have to roll the windows up. He also knows that the only place to eat that is open in Abilene on a Sunday afternoon is the Good Luck Cafeteria. The food there leaves much to be desired, but he thinks, "If my father-in-law wants to go to Abilene, I guess it's all right."

So the son-in-law says, "That sounds fine to me. I mean if Beth (his wife) wants to go."

And Beth says, "Well, yes, if everyone wants to go to Abilene, that's fine—if Mother really wants to go."

Mother replies, "Oh, yes, if you all want to go, well, that's where I want to go."

They all put on their Sunday clothes, climb into the old Buick, and take a long, hot, dusty trip to Abilene. Sure enough, the only place open is the Good Luck Cafeteria. They have a greasy meal, crowd into the automobile, and drive 53 miles home.

Finally, worn out, hot, tired, dusty, irritable, they struggle back into the house, and find another glass of lemonade. The father-in-law says, "Boy, am I glad that's over! If there's anything I didn't want to do, it was to go to Abilene. I sure wouldn't have gone, if you three hadn't pressured me into it!"

The son-in-law says, "What do you mean, you didn't want to go to Abilene? And what do you mean, we pressured you into it? I only went because the rest of you wanted to go. I didn't pressure anybody."

His wife speaks up, "What do you mean? I didn't want to go to Abilene. The only reason I went was because you, Mama, and Daddy wanted to go."

Mother chimes in, "I didn't want to go to Abilene. That's the last place in the world I wanted to go. I only went because Father and the two of you said you wanted to go."

Father expands on his previous statement. "As I said before, I didn't want to go to Abilene. I just suggested going because I was afraid everybody was really bored sitting around playing dominoes, and I thought you might prefer to do something else. I was just sort of making conversation, hoping you'd suggest something better, but I really didn't expect you to take me up on my idea."

SUMMARY

Modern organizations require collaboration in the form of teamwork to make decisions or plans, set goals, and accomplish work. Effective teamwork is characteristic of successful organizations. Therefore, modern managers must develop the capacity to manage effective teams to succeed.

Different activities require varying levels of teamwork. The greater the number of people involved and the more interrelated the task, the higher the level of teamwork required.

A number of instruments are available to help managers spot symptoms of team ineffectiveness, to gauge how effectively their teams are functioning, to know when to devote more time to team building, and to know how much effort will be required to make their team become effective.

A shuttle crew operates on a high level of teamwork.

Douglas McGregor has shown that unity of purpose is the main distinguishing characteristic of effective teams. Rensis Likert has shown that participative group action is the most effective way to deal with the complex problems facing modern organizations.

Research into group dynamics indicates: (1) consensus decisions for some types of situations are consistently better, are more accurate, and command greater commitment than individual decisions or those based on majority rule or compromise; (2) group norms possess powerful control over individual action; (3) decisions reached through active participation of group members are much more effective in achieving change than decisions reached as a result of exhortation to change; (4) effective feedback is necessary for groups to bring about needed change but requires an open and accepting climate within the group; (5) a healthy group climate is the result of acceptance of individual differences, sincere interest in group members, honest evaluation of performance, listening by leaders to group members, and allowance for mistakes; and (6) groups need time to perform maintenance functions that pay attention to the feelings and emotions of members.

Problem solving, process analysis, and role and expectation clarification are three of the most widely used methods of team building. Each has strengths and weaknesses. Regardless of the approach used, the shared, verbal commitment of leaders and team members is the most important factor determining successful team building.

KEY TERMS

Collaboration
Teamness
Team development
Overdependency
Lost decisions
Self-interest subgroup
Unity of purpose

Feedback
Group climate
Problem-Solving approach
Role and expectation clarification
Task functions
Relationship functions

REVIEW QUESTIONS

1. What factors determine the level of teamness required in an organization?

2. Name three characteristics of a mature team.

3. List the seven symptoms of ineffective teams discussed in the chapter.

4. What is the main distinguishing chartacteristic of successful teams?

5. What type of group action is most effective for dealing with the complex problems of modern organizations according to the research conducted by Rensis Likert?

6. According to Blake and Mouton, what question should organizations that recognize the importance of team action ask themselves?

7. What happens to the quality of decisions in groups that are not working well together?

8. What influence is likely to affect team members more, the team leader or group norms?

9. What effect does participation in goal setting and group procedures have on team productivity?

10. What is necessary for effective feedback in a group or team?

11. What are six things that a team leader can do to improve the group climate of a team?

12. What are three methods that are used to build teams? What are the strengths and weaknesses of each?

13. Why do informal leaders emerge in groups or teams?

14. What are three task functions? How do they differ from relationship functions?

CHALLENGE QUESTIONS

1. To what do you attribute the remarks about team effectiveness listed at the beginning of the chapter? Why is stated organizational support of teamwork not enough to produce good results?

2. How would you rank the following in order of teamness required in successfully completing the task involved:
   A. A student study group
   B. A group project for class
   C. An intramural basketball team
   D. A school debating team

3. How do the instruments listed in the chapter help team leaders discover problems and identify areas for concentration in team-building efforts?

4. How would you develop unity of purpose in a team?

5. If consensus decision making yields improved decision making in many situations, what implications does this have for labor relations in business?

6. How would you prevent a group that you are leading from developing overdependency on you?

7. What factors in a group climate can prevent or distort accurate feedback?

8. Explain the concept of the "good leader" as expressed by Lao-tzu and how it relates to team leadership.

9. How does delegation facilitate the accomplishment of task and relationship functions in teams? Give an example of delegation that accomplishes each separately and one that facilitates both at the same time.

CASE AND RELATED QUESTIONS

1. Name an action that Jim Thomas could take to overcome each of the eight problems listed in the case at the beginning of the chapter.

2. Why is it easier to analyze the failings of sports teams than to understand the dynamics of work teams? Why do managers fail to see themselves as team leaders?

3. What process did the Intel group use to come up with a solution to the problem they faced?

4. At Intel, what types of disagreement are encouraged? What is the inherent danger in this type of situation? How would you prevent the types of problems you foresee with Intel's approach from becoming disruptive of team goals?

5. What was the problem with how the group in the end case related to each other? Did anyone really want to go to Abilene?

6. Cite an example from your own life in which you or someone you know became involved in a "Trip to Abilene."

7. Why would this family team agree to something no one really wants to do?

8. Have you seen examples of teams taking a "Trip to Abilene"—doing things that people don't feel good about?

9. Why do teams make these types of dysfunctional decisions?

ENDNOTES

1. Case from William G. Dyer, *Team Building: Issues and Alternatives*, 2nd ed. (Reading, MA: Addison-Wesley, 1987), pp. 3–6.

2. Rensis Likert, *New Patterns of Management* (New York: McGraw-Hill, 1961).

3. M. Mascowitz, "Lessons from the Best Companies to Work for," *California Management Review* (Winter 1985), pp. 42–47.

4. Seminar conducted by William G. Dyer.

5. "Constructive Confrontation at Intel," *Business Week*, April 5, 1987.

6. Douglas McGregor, *The Human Side of Enterprise* (New York: McGraw-Hill, 1960).

7. Henry Mintzberg, *The Nature of Managerial Work* (Englewood Cliffs, NJ: Prentice-Hall, 1973).

8. William W. Whyte, *The Organization Man* (New York: Simon and Schuster, 1956).

9. McGregor, p. 227.

10. R. R. Blake, J. S. Mouton and M. G. Blansfield, "How Executive Team Training Can Help You," *Training and Development Journal*, January 1962.

11. Ibid.

12. Ibid.

13. The following sections are based on and some of the material quoted verbatim from William G. Dyer, *The Sensitive Manipulator* (Provo, UT: Brigham Young University Press, 1972), pp. 50–58.

14. Kurt Lewin, "Group Decision and Social Change," *Readings in Social Psychology*, eds. Macoby, Newcomb, and Hartley (New York: Henry Holt and Co., 1958), pp. 197–212.

15. Paul R. Timm and Brent D. Peterson, *People at Work: Human Relations in Organizations* (St. Paul, MN: West Pub. Co., 1982).

16. For a more recent review of these studies, see Ronald Greenwood, Alfred A. Bolton, and Regina A. Greenwood, "Hawthorne a Half Century Later: Relay Assembly Participants Remember," *Journal of Management*, Fall–Winter 1983, pp. 217–31.

17. M. Sherif, *The Psychology of Social Norms* (New York: Harper, 1936); Later works include M. Sherif and C. Sherif, *Groups in Harmony and Tension* (New York: Harper and Row, 1953); and M. Sherif and C. Sherif, "Experiments in Group Conflict," *Scientific American*, March 1956, pp. 54–58.

18. Lewin, p. 201.

19. William G. Dyer, *Insight to Impact: Strategies for Interpersonal and Organizational Change* (Provo, UT: BYU Press, 1972).

20. This study is from unpublished research conducted by Jack Gibb.

21. Sidney M. Jourard, *The Transparent Self* (Princeton, NJ: D. Van Nostrand, 1964).

22. For more information concerning forcefield analysis as a change strategy, see Lewin.

CHAPTER 12

ORGANIZATION DEVELOPMENT AND CHANGE

LEARNING OBJECTIVES

■ Identify the basic steps of the planned change process.

■ Understand why evaluation of the change after implementation is critical to successful change.

■ Explain the difference between individual change and collective change.

■ Discuss the contribution of the Hawthorne studies to change strategy.

■ Explain the different methods by which change is attempted through force-field analysis, and know which one of these methods is most critical to successful change.

■ Understand the basic elements of Dalton's Model and why all of these elements are essential for successful change.

■ Explain why intervention reinforcement is important after a change has been implemented.

■ Recognize both the differences and similarities of system and culture change.

■ Discuss the ethical problems involved in change strategies, and how ethical change is attempted.

■ Understand what manipulation is as it relates to change, and how it can be avoided.

■ Explain why it is critical that problems be identified correctly before change is attempted.

■ Understand the concept of spread effect, and why it is necessary to plan for it when attempting change.

Nyloncraft Inc. was plagued by absenteeism, and its turnover rate was approaching 400 percent when senior manager Ken Harkleroad decided it was time for a change. Instead of hiring a highly paid consulting firm, Harkleroad decided that face-to-face interviews with Nyloncraft's 450 employees, 85 percent of whom are women, would be more useful. Harkleroad described his method and what he learned as follows: "I spent a lot of time out on the floor talking to them about their problems, and there was a constant worry about children." This worry had resulted in the company having to write over 900 W2s for 1978, a year in which Nyloncraft employed about 250 people and, given the cost of training—about $2,000 per employee—the problem was a $1.3 million drain on earnings.

Harkleroad and Bob Tennyson, the other manager hired by owner Jim Wyllie when he took over the company after buying out relatives, were convinced that some sort of day-care arrangement might make good business sense. A company survey revealed that employees could afford day-care but could not find a reliable provider.

The company thus decided to provide its own day-care facilities and committed itself to a quality program. Suzanne Colley, director of the center, says Wyllie, "wanted the day care to be something they could really monitor and control. They didn't want any excuses from employees about why they weren't using it."

The implementation of day care was more difficult than merely making the decision to change. "In our ignorance," Harkleroad says, "we thought that there was nothing more to this than padding a room and putting kids in it." Nyloncraft's management soon learned that companies choose not to have their own centers for some very good reasons.

The company's plants in Mishawka and South Bend, Indiana, run 24 hours a day while Indiana day-care regulations apply only to centers open 8 hours. State regulations forbade cleaning while children were on the premises—not an easy rule to keep for a facility operating night and day. The state took a hard line at first. Finally, Wyllie told the representative that since the regulations did not apply to a 24-hour facility he would just go ahead and take his chances. When Wyllie contacted then-Governor Otis Brown his problems with the Welfare Department disappeared. Still to come were fire, health, and sanitation checks, and certification by the Department of Public Instruction (the center planned to offer preschool and kindergarten programs). Finally, in June of 1981, the Nyloncraft Learning Center opened its doors.

How has the center fared in helping the company achieve its objectives? In 1984, the company wrote just 26 more W2s than it had jobs and absenteeism dropped to less than 3 percent. Of the employees eligible to use the facility, 75 percent of them do so. The center costs the company approximately $50,000 per year, but the after-tax consequences are much less severe, and reduced training costs have made the investment back many times over.

A company's decision to provide its own day-care facility for its employees is an example of corporate change.

While the company underestimated the problems of opening the center, it likewise underestimated the benefits. The following is a partial list of benefits linked directly to the center:

1. Improved community relations. The company obtained approval to build a factory on land obtained for a song at a public auction, but not zoned for manufacturing. When some members of the town council and zoning commission visited the plant and saw the learning center, a zoning change was made without a dissenting vote.

2. The learning center has become a sales tool. Says Wyllie, "It wasn't intended, but you bring somebody to the learning center and their whole attitude toward us is, if this company is this progressive, then they must be somebody I want to do business with." Milt Bukes, purchasing agent for Ford Motor Co. says, "The bottom line is that any company that cares about their people like that has to be one hell of a company."

3. Higher quality. Lower turnover goes hand-in-hand with higher quality. Ford recently presented Nyloncraft with its Q-1 Preferred Quality Award for outstanding performance.

4. Employee recruitment has benefitted. Betty LaSalle, Nyloncraft's personnel manager, notes, "People know this is a progressive company because the president feels so strongly about the center. They enjoy working for a company that really cares about its people. That, in effect, has made my job easier."

While a day-care center in isolation would be insufficient to produce the benefits experienced at Nyloncraft, how the company assessed its turnover and absenteeism problems is symptomatic of how it approaches all its people problems. The bottom line is that Nyloncraft listens to its employees' problems and tries to help them. The message is clear: Listening to employees is a very good, very cheap source of data in evaluating problems and in implementing change. ⬛

INTRODUCTION

A strong case can be made that a manager's most critical function comes when key goals or objectives of the organization are not met and something must be changed. There are times when a condition arises that requires a modification or improvement if the goals of the organization are to be achieved. Organization development is the term used to describe the systematic action taken to deal with those conditions that reduce worker effectiveness in the organization.

In the Nyloncraft case, the creation of a child day-care center is an example of the organization development process. A problem is identified and analyzed, and action is taken that improves the problem condition. Employees are now able to stay on the job and feel secure that their children are being well-cared for.

This change by adding a day-care center did not disrupt anything in the on-going organization. Sometimes changes occur in organizations that are so wide spread and impactful that the whole organization requires adjustment. In 1986, Exxon Oil Company, the largest oil company in the world at that time, made a decision to "downsize" its organization. This meant reducing total manpower by about 30 percent, combining some divisions, eliminating others, and generally revamping the total organization in the interest of reducing costs at a time the world was experiencing an oil glut. These major changes are different in scope than a more limited organization development action, but the goals are the same—to diagnose an organization's problems and take actions that are designed to solve the problem condition.

Planned change is the term used to describe this process of systematically going about solving an organization's problems, whether the problem is relatively small or organization-shaking. Since managers are the ones to direct a planned change effort, let us look at what is involved in this process.

PLANNED CHANGE

In planning for change, the distinction between *planned* and *unplanned* change should be noted. Unplanned changes occur frequently, often randomly, in all organizations. One cannot predict most accidents, deaths, economic reversals, wars, etc., that may impact an organization and its outputs. Planned change represents a conscious, predetermined strategy of action to bring about desired consequences. It is the management of planned change that is the manager's challenge.

Steps in the Planned Change Process

Planned change usually begins with a problem or condition that requires some adjustment or improvement. A general strategy of change is shown in Figure 12-1, which outlines seven steps ordinarily considered important in the change process.

STEP ONE: IDENTIFY THE PROBLEM   All planned change strategies begin with a condition that someone feels needs improvement. As will be discussed later, the success of the change plan depends on the degree that everyone involved realizes that a problem exists, defines it the same way, and agrees that improvement of the condition is desirable.

Change programs get bogged down quickly if some people see the problem one way but others either see it differently or do not admit a problem even exists. Problem identification includes a general consensus regarding what the problem is as well as its cause. The strategy begins with identifying the problem as clearly as possible; step four in the process allows for redefinition after some data gathering and analysis has occurred.

STEP TWO: GATHER DATA   Accurate data is central to the creation of change because it tells us what the problem is and why it exists. At Nyloncraft, the company had data on employee turnover and absenteeism; it did not have data on what was the cause of the problem. While primary and secondary sources of data exist, the information collected from primary sources tends to be more accurate.

Primary Sources of Data   The best **primary source of data** is direct observation. This method cannot be applied to some problems, but it was very useful in helping Harkleroad determine why many of his Nyloncraft employees were often late and why they so frequently left the company altogether. This approach has already been referred to as MBWA—Managing by walking around—and is aimed at gathering direct information about what is actually going on. Using this approach, Harkleroad went out into the plant and talked directly to the employees, asked them what their

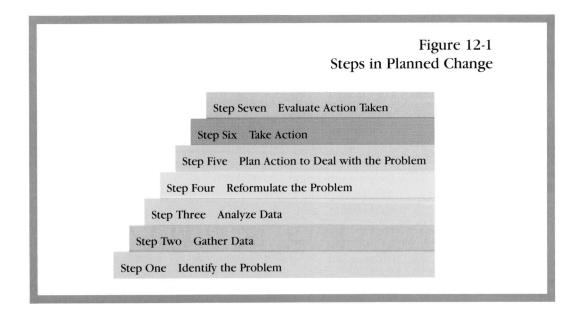

Figure 12-1
Steps in Planned Change

Step Seven   Evaluate Action Taken

Step Six   Take Action

Step Five   Plan Action to Deal with the Problem

Step Four   Reformulate the Problem

Step Three   Analyze Data

Step Two   Gather Data

Step One   Identify the Problem

problems and concerns were, and listened to their responses. While not very sophisticated, direct observation by a competent observer is often all that is needed to discover the cause of a problem.

Interviews or written comments from those directly involved in the situation under examination constitute a primary source. Yet the use of interviews, questionnaires, or surveys does not always elicit the total truth. If the data giver feels threatened by the interviewer or fears that the data may be misused to his or her detriment, the information may not be accurate. Sometimes, those in superior positions are sources of threat and should not be gathering data. Under such circumstances, it would be best to have an outside person (a consultant or personnel specialist) conduct the interview or survey.

Secondary Sources of Data   **Secondary sources of data** include anything other than direct observation or input from those involved such as, for example, input from an informant who has talked to someone directly involved but has not been personally involved in the problem. Secondary sources are often used with good reason but may be inaccurate. Records and reports are secondary sources that reflect reality but may be falsified, left incomplete, or slanted to reflect a particular bias.

Too often, managers plan action based on inadequate secondary sources of data. When a problem is raised at a management meeting (such as may have occurred at Nyloncraft), someone usually asks, "Why does the problem exist?" At that point, people supply secondary data that may be totally biased or inaccurate: "What I've heard is that a lot of our female employees just work for as long as it takes them to qualify for unemployment."; or "Some people have told me that the women don't like the foremen." It is wise to arrange more direct data gathering before action is planned or taken.

STEP THREE: ANALYZE DATA   A frequency tabulation—how many people said what, or how many times something occurred—and an intensity tabulation—how strongly people feel about something—are often helpful in diagnosing a problem. Surveys and interviews often indicate that a certain action occurs rather infrequently but has strong impact when it does. One organizational study reported that workers were very threatened by the possibility of an emotional explosion from a certain key executive. Such outbursts happened only once every year or so, but the unpleasant consequences were remembered for a long time. These incidents became a part of the organization's mythology, and all newcomers heard about this particular manager. In determining why this manager is not as effective as desired, it would be important to find out the intensity of feelings of subordinates regarding the manager's behavior—not just the frequency of the outbursts.

Following the tabulation by frequency and intensity, it is useful to sort the data into three categories: (1) Type A—a condition that can be changed or acted upon directly; (2) Type B—a condition that can be handled by someone whom the data gatherer must influence; and (3) Type C—unchangeable conditions that must be coped with.

CASE
Intermountain Metals Company

 The Intermountain Metals Company had a serious problem with its Edgemont plant, which had been in operation for a year without producing the projected output; moreover, nearly half the first-line foremen had resigned. After a major change program was instituted, a team of outside and inside change specialists spent a month gathering data. They interviewed all currently employed and former managers and administered an organization analysis survey to all current and former employees. In the data analysis phase, the information about why people quit and why they felt production was down was sorted out this way.

Type A Factors   Those that can be handled directly—targets of change:

1. The production process was completed and new workers were shoved into the line before they were adequately trained.

2. Departments were in conflict with one another, particularly production and maintenance, and production and supply.

Type B Factors   Those someone else must handle—targets of influence:

1. The plant was required to use certain equipment designed by people who were not located at the plant. The equipment was seen as dysfunctional.

2. The budget for training new employees was drastically cut by the corporate training department.

Type C Factors   Those that are not amenable to change—targets for coping:

1. The plant was located a long way from the community where most workers live. They did not like the long commute.
2. Other companies located close to the live-in community began to hire and attract company employees.

The data sorting shows that the Type A factors can be targets of change for the Intermountain Metals Company. Solving the first Type A problem may be dependent on influencing the corporate training department to restore funds for training (the second Type B factor). Sharing with corporate headquarters new data showing that the lack of training has influenced output becomes a logical plan of action in this case. Within the plant, some types of interdepartmental team building could be initiated to deal with the second Type A problem.

    The two Type C factors are difficult to solve. It is not possible to move the plant close to the community or move the community close to the plant. It is possible for management to create some conditions that would allow employees to accept the situation better. For example, the company could institute paid travel time, allow company transportation, or give proof of how company benefits compensate for the extra travel. In addition, while the company cannot stop its competitors from hiring away personnel, it can make its own working conditions such that people will want to stay.

STEP FOUR: REFORMULATE THE PROBLEM   Following the analysis of data, the original or presenting problem becomes refocused because of greater information. In the metals company case, the initial problems were a low production rate and a high turnover of personnel. Although these conditions remained the central issues, data-gathering and analysis showed that the factors behind these problems were inadequately trained workers and departmental conflicts, both of which made competitive employment opportunities more attractive. The reformulation of the problem showed that the action plan should address technology issues, departmental conflicts, and inadequate training.

STEP FIVE: PLAN ACTION TO DEAL WITH THE PROBLEM   Having determined why the problem exists, it is possible to begin developing a plan of action to deal with the problem condition. For example, if the problem is located in the social system at an intergroup level (interdepartmental conflict), the action plan should include some action that would reduce the difficulties between departments.

    Action planning is often a mix of empirical and creative processes. The empirical aspect involves studying the literature and examining the types of change actions that have been used in the past on similar problems and their degree of success. Sometimes past experience is unavailable to draw upon. The creative process addresses the kind of change action that would have to be created to have the best chance of reducing or eliminating the problem.

STEP SIX: TAKE ACTION   After the plan has been carefully developed, it must be implemented. Success in the change program is often dependent on support through sufficient resources, time, and commitment of key personnel to ensure optimal impact. Experienced managers often describe this phase as the most difficult. Just as a perfectly diagrammed football play gains no yardage without proper execution, a planned change will fail without proper implementation.

STEP SEVEN: EVALUATE ACTION TAKEN   Too often change programs omit advance determination of how success or failure will be measured; ideally, the plan should be monitored carefully to assess the actual impact of the action on those involved. Evaluation may mean a review of production records for a period of time, looking at turnover or grievance rates, or administering another climate or attitude survey. The evaluation may indicate that the problem still exists because the original diagnosis-action planning sequence was faulty or new factors have emerged that require another plan.

Change Actions

Individuals often refer to steps five and six above—the planning and taking of actions—as planned change, but effective change includes all seven steps. It is important for managers to ask the "Why" question before the "What" question, but too often they fail to do so. When a problem occurs, managers should ask, "Why is this problem occurring?" and seek to find an answer before asking, "What action should we take to deal with the problem?"

It is also important to consider the target of change.

INDIVIDUAL VERSUS COLLECTIVE CHANGE   A manager may be interested in altering the performance of a specific person or in changing the rate or average performance of a group of people. If an individual is the target of change: "How can I get Joe to improve the quality of his work?", the change effort may be quite different than that required for collective change: "Is it possible to improve the attendance at the meeting of our club?"; or "How can we increase the sales of our entire sales department?"

In attempting to change the behavior of a specific person, it is necessary to know something about that individual and gear the change plan to take into account his needs, goals, values, interests, and background. However, if the target of change is group performance (daily work output, attendance, grievance rate, breakage, and turnover), the strategy focuses on the collective change of a number of people.

The issue of collective versus individual change is one that faces many people and organizations. For example, traffic safety officials are concerned with reducing the accident and death toll over the Christmas holidays or Labor Day weekend. At the same time, traffic officials also may be concerned that their own teenagers are safe on a holiday trip.

Strategies for change, whether at the individual or collective level, are always geared to people. When change occurs it is because people have altered their performances. Sometimes people talk and write as though "the organization" is a tangible entity apart from the people who comprise it. It is not uncommon to read "the organization had a drop in sales or production." But an organization is an abstraction—organizations do not change their behavior, although a change in organization structure or process can impact behavior. What actually occurs is that a collection of people who share common orientations consciously or unconsciously decide to change their behavior. A strategy to produce change is always directed at affecting human behavior.

GROUP VERSUS COLLECTIVITY   In thinking about collective behavior, it is important to differentiate between a collection of people who are connected in some interactive way in a system called a "group" and a collection of people who share some common condition but have no group ties or interactions (**collectivity**). Employees who work together producing a product, who talk together, plan together, and make decisions, whether formally or informally, are a group. The millions of people driving cars over a holiday are part of a common collectivity but are not part of a group. Strategies for change applicable to a group may not even be possible with general collectivities. For example, group members may be able to discuss an issue and influence each other, but the collectivity usually must be reached through different processes of influence such as mass media (television, radio, newspaper articles, etc.).

Starting with the famous Hawthorne studies around 1930, it has been found that groups can and often do influence individuals in their judgments, decisions, and actions by the way group members behave toward individuals. Although the group may be a strong force in creating change, it is not always possible to predict the change of a *specific* group member, and group pressure is a method that cannot be used in the unconnected collectivity. Thus, the strategy for change is dependent on the target of change—an individual, a group, or a general collectivity of people.

ACTION STRATEGIES: MODELS AND RESEARCH EVIDENCE

The Hawthorne studies discussed in Chapter 2 were not planned change programs, but research efforts to determine what forces affected worker performance. These pioneering studies showed that changes in worker performance could not be accurately predicted by altering external stimuli such as lighting, rest periods, or pay. A key factor was how the group of workers felt about the changes and the decisions they agreed to implement. These studies demonstrated that worker performance could be improved if workers were allowed freedom to control their own work, were treated with respect, and were able to build group support. This section examines the various action strategies and change models available to managers wishing to rectify a problem situation.

Force-field Analysis

During World War II, the United States government became involved in planning change. At that time, meat was rationed, and scarce ration stamps were required to secure the choice cuts of meats—roasts, steaks, and chops. Other cuts of meat, such as liver, brain, tongue, and heart, were not rationed, but were hardly being used. Kurt Lewin, a professor at the University of Iowa, was asked to determine whether it was possible to get housewives to change their meat-buying and eating habits and to start using these nonrationed products.

With his assistants, Lewin set up experimental conditions. Some housewives were put in groups that listened to "attractive lectures . . . which linked the problem of nutrition with the war effort, emphasized the vitamin and mineral value of the [nonrationed] meats. . . . Both the health and economic aspects were stressed. The preparation of these meats was discussed in detail. . . . Mimeographed recipes were distributed."[2] Yet despite these extensive efforts, only 3 percent of the audience served any of the nonrationed cuts of meats.

Other housewives were asked to participate in discussion groups regarding food, nutrition, the war effort, and what they could do to assist. Following these sessions, it was found that 32 percent of the women served at least one of the previously avoided products. Apparently something that prompted change was present in the group sessions but not in the lectures. Lewin's own analysis indicates that he believed the differences were due to (1) the degree of involvement of people in the discussion, (2) the motivation in actually being a party to the decision to use nonrationed meats, and (3) group influence and support in reinforcing the decision.

From this and similar research, Lewin developed a model for analyzing the planned-change process. He visualized the existing conditions as a state of balance or equilibrium (with some fluctuation) between two sets of forces—**restraining forces**, which maintained the status quo and **driving forces**, which moved toward change. He called his model of counterbalancing forces "force-field analysis." Figure 12-2 illustrates Lewin's model.

In Lewin's meat-eating problem, the restraining forces that kept housewives from using the nonrationed meats seemed to be the taste, smell, and appearance of the meats, family reactions, the low status attached to eating these meats, the lack of approval by others, and the lack of information about preparation. The driving forces that pushed toward change were patriotism, hunger, nutrition, the requirement of no food stamps, and the new experience. Apparently, the drive for change was not enough to overcome the strength of resistance for most of the women involved in the Lewin study.

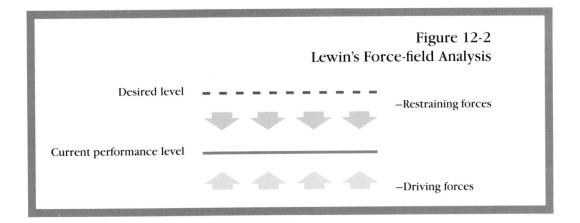

Figure 12-2
Lewin's Force-field Analysis

CHANGE STRATEGIES   The force-field model provides three basic **change strategies**:

1. *Increase* the driving forces.
2. *Decrease* the restraining forces.
3. Do both.

Ample research evidence suggests that just increasing the driving forces also results in a degree of increased resistance, and change will not be maintained unless pressure is constantly applied. According to Lewin, change occurs when the existing situation is "unfrozen," moved to a new level, and then "refrozen" at the new position. Just applying more pressure does not seem adequate to refreeze the change at the new level. In the meat-eating case, the lecturer attempted to increase pressure by appealing to patriotism in helping the war effort and by reducing the lack of preparation knowledge by passing out recipes.

More appropriate is the strategy of reducing or eliminating restraints or, even better, converting restraining forces into driving forces. The group discussion-decision method changed peer-group pressure from a restraining force to a driving force. Women who formerly had been uneasy about the reactions of their peers were now getting support from those very peers. Yet the group-process method was not strong enough to overcome certain resistance forces. More than 65 percent of the women still would not use the undesirable cuts of meat.

Even those who are excited and exhilarated as the result of change need a chance to let go of the past, to mourn it, and say their good-byes. Institutions, rituals, and traditions that help us to accept change are well worth the few hours it takes to help employees over the hump of organizational change. No skill may be more important to the effectiveness of tomorrow's managers than helping people cope with change. (See Box 12-1 on pages 382–83 for methods of reducing resistance to change.)

FORCE-FIELD ANALYSIS PROCEDURES   Force-field analysis follows a set of procedures that represents a method of organizational problem solving and is an important change process. There are six major steps.

Box 12-1
Overcoming Resistance to Change

Rosabeth Moss Kanter, author of *The Change Masters*, offers the following reasons for the resistance to change experienced by managers and, more importantly, what can be done to lessen it:

1. **Loss of Control**   Change is exciting when done by us, threatening when done to us. The more choices that a manager can give people, the more they will feel in control, and the less they will resist change.

2. **Excess Uncertainty**   Simply not knowing what the next step is going to be or feel like makes comfort impossible. Sharing as much information as possible, dividing change into a number of manageable steps, sharing a vision of and commitment to change are all ways of reducing resistance to change due to uncertainty.

3. **Surprise**   People are easily shocked by decisions or requests suddenly sprung on them without groundwork or preparation. A manager might come to work one day to find a list of people she must inform, immediately, that their jobs are being changed or eliminated. Timing of the release of information regarding the change is important.

4. **Difference**   People are required by change to be conscious of, and to question, familiar routines and habits. Minimizing the differences in a change situation is one way to reduce this effect. Invoking tradition, not the revolutionary nature of the change, and maintaining as many familiar routines and surroundings as possible are important. The words of Roger Smith, chairman of GM, as he launched one of the most revolutionary periods of change in GM's history are exemplary: "I'm going to take this company back to the way Alfred Sloan intended it to be managed."

5. **Loss of Face**   If accepting change means that the way things were done in the past was wrong, people are sure to resist. Instead, put the past in perspective by recognizing past actions as right for the past, but no longer right for the future. This way people do not lose face for changing; instead, they look strong and flexible.

6. **Concerns about Future Competence**   Can I do it? How will I do it? Will I make it under the new conditions? Do I have the skills to operate in the new way? Positive reinforcement, training, and the chance to learn new skills without being made to feel stupid are essential.

7. **Ripple Effects**   These are changes that are anticipated outside of the job situation, in personal or family life. Introducing change with enough flexibility to take into account ripple effects will help people go through the transition and feel committed, not resistant, to change.

Rosabeth Moss Kanter examined resistance to organizational change in *The Change Masters*.

8. **More Work** The effort that it takes to manage things under routine circumstances is multiplied when things are changing. Providing recognition and rewards—from cash bonuses to special celebrations—and support—such as making sure that families are informed and supportive of the extra effort—help make the extra effort "worth it."

9. **Past Resentments** People often dredge up past gripes and want redress as their price for going along with change. Going forward can mean going back—listening to past resentments and repairing past rifts.

10. **The Threat Is Real** Change can produce winners and losers. Avoid pretense and false promises. If some people are going to lose something, they should hear about it early, rather than worrying about it and infecting others with their anxiety and antagonism. And if people are going to be let go or moved elsewhere, it is more humane to do it fast.

SOURCE: Adapted from Rosabeth Moss Kanter, "Managing the Human Side of Change," *Management Review*, April 1985, pp. 52–56.

Step One: Define the Problem and Determine the Change Goals   In planned change, one begins with the "problem" or condition to be altered. Lewin's model suggests the same beginning but emphasizes defining clearly the existing condition as well as the desired condition to be achieved.

Step Two: Gather the Data   In order to identify the *real* forces in the situation, it is important to gather accurate information about both resistance forces and driving forces. If possible, learn which forces are most critical and which are amenable to change. Some factors may be open to change but are really not important, while some very important forces may be outside the ability of people to change to any great degree. As indicated earlier, data gathering may be accomplished by interviews, questionnaires, or direct observations. However acquired, results are fed back into the system as the basis for achieving change.

Step Three: Summarize and Analyze the Data   Accumulated data are put into summary form. For larger amounts of data, sophisticated computer and statistical analyses may be necessary. For interviews or direct observations, dominant "themes" or issues mentioned by several respondents should be identified. In force-field analysis, the emphasis should be on understanding the complexity of the factors, including a determination of which factors are most important, which are amenable to change, which cannot be influenced or modified, and which have the greatest probability for lending themselves to a successful change endeavor.

Step Four: Plan the Action   In a good action plan, the following matters are considered:

A.   Who are the significant people who must support a change program?

B.   Where should action taking begin?

C.   Who should be assigned to take what specific action?

D.   When should first reports of action be prepared for review?

E.   What resources (time, money, equipment, and personnel) are needed for the change program?

F.   What is the estimated completion time?

Step Five: Take Action   In putting the plan into effect, Lewin's model suggests the following in the action-taking stage:

A.   Work on reducing restraining forces.

B.   Involve people in planning their own change.

C.   Develop social supports for change.

D.   Get people to make their own decisions to change.

Step Six: Evaluate   Any good action research program contains the criteria for its own success. How do you know if you have reached your goals? Goals should be stated in such a way that evaluation criteria are evident and easily applied. For example, if an organization stated its change goal as "improving communications," success would be very difficult to measure. Any increase in talking could be said to "improve communications." A more measurable goal would be: "Have every manager conduct a sharing and evaluation session with each of his subordi-

Box 12-2
Minimum and Maximum Positions in Selected
Management Theories

THEORIST	MINIMUM POSITION	MAXIMUM POSITION
Douglas McGregor	Theory X: Assumes that people dislike work, need coercion, want security, and want direction.	Theory Y: Assumes that worker likes work, is self-motivated, and accepts responsibility.
Rensis Likert	System I: Exploitative, authoritative management. High control of people by the manager.	System IV: Participative group. Manager allows worker to participate in organizational matters.
Robert Blake and Jane Mouton	1,1 Style: Low concern for both production or results needs	9,9 Style: Optimum concern for both production, goal results, and people.
Abraham Maslow	Management concerned with only physiological or safety needs.	Eupsychian Management: Self-actualized managers dealing with self-actualized people.

nates every three months." Measurement of this change goal is possible. If it has not been achieved, the action-research model must be recycled: gather new data, analyzing it, and repeating the whole process.

Disparity Models

Most of the popular theories or models of managerial behavior have a disparity condition built into their formulations. All **disparity models** are based on the assumption that a change strategy must create a recognition of the difference between what an individual's ideal or objective is and what she is actually doing, thinking, or accomplishing. When a model presents an "ideal" state or style of management performance that either explicitly or implicitly is presented as a goal, persons examining the model cannot help but compare their own state with the ideal. If the actual performance is perceived as less than the ideal, a disparity condition has been created that presumably will inspire improvement. A number of current management theories are reviewed in Box 12-2 with their minimal and maximal conditions. All of these popular models display a disparity quality. Presumably, all managers fall somewhere between the high (ideal) and low types and thus will be motivated to improve.

Management-development programs based on one or more of the above theories usually attempt, by a variety of methods, to get managers to see themselves at some point between the low and the high positions and then try to move closer to the ideal level. Currently, several methods are used to create an awareness of the disparity between existing and ideal conditions:

Cognitive Insight   Most readings, lectures, and training films use a disparity orientation to move the reader, hearer, or viewer to engage in personal analysis and change in the preferred direction (**cognitive insight**). Managers, through their own internal dialogue, gain insight about themselves and see themselves somewhere below the ideal. Merely presenting information cannot ensure that the respondent will see himself or herself accurately; the information may create a disparity that is not consistent with reality. Key executives reading about a new management tool such as team building, job enrichment, or management by objective (MBO) often embark on an improvement program that may not be what is really needed in the organization. Cognitive insight from the sources listed above is not usually adequate by itself as the basis for a change program.

Interpersonal Feedback   A second disparity-producing method is to arrange for a person to obtain direct, immediate, accurate, and helpful feedback about his management style or performance from those who have interacted with him (**interpersonal feedback**). The open exchange of verbal feedback is commonly regarded as the most personal of the disparity models and the one with the most impact. The assumption is that either the person receiving the feedback is unaware of his impact on others, or his self-perception is at odds with reality. In either case, feedback should reveal enough disparity to move him toward change.

Surveys or Data-gathering Instruments   A number of data-gathering instruments give people extensive and sometimes statistically precise data about their performance, style, and impact on the performance or attitude of others in the organization. These instruments are circulated to co-workers; the data are then tabulated, summarized, and given to the subject on the assumption that the data will reveal a disparity and inspire change. Surveys are also used to gather organizational data; indications that conditions are less than optimal may create a need for organizational change.

Reports   Most reporting systems assume a disparity orientation. If a report shows that performance is down from the previous quarter or is below what was projected, this disparity ideally will create energy for change.

Dalton's Model

Gene Dalton, an organization analyst, reviewed the research on those factors connected with behavior change.[3] He found that the following two conditions are present when people initiate change:

Felt Need   People do not engage in any changed behavior unless they experience a felt need for change. The felt need is a sense of emotional discomfort that only decreases as the need is addressed. One of the important issues in change comes when a manager feels a need to improve outputs, but subordinates do not feel the same need. Is it possible to create a felt need in other people? In the past, managers have tried to get people to feel a need to change by trying to create conditions of fear, guilt, crisis, or reward-punishment. When these forces are brought into play, the need is to handle the induced conditions, not to change behavior to improve outputs. It is easier to produce a felt need to change the outputs if the manager: (1) shares clear, accurate information about the need for change; (2) allows others to be involved in planning the change; or (3) allows people to experience some form of reward for engaging in the change.

Involvement of a Respected Other   Other evidence suggests that people will begin to change when the felt need is supported by someone they respect. It is not often that people will engage in behavior change all alone. This is especially true in organizational behavior. Unless workers know that significant people in the organization support the change, they would be very reluctant to change alone.

Dalton also discovered the following additional factors that are present when change was maintained:

Move from General to Specific Plans   Even though change is started, significant change requires the continuation of the change behavior once it has begun. It is important to make sure the change plan is clear and specific. Often the change plan begins at a very general level: "We need to communicate more."; or "I need to have better staff meetings." Such plans are unlikely to be successful unless they are translated into specific action steps. Staff meetings will not improve unless the steps are laid out—clear agendas, written minutes and summaries, assigned responsibility for items, clear meetings goals, etc. Managers should identify exactly what should be done, by whom, and in what time frame for each aspect of change plan.

Move from Lower to Higher Self-Esteem   Unless people can clearly see that the change is going to result in a better feeling about themselves, it is not likely the change will be continued. In some respects it is not so much that people avoid change as it is they avoid the pain that often accompanies change. Some evidence that the change will result in greater individual or group satisfaction is needed or it is likely to be abandoned.

Move from Old to New or Revised Social Ties   Even if people begin to change, the behavior will be abandoned if the social support system does not reinforce the new behavior. Management training programs often result in some immediate change that is discontinued because those in the social system do not support the change. Consequently, the total team or, at a minimum, the immediate social system should be involved in change efforts.

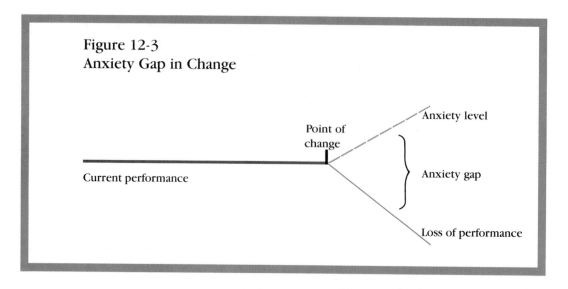

Figure 12-3
Anxiety Gap in Change

Move from External to Internal Commitment   People may begin to change at the request of others, but unless they become committed to the change goals, it is unlikely that new behavior will be continued. Personal commitment results as people think through the change program, are involved in developing the action steps, and wind up feeling the change is "owned" by them.

Change and Anxiety

An important consideration in implementing a change plan is coping with the resultant anxiety, particularly when the change initially decreases productivity. Lester Coch and J. R. P. French found that even under the best of change conditions, production falls off wl.en workers are asked to change assignments and begin new, unfamiliar work.[4] This drop-off in performance is usually acompanied by an increase in anxiety on the part of those who began the change program. See Figure 12-3.

At the point of heightened anxiety and decreasing performance, there is a strong desire to cancel the whole change effort and return to the earlier state. At this point, even if the old state was intolerable, it seems better than the new condition. Sometimes a change program is poorly conceived and should be cancelled. But if the plan has been based on data, those involved have chosen the change, plans have been thought through, and people are committed to them, the major issue then is to manage the anxiety—not the change. The Coch-French study found that it takes about two weeks for a turnaround in motor skill performance to occur. In other areas it may take many months before improvement is noticeable.

People manage anxiety best by talking honestly about their concerns, reviewing their progress and plans, and making modifications as needed. No one can guarantee the success of a change program. The elements of risk, surprise, and failure are always present. A manager plans for change because action seems a better course than inaction. If the plan is well-conceived, initiated, and carried out, the chances for success are better than the slow erosion of a deteriorating situation where nothing is done.

SELECTING A CHANGE INTERVENTION OR ACTION PLAN

It is likely that for any problem, even following a good diagnosis, more than one action plan could be implemented. How does a manager decide what change action to choose if more than one option is available? Following are some considerations:

1. **Root Cause**   If a single **root cause** is present, it is important that the change plan address this issue.

2. **Time Constraints**   Some change actions may take too long to start, or may take too long to complete. For some problems, it may be critical to get started immediately rather than waiting until people are less busy or some other factors are more favorable. The actions that could be started soonest may be the most effective.

3. **Financial Resources**   Some change plans might be considered to be more effective, but they may be too costly to implement given the realities of the existing budget. Managers must always take financial realities into account.

4. **Support from Key People**   Since the evidence is that change gets started when significant others support it, and is continued when the social system is behind it, an important selection criterion is: "Which actions will get the widest support?"

Individual versus System Intervention

If the constraints described earlier concerning time and available resources are important factors in intervention selection, a critical examination of interventions at the individual versus the larger organization or system level is necessary. To focus on the alteration of individual behavior or performance is usually a costly and time-consuming direction to produce change.

For example, how does a university initiate a program to reduce the amount of cheating among students? The reasons for cheating include the need for students to get grades to meet expectations of parents or peers and to gain competitive advantage in the quest for jobs or admission to graduate schools. Some pressures to cheat also come from peers because "everyone does it." How does a university devise an action plan to reduce cheating? On the individual level, one method is to identify each student who cheats and then engage in an individual counseling program—a long, laborious process. Intervention at the group level might be more efficient—some type of group counseling to establish new norms for peer group behavior. Another possibility is to strengthen controls on the students—alternate exams, monitoring, spaced seating, etc. Still another approach is to change the whole policy and program about testing and grading.

Each alternative presents different problems and possibilities. If grades in the ordinary sense are eliminated, the need for cheating is not present; or if it is possible to shift to an individual oral examination, then cheating possibilities would be seriously reduced. To alter the seating or monitoring systems is fairly easy to introduce with little change in existing organization processes for evaluation and grading. The motive for cheating still exists, and such changes could be expected to lead to more innovation on the part of students to try to "beat the system." To change the overall administrative policy about grades would, undoubtedly, reduce cheating most directly; but getting a change of policy of that magnitude may not be feasible given the realities of university policies and administration. The issues are important regardless of the alternative chosen.

Generally, interventions at the individual level take more time and resources than making appropriate adjustments in larger aspects of the total system. However, programs centered on altering individual behavior are often easier to "sell" to administrators of an organization. This results in starting change programs at the individual level that often produce poor overall results. Some individuals may change, but the system factors connected with the problem remain unchanged.

The Spread Effect

Another significant issue in the selection of an intervention into one part of the system centers on the reaction of others in the larger system to the change (**spread effect**). In a classic case Hovey and Beard introduced change to a toy assembly line.[5] The target of change was the paint unit, where the only bottleneck in the whole assembly line was occurring. A change program was begun, and after much negotiation and resistance from others in the organization, the paint crew was allowed to make a major change in the technical system. The intervention called for a switch that controlled the speed of the conveyer belt that brought the toys through the paint shop. This switch allowed the paint crew to control their speed of work during the day. From the perspective of the paint crew, the technical intervention was a smashing success. Production jumped markedly and morale was high. Unfortunately, the spread effect was not so positive. The other units on either side of the paint crew were now under pressure to increase their productivity to meet the standards of the revitalized paint group. These units felt pressured and resentful. The intervention was selected without thoughtful concern about the spread effects on other parts of the organization as a result of the intervention.

Some interventions can be correctly anticipated to have localized impact with little or no spread effect on other parts of the system. Other interventions might be

Workers at Honda's Ohio plant informally discuss change.

accurately predicted to have a wider spread effect. Still other interventions may be quite unpredictable. Some interventions are rejected because of anticipated negative spread effects, while others are rejected because they do not have enough positive spread-effect potential.

Spread effects can occur through both the formal and informal systems. Change is not created in a vacuum. People talk. Managers should anticipate spread effects and get all the people who might be impacted involved in at least understanding the change and giving their support before the change effort begins.

The concept of **stakeholders** was formulated to account for this spread effect. Stakeholders are those who can affect or are affected by organizational decisions. Recent research in the field has focused on the analysis of stakeholders in reference to specific change strategies. For particular decisions, a manager should ask herself not only who is affected but who of those affected cares most about the change, who has the power to promote or obstruct the change process, and who could possibly influence those in these positions of power.[6] It is important to remember not to assume the support or resistance of stakeholders. Notify them of the change; find out how they feel. Stakeholders may resist change just because they were not consulted before the change was announced.

INTERVENTION REINFORCEMENT

A significant factor in achieving positive results from an intervention is reinforcement from other parts of the system (**Intervention reinforcement**). Most people who have been involved in training have experienced the unhappy situation where the learning of an apparently successful training program was not applied in any significant sense on the job. The evidence shows that behaviors emphasized in the training program may not be accepted and supported by co-workers in the social system nor acknowledged and rewarded in the pay-advancement part of the administrative system. A person would have to be an absolute idealist, a fool, or a dunce to persist in behaviors that are not accepted or rewarded elsewhere in the organization. Too often interventions are planned and implemented without carefully building into the change plan the reinforcement that will be needed from other parts of the system to sustain and support the new actions.

Many organizations get excited about team building, job enrichment, or MBO and begin the new activity. However, as the regular processes of the organization move along, it often becomes apparent to the manager engaging in the team-building activity that his efforts are not acknowledged or rewarded. His boss does not ask him about the team building effort, and the success or failure of this activity is not reflected in his raises or promotions. Experience with team building has shown that managers will engage in this activity with greater commitment if they feel supported and rewarded generally by others in the organization.

Culture Change versus System Change[7]

Change experts are concerned with whether a change program tries to change the culture of the organization or just some parts of the system. Does it make any difference to anyone but the pure organizational theorist whether a change attempt is geared toward changing something in the system or something in the culture? The answer is "yes," it does make a difference depending on the kind of change that is desired. If a new CEO coming into a position of power felt that some very basic things were amiss in the organization—people were not loyal to the organization, a low concern about quality was present, people manipulated each other to gain personal or departmental advantage, and falsehoods or half-truths were released through the media to help maintain a positive public image—and if the CEO wanted to turn these very fundamental beliefs and values around, she would need to be concerned with the tough issue of culture change. The ending case in this chapter examines how the UAW-GM Human Resource Center is an attempt to change the relationship between management and labor at General Motors. The amount of funds and variety of programs undertaken to implement this change indicate the type of effort that is required to implement **cultural change**. Despite these efforts, the culture at GM may be so embedded that even more radical measures are required.

A **systems change**, or change in an organization's structure, is a very different issue from a cultural change. General Motors conducted a massive reorganization of its structure in an attempt to streamline operations and exploit more effectively market opportunities. Such change is fundamentally different than the efforts of the Human Resource Center in that they can be made independent of any cultural change.

Culture and System Overlap

Do the concepts of culture and system **overlap**? Of course. The collaborative problem-solving process combines elements of both culture and system. The organization formally incorporates the cultural value of collaboration while using a number of programs, that is, systems changes, to achieve the result. Conceptually, culture and systems are not so well refined as to make neat distinctions possible.

SYSTEMS REFLECT CULTURE   Many aspects of an organization's social, technical, and administrative systems reflect the deeper assumptions of the culture. For example, the UAW-GM Human Resource Center's efforts to democratize the workplace are undermined by such things as reserved parking spaces, separate lunch rooms, and a host of other management perks and prerogatives that serve to accentuate the differences between management and labor. The presence of such perks reflects a deeply held belief of management that workers are not really the equal of management. Until many of these barriers are removed, the programs of the Center will have little effect in terms of actually changing the culture at GM.

CULTURE CHANGES AFFECT SYSTEMS   If a manager who does not hold meetings and makes mostly authoritarian decisions or one-on-one decisions with subordinates learns through some insight process how to conduct effective meetings and involve subordinates as a group in planning and decision making, has the social system or the culture been changed? Perhaps both. It may be that the manager held a belief about the value of people and the need for their involvement and growth but did not know how to translate the belief into action. Management training in holding meetings or team building in this case might then allow the manager to change the social system and allow the core beliefs to be expressed. The manager may also have changed a core belief about people and then changed his meeting practices. Thus, a culture change would have led to a change in the social system.

How Cultures and Systems Are Changed

Most current organizational change is system—not culture—change. Most change interventions stem out of problems that are observed because of some malfunctioning in the system. The seven-step **change cycle** presented at the beginning of this chapter still represents an appropriate system change model for organizations.

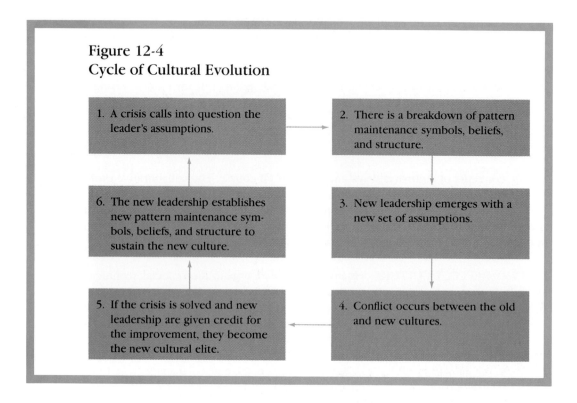

Figure 12-4
Cycle of Cultural Evolution

1. A crisis calls into question the leader's assumptions.

2. There is a breakdown of pattern maintenance symbols, beliefs, and structure.

6. The new leadership establishes new pattern maintenance symbols, beliefs, and structure to sustain the new culture.

3. New leadership emerges with a new set of assumptions.

5. If the crisis is solved and new leadership are given credit for the improvement, they become the new cultural elite.

4. Conflict occurs between the old and new cultures.

Data gathering and analysis allows the manager to identify when the subsystems are malfunctioning and to begin to suggest the kind of actions to be taken. Culture change is a far different venture. This means engaging in some action that gets at basic beliefs, values, and perspectives.

It is not clear if culture change is a two-way street. Can the core assumptions of an organization be changed by starting with some system change and slowly moving toward the core of the culture? Research shows that if the core is changed, the outward aspects will also change. It is not so clear that you can change the core by changing the outward systems or artifacts. The best evidence about culture change deals with a significant change in key leaders.

In a recent study of culture change, the key conditions under which cultural change takes place were discovered.[8] Figure 12-4 presents the six stages of the "cycle of cultural evolution." This model of culture change suggests the culture of an organization changes during a crisis that occurs in concert with the undermining of the power bases of the organization's leadership. New leadership arises to resolve the crisis and after a period of conflict, the new leadership becomes the new "cultural elite" after demonstrating their ability to resolve the crisis. The "old guard" is frequently purged in the process. Finally, the new leaders must reinforce this new culture with symbols, beliefs, or structures that support their belief system.

While the organization change cycle outlines a series of steps that can be followed to initiate change, the "steps" in the cycle of culture change are not as easily

---

Box 12-3

Differences between System Change and Culture Change

System Change	Culture Change
1. Problem oriented.	1. Value oriented.
2. More easily controlled.	2. Largely uncontrollable.
3. Involved in making incremental changes in systems.	3. Concerned with transforming basic assumptions.
4. Focus on improving organization outputs or measurable outcomes.	4. Focus on the "quality of life" in an organization; difficult to measure progress.
5. Diagnosis involves discovering "nonalignments" between systems.	5. Diagnosis concerned with examining dysfunctional effects of core assumptions.
6. Leadership change not essential.	6. Leadership change is crucial.

---

controlled by the manager, for the process is often one of revolution and conflict—not of incremental change.

Major shifts in an organization's culture often appear to make the organization more adaptive to new environmental conditions. However, such revolutionary changes are not easily programmable and the end result is not often determinable at the outset. Although the selection of new leaders is one phase of the cycle that can be "managed," the process is fraught with uncertainty.

Culture Change versus System Change

As has been suggested, some significant differences exist between culture change and system change. Box 12-3 outlines some of these differences. System change is concerned with diagnosing the problems that result from the malfunctioning in and between systems. After diagnosing the problem, a series of incremental steps are then taken to bring the systems into "alignment" and solve the problem. Generally, leadership changes are not required using a systems approach.

Culture change, however, is "value oriented"; that is, the change effort is directed toward socializing individuals to adopt new values and assumptions so they will behave "appropriately," and thus improve the quality of work life in the organization. Such changes are deemed necessary if harmful consequences arise from the basic assumptions of the culture. The change process involves major crises and conflicts and is often not predictable. Leadership change is not directed solely at improving outputs but in getting people to behave in accordance to the "correct" perspectives, values, and assumptions.

Culture change studies describe the crises, leadership transitions and power struggles accompanying culture change. Indeed such descriptions highlight the revolutionary process of culture change and the difficulty in controlling such a process. It may be instructive to look in some detail at two famous studies—one that clearly represents system change and another that shows a change in culture.

CASE ONE
System Change: The Coch-French Study[9]

 The Coch-French study is a famous work that was first published in 1948 in an article titled "Overcoming Resistance to Change." The interventions described were clearly problem-focused. The issue at the pajama-making Harwood plant was the recurring problem of workers asking to change from one kind of job to another—production and morale both dropped. The authors describe the culture of the company as follows:

> The policies . . . in regard to labor relations are liberal and progressive. A high value has been placed on fair and open dealings with the employees and they are encouraged to take up any problem or grievance with the management at any time. Every effort is made to help foremen find effective solutions to their problems in human relations using conferences and role-playing methods. Carefully planned orientation . . . is used. Plant-wide votes are conducted when possible to resolve problems affecting the whole working population. The company has invested both time and money in employee services such as music, health services, a lunchroom, and recreation programs. . . . Management has been conscious of the importance of public relations in the local community.

This statement clearly represents a strong set of assumptions about the importance of the worker and the values of management regarding worker involvement. In fact, the whole intervention in the case is consistent with these basic assumptions and values held by management.

The problem data were these: When operators were required to change over to new work, turnover jumped from 4½ percent to 12 percent. Additionally, among those workers who had to change, 62 percent either became chronically substandard operators or quit during the relearning period. Interviews with the changed operators showed feelings of resentment against management for changing them, feelings of frustration, loss of hope of regaining their former level of productivity and status, feelings of failure, and low levels of aspiration.

The change intervention consisted of three different degrees of participation in the change—no participation, participation through representation, and total participation.

The results are widely known. The nonparticipation group continued the pattern of high turnover, low performance, and negative feelings. In the participation through representation group, morale was good and relearning was high, reaching the old level in 14 days. The total participation group recovered faster than others, returning to prechange levels after the first day and then showing a 14 percent increase in output.

Clearly the action follows the change cycle. A problem was identified, data were gathered about why the problem existed, intervention was planned and implemented, and the problem was eventually solved. The evidence is that the culture was unchanged. In fact, a case could be made that this change in the social system (a participative process in dealing with changeover) was more consistent with the culture than the old, nonparticipatory process of changeover.

CASE TWO
Culture Change: The Guest Case[10]

Robert Guest conducted his famous study of cultural change at an automobile assembly line between 1953 and 1956. The introduction to his report begins this way: "This is a study of a patient who was acutely ill and who became extremely healthy." The impetus for the whole intervention was a plant crisis. Guest calls the time for the automobile plant during 1953 "The Period of Disintegration." Of the six plants in the same division, Plant Y was lowest in efficiency, quality, and safety, and the highest in grievances, costs, absenteeism, and turnover. Guest describes the conditions in the organization showing the nature of the total plant culture. The plant was depicted as being a place of high pressure, being "on the spot," and having slavish obedience to division directives. It was a place of threats, verbal abuse, crisis meetings, no planning, no listening to people, fear, suspicion, confusion, ignorance of the chain of command, inconsistent orders and treatment, and bottlenecks. The descriptive data supplied by Guest indicated that these conditions were present at all levels of the plant, in all units. It was an organization-wide condition and seemed to clearly represent the culture of the plant. The basic assumptions of the organization could have been interpreted as follows: (1) obey division management at all costs, (2) production is gained through pressure, (3) people are expendable, and (4) people should obey and not question.

In the cycle of culture change, first a crisis occurs that calls into question the leader's assumptions. This was clearly the case at Plant Y in 1953. The crisis situation is followed by a breakdown of the basic patterns in the organization. In the cycle, as in Plant Y, this was followed by the emergence of a new leader with a new set of assumptions. A new plant manager (Cooley) was introduced to people at Plant Y, and he brought with him a new approach. As one worker said, "He was inviting us personally to see him any time about ways to make the plant better. He said he welcomed any suggestions. This was a completely new approach to [us] and although some of the boys were skeptical, most of us felt that this man meant what he said."

It is important to note that the new manager followed up his declaration of beliefs about the people being good people and worthy of being heard with a set of prescriptions and actions (perspectives and artifacts) consistent with the assumptions. Meetings were held to get data and make decisions. People were involved in planning. Some people who could not adapt to the new values were replaced. It was not so much that people were fired, but were shifted to other places and people moved into supervisory positions who were more committed to the new values. Later, changes were made in the technical system but these came after the new culture had been introduced. The technical changes were all consistent with new assumptions and values.

Guest says this about the plant under the new manager: "The reaction of supervisors to the improved situation was entirely favorable: it may even be described as 'euphoric.' Members not only felt different about their 'new life' at Plant Y; they behaved in a different manner."

This seems to be clearly a case of a change in the total culture of the plant. In the Coch-French case a change was made in the social-administrative systems (change in decisions about how changeovers would be effected), but the culture remained almost entirely the same. Guest shows us what goes on when a total organization culture changes. ▼

THE ETHICS OF CHANGE

Before a manager tries to get others to change their behavior or performance, certain ethical issues should be addressed. Probably the most fundamental of all ethical questions is: "Does anyone have the right to try to change the behavior of another person?" In the past labor unions have resisted change efforts on the part of management to increase worker output if the workers do not share in any gains that result from the changes. The matter of ethics involves the question of "rights" in the management-worker relationship. Does management have the right to try to create conditions to improve the productivity of workers? Do workers have the right to resist efforts to get them to be more productive? This issue of "rights" has been at the heart of labor-management disputes for many years and a universally agreed on answer has not been devised.

Prerequisites for Ethical Change

Those who have wrestled with the issue of changing worker performance have generally agreed that if the following conditions exist, management has an ethical right to try and achieve a change in performance:

1. If people involved in the change understand what is wanted, and are free to make a choice whether or not to participate in the change plan.

2. If all relevant data about the decisions and actions involved in the change plan are shared with all parties.

3. If those involved in the change find that the plan is not functioning as expected, they have a right to withdraw from the change effort.

It should be noted that certain kinds of changes would probably not be resisted by anyone—in fact would be welcomed. If workers were disgruntled by a restrictive policy that negatively affected their work, and management changed the policy to remove the restrictions, nobody would resist the change. The change that might be resisted would be one designed to improve worker output by 10 percent with no thought of compensating workers for the gain of productivity.

Ethics and Manipulation

Manipulation usually has a negative, unethical connotation. Usually when people feel manipulated it is a result of being put in a situation where they take action without (as they find out later) being given all the information.

If management wanted workers to shift to a ten-hour, four-day workweek and gave them only the positive consequences of such a change and did not share what they knew of the negative effects, the workers would feel manipulated. Generally, manipulation refers to one party handling the information flow for its own benefit. If management withholds information, or distorts data and workers then make decisions based on the biased information, they would usually feel manipulated. Management can usually avoid being branded as being manipulative if they share accurate data, and allow others the right to participate in decisions that affect them.

ENDING CASE
Changing the Culture at General Motors[11]

A major business trend in the 1980s has been the steady increase of Japanese market share in many basic U.S. industries. Nowhere has this been felt more strongly than in the automobile industry where each percentage point in market share is worth almost two billion dollars. High cost and low quality have been identified as the major culprits in this trend.

General Motors, the world's largest automaker, has more to lose in the struggle against foreign competition than any other U.S. company. The opening case in Chapter 2 talked about the innovations taking place at GM's new Saturn Corporation. This case covers GM's attempt to build a cooperative relationship with the United Automobile Workers (UAW) to replace the adversarial nature of labor relations that has characterized its previous relationship with the union. The trauma of the early 1980s is the reason given for the change.

The fundamental difference between the new approach and the company's traditional method of manufacturing lies in its vision of employees as partners in progress instead of as adversaries. By building on mutual concern and trust, synergy is released in the work environment and the result is greater productivity. However, more than just words are necessary to achieve a change that amounts to a change in the total culture of the company, and the support of the union is needed to achieve the desired results. For these reasons, the collective bargaining agreement of 1982 set up the UAW-GM Human Resource Center, a jointly funded and staffed organization devoted to fostering cooperation between the old adversaries. The venture is funded through deductions from the paychecks of workers and contributions from the company. Basically, it signifies a major investment ($200 million per year)[12] in the cooperative model of labor relations.[13] The agreement establishing the Human Resource Center states:

> There is mutual recognition that these challenges require a fundamental change to maximize the potential of our human resources. This change can only occur by building on our current joint efforts and by fostering a spirit of cooperation and mutual dedication that will permit the full development of the skills of our people and meaningful involvement in the decision-making process.[14]

The Human Resource Center attempts to fulfill its mission of change through eight ongoing programs:[15]

1. **Health and Safety Program**   A five-day program of classroom and hands-on workshops designed to eliminate job-related injuries and fatalities.

2. **Quality of Worklife Program**   A program to "democratize" the workplace by encouraging all employees to participate in decision making.

3. **Attendance Procedure Program**   A program to reduce absenteeism by awarding bonuses to workers with perfect attendance and proportionately decreasing benefits to workers with less than 80 percent attendance. Peer counseling is also provided for employees with problems.

4. **Tuition Assistance Plan**   Provides from $50 to $5,000 for employees seeking to improve their skills through education. Since its inception in January of 1984, approvals have been granted to 72,000 applications.

5. **Paid Educational Leave**   Pays union leaders while they examine and discuss the major issues facing the automotive industry. The program emphasizes strategic planning with special emphasis on the forces shaping the collective bargaining environment.

6. **Preretirement Program**   A program to assist workers facing retirement deals with their concerns in such areas as financial planning and health and well-being.

7. **Joint Skill Development and Training** Committees at the plant level are charged with providing a comprehensive training plan based on the needs of the local work force. Assistance is also provided to displaced and laid-off workers.

8. **Area Centers for Skill Development and Training** Originally established to provide job placement and training services to dislocated workers (those laid-off without likelihood of reemployment by GM), the area centers have shifted their focus to provide training to active workers.

The funding level and the scope of the programs offered by the Human Resource Center indicate that the commitment to changing the culture at GM is more than just words and more than just a question of throwing money at a problem. In fact, a substantial commitment to change has been made. All of the programs run by the Human Resource Center are jointly funded and administered by GM and the UAW, indicating that a level of cooperation that would have been unthinkable even ten years ago has already been achieved. Projects like Saturn, the joint venture with Toyota at Fremont, California, and the Buick City plant renovation are the logical outgrowths of the commitment to change that started with the Human Resource Center.

SUMMARY

Management plays one of its most critical roles when things are not going well and changes must be made. This chapter examined how the process of planned change is managed.

For change to be effective, it is critical that problems be correctly identified and the results of any change action properly measured. Proper data gathering and analysis allow the problem to be reformulated so that central issues can be addressed in the action planning and action-taking stages. By deciding the criteria for success ahead of time, the change actions can be analyzed in terms of their results.

Change can take place at the individual or group level. Regardless of which level a change action is aimed at, change strategies must always take into account the needs of people.

Change often involves a great deal of anxiety. While a number of reasons may explain resistance to change, anxiety may persist despite total agreement as to the need for change and the action being taken. In this case, the management of anxiety is as important as managing the change itself.

Sometimes a manager is aware of the need for change but others in the organization lack the needed insight. Disparity models are one way of creating the desired awareness of the difference between existing and ideal conditions. Effective tools for creating this awareness of disparity include films, lectures, literature, interpersonal feedback, surveys, and reports.

Two conditions are needed to initiate change: (1) a felt need for change, and (2) the involvement of a respected other. Four conditions are required to maintain change: (1) plans are specific, (2) higher satisfaction for those undertaking the change action, (3) reinforcement of the change in the social support system, and (4) commitment to change is internalized.

When selecting an action plan it is important to address the root cause of the problem, to observe constraints on time and financial resources, and to gain the support of key people. It is also important to realize the planned change may have side effects. It is useful to anticipate this spread effect.

Most change actions involve changes in the systems of the organization. Systems include all of the various ways in which an organization achieves its results. Culture, on the other hand, reflects the deeply held beliefs of the organization. While changes to an organization's systems are relatively easy to make, changing culture involves tinkering with values and is a much more difficult process.

Finally, the ethics of change were discussed. Access to information and recognition of the rights of others to accept or reject the change are key to management's ethical right to achieve change. Failure to observe these rights results in feelings of manipulation.

KEY TERMS

Primary source of data	Interpersonal feedback
Secondary source of data	Root cause
Problem reformulation	Spread effect
Collectivity	Stakeholders
Restraining forces	Intervention reinforcement
Driving forces	Cultural change
Change strategy	Systems change
Disparity model	Overlap
Cognitive insight	Change cycle

REVIEW QUESTIONS

1. What is the difference between planned and unplanned change?
2. What are three prerequisites for a successful change plan as discussed in the chapter?
3. What type of data is most accurate?
4. What are some of the problems experienced in obtaining primary source data?

5. What are some of the problems that lead to inaccuracy of secondary source data?

6. Of what use are intensity and frequency tabulations?

7. Why is reformulation of a problem after data has been gathered and analyzed important?

8. In what three organizational systems are problems manifested?

9. Why is the determination of how success or failure will be measured an important part of implementing a change action?

10. What factors do you look at when a change action is directed at changing the behavior of an individual?

11. What is the difference between a collectivity and a group?

12. What are three effective strategies for producing change within the framework of force-field analysis?

13. What are the six steps of problem solving used in force-field analysis?

14. What was discovered by Coch and French in their study of garment workers?

15. How do people best manage their anxiety in work change situations?

16. What is the basic assumption that is built into all disparity models?

17. Name four ways of creating awareness of disparity.

18. Explain the conditions needed to initiate and maintain change as developed by Dalton.

19. What factors are considered in choosing between alternative change plans?

20. What causes the spread effect?

21. What are some of the differences between cultural changes and systems changes?

22. Under what conditions is it generally conceded that management has an ethical right to attempt to achieve a change in performance?

CHALLENGE QUESTIONS

1. Why is consensus important in terms of problem definition?

2. What are some of the problems with failing to determine how success or failure will be measured?

3. What might be some problems inherent in using force-field analysis to obtain changes in the work habits of subordinates? Why might people feel manipulated?

4. How would you handle the problem of measuring change given that your efforts might be perceived as "more paperwork required by the boss"?

5. How does Dalton's model tie in with the various disparity models used to create a desire for change?

6. How should the spread effect be taken into account in planning change actions?

7. How would a cultural value of "high quality" manifest itself in a company's operating systems?

8. How would you go about measuring the effectiveness of change actions to produce the following cultural values:
   A. Better labor-management relations?
   B. Stronger commitment to quality?
   C. More effective communications?
   D. Better customer relations?

9. Why are cultural changes often connected with new leadership?

10. Why might it be unethical to demand change of workers without making them party to the data upon which the change action is based? Without allowing them the freedom to choose whether they will participate?

11. What is gained and what is lost in a decision to pursue a change action at the group as opposed to the individual level?

CASE AND RELATED QUESTIONS

1. What kind of data did Nyloncraft base their decision to provide a day-care center on?

2. In terms of force-field analysis, what kind of change action did Nyloncraft initiate? Was the result a systems change or a cultural change?

3. Assuming a tax rate of 50 percent, what is the after-tax consequence in terms of training costs alone of the Nyloncraft day-care facility?

4. How might Intermountain Metals Company treat each of the problems identified in the case?

5. What does Rosabeth Moss Kanter's approach to overcoming resistance to change suggest about the implementation of change strategies?

6. What shock led to the need to change GM's culture? How would you analyze this in terms of force-field analysis? Dalton's model?

7. How would you use Dalton's model to analyze the change action being pursued at the UAW-GM Human Resource Center in terms of:
   A. The individual worker?
   B. Top management?

8. Explain how the systems introduced at UAW-GM Human Resource Center support the new culture that is being introduced.

9. Explain the results achieved in the Coch-French case in terms of systems and culture change. How do the two interact?

10. In the Guest case we see that some people could not adjust to the new values. Why do you think that some managers have a difficult time adapting themselves to a collaborative style of management?

ENDNOTES

1. Adapted from, "The Kids Are All Right," *Inc.*, January 1985, pp. 48–54.

2. Lewin, K., "Group Decision and Social Change," *Readings in Social Psychology*, eds. E. E. Macooby, T. M. Newcomb, and E. L. Hartley (New York: Holt, Rinehart & Winston, 1958), pp. 197–211.

3. G. W. Dalton, L. B. Barnes, and A. Zaleznik, *The Distribution of Authority in Formal Organizations* (Boston: Division of Research, Harvard Business School, 1968).

4. Lester Coch and J. R. P. French, "Overcoming Resistance to Change," *Human Relations*, August 1948, pp. 512–32.

5. Hovey and Beard, Harvard Clearing House, 1970.

6. Reba L. Keele, Kathy Buckner, and Sheri Bushnell, "Identifying Stakeholders: A Key to Strategic Implementation." *BYU Management Papers*, 1986.

7. Adapted from W. G. Dyer and Gibb Dyer, "Organization Development: System Change or Culture Change?" *Personnel*, February 1986, pp. 14–22.

8. Ibid., p. 20.

9. Ibid., pp. 21–22.

10. Ibid.

11. This case was developed with the cooperation of the UAW-GM Human Resource Center and is based on materials supplied by that organization.

12. *UAW-GM Human Resource Center Backgrounder* (Auburn Hills, MI: UAW-GM Human Resource Center, 1986).

13. Ibid.

14. *Memorandum of Understanding: Joint Activities,* GM-UAW 1984 National Agreement (Auburn Hills, MI: UAW-GM Human Resource Center, 1986).

15. The following material summarizes the program descriptions contained in, *UAW-GM Human Resource Center Booklet* (Auburn Hills, MI: UAW-GM Human Resource Center, 1986).

PART IV

THE CHALLENGE OF LEADERSHIP

CHAPTER 13

LEADERSHIP

CHAPTER OUTLINE

LEARNING OBJECTIVES

■ Identify the four competencies of strong leaders, and explain why each is important.

■ Describe the effects of empowering (how employees act when given power).

■ Identify the various approaches to leadership, their differences and similarities.

■ Understand the major characteristics of effective managers.

■ Describe the major aspects and assumptions of Douglas McGregor's Theory X and Y.

■ Explain the various parts of Blake and Mouton's managerial grid, and why it is a useful way to frame managerial style issues.

■ Understand the major reasons that top managers are derailed, and which of these are most damaging.

■ Describe what training might do to cultivate more effective leaders.

■ Understand the relationship between moral values and effective leadership.

■ Discuss the differences between the terms "management" and "leadership."

■ Understand the importance of teams or participative management in the major theories of management behavior.

■ Indicate how Likert's Systems I to IV theory differs from other theories of management behavior.

College students were asked to evaluate the eleven major M*A*S*H characters and to rank them in order of their preference as to whom they would like to have as a superior. Colonel Sherman Potter is a runaway first choice of students as the preferred superior, followed by Hawkeye as a distant second.

Why is Potter the prototype of the desirable organizational leader? The first reason is apparently the contrast between Potter's leadership style and that of the unit commander he replaced—Henry Blake. (Blake was the first member of the cast to leave the M*A*S*H series. The script had him rotated back to the states and killed in an airplane crash on his way home). Blake was a very unorganized, easily manipulated, often slow-witted commander whom everyone liked. While they also respected his skill as a surgeon, everyone manipulated him to get what they wanted.

He was replaced by Colonel Potter, who possessed a very different leadership style. Potter, a career army doctor, may chafe against the seemingly nonsensical red tape that surrounds him, but he understands its place and has learned to work with it. He establishes order in the schedules and routines. Although Radar is still his orderly, he cannot be diverted by Radar into signing orders without understanding what he is signing—an action that was characteristic of Blake. He portrays the crusty old colonel whose bark is much worse than his bite, and who respects his junior officers and relates to them as a friend without becoming so familiar that they lose their respect for him and his position. He is very approachable and exhibits a high level of concern for the well-being of all his subordinates. His subordinates also see his human side. They understand his devotion to his wife and his strong feelings for his daughter and grandchild. He can admit to being tired, frustrated, and sick of war, yet retain the ability to give orders that are respected and obeyed. ▨

INTRODUCTION

Leadership is an intriguing, sometimes elusive attribute of a manager. Warren Bennis, behavioral scientist, management theorist, and writer has this view about leadership:

> My goal (in studying 60 top corporate executives) was to find people with leadership ability, in contrast to just "Good Managers"—true leaders who affect the culture, who are the social architects of these organizations and who create and maintain values.
>
> Leaders are people who do the right thing; managers are people who do things right. Both roles are crucial, and they differ profoundly.[2]

Peters and Austin make the same point in referring to the management revolution they see in progress: "The concept of leadership is crucial to the revolution—so crucial that we believe the words 'managing' and 'management' should be discarded. 'Management,' with its attendant images, connotes controlling and arranging and demeaning and reducing. 'Leadership' connotes unleashing energy, building, freeing, and growing."[3]

There are some who feel that the terms "leader" and "manager" are synonymous and they use the terms interchangeably. However current research and writing present leadership and management as different dimensions of one in a superordinate role. In this context a manager is a person who achieves organization goals by effectively planning, organizing, and moving work to its conclusion. Leadership is a different dimension and represents the ability to move people to action. Thus one might be an effective manager without having much leadership capability. More attention is being given currently to helping people in management improve their leadership.

WHAT MAKES A LEADER?

The issue of leadership has attracted interest for many years. Who are these people who emerge and provide direction and vision and influence important activities? Is this a quality you are born with, or can leadership ability be acquired?

A great deal of research has been done trying to discover what makes a leader. The lives of great men and women have been analyzed. Some studies have tried to identify the leadership qualities of those selected by voting or peer selection. But trying to identify what is common to all leaders has not been a very fruitful path. The early leadership studies showed that about all leaders had in common was that they were above average in intelligence, scholarship, dependability in exercising responsibility, activity, sociability, and social participation.

Four Competencies of Strong Leaders

Bennis, quoted at the beginning of the chapter, interviewed 60 top corporate leaders. The median age was 56. Most were white males, with six black men and six women in the group. He found something unusual: all were married to their first spouse and all were enthusiastic about the institution of marriage. Bennis, through his own subjective analysis, identified four competencies he felt were found to some extent in every leader:

1. Management of attention
2. Management of meaning

Mohandas Gandhi provided India and the world with new vision and direction: Is a person born with this leadership quality or can it be acquired?

3.   Management of trust

4.   Management of self

The commands of Henry Blake and Sherman Potter provide an excellent backdrop to the analysis of these competencies.

MANAGEMENT OF ATTENTION   Management of attention refers to an ability to draw people to the leader by creating a vision, communicating that vision to others, and, through the leader's energy and commitment, making others want to join together in trying to achieve that vision. Bennis says, "The first leadership competency is the management of attention through a set of intentions or a vision, not in a mystical or religious sense, but in the sense of outcome, goal, or direction.[4]

Dubbed the "Great Communicator," Ronald Reagan as president effectively communicated his vision of government.

Henry Blake draws no one to him, or even tries, preferring instead, according to Hawkeye, "to go through the war anonymously." On the other hand, through his example, Sherman Potter is able to create a vision of what a MASH should be.

MANAGEMENT OF MEANING   This competency is the ability to communicate the vision to others so they can understand the meaning of the goals, directions, or issues. Leaders have an ability to integrate facts, concepts, and anecdotes into meanings that others can clearly understand, "to connect the seemingly unconnected."[5] When Ronald Reagan was President he was called the "Great Communicator." While some may have disagreed with his policies or programs, everyone agreed that he had a great ability to take rather complex matters and present them in ways that people felt they understood.

Potter is able to cut through army red tape, because he knows how to work with junior officers. He is able to simplify complicated problems for his subordinates. Blake confuses even himself, and will on occasion ask Radar what he himself meant or intends to say.

MANAGEMENT OF TRUST   Effective leaders generate trust in others. A fundamental part of building trust is reliability or consistency. People like to follow a leader they can count on, a person whose positions and approaches to issues they know. People prefer to follow such leaders, even if they disagree with their viewpoints, rather than leaders they agree with but who shift their positions. Trust also includes being trust-worthy—doing things you say you will do, keeping confidences, and maintaining your values.

Blake is never consistent. He vacillates among opinions of those in his charge. Potter is highly predictable. Although he is firm and consistent in his control of the MASH unit, his doctors can also trust both his medical judgment and his people sense.

MANAGEMENT OF SELF   Effective leaders understand themselves—their strengths and weaknesses—and operate consistently within the bounds of their capabilities. Because of self-understanding, leaders have confidence in themselves. They do not see mistakes as failures; they refer to them as errors, false starts, bloops, flops, foul-ups, bungles, but not as failures.

Blake is constantly afraid of getting in trouble with higher authorities, while Potter is not afraid to say what he thinks to superiors. He is quite capable of making mistakes, but accepts this trait as part of his humanity.

In Bennis' analysis, the above four factors result in a type of energy being transmitted from the leader to the followers. People feel empowered—contact with the leader makes them feel able to achieve. When people feel empowered they:

1. **Feel significant**   What they do makes a difference in the outcome of the organization or enterprise.
2. **Feel competent and confident**   People feel good about themselves; they can make mistakes and yet not fail.
3. **Feel a part of a whole—a unity, a team**   They feel a sense of community; they belong to something that is important and will make a difference.
4. **Find work challenging and exciting**   The leader "pulls" people along. They identify with the leader and are motivated by the attraction of the work and the vision rather than by rewards and punishments.

The reverse can also be true when these competencies are missing.

Approaches to Leadership

Warren Bennis presents a current view of the issue, "What is leadership and who are the leaders?" In the past, four major approaches or theories have dominated the study of leadership.[6]

THE GREAT MAN THEORY   This approach to leadership is based on the assumption that certain people are either born to become leaders, or leaders emerge at the right historical time when events thrust them into the leadership positions. This notion leads to an old question: Does history make the man (leader), or does the man (leader) make history? Implicit here is the idea that something in the makeup of leaders propels them to the forefront, and others are attracted to and willing to follow these "natural-born leaders."

Those who hold to this position would maintain that Gandhi, Hitler, Lenin, Jefferson, and others were born with certain traits and by the force of their presence altered the course of history. Others who accept the Great Man theory also feel that situational factors influence the impact of the Great Man, and would want to incorporate the following approach.

THE SITUATIONAL APPROACH   In contrast to the Great Man theory, situationalists claim that the demands of the situation determine who will lead. Proponents of this position would claim that the situation in India before and after World War II was ripe for someone with the attributes of Gandhi to emerge. Had Gandhi been born 100 years earlier, he would have lived and died without causing a ripple in the waters of history. It is easy to blend these two approaches—the leader is that person who has the right kind of attributes to take advantage of the demands of a particular situation.

These first two approaches to leadership are closely allied to the following approach based on the charisma of the leader.

THE CHARISMATIC LEADER APPROACH   This orientation is somewhat like the Great Man theory, for the assumption is that some people are endowed with certain extraordinary powers—even selected by divine intervention—to be the person others should follow. Moses, Jesus Christ, Mohammed, Buddha, and Zoroaster are some figures that people believe to have been divinely endowed to lead.others.

In the modern era, the concept of **charisma** is more concerned with the attributes of the charismatic individual's personality than with being touched by the Divine hand. Generally, the charismatic attributes are charm, vision, enthusiasm, personal attractiveness, ability to speak, personal energy, and intelligence. Bennis' approach is close to being in the charismatic camp—certain people have these qualities of energy and vision that push them to the forefront.

It is common to hear people talk about the charisma of various national figures. John F. Kennedy has often been described as a "charismatic personality" as has Ronald Reagan, while Richard Nixon and Lyndon Johnson have been described as astute politicians but lacking in "charisma."

THE BEHAVIORAL APPROACH   The behavioral approach has been most widely used in leadership research. The basic question is: What do effective leaders do? What functions do they perform that meet needs or accomplish goals? How do they motivate others? Instead of looking for personal traits or characteristics, the focus is on behaviors—activities, actions, and functions. The advantage of this approach is that "inborn" traits are irrelevant; observable actions are all important. If effective leadership behaviors can be identified, they can be taught. If inherited qualities are required, then people who already have these qualities must be selected and training is immediately irrelevant.

Part of John F. Kennedy's presidential appeal was his charisma: his charm, humor, speaking ability, energy, and
intelligence.

RESEARCH ON LEADERSHIP-MANAGEMENT BEHAVIOR

Using a behavioral perspective, researchers identify work units that have either high
or low productivity and morale. The researcher then asks workers in these high and
low units to describe what their leader (supervisor or manager) does, or does not do.
Comparisons are made to detect any differences in the behavior of the leaders or
managers within the two groups.

The University of Michigan Survey Research Center has investigated effective
management behavior for many years. Two University of Michigan researchers, Robert Kahn and Daniel Katz, summarized their findings from studies of a number of

companies from various industries.[7] At the time of this research the term "manager" was in vogue so they described effective managers as those who:

1. Spend more time managing than less effective managers, who are more involved with their own work or in the clerical aspects of their jobs. Better managers spend their time planning, talking with and training subordinates, dealing with the interpersonal aspects of the job, and keeping people informed about their work and the company.

2. Spend more time managing and do not supervise as closely as the less effective managers, delegating more readily. They give people more freedom to do their jobs. Lower-level managers are influenced by higher-level managers; managers who were closely controlled by their bosses also tended to control their subordinates.

3. Are seen by subordinates as taking a personal interest in them, trying to understand them, and keeping them better informed on their performance.

4. Inspire higher productivity and morale as well as more pride in and involvement with the work unit. Productivity and pride in the work group are probably interactive variables—an increase in one tends to increase the other. As a result, the trend is to encourage team building.

Another study by Jay Hall analyzed data on over 11,000 managers from a variety of organizations, job levels, and situations.[8] He broke his sample into high, medium, and low achievement managers based on achievement criteria. High achievement managers:

1. Make wide use of participative management practices. Low achievers make minimal use of such techniques.

2. Are rated high in interpersonal competence, and are described as open in communications and willing to experiment with new ideas and concepts by subordinates.

3. Concentrate on creating challenge and giving greater responsibility to subordinates. Low achievers are more likely to use security issues having hygiene significance in attempting to motivate others.

4. Are rated by subordinates as having a high task/high relationship orientation. Average achievers are low in both areas. High-task orientation indicates that efforts center on results-producing activities—planning, making assignments, setting goals. High-relationship orientation indicates that a manager permits subordinates to influence work activities and is willing to participate with subordinates in planning, goal setting, and decision making.

Management theorists have created management models to present these and other findings in a way that clarifies and simplifies research results and makes them easier for managers to use. These models use the terms "effective management" and "effective leadership" as almost synonymous terms.

Box 13-1
Assumptions of Theory X and Y

THEORY X ASSUMPTIONS

1. People have an inherent dislike of work and will avoid it if they can.

2. People will need to be coerced, controlled, directed, and threatened to get them to produce.

3. People prefer to be directed, want to avoid responsibility, have little ambition and want security above all.

THEORY Y ASSUMPTIONS

1. Work is as natural as play or rest—people do not inherently dislike work.

2. External controls and threats are not the only ways to influence behavior.

3. Commitment to objectives is a function of the rewards associated with their achievement. Ego satisfaction is the most important of these rewards and can be achieved through the work of the organization.

4. People, under the right conditions, learn not only to accept, but to seek responsibility.

5. The capacity to exercise a relatively high degree of imagination, ingenuity, and creativity in solving organizational problems is widely, not narrowly, distributed in the population.

SOURCE: Douglas McGregor, The Human Side of Enterprise (New York: McGraw-Hill, 1960).

THEORY X AND Y   Douglas McGregor divided the behavior into effective and ineffective management.[9] Effective managers had one theory of management, which he labelled Theory Y, and ineffective managers had a quite different theory, which was called Theory X.

McGregor postulated that leaders holding Theory X assumptions overcontrol subordinates, pay little attention to employee involvement, and exhibit low concern for employee growth and development. Conversely, managers holding Theory Y assumptions allow people more responsibility, involve them in goal setting and decision making, and show high concern for employee development. Box 13-1 illustrates the different assumptions in these theories.

Some managers who accepted McGregor's notions felt he was saying that the leader should never exert authority, and that people would naturally work hard if treated fairly. What McGregor did say was, "The assumptions of Theory Y do not deny the appropriateness of authority, but they do deny that it is appropriate for all purposes and under all circumstances."

The Managerial Grid

Robert Blake and Jane Mouton at the University of Texas developed a more elaborate model to measure managerial effectiveness than McGregor's.[10] Their managerial grid measures a manager's concern for two essential activities—work results and concern for the people who must do the work. Both of these activities are rated on a scale of one to nine, and then charted on a two-dimensional grid as shown in Figure 13-1. The problem in leadership is to integrate the concern for results with the concern for people. Blake and Mouton identified some common leadership styles:

1. **9,1**   High concern for results—low concern for people. The issue is integration—concern with results should not result in neglecting the people who must achieve the results.

2. **1,9**   High concern for people—low concern for results. Out of balance in the other direction; too much concern for people at the expense of dealing with legitimate work activities.

3. **1,1**   Low concern for either results or people. Indicates passive or apathetic leadership.

4. **5,5**   The most prevalent leadership style in Europe and America; essentially a compromise approach in which something in each dimension is sacrificed through accommodation to the status quo.

5. **9,9**   The model's "ideal" or generally most effective style. Here the leader tries, through building a team effort, to deal with both concerns at the same time. In teamwork, everyone in the team is responsible for both concerns, not just the leader.

In Blake and Mouton's management grid, the preferred style in most (not all) situations is 9,9 management. Here productivity and morale are in balance with each other at an optimum level. This high level of balance is usually achieved by building a team with all employees involved. Work is shared and the manager involves as many people as possible in planning, goal setting, and decision making. People are given all relevant information, trusted with important work, and feel useful and needed. This pattern of management requires a certain "philosophy" as to what management is about and an effective strategy for implementing the philosophy. The 5,5 style creates balance, but not at the highest level.

Systems I to IV

While McGregor divided managerial style into two camps, X and Y, Rensis Likert thought of the data as being on a continuum.[11] At one end he saw one highly authoritarian system or style of management, which was called System I, and at the other end was a participative management style called System IV (see Figure 13-2). Between

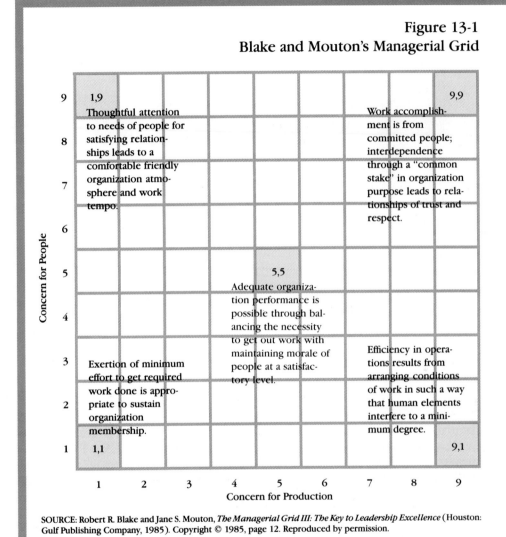

Figure 13-1
Blake and Mouton's Managerial Grid

SOURCE: Robert R. Blake and Jane S. Mouton, *The Managerial Grid III: The Key to Leadership Excellence* (Houston: Gulf Publishing Company, 1985). Copyright © 1985, page 12. Reproduced by permission.

these two extremes are two other systems. System II is authoritarian, but takes a benevolent or paternalistic stance with subordinates. System II leaders still want things done their way, but they are nice about it. System III (the most common style found by Likert) leaders are consultative. System III leaders consult with subordinates, but retain final control and the right to make final decisions.

Theory Y, 9,9 management, and System IV have some common elements. All of the models emphasize the **participative** stance of people in leadership positions. These leaders will try to work with people, get them involved in the decisions

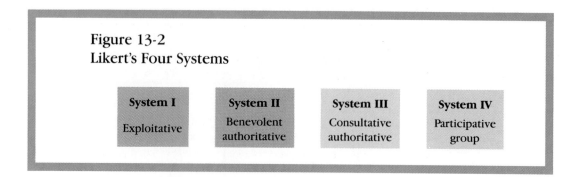

Figure 13-2
Likert's Four Systems

System I	**System II**	**System III**	**System IV**
Exploitative	Benevolent authoritative	Consultative authoritative	Participative group

and activities of the organization, and try to help them grow and develop through their work.

As advocates of these models presented them to students and new managers, it often appeared that they presented a universally good style (Theory Y, System IV) and a universally bad style (Theory X, 1,1, System I). Later, the rise of contingency theory began to emphasize the importance of understanding the demands of the situation. Perhaps in one situation a System I, or 9,1 management style might be appropriate and effective, but not in a different situation.

Contingency Theory of Leadership

Influenced primarily by the work of psychologist Fred Fiedler, the **contingency theory** model has received much attention. The main contention is that there is no one leadership style that is effective in all situations—you must look at the nature of the task, the kind of people and the time frame involved, and the goals of the organization to determine what leadership style would achieve the best results. In a crisis situation with a short time frame, an authoritative style might be more effective than a more relaxed participative style.

Path-Goal Model

A type of situational leadership model was developed by psychologist Robert House.[12] The critical role of the leader in House's model is to understand the situation and the subordinates, to make sure the path to achieving goals is clear, and to supply rewards that are important to the workers.

The first concept in this model is the necessity of the leader motivating subordinates to accomplish work goals by clarifying the personal rewards they will receive. If obstacles or uncertainties exist, the leader is to remove them and smooth the path to personal rewards.

Secondly, if the path to the goal is clear and adequate structures are in place, the leader must see that additional structure is not added since too much structure leads to reduced performance.

The final concept in this model is relating the reward to goal attainment. the leader offers a reward only if the task is accomplished. The leadership style that is most effective is one that clarifies the kind of behavior most likely to result in goal accomplishment and the earning of the reward.

This model is situational since the goal for one group may be different than another, and subordinates' needs may also vary. The leader should understand the goal of the organization or work unit, the people involved, and clarify the path to achieve the goal.

CASE

Management by Intimidation

James L. Dutt's efforts to transform Beatrice from a loose confederation of regional operations to what he called "the premier worldwide marketer" took their toll on both him and the organization that he led. Beatrice's 1984 purchase of Esmark, another Chicago food and consumer products giant, made Beatrice about as large as Procter & Gamble in terms of revenue. The strains of this and other acquisitions changed the management style of Dutt from one described as easygoing and amiable to that of a fiery-tempered autocrat, according to more than a half dozen people who observed him in action.

Dutt's behavior suggested a monumental impatience with anyone who failed to catch his vision of what Beatrice should be. At management meetings he was reported to deliver tirades that demoralized rather than inspired. He waved his arms and harangued his followers, insisting that they did not work hard enough and that only he could muster the drive, intelligence, and skill to bring his vision for Beatrice to reality. At a meeting of industry analysts in St. Petersburg, Florida, Dutt gestured toward three top executives seated behind him on the podium and declared that they would lose their jobs if the financial goals he had outlined to the analysts were not met.

Dutt was portrayed by employees as vindictive: a man who would ruin the career of one who openly criticized him or the company. Some employees, however, saw Dutt in a different light. Richard J. Pigott, executive vice-president and chief administrative officer, offers a typical comment from this group, "I would evaluate his leadership as very effective. I don't think he has any shortcomings worth mentioning." Alexander Brody, a director, says, "Impatience is a quality of leadership."

Executive turnover became extraordinarily high. Of Beatrice's 58 top corporate officers at the end of fiscal 1980—Dutt's first year as CEO—only 21 remained with the company in the summer of 1985. Many of those who left were fired or resigned in anger. Among this group was former President Donald P. Eckrich, who has never been replaced. The La Choy Oriental foods division had three presidents in just three years and Tropicana Products, a fruit juice division, had three presidents in just one year. The Esmark division came under fire from Dutt in 1985, with dozens of firings and resignations, including the two principal operating managers of the Swift/Hunt-Wesson food business and the International Playtex operation, individuals credited with being the glue that held Esmark together.

Some people complained that Dutt was either too much in the picture or impossible to reach. His hands-on style of management meant that he got involved with the nittiest and grittiest of details, especially in food products where he rose through the ranks, and that he initiated management changes at almost every level of the organization. It is also said that he sometimes retreated into Howard Hughes-like seclusion and that a personal request had to be submitted to his personal secretary when he was needed for consultation.

Dutt's efforts resulted in a marked increase in the awareness of Beatrice. Critics claim, however, that this did not lead to increased shelf space at retail. Studies have shown no boost from the increased recognition of the Beatrice name. Over the period of Dutt's tenure as CEO, Beatrice stock has risen 51 percent while the Standard & Poor's 500 index rose 80 percent. Long-term debt rose to 108 percent of equity after the Esmark merger and interest costs were running at $382 million per year.

Beatrice has been able to use the in-house sales and distribution force of Esmark, one that deals directly with retailers (Beatrice's own sales and distribution were handled largely by brokers). The Beatrice advertising budget of $800 million now ranks with that of Procter & Gamble. While some gains were certainly made by Dutt, his problems with personnel and management turnover were perceived as destroying any competitive advantage that he hoped to gain. The result was that the Beatrice board of directors was finally forced to act, calling for Dutt's resignation before he had a chance to see his vision become reality. The board agreed with his strategy; however, they decided that Dutt was not the one to make it happen. ▨

Leadership Failure

What causes a corporate leader to fail? If a leader fails to produce results over an extended period, the leader is probably assessed a failure and is normally terminated, as was Dutt at Beatrice. But what causes the leader to fail to produce results?

One answer to this question has been supplied by a study completed by the Center for Creative Leadership in North Carolina. A cross section of large companies on the East Coast was selected and corporate leaders who had been moving up in the organization and then got **derailed** (fired, demoted, or held back in some way from further promotions) were identified. Why were these formerly promising executives derailed? People who knew them were interviewed and the following pattern of behavior emerged. Box 13-2 lists the ten most common reasons given for derailment roughly in order of importance. No person was derailed for just one factor—usually it was a cluster of reasons.

Box 13-2

Fatal Flaws: Ten Reasons for Derailment of Top Managers
in Order of Frequency

1. Insensitive to others, abrasive, and intimidating.

2. Cold, aloof, and arrogant.

3. Betrayal of trust—failure to meet commitments.

4. Overly ambitious—plays politics and pushes too hard to get ahead.

5. Failure to handle specific performance problems, and trying to cover up problems or shift blame.

6. Overmanaging—unable to delegate or build a team.

7. Unable to select and develop own effective staff.

8. Unable to think broadly or strategically—too much attention to detail and technical problems.

9. Unable to adapt to a boss with a different style.

10. Overdependence on a boss or mentor.

SOURCE: Adapted from W. McCall and R. Lombardo, "What Makes a Top Executive," *Psychology Today*, February 1983.

The inability to work effectively with others was a major factor in the failure of these individuals. Leaders require a power base to move ahead on the career ladder. **Power** is the ability to influence the behavior of others in predetermined directions. Therefore, the ability to influence a network of others in the organization is a requisite of power.

Wise leaders pay attention to the network of support that enables them to achieve results. Derailed leaders alienate people, destroying their support base and bringing their career to a standstill. None of the ten major reasons for derailment had to do with technical incompetency. As people move from lower to higher management they must move from technical management to handling people, from a narrow task focus to broader administrative matters. The derailed leaders failed to make this transition. Dutt, in the Beatrice case, for example, was technically competent, but an inability to work with others, not as easily noticed in, or essential to the success of, a lower-level manager, led to his downfall.

Leadership Development

Since so much of the success of the enterprise depends on the effectiveness of leaders or managers, almost all organizations of any size provide training and development programs for their managers. The basic assumption is that people can change their behavior and can improve in their ability to work with others.

Whether training programs can change behavior significantly is an issue still strongly debated. Some theorists, primarily Fred Fiedler of the University of Washington, contend that most adults are strongly locked in to their personality and styles of behavior; consequently, the fit between the existing attributes of the person and the requirements of the job are the major consideration.[13] Dutt's story provides support for this theory, because he could not change his behavior. A nonpeople person should be put into a job requiring task competence, not one requiring people skills. Others believe that people can learn and change if exposed to a sound development program.

VALUES AND THE LEADER

There is growing evidence that effective leaders are value-driven. They hold to a body of ethics and principles that emphasize the importance of people, the community, and the environment.

A major study, *Managerial Values and Expectations*, was published by the American Management Association in 1982.[14] The following findings were obtained by Warren Schmidt and Barry Posner, from their study of 1,460 managers:

1. Asked to pick one statement as the basis for improvement in the quality of life in our country, 61 percent chose "a return to basic values." This includes an emphasis on "cooperation and the improvement of the total human community."

2. The qualities most admired in subordinates, colleagues, and superiors were integrity and competence.

3. Sixty-nine percent felt they were confident they understood the values of those with whom they worked. They also felt people worked better together if they shared similar values.

4. Managers' priorities seem to be shifting from career to private life. No longer are they automatically willing to forego an important home life for the office.

5. Female managers were found to be more career-oriented than their male counterparts. Sixty percent of the women chose career as the most important source of satisfaction compared to 37 percent of the men.

6. Nearly 80 percent agreed with the statement that they were clearer about their personal values now than they were five years ago.

7. Of those people considered important to an organization, the respondents felt they, themselves, were most important, followed by customers, subordinates, then superiors, and colleagues.

Box 13-3 on pages 428–29 gives a summary of this study, showing what some common beliefs are and what the evidence actually shows.

ENDING CASE
Even Leaders Have Limits[15]

Even the President of the United States, with the august power of that imposing office, can be overwhelmed by the incredible inflexibility of the organization. The *New York Times* relates how, after assuming office, Carter detected mice in the Oval Office; the very focal point of the presidency. He called the General Services Administration (GSA) who then came and handled the matter. Shortly after Carter continued to hear mice; but worse, one died in the wall and the stench was quite noticeable during formal meetings. However when he again called the GSA, he was told that they had carefully exterminated *all* the mice; therefore, any new mice must be "exterior" mice, and exterior work was the province of the Interior Department. The Interior Department at first demurred, but eventually a joint task force was mounted to deal with the problem.

SUMMARY

Leadership is a much desired but often elusive characteristic that organizations look for in managers. Bennis found that leaders are able to draw people to them by creating a vision and communicating it to others; leaders generate trust in others and have great faith in themselves, enough faith to believe that mistakes are just another distraction on the road to success. People feel empowered by effective leaders, they feel more competent and confident in themselves, and thus they find work exciting and challenging.

A number of theories have been developed to explain how leadership arises: Are leaders great men or does some other factor such as the need created by the situation determine who will be the leader? Some theorists believe that possession of charisma results in leadership, while others believe that leadership results from the sum total of a person's behavior and can be learned.

Researchers have found that effective management leaders spend more time in management functions such as planning and training others, exhibit more faith in their subordinates, and are more people-oriented than their less successful counterparts. Students of management have developed a number of theories to explain the orientation of managers to their employees and to competition. How a manager attempts to lead is largely explained by the attitudes brought to the task.

Leadership and advancement are directly affected by the ability to influence people's behavior in predetermined directions through the use of a power base. A study of derailed leaders showed that they had leadership styles that alienated people,

Box 13-3
Understanding the American Manager

SOME COMMON BELIEFS	WHAT 1,460 MANAGERS TELL US
About Organizational Values and Priorities	
Managers rate profitability as the most important of all organizational goals.	Profitability ranks seventh—after organizational effectiveness, high productivity, organizational leadership, high morale, organization reputation, and organizational efficiency.
Managers regard stockholders as being more important to the organization than customers.	Not true! Customers are seen as being significantly more important than stockholders.
Managers feel a strong pressure to conform to organizational standards	True. More than 70 percent feel these pressures (and very few see these pressures diminishing).
Managers regard service to the public as one of the most important goals of an organization.	An important goal for some, but it ranks behind 12 other organizational goals in the overall sample.
Managers at the supervisory level have very different value priorities than executives.	Managers at all levels, from supervisors to executives, have a fairly consistent set of values.
About Work and Home	
Most managers get more personal satisfaction from their career than from their home life.	Not true! Home life is a slightly greater source of personal satisfaction.
Most managers give a higher priority to their work responsibilities than to their family responsibilities.	Generally true—unless the job requires a change in lifestyle. Then the balance is almost even.
Most managers have jobs that prevent them from spending as much time as they would like with family and friends.	For half of the managers this is true; for half it is not true.
Work causes a great deal of stress in the home life of most managers.	Almost an even split—half feel the stress and half are not bothered.
Male managers are much more career-oriented than female managers.	No! Exactly the opposite proves true when we compare male and female managers who have similar positions and backgrounds. Women are more career-oriented than men.
About Bosses and Subordinates	
Managers want their superiors to be, above all, thoughtful and helpful.	No! The most important quality of a good boss is integrity—followed closely by competence.

About Bosses and Subordinates

Managers want their subordinates to be, above all, loyal and cooperative.	No! Managers want subordinates to have (1) integrity, (2) determination, and (3) competence.

About Personal Values

Ambition is number one on most managers' list of "most desired personal qualities."	Ambitious rates well below responsible, honest, capable, imaginative, and logical as the most desirable personal quality.
Most managers are less clear about their personal values today than they were several years ago.	Not true. Most are much clearer about their values now than they were five years ago.
The congruence between a manager's personal values and the values of the organization increases with age and rank.	This is true!

About Ethical and Unethical Behavior

Few managers would actually resign if they were asked to do something unethical by their boss.	Three out of the four managers say they would resign rather than carry out an unethical order. The lower levels feel more pressure to comply.
Most managers believe that the moral climate of society is the major influence on unethical behavior at work.	Not true. Most believe that unethical behavior is largely dependent on organizational climate—especially the actions of one's immediate boss.
When faced with an ethical problem, most managers go to a close friend or clergyman for guidance.	No. Most would discuss the problem with (1) their spouse, or (2) their boss.

On the Future

Managers tend to be optimistic about future trends.	It all depends. They are mixed about economic, social, and political trends, but optimistic about the future of themselves and their organizations.
Younger managers have very different views of social and political trends than older managers.	Age does not seem to affect managers' feelings of optimism or pessimism about these trends.
Most managers believe that the quality of life in America depends most heavily on technological advances.	No! Much more important would be a return to basic values emphasizing individual initiative.
Managers feel that trends in human affairs are pretty much out of control.	Not so. Most managers feel that the future has many challenges, but the challenges can be managed.

SOURCE: W. Schmidt and B. Posner, *Managerial Values and Expectations*, AMA Survey Report, (New York: American Management Association, 1982).

undercutting their power base and bringing their careers to a standstill. Of ten factors responsible for derailing this group's careers, none involved technical competency and only one had to do with analytical skills—people skills were the most important.

While leadership skills can be taught, it is a mistake to attempt to train people who do not see a need for change or improvement in their leadership skills. Likewise, the organization must support the changed behavior of those trained. Training programs should be aimed at on the job experiences to be effective.

Finally, the results of a study of managerial values debunk a lot of myths about the values and priorities of managers.

KEY TERMS

Management of attention
Management of meaning
Management of trust
Management of self
Great Man theory
Charisma
Theory X
Theory Y

Managerial grid
Systems I to IV
Participative management
Contingency theory
Path-goal model
Derailment
Power

REVIEW QUESTIONS

1. What four competencies did Bennis find in every leader?

2. In Bennis' analysis, what manifestations in followers indicate effective leadership?

3. What similarities exist between the views of those supporting the Great Man theory and the situationalist theory?

4. What characteristics did John F. Kennedy have that have caused him to be described as charismatic? Does charisma in a political leader depend on agreement with the leader's policies?

5. Why is the behavioral approach more useful in terms of researching the subject of leadership?

6. What implications does the behavioral approach to leadership and leadership training have for managers that sets it apart from the other three theories?

7. What four traits of effective managers were determined by University of Michigan researchers Robert Kahn and Daniel Katz?

8. What four traits of high achievement managers did Jay Hall identify?

9. Would you rather work for a manager who held the assumptions of Theory X or Theory Y? Why?

10. Can you think of a situation in which Theory X leadership would be preferable to Theory Y leadership? What does contingency theory suggest about your answer?

11. Compare and contrast System IV, 9,9 management, and Theory Y leadership.

12. Identify three traits in your personality that could lead to your derailment in a management career if you fail to control them.

CHALLENGE QUESTIONS

1. What similarities between top corporate leadership and marriage in terms of Bennis' four competencies suggest themselves from his study?

2. How would adherents of the following approaches to the study of leadership answer the statement: "Leaders are born, not made." True or false?
   A. Great Man
   B. Situational
   C. Charismatic
   D. Behavioral

3. A number of companies that have managed to make or are trying to achieve a major cultural change in their manufacturing operations have found themselves retaining workers while making wholesale changes in management personnel. Can you offer an explanation of this phenomenon in terms of Theory X and Theory Y?

4. Contingency theory suggests that different management styles might be appropriate depending on the demands of the situation. How do you explain the emphasis on management by consensus in large organizations?

5. Analyze the public's perception of Ronald Reagan and George Bush as you see them in terms of the factors found to derail top managers (treat the voters as the president's boss). Who do you think rates higher in each category? Does your analysis help explain election results?

CASE AND RELATED QUESTIONS

1. From the description provided of Colonel Potter, how would you assess his style in terms of the Blake-Mouton model? Where would Potter fit on Likert's Systems I to IV continuum?

2. Of the four characteristics common to high achievement managers identified by Jay Hall, which best describes the perception of Colonel Potter by the college students in the case?

3. What management style (authoritarian, democratic, laissez-faire) best describes former Beatrice Chairman James L. Dutt?

4. What expectations did Dutt have of his subordinates?

5. Given that Dutt was derailed, what factors led to his derailment? (Use the criteria suggested by the Center for Creative Leadership).

6. Dutt apparently convinced the Beatrice board of directors that his vision was correct because the company did not change directions after his departure. How do you explain his firing given this fact?

ENDNOTES

1. W. G. Dyer and J. H. Dyer, "The M*A*S*H Generation: Implications for Future Organizational Values," *Organizational Dynamics,* Fall 1984.

2. W. Bennis and B. Nanus, *Leaders* (New York: Harper & Row, 1985).

3. T. Peters and N. Austin, *A Passion For Excellence* (New York: Random House, 1985).

4. Bennis and Nanus, p. 17.

5. R. B. Smith, "Humanities and Business: The Twain Shall Meet—But How? *Management Review*, April 1985, p. 36.

6. C. G. Browne and T. S. Coltor, *The Study of Leadership* (Danville, IL: The Interstate Pub. Inc., 1958).

7. R. L. Kahn and D. Katz, "Leadership Practices in Relation to Productivity and Morale," *Group Dynamics*, ed. D. Cartwright and A. Zarrar (Evanston, IL: Row, Peterson & Co., 1960).

8. J. Hall, "To Achieve or Not: The Manager's Choice," *California Management Review*, Summer 1976.

9. D. McGregor, *The Human Side of Enterprise* (New York: McGraw-Hill, 1960).

10. R. R. Blake, J. S. Mouton, and B. Fruchter, "A Factor Analysis of Training Group Behavior," *Journal of Social Psychology,* October 1962, pp. 121–30; and R. R. Blake and J. S. Mouton, *The Managerial Grid* (Houston: Gulf Publishing, 1964).

11. R. Likert, *New Patterns of Management* (New York: McGraw-Hill, 1961).

12. R. J. House and T. R. Mitchell, "Path-Goal Theory of Leadership," *Journal of Contemporary Business*, Autumn 1974, pp.81–98.

13. F. E. Fiedler, "The Leadership Game: Matching the Man to the Situation," *Organizational Dynamics*, Winter 1976, pp. 6–16.

14. W. Schmidt and B. Posner, *Managerial Values and Expectations*, AMA Survey Report (New York: American Management Association, 1982).

15. *New York Times Magazine*, January 8, 1978, p. 29.

CHAPTER 14

MOTIVATION

LEARNING OBJECTIVES

■ Understand what managers can do to influence employee motivation.

■ Describe the various ways employees may react to a perceived threat.

■ Indicate the different methods used by managers to reduce or control the perception of a threat.

■ Explain how guilt is used to motivate, and why it is a form of internal disparity.

■ Describe the elements of Maslow's needs theory, and identify which needs are more basic and which are less essential.

■ Understand Alderfer's ERG theory—how it is similar to yet different from Maslow's needs theory.

■ Discuss what expectancy theory is, how it differs in its orientation from either the needs or ERG theory, and why it does not recognize internal needs.

■ Explain how reinforcement theory may be applied in an organizational setting.

■ Describe various strategies to directly motivate or influence employees.

■ Understand the relationship between a manager's value system and his or her direct influence strategy.

■ Explain how a manager can influence an employee by altering the work environment.

■ Recognize the problems associated with the use of competition as an internal motivation strategy.

One thing for sure, Arthur Friedman will never become the chairman of the board at General Motors.

It is not just because the modish, easygoing Oakland appliance dealer does not look the part—Hush Puppies, loud shirts, and denim jackets tend to clash with the sober decor of most executive suites. And it certainly is not because he is an incompetent administrator—the Friedman-Jacobs Co. has prospered during the 15 years of his stewardship.

It is mainly because Art Friedman has some pretty strange ideas about how you run a business.

Five years ago, he had his most outrageous brainstorm. First he tried it out on his wife Merle and his brother Morris.

"Here he goes again," replied Merle with a sigh of resignation, "another dumb stunt."

"Oh, my God," was all that Morris could muster.

His idea was to allow employees to set their own wages, make their own hours, and take their vacations whenever they felt like it.

The end result was that it worked.

Friedman first unleashed his proposal at one of the regular staff meetings. Decide what you are worth, he said, and tell the bookkeeper to put it in your envelope next week. No questions asked. Work any time, any day, any hours you want. Having a bad day? Go home. Hate working Saturdays? No problem. Aunt Ethel from Chicago has dropped in unexpectedly? Well, take a few days off, show her the town. Want to go to Reno for a week, need a rest? Go, go, no need to ask. If you need some money for the slot machines, take it out of petty cash. Just come back when you feel ready to work again.

His speech was received in complete silence. No one cheered, no one laughed, no one said a word.

"It was about a month before anyone asked for a raise," recalls Stan Robinson, 55, the payroll clerk. "And when they did, they asked Art first. But he refused to listen and told them to just tell me what they wanted. I kept going back to him to make sure it was all right, but he wouldn't even talk about it. I finally figured out he was serious."

"It was something I wanted to do," explains Friedman. "I always said that if you give people what they want, you get what you want. You have to be willing to lose, to stick your neck out. I finally decided that the time had come to practice what I preached."

Soon the path to Stan Robinson's desk was heavily traveled. Friedman's wife Merle was one of the first; she figured that her contribution was worth $1 more an hour. Some asked for $50 a week, some $60. Delivery truckdriver Charles Ryan was more ambitious; he demanded a $100 raise.

In most companies, Ryan would have been laughed out of the office. His work had not been particularly distinguished. His truck usually left in the morning and returned at five in the afternoon religiously, just in time for him to punch out. He dragged around the shop, complained constantly, and was almost always late for work. Things changed.

"He had been resentful about his prior pay," explains Friedman. "The raise made him a fabulous employee. He started showing up early in the morning and would be back by three, asking what else had to be done."

Instead of the all-out raid on the company coffers that some businessmen might expect, the 15 employees at Friedman-Jacobs Co. displayed astonishing restraint and maturity. The wages they demanded were slightly higher than the scale of the Retail Clerks Union, to which they all belong (at Friedman's insistence). Some did not even take a raise. One serviceman who was receiving considerably less than his co-workers was asked why he did not insist on equal pay. "I don't want to work that hard," was the obvious answer.

When the union contract comes across Friedman's desk every other year, he signs it without even reading it. "I don't care what it says," he insists. At first, union officials would drop in to see how things were going, but they would usually end up laughing and shaking their heads, muttering something about being put out of a job. They finally stopped coming by. It was enough to convince George Meany to go out to pasture.

The fact is that Friedman's employees have no need for a union; whatever they want, they take and no one questions it. As a result, they have developed a strong sense of responsibility and an acute sensitivity to the problems that face the American worker in general that would have been impossible under the traditional system.

George Tegner, 59, an employee for 14 years, has like all his co-workers achieved new insight into the mechanics of the free enterprise system. "You have to use common sense; no one wins if you end up closing the business down. If you want more money you have to produce more. It can't work any other way. Anyway, wages aren't everything. Doing what you want to do is more important."

Roger Ryan, 27, has been with the company for five years. "I didn't know about the big inflation in '74, but I haven't taken a raise since '73. I figure if everybody asks for more, then inflation will just get worse. I'll hold out as long as I can."

Payroll clerk Stan Robinson: "I'm single now. I don't take as much as the others, even though I've been here longer, because I don't need as much. The government usually winds up with the extra money, anyway."

Elwood Larsen, 65, has been the company's ace serviceman for 16 years. When he went into semi-retirement last year, he took a $1.50 cut in pay. Why? Larsen does not think a part-timer is worth as much: "I keep working here because I like it. We all know that if the Friedmans make money, we do. You just can't gouge the owner."

In the past five years, there has been no turnover of employees. Friedman estimates that last year his 15 workers took no more than a total of three sick days. It is rare that anyone is late for work, and even then there is usually a good reason. Work is done on time, and employee pilferage is nonexistent.

"We used to hear a lot of grumbling," says Robinson. "Now, everybody smiles."

As part of the new freedom, more people were given keys to the store and the cash box. If they need groceries, or even some beer money, all they have to do is walk into the office, take what they want out of the cash box, and leave a voucher. Every effort is made to ensure that no one looks over their shoulder.

There has been only one discrepancy. "Once the petty cash was $10 over," recalls Friedman. "We never could figure out where it came from."

The policy has brought about some changes in the way things are done around the store. It used to be open every night and all day Sunday, but no one wanted to work those hours. A problem? Of course not. No more nights and Sundays. "When I thought about it," confesses Friedman, "I didn't like to work those hours either."

The store also used to handle televisions and stereos—high profit items—but they were a hassle for all concerned. The Friedman-Jacobs Co. now deals exclusively in major appliances such as refrigerators, washers, and dryers.

Skeptics by now are chuckling to themselves, convinced that if Friedman is not losing money, he is just breaking even. The fact is that net profit has not dropped a cent in the last five years; it has increased. Although volume is considerably less and overhead has increased at what some would consider an unhealthy rate, greater productivity and efficiency have more than made up for it.

None of this concerns Friedman, though. He keeps no charts, does not know how to read cost-analysis graphs, and does not have the vaguest idea what cash flow means. As long as he can play golf a couple of times a week, and make money to boot, he could not be happier.

Encouraged by his success, Friedman decided to carry his revolution beyond labor relations. If it worked there, he figured, it should work with customer relations as well. So policy changes resulted in such innovations as the following "last bill" notice, that dread purveyor of bad tidings:

"For some reasons which we really cannot understand, you have decided not to pay the bill that you owe us.

"This letter officially cancels that bill and you are no longer under any obligation to pay us. We have decided not to give this bill to the collection agency, as our gain would be small compared to your loss.

"We would appreciate it, however, if you would take a moment to tell us why you made the decision not to pay us. It would be very helpful to us and the rest of our customers."

As cute as this may appear, it could hardly be expected to work. But Friedman claims that delinquent accounts are no more frequent today.

"We don't collect any more money than we did before, but we don't collect any less either. The difference is that you learn a lot more about the problem. Anyway, it's a lot more pleasant way of doing business," Friedman says. ▼

One of the most common managerial strategies for increasing performance is rewarding employees.

INTRODUCTION

Perhaps no question is raised more often by managers than, "How can I motivate (influence) my people to improve their performance?" While the strategy outlined in the opening case may be effective in some small business settings, it obviously is not possible to handle General Motors this way. The case does, however, show one innovative way to try to motivate people to higher performance. The basic presumption is that a manager can do something that will have an effect in altering either the quantity of performance, the quality of performance, or the direction of the performance. For example, a manager's concern may be: "How can I get employees to produce more?"; or "How can I get my people to do a better job—improve the quality of their work?"; or "How can I motivate my people to shift from spending so much time on recreation and spend more time in thinking about their work and their careers?"

The power to change behavior is always in the domain of the person whose behavior management is trying to influence. This means that motivation is something that goes on *inside* the person. The manager's problem is to find a strategy that will connect with this internal state in such a way that an employee feels motivated to act out of his or her own feelings. To Charles Ryan, Art Friedman's lazy driver, more pay (or at least the ability to set his own pay) is a motivator; to others in the case, money is not as important. While managers often use the phrase, "How can I motivate someone?" managers really do not motivate subordinates. People are motivated or not depending on their own internal state of affairs. Managers often try to influence this state of affairs, and the more appropriate phrase is probably, "How can I influence the motivation of my people?"

In order to function and stay viable in our competitive world, organizations must "motivate" people to do the following:[2]

1. To join the organization and to remain in it.
2. To perform tasks for which they are hired, and to do this in a dependable manner.
3. To go feasibly beyond this dependable behavior and to engage in more creative, spontaneous, and innovative behavior.

If all organizations have similar technology in the same market area, the organization that can solve the motivation problem best would appear to have a significant advantage. If employees at all levels are motivated to stay with the organization, do their jobs at their most effective level, and try to do things better, that organization would be more effective than one where turnover is high, performance is below standard, and no one tries to innovate or find ways to improve work performance.

Common Managerial Strategies

From almost the beginning of human society, superiors (parents, priests, kings, and, finally, managers) have used certain methods to impact the internal motivation of subordinates. Superiors have used some of the following methods over time because they were thought to be effective.

FEAR   Superiors have long assumed that fear can induce a change in performance. If people experience enough fear, they will alter their actions. The superior using this approach attempts to engage in some type of fear-inducing action, such as threats of bodily harm, loss of status or acceptance, or possible eternal consquences (going to hell or being reincarnated into a lower condition). If people are fearful and discomforted enough, it is thought that they will behave in ways prescribed by their superiors in order to reduce or eliminate the fear.

PUNISHMENT   Closely allied to use of fear is use of punishment. People fear many things (ghosts, the unknown, heights) that are not exactly punishments. But most people also fear being punished or even the threat of punishment. One can be physically punished—a spanking or a physical beating—or emotionally or psychologically punished—being rejected by a person or group or losing a promotion or raise. A superior using this strategy actually inflicts punishment until the person changes or threatens to inflict a punishment unless the person complies.

REWARD   Giving or promising a reward is one of the most widely used practices in trying to motivate people to improve performance. It is based, in part, on one of the oldest principles in the field of psychology: the **pleasure-pain principle**. In short, this commonsense principle states that people will tend to seek pleasure and avoid

Box 14-1
Motivation Quiz

What would "motivate" you to change your work performance in the following ways? Match up all the motivators with the performance changes to gain an idea of your own personal priorities.

PERFORMANCE CHANGES	MOTIVATORS
1. Start coming to work earlier.	A. An increase of salary. (How much increase would be needed?)
2. Start staying longer at work.	
3. Take less time at coffee breaks or lunch hour.	B. A bonus at year's end. (How much would be needed?)
4. Work harder (longer or with more intensity) on assignments.	C. A chance to select your assignments.
5. Start to read more in your field.	D. Informal praise and encouragement from your boss.
6. Take a night class to upgrade your skills.	E. Formal recognition (an award certificate, dinner, or picture in paper).
7. Take on an extra assignment.	
8. Take work home so you can get it done before the due date.	F. Chance to work with colleagues of your choice.
9. Spend time helping someone else.	G. Opportunity for promotion.
10. Volunteer your services to your boss for anything that needs to be done.	H. Freedom to do the job the way you want to.
11. Ask for suggestions as to how you can do your job better.	I. Some time off when you need it.
	J. More resources or help to do work.
12. Seriously try to organize your time better and try to become as efficient and effective as possible.	K. Have the company tell your family you are appreciated at work.
	L. A chance to attend professional meetings at company expense.

pain. Culture often defines what is rewarding or painful for a group of people. Almost everyone tries to avoid those things that are painful and increase rewards or "pleasure." Working harder to get a good grade, expending great effort to get on an athletic or drill team, putting in extra effort to get a higher score on a graduate admission test, or working extra hard for a raise or promotion are all examples of this principle.

GUILT   Another old-line strategy to induce motivation in others is guilt. Guilt is a form of internal disparity. If people are made to see that their performance is less than

PERFORMANCE CHANGES	MOTIVATORS
13. Set goals for yourself and have daily goals you are trying to achieve.	M. A chance to work on something new or different that would help you get new experience or skills.
14. Write up your suggestions and submit them showing how the company could get things done better or could save money.	N. An opportunity to be invited to make a presentation to upper management.
15. Take initiative to ask your boss how you might improve your performance.	O. To be chosen to attend a special training program.
16. Take time to show someone else how they might improve their work.	P. A threat of a poor evaluation or even termination.
17. Increase your participation in meetings, giving more suggestions, and offering to help move some new ideas along.	Q. A threat of a loss of salary or a demotion.
	R. An appeal that the company faces a crisis and needs your extra effort.
	S. Working with a team and doing whatever makes sense to the team.
	T. Clearly understanding what your career is and how this will help your career.
	U. You feel you are not able to do this much more regardless of the motivators.

promised or less than that done for them or expected from them, the imbalance results in feelings of guilt for most people. Increased performance is one way to reduce guilt feelings.

A sense of duty or reciprocity is often present in inducing guilt feelings. A boss may say: "Look what the company has done for you."; or "You owe it to the company to work more, one should produce a fair day's work for a fair day's pay."

As in most of the traditional strategies, even if guilt is induced, the resulting action may not be improved performance. Rejecting the claims of those trying to induce guilt will reduce the disparity as easily as increased performance. Workers could say (as unions have done in the past): "You have not given me a fair day's pay for my work, and I owe nothing to the company until they come up with equity in wages."

CRISIS   This strategy is based on the premise that if a crisis demands increased performance, people will respond to the crisis and produce the extra work. A manager might say: "We have just received an unexpected set of orders that require additional effort to meet. Will you help get the work out?" The premise is that the crisis creates an internal imbalance in the subordinates (they can see the need that created the crisis) and as a result they are motivated to engage in the extra effort.

However, workers could also reject the premise of a necessary crisis. They could claim that management was using the crisis as a means of getting more work for the same pay, or that it was management's lack of foresight and planning that caused the crisis. Workers could argue that if they have to work more they should be paid more.

MOTIVATION THEORY

Having reviewed some of the traditional motivational strategies, we will now examine what are currently considered the important issues to address in trying to understand human motivation.

Maslow's Need Theory

Need theory postulates that human beings have characteristic drives or needs. This theory postulates you can motivate people by providing something they need in exchange for effort. In other words, people are "motivated" to satisfy those needs that are most dominant in their lives. Abraham Maslow, an important American psychologist, developed a model called the need hierarchy[3] (see Figure 14-1). Maslow felt that certain of the internal needs were more fundamental than others, and that you would have to achieve some satisfaction of the lower or more basic needs before you would be able to exert energy in filling higher order needs.

PHYSIOLOGICAL NEEDS   At the lowest level in Maslow's hierarchy are basic biological or physiological needs. The body in its very makeup requires oxygen, food, water, rest, etc. The model suggests that if people are starving or threatened with a loss of the basics of human existence, they will have little concern for social life or meeting ego needs. Only when these fundamental biological needs are satisfied are people able to move on to other needs that have been latent, waiting upon the fulfillment of these lowest needs. Art Friedman's employees, for example, first value em-

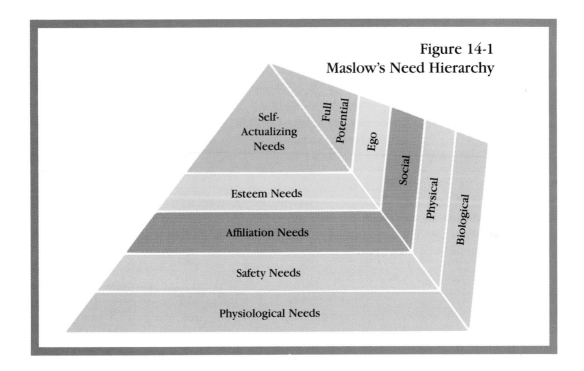

Figure 14-1
Maslow's Need Hierarchy

ployment itself—especially if it is perceived as the only way to meet physiological needs—before they value nights and Sundays off.

SAFETY NEEDS When biological, life-sustaining needs are met, people become concerned about their physical or psychological safety. In some respects your safety is threatened if a danger exists that you might die of hunger, thirst, or lack of air. But safety here represents certain conditions that threaten a person's physical well-being. Were an earthquake to hit the Bay Area again, Art Friedman's employees would probably be more concerned with their lives than the care of the inventory, even if a lack of care would cost them their jobs. This concern for safety preempts other motivational concerns. However, the Maslow hierarchy suggests that if employees were physically deprived for a long enough time, they would care for the inventory first, even in an earthquake, if there were no other way to meet their physiological needs.

AFFILIATION NEEDS When one is physiologically satisfied and feeling safe, it is then possible to try to satisfy a need for social contact. The model indicates that people have a need to interact with others, and find social support. If people are isolated and lonely, the social need would be deprived and energy would be expended to try and fill this need.

The social need is probably more culturally conditioned than needs for safety or psychological satisfaction. Some cultures require much more social contact than others, and people learn to "need" more social interaction and support. In almost every culture, however, the hermit—the one who isolates himself from human contact—is seen as a deviant.

ESTEEM NEEDS   Esteem needs refer to the need to be thought well of by others, and the need to feel that one is a worthwhile, respected person. The ego is bruised, and ego needs are unmet if you are ridiculed, slandered, disparaged, or evaluated negatively. In modern organizations, where the more basic needs are met, ego needs demand a great deal of the attention and energy of managers. Art Friedman, for instance, is very concerned with his employees' ego needs, and shows trust and appreciation through his management strategy.

A great many situations are potentially ego-threatening—yearly or semiannual performance reviews, promotions and raises (or the lack), type of assignments given, and all kinds of critical feedback. An astute manager recognizes the ego needs of employees.

SELF-ACTUALIZING NEEDS   Maslow postulated that if the prior needs could all be satisfied—which is not often the case—then people would be in a position to develop their full potential. They would have a need to actualize their potential and achieve their highest goals and aspirations. Maslow found that many people, when they thought about their own potential, became fearful of what they could become. Some of these people try to run away from their own potential development or sense of personal mission or goal. Maslow called this tendency to run away the "Jonah Complex" after Jonah of the Old Testament, a prophet who tried to run away from his mission but was swallowed by a whale and later released to fulfill his personal destiny.

Some interesting implications arise from need theory for managers. If people do in fact have internal needs that push for some type of satisfaction, a series of problems may arise in organizations that do not provide the means whereby these needs might be met.

Chris Argyris of Harvard has argued that since social and ego needs are often ignored in organizations and the only area open for bargaining is salary and benefits, the workers bargain hard in these areas.[4] It is as if they are saying: "You may keep me from filling any higher-level needs I have but it will cost you. You will have to pay for it." It is easier to bargain for money, time, and benefits than it is for social interaction, status, esteem, and personal fulfillment. Managers sometimes feel that because workers bargain mostly for tangible factors, then those are the matters of greatest importance. It is possible that if managers were to pay more attention to the satisfaction of social, ego, and self-fulfillment needs, less conflict over the symbols of the lower-level needs would result.

Alderfer's ERG Theory

A more recent variation of need theory has been the work of Clayton Alderfer and his **ERG theory**.[5] In his approach, Alderfer reduces Maslow's hierarchy into three needs:

existence (E), relatedness (R), and growth (G). His model is an attempt to make needs more applicable to organizational settings.

EXISTENCE NEEDS   In his existence needs, Alderfer includes the two most basic need levels of the Maslow model but translates these into the organizational setting. These include the need for pay, benefits, and decent working conditions.

RELATEDNESS NEEDS   These are similar to Maslow's social needs, and in the work environment refer to needs for social interaction and contact with others.

GROWTH NEEDS   A combination of Maslow's ego and self-actualization needs, growth needs refer to the needs to be creative and to experience growth and development on the job.

DIFFERENCES BETWEEN ALDERFER AND MASLOW   Two major differences separate the Maslow and Alderfer models. Maslow sees the need hierarchy as a satisfaction-progression process. That is, as one level of need is satisfied one moves on to a higher-level need. Alderfer postulates not only the progression of needs, but a regression component as well. This means that if a higher-level need is frustrated, a person will regress to an increased concern for a lower-level need—partly as a compensation of the loss of the higher-order condition.

The second major difference involves the number of needs operating at one time. Maslow's hierarchy indicates that people move from one level of need to another and experience only one need at a time. The ERG model claims that people in organizations experience more than one need at a given time. Thus, a person may have a need for both a pay increase and a more growthful job.

Expectancy Theory

As discussed above, one way to think about human motivation is to consider an individual as a cluster of needs. People are "motivated" to have their various needs fulfilled. Another way to think about motivation is in terms of expected outcomes or rewards. This orientation, developed mostly by Victor Vroom, is called **expectancy theory**.[6] This model postulates that people take into account the outcomes that can be expected and the strategies that can be expected to achieve desired outcomes. People will then be motivated to choose the most appropriate strategies that will produce the most favorable results. In this model, if a person desires a promotion and expects that to get a promotion extra hours and extra work are required, then she will be "motivated" to do the extra things to produce the desired outcomes. In the Vroom model, the important factors are the following.

EXPECTANCY   **Expectancy** is the perception that you expect a certain outcome to happen as a result of a certain action.

VALENCE   **Valence** is the strength of preference you hold for a particular outcome. Valences can either be positive or negative. Pay, promotions, and interesting assignments would all have a positive valence while reprimands, transfers, or a demotion would have a negative valence.

OUTCOME   **Outcome** refers to the end result of the behavior chosen. First- or second-level outcomes are possible. A first-level outcome is usually some type of performance and the second-level outcome is the result of that performance. For example, a worker might say, "If I work extra hard I will get my work done early (first-level outcome) and this should result in a superior evaluation (second-level outcome).

INSTRUMENTALITY   **Instrumentality** is the perceived relationship between first- and second-level outcomes. This can be quantified to fall somewhere between + or − 1.0. If the first-level outcome (getting work done early) always leads to a positive evaluation (second-level outcome), the instrumentality of the one towards the other is + 1.0. This value can approach zero when no perceived relationship or instrumentality exists, or to a − 1.0 if it is perceived that the second-level outcome cannot be reached by the first-level outcome.

ABILITY   **Ability** is the capacity a person has for performing the task that leads to the various outcomes. Lack of ability may affect motivation. For example, a person who has an expectancy of outcome for a certain action, may choose not to perform the action because he knows he does not have the ability to perform it successfully.

CHOICE   **Choice** is the prerogative a person has to select the most advantageous behavior to achieve a desired outcome given the probability the desired outcome can be achieved.

The processes involved in expectancy theory include looking at a situation and determining the valence or value of certain outcomes. If valence is high, and a person sees a high relationship between an action and the desired outcome, and she feels that she has the ability to carry out the action, she would predictably have high motivation to choose and carry out the selected action. On the other hand, even if the valence for a certain outcome is high, but a person cannot see that a recommended action will achieve the outcome, or if he feels the action suggested is outside his abilities, the motivation to engage in the action would predictably be low.

According to expectation analysis, many job-related problems arise because role expectations are at variance with role performance. If what the boss expects of a subordinate differs from what the subordinate thinks should be done, a violation of the boss's expectations is likely to occur, especially if the boss has not spent adequate time in defining his or her expectations to the subordinate. Times of changing organizational membership (adding new staff, new leadership coming in from the outside) are especially likely to lead to mismatched expectations. In cases of serious mismatched or violated expectations people may become seriously demotivated even to the point of leaving the organization.

CASE
Jerry and Tim Hartley[7]

Jerry cannot understand what is happening. For the past two weeks it seems he can never do anything right. He does not know why. His boss, Tim Hartley, is on his back all the time. Jerry is trying to do a good job. He tries to stay out of Hartley's way and does his own work without bother- ing anyone. He is expediting his work to prove that he is a good employee who takes the initiative, does not have to rely on the boss for everything, shows results even if others are not doing a good job. But for some reason that does not seem to be enough.

Tim Hartley is also perplexed. He likes Jerry and considers him a valuable employee. But Jerry is also a problem. Tim thinks to himself: "Why won't he ever check things out before he moves ahead on his own? This would keep me informed and keep him from making unnecessary mistakes. Also, a good employee fits into the team, and he is always working by himself, showing other employees up and creating a lot of resentment."

Jerry and his boss suffer from a case of mismatched expectations. Jerry expects himself to behave in certain ways consistent with his definition of a "good" worker. Although Jerry is behaving consistently with his definition of a good subordinate, his performance never will be adequate unless Tim's expectations change. Tim's negative sanctions (criticism, yelling, "being on" Jerry) violate Jerry's expectations about how a boss should behave; Jerry feels that a good boss should not criticize unjustly or without explaining. If Tim continues his pressure, Jerry may react in negative ways. In fact, he is already starting to avoid Tim. This cycle of negative action and reaction can build until a crisis occurs. If open conflict results, the consequence may be the loss of a good employee. ▼

Reinforcement Theory

Reinforcement theory is the modern version of the pleasure-pain principle, and is also known as **behaviorism** or **operant conditioning**. Its strongest current advocate is B. F. Skinner, a Harvard psychologist, and its central tenet is that behavior is a direct result of the stimuli to which a person is subjected.[8] If you can control the stimuli, you can control the subsequent behavior. Reinforcement theory does not recognize internal needs, motives, drives, or attitudes; they cannot be seen. Only behavior can be seen and observed. Therefore, the important matter is to find what kinds of stimuli will produce the desired behavior. For Tim Hartley, the manager in the preceding case, it means modifying the behaviors that elicit Jerry's undesirable responses. Skinner produced some remarkable achievements with animals—for

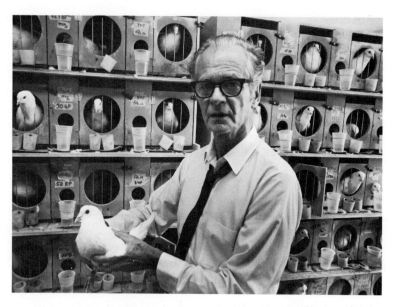

Reinforcement theory, as developed by behaviorist B. F. Skinner, relies on rewarding or punishing observable behavior.

example, getting pigeons to play a tune on a piano by constantly reinforcing or rewarding the desired behavior.

In organizations, managers apply this theory by clearly identifying desired outcomes or actions and then systematically rewarding the desired behaviors. Conditioning can be achieved either by **positive reinforcement** (a form of rewarding the behavior), punishment (actually punishing the behavior), or avoidance (essentially ignoring the behavior). If behavior is constantly rewarded, it is reinforced and will likely continue. If behavior is punished or ignored, it will likely cease. **Negative reinforcement** is a special case. Some evidence suggests that if a person wants attention and a certain behavior always results in attention, even if it is negative, the attention is perceived as a reward and results in a continuation of the behavior.

STRATEGIES OF MOTIVATION/INFLUENCE

Having looked at the more modern explanations of motivation, we will now examine those strategies a manager can use to tap into or influence this internal state of affairs in others.

Two major strategies by which a manager can attempt to influence another's behavior present themselves: (1) direct influence—those strategies that represent a direct interaction between managers and those they desire to influence; and (2) situational adjustments—those strategies designed to alter the nature of the situation within which a person works assuming that the altered situations will affect the internal motivation of others.

Direct Strategies

REWARD/PUNISHMENT   Probably no method is better understood and practiced than an approach similar to the following: "Jane, if you will improve your performance I will see that you are rewarded (raises, bonuses, promotions, etc.). If you do not improve, I will see that you are punished in some way (being fired, transferred, refused raises or promotions)." This is an exchange of commodities. The worker essentially says, "I will exchange my improved behavior for your rewards." To engage in such an exchange, it is vital that the worker be able to offer an improved performance, and that the manager be able to deliver the reward or carry out threatened punishment.

Pay as Reward   There has always been the interesting issue of pay as a motivator. Do people work harder if they are paid more money? Frederick Taylor used pay as a basic part of his early scientific management model. However research soon showed that other factors were more important—people worked harder under conditions of more autonomy, more ability to influence work conditions, more satisfying work. As a result research on money as a motivator was almost nonexistent for years. However, more recent research shows that money is important for two reasons—what it ultimately can buy in goods and services that are important to people, and as a symbol of a person's ranking and value in the organization. Money can be used as a motivator under certain conditions: (1) if it can be shown that performance is tied to pay (instead of seniority or loyalty); (2) if pay is truly important to people; and (3) if good performance is recognized and rewarded.[9]

Money, particularly in amounts often available to managers, is motivating to some people and not to others. A manager must understand the need system of subordinates and have the ability to meet these needs inside the constraints of the organization.

Sometimes managers use rewards and punishment without really determining if the worker can deliver the improved performance or if the manager can, in fact, control the rewards or punishments. Even assuming that both of these conditions are possible, an additional question presents itself: Are these rewards or punishments important enough to the worker that she will be willing to exchange improved performance for them? In times of affluence, easy job mobility, and values emphasizing freedom and autonomy, many people are not willing to make such an exchange because rewards and punishments do not motivate them very much. Strategies that emphasize fear, guilt, or threat are all punishment-oriented and fall into this category.

The research evidence in behavior modification clearly shows that engaging in consistent rewards for behavior improvement does make a difference, but punishment strategies are not motivating. Currently, a number of companies are using the behavior modification approach with success. In this approach, the manager tracks the performance of the subordinate and uses both formal and informal rewards (praise, pats on the back) to reinforce the improvement.

PERSONAL RELATIONSHIPS   While almost all influence strategies have some type of reward attached, the difference between offering a set of external rewards or punishments and appealing to something in the relationship is significant. The classic statement of interpersonal relationship influence is found in the New Testament when Jesus says, "If you love me, keep my commandments" (John 14:15). Most people have experienced the situation where someone has asked them to do something and they agree to the request because: "I respect Jim. He never asks unless it's really important." You also see a form of interpersonal exchange: "I owe Kathy a favor and I'll do it, but this puts us even."

The issue of interpersonal exchange is interesting. It is almost as if when a person asks or does a favor that he or she adds or subtracts from an interpersonal bank account. It is not uncommon to hear someone who is sensitive to this issue say: "No, I don't want to ask for that. It would use up my 'credits' and I want to save them for a more important issue."

It is important to remember that a manager can use interpersonal influence only if it has already been established in a relationship. It will not be very effective if a manager calls for improved performance based on personal liking, trust, and loyalty if these ingredients are not already present.

It is possible to combine interpersonal influence with reward and punishment. In various ways, the supervisor (manager, parent, teacher) could communicate to the subordinate: "If you don't do as I ask, I won't like you as much anymore." If the relationship is important, the threat of a loss of friendship or respect is very powerful; however, it probably produces as much hidden resentment and anxiety as improved performance.

LEGITIMACY OF THE REQUEST   Sometimes people are influenced to alter performance because the request is presented in such a way that it "makes sense." It agrees with their values or goals, and since they understand the request, they engage in the appropriate behavior change.

Recently the automobile industry has been involved in unprecedented agreements between the manufacturers and the unions to reduce rewards and to improve performance. It was clear that unless adjustments were made the industry would lose even more market share to foreign competition and many people would lose their jobs. The threat of loss or punishment was present, but the influential factor was that the request made sense to everyone.

In order to use the "makes sense" strategy, the manager must have data or information or be able to present the reasons for change. The reasons must be understood by people if they are going to change. The old authoritarian boss who wants people to change because he says so might find it hard to adjust to a new strategy where he must make sure that the workers understand and accept the request.

Some managers use the rational data-based approach first. They present the information upon which the request for change is based, but if the subordinates do not "buy" the rationale, the manager shifts to a backup strategy: reward, punishment, or interpersonal influence. If this occurs very often, workers may appear to accept the manager's position because they feel they will be coerced later, but the change in their behavior will not be a lasting one.

Values and the Influence Strategy

In part, the kind of direct influence strategy a manager employs is a function of the manager's value system. If the manager values the personal relationship, she may consciously or unconsciously use this point of leverage as the basis of influence. Another manager may feel that a good boss is one who "keeps aloof from the troops" and would never try to use personal relationships as a means of influence.

The reverse side of the issue is the value system of the subordinate—or the person who is the target of influence. If subordinates value being given accurate data and being allowed to participate in making the decision to change performance, they will likely resent rewards or punishments as inducements to change. For example, one company offered mementos of various kinds as a reward for faithful service: a five-year pin, a wall plaque for 10 years service, and a gold watch and dinner after 25 years. Some employees valued these mementos and were motivated to stay with the company and give faithful service. Other employees scoffed at such rewards; they felt they were juvenile and inappropriate symbols of recognition. In the preceding case, Tim Hartley will have difficulty motivating Jerry, because of a difference in value systems.

A kind of values progression may also take place. When people are young, struggling, and insecure, they may value those things that represent Maslow's lower-level needs. As they get these needs under control, they may begin to value attention paid to higher-level needs. If managers are not aware of this, they may continue to deal with lower-level needs that do not address current employee concerns. For example, one executive in a volunteer community service organization made it a practice to give a dinner or offer a prize to those who contributed a given number of service hours. Newcomers enjoyed these rewards, but many veterans felt resentful because they felt service should be for the improvement of the community—not for a dinner. They were more motivated by the legitimacy of the goals and not by immediate, short-term rewards.

CASE
Motivation Problem

Jack Wixom has been a member of your work unit for nearly three years. He is something of a puzzle to you. Everything about him seems to indicate that he should be one of your best employees, but he continues to come out as an average performer.

The information you have indicates that he has all of the necessary educational training needed to do the work required. He is bright enough and has had enough experience. But somehow he never seems to improve his performance. His work stays about the same. Currently, he shows little drive to move ahead either on a management track or a professional track. There have been several others who have been promoted over him. He just seems to drift along.

You wonder: Is it possible to light a fire under Jack and get him excited about his work and his long-term career in the Company?

What kind of actions could you, as his supervisor, take that might help move Jack into a different level of performance? 🔳

Situational Adjustment Strategy

Instead of using face-to-face interaction, a manager can also influence employees by altering the nature of the work environment. The assumption is that the factors in the changed situation will connect with the motivational forces inside the worker and result in improved performance.

INVOLVEMENT/PARTICIPATION   A major way of changing the work environment is to increase participation in planning, goal-setting, and decision-making processes. MBO, discussed in detail in Chapter 5, is one such system. When participation is real, not just a form used in an interview and discarded later, MBO has been shown to be very effective.

JOB ENRICHMENT   Another way of improving a work environment that is monotonous, unchallenging, and unmotivating is the job enrichment program of Herzberg,[10] which was discussed in Chapter 10. Herzberg's analysis broke job factors into "satisfiers" and "motivators." People could become satisfied or dissatisfied with such factors as pay, benefits, or working conditions, but these would not motivate a worker. Motivation has to connect with deeper feelings of growth and development. Spending more time on the "satisfiers" in the situation (pay, working conditions, human relations) may make people more satisfied (or less dissatisfied), but will not improve performance unless the work is altered or "enriched." The job change must be seen as providing more challenge, more personal or professional growth, more recognition, and a greater sense of contribution.

The manager is faced with a strategy decision in trying to influence performance change: "Should direct influence be used or would it be more effective to work on job enrichment?" The answer generally depends on the situation.

If job enrichment is chosen, the manager must further decide whether to allow people to review their work and to see if they can create a more enriched work environment on their own or to hire a job enrichment expert. Research in value

The Japanese pioneered the use of quality circles for increasing worker participation in decision making.

system psychology has shown that people differ in what they value. What is seen as job enrichment to one may not be enrichment to another. This being the case, the more effective process in job enrichment is to allow people themselves to determine what job changes are the most challenging to them.

Asking workers to deal with the issue connects them with two "motivating" processes—involvement and job enrichment. If the manager chooses this route, it is imperative that he be prepared to accept the work changes recommended. Nothing is more deflating than to expend time and energy coming up with some new ideas and then have those in authority reject them. The limits, if any, to the changes to be made, should be spelled out in advance so that people know the parameters within which they are expected to work.

QUALITY CIRCLES   The use of quality circles, which was also briefly discussed in Chapter 10, with worker involvement, represents a major situational change. Instead of using quality circles for management groups, workers are allowed to form into teams of eight to twelve people, usually under the direction of a trained group leader (a regular work supervisor who has been given special training in advance). The worker team or "circle" meets on a regular basis to consider the company, the department, the job, or specific problems, to investigate the factors that are reducing output or work effectiveness, and to make recommendations to management. Nearly all quality circle programs require that all worker suggestions be treated seriously and that management inform the circle of the disposition made of their suggestion. Quality circle programs include the involvement/participation dimension and may also lead to work changes consistent with job enrichment orientations.

COMPETITION   A common strategy used in certain areas of organizations is to put units or individuals into competition with each other. The assumption is that people will be motivated to increase performance when they have an opportunity to win.

The evidence as to the effectiveness of internal competition is inconclusive.[11] Very competitive individuals are motivated by opportunities to test themselves against others and to win. Others are intimidated by competition, get very anxious, and perform poorly in competitive situations.

The effects of win/win versus win/lose approaches to competition have been studied. A win/lose competition is one in which for someone to win, someone else must lose. Sales competitions are often this way. If the top 30 percent of the sales staff goes to Hawaii, the other 70 percent lose—they do not go.

Win/lose competitions can easily degenerate into lose/lose situations when some of the competitors decide that if they must lose, they will make sure that everyone else loses too. They do this by failing to share information about customers, about sales techniques, etc. While some salespeople win, the company loses since nobody has worked to help others do their best. By contrast, in sales organizations adopting a collaborative strategy of high support, sharing at sales meetings, and effective planning, sales increase for everyone.

An alternative strategy is to create win/win opportunities. In a **win/win competition** everyone has a chance to win. For example, a sales contest could be structured so that all salespeople who improve their sales performance over the previous period (either by writing more total business or by improving in some other area such as obtaining new customers) will be eligible for the reward. Such a program makes it possible to collaborate without being personally personalized. Win/win competitions are consistently used by companies such as McDonald's (service), Procter & Gamble (product management), and Tupperware (sales).

FEEDBACK OR DATA-SHARING STRATEGIES   Another way to alter the situation is to move from a data-deprived condition to a data-enriched situation. One of the factors in the early Hawthorne studies was to give the women workers in the test situation clear, frequent data about their work output.

Data sharing can form the basis of a kind of informal competition either between units or within the person herself, or it can be the basis of reward to those involved who can experience the satisfaction of seeing performance improved. Andrew Carnegie set up a kind of informal competition between the day shift and night shift in steel-making crews by merely writing on the floor in chalk the production record of the day shift. When the night shift saw the report, they tried to beat the record and wrote their production in the same place for the day shift to see.

Most behavior modification programs use increased data sharing as an important element in achieving improved performance. As people set goals for improvement, the supervisor tracks the change in output, shows the worker the record of change, and conveys personal expressions of encouragement, praise, and support. The usual practice of combining praise and recognition with data sharing represents a change in supervisory style for most managers, and they spend more time interacting with subordinates. This alone may explain the success of behavior modification programs.

Another form of data sharing that can be combined with the direct interaction approach is direct feedback from supervisor to subordinate, as in a performance review session, or survey or instrumental data that is gathered from subordinates, peers, and superiors about the person's performance, and is used as a basis for performance planning. General Electric's plant experience indicates that direct verbal feedback, either positive or negative, that was not accompanied by an objective review of performance, and planning for specific improvements did not result in improved performance.

The assumption behind data sharing is that feedback creates a certain amount of disparity or tension inside the person receiving the feedback. If the feedback indicates that the person is doing less than the person had thought he or she was doing, tension is created and an improvement in performance is required before it is reduced. More research is needed to pinpoint the answers to the following questions: (1) Does all feedback from any source create tension to change? (2) Can a person get too much feedback? (3) When should feedback be given, by whom, and in what manner? While feedback can create a motivation to change, the unanswered questions make it important to caution that this strategy should be used carefully.

ONE-ON-ONE INTERVIEWS   Another way of altering the situation (with some elements of direct influence) is to begin to hold regular one-on-one, face-to-face interviews with subordinates. Wayne Boss of the University of Colorado, conducted a series of experiments on the impact on performance of a regular interview. He devised a process he called the "Personal Management Interview" (PMI) and had some managers hold the PMI while others did not. Boss found that in every case where an effective PMI was conducted, performance improved, and the improvement was maintained over a period of years. When the PMI was not held, performance always dropped off.[12]

In order for the PMI to be effective, Boss found it had to be held between manager and subordinate on a regular basis (no less than once a month, preferably once a week or biweekly) and it had to follow a particular flow. The format of the PMI included the following:

1. In the first session, the manager and subordinate share and agree on mutual expectations. What do they expect of each other on the job and in the PMI? They need to agree on what constitutes reasonable expectations of each other in each area.
2. Following the agreement on expectations, the manager and subordinate identify and discuss any problems currently facing the subordinate.
3. **Coaching-training**. After identifying current problems, the manager presents suggestions and ideas, and even role-plays methods of dealing with the problems.

4. After looking at job problems and ways of handling them, the manager and subordinate look at any problems or issues that exist between the two of them and attempt to resolve them.

5. Information sharing. The manager shares any information about the organization or work unit that might be important for the subordinate to understand.

6. Discussion of personal needs or concerns. The subordinate is given the opportunity to talk about any concerns, and managerial help is given to the extent possible.

7. Assignments are made and reviewed. In each session, the manager and subordinate spend time writing down what assignments, actions, and goals are to be carried out between this session and the next PMI. At the next session, the progress made with regard to these items is reviewed and new assignments are agreed upon.

One of the initial complaints from managers when the PMI procedure was started was that they did not feel that they had the time to conduct the sessions. Time is a real constraint in management, but when managers finally learned to conduct effective interviews that resulted in higher motivation and improved performance, they began to realize that the interviews were saving them time in the long run.

With an understanding of the perceptions individuals bring to their jobs and some useful ways of utilizing that information to enable them to become more motivated, the discussion turns to how leaders use this information and other techniques to enable organizations to meet their goals successfully.

ENDING CASE
Motivation—In the Eye of the Beholder?[13]

 Vince Flowers, senior partner of the Values Institute, Dallas, Texas reports the following experience when he was an engineer working for Texas Instruments. Engineering ceased to be a challenging career and he began to be more and more interested in the human factors in organizations. With this interest in mind, he asked his superiors if he could spend time investigating the interesting question, "Why do people stay on a job with a company?" The reverse question, "Why do people quit?" had received a great deal of attention in much research.

The company was responsive to the request and gave him time, an office, and access to a variety of people who had been with the company for years to interview. Flowers developed a set of ten questions designed to cover the important issues of employment. For the next several weeks he interviewed a number of people each day and got increasingly excited as answers to his questions began to emerge. He worked long hours, interviewing more people.

One time in the late afternoon he was conducting his last interview of the day with an operator who had been with the company for many years assembling component parts for computers. His job consisted primarily of putting together the same six parts, over and over again, day after day. It was a surprise to Flowers that the man always talked with pride and enthusiasm about his work. He obviously liked what he did and anticipated staying with the company until retirement, probably doing the same routine job of assembling the same six parts.

At the end of the interview, Flowers said, "Ed, this is not one of my ten questions, but tell me, don't you get bored to death assembling the same six parts day after day?"

Ed looked at him with amusement and responded, "Vince, I have been wanting to ask you the same question: Don't you get bored to death asking the same ten questions over and over again day after day?"

This experience led Flowers to shift his whole career into examining the impact of values on motivation—what motivates a person seems to depend to some considerable extent upon what a person values. ☒

SUMMARY

In order to understand motivation, managers must first understand why individuals behave the way they do—how they react to threat and attempted influence. Motivation is, after all, an internal process, not an imperative that can be imposed externally. With this key concept in mind, managers can utilize methods of reducing the number or degree of threat reactions among their employees.

Managers should also understand traditional managerial strategies—how they succeed or fail, based on how they motivate internally. Human needs theories, among them, Maslow's need theory, provide valuable insight concerning motivation and these traditional strategies. According to Maslow, certain internal needs are more basic than others, and human beings satisfy higher needs only when the more basic needs are met. Managers must therefore provide avenues of self-fulfillment or employees will remain unmotivated.

Motivation strategies fall into two basic groups: direct influence and situational adjustments. Herzberg's motivation theory is helpful in understanding these strategies. He postulates that pay and benefits are merely satisfiers, not motivators. Motivation is related to deeper feelings of growth and development. Increasing participation (for example, through quality circles) can help to boost employee motivation levels.

KEY TERMS

Fear	Outcome
Punishment	Instrumentality
Reward	Ability
Pleasure-pain principle	Choice
Guilt	Behaviorism
Need theory	Positive reinforcement
ERG theory	Negative reinforcement
Expectancy	Win/win competition
Valence	Coaching-training

REVIEW QUESTIONS

1. How is data sharing used to motivate employees? What does the concept of data sharing assume about human nature?

2. How is the pleasure-pain principle related to the motivational strategy of rewarding for performance?

3. According to Maslow what physiological needs do human beings have? If these needs are filled, what needs do human beings seek to satisfy next?

4. What implications arise for managers from Maslow's needs hierarchy?

5. According to Chris Argyris why is bargaining for salary and benefits emphasized so heavily in a organization?

6. What role do expected outcomes play in Vroom's expectancy theory?

7. What are first- and second-level outcomes according to expectancy theory?

8. What is the relationship between role expectation and role performance? Why does a discrepancy between them cause problems?

9. What is negative reinforcement? How does it differ from avoidance or punishment?

10. What factors must be accounted for in successful reward/punishment motivation strategy?

11. Why is it important for managers to respond to the recommendations of quality circles?

CHALLENGE QUESTIONS

1. Why is it necessary to look inside someone, or understand his or her internal state, in order to motivate them?

2. Why do you suppose people run away from their own potential development, or from self-actualization? Why are they fearful of what they can become?

3. Why are tangible (wages, bonuses) needs perceived to be more important than intangible ones (status, esteem)?

4. Which one of the human needs theories most closely resembles your own needs experience? Take into account factors like Alderfer's claim that people experience more than one kind of need at a time, not necessarily in the sequence suggested by Maslow.

5. Explain Herzberg's motivation theory in terms of Maslow's needs hierarchy. What does Herzberg say people are motivated by, and how does this compare with the implications of need theory concerning motivation?

CASE AND RELATED QUESTIONS

1. What influence strategy most closely resembles that of Art Friedman?

2. In terms of reinforcement theory, what accounts for truckdriver Charles Ryan's change in work habits, or in the development of a strong sense of responsibility among the employees in general?

3. What situational adjustment strategies can be seen in Art Friedman's policy changes?

4. What need level (of Maslow's hierarchy) do you think Jerry has been unable to satisfy? How would Alderfer's ERG Theory categorize Jerry's unsatisfied need?

5. How could Tim benefit from an understanding of the individual behavior orientations outlined in the chapter? How is Jerry's reaction to Tim's management style explained by these orientations?

ENDNOTES

1. From Martin Koughan, *The Washington Post*, February 23, 1975.

2. R. M. Steers and L. W. Porter, *Motivation and Work Behavior*, (New York: McGraw Hill, 1975).

3. A. H. Maslow, "A Theory of Human Motivation," *Psychological Review* 80 (1943), pp. 370–96; and A. H. Maslow, *Motivation and Personality* (New York: Harper & Row, 1970).

4. C. Argyris, *Personality and Organization* (New York: Harper & Row, 1957).

5. C. P. Alderfer, *Existence and Relationships and Growth* (New York: Free Press, 1972).

6. V. H. Vroom, *Work and Motivation* (New York: Wiley, 1964).

7. W. G. Dyer, *Strategies for Managing Change* (Reading, MA: Addison-Wesley Pub. Co., 1984), chap. 12.

8. B. F. Skinner, *Beyond Freedom and Dignity* (New York: Alfred A. Knopf, 1971).

9. See R. M. Steep and L. W. Porter, *Motivation and Work Behavior* (New York: McGraw-Hill, 1975), chap. 15.

10. F. Herzberg, "One More Time: How Do You Motivate Employees," *Harvard Business Review* 46 (1968) pp. 53–62.

11. D. J. Cherrington, "Satisfaction in Competitive Conditions," *Organizational Behavior and Human Performance* 10 (1973) pp.47–71.

12. R. W. Boss, "Team Building and the Problem of Regression: The Personal Management Interview as an Intervention," *Journal of Applied Behavioral Science* 19, No. 1 (1983).

13. Personal interview with Dr. Vince Flowers.

CHAPTER 15

COMMUNICATIONS

LEARNING OBJECTIVES

■ Discuss the reasons communications often break down.

■ Explain strategies for improving communications skills.

■ Describe the characteristics of a successful communicator.

■ Realize how unconscious intentions can be displayed in our communications.

■ Understand the different communications strategies, how one may be organized, and when they can be used.

■ Indicate how communicating too much or too little can be detrimental to the communication process.

■ Explain the elements of the Johari window and how it can be used to better understand communications.

■ Develop the pros and cons of the "open door" policy—why it can be counterproductive and what is needed to make it successful.

■ Understand the strengths and weaknesses of both written and oral communication.

■ Explain the principle of feedback and how it relates to the communication process.

■ Identify the different ways by which feedback may be obtained.

■ Understand proper methods of giving feedback.

John Holland, controller of Lawton Pharmaceuticals, Inc., contacted Harry Triemstra, partner of Froehling, Winthrop, and Triemstra, public accountants. Holland wanted an audit of one of Lawton's divisions, and because of a current profit squeeze, at the lowest possible fee. Triemstra assured Holland that the job would be done competently and as inexpensively as possible.

Triemstra assigned Nils Swenson, a capable and experienced senior, to the account, emphasizing Holland's concern about the fee.

"Let's make a good impression, Nils," Triemstra said, "Lawton could be a big account for us."

Jeff Watkins, a bright but inexperienced young junior, was also assigned to the job, under Swenson's supervision. Swenson and Watkins began their examination on Monday, and despite the fact that this was Watkins' first audit, the work went smoothly. Swenson was eager to complete the assignment quickly, not only to please the client but to be free to attend a technical seminar in Chicago the following week. Late Friday afternoon he reviewed the work and determined that the examination had been completed except for analyzing a few small expense accounts.

"Jeff, it looks to me as if we've just about wrapped this one up except for vouching the expense accounts. So why don't you do those, and I'll be back from the seminar a week from Monday to review the work papers. And, incidentally, Jeff—you've done a very good job, considering this has been your first audit."

Jeff was obviously pleased with the compliment. "Thanks, Nils, it was a pleasure working with you. I'll have those accounts ready when you get back."

The following Friday, Harry Triemstra received another call from John Holland.

Holland: Say, Triemstra, I thought we were in agreement that the costs on this job would be minimal.

Triemstra: Exactly, what's wrong?

Holland: Then why has this greenhorn accountant of yours been spending a solid week vouching all our expense accounts? I can tell you there's no way we're going to pay for those 40 hours of vouching work!

Triemstra: He's been vouching expense accounts all week? Frankly, this baffles me. I'll check with our senior, Nils Swenson, and find out why he decided to extend their tests. I'll get back to you.

As soon as he finished his conversation with Holland, Triemstra buzzed his secretary: "Diane, get hold of Swenson immediately. He's in Chicago at the [expletive deleted] seminar!"

Miscommunication between President Truman and General MacArthur almost resulted in a World War.

INTRODUCTION

Ask any manager what are the top five problems he or she faces, and communications is sure to be listed as one of the top issues of concern. This is not surprising because, as Roger Smith, CEO of General Motors, puts it: "Communication is the vehicle for all other forms of business competence. Everything we do depends on the successful transfer of meaning from one person or group to another."[2]

Communication is a major problem in many management situations. In the opening case the essential problem is that Jeff did not understand clearly what was expected of him. The communication between Nils Swenson and Jeff Watkins left a lot of ground for misunderstanding. This is not unusual and miscommunication can lead to far more serious problems than outlined in the case. The most striking evidence is the hot line between Washington and Moscow, which was installed to prevent a communications misfire from triggering a nuclear holocaust.

Richard Neustadt documents a famous case of misunderstanding between President Harry S Truman and General Douglas MacArthur when the two met in Guam to discuss the Korean War.[3] Truman came away from the meeting convinced that they had agreed to limit the conflict to the country of Korea, while MacArthur came away with a clear understanding that he had permission to send American aircraft over the Yalu into Manchuria and bomb the People's Republic of China. The stakes involved a possible World War.

People communicate with each other verbally (face-to-face or by telephone), by written messages (letter, memos, or reports), or nonverbally (facial or body gestures), or through a third party (via a messenger of some kind). A variety of snags can occur as one person tries to let others know what is on his or her mind. These may lead to a true communication problem.

In addition, what people sometimes refer to as communications problems are actually symptoms of other problems. When asked what the problem is, people often say, "We don't communicate." The reason they do not communicate, however, is that they have not worked through the collaborative process—they have not agreed on schedules, they have not made common decisions together, they blame others for failures, and they avoid each other as much as possible. Lack of communications, therefore, is often a symptom of other problems.

Communication skills are not only important, but the need for them is pervasive. Everyone needs to communicate effectively with others. In this chapter the major goals of communication are discussed. The reasons communications break down are also outlined. The last half of the chapter introduces strategies for improving communications skills and for gathering feedback to measure improvement.

THE GOAL IN COMMUNICATIONS

The goal in communications is to achieve our intentions through interaction with others. Generally, a manager is a successful communicator if:

1. People feel they have received enough information. This usually means that subordinates feel they know what is happening in the organization and their unit, particularly anything that affects their job.
2. People feel the messages and information they receive are clear and accurate.
3. People feel the manager listens to them and understands what they have to say.

Conversely, it can be said that a manager's communications are inadequate or ineffective if the following conditions prevail:

1. Not enough information is shared. People are confused and feel they are "in the dark"; changes occur or decisions get made or actions taken they do not know about or understand.
2. Messages are given that are unclear, confusing, or contradictory. When assignments or directives come out people do not feel they really understand what is being said. They may also feel that they have no opportunity to clarify the message.

3. The communication flow is uneven. Some people get the word about happenings, events, or changes and others do not.

4. Actions are not consistent with the communicated message. Distrust results when people are told one thing but observe actions that contradict what they were told.

5. Communications get blocked. High frustration results when a request for information or a decision is sent up "through channels" and nothing happens. Somewhere in the communication pipeline the request was blocked, lost, or diverted into oblivion.

6. No one listens. Since communication means both someone telling and another hearing, the communication flow is blocked if a listening ear is unavailable—someone who is willing to spend time listening to others.

Communication Directions

Communication can come from a number of directions—downward, upward, and sideways. Downward communication is used to convey the messages of superiors and may be found in a variety of forms, such as memos, policy manuals, bulletins, direct orders, and mission statements. These communications are essential to the proper functioning of an organization, but can also be detrimental to survival if they become the only acceptable means of transmitting information. This type of one-way communication could stifle innovation or increase worker dissatisfaction.

A balance has to be struck between downward communication and upward communication. Frontline employees are most familiar with various aspects of the organizational environment and need to have some avenue through which their knowledge may be shared with superiors. Many of these avenues will be discussed later on in the chapter from the manager's perspective—as ways to elicit feedback from subordinates. Recent evidence suggests that managers who regularly seek feedback from subordinates are more effective in accomplishing their tasks than managers who do not.

Horizontal and diagonal communications can also occur in an organization. These avenues can serve to increase coordination among various organizational departments. Production may need to coordinate activities and share information with engineering, therefore creating a necessity for horizontal communication—communication between equals in the hierarchy. Diagonal communication is the least used of communication directions, because it bypasses traditional hierarchical lines of authority. Employees of unequal rank in different departments, however, may feel the need to communicate directly with each other—especially when time needs to be saved. Diagonal communication linking the sender directly to the receiver may therefore be more efficient and accurate in certain circumstances than more traditional means of communications.

What are the conditions that foster good communications or lead to a breakdown of this important process? Managers usually communicate personally through direct, interpersonal contact, or more formally through memos, directives, speeches, or other methods that reach a number of people. Let us look at both of these processes.

INTERPERSONAL COMMUNICATIONS: INTENTION TO IMPACT

Communication usually begins with a person who initiates contact with others to achieve some purpose or goal. A manager may call in an employee to clarify an assignment or to give instructions. Later he may want to instruct, stimulate, encourage, or support the same employee. The goal in communication is to achieve the actual impact or result we intend—to have our message impact others in a way that will result in the desired outcome (**intention to impact**).

Intention and Impact

Intentions are the end results or goals that are desired through communication. Nils Swenson wanted to encourage Jeff Watkins by complimenting his good work. He coupled his instructions to vouch the expense accounts with the statement that he would review Jeff's work when he got back. His intended impact (the message he really wanted to impart) was that he had confidence that Jeff could finish the expense accounts quickly and he would review Jeff's work upon his return.

Behavioral Gaps

However, between your intention and the impact—the actual effect of your communication—are two major gaps that must be considered and to some degree managed (see Figure 15-1). Nils needed to translate his intentions into behavior. For most people this is a major difficulty much of the time. Nils expressed his intentions clumsily and Jeff thought he had a week to vouch the expense accounts thoroughly.

SENDING THE WRONG MESSAGE   Subordinates of some managers feel hostile, defensive, and resistant to their boss. A conversation with the boss would disclose that the boss is distressed with how the workers feel; this negative reaction is certainly not what the boss intended. When managers send wrong messages, they generally do not mean to. In complimenting Jeff Watkins, for example, Nils Swenson said, "You've done a very good job, considering this has been your first audit." Jeff may have heard, "For a rookie you are okay, but of course you can't measure up to us professionals." Jeff may well have decided, "Oh yeah, well I'll show him I can do a job as well or better than anyone else."

Figure 15-1
The Cycle of Interpersonal Communication

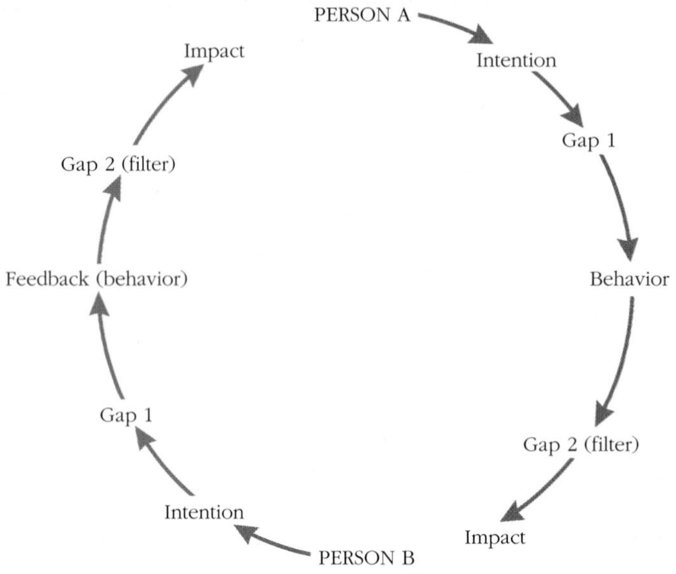

PERSON A

Impact — Intention — Gap 1 — Behavior — Gap 2 (filter) — Impact — Intention — Gap 1 — Feedback (behavior) — Gap 2 (filter)

PERSON B

1. Gap 1 is the difference between one's intentions and the behavior that represents them.

2. Gap 2 is the difference between one person's behavior and the other person's perception of it (filter system).

3. Feedback is finding out how our behavior has been received by others.

A person's unconscious intentions are sometimes displayed exceptionally well. The person would really like to say some things, but since they are often not socially (or personally) acceptable or desirable, they are kept hidden. A manager, for example, may at some deeper level distrust his subordinates, and his behavior communicates his distrust very accurately. At the conscious level he would say that the communication of distrust is not his intention. One of the important reasons for getting feedback is to help the communicator examine, honestly, his total intention system—both conscious and unconscious.

"FILTER" SYSTEM: RECEIVING THE WRONG MESSAGE   The point of distortion between intention and impact may also be in the "eye of the beholder." Nils may very clearly represent his intentions to Jeff, but if Jeff has a clogged **filter system**, or perceptual screen, and perceives the message quite differently than was intended, the resulting impact will not be what Nils desired. For example, Jeff may have a thick antiauthority filter, which causes him to resent any implication that he is not Nils' professional equal. He interprets attempts to clarify or encourage as disapproval or control. All people have filters and are usually aware of some of them and blind to others. Filters are made up of biases, prejudices, values, experiences, and feelings.

Filters and Attribution

Filters shape our perceptions of sensory data. The message from the sender is seldom the same as that experienced by the receiver. Each has had a different set of background experiences and that can distort the communication. For this reason it is important for managers to consider the intended receiver before sending any message, gearing that message specifically for those intended.

Because filters shape how we perceive others, we can only know what exists as we interpret it, never what really is. Weir sums it up this way: "Each of us is continually perceiving and organizing his world in his unique way, never precisely the same as anyone else. I am 'doing' myself and you are 'doing' yourself. Your 'existence' is for me always my perception of you, the 'you-in-me.'"[4]

In either event, whether the problem of the undesirable impact results from sending the wrong message or receiving the wrong message, the result for Nils is the same: He has not achieved the consequence he intended.

Competency in Communication

THE COMPETENT COMMUNICATOR   The competent person (in this framework) is one who is capable of rather consistently achieving the impact intended. If he wants issues clarified, they become clarified. Should he desire to encourage or motivate others, they feel encouraged or motivated following the communication.

THE INCOMPETENT COMMUNICATOR   On the other hand, the incompetent communicator is one who regularly and consistently impacts others in ways that are not intended. He finds that for some reason he is fighting a series of unintended and unanticipated consequences. People are resistant, overly dependent, apathetic, hostile, fearful, frustrated, or cautious when he really would like them to be open, innovative, collaborative, and enthusiastic. Something is going on between the intention and the impact that requires some modification or adjustment in the communication process.

HOW TO DEVELOP AN EFFECTIVE STRATEGY   It is not possible for anyone to be so all-wise, sensitive, and skillful as to always know exactly the right things to communicate to produce the exact impacts or results desired. However, it is possible to develop a strategy for improving your effectiveness. Following is an outline of how a manager might develop an effective **communication strategy** in collaboration with those she wants to influence.

Declare Intentions   Instead of moving directly into the implementation of intentions, the manager could bring together the people she is trying to influence to talk with them about what she would like to achieve. As a result of this discussion they would understand her intentions and would not need to guess at what they are by interpreting her behavior. If subordinates have not yet experienced this discussion of intentions before, their filter systems may cause them to look upon this action with suspicion—as another "gimmick" or trick. The leader must be completely candid in declaring her intentions and, when this is accomplished, she should invite the next step.

Elicit Suggestions for Action   The next step is to ask people for their ideas, suggestions, and insights about how to achieve the desired results. If a manager's intentions are to motivate her subordinates to greater productivity, she might bring them together and honestly explore her intentions, what she desires, and why she desires it. She may find in that process that the views of her subordinates are quite different from her own. This discovery might cause her to revise her intentions. But, assuming the subordinates accept her intentions as valid, they could then offer their suggestions about what would be necessary or important in motivating them to increase their production. All of this requires an opening of the channels of communication so that everyone is sharing important information with each other. The leader should check to be sure that she understands her subordinates by reflecting back their statements with comments like, "I understand that you feel this way, is that correct?" She should also make sure her subordinates understand the matter as she intends. A useful question to ask is, "What have you just heard me ask of you?"

UNACTED INTENTIONS   It should be obvious that you cannot achieve desired impacts unless action is taken. The behavior of some people does not appropriately reflect their intentions because they lack skill, are inexperienced, or are ignorant regarding useful strategies. Other people are afraid to take action and sit silently on their intentions wishing that something could be done, having fantasies of the great accomplishments that might be, but in the final analysis doing nothing.

In the real sense inaction is a strategy—it is one way of coping with a situation—and it will certainly have an impact on others. It may not have the impact one desires, however, and if you are going to be an effective manager a more appropriate strategy to achieve the desired impact is needed.

UNINTENDED COMMUNICATIONS   Very simply, communication is the process whereby one person, through the use of symbols (words, actions, and gestures), makes others understand how he thinks and feels. Sometimes people send out unintentional signals that let people know how they feel when they might have preferred to keep their feelings hidden. A case in point is the Freudian slip—what we really think just slips out unintentionally.

COMMUNICATING TOO MUCH   One problem in most organizations is that in certain areas the communication system is too good; that is, more is communicated than is really intended. People are able to pick up each other's signals much like a radio antenna plucks radio signals from the air. One early study of very young babies found that, if a baby was fed orange juice by a nurse who did not like orange juice, in a short time the baby did not like it either. However, if the nurse liked orange juice, so did the baby. Somehow, the nurse was able to communicate to the child her distaste for orange juice via tenseness, grimacing, or shuddering at the sight of the baby drinking the "nasty stuff."

Subordinates and bosses, too, pick up all the communicative signals given by each other—not just what is spoken directly to them. What about the following exchange?

Subordinate: "Will you come and help me with this report?"

Boss: "Just a minute, I'm busy right now preparing some letters."

Boss (later):   "Come and look over this material."

Subordinate: "Just a minute, I'm still working on my report."

Boss: "Not in 'just a minute.' When I call you I want you to come right now."

What is the boss unintentionally communicating to his subordinate? Does the employee "hear" the boss expressing two standards—one for him and another for his boss. Or does he hear that his superior's work is more important than helping him with his problems. If someone were to ask the boss: "What is more important, your work or your subordinate's problems?", he might insist that he is more concerned about his subordinate. But in subtle ways he has communicated to his subordinate that the concerns of the subordinate come after his own.

Subordinates can also unintentionally communicate attitudes to their bosses, often with disastrous effects on their careers. Peter Drucker points out that the worst mistakes made by talented managers in their early years are ones of communication—underrating the boss and failing to understand how the boss receives information best. Even though the young manager never overtly says or does anything to indicate that he feels his boss is incompetent, the boss will almost always detect this attitude. For example, the young manager prepares a brilliantly written, lengthy report and submits it to the boss. When she does not get a reaction, she loses respect for the boss. The subordinate, however, has failed to realize that the boss in this case maybe a listener, not a reader.[5]

LOPSIDED COMMUNICATIONS: COMMUNICATING TOO LITTLE   If a baby is sensitive enough to pick up from his nurse how she feel about orange juice through her subtle body actions, what messages do subordinates receive from managers in incidents like the following?

Boss talking to subordinate in the car on the way home from a company meeting: "What a boring meeting that was! I don't know the last time we had a really good speaker. I'd have gained more from staying home and reading a good book."

A week later, the same manager says to his subordinate, "What! You don't want to go to the company meeting? I can't understand that. You never see me staying home from those meetings! I think they are important to understand what is going on here!"

You might guess that the manager has unintentionally communicated his true feelings about such meetings: Namely, that the good meeting (not found very often) is one having a speaker who is interesting and entertaining (to the manager).

Another interpretation may be that the manager has both positive and negative feelings about going to company meetings. He may enjoy the topic and the general discussion but dislike the speaker. However, his pattern of communication, developed over a long period of time, is to talk only about things he dislikes. Thus the subordinate is unaware of his other feelings. The result is unbalanced communication—the manager has communicated his negative feelings but not his positive feelings.

The above cases indicate that people unintentionally communicate to other people their likes, dislikes, preferences, and disgusts. It appears that at least one important basis of "good" communication is not to learn how to say the words better, but for people to examine themselves and begin to alter those attitudes, feelings, and reactions that they do not like to see in others, or make sure they explain the whole range of their feelings.

Sending Nonverbal Messages

The study of unconscious and nonverbal communication has risen dramatically, paralleling even the expansion of other forms of communication through modern media.[6] In fact the primary task in the field of social perception is to identify nonverbal messages, to accurately read another's thoughts, feelings, and behavior. Recent evidence suggests that spontaneous facial expressions of emotion and body movements are innate, and hence easily decipherable.[7] Many classes of messages can be derived from these two basic forms of communication, ranging from those very specific in meaning (for examples, gestures that may clearly replace a word or other audible expression), to very vague expressions subject to interpretation.

Despite all we know, however, this area of communication continues to be misunderstood. Soucie confronts two major fallacies concerning nonverbal communication. First, nonverbal communication is only a minor part of interpersonal communication. This perception is probably because nonverbal communication operates on a lower level of consciousness than verbal communications. Although we may speak to few people we pass every day, we will unavoidably communicate nonverbally to every one of them. It is also not true that most of us already know how to communicate perfectly well nonverbally. This fallacy assumes that we are naturally good at what we have done for years, and this is not the case even in reference to verbal communication. The old adage—what we practice becomes permanent, not perfect—certainly applies here.

So it becomes essential to have a basic knowledge of nonverbal signals in business also. Evidence suggests that nonverbal communications, such as those during a

A powerful form of communication, body language often sends out unintentional messages.

business interview, are just as damaging or impressive as verbal ones.[8] Certainly there is something behind the "dress for success" craze of recent years. Richard Nixon could have gained from the study of nonverbal signals, especially in the presidential debates with John Kennedy, where he looked tired and haggard. Although some people felt Nixon was the better debater, Kennedy's energetic and confident appearance helped him to win widespread support and come out the perceived victor.

THE JOHARI WINDOW

Joseph Luft and Harry Ingham developed a model for depicting the pattern of communications between two (or more) people. Because it resembles the panes of a window, Luft and Ingham combined their two first names and called their model the **Johari window**.[9] Figure 15-2 shows their basic model.

Quadrant 1 (Q1) represents the arena of open communications—ideas, events, attitudes, and feelings that the person and others both know about and feel free to discuss. Some things may be known but the parties deliberately avoid them, such as a painful fight or distressing situation; as a result, some matters are unavailable even in this quadrant.

Quadrant 2 (Q2) indicates those things known to the self but unknown to the other(s): true feelings, ideas, creativity, warmth, and experiences. Something in the relationship or the situation keeps this information from being shifted into Q1. For

Figure 15-2
The Johari Window

	Known to Self	Unknown to Self
Known to Others	**Q1** Open communications	**Q3** Blind area
Unknown to Others	**Q2** Hidden area	**Q4** Unknown part of relationship

Box 15-1
Risks versus Rewards in Sharing

RISK	REWARD
1. If I share my problems, others may think I am dumb or stupid for having such problems.	1. If I share, others may understand and help me deal with my problems.
2. If I share, others may get angry or offended.	2. If I share sincerely, others may appreciate what I say and we will become closer.
3. If I share, I may get hurt or rejected.	3. If I share, I may get greater acceptance.
4. If I share, I may be putting my burden on others.	4. If I share, others may be willing to share their burdens with me; maybe we can carry them together.

example, subordinates often hide information from superiors because of fear of what might happen if they knew.

The third quadrant (Q3) is the flip side of the coin from Q2, things kept hidden by others: their feelings, backgrounds, experiences, and attitudes. Q3 represents all that others know about themselves but do not share with others.

Finally, the fourth quadrant (Q4) is the hidden or unknown part of the relationship. Everyone has feelings, attitudes, or resources that he or she keeps repressed from himself or herself and others, perhaps a rich area of potential that is yet untapped. For example, a man might have deep fears about becoming too close to anyone, fears kept so well hidden from himself and others that they do not emerge into Q1 until he is married and suddenly feels threatened. A more positive example of Q4 is a girl, an only child, who has never been around children but who finds with the birth of her own child a great capacity within herself for loving and caring for children, a potential waiting to be released.

Using this model, the goal of interpersonal communications is for all parties to put as much information as possible into Q1 so they can understand each other and work more effectively together. However, putting information out in the open means taking a risk. Risks as well as rewards accompany sharing. Look at the risks versus rewards table in Box 15-1 to see if the rewards outweigh the risks. If they do, sharing may be worth the risk.

ORGANIZATIONAL COMMUNICATION

Attention is now shifted from interpersonal communications to the larger, often more formal and structured communications encountered in organizations. In addition to the formal channels of getting information up, down, and sideways in the organization, the informal network usually referred to as "the grapevine" is also present. Both the formal and informal channels will be examined.

A number of facts about communication have been determined through research. Openness in communications is directly linked to organizational effectiveness[10] and open communication between superiors and subordinates is a vital element in organizational climate.[11] Subordinates typically distort information as they pass it on to their bosses[12] and fear reprisals if they share unfavorable information with their superiors.[13] Although subordinates greatly prefer the consultative style when dealing with their superiors, they also believe that this style is less likely to obtain results than a direct threat when they are the boss.[14]

Strategy and Organizational Communications

As in interpersonal communication, the manager must also think about the desired impact and strategy when communicating through organizational channels. A manager's intentions may not be communicated in the memo or message she sends, and the message may be distorted or misperceived even though clearly presented. In designing a strategy for effective organizational communications, the following issues should be taken into account:

ONE-WAY VERSUS TWO-WAY COMMUNICATIONS   Too often managers do not plan, as part of their communications strategy, to open up the possibility for people to ask questions and clarify formal information. It is easy to understand how a busy executive, in a desire to get instructions out to a number of people, could send out a memo without thinking that the memo could be misinterpreted or misunderstood and people would not know how to get a clarification. For example, consider the memo in Figure 15-3, which was sent to all members of one organization. The memo was received with an immediate, angry reaction. People began to cluster in offices, in restrooms, and in the eating and coffee-break areas to give vent to their feelings. The memo elicited the following reactions:

1.   If we can't get information in to finish our report should we leave it out, falsify the data, or make a guess so it can get in on time? What does it mean to avoid a late report "at all costs?" Should a person be threatened with termination if his report is not in on time? Why not change the date for getting reports in if they are late for legitimate reasons?

2.   What is a legitimate reason to come late or leave early? Is it better to call in sick than come late? What does the CEO mean to complete the job before leaving? Is a person expected to work all night? Does the company have a responsibility to compensate us in some way for overtime? Can the company demand any number of hours from us?

3.   What is personal use of company equipment? If a person spends time on the computer to increase her skills, is that personal use? What time is "company time?" If I use the equipment during my lunch time is that "company time?" Does this mean one cannot use equipment even if your supervisor gives permission?

It is obvious that the memo potentially raises many more questions, issues, and concerns than it solves. The above problem exemplifies one-way communication where information comes down but there is no way to clarify the unclear parts of the message. Even talking with a person's supervisor or a manager may not help since they may not know what the CEO intended.

The end result of this memo was anger, resentment, guilt, blame, and suspicion, along with resolves to lie, look for a new job, protect oneself, and put the blame on others. No CEO deliberately intends to impact all employees in this way. This CEO may have had some legitimate concerns to raise, but a one-way memo to all employees without a chance for a two-way dialogue is not the way to raise or solve these concerns.

THE FALLACY OF THE "OPEN DOOR" POLICY   A strategy sometimes adopted as a means of opening up channels of communication is the **open door policy**. A manager announces or sends out a written notice that a new policy has been estab-

> ## Figure 15-3
> ## Sample of Misunderstood Memo
>
> TO: All Personnel
>
> FROM: C.E.O.
>
> RE: Improving Personal Performance
>
> DATE: Today
>
> It has recently come to my attention that a number of people have been engaging in practices that create problems for the company. These are:
>
> 1. Reports have not been getting in on time. Too often a critical report is two or three days late. This should be avoided at all costs.
>
> 2. It has been observed that many salaried people are leaving their offices early or arriving late. One should not consider leaving until the job is completed.
>
> 3. Some people are taking company equipment home for personal use or using equipment for personal use on company time. This increases wear and tear on the equipment and shortens its usable life. This practice should not be continued.

lished—such as from now on the manager's door will be open to anyone who has an issue they want to discuss. Having announced the policy the manager may mistakenly assume the communications problems have been solved.

This is somewhat akin to the old tale of the rabbit who found himself at the edge of a large lake and was unable to get across. He went to the wise old owl with his problem and asked if the owl knew of a way across the lake. After a moment of thought the owl declared, "All you have to do is sprout wings and fly across." The perplexed rabbit then asked, "How do I sprout wings?" To which the owl replied: "I've given you the general principle. It's your job to work out the details."

An open door policy without all of the details in place puts people in the same kind of dilemma as the rabbit. An open door policy will *not* solve communications problems if the following conditions exist:

Mistrust   If people mistrust the manager, they will not step through the open door. People must feel the manager honestly wants to hear from them, will spend the time, and will respond to what is shared. If they mistrust the manager's intentions in establishing an open door policy or mistrust his commitment to implementing it, then the policy will not increase communications.

Unavailability   If people feel that the manager is never available—is always too busy—then a policy has no real impact on activities. A manager must set aside reasonable time so he or she can get work done, and also set aside time to listen to subordinates.

Subversion of the Chain of Command   The open door policy may subvert the existing chain of command. If people at any level in an organization feel the open door policy gives them the right to go over the head of their immediate supervisor, they could adopt the practice of by-passing their supervisor and taking every issue higher up. Such a practice would soon *overburden* the manager and rob the supervisor of legitimate decision-making activity.

The chain of command is a real issue when an open door policy is used. If people feel they are not getting fair treatment from their own superior, a process that allows the person to get a hearing from another person at a higher level is needed. A common policy is to allow a person to have access to a person at a higher level if a request for an appointment is made in advance. Sometimes it is also required that the immediate supervisor be notified of this meeting. IBM has made such "skip-level" interviews a part of its corporate culture, and combines them with informal contacts between senior managers and lower-level employees in an attempt to discover employee morale problems in their early stages.[15]

ORAL VERSUS WRITTEN COMMUNICATIONS   Another communications strategy issue is the decision to communicate via the written or spoken word or both. In addition is the decision to communicate one-on-one or with a larger group. It is possible, for example, to send a personal, written message to every person with whom you wish to communicate, but this takes a great deal of time. The alternative is to send the same written message to every person. With modern data processing equipment the latter procedure takes very little time but it loses the personal impact the one-on-one message usually has.

Likewise it is possible—if you choose to adopt an oral strategy—to talk to each subordinate one-on-one. Or a manager could decide to call all people together and give them the information in one, large meeting.

Pros and cons for these strategies—written or oral, one-on-one or total group—exist. If one has an open, oral procedure talking to the total group, the obvious advantage of two-way communications is lost if no time is allowed for questions or clarifications. The manager should look at the following factors in making this strategy decision: (1) the time available, (2) how critical the message is, (3) the receptivity of the receiver(s), and (4) the manager's skill at written versus verbal presentation.

Sometimes it is wise to send a particularly important message to people in advance of an open meeting. This allows people to read the message and prepare themselves to discuss it at the meeting. Such a procedure could also be followed in a one-on-one session.

Another common procedure is to have an open discussion of an issue first, clarify and reach an agreement on it, and follow it up with a written summary of the agreement.

USE OF THE "GRAPEVINE"   Almost from the beginning of human history, people have informally passed information on from one to another. This has been referred to as gossip, informal communications, tale bearing, rumor spreading, and the **grape-**

Box 15-2
Communication Situation

The following memo was put on the employee bulletin board of a state hospital:

TO: All Employees

FROM: Hospital Administrator

RE: Personal Hygiene

It has come to my attention that some hospital employees are neglecting their personal hygiene. This is offensive to patients and fellow employees. Would all personnel negligent in this area please improve as soon as possible.

Questions

1. What does this memo communicate to employees?
2. If you were an employee what would your reaction be?
3. How would you improve communications in this sensitive area?

vine. This process occurs in military units, church congregations, schools, neighborhoods, and organizations.

If a message is given to one person and passed on to another with no opportunity to get the message repeated or clarified, the message becomes shorter and distorted. Certain elements become heightened and these distorted, high impact items will be the ones conveyed.

Elements of truth are often present in the grapevine message. Someone overhears a conversation, reads a confidential memo, or sees a document and then passes along both fact and fancy. Sometimes the information flow process itself creates the problem. In one organization the CEO met every Monday with his staff. Information was shared and no restrictions were imposed as to what information could be passed along. Some of the meeting participants shared everything with their staffs. Others did not. Those people who got the word, passed it on to those who did not. Sharpening, shortening, and distortion took place and soon people began to be upset with information they got via the grapevine that was not factual. The CEO achieved impacts he did not intend. The method of sending down information did not get clear, accurate data down in the organization. The problem was overcome by sending written summaries of the staff meetings to all departments for anyone to read.

The grapevine can be used constructively by feeding in accurate data on a regular basis. In one method called **sharing meeting**, the manager invites a cross section, from 6 to 12, of subordinates to a two-hour meeting. Each person is asked to share what is going on in his or her area—the things people are doing, the questions they are asking, the problems they are facing. This allows the manager both to find out what is going on by tapping into the grapevine, and to share accurate data that can be passed on by those attending the sharing meeting.

The Use of Listening Skills

We often put too great an emphasis on speaking instead of listening abilities. Effective communication in our society is often equated with effective speaking, but communication is a two-sided coin. Just about everyone fails to use the listening side to their advantage. Reasons for this are varied, including many external (the telephone ringing) and internal (pressures at home) distractions. In addition, listening is hard work, calling for more effort than speaking—it is an active, not passive, process.

The fact is that we unintentionally work hard to become poor listeners. We do not want to be impolite, so we master the art of pretending—giving meaningless aahs and oohs, empty nods of the head, etc. In short, we master the art of sleeping with our eyes open.

Methods to overcome poor listening habits include the following:

1. **Listen for Meaning—the Whole Meaning**   Hearing what someone says is not the same as understanding what someone means. Be an active listener.

2. **Refrain from Evaluation**   An effective listener does not comment evaluatively on the speaker's ideas. Evaluation should come after the full expression of an idea. Evaluation before this time distorts the speaker's ideas.

3. **Work with the Speaker**   Be patient, and help the speaker express his ideas. Speech is an inexact process for communicating; meaning is best facilitated in conversation through active interaction of speaker and listener.

4. **Prepare to Check Your Grasp of Meaning**   This allows checking for accuracy in listening. A speaker can then rephrase and fill in what lacks in the communication of ideas.

Ralph Nichols specifically emphasizes the importance of listening for managers, identifying bad habits managers must overcome in order to be effective communicators. He recommends three mental manipulations that may facilitate effective listening:[16]

Developing good listening skills is critical for effective communication.

1. **Anticipate the Speaker's Next Point**   This ensures aggressive listening and learning by comparison and contrast.
2. **Identify Key Elements of a Conversation**   Identifying supporting elements of main points will enhance the listener's ability to grasp the main idea.
3. **Make Mental Summaries**   When the speaker breaks momentarily, the effective listener recapitulates what has been said, organizing in his mind the ideas expressed.

FEEDBACK: A METHOD OF IMPROVING YOUR COMMUNICATIONS

In current organizational life, people have learned to mask, hide, and cover up their feelings, particularly toward people in positions of power and influence. Because of this, it is often difficult to know what your true impact on others has been. You may see only the polite smile, the ready agreement, and the apparent consensus and assume, falsely, that these external feedback cues represent the truth. A person with good interpersonal skills has ways of checking to determine his or her actual impact and to ascertain whether the problem, if any, derives from an inability to communicate accurately or whether it lies in the filter systems of others.

In the process of improving performance, probably no skill is more important than the ability to gather accurate and honest feedback about your impact on others. This requires sensitivity, because most people feel fearful and inept confronting someone directly with their feelings about his or her performance. It is not easy for a person in a lower-status position in an organization to face a more powerful, higher-status person with feedback that is unsolicited and presumably unwanted. The risks involved, from the lower-status person's perspective, are so great that unless the situation becomes intolerable, the safest course is to remain silent and hope the passing of time will improve conditions.

This silent minimal-change strategy, widely used for coping with those who have negative impacts on us, masks reality and keeps frustration underground. But until the truth surfaces, the negative consequences of a poor relationship are difficult to manage. The role of communications consultants sometimes may be to persuade members of the client system to gather feedback data in an effort to bring the truth to the surface.

Techniques for Eliciting Feedback

By creating a climate where others feel safe or even rewarded for sharing information, you are more likely to receive sensitive feedback. How do you go about doing this?

INDIVIDUAL DIRECT REQUEST   The simplest method is to invite the subject to a private one-on-one session. Ideally, this is preceded by a written memo or verbal request stating the purpose of the meeting, giving the person time to prepare. For example:

Dear Ed,

I would like very much to get your reactions to my management perform-ance. Do you see anything I do that creates problems for others? Do you have any suggestions as to how I might improve my effectiveness? Specifi-cally, I would like your ideas about how I could improve our performance appraisal sessions, our method of giving out assignments, and our pro-cedures for setting goals. I'd like to get together with you next week to talk about it. I'll have my secretary call and set up a time when I can come to your office for a discussion.

Thanks,

Don

Many managers prefer their boss to come to their office for such a discussion. Others feel it is appropriate to discuss the matter in the boss's office at a regular discussion meeting. People can prepare for such a session best if they know the specific issues and areas on the agenda.

WRITTEN FEEDBACK   A second method is to request (either verbally or by memo) that the subject write down his or her feelings about specific matters. For example:

> Dear Ed,
>
> I'm trying to improve my management effectiveness. Would you be willing to take the time to write down any suggestions you have, particularly in the areas of performance review, assignment giving, and goal setting? Try to be as honest as possible. I feel it's important to determine my impact on others, both positive and negative.
>
> Thanks,
>
> Don

In a direct request for either verbal or written feedback, the person asked may feel put on the spot. If a boss is making the request, the subordinate may feel obligated to cooperate but uneasy because of the risk involved. Because such direct request data are not anonymous, the subordinate may wonder how direct he or she can be without creating ill will. It is generally less threatening to give feedback through suggestions rather than by declaring negative feelings.

SUBGROUP MEETINGS   More anonymity results from dividing the staff into subgroups of three or four people that meet for thirty to forty-five minutes following a request like this:

> I am very much concerned about my effectiveness as a manager. I would appreciate it if all of you could help me at the next staff meeting by forming subgroups to identify my behaviors or any procedures that seem to reduce the effectiveness of our operation. I'd also like a list of things that you approve of and want me to continue. It would be helpful if you could give me concrete suggestions for improvement (identify the specific areas to be considered). I won't be present while you meet. You can turn in a written summary to my secretary. No names need to be attached—I'm more interested in the information than in knowing its source. If any subgroup would like to talk with me directly, I'd welcome that opportunity.

TOTAL GROUP MEETING   A manager can also meet with the entire staff to solicit suggestions for improvement. Such discussions are usually preplanned and the dialogue is more open than in the subgroup format; an atmosphere of concern and mutual assistance will lead to the most useful exchange. A useful method is to have the manager share his or her own impressions of problem areas and then ask for the opinions of subordinates.

The format can vary. The manager can summarize his impressions of his style and ask for reactions from each person. The staff can form temporary subgroups and then resume a general discussion. When a manager and/or subordinate feel(s) uneasy about sharing sensitive information, it is advisable to bring in a facilitator (consultant acting as a change agent) to help direct the activities and prevent the group from moving into unproductive or difficult areas.

QUESTIONNAIRES   Written instruments provide another avenue for anonymous feedback. Here, the manager or personnel department circulates a questionnaire to gather data about a manager's performance as experienced by peers or subordinates. Available instruments include the Blake-Mouton grid, Likert's Systems I to IV, Hall's Telemetrics Instruments, and the Behavior Science Resources' Management Profile.[17]

Instrumented data can identify how the manager is perceived and how his or her management style could improve. Some instruments contain open-ended questions ("What does this person need to do to improve in this area?") that provide specific change alternatives.

The advantages of the instrumented process are that it can be widely administered, it focuses on common problems, it can be repeated at a later date, and it protects the anonymity of the respondents. Sometimes it is appropriate to hire an external change team to gather the data and then share it with those in the system for use in planning the change program.

SHARED ASSESSMENT   With this technique, the manager writes an assessment of his or her performance and asks others to confirm or deny it, to share additional reactions, and to make suggestions for improvement. The memo in Figure 15-4 might be used. Space should be left under each of the comments for the reviewer's reactions and suggestions.

A form of shared assessment is used in performance review when the employee assesses his or her own performance and the superior reviews it. This becomes the basis for planning improved performance.[18]

OUTSIDE CONSULTANT   An external consultant commonly is used for gathering feedback data. This person can come from outside the organization or from the company's training or personnel department, but rarely from the manager's department.

The consultant can use a variety of methods to gather feedback. He or she can observe the manager in action at meetings, in problem-solving sessions, or in the work setting. The consultant can also interview peers and subordinates or administer instruments and tabulate a summary profile.

The advantage of an outsider is that he or she often can see things to which insiders have become oblivious and can probe in areas not accessible to the manager. A disadvantage is that the manager and subordinates may become dependent on the consultant and never learn to give and receive helpful feedback as part of their ongoing relationship.

> ## Figure 15-4
> ## Sample Memo
>
> I have written the following assessment of my performance as a manager. Would you please indicate whether you agree or disagree with the various points and what your reactions are. I feel I do the following things well:
>
> 1. I am punctual and never miss appointments or keep people waiting.
> 2. I am dependable in fulfilling assignments or requests.
> 3. I am a hard-working person with great loyalty to the company and its goals.
>
> I also see the following negative things about my performance.
>
> 1. I am a rather closed person, and I don't communicate very much or very easily. I want to improve this, but I'm not sure exactly how to do it.
> 2. I tend to cut people off in staff meetings and tend to reject new ideas. I'm not exactly sure how people see or react to this.
> 3. People are a little afraid of me and feel a bit uncomfortable talking with me. (I don't know what causes this or what I can do to reduce it.)

After Feedback

For most people, sharing data with a superior is an especially high-risk activity. When it is first attempted, the employee usually watches closely to gauge the superior's reaction. This reaction usually determines whether such feedback will be given again.

LISTEN, DON'T EXPLAIN OR JUSTIFY   The tendency to explain or justify actions when feedback is received that seems unwarranted or stems from a misunderstanding should be avoided. When asking for feedback, the burden is on the manager to listen and comprehend. This does not mean the manager is obligated to believe or accept the information; his or her responsibility is to try to understand why the other person feels and reacts that way. Defensive behavior stifles the flow of communication because it tells people the manager is more interested in justifying himself than in understanding his impact on others.

ASK FOR MORE   Especially in the open verbal feedback process, additional information might be forthcoming if the person eliciting the data can honestly keep saying: "That's extremely helpful. Tell me more. Is there anything else I should know about that?" This will support and encourage the continual flow of feedback.

CHECK OUT THE DATA   To make sure the manager has understood what the other person meant, it is helpful to summarize what she has heard and to ask if she has understood correctly.

EXPRESS APPRECIATION AND PLAN FOR THE FUTURE   Following feedback, the manager should acknowledge the risk that was involved for the person giving it and express appreciation for his efforts. It also is a good time to plan future feedback sessions, which are likely to be less disturbing and more productive than the initial encounter.

Giving Feedback

Managers are often involved in giving feedback to subordinates as well as receiving it.

From time to time, despite management's best efforts in hiring and training employees, an employee fails to meet the minimal objectives necessary for continued employment. The performance appraisal interview is one appropriate setting to communicate this type of information. The interview should include a definition of the course of action to be taken to remedy the shortcomings. Clear objectives should be set and a procedure established to monitor the employee's progress. The ideal situation is for the manager to identify the employee's strengths as a basis upon which to build. Care must be taken not to overwhelm the employee with a sense of impending doom while at the same time conveying the relevant concerns. The objectives determined and the consequences of failing to meet them should be put in writing with copies to the employee, the manager, and the personnel department for inclusion in the employee's file (important for legal as well as sound management reasons). The approach to this meeting should be consultative; however, for some, it may require clearly spelling out the possible consequences in order to achieve the desired change.[19]

ENDING CASE
Open Communication Increases Goal Achievement[20]

If you are going to make a New Year's resolution this January, you will be more likely to keep it if you tell someone else.

Psychologist Steven Hayes wanted to see if social pressure would help people stick to their goals. He and his co-researchers recruited 21 students interested in improving their study skills. Students were told they would be part of a self-directed program in which they would read study packets that taught methods for improving study skills and increasing their vocabulary.

Before they began studying this material, students were divided into three groups. Each group took a true-false, multiple-choice test covering vocabulary and study skills. All participants were told their scores. Members of two of the groups then estimated how many of the 12 packets they would read over the next five weeks and how well they would do on another test at the end of that time.

One group made their goals public by writing them on a signed sheet of paper and announcing them to their classmates. The second group was told not to discuss their goals with anyone, just to write them down, unsigned, and turn them in. Unknown to the students, their unsigned papers had been premarked so the researchers could keep track of their goals. The last group was not told to set any goals.

Five weeks after setting their goals, students took another test. Those who had publicized their goals did significantly better than those who had not. Eighty-six percent of the students who had publicized their goals improved their scores by 20 points. Among the two other groups, only 14 percent improved by that much. There was no difference between the students who had privately set goals and those who had not made any at all.

Both goal-setting groups had made similar commitments to how many packets they would read and how well they would do on the final test, but the public group came closer to meeting their goals.

"Apparently, the public goal-setting subjects studied more effectively, but not necessarily more often than the other groups," Hayes writes. "Overall, the effects of public goal setting were relatively strong, long lasting, and highly consistent across subjects."

Hayes believes that private commitments are rarely successful, unless they concern something of extreme importance. But for those things that everyone hates to do, imposing a little social pressure on ourselves may help.

"If we tell people we're going to do something and don't do it, we believe something bad will happen to us," Hayes speculates. "We're very social creatures and social consequences are important to us."

SUMMARY

Communication is one of the most difficult aspects of the manager's world. The source of most communications problems is the difference between the impact or message intended by the manager and how others in the organization receive what is communicated. This chapter discussed some ways that managers can reduce the difference between their intended message and the message actually received by employees.

One of the best ways for a manager to become more effective is to learn how actions and words impact others. What are managers communicating to those around them? The key to discovering the impact you are making on others is to elicit their feedback; however, giving and receiving feedback involves risk. In personal relationships, people open up to each other slowly and share more of themselves with others as they become more comfortable with their relationships. In the organzational context, the problem is exacerbated by the power that managers have to impact subordinates negatively in terms of pay, promotions, privileges, and recommendations, and by the distortions in information as it is passed through informal channels, otherwise known as the grapevine. There are methods for developing an effective communications strategy that assist managers in making sure that what they intend to communicate is actually the message received, and methods for obtaining needed feedback.

Managers also give feedback to other managers and subordinates. When dealing with superiors, managers face many of the same problems their subordinates face in giving feedback to them. When dealing with subordinates, managers need to be clear about the standards subordinates are expected to meet, the degree to which the employee needs to improve, and the consequences of failing to improve. Communication about performance expectations should begin before the subordinate is even hired.

KEY TERMS

Intention to impact	Johari window
Behavior gap	Open door policy
Filter system	Grapevine
Competent communicator	Sharing meeting
Incompetent Communicator	Written feedback
Communication strategy	Subgroup meetings
Unacted intentions	Total group meetings
Unintended communications	Shared assessment

REVIEW QUESTIONS

1. What must a manager do to be considered a successful communicator?

2. What is the goal in human interaction?

3. What is the behavior gap and how does it impact our abillity to communicate?

4. What is a filter system and how does it influence our perception of the messages others communicate to us?

5. How would you define an incompetent communicator in terms of intention and impact?

6. What does the relevant research indicate about communication style and effectiveness as a manager?

7. Can people with different communications styles successfully implement similar communications strategies?

8. Why is inaction a strategy? Is it likely to be effective?

9. What are the steps in building a successful communications strategy?

10. What are unintended communications and how do they reflect our feelings?

11. What are some of the most damaging unintended communications that young managers make in their early years according to Peter Drucker?

12. Explain the Johari window.

13. Explain sharing in terms of the Johari window.

14. What are some of the ways a manager can overcome subordinates' fear of sharing unfavorable information with their superiors?

15. What do some managers assume when they institute an "open door" policy? What is necessary to make this policy work?

16. How does the chain of command issue conflict with the open door policy? What has IBM done to solve this problem? Do you agree with IBM's approach?

17. What is a "sharing meeting" and what is its purpose? What advantages does it have over pure reliance on the "grapevine"?

18. What are the three situations in which managers are normally required to give feedback? What role does the performance appraisal interview have in each?

19. What are four factors to consider in an employee termination and what do they have to do with communication?

CHALLENGE QUESTIONS

1. Consider a manager that you are aware of in terms of competence in communication. What does this person do correctly in your estimation? Incorrectly?

2. What filters influence the perception of people about the work they do and the organization they work for?

3. Following are some perceptual filters. Rank them in terms of their probable strength and durability. Does this tell you anything about communicating with people having such filters?
   A. Political ideology
   B. Religious belief
   C. Economic status
   D. Membership in a social club
   E. Relationship with parents

4. What does the underlying need structure of the individual have to do with unintended communications and unacted intentions?

5. What challenges does a manager face with regard to the trust limit? How would you define "all needful matters"?

6. Consider the impact of communications on decision making. Does this help you with regard to your answer in Question 5 above?

7. How would you communicate the information in the memo sent by the CEO in Box 15-2 to eliminate the weaknesses of the approach used? Is a memo the correct way to communicate the type of information in the memo? What would work better?

8. How could the termination of an employee lead to goodwill for the company? Assume that this goal is achievable. What communication strategy would you employ to achieve this goal?

CASE AND RELATED QUESTIONS

1. What filters appear to have affected the quality of communication between Nils Swenson and Jeff Watkins? Consider the filters of both Nils and Jeff in your answer.

2. How could Nils have made certain that Jeff understood him? What did Nils assume about Jeff's understanding of the job?

3. Harry Triemstra emphasized John Holland's concern about the fee to Nils Swenson. What concern about the fee did Nils pass on to Jeff Watkins?

4. In terms of eliciting feedback, do the examples given in the chapter strike you as something you would be comfortable doing? If so, with whom? How would you develop a relationship that would enable you to feel comfortable eliciting feedback?

ENDNOTES

1. William V. Haney, *Communications and Interpersonal Relations*, 5th ed. (Homewood, IL: Irwin, 1985), p. 299.

2. Roger B. Smith, "Humanities & Business: The Twain Shall Meet—But How? *Management Review*, April 1985, pp.36–37.

3. Richard Neustadt, *Presidential Power: The Politics of Leadership from FDR to Carter*, (New York: Macmillan, 1980).

4. John Weir, "The Personal Growth Laboratory," in *NTL Handbook*, 1982, chap. 13.

5. "From Peter Drucker's Wealth of Experience . . . Mistakes Managers Make," *Boardroom Reports*, May 15, 1985, p. 3.

6. Robert M. Soucie, "Common Misconceptions about Nonverbal Communication: Implications for Training," *Nonverbal Behavior: Applications and Cultural Implications*, ed., Aaron Wolfgang (New York: Academic Press, 1979), pp. 209–18.

7. Saul M. Kassin and Reuben M. Baron, "Basic Determinants of Attribution and Social Perception," *Attribution: Basic Issues and Application*, ed. John H. Harvey and Clifford Weary (London: Academic Press, 1985), pp. 37–58.

8. Walburga Von Raffler-Engel, Keith Norman, Robert Foster, and Frank Gantz, "The Relationship of Nonverbal Behavior to Verbal Behavior in the Evaluation of Job Applicants," *Aspects of Nonverbal Communication*, ed. Walburga Von Raffler-Engel (London: Swets and Zeitlinger, 1983), pp. 357–75.

9. J. Luft, *Of Human Interaction* (Palo Alto, CA: National Press Books, 1969).

10. B. P. Indik, B. S. Georgopoulos, and S. E. Seashore, "Relationships and Performance," *Personnel Psychology*, 1961, pp. 357–74; and R. D. Willits, "Company Performance and Interpersonal Relations," *Industrial Management Review*, 1967, pp. 91–107.

11. W. V. Haney, *Communication and Organizational Behavior*, 2nd ed. (Homewood, IL: Irwin, 1967); and R. Likert, *The Human Organization* (New York: McGraw-Hill, 1967).

12. W. H. Read, "Upward Communication in Industrial Hierarchies," *Human Relations*, 1962, pp.3–15; A. Downs, *Inside Bureaucracy* (Boston: Little, Brown, & Co., 1967); and K. Roberts and C. O'Reilly, "Failures in Upward Communication: Three Possible Culprits," *Academy of Management Journal*, 1974, pp.205–15.

13. P. B. Blau and W. Scott, *Formal Organizations* (San Francisco: Chandler, 1962).

14. L. McCallister, "Predicted Employee Compliance to Downward Communication Styles," *The Journal of Business Communication*, 1967.

15. Richard Pascale, "Fitting New Employees into the Company Culture," *Fortune*, May 28, 1984, pp. 28–34.

16. P. R. Timm and B. R. Peterson, *People at Work* (St. Paul, MN: West Publishing, 1982), p. 303.

17. For more information on these instruments, see individual bibliographic entries.

18. G. Myers, in A. Marrow, *The Failure of Success* (New York: American Management Association, 1972).

19. L. McCallister, "Predicted Employee Compliance to Downward Communication Styles," *The Journal of Business Communication*, pp. 20, 67.

20. *Psychology Today*, October 1985, p. 11.

CHAPTER 16

HUMAN RESOURCES MANAGEMENT

CHAPTER OUTLINE

LEARNING OBJECTIVES

■ Illustrate the problems of adequate staffing in an organization.

■ Discuss the role of human resources planning and its relationship to organizational planning.

■ Discuss how organizations meet their staffing needs through recruitment and selection of qualified applicants.

■ Understand why people in human resource management must understand current laws at the federal, state, and local levels.

■ Evaluate the results of research findings on the job interview process.

■ Describe how to prepare for successful job interviews.

■ Discuss employee training and development and the key considerations in the training and development process.

■ Explain the purposes served by performance review, the reasons that it often fails, and a proven method to overcome these deficiencies.

■ Discuss the issues that should be considered in decisions regarding rewards and compensation.

■ Discuss the impact of various laws on the conduct of human resources management.

The planning process, in addition to supplying a firm with a competitive edge in areas as different as products and distribution, can have a great effect on employee morale. At IBM long-term manpower planning en- ables the firm to practice a policy of no layoffs.[2] This policy is achieved by matching work force requirements throughout the company with the available personnel. Where skills and skill requirements do not match, the company retrains the individuals involved. This practice is especially important at a time when technology is changing so rapidly within the computer industry that today's skills become quickly obsolete.

An example of IBM's planning process at work can be seen in the automation taking place at the company's typewriter plant in Lexington, Kentucky. When hand assembly operations became obsolete, the workers trained in these operations became redundant. The company initiated training programs to teach the displaced workers the skills that were still in demand at Lexington and at other sites where the employees would be willing to relocate.

At another plant where the work force was heavy in high-level printing skills, the company changed the facility to a distribution center. Employees were retrained in the skills that the changed-over facility would require. The results of a worker survey showed that morale actually increased during the changeover.

Four steps have been identified by IBM as critical to meeting long-term manpower planning goals:

1. Determine the skill needs.
2. Communicate the program.
3. Select the participants.
4. Conduct the program.

The first step is the most difficult and requires that each business unit look at future skill needs, identify potential imbalances, and put into place programs to meet requirements or fix the imbalances. IBM has developed a company-wide data bank that inventories employee skills as well as forecasts of future needs. By matching the two lists, the company can determine what programs it needs to establish.

Managers are given all the details of each program before it is announced. The requirements, selection process, and details of the training are fully laid out. Program announcements are then made on bulletin boards and interested employees are invited to a meeting in which the work is realistically described and questions encouraged. Interested employees who meet the requirements are then nominated by their managers.

The selection process consists of management review of the candidates' experience, performance, and education. Tests are given where appropriate.

Training programs vary according to the type of job offered. Colleges and universities are often used in combination with on-the-job training. Retraining programs may take as long as two years. Unsuccessful trainees are returned to their old or comparable jobs without penalty.

Overall, the IBM program provides a workable solution to the problem of manpower planning. ▼

INTRODUCTION

Any organization, as it grows in size, finds itself faced with a set of critical issues concerning human resource or personnel needs.

If the organization is growing, methods of finding and hiring workers who have the required skills are needed. This usually results in some form of human resource planning: Someone looks at the organization and projects the trends over the next few years and estimates the number of people who will be needed, and the kinds of skills and abilities required for the positions that will be open. Part of this is succession planning—determining how many managers will be retiring and how their positions will be filled with high-caliber people.

Following the development of the human resource plan, a series of steps is necessary to implement the plan. The first major part of this implementation is **staffing**, including a determination of how many people, with what needed skills, will be required at what particular time. The next step is **recruitment**—a procedure for attracting qualified people to apply for positions in the organization. After people have been attracted to apply, the **selection** procedure is used to determine the individuals who will actually perform the tasks of the organization—which applicants will be hired.

Newly hired people need to be taught the rules and standards of the organization in some type of orientation program. After people have been oriented to the system, it is often necessary to help people bring their skills, attitudes, and general competencies up to what is considered to be an appropriate level for effective work. Training is generally necessary to help people achieve the needed level of effectiveness. When people are in the organization and functioning at an appropriate level the additional problem of reward or compensation arises. What is a fair wage or salary for people with different skills and job responsibilities? What is an appropriate procedure for evaluating performance, so management can make a fair judgment about the rewards offered either in salary or promotion?

As people establish themselves in an organization, they are concerned about the **benefits** (nonmonetary compensation) that are offered. What can a person expect in terms of health insurance, sick leave, vacations, and retirement?

Many businesses recruit prospective employees at college job fairs.

This whole range of activities is variously called human resource management, personnel management/administration, or some variation of these titles. Usually a larger firm will have a special department or unit that has responsibility for handling all personnel and human resource functions.

Some students interested in a management career may focus their attention on the entire field of human resource management. This means developing skills in staff functions—planning, staffing, recruiting, training, wage-salary administration (compensation), labor or union relations, and benefits. Smaller organizations may have generalist human resource employees experienced in many of these functions, while larger organizations may require specialists in each. In the opening case, for instance, IBM manpower planners may be specialists in any one of these staff functions. This chapter considers human resource management functions in greater detail.

Traditionally, there has been some disagreement over what should be line functions and what should be staff activities (see Chapter 10 for discussion of line and staff functions). Some feel that recruiting, selecting, training, and evaluating performance and the allocation of rewards should all be a part of what line managers do. These people define the staff functions very narrowly and place the primary burden of human resource management on line managers. Others take the position that line managers are too busy with output responsibilities and should be able to rely on the staff specialist to ease the management burden and perform these needed functions for line managers. However, it would be wise for every line manager to understand the human resource policies and procedures existing in the organization.

HUMAN RESOURCE PLANNING

An important part of human resource management (HRM) is **human resource planning** (HRP). Since the human resource is the most vital resource in determining the long-term effectiveness of any organization, it is important that systematic plans be prepared to identify short- and long-term personnel needs. These personnel needs should be considered in connection with the overall long-range and strategic plans of the organizations. IBM's long-term manpower planning goals, for example, would be useless if not set within the context of strategic planning. In this context, HRP is an integral part of the larger organization planning process. Too often organizations look at strategic planning only in light of the marketplace—the demand for the product, cost of production, and expansion and development of the marketplace—and only incidentally look at the manpower requirements of an expanding organization.

Figure 16-1 shows the integration of organization and human resource planning. While the organization's planners are looking at the long-range strategic plans and the short-term operational plans, the human resource planners are taking inventory of the current supply of human talent available in the organization.

Organizational planners review the environment, looking at the opportunities present as well as the political, social, and economic factors that may have a positive or negative influence on future plans. Human resource planners look at the current jobs in place and the skills needed to meet those jobs, as well as the ages and current productivity of existing personnel.

At this point the two planning processes must come together. The future plans of the organization must mesh with the work of HRP. If the organization plans to expand its output or move into new areas or products, then these considerations must be reviewed in light of the people who will be needed to move the plans ahead. IBM's computerized skill-job matching system mentioned in the opening case fills this important need. It may be the new plans call for an expansion of scientific or engineering people. Currently in the U.S., a serious shortage exists in certain of these areas, and the HRP people will advise the organization planners what they can realistically expect to achieve in the human resource area. Thus, the planning process achieves a balance between the needs of the organization and its capability of finding and preparing the necessary human resources.

The total plan is completed as the future plans are implemented. Data are gathered on the effectiveness of the plan, and perhaps as a result of this evaluation, the plan is corrected or redesigned to ensure the appropriate achievement of goals. At IBM, the process of balancing human resources with the needs of the organization has resulted in the company being able to offer virtually guaranteed employment with a resultant increase in employee morale.

Figure 16-1
Integration of Organization and Human Resource Planning

Organizational Planning

Strategic planning
Operational planning
Organization goals and objectives
Economic conditions
Political environment
Labor conditions

Human Resource Planning

Human resource inventory (assessment of
    jobs needed)
Skill inventory (skills required for jobs)
Current performance level
Ages of current employees
Productivity of employees

Integration of Both Types of Planning

1. Assessment
   - Human resources versus organizational needs
   - Forecast of future human resource needs
       Numbers required
       Characteristics of required workers
       Budget needed
2. Implementation
   - Research
   - Identification of new replacements
3. Evaluation/Redesign
   - Cost/benefit analysis
   - Degree objectives were met
   - Redesign based on data

Staffing

Having first developed an overall plan for the human resource needs of an organization, staffing becomes the first part of implementing the plan. In the skill inventory,
the number of jobs and the skills needed for carrying out those jobs has to be determined. This usually means the development of some form of **job description** where
the various positions are described in some detail. Job descriptions include both the
requirements of the job and some assessment of the kind of skills needed to fulfill
those requirements.

As vacancies occur, people with adequate skills to meet the requirements of the
jobs available must be located and recruited. It should be kept in mind that given the
current emphasis of federal and state legislation, a wide range of factors must be
considered in the recruitment and selection of applicants. These factors are discussed
in some detail later in this chapter.

Currently almost all large, technologically based companies, such as companies in the oil, automotive, telecommunications, finance and investment, heavy industry, and high technology areas, send recruiters to college campuses. Almost every college and university will have an employment service that links up recruiters with interested students.

Selection

Following the recruitment process, the challenging matter of selection must be faced. How does a Personnel Department make a choice among several qualified candidates for the same position?

Several methods are currently employed to help in the selection process. Many companies use aptitude, interest, and personality tests to match the needs of the job with the characteristics of the applicants. Usually the applicants will also be asked to supply a personal resume, which gives important information about their background and experiences. Along with the resume, **letters of reference** from previous employers or others who have knowledge of the applicant's abilities are usually requested.

A key activity in the selection process is the **interview**, the face-to-face questioning of the applicant. An applicant may go through a series of interviews before a final selection is made. If the recruiting method is used, the first interview is with the recruiter. If the applicant "passes" this interview, the candidate may then be invited to visit the company and interview with others in the organization, especially the manager or supervisor under whom he or she might work.

A good deal of research on the effectiveness of the interview as a method of selection has been done.[3] See Box 16-1. Since the interview is a human encounter, a certain degree of bias and human error in the process are inevitable. Some candidates with good technical skills may interview poorly; they get nervous and anxious and present themselves inadequately. Others may present a very positive appearance in the interview. The research evidence shows that the more experience the interviewer has, the more able he or she will be in looking through those factors that might bias the interview results.

Candidates might expect such questions as: (1) "Tell me what you know about the industry of this company."; (2) "What contributions can you make to our company?"; (3) "What problems do you see facing the economy and our industry in the next few years?"; and (4) "What are your special strengths? Weaknesses?"

After all of the evidence has been considered—resume, tests, letters of reference, interviews—a decision to hire is finally made. An offer of employment is made to the candidate selected that the candidate can either accept or reject. In the hiring process a strong attempt is made to match the requirements of the job with the skills and abilities of the applicant to ensure as far as possible the success of the person in the position.

Box 16-1
Major Findings from Research on the Job Interview

1. Structured interviews are more reliable than unstructured interviews.

2. Interviewers are influenced more by unfavorable than by favorable information.

3. Interrater reliability (agreement between different interviewers of the same candidate) is increased when a greater amount of information about the job to be filled is available.

4. A bias is established early in the interview and this tends to be followed by a decision in accordance with the bias.

5. Intelligence is the trait most validly estimated by an interview, but the interview information adds nothing to test data.

6. Interviewers can explain why an applicant is likely to be an unsatisfactory employee but not why the applicant may be satisfactory.

7. Factual written data seem to be more important than physical appearance in determining judgments. This increases with the interviewer's interviewing experience.

8. An interviewee is given a more extreme evaluation when preceded by an interviewee of opposing value.

9. Interpersonal skills and motivation are probably best evaluated by the interview.

10. Allowing the applicant time to talk makes rapid first impressions less likely and provides a larger behavior sample.

11. An interviewer's race affects the behavior of the person being interviewed.

12. Experienced interviewers rank applicants in the same order although they differ in the proportion of interviewees that they will accept. Experienced interviewers tend to be more selective than inexperienced ones.

Selection and the Law

In the last decade the area of employee selection has been altered by new legislation. Affirmative action and the concept of preferential treatment, meaning the preference of a certain group or groups instead of mere neutrality, is an issue for all managers. The rationale behind preferential treatment is easy to understand: Preference is needed as long as prior discrimination continues to affect certain groups. Until those

Managers should be acquainted with the Vocational Rehabilitation Act of 1973, which promotes the employment rights of the disabled.

effects are no longer felt, neutrality cannot guarantee true equality.[4] Three traditional types of arguments have been used to justify this policy: (1) utilitarianism, (2) distributive justice, and (3) compensatory justice. Utilitarian arguments claim the preference policy simply is best for mankind or for the majority. Distributive justice is an egalitarian concept based on the importance of equality. For example, men and women are not equal in the marketplace; therefore, some sort of action must be taken to guarantee equality. Compensatory justice arguments center on the responsibility of society to provide restitution for past injuries.

Managers must be familiar with the laws that support this policy. The Civil Rights Act of 1964 seeks to prevent discrimination on the basis of race, color, religion, sex, or national origin. The Equal Employment Opportunity Commission (EEOC) investigates selecting practices reported to be in violation of the act. As interpreted by the Supreme Court, Title VII of the act has been held to forbid certain tests and job requirements not because of their discriminatory intent, but because of their discriminatory impact on blacks, women, and other minorities where the qualification is shown not to be required for effective job performance. Allowance is made in cases where the employer can demonstrate a specific need to discriminate (such as requiring a black actor to play the lead character in a portrayal of the life of Martin Luther King); such qualifications are known as **bona fide occupational qualifications** (BFOQs).

Not only has the federal government acted, but every state also has fair employment practice statutes. Furthermore, in 1978 the Pregnancy Discrimination Act was passed, which prohibits employers from forcing pregnant women to resign, or to take leaves of absence. Other Supreme Court decisions, especially *University of California* v. *Bakke* (1978), have further defined organizational responsibilities and options concerning affirmative action. In the Bakke decision, the Court held it permissible for a state medical school to include race as a factor in competitive admissions, and the Court also held in another case that Title VII permitted the private sector voluntarily to apply a compensatory racial preference in employment.[5]

Other legislation has focused on the rights of the handicapped and elderly. The stated goal of the Vocational Rehabilitation Act of 1973 is to promote and expand employment opportunities in the public and private sector for handicapped individuals. Studies show that 91 percent of organizations fail to comply with the regulations of the act, and only 24 percent have affirmative action programs for handicapped. This act requires affirmative action in the employment of the handicapped for anyone under a federal government contract. Because the act is complicated and compliance is often difficult to determine—even the definition of the "handicapped" is very slippery—managers should read Department of Labor publications concerning the act, which are issued free to interested organizations.

EMPLOYEE TRAINING AND DEVELOPMENT

Following the selection process, most organizations have a program for helping the employee continue to upgrade his or her skills and to try and ensure the optimum effectiveness of performance. Most companies first try to orient the new person to the expectations, requirements, standards, and programs of the company. This **orientation** program may be a few hours or several days depending on the level of the position and the importance the company puts on the orientation program. The orientation program usually includes some background on the mission and goals of the organization, its philosophy, the rules and regulations, and a review of the various programs and benefits of the company.

Types of Training

After an employee has been in place in a position, some types of **training** are usually supplied to help upgrade his or her skills. For some, the major emphasis will be on technical training—helping the person to improve skills in handling technical equipment or programs. For others, training involves interpersonal skills—the ability to work effectively with others, or **cognitive** skills—the ability to think clearly, plan, or solve problems. Other programs are often called training, but are really educational in nature. Their purpose is to expand a person's vision or understanding of issues and problems and they are often critical for the development of people moving up in management or into certain positions within the organization.

Training programs are important change activities in many organizations. Training directors and specialists are professionals whose job it is to plan and carry out training programs to increase the effectiveness of people at all levels. Because a training program can be time-consuming and expensive without producing results, the nature of effective training must be examined. (See Chapter 13 for a discussion of how training relates to the development of leaders.)

The Goals of Training

Training, as presently used, refers to any type of education program that leads to an improvement in performance by a person or persons engaged in an ongoing activity. Improvement is generally seen as behavior or performance that is more efficient— producing more output with less expenditure of resources—or more effective— achieving goals with better qualitative or quantitative results. In the case of managers, training in the first sense might make them more efficient; that is, they might be taught to organize their time in such a way that they accomplish the same amount of work more quickly. Alternatively, they might become more effective; that is, they might be taught to handle counseling problems in such a way that people feel better or work more productively after consulting with them.

When to Train People

The question of when to engage in training should be considered seriously. One of our cultural values maintains that everyone can improve, that no one is perfect. Implicit is the notion that everyone could benefit from training concerning every facet of his or her life. Taken to absurd limits, this belief would result in people spending all their time being trained. Realistically, the question is the level of performance (either a minimum level or an optimum level) that people should achieve. If they have not reached this level, should some type of training be instigated?

Often, those responsible for training decisions have not thought through what levels or limits must be reached, but still persist in initiating all kinds of training programs. Undoubtedly the success of the training at IBM is partially because the programs are clearly defined, and details are laid out before the selection of those to be trained is even attempted. Moreover, most training programs include little or no evaluation to determine if the training has accomplished its proposed goals. If realistic performance levels have been established, however, and if people have not achieved these levels, some type of training might be appropriate.

Training is necessary as a means of improving performance when a person is inexperienced in the role or job demands. Thus, new employees often go through a training program to prepare them to perform their jobs at the required level.

The training of leaders, however, is a quite different issue. For them, training is not simply an issue of learning to perform a new skill, but of learning to manage people. Can this be done? The whole area of management training or development commands considerable attention in almost all organizations. Not only does research show that productivity and morale are impacted by management behavior, but the future of the organization often depends on people who are prepared to take over key positions in the company. It is estimated that over $10 billion are spent each year on management development. Some companies like General Motors and Apple Computers even have their own faculties of their training programs, which are organized like a small university.

When Not to Train People

Despite the cultural value that anyone can improve, training should not be utilized when:

1. The time taken for the training program would not be worth the benefits that would accrue.
2. The beneficial results of the training program are questionable in terms of the expenditures of resources.
3. The resulting behavior change is not functional or useful to the goals of the organization.
4. More effective results can be achieved by simpler (less time-consuming, less costly) methods. In a managers' program, a company might try to train all managers in the art of counseling when it actually would be simpler to refer people with problems to a professional.
5. The reasons for inadequate performance are location, low motivation, or organizational constraints. Under these conditions, training will not improve the performance level; what is needed is intervention at a different level in the organization. It has been suggested that the following question be asked: "If the employee's life depended on it, could he or she perform the desired behavior at the desired level?" If the answer is no, then training is needed. If the answer is yes, it is not a training matter. Other factors reducing performance must be addressed.

Coaching

Coaching, an old principle of training, derives from the work of the athletic coach, who watches his players practice, assesses their performance during a game, takes people out of the game, gives them instructions, and then puts them back in. After-ward, performance is reviewed, more practice is undertaken, and another game is played.

This old principle is losing ground because in many situations it is awkward to have a coach present. Even so, many organizations are experimenting with coaching; some are assigning new people to experienced older managers who act as coaches or mentors for a period of training. A major activity for an effective manager is coaching subordinates. Wayne Boss of the University of Colorado has described the use of a regular personal management interview (PMI) in which a range of issues are dis-cussed, including the opportunity for coaching.[6] Boss presents clear evidence that a regular interview maintains the gains that come from team training in addition to leading to consistently high performance. (See Chapter 14 for Boss' theories on im-proving performance.)

Job Rotation

One form of training is **job rotation**, in which a person spends time in a variety of jobs to gain specific first-hand experience, often with coaching by a qualified person.

Modeling

Recently, many training programs have employed a **modeling** format. The usual practice is to videotape either an actual performance or an enacted scene to demon-strate desired or undesirable behaviors. Trainees practice via role-playing the behav-iors they have observed. Poras, who describes the use of modeling in an industrial setting, has evidence that improved performance results.[7]

The following case raises many of the issues discussed in this chapter. Note, especially, the letdown that resulted when the company failed to utilize the new skills that it paid to have Ralph Delafino develop.

CASE
Training and Expectation

Ralph Delafino was surprised and elated when he was selected to attend a Residential General Management Program by the Boston-based insur-ance company for which he worked. As his wife expressed it, "It meant great things in the future!" The separation that resulted from Ralph's attendance at the program was a small price to pay for the chance to advance in his career. As a black from a small town in Texas who had attended segregated schools for most of his life, Ralph was eager to expand his horizons.

Ralph was apprehensive about the program, having heard from others that it was a stressful experience. It turned out not to be as stressful as predicted, although the first few weeks were very tough. "During the first three or four weeks, I was really scared. The peer pressure is enormous. It is a very competitive environment, and I was struck by the well-roundedness of the other participants. I felt that I was not at the level of the program, that I did not have enough experience compared to the others. . . . But then I started to realize that these guys put on their pants the same way I do, and from there on everything became much easier and I enjoyed the program."

The greatest learning experience for Ralph was the exposure that he received to other lifestyles and to the personalities of the other participants. "That gave me a different perspective on things, living with these guys in this competitive environment. It really affected me." Ralph found himself actually enjoying subjects that he had always disliked, such as finance. His new skills increased his self-confidence: "I am now more confident of my skills as compared to others."

Back on the job, Ralph is not able to use all of the skills that he has learned. This is due, Ralph says, to the management strategy in his organization. "There isn't really a clear statement of philosophy in the company. It is more a day-to-day operation, but they are very successful. Also, there is little delegation. The power basis is very small, and the decisions are made centrally at a high level. The general atmosphere is one of not rocking the boat."

Coming back to work was very frustrating for Ralph after the excitement and growth of the training program. He felt that he was not given any significant new responsibilities, and he wanted the chance to use the newly acquired skills. His wife Susan confirmed his sense of frustration: "Ralph had a most difficult time after the program. He had a management job in mind; nothing happened. And they weren't using his abilities. He got depressed about it, and he talked to his superiors about it. They reassured him. Finally, he got a promotion, but I think he's at a plateau now. He isn't as excited about it as he was in his first few job changes." Ralph has considered leaving the company, although he is somewhat afraid to gamble on a new employer at this point. ▨

PERFORMANCE REVIEW

After people have been selected, oriented, and trained in their positions, some type of process to review their work effectiveness is needed. This **performance review** is needed for two vital purposes:

Managers usually conduct performance reviews in private one-on-one sessions.

1. To help a person see areas of deficiency so he or she can engage in a program of improvement.
2. To evaluate a person's contribution in order to establish a fair reward, either in promotion or compensation.

Here again managers must be careful not to violate civil rights legislation. If groups that are protected by civil rights legislation are consistently rated inferior, an employer may face legal action initiated by those groups. Performance evaluation must be as objective as possible, based on criteria directly related to the job.

Almost all organizations have some type of performance review or evaluation system. Usually, a manager is required to get together with all subordinates once or twice a year and review their performance with them, most often in a private one-on-one session.

Performance review can be found in a variety of forms. Graphic scales of performance are most common. These graphics provide the evaluator with some form of continuum—high–low, good–bad,1–10—within which those being evaluated are placed according to performance. It is also common to evaluate workers against one another, ranking them in terms of some criterion such as output or attitude. Although not as common as these two more graphic representations, written statements can serve as performance evaluation. These statements may not have any predetermined format, as do the two methods above, allowing for greater flexibility in evaluating. This flexibility is limited, however, when the interviewer is given a set of questions concerning performance to which she must address her written statement.

Other evaluation methods exist, but they too are limited in their ability to measure accurately the contributions or worth of employees. The evaluation process is a human encounter, and, as such, is subject to human biases. In other words, the medium by which performance is evaluated may vary, and may display signs of objectivity, but the inputs of that medium will always be subjective.

The research evidence on the effectiveness of such activities is not encouraging. Performance review systems are often found not to lead to an improvement of performance, and employees are also not convinced that the resultant evaluation leads to a fair allocation of the promotion or compensation rewards.[8]

The reasons that many performance review programs do not produce positive results are:

1. Lack of consistent feedback, review, and support. For performance improvement, these things need to take place more than just once or twice a year.

2. Managers do not feel they know how to conduct such sessions effectively.

3. The requirement to make evaluations produces anxiety and managers want to handle the matter as quickly and painlessly as possible.

4. Managers have a tendency to want to tell people they "are coming along fine" rather than to deal with the matter of tough, honest feedback that may be critical.

Research done at General Electric on performance review is instructive. These findings showed that a review giving only criticism or negative feedback results in people becoming defensive and did not lead to improvement. When the review consisted of only praise, people liked the process but did not improve. Performance improved when the review session concentrated on the manager and employee engaging in mutual goal setting and then following up with a more regular interview to see how the person was coming along with the goals established.[9]

REWARDS AND COMPENSATION

In some respects the most sensitive of all the human resource management issues is that of organizational rewards, including promotions and compensation. People at all levels in an organization keep careful track of their financial and nonfinancial rewards particularly as they compare themselves with others.

Compensation in its various forms—wages, bonuses, stock options, or profit sharing—has two important impacts on people. The first is the actual amount of money received and the lifestyle the individual can achieve as a result. The second is the symbolic value of compensation. This represents how one is valued in an organization, particularly as compared with others.

Many organizations have found that people react fiercely to a raise if they know that a peer received just a few hundred dollars more a year. The amount of money actually available for spending is negligible, but the employee sees the raise as an indication that the other person was evaluated more positively. Unless the method of determining wage and salary increases is open and clearly objective, people will often feel the evaluations and resulting rewards are unfair. You can understand the reason why many organizations have used seniority only as the basis for increases. This measure is clear and it is eminently objective even if not fair in terms of the real contribution an employee makes.

Managers are involved in rewards at two levels. On the one hand they make judgments and allocate rewards to those who work under them. In this role they need to understand the emotional forces surrounding the giving of promotions or raises. On the other hand, managers are also the recipients of rewards as a result of their evaluation by their superiors. In these circumstances they are subject to the same emotions as their subordinates.

Various types of compensation are seen in different organizations. Sometimes promotions and raises are given as an exchange—an employee receives a reward in exchange for service. At other times, managers may want to use forms of compensation as an incentive system. It is assumed that if people are offered greater rewards, they will be willing to increase performance to gain the reward. If used in this way, it is important to understand what people see as a reward. What may be rewarding to one person may not be rewarding to another.

Compensation can also be a form of punishment, a form of negative control. Some managers use the threat of a **demotion** (usually a vertical move in the organization to a job with lower responsibility and pay), the loss of a bonus, or the possibility of no raise as a means of controlling the behavior of others.

Promotions (opposite of demotion), raises, and bonuses have a variety of uses and have great symbolic and emotional impact. Managers want their superiors to use rewards in a just and fair manner and need to behave equally so with those under them.

Employees may value a generous benefits package as much or more than a high wage, so managers must be familiar with different benefits options. Benefits have been used increasingly over the last few decades as tools to attract and retain employees with needed skills. Some human resource managers may seek to implement benefits plans, assuming benefits would increase productivity or employee satisfaction, but studies show that this idea is unsound.

Despite this, however, benefits packages are in heavy demand, and come in a variety of forms. Managers can choose from a multitude of insurance policies, pensions, or other services. In addition, employers must participate in benefits programs like workers' compensation. All benefits options are influenced by current state and federal laws, such as the Employee Retirement Income Security Act (ERISA) of 1975, which are altered frequently, so managers should consult with their local government officials before committing themselves to any particular option.

THE EMPLOYEE-MANAGEMENT RELATIONSHIP

Labor/Union Relations

Managers will sometimes have to face labor problems, and possibly deal with a union in order to solve those problems. Recently labor has lost some of its former strength, which had been increasing steadily throughout this century. The percentage of workers represented by unions has dropped to below 25 percent in the last several years, partly because of the "deindustrialization" of the economy—the movement of jobs out of heavy industries, such as steel, rubber, mining, and automotive, where the drive to organize workers had been particularly effective in the past. Despite this trend, however, unions have recently penetrated once overlooked labor categories (education, medicine, and public service).[10]

To deal with labor problems, a union will first go to its client's frontline supervisor. Grievances that are not settled on that level are taken to the human resource or personnel manager, who regularly meets with union officials. Prior to these meetings, grievances are placed in written form. Grievances can be taken further up the organizational ladder if they cannot be settled at that level, possibly reaching top management or an independent arbitrator. Because of the complexity of the labor-management relationship and the specialized nature of the procedures involved (such as grievance settlement, arbitration, and other legal issues), organizations often retain expert help in this area in the form of labor lawyers and labor relations specialists.

Legislation

In the 1930s the United States Congress passed two major pieces of legislation that significantly affect the labor and union relations with management: The National Labor Relations Act and The Fair Labor Standards Act. In The National Labor Relations Act (NLRA) of 1935, the United States government formally recognized labor's right to organize and defined unfair labor practices. The act also established the National Labor Relations Board, an enforcement body designed to investigate and rule on unfair labor practices. If workers attempt to unionize, the Board will supervise the process, making sure that the proceedings are fair to both labor and management. Because over 90 percent of all unfair labor practice charges concern union organizing and certification procedures, managers should be familiar with the act.

The NLRA has been amended several times, most notably by the Labor Management Relations Act (Taft-Hartley Act) of 1947, which was passed to regulate abuses by unions and permitted the passage of state right-to-work laws. Taft-Hartley defines union unfair labor practices (such as refusing to bargain in good faith) and allows for the President, under the National Emergency Strike Provision, to obtain a court injunction to end a strike that endangers the national health or safety. The injunction is good for 80 days, by which time it is hoped that a settlement can be reached. The democratic rights of workers to fair union elections and financial disclosure of union finances are guaranteed by the Labor Management Reporting and Disclosure Act (Landrum-Griffin Act) of 1959.

Under the NLRA if 30 percent of an organization's employees sign election authorization cards, a representation election must be conducted. If a simple majority of the applicable bargaining unit vote in favor of union representation, then the employer must recognize the union as the exclusive bargaining agent for that unit.

Many companies prefer to remain nonunion because management feels that efficiency and flexibility in meeting organizational goals are often thwarted by unions. Consequently, management and labor often find themselves in an adversarial relationship. Recently a number of unions and companies have attempted to reform their relationship by behaving more cooperatively. This trend is exemplified by the GM-UAW Saturn Agreement discussed in Chapter 2.

Managers should also be familiar with the Fair Labor Standards Act (FLSA) of 1938 and its subsequent amendments. Regulations concerning record keeping, basic wage standards, overtime pay, child labor, and other human resource-related practices are covered in the act.

In 1963 a significant amendment was added to the FLSA. This was the Equal Pay Act, which prohibits discrimination because of sex. Men and women performing the same job must be paid the same wage or salary. The courts look to the substance of the work performed and will disregard certain forms such as different titles used to cover up illegal discrimination. In addition, the Age Discrimination in Employment Act (ADEA) of 1967 prevents discrimination based on age. In 1986, ADEA was amended to prevent discrimination against anyone 40 or older, meaning that workers cannot be forced to retire at any age. Exceptions were made for tenured university faculty, police, and firefighters for whom the amendments will be phased in gradually. ADEA does not apply to executive personnel, which generally means salaried employees earning more than $44,000 per year.

For more information concerning the FLSA and related acts, consult the Wage and Hour Division of the U.S. Department of Labor's Employment Standards Administration. They are responsible for enforcement of the standards set in the FLSA and can answer a wide range of questions concerning the responsibilities of management to their employees—from how long time card records must be kept, to how much overtime should be paid in a given situation.

Management Responsibilities

Human resource managers must have an accurate perception of worker attitudes and needs. Because many people are not fully satisfied with their jobs, an organization that upgrades working conditions and benefits will gain an advantage in the competition for needed skills. There are many ways in which managers attempt to upgrade worker satisfaction—enriching job requirements, redesigning work, reforming objectives, teaching a manager how to deal more effectively with subordinates—but the exact effect of these programs is unknown. Most of these interventions are designed around the fundamental concepts of organizational change (a topic that is handled independently in Chapter 12).

Employee Assistance

Because we believe that management must take responsibility for their employees, we feel employee assistance in the form of counseling, drug rehabilitation, and other programs is very appropriate. The proliferation of such programs suggests that others also recognize this responsibility. In 1959, for instance, only about 50 U.S. companies were operating occupational alcoholism programs, but by 1977 that number had risen to 1,000. Today over 3,000 of these programs exist,[11] the most successful of which offer services to all "troubled" employees, not just those with an alcohol problem. A manager's responsibility in this broader type of employee assistance program is not to look for symptoms of alcoholism, but only to identify lagging productivity—a job which he or she is much more capable of performing—and refer the employee to assistance personnel.

These programs simply make sense—healthy employees are more productive employees. Employee assistance programs have been shown to reduce absenteeism, weekly indemnity, hospital, medical, and surgical costs. General Motors estimates that for every dollar spent in their program more than two dollars was being returned within a period of three years.[12]

Legislation

Despite the advantages of taking an active role in providing for the welfare of employees, however, many employers continue to ignore employee needs. To compensate for this, legislation has been passed in addition to those mentioned above that set a minimum standard of fairness. In 1970 Congress passed the Occupational Safety and Health Act (OSHA), to ensure safe and healthy working conditions. The Occupational Health and Safety Administration was created to see that safety standards are enforced. Employers must give evidence that they are in compliance, and penalties and heavy legal damages can result if a company is not. In addition, OSHA inspectors are empowered to conduct on-site inspections of plants and facilities to determine compliance if a complaint has been filed or a serious accident or injury has occurred. Safety programs are therefore common in most organizations.

The Social Security Act, passed in 1935, is essentially an insurance plan designed to cover people against the loss of earnings due to retirement, unemployment, disability, or death. Old age and survivors insurance (OASI) is the backbone of the Social Security system and provides retirement benefits to most workers and their spouses. Most employers are covered under this Act and must pay a portion of the costs.

In addition to these laws, a growing body of case law (as distinguished from legislation) has held employers liable for damages for wrongfully dismissing an employee. Remedies include reinstatement, payment of back wages or salary, and in some jurisdictions, punitive damages. A wrongful dismissal claim under state law will often accompany a claim under the federal Civil Rights statutes or the Fair Labor Standards Act if the employee has been fired.

ENDING CASE
The Bakke and AT&T Cases

 When Allan Bakke applied to the University of California Medical School at Davis, he was turned down. At the same time, under a special quota program to help disadvantaged minority students, the school accepted sixteen Hispanic, black, and Asian-American students. According to Bakke, the sixteen minority students were less qualified than he was. Thus the school's acceptance of them was a violation of his civil rights.

Bakke sued the University of California. The case went all the way to the United States Supreme Court, which heard oral arguments in late 1977. The primary issue before the Court was whether, under the Constitution, universities can give preference to minorities over whites in order to remedy the evils of past discrimination.

The case had far wider importance, however, than the narrow question of university admissions. For example, more than fifty *amicus curiae* (friend of the court) briefs were filed by various organizations. The written argument of the U.S. government, for example, listed fifteen major programs that might be affected by the case. These ranged from grants to assist businesses owned by minorities to National Science Foundation grants to improve education in colleges with a majority of black and Spanish-speaking enrollments.

The Supreme Court also had under advisement another case. This one involved American Telephone & Telegraph Company, which had agreed in 1973 to make payments of $15 million to compensate 15,000 workers, mostly women, who were alleged to be victims of past salary and promotion discrimination. AT&T had also agreed with the federal government to set percentage goals in a number of job categories as well as to promote a large number of women and minorities. For example, women and minorities got more than two-thirds of the 61,000 new jobs and promotions offered by the company in 1977. Three unions challenged the quotas as **reverse discrimination**—the selection of minority persons or women for jobs or education in place of better-qualified whites and men. The unions also claimed that the affirmative action plan violated seniority rights clauses that were previously established in contracts with AT&T.

In mid-1978, the Court ruled on both cases. In the Bakke case, it decided that rigid quotas based solely on race were forbidden but that race could legitimately be an element in judging students for admission. In the AT&T case, it let stand the "model" affirmative action plan by refusing (without explanation) to review a lower-court ruling that had approved the establishment of numerical goals for employment and promotion of minorities and women. The two rulings were generally seen as supporting affirmative action programs in both education and industrial hiring and promotion policies. ☒

SUMMARY

As organizations grow they face a number of critical issues with regard to the handling of human resources. Companies usually develop a plan to attract and retain individuals possessing the skills needed by the organization. The implementation of the plan involves recruitment, selection (staffing), training, compensation to reward effective performance, selection of appropriate employee benefits, and constant performance review to ensure that organizational objectives are met. These activities are referred to as human resources management.

The human resources plan is developed in conjunction with the organization's strategic plan. As the organization determines available growth opportunities it is necessary to correlate those opportunities with the skills that will be needed to capitalize on them. Recruitment, training, and compensation programs are then developed to obtain and retain the necessary skills.

The development of personnel involves a process of training people to perform the tasks needed by the organization. The problem is to know how much and what kind of training to give to which employees. All training decisions should take into account the motivation of the trainee. There are a number of training techniques and elements required for a training program to be effective.

The issues involved in the performance review process were discussed, especially as they relate to compensation and rewards. It is important to evaluate both effective and ineffective behavior, and that the perceived fairness of the distribution of rewards is essential to employee support.

Finally, the legal issues facing companies as they work with and develop their human resources were discussed. A host of health, safety, and other laws govern the employment relationship. Managers need to be aware of these laws to avoid improper decisions and legal liability.

KEY TERMS

Staffing	Orientation
Recruitment	Training
Selection	Cognitive
Benefits	Training programs
Human resource planning	Job Rotation
Job description	Modeling
Resume	Performance review
Letter of reference	Demotion
Interview	Promotion
BFOQ	Reverse discrimination

REVIEW QUESTIONS

1. What is the purpose of an orientation program?
2. Define human resources management.
3. What is the relationship between performance review and compensation?
4. What skills must be developed to pursue a career in human resources management?
5. Define strategic human resources planning.
6. How would you assess human resource needs?
7. What is the role of a job description?
8. What are major issues that an organization must face in the recruitment and selection of personnel?
9. When is training useful? When is it better not to train people?
10. Name three types of training programs and one advantage of each.
11. What are seven attributes of a good training program?
12. What is the purpose of a performance review? Why do performance reviews often fail to meet their objectives?
13. What are the two impacts that compensation has on people? Of what importance is each?

CHALLENGE QUESTIONS

1. How is human resource planning tied to strategic planning, and why is this tie-in important to the organization?

2. Is the emphasis on improved efficiency that is characteristic of most training programs justified at a time when concerns with such things as product quality are paramount?

3. What factors would you take into account in deciding what type of training program to undertake?

4. Is affirmative action as defined in the chapter "reverse discrimination?" Why or why not?

5. How do the characteristics of a good training program compare with MBO as discussed in Chapter 4?

6. Why do you think that compensation often has a higher symbolic impact on people than the amount of pay itself?

7. Given the various laws governing the employment relationship, what information would it likely be illegal to solicit on an employment application? Could a firm request a picture of an applicant? If so, under what conditions?

CASE AND RELATED QUESTIONS

1. What is the key to the effectiveness of IBM's HRP program?

2. On what basis does IBM decide which workers will be retrained? Do the criteria used match the chapter's description of when to train people?

3. What benefits accrue to IBM as a result of its program? How does the program benefit employees?

4. What principles discussed in the chapter did Ralph Delafino's company violate when it sent him to the training program?

5. What role did the training program play in raising Ralph Delafino's expectations? Were those expectations eventually realized? If so, why is Ralph contemplating leaving the company?

6. Should the company have sent Ralph Delafino to the training program? Was the mistake mainly one of timing?

ENDNOTES

1. Adapted from Hastings H. Huggins, Jr., "IBM's Retraining Success Based on Long-Term Manpower Planning," *Management Review*, August 1983, pp. 19–20.

2. While IBM has resorted to early layoffs and attrition in recent efforts to trim its work force in the face of a computer industry slump, career employees remain protected from layoff.

3. See Thomas L. Moffatt, *Selection Interviewing for Manager* (New York: Harper & Row, 1979).

4. See James Hollander, "A Step-by-Step Guide to Corporate Affirmative Action," *Business and Society Review*, Fall 1975.

5. L. S. Kleiman and R. L. Durham, "Performance Appraisal, Promotion and the Courts: A Critical Review," *Personnel Psychology*, Spring 1981, pp.103–121.

6. R. W. Boss, "Team Building and the Problem of Regression: The Personal Management Interview," *Journal of Applied Behavior Science* 19, 1983.

7. J. Poras and B. Anderson, "Improving Managerial Performance through Behavior Modeling," unpublished paper, April 1980.

8. R. E. Lifton, "Performance Appraisals: Why They Go Wrong and How to Do Them Right," *National Productivity Review*, Winter 1986, pp.54–63.

9. H. H. Meyer, Kay, J. R. P. Frence, Jr. "Split Roles in Performance Appraisal," *Harvard Business Review*, January–February 1965, 123–29.

10. See H. Chruden and A. Sherman, *Managing Human Resources*, 7th ed. (Cincinnati: South Western Publishing Co., 1984), part 5; and S. Cohan, *Labor Relations in the United States*, 4th ed., (Columbus, OH: Charles E. Merrill Pub. Co., 1975).

11. See J. A. Belohlov and P. O. Popp, "Employee Substance Abuse: Epidemic of the Eighties," *Business Horizons*, July–August 1983, pp. 29–34.

12. E. G. Busch, "Developing an Employee Assistance Program," *Personnel Journal* 60 (1981), 708–711.

CHAPTER 17

THE MANAGER, STRESS, AND THE FAMILY

CHAPTER OUTLINE

LEARNING OBJECTIVES

■ Understand how spousal support affects an employee.

■ Discuss the types of conflict that arise between job and family.

■ Explain how role expectations can cause conflict among a manager and his family members.

■ Understand how various marriage patterns can affect a manager's behavior in the office.

■ Explain the ways in which stress can affect a manager's job performance.

■ Recognize the various types of stress and how they may be controlled.

■ Explain ways in which organizations strive to reduce individual employees' stress levels.

■ Understand what a "wellness workplace" is and why organizations will be implementing more of them in the future.

■ Identify the differences between Type A and Type B personalities, and why one type experiences lower levels of stress than the other.

■ Explain why two-career families may possibly be subject to more stress than other families.

A major stressor in corporate life is caused by the periodic **relocation** (a change in job responsibilities accompanied by a change of domicile) of managers as they move up the corporate ladder. A move can come at times that are not convenient for the manager, the spouse, or the family. Nowhere is this more evident than in the case of the **two-career family** (husband and wife in separate career paths).

Merrill Lynch Relocation Management, Inc., the country's largest relocation firm, found that 60 percent of corporate moves involve dual-career couples. By 1990 the rate is projected to be 75 percent. As a result, MLRM now offers a "trailing spouse service" as part of its program. A **trailing spouse** is defined as someone who pulls up roots to follow a transplanted mate. As companies have watched the decline rate (the percentage of managers refusing a transfer) increase, the rationale for such a service has become compelling. The Merrill Lynch program is a reflection of what many companies were already doing informally.

For example, Ken Moelis, 27, a vice-president of corporate finance at Drexel Burnham Lambert, Inc. in New York, was offered a move to Los Angeles. Ken's wife, Julie Taffet, who worked in retail sales management for Drexel, objected to the move unless it was accompanied by "an incredible opportunity." As Julie put it, "I loved my job. All our friends and family are in New York."

Drexel decided that the best way to get Ken to move was to help Julie. So the company arranged interviews for Julie with several southern California companies, including Columbia Savings & Loan Association in Beverly Hills. Columbia offered her a post as vice-president and investment department manager. "It worked out really well," says Taffet. "It's a nice lifestyle out here."

Older couples often need such a service more than younger ones. When AT&T promoted James C. Nelson, 43, from local to regional supervisor, it was the fourth time in 18 years that his wife, Virginia, faced the prospect of moving—this time to Kansas City, Missouri, from St. Louis. Formerly a nurse, the earlier moves had been no problem for Virginia, but this time she was an education coordinator at Missouri Baptist Hospital, a harder job to replace. The career counselors at AT&T coached her with tips on constructing a resume and handling interviews. The result was a job in Kansas City with the same title but greater responsibility than her former position.

A growing trend is the husband who trails his wife as she takes advantage of career opportunities. When Ann Kramer, 28, went job-hunting before getting her MBA at Indiana University in 1982, she asked interviewers about job prospects for her fiance, an Indiana MBA then employed by a South Bend brokerage house. One company handed her the telephone directory. Another said, "He'll have no problem, it's a big city." The Leo Burnett advertising agency, however, offered advice and assistance. Ann, now a Burnett account executive, says that she and her husband will not forget the agency's efforts.

Corporate relocation can be especially stressful for the two-career family.

Such assistance makes a lot of economic sense for the companies involved. Not only do they attract people like Ann Kramer, they retain them longer and find that upon arrival at the new location they become productive more quickly. With the average cost of an employee move approaching $35,000, such assistance often protects that investment to say nothing of the much greater investment already made in training the employee the company wishes to move (an estimated cost of five times salary to recruit, train, and bring a new manager up to speed). ◿

INTRODUCTION

We have already mentioned how all organizations are open systems that are continually interacting with forces in the environment. One of the key interfaces for any manager is the interplay between work and home and the family. These two important social organizations come into contact through the manager almost every day. Figure 17-1 illustrates the influence of these two systems on the manager, and possible resolutions of the work-family conflict.

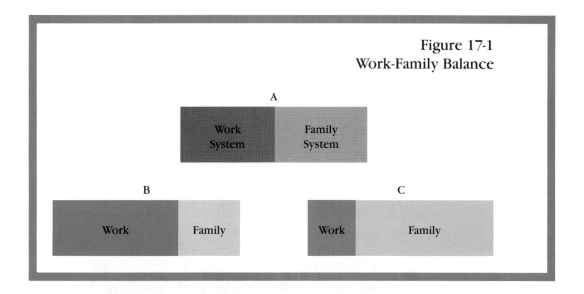

Figure 17-1
Work-Family Balance

A

Work System | Family System

B

Work | Family

C

Work | Family

Figure 17-1(A) shows a manager who is rather equally **balanced** between the demands of the workplace and the home situation. Figure 17-1(B) illustrates a manager who is dominated by work concerns and allows them to overshadow the influence from the home setting, while Figure 17-1(C) shows the manager who lets the family have the greater influence in activities and decisions.

Research shows that behaviors as a husband and father or mother and wife are influenced by the individual's job, and, conversely, job performance is affected by what is happening at home.[2] In the opening case, for instance, the Leo Burnett advertising agency acted in its own best interest, as well as in Ann Kramer's. Because the firm offered to assist her husband in finding a job, they were able to hire Ann, foster in her a sense of loyalty to the firm, and create a more stable home life for her and her husband, thereby helping to raise her level of productivity. Currently, in American society, more and more women and mothers work outside the home—some from necessity and some because more and more women feel that a career and a family are activities that should be available to both men and women. The two-career family is a common American phenomenon, but balancing a career and a family for both husband and wife creates additional pressures and strains not observed in a single-career family.

INFLUENCES BETWEEN FAMILY AND JOB

When all family members are interviewed, it is very apparent that family members (with the possible exception of very little children) are very conscious of the impact the parents' jobs have on the family. However, family members may not be as aware of the impact the family has on the parents' performance on the job.

One wife remarked about her husband who was going through a difficult period in his work position: "He is very unhappy with his job and it naturally reflects in his attitude and conversation at home. His naturally happy-go-lucky attitude is disappearing." Children also observed the job impact and one said: 'Daddy is cranky all of the time now. He used to take me to the movies but now he doesn't any more.'"

Spousal Influence

Maccoby found in his interviews with top male executives that they are generally very aware of the impact the wife has on a male manager's career. One executive describes his wife as being "flexible and supportive" and said: "It is very unusual for someone to get ahead in the corporate world if his wife does not support him. They seldom get to the very top. People at the very top generally have very attractive wives who are respected. They are the kind of people others want to emulate."[3] Maccoby further states,

> The executive wives we interviewed are women who like men. Most of them enjoyed close relationships with their fathers who also liked them. Although they support the women's movement for equal rights, they disapprove of the "Extremists" who hate men or practice lesbianism. They feel at home in a world dominated by men, and they admire their husbands.[4]

Clearly, Maccoby's study shows that wives are an important influence in the career of the husband; in fact, without the right kind of wife it is doubtful that the husband who plans a career in management can move to the very top.

The person who selects management as a career may also find that career selection also influences the kind of lifestyle you wish to have and even the kind of behavior you want in your children. Often this means wanting children to be successful in sports and school affairs. In one family the executive father was pleased with an older son who took after the father in sports and school politics, but the father had a difficult time relating to a younger son. This boy was reserved, affectionate, and artistic. With him the father felt powerless and the boy escaped into compulsive eating and TV watching. His father countered by bringing home a TV camera and suggested his son become a director.

Conflicts between Job and Family

Many people trying to balance both a career and a family report a great deal of stress in their lives resulting from conflicts between these two systems.

It should be pointed out that a person experiences personal, internal conflict or stress when the same behavior is simultaneously rewarded and punished. This sense of being in a double bind is the basis of personal conflict. For example, if a working wife and mother is needed at work to spend additional time in her job, she will be rewarded by her work associates. But at the same time, she may find that her absence from the home is resented and punished by her husband and children.

TIME   Working spouses may find themselves in relationships in two systems with incompatible expectations. Time is certainly one area where conflicting role demands and expectations often occur. A person has only so much time—no one has more than 168 hours every week. When you have multiple roles and relationships, you are subjected to multiple **role expectations**. Each group or person has legitimate demands on your time. A great deal of tension, stress, and frustration can result when a person feels bombarded by conflicting time demands.

PRIORITIES   Which set of roles in which system should have priority? This is another conflict related to time considerations that must also be resolved. A trailing spouse, like those mentioned in the opening case, experiences this type of double bind. Following a spouse in a geographical move means leaving a job, often one that is very satisfying. If a relocation agency can find a suitable job for a trailing spouse, then the double bind, and the corresponding stress, is eliminated. Should the job have priority over the family? Many people seem to feel that the father's job may take precedence over the family, but if the mother also works, for some reason the family should come first for her. One early study by Blood and Hamblin showed that in families where the wife did not work, the husband was involved in about 15 percent of the basic household chores (doing dishes, cleaning, doing the laundry, etc.), but when the wife worked the amount only increased to 25 percent.[5] Obviously the wife was still expected to be responsible for the majority of household work even though she also worked full time.

VALUES   A **value conflict** between job and the family may also be a factor creating stress. The job may expect the husband or wife to value social drinking, cocktail parties, dressing well, eating out each day for lunch, and entertaining business associates in the home. These may all be at variance with personal values in the family where drinking is not an accepted pattern; money is to be saved, not spent on clothes, lunches, or social life; and entertaining is primarily for family and close friends. Again, conflict results when behavior is rewarded in one system but negatively sanctioned in the other.

In a two-income family some tough differences in expectations about income can surface. For example, when both husband and wife work, is the money earned considered joint income? Some wives feel that if they work the income they earn is theirs alone while the husband's income is "family" money. In other families, each contributes so much money into a family pool and considers the rest as their own income to be spent as they see fit. Still others pool all income. It is apparent that differences in expectations about income could be a major source of conflict and stress in a relationship. Some of the common areas of conflict that result from the interrelationship of a manager's home and work life are listed in Figure 17-2.

Figure 17-2
Conflict Areas between Home and Work

- Role expectations
- Emotional demands
- Time demands
- Physical demands (fatigue)
- Value conflicts
    Definition of success
    Personal standards
    Personal preferences
- Financial expectations
- Periodic relocation

The Influence of Marriage Patterns

A common perception is that a "man's home is his castle." The inference is that at home a person (traditionally the man) can shed the cares of the world, relax, and get support, comfort, and renewal. If people marry with this ideal in mind, does the home in fact become the "castle" of their fantasies? The evidence is mixed. On the one hand, for certain marriages the desired support is present, but other families demonstrate a different pattern.

FIVE MARRIAGE PATTERNS   One study of marriages of highly educated, financially successful, articulate couples found five different marriage patterns.[6]

Conflict-Habituated Relationships   The **conflict habituated relationship** is characterized by chronic conflict, but it is kept under control. The conflict itself seems to be the main basis of the relationship, constituting the cohesive factor in the marriage.

Devitalized Relationships   **Devitalized relationships** are characterized by the lack of real zest or vitality. The couple stays together out of legal or religious requirements. "The relationship between the pair is eventually devoid of vital meaning by comparison to what it was when the mating began." This type of relationship was found to be exceedingly prevalent.

Passive-Congenial Relationships   **Passive-congenial relationships** can be described as "comfortable adequacy" and are very prevalent. The couple shares some

Depending on the marital relationship, the home can either be a source of support or stress for a couple.

interests in common but they are not vital nor do they require much joint participation. The couples are passively content but the relationship shows little vitality.

Vital Relationships   In **vital relationships**, the husband and wife exhibit a vitality based on the vibrant and exciting sharing of some important life experiences—children, work, or some creative activity.

Total Relationships   The **total relationship** is like the vital relationship, but, in addition, it is multifaceted. The partners share a wide range of experiences together. The researchers say that this total relationship is quite rare but "one will occasionally find relationships in which *all* important aspects of life are mutually shared and participated in. It is as if neither partner has a timely private existence."

IMPLICATIONS FOR MANAGEMENT   If this analysis is correct, it means that for many managerial-professional marriages the home is not the source of great support and renewal. In fact, the home environment may tend to intensify feelings of conflict and stress experienced at work rather than reduce them.

Often the home and office situations are working against each other. For example, strategies are often developed in the workplace to try and increase the commitment of people to the job. Various actions are taken to try to increase worker motivation—get them to identify more with the work, and become more totally involved. In one company, after one year of a successful motivational program, many of the women involved said that they would have to quit the job if they were not allowed to leave the program. They said the increased commitment to the job was interfering with their family life. When they were home they were too concerned about issues at work, which hindered their activities as a wife and mother.

This raises the important issue of **intersystem planning**. In the past, work organizations have not often taken the family system into account when they have planned new developments to "motivate" workers. In the future it is expected that more enlightened companies will plan improvement programs taking the family and other external systems more into account.

Organizations have, at times, wisely considered the family setting and made appropriate modifications. In an early study of the restaurant industry, one case study described a woman worker who was in charge of preparing fish in a restaurant and who suddenly came in and quit her job.[7] When asked why she wanted to quit, management was told that she was referred to both on and off the job as the "fish woman." In a family argument, family members had referred to her in a negative way as "you old fish woman." Management wisely asked her if she would stay on the job if they officially gave her the title as "Manager of the Seafood Station." This change of title allowed her to represent herself more favorably to important others off the job and she stayed in her position. The point here is not that companies can improve everyone's morale just by cosmetically changing job titles, but at some point understanding family-job connections and a willingness to alter **job connections** (where the family system intersects the job system) can be an important boost to employee job satisfaction.

STRESS

In this chapter it is important to look at the issue of stress as it affects individuals. Considerable evidence shows that certain job conditions create a great deal of stress for employees. If the employee feels that the family is the place to reduce tensions and stress but instead of reduction, stress is increased, the negative consequence of stress is intensified to the detriment of both the work organization and the family. Consider stress in light of a well-known piece of research concerning the small Pennsylvania town in the following case.

CASE
Changing Levels of Stress in Roseto, Pennsylvania[8]

 Roseto, Pennsylvania, is a small town at the base of the Pocono mountains in the east-central portion of the state, less than an hour and a half drive from New York City. It is of interest because of the results of extensive medical and sociological studies undertaken in Roseto and neighboring communities during the last two decades. The Roseto story provides a vivid illustration of the rapid onset and the severe consequences of stress in modern life.

The most striking aspect of what sociologist John Bruhn and his research team uncovered was that the Rosetans enjoyed virtual immunity from coronary heart disease.[9] The heart disease rate was less than a quarter of the prevailing rate in surrounding communities in spite of the fact that obesity rates in Roseto were higher than average, and that Rosetans' dietary, drinking, and smoking habits did not differ appreciably from those of other American urban dwellers.

Roseto was different from other typical American communities in several additional respects. Family relationships were extremely close and mutually supportive, and this cohesiveness extended to social and community relationships. Virtually everyone who lived in Roseto worked in the town. Roseto had no freeways, no commuting, no traffic. A ten-minute drive to work was considered long. Family units tended to stay intact; two or even three generations often shared the same house. When children left home, they invariably remained in the community. Work in Roseto was steady and unemployment low. Most of the men in the town worked in jobs associated with the numerous slate quarries situated throughout the town. The tasks they performed were relatively straightforward, routine, and did not require a great deal of complex problem solving or decision making. Nor were the jobs brought home with the men in the evenings; at the end of the day work was forgotten until the following morning.

This, then, was Roseto in the early 1960s. By the 1970s when the research team returned, the picture had been significantly altered. Family units were no longer as tightly knit. Children were leaving town to attend college, and either did not return or returned with a value orientation different from their parents'. Traffic congestion had become a problem. Television significantly decreased the amount of social interaction within family units. Many of the men commuted to work in Bethlehem and other cities, including New York. A new concern among workers for upward mobility had surfaced. Civil involvement had decreased and with it the mutual support that Rosetans had previously given each other. In short, within a decade, Roseto had become modernized. It had been brought—somewhat unwillingly—into the 1970s.

For the first time, stress had become a factor in the lives of the Rosetans—stress in the form of changing values, shifting work patterns, increased life pace, loss of sources of support in the form of declining family and civic ties, traffic congestion, and a host of other alterations associated with modern urban living and "progress." This progress and the stress that accompanies it had a price. By 1971 the town had recorded its first heart-disease deaths in men under the age of fifty. By 1975, formerly relatively stress-free Roseto had lost its immunity to heart disease, and its death rate from it had reached that of neighboring communities. While the Roseto research was primarily concerned with heart disease, no doubt other stress indicators would have exhibited important changes had they been examined closely. Heart disease is simply one of a plethora of possible physiological and psychological consequences of stress.

Roseto is important because it is a stress microcosm of the United States—what took place in Roseto in a decade has been developing elsewhere for many decades. Change is a potential source of stress; the sheer volume of change is itself a potent stressor. Many changes and sources of stress are related to jobs, careers, and the organizations in which Americans spend their time. Everyone—particularly managers—must understand the pandemic nature of work stress and its detrimental role in individual and organizational health and effectiveness. ⬛

Issues and Definitions

In understanding the matter of stress, it may be profitable to look at some issues and definitions. For example, is "stress" a causal factor or the result of a causal factor? When a manager is overloaded with too much work is the overload the stress or is the manager's response to the overload the stress? It may be useful to differentiate these two views. Let us call the causal factor a **stressor** and the resultant response **stress**. Thus, a person who is subjected to work overload (the stressor) may experience an internal condition of upset (stress). Stress is then the physiological or psychological response an individual makes to an environmental stressor. In the preceding case, then, the stressor was originally absent in Roseto. Life was relatively uncomplicated and community members were content. Only after stressors in the form of increasing complexity were introduced were levels of stress that caused an increase in heart disease experienced.

How the Body Reacts to Stress

One of the physiological difficulties human beings have with current forms of stress is that the body generally prepares itself for **fight or flight** but modern situations do not allow these responses easily. If one is accosted on the street by a potential mugger, one can either stay and fight or can engage in flight and run away. In either case the body engages in physiological preparations for action (an increase of adrenalin for example).

Following the encounter with the stressor, the body begins to return to normal. But what if the stressor does not go away and the norms of the situation will allow neither fight nor flight? If a person is given a disagreeable assignment, is overloaded with work, or is transferred to an incompatible situation, it may not be possible to fight or run away. But the body is still mobilized to deal with the stressors and remains so until the stressors are removed.

The work of Hans Selye is important here. He did much of the current research and thinking about the matter of stress.[10] Selye considered stress a nonspecific response to any demand made on the individual. He identified three stages of the nonspecific defense reaction.

Stress is the physiological or psychological response of an individual to an environment stressor.

ALARM STAGE   When the stressor is encountered the "alarm" is sounded and the body prepares for action. Virtually every major organ of the body is involved. Hormone secretions are drastically increased. Adrenaline acts on the muscles and fat tissues causing them to release chemicals they store. The liver converts these chemicals into glucose that is used as a source of energy. During the alarm stage the heart rate increases, respiration and blood pressure are up, blood cholesterol increases and blood clotting secretions also are activated. The body gets prepared for action.

RESISTANCE STAGE   In this stage resistance to the stressor increases. The organ or system best able to deal with the threat is mobilized. Thus, resistance to a fight or primary stressor is high but resistance to secondary or unrelated stressor is low. This helps explain why individuals are more illness-prone during periods of emotional strife than at other times.

EXHAUSTION STAGE   If the body is faced with the same stressor too long, it may use up the adaptive energy available and the system becomes exhausted. At this point, many of the activities of the alarm stage return and the defense may be shifted to an alternative system. If the system is totally depleted of an alternative defense system, the person may collapse—even die.

Box 17-1
Consequences of Stress

Subjective effects   Anxiety, aggression, apathy, boredom, depression, fatigue, frustration, guilt and shame, irritability and bad temper, moodiness, low self-esteem, threat and tension, nervousness, and loneliness.

Behavioral effects   Accident proneness, drug use, emotional outbursts, excessive eating or loss of appetite, excessive drinking and smoking, excitability, impulsive behavior, impaired speech, nervous laughter, restlessness, and trembling.

Cognitive effects   Inability to make decisions and concentrate, frequent forgetfulness, hypersensitivity to criticism, and mental blocks.

Physiological effects   Increased blood and urine catacholamines and corticosteroids, increased blood glucose levels, increased heart rate and blood pressure, dryness of the mouth, sweating, dilation of the pupils, difficulty in breathing, hot and cold spells, lump in the throat, numbness, and tingling in part of the limbs.

Organizational effects   Absenteeism, poor industrial relations and poor productivity, high accident and labor turnover rates, poor organizational climate, antagonism at work, and job dissatisfaction.

SOURCE: T. Cox, *Stress* (Baltimore: University Park Press, 1978).

Ivancevich and Matteson claim: "The more the (body) is activated and the longer it remains in operation, the more wear and tear the body is subject to. Like any machine, the body has limits beyond which it cannot continue to function. The more frequently the individual is in a fight-or-flight mode, the more susceptible that individual is to fatigue, disease, disability, aging, and death."[11]

Cox has identified a number of consequences of stress, which are summarized in Box 17-1.

Stressors at Work

Having identified the issue of stress and some important consequences of stressors on the individual, the conditions in the workplace that create stress need to be addressed. Ivancevich and Matteson identify five main categories of stressors that affect performance at work, which are listed in Box 17-2.

Given the wide range of possible stressors in a person's life, it is no wonder that many people suffer severe physical and emotional illnesses stemming from stress overload. Meyer Friedman and Ray Rosenman have identified two types of individuals, one more prone to heart disease than the other. Those most likely to have heart

---

Box 17-2
Stressors in the Work Environment

1. **Physical Environment Stressors**
   Lighting
   Noise
   Temperature
   Vibration and motion
   Air pollution

2. **Individual-level Stressors**
   Role conflict (demands of one set of pressures make compliance with another difficult or impossible)
   Role ambiguity (lack of clarity about your job, goals, or responsibilities)
   Work overload (quantitative—too much work for the time allowed—and qualitative—standards are too high for your level of competence)

3. **Group Stressors**
   Lack of group cohesion (group is splintered)
   Inadequate group support (group members do not support each other)
   Intra- and intergroup conflict (antagonistic action inside or between groups)

4. **Organizational Stressors**
   Organization climate (feelings of being overcontrolled, regulated, and punished)
   Organization structure (inappropriate divisions; too flat or too high structure)
   Organization territory (people working in alien territory where they are not known or accepted)
   Task characteristics (not enough autonomy, variety, or identity)
   Leadership influence (style and impact of the leader)

5. **Extra Organizational Stressors**
   Life events (marriage, divorce, death, or job change)
   Family (conflicts or parent-child problems)
   Financial matters (lack of income, or debt)
   Residence (problems with neighbors, schools, or church)

SOURCE: J. M. Ivancevich and M. T. Matteson, *Stress and Work: A Managerial Perspective* (Glenview, IL: Scott, Foresman, 1980), chaps 5, 6, 7.

---

disease they called **Type A** and those less likely to have coronary problems are **Type B**[12] (see Figure 17-3).

Friedman and Rosenman studied 3,500 males between the ages of 39 and 59. In 1960, none of these had a known history of heart disease. One half were classified as Type A—the other half as Type B. As of 1972, 257 of the subjects had developed some form of heart disease. Of these, 70 percent were Type A.

Figure 17-3
Stress Typology and Heart Attacks

Type A Behavior	**Type B Behavior**
Heart attack prone	*Not prone to heart attack*
• High degree of drive and ambition	• High level of patience
• Extremely competitive	• Allows time for leisure
• High level of aggressiveness	• Works at leisurely pace
• Constantly working against time	• Not preoccupied with status and social achievement

The History of Stress in the Workplace

For decades now the trend in business operations has been toward increasing specialization, automation, and computerization, resulting in higher levels of stress in the workplace. Scientific management, discussed in an earlier chapter, must take some of the blame for this trend. Part of the effect of these principles of management has been to mold human beings into efficient machines attuned to "a new rhythm of methodical specialization." Technological advances have pushed workers into dehumanized jobs of high psychological demand and very little decision latitude—the two job factors that appear to be most conducive to stress in the workplace.

Increasing bureaucratization focusing on efficiency—improving productivity by cutting costs and controlling the work process through rational management—also contributes to mounting levels of stress. Workers are often forced into taking specialized processing jobs, such as keyboard operator or assembly line worker, which delegate to machines the bulk of old job responsibilities. Workers in these jobs are reported to suffer from exhaustion after work, trouble awakening in the morning, depression, nervousness, anxiety, and insomnia or sleep disturbance.

Managing Stress

Stress is a condition that can seriously reduce the effectiveness of people at all levels of an organization. Managing stress is an issue for both the individual and the organization. John Naisbitt, the social forecaster, in his book *Re-Inventing the Corporation*, predicts that organizations of the future will strongly emphasize the maintenance of employee health. Naisbitt claims that even now the cost of health care through company health plans is $100 billion a year. For example, he states that Hewlett-Packard's cost of health care for each employee has risen from $500 to $1,500 per year in a decade.[13]

At the same time corporations try to reduce health-care costs, they will also be more active and effective in developing the company into a "wellness workplace." Companies will be doing more and more of the following programs.

REDUCTION OF CORPORATE STRESS   At the corporate level, there is much that can be done to alleviate areas of stress, such as:

1. **Task redesign**   If stressors result from unclearness over tasks, or tasks put people into role conflicts, more task diagnosis and redesign will be undertaken.

2. **Worker autonomy**   Increased use of participative management—organizations will increase the level of autonomy and control people have over work so they will feel less stress in the sense of feeling their work controls them.

3. **Flexible work schedules**   The practice of flextime—people having flexible work hours—is already practiced in many organizations. People can set work schedules more consistent with the demands in the home and community.

4. **Career development**   More and more companies are putting career-development programs in place. One of the great stressors for many people is the feeling that they are locked into a job with no future growth potential. Career-development programs will help people plan for an expanded future.

5. **Design of physical work settings**   Increased concern will be paid to reducing excessive heat, noise, and light. Work settings will provide a more suitable work atmosphere, such as less confining open office designs.

6. **Team building**   To ensure social support, organizations will undertake more team development. Identification of interpersonal problems will become more systematic as organizations attempt to improve team performance.

INDIVIDUAL STRESS REDUCTION PROGRAMS   Besides actions at the corporate level, companies in the future will encourage and facilitate more individual stress reduction in the following areas:

1. **Physical fitness**   Companies will not only support individual fitness programs but provide such things as a gymnasium, weight room, swimming pool, exercise equipment, and jogging track. Employees will be encouraged to use these daily. This trend is already apparent.

2. **Relaxation training**   Stress can be effectively reduced if people can learn to relax. Relaxing is a learned response and companies are now teaching people to relax—some to meditate.

3. **Time management**   Since many people overload themselves with too many activities for the time available, many companies already have in place programs for teaching people how to manage their time more effectively.

Company fitness programs are becoming more common in the drive to reduce stress.

4. **Individual and group therapy**   For those who have some serious problems in stress overload, it may be necessary to provide individual therapy. Groups oriented to helping each other cope with the problems of a complex world will also be formed and supported by the company.

An exemplary company stress reduction program is found at Kimberly-Clark, which is discussed in the following case.

ENDING CASE
Stress Reduction at Kimberly-Clark

Kimberly-Clark's Health Management Program began full operation in 1977 with the stated goal of significantly reducing absenteeism, health-care costs, and cardiovascular risk factors within ten years. The home of the program is a $2.5 million health services center at the corporate office in Wisconsin's Fox Valley. It is available to the 2,600 salaried and 1,900 hourly employees of the office. The center includes a 7,000-square-foot multiphasic health-testing center and a 32,000-square-foot fitness center featuring a 25-meter Olympic pool, a 100-meter suspended track, exercise equipment, a sauna, and a lounge and dining area. A staff of 40, including 17 health professionals, is responsible for the evaluation, counseling, fitness training, and lifestyle modification programs.

Participants enter the program through a series of five steps. First, participants are asked to complete a comprehensive, computerized health history. Next, the employee is given a series of laboratory tests to assess liver, heart, kidney, and lung functions as well as hearing and vision. The third step is a complete physical examination and a treadmill test. A periodic follow-up examination is offered every two to three years, depending on age. Fourth, following the initial evaluation, the results are reviewed and recommendations are made for health promotion and, where necessary, further medical care. A health prescription is prepared with the approval of the employee's personal physician. The health prescription includes an exercise program which usually offers swimming, jogging, cycling, or walking. The fifth and final step is admission to the fitness facility.

The center opened with a large promotional effort, including three weeks of presentations to employees. The medical director kept an open telephone hotline in his office to answer questions and receive feedback about the program. Initially, 60 percent of the salaried employees signed up—10 percent more than expected. To date, over 90 percent of the employees have been through the health screening, 50 percent have received exercise orientation, and 25 percent use the facilities regularly.

The screening program has uncovered a significant number of treatable health conditions and has already succeeded in lowering blood pressure and triglyceride levels. The Employee Assistance Program provides counseling services. About one-half of its clients have alcohol or drug problems, and it reports a favorable rehabilitation rate of 65 percent. Over 200 employees and family members have received training in cardiopulmonary resuscitation.

In addition to the screening, exercise, and counseling programs, the center has a full schedule of health education classes on stress management, obesity, nutrition, and alcohol and drug abuse.

The services and facilities are available to employees on a voluntary basis and without charge. The estimated cost is about $435 per person per year. On the basis of current operations, and projected reductions in absenteeism and use of medical services, it is estimated that the overall break-even point will be 8½ years—3 years for the Employee Assistance Program and about 6½ years for the remainder of the program.

The entire range of services has been well received by employees, the company's public image has been enhanced, and recruitment efforts have been more successful. The cooperation and participation of local physicians has also been obtained. The ten-year goal for reducing absenteeism, health-care costs, and cardiovascular risk factors also is within reach.

SUMMARY

This chapter began by examining again the concept of the organization as an open system. In the future, it is likely that the boundaries between the workplace and other parts of a person's life—family, community, personal development, lifestyle—will be less well defined than ever before.

Organizations in the future will be more active in managing the linkages between the world of work and other parts of a person's life. Some very innovative measures are already being taken. Some companies hire both husband and wife who share a job so that both can work and be at home with young children. More workshops, orientation programs, and conferences are helping to integrate the total family into the goals and responsibilities of the organization.

Since stress has been shown to be a major health problem that reduces the efficiency and effectiveness of employees, more and more companies are developing stress management programs. The total well-being of employees will be a concern of the manager of the future. Health maintenance programs that serve both to reduce stress and increase physical fitness can be justified on a cost basis in that employee absenteeism, turnover, and use of company-provided health services are all reduced as a result.

KEY TERMS

Relocation	Stressor
Two-career family	Stress
Trailing spouse	Fight or flight
Balance	Alarm stage
Role expectations	Resistance stage
Value conflicts	Exhaustion stage
Conflict-habituated relationship	Type A
Devitalized relationship	Type B
Passive-congenial relationship	Task redesign
Vital relationship	Worker autonomy
Total relationship	Flexible scheduling
Intersystem planning	Relaxation training
Job connection	Time management

REVIEW QUESTIONS

1. What is meant by a work system/family system balance?

2. How does the family situation impact the manager's performance at work? How does the manager's work impact the family?

3. Do top executives characteristically have strong or weak marriages according to Maccoby's research?

4. What kind of women are typically married to top male executives?

5. How do home-work conflicts result in stress?

6. How do incompatible expectations influence the manager's home life?

7. What did Blood and Hamblin find with regard to role expectations that is of significance to dual-career families?

8. Name seven common areas of conflict that result from the interrelationship of the manager's work and home life.

9. What are the five types of marital relationship discussed in the chapter and what attributes characterize each?

10. What is often one unexpected result of management efforts to increase the commitment level of subordinates?

11. What does it mean to plan improvement programs that take the family and other external systems into account?

12. How does stress affect bodily systems, and what differences are there between bodily reactions during the various stages of stress?

13. What are the five major categories of stress consequences as identified by Cox?

14. Describe a Type A individual and explain the risks this person faces and why.

15. What are some of the ways companies can help to manage stress at the corporate level? The individual level?

CHALLENGE QUESTIONS

1. The imbalance between home and work life is often hard to detect because the decisions affecting the outcome are almost always made at the margin (I'll just work weekends this month to finish this project). What are some methods a manager can use to make sure that balance is maintained?

2. How do you explain the health of top executive marriages given the time commitments of most senior managers?

3. What steps can dual-career couples, especially the women partners in a marriage, take to avoid serious conflict over the division of home responsibilities?

4. What role expectations do you have with regard to marriage? How would a frank discussion of such expectations help or hinder your relationship with your spouse or prospective spouse?

5. Why is it important for managers to take into account the forces outside the workplace that affect performance? What advantages would accrue to a company that paid careful attention to such forces? What disadvantages could result?

6. If the majority of managers are aware that stress can actually lead to life-threatening illness and even death, why do you think so few of them are involved in an

active program of stress reduction? What kind of relationship would you expect to find between stress and the consumption of coffee, tobacco, alcohol, and drugs? What can you do to protect yourself? Do you really expect things to become easier after you have left school?

7. Does your personality more closely reflect Type A or Type B? Would it be to your advantage to know with some certainty what type you really are? How would you react to the knowledge that you are a Type A personality? Type B?

8. In the context of a job interview what indirect methods and questions would help you determine the organization's efforts to help employees deal with stress?

CASE AND RELATED QUESTIONS

1. What factors in family life do you feel are responsible for the rise of the "decline rate" in the area of corporate relocations? What suggestions would you make to a corporate relocation manager to overcome your concerns?

2. What advantages accrue to a corporation by transferring employees? Do you think that they are worth price tags averaging in excess of $30,000 per transfer?

3. What is a "trailing spouse" service and why has it become such an important part of relocation in North America?

4. What factors contributed to the relatively stress-free environment of Roseto, Pennsylvania, in the early 1960s? What changes resulted from Roseto's introduction to the modern world of the 1970s?

5. What steps can a manager take in the marriage and family context to reduce stress? What effects are likely results of this effort?

6. What are the five steps that participants in Kimberly-Clark's Health Management Program go through? Who does the Employee Assistance Program help?

7. Can health improvement facilities be adequately costed on a direct basis? How about the measurement of benefits? What are some benefits that cannot be adequately measured?

ENDNOTES

1. Adapted from Irene Pave, "Move Me, Move My Spouse: Relocating the Corporate Couple," *Business Week*, December 16, 1985, pp. 57–58.

2. M. Maccoby, *The Gamesman* (New York: Simon and Shuster, 1976).

3. Ibid., p. 119.

4. Ibid., p. 120.

5. R. Blood and R. Hamblin, "The Effects of the Wife's Employment on the Family Power Structure," *Social Forces* 36, May 1958, pp. 347–52.

6. J. F. Cuber and P. B. Harro, "The More to the View: Relationships Among Men and Women of the Upper-Middle Class," *Marriage and Family Living* 25 (May 1963), pp. 140–45.

7. W. F. Whyte, *Human Relations in the Restaurant Industry* (New York: McGraw-Hill, 1948).

8. J. M. Ivancevich and M. T. Matteson, *Stress and Work: A Managerial Perspective* (Glenview, IL: Scott, Foresman, 1980), pp. 2–3.

9. J. G. Bruhn and S. Wolf, *The Roseto Story: An Anatomy of Health* (Norman, OK: University of Oklahoma Press, 1979).

10. H. Selye, *The Stress of Life* 2nd ed. (New York: McGraw-Hill, 1976).

11. Ivancevich and Matteson, p. 13.

12. M. Friedman and R. Rosenman, *Type A Behavior and Your Heart* (New York: Alfred A. Knopf Inc., 1974).

13. J. Naisbitt and P. Aburdene, *Re-Inventing the Corporation* (New York: Warner Books, 1985).

PART V

THE CHALLENGE OF CONTROL

CHAPTER 18

CONTROL

LEARNING OBJECTIVES

■ Understand the role and purpose of control in an organization and its relationship to other management functions.

■ Identify the organizational characteristics that make control necessary.

■ Recognize the control process, its main elements and obstacles to success.

■ Discuss ways of overcoming obstacles to effective control.

■ Understand the tools and techniques of control and their various strengths and weaknesses.

■ Develop a basic understanding of control as key element of a manager's responsibility.

"What price creativity?" is far from an academic question. Movies are the art form of the twentieth century. As Stephen Bach, former executive vice-president of United Artists puts it: "Movies matter. Because they do, and because they are created and manufactured in both artistic and in-dustrial contexts, their costs matter, too. Signs that those costs are once again escalat-ing wildly and could one day make movies simply a prohibitively expensive 'luxury' should be deeply sobering to those who care about them . . ."[2]

Bach speaks as one who should know. It was during his tenure that Michael Cimino directed the biggest financial disaster in movie history, *Heaven's Gate*, an epic Western about a range war in Wyoming. In the aftermath of the debacle, Bach and all of the executives associated with the movie's production were fired. TransAmerica, UA's corporate parent, decided it was time to sell out to MGM.

Michael Cimino was what is known as a "hot property" in movie circles in 1979, the year *Heaven's Gate* was filmed. A perfectionist, Cimino had fought tooth and nail with Universal Studios over cuts it wanted to make in his film version of the Viet Nam War. Cimino won that battle and was vindicated when the *Deer Hunter* won six Os-cars, including "Best Picture."

United Artists, on the other hand, was on the defensive in 1979. Critics attacked the firm as being run by accountants and pencil pushers from TransAmerica. UA was desperate for a big hit for the upcoming Christmas season. UA executives saw Cimino and *Heaven's Gate* as a way to solve both problems.

Michael Cimino played on United Artist's needs like a virtuoso. His lawyers wrote UA a letter in which Cimino laid down the gauntlet: "It is agreed . . . that any and all monies in excess of the approved cash budget . . . to complete and deliver the picture for a Christmas 1979 release shall not be treated as over budget expenditures . . . even if it is finally decided that it is not feasible to complete and deliver the picture in time for such a release."[3] UA did not have the nerve to call Cimino's bluff, if a bluff it was. Cimino was firmly in control.

The approved budget was $11,580,771 and the executives at UA privately agreed that something closer to $15 million was more likely. They did not tell Cimino, how-ever, hoping that he would work to the lower figure. Those hopes proved to be mere dreams; Cimino had the right to charge all overages to UA. The only thing Cimino had agreed upon for certain was to complete a movie that would be between two and three hours in length.

Filming was to take place at Kalispell, Montana, near Glacier National Park, a site of stunning mountain scenery. Cimino, however, liked a tiny town called Sweetwater, two hours away, a little better. The cast and crew thus spent four hours of an eight-hour day travelling to and from the site and the rest of the time on overtime. Need-less to say, they loved their director and sided with him when UA tried to rein in the expenses.

During the filming of *Heaven's Gate*, United Artist had no effective control on director Michael Cimino's spending.

Cimino's artistry can best be appreciated by the fact that he would take up to seventy-five takes of a single scene, sometimes waiting until twilight for perfect lighting. The production fell ten days behind in the first twelve days of shooting and the snail's pace continued at $200,000 a day for three months. Cimino seldom talked to UA executives and threatened to take the movie elsewhere if they interfered. By the time Cimino was brought under control, the film's cost had skyrocketed to about $36 million and box office receipts of $100 million were required just to break even.

The worst was yet to come. Cimino's three-hour movie was previewed for UA executives. Before it began Cimino stated that it was a little longer than the final version would be and that fifteen minutes could probably be cut. Five hours and twenty-five minutes later the film was over.

By opening night the film had been cut to three hours and thirty-nine minutes. The critics panned it. The scenery was beautiful but the film failed to tell a story. Vincent Canby of the *New York Times* wrote, "*Heaven's Gate* is something quite rare in movies these days—an unqualified disaster."[4]

United Artists then took drastic action; it withdrew *Heaven's Gate* from the market. The company hoped that by cutting it down to two and a half hours it could be resuscitated. The new version was more watchable. It was no longer a disaster, just a flop. When all costs, including promotion, had been tallied, the firm wrote off $40 million for a piece of art no one wanted to see. ▼

INTRODUCTION

As can be seen from United Artists' experience in the making of *Heaven's Gate*, organizations seldom execute their plans in a perfect fashion. As a result, management needs to monitor performance and compare operating results with planned results constantly. In monitoring these deviations from plans, and making sure the organization is functioning as intended, management is performing the **control** function.

Control is the last of the basic management functions discussed in Chapter 2 and is closely linked with the planning function discussed in Chapters 5 and 6. Control can be defined as "the activity of insuring that activity and events conform to plans."[5]

This chapter will begin with an overview of the control process. Following the overview, the control process found in effective organizations is described, and key considerations in making the control system effective are analyzed. A number of useful control techniques and methods are then summarized with particular emphasis on financial control. Chapter 19 discusses operations management techniques that can be used to control both manufacturing and service production activities. Chapter 20 describes new developments in management information systems and how they can be used to improve managers' control.

AN OVERVIEW OF ORGANIZATIONAL CONTROL

Organizational control is largely a matter of structure. A control system consists of "those components of the organization that constrain and direct the behavior of members." Control systems include policies, procedures, wage and salary structures, incentive plans, information systems, authority relationships, selection processes, and the nature of the work itself.[6]

Any organizational activity can be controlled. One helpful way to visualize control activities is in terms of the basic types of organizational inputs: human resources, physical resources, information, and financial resources.

Human Resources   Control of human resources includes the selection, placement, and development of employees, systems of performance appraisal, and compensation practices. As United Artists discovered, when Cimino had no real check on his activities, he could justify just about any expense as part of a plan to make the Christmas deadline. In recent years, human resource accounting has been widely discussed as an approach to recognizing the value of the human resources within an organization. More will be mentioned of this topic later in the chapter.

Physical Resources   Control of physical resources includes inventory control (keeping the right amounts of inventory on hand), equipment control (having the necessary physical equipment including buildings and office equipment), and quality control (maintaining the appropriate levels of quality output). In movie making, physical control includes the selection of the location for filming. Lack of control over this issue meant that most people on the set of *Heaven's Gate* spent half their day travelling. Shooting in Sweetwater instead of Kalispell would not have been a problem, however, if the company had first assured itself that even temporary quarters were available for the cast and crew at or near Sweetwater. The excessive retakes during the filming were an example of quality control gone wild.

Information Resources   The control of information resources involves such things as economic forecasts, environmental information, and sales and market forecasts. Appropriate information is critical to the decision-making process and to the accomplishment of goals. United Artists had tremendous problems in getting Cimino to divulge what was going on up in Montana. The company also ignored market information that suggested that Westerns were no longer very popular with moviegoers.

Financial Resources   Financial controls typically receive the primary emphasis in control systems as illustrated in Figure 18-1. Not only are financial resources important in their own right, but they are related to each of the other inputs. Poor control of financial resources results in inappropriate levels of spending on human, physical, and information resources. Poor selection and placement activities result in increased training costs or termination and rehiring expenses. Poor economic and marketing forecasts are harmful because of deviations in planned cash flow. Finally, excess inventory is expensive because of the costs of storage as well as the opportunity cost of having funds tied up in unused assets. Thus, financial controls tend to be the most common of all control techniques and tools.

The Importance of Control

In the minds of some people, organizational control may be a negative force—necessary perhaps, but, in light of today's emphasis on personal freedom and participative

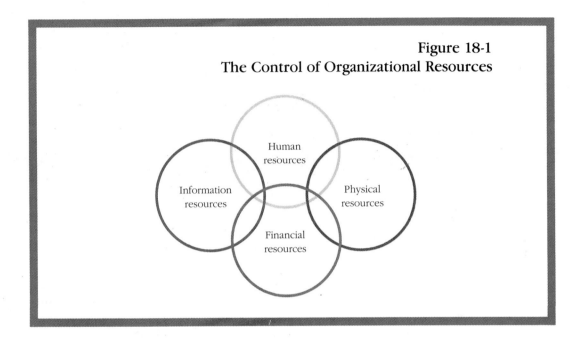

Figure 18-1
The Control of Organizational Resources

management, unpleasant. Others view it more positively, as a function that helps an organization achieve its goals and objectives. Control is a positive and important function, and several major factors make it necessary.

CHANGE   In today's complex and turbulent environment, all companies must learn to manage change (Chapters 12 and 20 discuss this issue in more detail). For instance, if *Heaven's Gate* had been produced in a static environment where audience tastes were the same from year to year and these tastes were known, all Cimino would have had to do to succeed was to produce a picture keyed to these tastes and watch the money pour in. He could have concentrated on content and not worried much about artistic expression. In such an environment, planning and controlling become automatic rather quickly. Control, however, is much more difficult when a company cannot be sure what will catch the public's fancy, especially in an area where public tastes are as mercurial as they are in motion pictures.

Even in industries viewed as stable, complete stability does not exist. Change is inevitable in all industries as new products are developed, competitors and strategies shift, new technological advances are made, consumer preferences change, and new levels of regulation are passed. With effective control systems, management is able to detect these changes and respond to them.

COMPLEXITY   Another factor underlying the importance of control is the increasing complexity of modern organizations. When firms have a simple structure, produce only one product from a single location, and have limited suppliers and a small

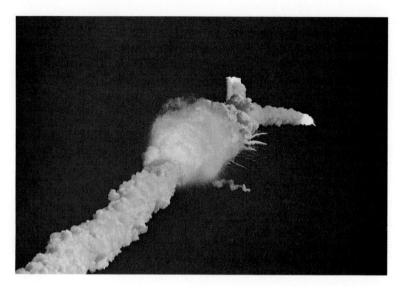

The absence of adequate control contributed to the space shuttle *Challenger* tragedy.

number of customers, a very informal system of control is sufficient. Today's large organizations, however, require a much more formal approach to control. Diversified product lines produced at multiple locations must be monitored closely to ensure that the necessary quality and profit standards are being maintained. Part of United Artists' problem was that its executives had better things to do than spend their time in Kalispell; many other movies such as *Rocky II* and the new James Bond thriller, *For Your Eyes Only*, were in the works.

Decentralization   One of the developments that has added significantly to the complexity of today's business firms is the increasing practice of decentralization. Many firms now have regional manufacturing and sales offices with the resultant emphasis of control at the local level. Thus, for decentralization to be effective, the control activities of the individual units must be precise. Performance against established standards allows general managers to assess more accurately the effectiveness of business units as well as allowing top-level management to evaluate the performance of the general managers.

Delegation   Related to the issue of decentralization is delegation. When managers delegate authority they are still held responsible for satisfactory performance levels. When tasks have been delegated, control systems are necessary to allow managers to monitor the successful completion of those tasks. One of the results of the *Heaven's Gate* debacle was a system of daily monitoring implemented by United Artists on all future projects.

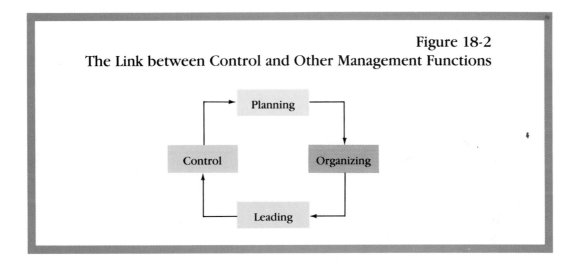

Figure 18-2
The Link between Control and Other Management Functions

MISTAKES   A third reason why control is necessary in today's organizations is the compounding effect of mistakes. Small mistakes might not seriously threaten an organization's strength. If not corrected, however, small mistakes can compound over time and become very serious. A wrong pricing decision, for instance, can have serious consequences over a period of time if not corrected. A control system allows managers to become aware of these mistakes before they become critical. The location decision in *Heaven's Gate* could have been rectified almost immediately if the executives had known of it early enough. Once filming began they were, in effect, locked into the site at a cost of $100,000 per day.

How Control Is Related to Other Management Functions

As has been suggested, the essence of control "is the process whereby managers assure themselves that actual activities conform to planned activities." As discussed in Chapters 5 and 6, goals and objectives are first established during strategic planning. The control system measures progress toward these goals and highlights deviations from the plan in time to take corrective action.

The link between control and the other management functions is illustrated in Figure 18-2. Planning is the first part of the management process. Then the organizing and leading functions get the actual work done, and the controlling function is tied directly into planning as feedback on performance is obtained.

United Artists' handling of *Heaven's Gate* is illustrative of poor linkage between control and the other management functions. The UA executive team analyzed their situation and decided that a film by Cimino would be of help. They then planned for the film, made a budget, and signed the contract. The control system was rendered ineffective, however, by Cimino's unrestricted right to bill UA for costs over budget. Feedback was uncertain and the failure to require contractually certain information of Cimino led to information that was not helpful by the time it was received. Consequently, UA executives made poor decisions.

The Control Process

The steps in the control process can be visualized in Figure 18-3. The major steps in this process are: (1) establishing standards; (2) measuring performance; (3) comparing measured performance with standards; and (4) taking corrective action if required.

ESTABLISHING STANDARDS   The first step in the control process, establishing standards, emphasizes the close relationship between the manager's function of controlling and planning. Standards are established through the process of planning and establishing goals. A **standard** is a yardstick that determines the adequacy of organizational performance. For example, par (the standard number of strokes for a golf hole—one that varies with the difficulty of the hole) is the standard against which a golfer measures his performance. A golfer who wants to shoot par for an entire course, knows that improvement is needed on later holes if par is exceeded on a given hole.

Goals in organizations can be developed into standards by making them measurable. An organizational goal to finish *Heaven's Gate* "under budget" could have been translated into a management performance standard of completing two pages of script per day (less than half this amount was achieved). This in turn might have been supported by specific goals for each page of script (a schedule for shooting each scene, for example).

Standards may be set in all functions of a business enterprise. Four common types of standards are financial, physical, human, and time.

- Financial standards include targets for the cost of products, the desired return on investment, the level of debt and liquidity, and profit margins.

- Examples of physical standards include the quality of products or services, their quantities, and market share.

- Human standards indicate types of attitudes that management strives to develop in its employees, and the types of training programs required.

- Time standards include productivity measurements such as the speed with which jobs should be done, and the deadlines by which jobs are to be completed or goals are to be met.

In many areas, however, the quantification of the objective or standard is difficult. Consider the areas of research and development and technological change. In evaluating these areas, management may not be able to establish measurable criteria.

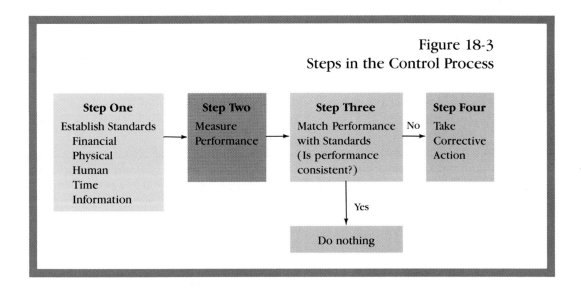

Figure 18-3
Steps in the Control Process

Inability to quantify the desired output does not mean, however, an absence of a conception of what constitutes satisfactory performance. For example, a consumer products company may have a standard for R&D of two marketable products per year even though the exact nature of those products is not known.

MEASURING PERFORMANCE   Measuring performance, the second step in the control process, has at least two aspects.[7] The types of measures used in the measuring process represent one aspect. A second major consideration is the timing and type of measurement system to be utilized.

Types of Control Measurements.[8]   Most systems used for measuring performance can be classified as feed forward, concurrent, or feedback.

    Feed forward   Feed forward controls, sometimes called steering controls, detect deviations from a standard before a major activity has begun. For example, if the purchasing manager of a manufacturing company becomes aware of a delay in the arrival of important parts, he would alert the production and marketing managers. The production manager would need to reschedule the production run while the marketing manager could negotiate a new delivery date. Feed forward data reduce the negative impact of deviations from standard before a major activity is begun.

    Concurrent control measurements   Control measures that are being performed as the work is being done are called concurrent control measures or screening control. These control measures relate not only to human performance but also to such items as departmental and machine performance. For example, agricultural commodities are often sorted as they are being washed or put through some other process.

One of the reasons for the strength of the Japanese automakers during the 1970s and 1980s is the active involvement of the production workers in screening controls. In the United States, inspection for quality generally occurs when an automobile has been completed. In Japan, however, each worker acts as an inspector and screens for defective parts as part of the process of completing his or her operation.[9] Because screening measurements are widely applicable and useful in identifying problems, they tend to be used more often than other types of measurements.

Feedback control measures   Control measures that concentrate on completed organizational tasks are called feedback control. Feedback measures are helpful because they permit managers to use information on past performance to bring future performance into line with objectives. This history concentrates on one factor at a time, such as inventory levels, customer complaints, or on the relationship between such variables as profit and sales revenue.

Timing   At least two time frames of performance measurements can be used—continuous and intermittent. A **continuous measurement** measures activities that occur on each unit (such as quality control checks on each car manufactured by Ford Motor Company). An **intermittent measurement** checks activities at specified time intervals, such as quarterly sales reviews or annual performance appraisals. Frequent measurements are more expensive to obtain. In selecting time frames, managers need to balance the costs of frequent measurements with the challenge of detecting performance problems in time to respond to them. United Artists decided after its *Heaven's Gate* experience that daily reports would best suit its need for cost information.

MATCHING PERFORMANCE WITH STANDARDS   The third step in the control process is comparing performance with established standards. In some ways this is the easiest of the steps because the complexities of measurement and the decision as to which variables to measure have been made in the previous steps. Performance may be higher, lower, or the same as the standard. The issue for managers is how much leeway is permissible before remedial action is taken. If it is judged that the performance meets the standard, the control process returns to the measurement stage as seen in Figure 18-3. If performance does not meet the standard, corrective action may be required.

CORRECTIVE ACTION   When performance measures have been compared with standards and significant deviations have been identified, it is important that managers take the necessary corrective action. Corrective action is managerial activity focused on bringing performance up to the level of performance standards. Without their focus on action, management would simply be monitoring performance rather than controlling and influencing performance levels. Several principles should be remembered when taking corrective action.

Identify the Underlying Problem   In taking corrective action, it is important that managers identify the underlying problem rather than focusing entirely on symptoms of the problem. For example, if a student sets a standard of scoring 90 on exams, and only reaches a level of 68, he or she must determine the underlying causes of this deficiency before taking the next exam. Were the assignments clearly understood? Was sufficient time spent in preparation for the exam? Was the wrong material prepared? Before improvement can begin, the underlying cause for the poor performance needs to be identified. Likewise, the reasons for poor performance on the part of an employee need to be identified before effective corrective action can be implemented.

Decide If Deviation from Standard Is Justified   Some deviation from standard may be justified because the standard may have been too high or too low to begin with. In the case of the university student, this would be apparent if large numbers of the class achieved a score of 90, or if no one ever reached that standard in the class. In other situations, a standard that was perfectly good when it was set may no longer be appropriate because of changed or extenuating circumstances. A sales increase standard of 15 percent may need to be altered when it becomes apparent that a major competitor has come up with an improved product or service. Thus, standards need to be evaluated in light of existing conditions.

Determine Whether Action Is Required   Finally, some processes are self-correcting. A common example is that of a heating system with a thermostat. If the thermostat is set at 70° (the standard), the heating system will be activated (corrective action) only when the temperature in the room falls below 70°. If the control system is working properly, no management action is required to correct it. Similarities might be found in inventory control systems where orders are placed automatically upon the achievement of a particular inventory level.

Resistance to Control

The word "control" has some unpleasant connotations for many people. The perceived loss of freedom and autonomy is one concern that is often expressed. Because of these and other human concerns, managers need to be sensitive to potential negative side effects or barriers to the control process.

OVEREMPHASIS ON THE SHORT RUN VERSUS THE LONG RUN   A possible consequence of control systems is the overemphasis on short-term goals. On occasion it is possible the short-run action encouraged by the control system would actually run counter to the long-run interests of the organization. Common examples might come from the manager's desire to achieve short-term profit objectives. Commonly cited examples might be to:

- Run machinery at full capacity for extended periods without stopping them to be serviced properly.

■ Reduce investments in research and development by eliminating all projects that have a longer payback than two years.

Such action by managers may ensure that planned for performance and actual performance are equal in the short run. The long-term negative consequences of these actions, however, should be obvious. In fact, the preoccupation of U.S. management with short-term profit performance is often cited as a major factor in the deterioration of the U.S. position in international trade.

One recent study of managers in six major companies found that managers who emphasize the attainment of short-term goals at the expense of long-term strategic goals do so for two reasons.[10] The first is that the manager's performance evaluation (control system), and thus his financial incentive, emphasizes short-term results. The second is that short-term goals are more visible and easily comprehended than long-range objectives.

NARROW PERSPECTIVE   Another possible undesirable impact of control systems is the tendency to narrow a manager's perspective. A manager may focus on a particular performance standard and not consider the possible consequences elsewhere in the organization of achieving that objective. A common problem is the emphasis of some production managers on pushing production out the door without regard to quality. Dissatisfied customers soon plague the marketing department, and the problem eventually comes back to haunt the production manager when goods are returned for rework or production lines are closed because of a drop in orders.

Cimino's obsession with perfect camera shots is an example of a narrow focus. In focusing so completely on technical perfection, he forgot that the first requirement of a good motion picture is to entertain, to tell a story that touches the emotions of the audience. The critics agreed that the film was technically virtuous, but they panned it for its failure to tell a story.

NEGATIVE EFFECT ON EMPLOYEE MORALE   If management does not allow a proper balance between freedom and control, then employees may become frustrated and unhappy with their jobs. When too much control is exercised or management is perceived to be too rigid, employees may feel that control systems are simply another tactic to pressure workers toward higher production. Sales quotas established simply by projecting an increase over sales of past years without taking into consideration changed economic or competitive conditions can be counterproductive. Perhaps sales should increase much more rapidly to stay even, but if the sales staff feels that "quota" is sufficient, sales will not jump. Likewise, such a system may demoralize a sales staff facing a serious downturn in business, and some sales personnel may actually resign rather than face the failure of not making quota. Employees subject to unreasonable standards or excessive managerial rigidity in their application are understandably critical.

IMPROVING EFFECTIVENESS OF CONTROL ACTIVITIES: OVERCOMING RESISTANCE

Managers, in establishing control systems, are obviously concerned about minimizing the possible negative side effects mentioned in the preceding section. Being aware of these potential problems and effective use of the following skills is important for managers at all levels.

Participative Management

In Chapter 12 we noted how employee involvement in the change process can overcome resistance to change. Similarly, when employees are involved in the establishment of a control system, the standards will more likely be considered fair by those whose performance is being controlled.

For example, a salesman who is taught how to make a proper sales forecast for a sales territory is much more likely to be committed to a sales objective derived from the forecast than to one handed down from the sales manager. In addition, the process of creating the forecast teaches the salesperson to think in an analytic fashion about economic, industry, and company conditions, the very skills needed for advancement within the organization.

MANAGEMENT BY OBJECTIVES   The use of management by objectives (MBO), discussed in Chapter 5, is another way to overcome employee resistance to control systems. When MBO is used appropriately, managers are involved in establishing their own goals or standards. They are also aware of the rewards that will come to them as they are successful in meeting these standards. By focusing on the accomplishment of these standards, control in the organization is accomplished as much by managerial self-control as it is by external controls. MBO, then, becomes a vehicle for facilitating the integration of planning and control.[11]

BALANCE BETWEEN CONTROL AND FREEDOM   The formality and nature of control can vary. With too much control, the workplace can become a restrictive and inhibiting place; with too little control, the organization can become inefficient and ineffective in accomplishing its goals. Thus, a major challenge for managers is to maintain the proper balance between controls and personal freedom.

Because organizations, people, and environments keep changing, control systems require constant review and modification in order to maintain their balance. One of the conditions that clearly needs to be considered is the level of competence and commitment of the employee. Where competence and/or commitment levels are low, greater control is required for the accomplishment of performance standards. Where competence and commitment levels are high, greater personal freedom can be allowed.[12]

CREATE EFFECTIVE CONTROLS   One of the best ways to overcome resistance to control is to have effective control systems in the first place. Reliable and effective control systems have certain characteristics in common.[13] Some of these qualities are:

Accuracy   Information on performance levels must be accurate. Inaccurate data causes management to take corrective action that either does not correct the problem or creates a different one. If sales estimates, for instance, are artificially high, management might cut advertising, thinking it was no longer needed. Making sure that the information they receive is accurate is one of the most important tasks managers can perform.

Timeliness   Information needs to be gathered and evaluated in a timely fashion if it is to be helpful in managerial decision making. Timeliness does not necessarily mean speed but rather it means obtaining information as often as needed to control a certain activity. In retail stores, sales may need to be evaluated daily to allow management to make necessary decisions concerning advertisement and promotions. On the other hand, physical inventory counts for retailers can be taken much less frequently.

Flexibility   Another characteristic of an effective control system is flexibility, the capability to accommodate change. As discussed earlier, all modern organizations face change in environment, technology, and human resources. Control systems must react quickly to take advantage of new opportunities or minimize adverse situations. An example of system flexibility can be found in the procedures used by universities to control class sizes. Classes frequently have enrollment limitations. When these limits have been reached no additional students are allowed admission. If some students need the course because they are graduating at the end of the term or if they have work schedules that must be kept, it is frequently possible to add these students to the class.

Objectivity and Comprehensibility   The information utilized in control systems should be understood by all parties and should be as objective as possible. The more objective the control system is, the greater the likelihood that managers will respond in appropriate ways. For instance, if a manager responds to a question about the level of employee morale by giving subjective responses such as "normal" or "fine," important information may not be understood by upper management. On the other hand, if the response to the query included objective data concerning turnover, grievances, and tardiness, management is more likely to respond knowingly and efficiently to the information that it receives. An easily understood control system will help to avoid unnecessary mistakes and confusion among employees.

Use of Strategic Control Points   The control system should be focused on those activities where deviations from standards are most likely or will do the most harm. In addition, control should be focused where corrective action is most likely to be effective. In the case of making automobiles, it would do little good to check quality when cars reach the dealer's showroom. Instead, quality is checked at strategic points along the production line.

Realistic Economics   In the implementation of control systems, great care needs to be given to an analysis of the costs versus the benefits of the system. Control systems and corrective action should be given to the minimum number of situations required to reach a distinct goal. If a sales manager has five regions with sales goals of $500,000 each, and only one region has a major deviation from goal, that manager should focus the greatest amount of attention on the area with the most significant deviation.

It is also critical to know what action is to be taken when the control system signals a warning. United Artists' major problem in *Heaven's Gate* was the timing of the information it received, but it also failed to set out in advance what it would do if the movie went seriously over budget.

TOOLS AND TECHNIQUES OF CONTROL

For many people in both the private and the public sector, control means budgeting. Yet the preparation of budgets is also an important and integral part of the planning process, and one of the end products of planning is a set of planned budgets.

Financial Control: Budgets

What is a budget? **Budgets** are formal statements of expected revenues, expenses and profits developed to control the use of an organization's financial resources. While budgets are generally expressed in financial terms, they may occasionally be expressed in terms of units of output, manpower, time, or other quantifiable factors.

Budgets are the foundation of most control systems. Because of their quantitative nature, budgets provide yardsticks for measuring performance and they make possible the comparison of performance versus plans from one time period to another.

Budgets serve four primary purposes: (1) they help coordinate resources and projects because they are generally stated in dollars; (2) they help define the standards needed for all control systems; (3) they provide clear and specific guidelines about resources and expectations; and (4) they facilitate the evaluation of managerial and unit performance.

THE BUDGETARY PROCESS   Budgets can be prepared by either a top-down or bottom-up process.[14]

Maintaining accurate records of revenues and expenses is part of the financial control process.

Top-Down Process   In the top-down approach, budgets are prepared by top management, frequently the financial vice-president, or the controller. Although lower-level managers may be given an opportunity to make suggestions, their major responsibility becomes one of implementation.

Although some organizations still follow this procedure, most organizations follow a process in which the budget is prepared with the active involvement of those managers responsible for implementing it, an approach offering a number of advantages over the traditional top-down process. First, managers who are responsible for implementation have a greater understanding of their needs and constraints. Second, the likelihood of overlooking important items is reduced. Third, when managers are involved in developing the budget they are more motivated to implement it.

Bottom-Up Process   The budgeting process for a bottom-up approach includes the following important principles:

Statement of Goals   This statement includes important economic and environmental forecasts and is communicated for the coming budget period (usually a year).

Preparation by Lower-level Managers   Budget preparation is initially the responsibility of lower-level managers. A frequent starting point is an analysis of current income and expenses. Typically, a manager (A) compares current income expenses against the previous budget, (B) states how the next period will differ from the current period, and (C) proposes the next period's budget based on the current budget, plus or minus expected changes. While this process sounds rather simple, in practice it can be quite complex. For cost estimates, a manager must cope with such uncertainties as inflation and interest rates; for revenue estimates, judgments must be made about such unknowns as competitor response, economic variables, and consumer preferences. Managers often handle this uncertainty by making what are known as "educated guesses."

TOP MANAGEMENT INVOLVEMENT   Review and budget approval brings top management into the process. Top managers or budget committees review the budgets of individual units. Overlapping or inconsistent requests are corrected and funds are allocated to the various departments. Allocation decisions are often among the most difficult that top management must make. In most firms resources are scarce and departments cannot be given what they say they need even though resources are crucial to success. Loss of essential resources can jeopardize a department's performance and damage the entire organization. Allocation decisions are so critical that a budget committee consisting of the president and executive vice-presidents often makes the final decisions.

EVALUATION AND CONTROL   Budget evaluation and control occurs as the unit performs during the budget period. Careful attention is paid to every variance from the budget, giving managers the information needed to take corrective action. This continuous check enables management to locate problems before they become too large to manage effectively.

Changes or adjustments to the budget may be necessary in some situations. However, if a department's budget can be revised at will, the initial effort in making and improving it is wasted. On the other hand, if conditions change and the assumptions on which the budget is based are incorrect, budget revisions are appropriate. Figure 18-4 demonstrates the relationship between budgetary control and planning.

ADVANTAGES AND LIMITATIONS OF BUDGETING   Budgets offer a number of advantages for managers, but they have some limitations as well. Both are summarized in Box 18-1.

Advantages   On the positive side, budgets aid in planning by forcing managers to develop specific goals and the plans to achieve them. Second, the use of budgets facilitates coordination and communication between departments. The interaction between managers and subordinates that occurs during the development of budgets helps define and clarify performance-related activities. Third, by specifying what resources are to be used, budgets help managers achieve goals by successfully implementing corporate strategies. Finally, from a control point of view, budgets assist in the efficient use of resources and establish a mechanism for periodic corporate evaluation.[15]

Limitations   On the other hand, some managers may apply budgets too rigidly. They may fail to consider that changing circumstances can justify some budget adjustments. Also, some managers are concerned that one of the strengths of budgeting—

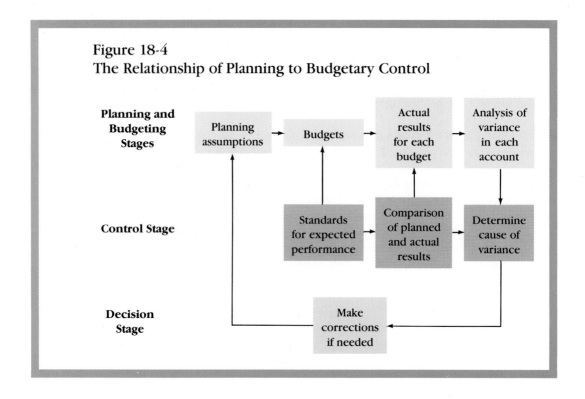

Figure 18-4
The Relationship of Planning to Budgetary Control

Box 18-1
Strengths and Weaknesses of Budgeting

STRENGTHS	WEAKNESSES
1. Aid to planning.	1. May be used too rigidly.
2. Facilitates coordination and communication between departments.	2. May cause only those activities that are measured in financial terms to be rewarded.
3. Assists in accomplishment of corporate strategies.	3. Budget variances may confuse symptoms with causes.
4. Facilitates effective control.	4. Budgets may limit innovation and change.

translating organizational activities into a monetary unit of measure—may become one of its weaknesses. This shortcoming occurs when only those activities that can be easily measured are rewarded; leadership, team building, and plans for organizational development may be ignored because they are not easily quantified in financial terms.

Box 18-2
Types of Budgets

OPERATING BUDGETS	Revenue Budget—focuses on expected revenue.
(Express plans for operations in financial terms.)	Expense Budget—identifies expected expenses.
	Profit Budget—combines the above two budgets.
FINANCIAL BUDGETS	Cash Budget—identifies short-run and current cash flows.
	Capital Expenditure Budget—identifies expenditures required for fixed assets such as buildings, machinery, and land.
	Balance Sheet Budget—focuses on what the organization's balance sheet will look like if all other budgets are met.

It is also possible in the analysis of budgetary variances to confuse symptoms with causes. If a drop in expected sales revenue is experienced, the remedy may not be to increase marketing efforts. Rather, the underlying cause may be product quality or a change in a competitor's strategy. Finally, the process of developing budgets may be very time consuming and limit innovation and change. When all available funds have been allocated in present operating budgets, it may be difficult to obtain the necessary funds to take advantage of unexpected opportunities.

TYPES OF BUDGET   So far, the discussion in this section on control techniques has been limited to budgets in a general sense. However, most organizations have two types of budgets: operating budgets and financial budgets. **Operating budgets** focus on goods and services the organization intends to utilize during the budget period. **Financial budgets** identify the financial resources that the organization intends to spend during the same period as well as the source of those funds. Box 18-2 summarizes these different kinds of budgets.

Operating Budgets   An operating budget is an expression of the organization's operations in financial terms. Thus, operating budgets outline what will be consumed and what will be provided. The following are the three major types of operating budgets:

Revenue Budgets   Revenue budgets focus on the income that an organization expects to receive during the budgetary period. If a firm expects to sell 100,000 units of its product at a price of $100, its revenue budget is $10,000,000. The revenue budget is a critical part of the profit budget and one of the most uncertain. If an organization produces its product on the basis of firm back orders or if it is operating in a stable environment, its revenue budgets are more certain than those of an organization that operates in an unpredictable and changing market environment. However, even organizations operating in an uncertain environment, can control the quality and quantity of the factors that affect revenues, such as advertising, service, and product quality. This control gives them some influence over the level of revenues achieved and allows them to make reasonable sales estimates.

Expense Budgets   An expense budget outlines the anticipated expenses of the organization in the coming time period. If a university department chairman has a supply budget of $24,000 per year, he or she knows that they must average no more than $2,000 per month on supplies. One of the advantages of expense budgets is that they allow managers to prepare for upcoming expenses. If a manager knew that a major fixed expense such as $20,000 in property taxes was due in October, the firm could prepare for this by setting something aside each month rather than trying to meet it out of the revenues of that month only.

Profit Budgets   A profit budget combines the revenue and expense budgets into one statement. If a firm expects revenues of $1,000,000 and budgeted expenses are $750,000, the manager has an operating profit budget of $250,000. If budgeted expenses and revenues are too close together, managers will need to take corrective action. Steps may be taken to increase the revenues by increasing prices or marketing expenditures or by cutting the expense budget.

Financial Budgets   Financial budgets deal with how the organization is going to spend its cash during the coming period and where it expects to obtain its financial resources. The major sources of funds are reducing assets, increasing liabilities by taking out loans, increasing equity by selling common stock or retaining profits. Common uses of cash are to purchase new assets, reduce liabilities by paying debt, or reducing equity by repurchasing stock or paying dividends. The following are the most common financial budgets:

Cash Budgets   Cash budgets are a projection of cash revenues and expenses for the budget period. They provide managers with information about the amount of cash flowing through the organization and the timing of the disbursements and receipts. If the owner of a small business knows that the business has a payroll obligation of $25,000 due on the last day of the month, she must be sure that sufficient cash is on hand to meet these obligations. Cash budgets are essential control tools in allowing managers to invest excessive cash on a short-term basis or to take the corrective action necessary to meet important financial obligations.

Capital Expenditure Budgets   Capital expenditure budgets indicate future investments in capital equipment or fixed assets such as buildings, machinery, or land. These investments are generally made to renew or expand productive capacity and thus are of significant importance to the organization. Capital budgets are therefore developed only after careful study of the external environment and the probability of certain events. Because these budgets deal with a longer time frame and large amounts of money, they are very helpful in providing management with information about financing requirements they will face in the future. Capital budgeting decisions are generally made by the highest levels of management and usually require approval by a company's board of directors.

General Motors' plans for its Saturn plant, discussed in Chapter 2, provide an example of capital budgeting on a major scale. GM had to forecast such things as disposable income, interest rates, the value of the dollar, competitive response, and consumer tastes before making the decision to invest. The number of factors considered and the uncertainty associated with the necessary forecasts make capital budgeting decisions among the most difficult that a business faces; incorrect decisions can lead to loss of competitive positions and even bankruptcy when debt financing is used.

Balance Sheet Budgets   A balance sheet budget is a combination of all other financial budgets and projects what the balance sheet will look like at the end of the budget period if actual results conform with planned for results. Sometimes called a pro-forma balance sheet, it becomes an important control document to ensure that the organization's objectives are being realized. Analysis of the balance sheet budget might suggest problems that managers will have to address, sometimes by altering other budgets. For example, an analysis of the pro-forma balance sheet might reveal that present budgets will result in an excessively heavy debt burden, requiring either a reduction of the capital expenditure budget or a decision to sell more common stock.

Fixed and Variable Budgets   Budgetary controls can be inflexible at times. If expense budgets are determined for estimated sales of $10,000,000 (a type of **fixed budget**), it is not likely that they would be sufficient if actual sales of $13,000,000 are achieved. Manufacturing costs are one of many expenses that increase as production increases to meet the demand.

To meet this potential problem, **variable budgets** (sometimes called flexible budget, sliding scale budget, or step budget) can be utilized. This technique ties standard costs to the volume of revenues, permitting managers to control expenditures as a function of sales levels. Table 18-1 is an example of a variable budget. Note the implicit assumption that expense items as a percentage of sales will fall slightly as sales increase, reflecting volume discounts and greater efficiency in resource use as volume increases.

The prerequisite for variable or flexible budgeting is the identification costs as either fixed or variable. Some costs are fixed costs in that they are unaffected by volume of sales. For example, in many organizations monthly salaries of managers, insurance payments, rent, and some utility costs are not altered by a change in the sales level. Variable costs are those costs such as raw materials, extra workers' wages

Table 18-1
Budget for Sales Expense for the Year 1987

Revenue per month	$50,000.00	$100,000.00
Variable costs		
Commissions	$ 2,500.00	$ 5,000.00
Long-distance phone expense	1,300.00	2,200.00
Car maintenance and repairs	300.00	400.00
Fuel	350.00	500.00
Advertising	700.00	1,000.00
Office supplies	200.00	400.00
Total Budget for Variable Costs	$ 5,350.00	$ 9,500.00

and supplies that vary directly with the volume of sales or output. Table 18-2 is an illustration of the variable and fixed components of total cost.

When developing a variable budget, managers need to account accurately for both categories of expenses. Fixed costs are, of course, the easiest to deal with. In estimating the variable costs, managers rely on their experience and judgment. Some forecasting techniques can also be helpful in estimating certain kinds of variable costs.[16]

CONTEMPORARY BUDGETING APPROACHES   In recent years many profit and nonprofit organizations have adopted new approaches to budgeting. Among the most popular are zero-base budgeting and human resource accounting.

Zero-Base Budgeting   In traditional budgeting approaches, yearly budgets are based on the previous year's budget, and the manager needs to justify any additional funding. It is assumed that past expenditures are appropriate and should be continued.

In **Zero-base budgeting** (ZBB), no such assumption is made. Each budgeting unit begins with a clean slate each year. With each new budget, managers need to justify every dollar expenditure as if they started from a "zero base." For example, a manager of research and development would need to justify funds for each new study as well as those funds that are required to carry over research projects from the previous period.

Zero-base budgeting was pioneered at Texas Instruments in 1970, and popularized by President Jimmy Carter when he used it in the federal government in the late 1970s.[17]

Zero-base budgeting allows an organization to allocate funds on the basis of a cost-benefit analysis of each of the organization's activities. The process includes three major steps. First, activities of the organization are broken down into decision packages that include all the information needed to evaluate and compare the costs

Table 18-2
Sales Department Variable and Fixed Costs

Fixed costs	
Salaries (2,500 per month × 3 salespersons)	$ 7,500.00
Office rental	2,000.00
Office equipment	300.00
Payroll taxes	500.00
Phone service	500.00
Secretarial salaries	2,000.00
Car leases	600.00
Insurance	100.00
Utilities	400.00
Miscellaneous	500.00
Total Budget for Fixed Costs	$14,400.00
Variable costs (revenue of $100,000 per month)	
Commissions	$ 5,000.00
Long-distance phone expense	2,200.00
Car maintenance and repairs	400.00
Fuel	500.00
Advertising	1,000.00
Office supplies	400.00
Total Budget for Variable Costs	$ 9,500.00
Total Fixed and Variable Costs	$23,900.00

and benefits of a program or activity along with the consequences of nonapproval. Second, the individual decision packages are ranked according to their benefit to the organization. Unit rankings are given to higher-level management who develop a rank order for the entire organization. Finally, resources are budgeted according to the final ranking that has been established.

The primary advantage of zero-base budgeting is that it forces managers constantly to examine each program carefully, eliminate low priority activities, and develop more effective programs. On the other hand, the process of continual justification creates more paperwork and managers may resort to inflating the importance of their programs to maintain the present level of funding and pet projects. Because it takes a total organizational viewpoint and stresses the effective use of resources, a growing number of organizations will be using zero-base budgeting as a technique for organizational control.[18]

Human Resource Accounting   **Human resource accounting** (HRA) attempts to acknowledge that human resources have a quantifiable value to an organization that should be considered in managerial decision making. The point has been made throughout this text that human resource management is important because so many managers feel that "our human resources are our greatest asset." Employees are the resource that produces profits; other resources facilitate the profit-making potential of organizations.

In Aesop's "Fable of the Goose and the Golden Egg," the profit-making capacity (the goose) needs to be nurtured and taken care of if the profit (golden egg) is to be long-lived. The proponents of HRA point out that if the importance of human resources to the organization can be dramatized, greater attention will be given to how they are managed.

Human resource accounting is an outgrowth of research done at the University of Michigan by Rensis Likert and his associates. After hearing that many top managers estimated that it would cost them about 3 times their annual payroll or about "24 or 25" times their annual earnings to replace their organization, Likert tried to develop a method for measuring the value of those human assets.[19]

A number of techniques have been developed to assess the value of human resources.[20] Four of the most useful are (1) historical cost, (2) replacement cost, (3) economic value, and (4) present value. The historical cost method capitalizes the costs of selecting and hiring personnel. These assets are then depreciated over some time period, generally the expected tenure of the employee. When the employee leaves the organization, the unamortized portion of the investment is written off as a loss in the accounting period of the separation. The replacement cost method uses estimates of the expenses that would be incurred to replace a particular employee. These costs include recruiting and training expenses as well as the opportunity cost of not having an adequate replacement for a period of time. The economic value method assumes that employees are compensated according to their worth to the organization. The result is a value equal to the salaries of employees. Finally, the present value method utilizes the present value of a stream of net future contributions of the employee to the organization. This approach uses expected salary, estimates of future contributions, and the probability of separation from the organization.

The use of HRA has not, as yet, been widely accepted by managers. As can be seen by the brief description of the calculations mentioned above, many estimates are required and the data is not as objective as is financial data. Nevertheless, the concept has great potential in that it calls the attention of managers to the importance of human resources.

Financial Controls: Financial Statements

Although budgets are the most commonly used method of financial control, other techniques are also used with great frequency. The financial control techniques discussed in this section include financial statements, ratio analysis, and break-even analysis. The use of these tools allows managers to evaluate an organization's performance in areas that are crucial to its survival.

Financial statements document, in dollar terms, the flow of funds to, within, and from an organization. They are prepared by the accounting staff and provide a method of controlling three very important dimensions of an organization's well being: (1) **liquidity**—the ability of the organization to pay its bills and meet its financial obligations; (2) **leverage**—the balance between debt and equity, and (3) **profitability**— the ability to earn profits over a period of time.

In the United States the major financial statements used for control purposes are the income statement, and the balance sheet. The reports are generally prepared on a quarterly basis.

INCOME STATEMENT   The purpose of the **income statement** (profit and loss statement) is to show the total revenues earned by an organization during a particular time period as well as the total expenses incurred during the same period. The difference between the revenues and the expenses is called the net income (earnings or profits) or net loss for the period. Table 18-3 illustrates a sample income statement.

BALANCE SHEET   The **balance sheet** reports the organization's assets, liabilities, and owners' equity at the end of the reporting period. The assets must balance with the sum of the organization's liabilities and equity, thus the term "balance sheet."

While the income statement summarizes financial performance over a given period of time, the balance sheet describes an organization's financial well-being at a given point in time. The managerial focus shifts from "how much money are we making," to "what is our financial condition." Table 18-4 demonstrates the balance sheet.

Analysis of Financial Statements

Although financial statements reveal such information as net worth, profit, and total debt, these numbers alone provide the manager with limited information. For this reason, ratio analysis is used to interpret the financial statements and give management more of the information it needs for control purposes. Ratio analysis involves selecting two significant figures from a financial statement and expressing their relationship in terms of a percentage or ratio. The resulting ratio is then compared with similar ratios for firms in the same industry or with ratios from the firm in a previous period.[21] The first comparison indicates how well the organization is performing compared with its competitors; the second type will suggest how the organization has been performing over a period of time.

When analyzing financial statements, the manager should keep several general considerations in mind. First, all accounting data are historic and the accuracy of projections is dependent on the forecaster's ability and the uncertainties of economic events. Second, the historical data were reported on the basis of some accounting conventions. Accounting systems may vary from one organization to the other and

Table 18-3
Honest John's Used Cars Income Statement

PERIOD ENDING DECEMBER 31, 1990		
Revenue		
Sale of vehicles	$2,250,000	
Income from service department	600,000	
Leasing revenues	400,000	
Warranty contract commissions	10,000	
Gain on sale of financing contracts	8,000	
Interest earned	11,000	
Total Revenue		$3,279,000
Expenses		
Cost of goods sold	$2,000,000	
Wages and salaries	650,000	
Commissions	80,000	
Lease of building and premises	250,000	
Utilities	30,000	
Insurance	25,000	
Bad debt expense	6,000	
Interest expense	14,000	
Advertising expense	100,000	
Total Expenses		$3,155,000
Profit (Loss)		$124,000

some financial figures, such as depreciation, may be based on definitions that are arbitrary or ambiguous. Finally, because of the variability of seasonal funds flows and requirements, the timing of the reporting cycle needs to be considered by the analyst. For companies in highly seasonal or cyclical industries, the timing of the financial analysis will have significant impact on the outcome of the ratios.

Managers use many kinds of ratios of many different types. The categories of ratios most commonly used are profitability, liquidity, asset-usage, and capitalization.

PROFITABILITY   This group of ratios focuses on the relative profitability of the organization. A healthy-sounding profit may not be as impressive when compared to the sales revenues generated or the total assets required to generate the profit. Commonly used ratios to measure a firm's profitability include the following (we will use Honest John's financial information as an example).

$$\textbf{Profit margin} = \frac{\text{Net income}}{\text{Total revenue}}$$

Table 18-4
Honest John's Used Cars Balance Sheet

	DECEMBER 31, 1988	DECEMBER 31, 1989
Assets		
Current		
Cash	$ 25,000	$ 32,000
Accounts receivable	100,000	130,000
Car inventory	240,000	240,000
Parts inventory	55,000	60,000
Prepaid expense	30,000	30,000
Supplies	7,000	10,000
Long-term		
Equipment	65,000	75,000
Total Assets	$522,000	$577,000
Liabilities		
Current		
Accounts payable	$110,000	$100,000
Salaries payable	10,000	10,000
Commissions payable	2,000	5,000
Long-term		
Bank debt	200,000	200,000
Owners' Equity		
Common stock	100,000	$100,000
Retained earnings	100,000	162,000
Total Liabilities and Equity	$522,000	$577,000

Honest John's profit margin for 1989 is thus:

$$\frac{124,000}{3,279,000} = 3.8\%$$

The return-on-asset ratio indicates whether or not the organization is realizing enough net profit in relation to total assets:

$$\textbf{Return on assets} = \frac{\text{Net income}}{\text{Total assets}}$$

The return on assets for Honest John's for 1989 is:

$$\frac{124,000}{577,000} = 21.5\%$$

The return-on-equity ratio indicates the rate of return the company is earning on the shareholders' investment:

$$\textbf{Return on equity} = \frac{\text{Net income}}{\text{Shareholders' equity}}$$

For Honest John's the return on equity is calculated as:

$$\frac{124,000}{100,000} = 124\%$$

LIQUIDITY RATIOS   Ratios that measure an organization's ability to meet its current obligations are called liquidity ratios. Current obligations are defined as those that are due within one year and they are generally paid off with the organization's short-term liabilities. In assessing the liquidity of a company, the analyst will generally calculate the following two ratios:

$$\textbf{Current ratio} = \frac{\text{Current assets}}{\text{Current liabilities}}$$

For Honest John's the current ratio is:

$$\frac{502,000}{115,000} = 4.36$$

Current assets include cash, accounts receivable, and inventory, while current liabilities include accounts and short-term notes payable, and any other accrued expense.

The acid test or quick ratio is the same as the current ratio except that it does not include inventory. Thus, it only includes the asset items that are assumed to be most readily convertible into money or securities:

$$\textbf{Acid test} = \frac{\text{Current assets} - \text{Inventory}}{\text{Current liabilities}}$$

The acid test for Honest John's is:

$$\frac{502,000 - 300,000}{115,000} = 1.75$$

Asset-Usage Ratios   These ratios, often called activity or "turnover" ratios, measure the company's effectiveness in using its resources.

One of the common concerns of managers is the quantity of the company's credit sales. The ratio of accounts receivable to net sales indicates the relative proportions of credit and cash sales. This ratio is used to determine the days sales outstanding and is also a measure of a firm's efficiency in collecting on credit sales:

$$\text{Days sales outstanding} = \frac{\text{Accounts receivable} \times 365 \text{ days}}{\text{Net sales}}$$

The days-sales-outstanding ratio for Honest John's is:

$$\frac{130,000 \times 365}{3,268,000} = 14.5 \text{ days}$$

Inventory turnover indicates the appropriate level of inventory for a given sales volume. A low or declining ratio may indicate excessive levels of inventory:

$$\text{Inventory turnover} = \frac{\text{Sales}}{\text{Inventory}}$$

Inventory turnover at Honest John's is:

$$\frac{3,268,000}{300,000} = 10.9 \text{ times}$$

Asset turnover is used to examine the effectiveness of the company in utilizing all of its assets in generating sales.

$$\text{Asset turnover} = \frac{\text{Sales}}{\text{Total assets}}$$

Asset turnover at Honest John's is:

$$\frac{3,268,000}{577,000} = 5.66 \text{ times}$$

CAPITALIZATION RATIOS   Capitalization ratios provide the manager with information about the long-term sources of financing that the organization has used. Since these long-term sources of money are either debt or equity, the capitalization ratios involve an analysis of these accounts. The following are some of the most commonly used ratios.

The debt-to-equity ratio focuses on the relative size of the debt and equity sources of funds. The use of debt creates "leverage" in that the profits are increased if the assets financed by debt produce more revenue than the cost of the debt. This ratio helps managers understand the level of risk they are assuming to achieve this "leverage" effect.

$$\text{Debt to equity} = \frac{\text{Total long-term debt}}{\text{Total stockholders' equity}}$$

For Honest John's the debt to equity is:

$$\frac{200,000}{100,000} = 2.0$$

The debt-to-asset ratio gives the percentage of assets financed by creditors. It also helps managers to understand the relative risk level incurred by the use of debt.

$$\textbf{Debt to assets} = \frac{\text{Total debts}}{\text{Total assets}}$$

For Honest John's the debt to assets is:

$$\frac{200,000}{577,000} = .35$$

The times-interest-earned ratio indicates the organization's ability to pay interest expenses directly from gross income:

$$\textbf{Times interest earned} = \frac{\text{Gross income}}{\text{Interest charges}}$$

For Honest John's the times-interest-earned ratio is:

$$\frac{124,000}{14,000} = 8.86 \text{ times}$$

Break-Even Analysis

Another financial control tool used by many managers is break-even analysis. This tool generates information that allows the manager to estimate potential profit or loss with various levels of production. Assume that Honest John's Used Cars sells only used cars (no leasing, service, or any other revenue source) and that each sale produces an average of $4,000 in revenue. The variable costs are $2,800 for the cost of the car and $200 in sales commissions. All other costs are fixed and the annual fixed costs are $1,000,000. **Break-even analysis** allows the manager to determine the point where the company's sales will cover its costs.

Figure 18-5 represents the key elements in the break-even analysis for Honest John's Used Cars. The relationship between fixed costs, variable costs, units sold, and profit are represented for a period of one year. The graph shows that a net loss will occur if sales are less than 1,000 units, but that at sales levels above that figure a profit will result.

Mathematically, the break-even point may be found by using the formula:

$$\text{BEP} = \frac{\text{TFC}}{\text{P-VC}} \quad \text{or} \quad \frac{\text{TFC}}{\text{Contribution margin}}$$

$$\textit{where } \text{BEP} = \text{Break-even point}$$
$$\text{TFC} = \text{Total fixed costs}$$
$$\text{P} = \text{Price per unit}$$
$$\text{VC} = \text{Variable cost per unit}$$

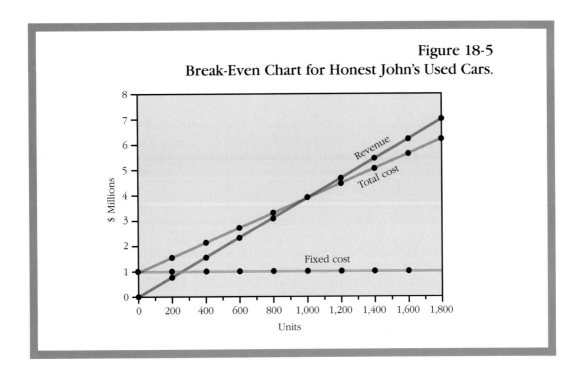

Figure 18-5
Break-Even Chart for Honest John's Used Cars.

Honest John's break-even point is thus:

$$\frac{1,000,000}{4,000 - 3,000} = 1,000 \text{ cars}$$

USES OF BREAK-EVEN ANALYSIS   Break-even analysis is a useful control tool because it helps managers understand the relationships between the key variables of fixed costs, variable costs, total costs and profit or loss. When these relationships are understood, managers can take steps to alter one or more of these variables to reduce significant variation between planned profit levels and actual profit levels.[22] In the Honest John's example, if fixed costs increase by 10 percent, the break-even level would increase by 100 units. Alternatively if the unit price of used cars drops to $3,500, the break-even point will move up to 2,000 units.

Break-even analysis can also be used by managers to identify the minimum sales volume necessary to meet established profit objectives and to provide information helpful in the capital investment decisions as well as decisions regarding additions to product lines.

LIMITATIONS OF BREAK-EVEN ANALYSIS   Break-even analysis, although a popular planning and control technique, suffers from some limitations that managers need to be aware of if they are to use it effectively.

Assumption Can Become Outdated   Managers may view the assumptions made in break-even analysis as lasting for long periods of time. Costs and prices change over periods of time. Even fixed costs may change as new equipment is purchased to support increased sales volume or additional staff are added. For break-even analysis to remain a useful tool, it needs to be updated continuously.

Variable Costs May Change Over Time   Managers sometimes view variable costs as being constant. If production facilities are used to capacity, then, large increases in overtime labor may be required. In addition, higher reject rates may be experienced because of reduced quality. In most situations as production levels rise or fall, variable costs will also fluctuate as a percentage of revenue.

No Substitute for Judgment   Managers may view break-even analysis as a quantitative and objective means for making decisions. This should not be the case however. As with any control tool discussed in this section, it only provides information which enables managers to make improved decisions. The element of managerial judgment remains very important and the use of any tool should not lead to mechanistic decision making.

Financial Control: Auditing

Another effective control method is auditing, which is the examination and verification of the accuracy of records. Traditionally, auditing has consisted of an independent appraisal of the organization's financial records by a certified public accounting firm. This concept has been expanded, however, to include audits not only of financial and accounting records but of operating systems as well. The two major forms of audits are the external audit and the internal audit.[23]

EXTERNAL AUDIT   External audits are conducted by outside experts who are not employees of the organization. These examinations of an organization's financial records seek to determine the degree of accuracy and the extent to which financial statements reflect fairly what they are designed to represent. Thus, audits are often regarded as ways of encouraging ethical behavior on the part of management as well as controlling and safeguarding the financial resources of the organization. Certified public accountants (CPAs) are most commonly used for this purpose.

External audits are generally very thorough. It is not uncommon for the auditors to take a physical count of inventory and personally check the sales records generating the accounts receivable to verify that the accounts on the balance sheets are accurate. The motivation for the great care that the auditors take is to establish and protect their reputations for honesty and accuracy.

INTERNAL AUDIT   Auditing can be an effective means of control as well as a means of verifying records. Internal audits are conducted by employees of the organization and are frequently wider in scope than the external audit. The internal audit is used to examine the effectiveness of the control system as well as to verify the accuracy of records. In some cases, an accounting system may be technically accurate but inefficient.

The General Accounting Office (GAO), the internal audit staff for the federal government, is an example of an internal audit staff. The scope of their audit function is extensive, ranging from reports on the efficiency of defense spending, the use of technology by defense contractors, the efficiency and cost effectiveness of governmental agencies, as well as the oversight on the use of funds received from the sale of excess material in national stockpiles. Many businesses have similar systems in place.

The challenge of proper control procedures is illustrated in the challenge facing Robert Campeau as he attempts to give direction to a far-flung retailing empire.

ENDING CASE
Can Campeau Control His Retailing Empire?

Will everyone go to the bank on the Campeau-Federated takeover? Some seem to think so with the money that is flowing to everyone as the deal closes. Golden parachutes total $167 million to executives of Federated, and investment banking, financing, and other fees are over $350 million.

The question is: Can Robert Campeau really pull it off? The Canadian real estate tycoon-turned corporate raider has acquired Allied Stores in 1986 and now Federated. The retailing empire should have revenues of $7 billion for 1988.

Campeau's plan is simple; cut overhead by $240 million per year to increase profits and sell off assets to pare down debt—the same basic strategy that other corporate raiders have used.

The reduction in overhead was to come from reducing employment by 6,500 employees. These firings have lowered morale and hurt customer service at even the up-scale divisions such as Bloomingdales. Waiting 40 minutes for a clerk is not the way to keep top-of-the-line customers. Bloomingdales was forced to discount merchandise during the Christmas season to make up for the poor customer service. The result has been no increase in profit as lower labor costs have been offset by lower margins.

Poor information control and wide-scale replacement of management has caused profit catastrophes at other chains in the empire. Goldsmiths, once the Federated profit leader, based in Memphis reported its first loss in decades. Six hundred of the twenty-five hundred employees were terminated including all executives when the takeover was completed. In an effort to consolidate purchasing, the stores were asked to clear out Goldsmith-tagged merchandise. A slashing of prices resulted, and the first loss was reported. The next few months large imbalances of merchandise hurt sales as the new management lacked knowledge in the type of merchandise that would sell in various stores.

Even the asset sales seem to be going awry. The Ann Taylor chain sold for $170 million less than expected. Gold Crown, a discount chain, went for $325 million, or nearly $200 million less than originally planned. Estimates of asset sales are around $600 million less than projected.

With the continuing losses at Federated and Allied, the pressure to sell assets to meet payments may increase. In the third quarter of 1988, the two retailing companies lost nearly $54 million. Robert Campeau has secured some of the debt with his vast real estate holdings and selling off shares in his own company. He now controls only 54 percent of the stock. If a recession arrives in the near future, Campeau could even lose control of the companies he now reigns over.

The capital markets are demonstrating their concern for the companies' operation by requiring a hefty 16 to 18 percent coupon on the junk bonds issued in conjunction with the takeover. Even at that lofty rate, First Boston is having a tough time lining up takers and could eventually take a loss on $400 million in junk debt it still has not placed. ☒

SUMMARY

Control is the name given to those activities designed to make sure that actual results conform to organizational plans. Any organizational activity can be controlled, but it is useful to visualize control activities in terms of the input of resources: human, physical, informational, and financial. For each of these resources it is necessary to develop a plan or budget for its use. The plan is based on standards and to be effective the standard must be quantifiable. As the organization goes about its business, actual results are compared to planned or budgeted results. Deviations from standard are analyzed and corrections and adjustments are made to the plans or budgets as needed. The great advantage of this system is that it allows management to detect mistakes or changes in the environment before the organization is irreparably injured.

A wide variety of control devices are available to aid managers: financial statements, ratio analysis, break-even analysis, and auditing. The purpose of all these tools is to aid managers in applying judgment to the analysis of business problems. Each tool has its limitations and it is important to realize that judgment, not the tool, will result in decisions about how to get performance back on track so that the organization may achieve its plans.

KEY TERMS

Control

Standard

Feed forward

Concurrent control measurements

Feedback control measures
Continuous measurement
Intermittent measurement
Budget
Operating budget
Financial budget
Revenue budget
Expense budget
Profit budget
Cash budget
Capital expenditure budget
Balance sheet budget
Fixed budget
Variable budget
Zero-base budgeting
Human resource accounting
Liquidity
Leverage

Profitability
Income statement
Balance sheet
Profit margin
Return on assets
Return on equity
Current ratio
Acid test/Quick ratio
Days sales outstanding
Inventory turnover
Asset turnover
Debt to equity
Debt to assets
Times interest earned
Break-even analysis
External audit
Internal audit

REVIEW QUESTIONS

1. How do human resources impact information, financial, and physical resources?

2. How does change affect the control process?

3. Why does complexity create a need for control?

4. How does control help a firm to find and overcome mistakes? Of what benefit is this to the firm?

5. Explain the link between control and planning.

6. What are the four steps in the control process?

7. What considerations should affect a manager's choice of a method to measure performance?

8. Why are some deviations from standard acceptable?

9. What are four negative consequences that can result from the use of controls within an organization?

10. What are some methods that can be used to overcome resistance to control?

11. What are six characteristics of effective control systems?

12. What are some of the advantages of a bottom-up budget process over a top-down process?

13. Why are resource allocation decisions among the most difficult decisions that top management must make?

14. What advantages does zero-base budgeting offer a firm?

15. Of what use is human resource accounting? Why has it not been more widely adopted? (Give your own views).

16. What kinds of information does financial ratio analysis give management and why is this type of analysis so useful?

17. What are some of the uses and limitations of break-even analysis?

18. How does internal auditing differ from external auditing and why is it important?

CHALLENGE QUESTIONS

1. What is the purpose of control within an organization?

2. The following items are key to the success of any business. What controls would you use to make sure that performance measures up to plans?
   A. Sales performance
   B. Quality of product

3. What are some methods by which management can overcome the negative impact that control methods often have upon employee morale?

4. How could a control system interact with a compensation system to lead to unethical employee behavior? Give an example.

5. How are budgets typically arrived at? Of what value is a stable environment to a business planning its activities?

6. What can top management do to prevent budgets from losing their usefulness to an organization? What type of training program does your answer suggest for managers who are involved in constructing or implementing a budget?

7. Of what benefit is a variable budget to a manager? What pitfalls can a manager fall into in constructing and implementing a variable budget?

8. What is the difference in terms of timing between an income statement and a balance sheet? Of what interest would this information be to an investor?

9. What is the difference between the current ratio and the quick or acid test ratio? Why would a bank loan officer be concerned with a large disparity between the two? Would it matter if the company had firm orders for the inventory?

10. What are two commonly used capitalization ratios? Who would be more interested in them? Rank in order of interest.
    A. Secured creditor
    B. Unsecured creditor
    C. Stockholder
    D. Bond holder
    E. Major customer

11. What types of decisions would you expect break-even analysis to be most used in conjunction with and why?

CASE AND RELATED QUESTIONS

1. What are some basic controls that were missing in the filming of the movie *Heaven's Gate*? Name three things that United Artists could have done to get better information.

2. How would pre-existing company policies have enabled United Artists to negotiate more effectively with Michael Cimino?

3. What costs in the making of *Heaven's Gate* were amenable to control once the contract was signed? Hint: What were the fixed and variable costs?

4. The management at United Artists developed several budgets with respect to the making of *Heaven's Gate*. What fatal flaw was present in all of these budgets?

5. What kind of control process (feed forward, concurrent, or feedback) would have been most effective in controlling the cost of the movie *Heaven's Gate?* What type of information is required for each type of control and what contractual provisions would have been necessary to enforce them?

6. Evaluate the control process instituted by United Artists in terms of standards and the criteria for effectiveness listed in the chapter (timeliness, accuracy, etc.).

ENDNOTES

1. Based on the book by Steven Back, *Final Cut: Dreams and Disaster in the Making of Heaven's Gate* (New York: William Morrow & Co., Inc., 1985).

2. Ibid., p. 416.

3. Ibid., p. 206.

4. Ibid., p. 363.

5. Henry L. Tosi and Stephen J. Carroll, *Management*, 2nd ed. (New York: John Wiley & Sons, 1982), p. 551.

6. Ibid., p. 551.

7. For a good discussion of performance evaluation, see Stephen J. Carroll and Craig E. Schneir, *Performance Appraisal & Review Systems*, (Glenview, IL: Scott, Foresman, 1982).

8. The discussion in this section is based on William H. Newman, *Constructive Control* (Englewood Cliffs, NJ: Prentice Hall, 1975).

9. Charles G. Burke, "Can Detroit Catch Up?" *Fortune*, February 8, 1982, pp. 34–39.

10. "Strategy: Trading Tomorrow for Today," *Harvard Business Review*, 57, May–June 1979, pp. 112–20.

11. Peter F. Drucker, *Management: Tasks, Responsibilities, Practices* (New York: Harper & Row, 1974), p. 494.

12. Ken Blanchard, *One Minute Manager and Leadership* (New York: Morrow, 1985), pp. 67–78.

13. William H. Schler, "Toward Better Management Control Systems," *California Management Review* 14, No. 2 (Winter 1971), pp. 33–39; and Peter F. Drucker, *Management: Tasks, Practices & Responsibilities* (New York: Harper & Row, 1979), pp. 489–504.

14. R. N. Anthony and J. Dearden, *Management Control Systems*, 3rd ed. (Homewood, IL: Irwin, 1976), pp. 453–75.

15. Ibid., p. 453.

16. For more discussion, see Anthony and Dearden; and Glenn A. Welsch, *Budgeting: Profit, Planning & Control* 4th ed. (Englewood Cliffs, NJ: Prentice-Hall, 1976).

17. Peter A. Pyhn, "Zero-Base Budgeting," *Harvard Business Review*, November–December 1970, pp. 111–21.

18. For recent reviews, see Stanton C. Lindquist and K. Bryant Mills, "Whatever Happened to Zero-Base Budgeting?" *Management Review*, January–February 1981, pp. 31–35.

19. M. R. Weisbord, "Management in Crisis," *Conference Board Record*, 7 (February 1970), pp. 10–16.

20. See R. B. Frantzub, L. T. Landau, and D. P. Lundberg, "The Valuation of Human Resources," *Business Horizons*, June 1974, pp.73–80; and M. M. K. Fleming, "Behavior Implications of Human Resource Accounting," *Human Resources Management*, Summer 1977, pp. 24–29.

21. For a more thorough discussion, see Eugene F. Brigham, *Financial Management: Theory and Practice* (New York: CBS College Publishing, 1982), pp. 207–21; and Diana R. Harrington and Brent D. Wilson, *Corporate Financial Analysis* (Plano, TX: Business Publications, Inc., 1983), pp. 8–18.

22. Robert J. Lambrix and Surendra S. Singhri, "How to Set Volume-Sensitive ROI Targets," *Harvard Business Review*, March–April 1981, p. 174.

23. Arthur W. Holmes and Wayne S. Overmeyer, *Basic Auditing*, 5th ed. (Homewood, IL: Irwin, 1976).

CHAPTER 19

OPERATIONS MANAGEMENT

CHAPTER OUTLINE

LEARNING OBJECTIVES

■ Develop an understanding of the critical role of operations management in the firm, and indicate why understanding operations is critical not just to operations managers, but to managers in finance, marketing, accounting, and general management.

■ Introduce the planning/production cycle and types of operations environments as methods of thinking about operations issues.

■ Understand the basic concepts and areas of operations management, where they fit in the planning/production cycle, and how they vary with the type of operation environment.

■ Examine inventory management issues, and introduce basic concepts of inventory analysis and control.

■ Compare the strengths and shortcomings of new approaches to operations control with more traditional methods.

■ Develop an understanding of the critical role of quality control in today's world, and discuss methods of improving quality.

Priority One is a rapidly growing, extremely successful mail-order electronics supply company located in Chatsworth, California (near Los Angeles). 1983 sales were approximately $8 million, and had grown nearly 100 percent per year for the previous three years. Heath Kline, the president, saw his success as coming from low prices, rapid service, and complete inventory, allowing customers to fill all their needs from one source. With the rapid growth, however, he was becoming concerned about the costs and performance of the operations side of the business.

Priority One has no manufacturing. Operations, in this case, consists of purchasing products from outside suppliers, and keeping them in stock for resale. When orders are received, either by telephone or by mail, proper items are picked from shelves, packaged, and shipped to the customer. The major tasks of the operations group are:

■ **Purchasing**   When an item gets low, it is time to reorder. Questions to be answered are: How much should be ordered? How far ahead of time should Priority One plan on placing the order? What prices and terms can it get from the suppliers?

■ **Stockroom management**   Incoming shipments should have a purchase order, and orders must match with the items received to make sure that Priority One gets what it is paying for. Then the items need to be put away—and there are a surprising number of decisions involved in deciding how that should be done. Finally, someone has to keep track of where everything is (in a large warehouse it is easy to lose items), and keep track of when stocks are getting low enough to place another order.

■ **Order filling**   A customer might request a single item, but more typically orders are for a half-dozen or more different items. Requested items are pulled from shelves, and the order is checked for completeness and accuracy, then packed and shipped. The way in which shelves are laid out can make a significant difference in efficiency and accuracy in order picking; the warehouse manager chooses how to organize the warehouse. There are several problems warehouse management must also be prepared to handle, such as what to do when an item is out of stock (so only part of an order can be shipped), and how to pick up outstanding orders for incoming items.

Although Heath was generally pleased with warehouse operations, he had noticed that many orders were being delayed awaiting the arrival of out-of-stock parts. To prevent too many such delays, replenishment orders had been placed more and more ahead of time, resulting in larger and larger investments in inventory. Despite

Warehouse management is a principal part of a business like Priority One Electronics.

the substantial amount of capital devoted to this purpose, the number of delayed orders seemed unacceptably high to Heath. As additional items were continually being added to the catalogue, the problem promised to get even worse in the future.

What should Kline do? He has developed a winning marketing plan, and has what appeared to be adequate financing. Growth and profitability have been excellent so far. However, these strengths will prove useless unless operations, the group responsible for actually filling and shipping orders, manages to get on top of their problems.

INTRODUCTION

All successful business enterprises share at least two characteristics—they must sell something, and they must have something to sell. **Operations management** deals with how the "something to sell" is made or provided. In most companies the largest portion of money invested goes to provide production or service facilities. Also, most of each sales dollar a company receives typically must be used to cover the cost of making the product or providing the service. Therefore, operations management is not only a necessary but an extremely important part of every business.

Operations appears very different in different companies. For example:

- A grocery store provides clean, well-organized, fully stocked shelves of items for sale. Operations deals with how shelves should be arranged, how frequently you should replenish shelves, and how much to order with each new reorder. Operations also deals with assigning people to checkout stands, stock handling, and cleanup.

- The product offered by an airline is seats going from point A to point B at specified times. Operations management schedules aircraft and crews, plans routes, provides fuel, meals, and supplies, and provides maintenance. Operations also includes reservations, luggage checking and handling, and boarding check-in. In short, anything to do with the physical operation of the airline is part of the operations area.

- In a manufacturing company, operations deals with making products—buying materials, specifying manufacturing steps, coordinating workers, and planning inventories.

Despite the differences in details, there are basic principles to effective operations management. In general, they are not difficult to grasp. At Priority One, the operations problems were solved by applying some simple ideas of operations management. Many such principles are covered in the remainder of this chapter.

The Impact of Operations Management

Heath Kline estimated the value of applying several straightforward operations management techniques to be at least $60,000 per year. In our experience, saving this much money in operations is not difficult in most companies. After all, most of a company's investment and most of the ongoing costs are in the operations area. As a result, even modest percentage savings in operations can have a strong influence on company profitability.

To illustrate, suppose a company has sales of $10,000,000 per year, and realizes a gross margin of 20 percent. Also suppose that fixed costs and overhead account for $1,500,000 per year. The before-tax profit is then $500,000:

Sales	$10,000,000
Cost of product (80%)	8,000,000
Gross margin (20%)	2,000,000
Fixed costs and overhead	1,500,000
Before-tax profit	$ 500,000

In an effort to increase profits, the company might try to increase sales. If sales were increased by 10 percent, the fixed costs and overhead would generally rise by about that amount as well. Perhaps a much larger sales force would be needed, or additional products would be added to give better market penetration. The net result, assuming that the gross margin stayed at 20 percent, is that profit increases by 10 percent:

Sales	$11,000,000
Cost of product (80%)	8,800,000
Gross margin (20%)	2,200,000
Fixed costs and overhead	1,650,000
Before-tax profit	$ 550,000

Now suppose that instead of increasing sales by 10 percent, the same amount of effort was put into cutting product costs by 10 percent. Product costs drop from the original $8,000,000 to $7,200,000 while the other figures stay constant:

Sales	$10,000,000
Cost of product (72%)	7,200,000
Gross margin (28%)	2,800,000
Fixed costs and overhead	1,500,000
Before-tax profit	$ 1,300,000

Note that increasing sales by 10 percent upped profits by 10 percent, but cutting costs by 10 percent increased profits by 160 percent! As illustrated by Priority One, such savings can be real, not simply theoretical.

We turn now to the "nuts and bolts" of operations management—the techniques that have been shown to be useful in practice. In the next section we present a framework for our remaining discussion.

Discussion Framework

Some decisions look far into the future, while others focus on immediate issues. Box 19-1 summarizes the major topics covered in the remainder of this chapter, indicating where each topic falls in the planning/production cycle.

TYPES OF OPERATIONS ENVIRONMENTS

The role of operations management can vary enormously from company to company.[1] Tasks that are critical in one environment may be of little consequence in another. However, there are patterns within the differences, and understanding the patterns helps in deciding where the major management problems probably lie, and which solutions may prove useful.

Figure 19-1 shows a continuum between job shops and continuous-process operations. Job shops provide a wide variety of services or make a wide variety of products. A hospital emergency room, for example, is a job shop. Each patient is a unique case. Some need x-rays, some need emergency surgery, others need medication, and

Box 19-1
The Planning/Production Cycle

TIME HORIZON	TOPIC
Years	Product or service design Forecasting
Months	Aggregate planning Inventory planning and control
Weeks	Production and materials planning Assembly-line management Scheduling
Days	Shop floor control
Throughout the cycle	Quality control Work force management Productivity measurement and management Project management

Figure 19-1
Job-Shop–Continuous-Process Continuum

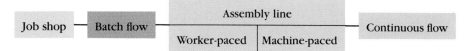

Job shop   Every product is unique, and has its own requirements. Each follows a unique path through the manufacturing or services process.

Batch flow   A wide variety of products are made or services provided. However, like products or services can be grouped and processed in a similar manner.

Assembly line   Work is divided into a sequence of steps that most products or customers need. Each step is performed at a different station, with the customer or partially completed work moving from station to station. A worker-paced assembly line is one in which each worker sets his or her own pace. A machine-paced line has a machine, often a conveyor, robot, or automated tool, setting the pace.

Continuous process   Large volumes of identical products are made or services performed.

Box 19-2
Contrasts between Job Shops and Continuous Processes

	JOB SHOP	CONTINUOUS PROCESS
Differences in Equipment and Layout		
Type of equipment	General purpose	Special purpose
Plant layout	Group machines of similar type	Locate machines according to demands of the manufacturing process
Ease of measuring capacity	Very difficult	Relatively easy
Cost and ease of increasing capacity	Small capacity increments can be made at moderate cost.	Capacity can be increased only in large increments at high cost.
Capital investment	Relatively low	Much higher
Degree of vertical integration	Low to moderate	Much higher
Differences in Process Management		
Supplier relationships	Short-term, flexible	Long-term, formal
Attention to detail	Relatively low	Very high, critical
Scheduling	Ad hoc, flexible	Formalized, rigid
Inventories		
Raw materials	Very low	High
In-process	High	Low
Finished goods	None	Low to moderate
Flexibility		
In scheduling	High	Low
In adding products	High	Low

some require a combination of services. A continuous process, on the other hand, provides a large number of identical services or makes many identical goods. Conducting routine medical examinations for army draftees is a continuous process. Everyone goes through exactly the same steps. In manufacturing, the classic example of a job shop is a small metal fabricating company. Equipped with machines for shap-

	JOB SHOP	CONTINUOUS PROCESS
Differences in Finance and Control		
Profit margins	High	Low
Basis for pricing	Bids	Published market prices
Job costing	Bid estimates	Standard costs
Internal control	Profit center	Cost center
Differences in Personnel Management		
Skills required of the manager	Wide range: estimating, bidding, personnel management, customer relations	High-level specialized expertise is required of the technical manager; good organizing and general management skills are required of the general manager.
Skills required of the workers	Initiative, imagination, technical expertise in several areas	Technical expertise is in limited areas, with the ability to follow detailed procedures accurately and to cope with routine duties.
Nature of worker duties	Changing, always different	Routine, well defined, must be accurate
Management-worker communications	Two-way	One-way (downward)
Evaluation of subordinates	Difficult, many individual factors	Relatively easy and routine
Use of individual incentive pay	Common, based on profits or cost control	Rare

ing, cutting, drilling, and welding metal, such shops can make an endless variety of unique shapes. An oil refinery is a continuous-process operation. Each barrel of crude is treated in essentially the same manner to produce final products.

As summarized in Box 19-2, job shops and continuous processes differ in many significant ways in the type of equipment used and the way they are physically arranged, in the concepts used in managing the production process, in financial ratios and tools used for financial control, and the required management and worker skills. However, the differences are not random, but systematic. Companies that fall between the two extremes have characteristics that are part way between job shops and continuous processes.

Strategic Considerations

In deciding how to compete, management has a bewildering array of choices. Should a major subcomponent be purchased or made in-house? Should service policies be designed to accommodate the most common customers quickly, making the unusual cases wait, or should service policies be custom fit to each customer's requirements? In a broader sense, where along the job-shop/continuous-process continuum should the production process be located?

The production or operations strategy of a company clearly affects the strategy of the entire company. Furthermore, company placement on the job-shop/continuous-process continuum has a profound impact on their business strategy. For once in place, the strengths and weaknesses inherent in the buildings, machinery, and systems of a production operation are difficult to change.

There are two essential factors to consider in determining strategic options. First, management must be consistent. All individual decisions interrelate, so they must be coordinated. Inventory policies, types of equipment and operating policies, wage and labor practices, and other similar areas, must work together consistently or the entire process will lose effectiveness.

The second concept is focus. Because it is impossible to optimize a production facility for all possible circumstances, manufacturing strategy is most likely to be successful when focused. An attractive market opportunity must be identified, key competitive factors defined, and the production facility optimized according to the key factors.

Figure 19-2 depicts the matchup between the design of a production facility and the demand on that facility. For short-run, low-volume products a job shop enjoys the flexibility necessary to shift quickly and easily from one product to another. As sales volume increases, more efficient production schemes become possible. Management can justify special-purpose machines, and it makes increasing sense to locate machines according to product-flow requirements. Workers can specialize, materials can be purchased in volume and stored in anticipation of production demands, and information flows can be tailored increasingly to the needs of the dominant process. In short, the process can move toward a continuous-process operation, as depicted by the diagonal in Figure 19-2.

As companies grow, production strategies often remain unchanged. On Figure 19-2, such a business would be located above the diagonal. As production volume increases, the *tried and true* methods that served so well in the job-shop phase may

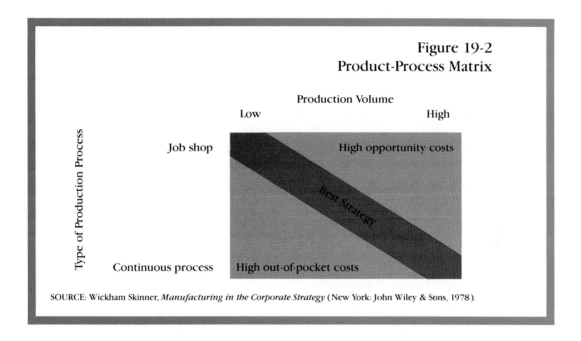

Figure 19-2
Product-Process Matrix

Production Volume

Low   High

Type of Production Process

Job shop   High opportunity costs

Best Strategy

Continuous process   High out-of-pocket costs

SOURCE: Wickham Skinner, *Manufacturing in the Corporate Strategy* (New York: John Wiley & Sons, 1978).

still work to a degree, but their structure becomes increasingly inefficient and difficult to manage. At best, the company loses the savings possible through more appropriate methods; at worst a job-shop-oriented management system is overwhelmed by
the sheer size of the expanded enterprise.

It is also possible to err in the opposite direction. When management builds a
high-volume production facility and the expected volume never materializes, it is
ordinarily very expensive to redesign the facility for an alternative product. Yet the
company must either continue to cover the high overhead inherent in such operations or abandon the facility. Either way, out-of-pocket costs are unnecessarily high.

If a facility is appropriate for its production volume, it would lie somewhere
along the diagonal in Figure 19-2. However, any given plant can cover but a small
portion of the total diagonal. Just as an automobile can be designed to maximize
either power or fuel economy—not both—factories can be designed to provide high
performance in limited areas only. The skills, facilities, and management techniques
required to manage job shops effectively are so different from those required to manage continuous-process operations effectively that there is considerable doubt that
such dissimilar functions can even be housed within the same facility. As a company's
product line grows and diversifies, it makes better sense to provide several facilities,
each focusing on a single segment of the diagonal. Focused factories can operate in
separate locations or can sometimes operate in separate parts of the same building.
However, it generally makes little sense to share any critical resource (labor, inventories, management) among the facilities.

THE PLANNING AND PRODUCTION CYCLE

Product or Service Design

A successful service or product meets a customer need. However, there are many different ways to meet most needs. For example, the need for food is satisfied by farmers, by grocery stores, and by restaurants. The first task of the manager is to define the business she or he intends to compete in, and to define appropriate products and services.

Heath Kline defined Priority One's business as supplying electronic components. Customer contact would be primarily by mail order, and Heath would offer a large selection, rapid service, and low prices. Notice that these decisions largely define the tasks of the operations side of the business. We can already see that operations will have to

- Manage a large inventory so as to provide reasonable assurance that items are in stock at all times, but also while keeping inventory investment under control.
- Provide for rapid, error-free order processing.
- Provide excellent quality control so orders are filled accurately, and at the least possible cost.

Design decisions do not stop here. Heath needs to decide what products will be stocked? Precisely, what will the pricing policy be? Will customers be offered truck delivery, air freight, or a choice? How fast does "fast delivery" have to be—same day, next day, within a week? Each of these decisions, plus countless others, affect and are affected by the workings of the operations side of the business.[2]

Capacity Planning

The price, speed, and flexibility with which a good or service is offered is as important as the product itself. How does a business choose to compete—as a job shop with service and custom design, or as a continuous process with price and uniformity? These questions affect the volume, which in turn affect the capacity needed in the production facility. Capacity planning requires the business to anticipate the expected volume and to plan for enough capacity to meet that demand. Further, there must be enough of each critical resource to meet demand. If there is adequate machinery but too few skilled operators, the business will fall short of its production plan.

Aggregate Planning

Many companies experience seasonal patterns in demand, or experience substantial growth from year to year. **Aggregate planning** is the act of looking into the intermediate-range future (generally a year or more in advance) to determine overall production levels and capacity requirements. The term "aggregate" indicates that planning is done on an aggregate, or combined, level. The business plans the total number of cars produced or customers expected, not the details of what models will be made or specific customer needs.

Demand for many products is strongly seasonal. One way to react to fluctuating demand is to allow capacity to fluctuate along with it. This is called a **chase strategy**. In some industries, particularly service industries, the only way to meet peak demands is to add temporary workers at busy seasons. For example, many retail stores add extra help for the Christmas season.

In many ways a chase strategy is expensive. The physical facility must be large enough to handle peak demands; during slack periods some of the physical capacity will not be utilized. It is costly to locate, train, supervise, and eventually discharge temporary workers. Since temporary workers do not have a strong commitment to the company, error rates, absenteeism, and interpersonal problems are often higher than for permanent employees.

In manufacturing industries there is another approach. Plan enough capacity to cover the average yearly demand, and produce at the average rate for the entire year. This is called a **level strategy**. A business builds up inventory during the slack season, and uses inventory to help meet some of the demand during the busy period. For example, soft drinks can be bottled during the winter for consumption during the summer. Although investment in physical capacity and personnel costs can be lower, the level strategy requires a large investment in the annual inventory. There is also some risk that part of the inventory will become obsolete or exceed its shelf life.

Most manufacturing companies follow some combination of level and chase strategies in order to minimize total costs. Unfortunately there is no method of finding the best combination of the two. Managers must consider their own unique costs, and find a reasonable plan by trial and error.

Inventory Planning and Control

In the previous section we saw an important use of inventories—to level production between periods of high and low demand. Inventories are also used for other useful purposes:

- Inventories provide a buffer between two work stations, so the pace of the two need not be identical at all times.

Businesses can use various inventory control techniques to reduce inventory costs.

- Goods are often purchased in advance of a price rise, or in anticipation of a strike.
- Seasonally available materials, such as farm produce, must be stored until they are needed.
- In order to realize economies in ordering and shipping costs, many goods are purchased in large lots. It takes some time to use the entire lot. So-called **cycle stock** inventories result.
- Since lead times and demand rates are uncertain, it is prudent to keep an extra supply on hand when running out of a product would be inconvenient or expensive. This inventory is called **safety stock**.
- Every production system has materials being worked on, waiting to be worked on, or in transit. These types of inventories are called **work in process** and **work in transit**.

Inventories clearly fill a necessary role. However, all inventories also represent investments; money tied up in inventories cannot be used for alternative purposes. Thus, investments in inventories can be analyzed like any other investment. They should produce a return in the form of savings or income, and the rate of return should be comparable to other business investments.

The major problems that Priority One Electronics experienced were inventory problems. Applying inventory control techniques was worth several tens of thousands of dollars per year to the company. Such savings are not unusual; inventory control is generally one of the most fruitful areas to find cost savings in companies that have substantial inventories.

ABC ANALYSIS   At Priority One, investigation showed that 50 items (1 percent of the total number of items stocked) accounted for 75 percent of all dollar sales. Obviously, management should pay special attention to those items to make sure they were managed as efficiently as possible. Although Priority One's experience was somewhat more dramatic than is usually seen, every inventory system has some expensive or fast-selling items, and some inexpensive slow movers. The "80/20 rule"— 80 percent of the dollars are accounted for by 20 percent of the items—is nearly universally true.

This observation forms the basis of **ABC analysis**. The total inventory is divided into three classes: A, B, and C items. The A items are the faster-moving and more expensive items that make up the bulk of dollar sales. Management is best advised to pay the extra costs of using sophisticated inventory management techniques for these items. The B items constitute a second layer of moderately important items. They are worth monitoring carefully, but less expensive and less precise techniques than are used for the A items should be used. The C items are the seldom used or low-cost items. Management can be content with the crudest of techniques, such as "order a one-year supply each January." Potential cost savings simply do not justify more accurate tools.

The cutoff points between the three classes depend on the value of inventory items, the rate of demand, and the management systems available to monitor inventories. A rule of thumb is to let items making up the top 10 percent of the dollars be A items, the next 40 percent being B items, and the remainder C items. However, a good deal of judgment should be exercised in setting the cutoffs. Ideas discussed later in this section have also proven helpful.

ORDER SIZES   When items are ordered, there is generally an **ordering cost**. Someone must initiate the paperwork, call possible suppliers, and place the order. There is a cost of shipping the order, then a cost to receive it, check it against the original order form, perhaps verify quality, and to put it away. Finally, the receiving documents must be processed and payment made to the supplier. Total costs for these steps can easily exceed $30 or $40 per order. When orders are placed for manufactured goods, there are additional costs for machine setups that can be much higher than that. Thus, it makes sense to purchase many units at a time. That way we have to order less often, and pay fewer order and setup costs.

However, there are costs of making orders too large. Large orders cost more money than small ones, and since it takes a long time to sell or use up a larger order, money is tied up longer. Money used for inventories is not available to repay debt or to earn interest. Also, larger inventories require more storage space. They are sometimes subject to deterioration, spoilage, or theft. Insurance costs may be higher. In some states, there are taxes on inventories. These types of costs, known as **inventory holding costs**, encourage businesses to keep inventories small.

The best order size is one that balances these two types of costs (**economic order quantity**). Figure 19-3 shows how each cost type behaves when we change the average order size. If the average order size is small the inventory costs are small, but since we place many orders the ordering and setup costs are high. As the average order size increases the inventory costs also increase, but we place fewer and fewer orders so the ordering costs go down. Total costs follow the pattern shown on the figure. The minimum occurs where the two lines cross, when the order size is given by

$$Q^* = \sqrt{\frac{2DS}{ic}}$$

where

     Q^* = the best order size
     D = annual demand for the item
     S = total ordering and setup costs
     i = the annual inventory holding costs
     c = the cost per unit for the item.

LIMITATIONS OF THE LOT SIZE FORMULA   The formula given above, although remarkably useful, covers only the simplest inventory situations. Specifically, it assumes that:

■   The entire order arrives at once.

■   Stockouts or backorders (orders arriving before goods are available) are not allowed.

■   All costs are known and do not vary.

■   Lead times between order placement and order receipt are known.

■   Demand is known and constant.

Some complications, such as the first two, can be handled through simple modifications to the lot size formula. The third problem is harder, particularly since it is difficult to estimate such factors as the cost of placing an order, but fortunately the lot size formula does not require much accuracy. A ball-park estimate is nearly always adequate. The last two problems are more important in practice, and are more difficult to address. If demand is not constant, the lot size formula does not yield good results, but there are several techniques that give good answers. If demand and lead times are uncertain, we have a second decision to make. In addition to deciding how large to make the order, we must also decide when we must place an order. In most cases, we must plan on having some extra stock (safety stock) on hand in case demand is unexpectedly high during the lead time.

     Finally, there are several important problems that cannot be solved mathematically. For instance, if you have several warehouses, there is no easy way to find the best method of coordinating stocks at each warehouse so as to make the overall

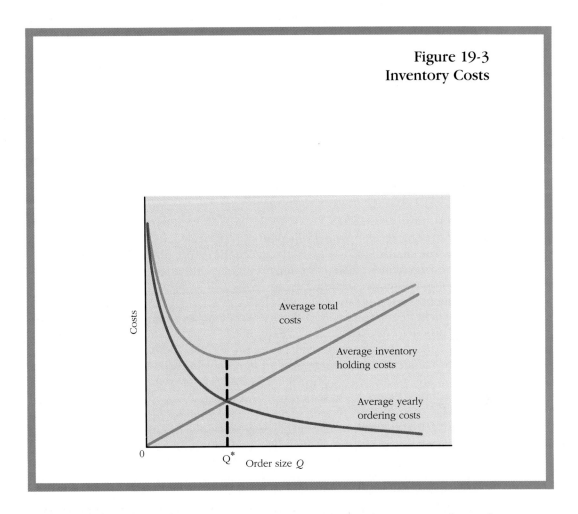

Figure 19-3
Inventory Costs

system perform as well as possible. If you order several items from one supplier and can combine orders to save on shipping costs, it is difficult to tell how best to do this. Despite these limitations, the inventory tools sketched above have proven to be extremely useful in practice.

Independent versus Dependent Demand

In our discussion so far, we have assumed that demand for each item is independent of demand for other items. For such companies as Priority One, this makes a good deal of sense. Demand for transistors is not affected by demand for disk drives. In some cases, however, demand for different items is closely tied together. For example, assume that you manufacture toy wagons, and purchase both sheet metal and rubber tires from outside suppliers. When demand for your wagons increases, you will purchase more tires and more sheet metal—the demand for the two items is tied together. We term this situation **dependent demand**, as opposed to the **independent demand** experienced by Priority One.

As a toy wagon manufacturer, it would make sense to coordinate your purchases of both sheet metal and tires, and to base purchases for both on your manufacturing plans. If you plan a heavy production schedule, you need to order large amounts of both products, and to time your purchases so that they arrive just as you will need them. Dependent demand items require coordinated purchasing decisions. The lot size formula makes no allowances for coordination, but another technique, material requirements planning, has come into wide use in recent years.

MATERIAL REQUIREMENTS PLANNING   Material requirements planning (**MRP**)[3] starts at the end result—with a schedule of how many final products you wish to produce. The final production schedule (called the master schedule in MRP) is determined by management after consulting forecasts, current inventories, and similar information. The master schedule usually gives daily or weekly production totals for several months into the future.

The next step is to see what parts and subassemblies have to be available to make the final product. For example, if we are making toy wagons, then to make one wagon we would need a body, a front-wheel assembly, a rear-wheel assembly, and a handle assembly. Frequently these assemblies in turn contain subassemblies. For instance, the rear-wheel assembly consists of a bracket, an axle, two wheels, plus various nuts, bolts, and pins. Figure 19-4, which lists this information, is known as the **bill of materials**.

In an actual application, the bill of materials would also show how long it would take to purchase or make each item. For example, suppose it takes three days to assemble a lot of wagons. If we want to have fifty wagons ready to ship on day 30, we must begin assembling them on day 27. If it takes another 10 days to make wagon bodies, then we must start making the bodies on day 17. This process, known as **lead time offsetting**, is the key to MRP. When we know exactly what goes into each final product and know how long it takes to make each component, we can coordinate purchasing and manufacturing so each part arrives just when it is needed in the process. Thus, even complex, highly interrelated processes can be coordinated, keeping expensive in-process inventories at a minumum.

Although the ideas behind MRP are quite simple, realistic MRP systems require enormous amounts of data. For starters, we must have complete, accurate bills of material for every product we make. Lead times must be realistic—neither too short nor too long. Then we must have current data on how much of each subassembly and part we have in inventory, so as to properly coordinate purchasing new material. None of these tasks appears too difficult on the surface, but in practice it is extremely difficult in a dynamic, changing world, to keep information up-to-date. In addition, MRP requires substantial investments in computers, computer programs, and all the people needed to keep the computers running. Thus MRP demands substantial investments in equipment and people. However, MRP has also proven to be an effective tool for increased efficiency, improved performance, and lower inventories.

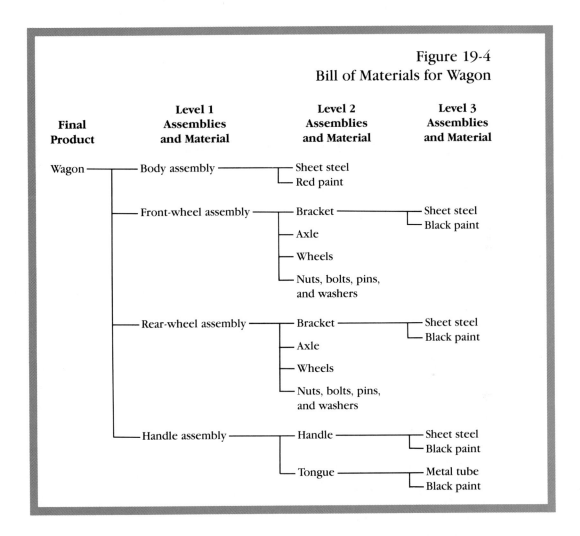

Figure 19-4
Bill of Materials for Wagon

<table>
<thead>
<tr><th>Final Product</th><th>Level 1 Assemblies and Material</th><th>Level 2 Assemblies and Material</th><th>Level 3 Assemblies and Material</th></tr>
</thead>
</table>

- Wagon
  - Body assembly
    - Sheet steel
    - Red paint
  - Front-wheel assembly
    - Bracket
      - Sheet steel
      - Black paint
    - Axle
    - Wheels
    - Nuts, bolts, pins, and washers
  - Rear-wheel assembly
    - Bracket
      - Sheet steel
      - Black paint
    - Axle
    - Wheels
    - Nuts, bolts, pins, and washers
  - Handle assembly
    - Handle
      - Sheet steel
      - Black paint
    - Tongue
      - Metal tube
      - Black paint

JUST-IN-TIME (KANBAN) CONTROL SYSTEM   As sketched above, MRP has proven to be effective in decreasing inventories and increasing productivity. However, MRP systems are invariably computerized, and require painstaking efforts to make sure that production and inventory data are completely accurate. In practice, the costs of ensuring accuracy in inventory data, bills of materials, and lead times are very high.

The Japanese have pioneered an alternative approach—just-in-time (JIT) manufacturing systems, also known as "kanban" systems.[4] The emphasis in JIT is on small lot sizes, short lead times, and simple management systems. To illustrate a simple form of JIT system for wagon manufacture, examine Figure 19-5. The final assembly area is to the right. Immediately adjacent are storage areas for each of the four components. Each storage area has enough space for only enough components to make one wagon—one each of the body assembly, front- and rear-wheel assemblies, and handle

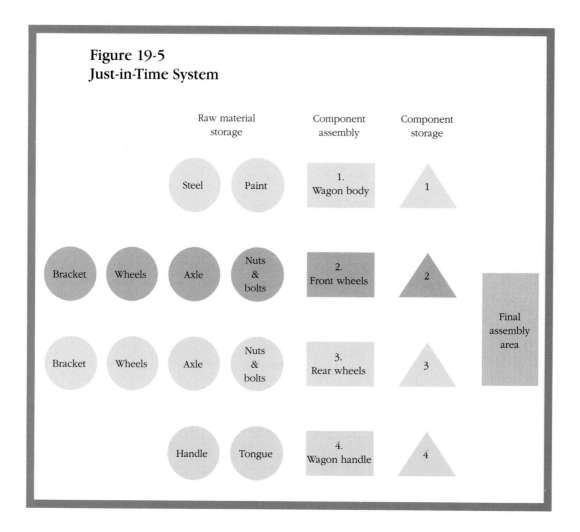

Figure 19-5
Just-in-Time System

assembly. Immediately to the left of the storage areas are the four component assembly areas, each in turn supplied with their own raw materials storage locations.

Suppose a wagon is now needed. The final assembly workers take the four components from the storage areas, and begin assembling the wagon. A JIT system is generally set up so that each component comes in a container with just enough room for the one component. As soon as the container is emptied, it is delivered to the appropriate component assembly area. For example, the empty box for the wagon body assembly is delivered to the body-assembly area. In JIT, an empty container is a signal to produce another unit. Workers in the body-assembly area remove sheet steel and red paint from their respective storage areas, and begin making the body. When finished, they put the newly completed body into the empty body container, and deliver it to the final-assembly storage area. In the mean time, empty sheet steel and paint containers are delivered to their respective supply points, where other workers or suppliers then begin work to replenish the body assembly supply locations.

This system is the most simple type of JIT system. In one common variation, a card is attached to each container. When the container is emptied, the card rather than the container is delivered to the next work station to signal the need for more product. The Japanese word "kanban" means card, hence the use of that term. In some systems, notably the kanban system at the Toyota automobile plant, two different kinds of card are used.

Note the extreme simplicity of this system. Demand for the final product triggers work flow through the entire system. No computers or elaborate inventory control systems are needed. Further, if demand drops off temporarily, the work pace throughout the entire area automatically adjusts itself to the new level. Another advantage is that quality problems show up very quickly. If the front-wheel assembly is made poorly, the next workers up the line detect the problem immediately, so corrective action can be taken.

However, also note the demands a JIT system puts on manufacturing design. First, JIT is most effective when only one unit at a time is made. If setup costs are high, it is costly to make products in this manner. A good deal of engineering time and capital investment is often needed to reduce setup costs. Second, the work must be well balanced in different manufacturing areas. Ideally, it would take exactly as long to make a body assembly as to assemble a final wagon. Then the new body assembly would arrive just as the old wagon was completed. A good deal of fine tuning is needed to balance the work loads. The fine tuning can be best done when the work load is steady and predictable. These considerations argue that JIT is best suited to situations where large amounts of product are made, and where demand is relatively constant.

Assembly-Line Management

The assembly line is one of America's major contributions to the art of manufacturing. When initially developed, most notably by Henry Ford, assembly-line techniques yielded dramatic improvements in productivity and costs. Recently, many service industries have made excellent use of assembly-line concepts. McDonald's, for example, has developed extremely efficient and effective methods for making hamburgers. To cite another example, routine health-care examinations can be performed on an assembly-line basis with significant improvements in both costs and quality of care.

To return to our example, we could obviously make wagons on an assembly line. We would examine each step in making a wagon, then divide the tasks into several groups, with each group being done at a separate assembly-line station. The worker at station 1 does all his or her tasks, then passes the partially completed wagon to station 2, where the second worker completes those tasks, and so on. The time spent completing all the tasks at one station is called **cycle time**. Assembly lines can be extremely efficient, particularly when large numbers of similar or identical products are being made.

There are also disadvantages to assembly-line production. From a technical standpoint, assembly lines always contain inherent inefficiencies. Since it is impossible to balance perfectly the amount of work at each station, and since humans do not work at exactly the same pace all the time, there are inevitably times when some people are idle (**balance delay**). Careful design of the line can minimize these problems, but can never eliminate them. A second problem relates to the role of the worker. In an assembly line, the human is treated essentially as a piece of machinery. Assembly-line work has been criticized as boring and dehumanizing. Continually repeating identical motions sometimes leads to hand and wrist problems, even if very little effort is needed. Various methods of redesigning assembly work and increasing use of industrial robots for some routine work have helped, but have not overcome these criticisms.

Scheduling

Frequently, several jobs wait for the same key worker or machine, and someone must decide which gets the highest priority. Managers usually have some information to aid this decision, such as the estimated time the job requires, the job due date, and the amount of work remaining after finishing a bottleneck step. Some guidelines exist to help us schedule work, but unfortunately no one method works best for all circumstances. Here, we describe five common scheduling rules,[5] and briefly discuss the strengths and weaknesses of each.

FIRST COME, FIRST SERVED   This is an easy rule to apply, and if job deadlines parallel starting times, the "first come, first served" rule does reasonably well in giving more urgent work higher priority. However, all information on due dates and estimated work times is ignored. A late or high priority job must wait in line behind less urgent work until its turn comes up.

DO THE SHORTEST JOBS FIRST   By giving shortest jobs the highest priority, the maximum number of jobs are done quickly, allowing work to proceed to further processing steps. This way workers do not hold up lots of work while doing the long jobs. This rule minimizes the average time taken to process all jobs. However, this rule also ignores due dates and priorities. Short jobs that are not due for several weeks take priority over long jobs that may be overdue. What is worse, if new work is continually arriving, the long jobs tend to be put off indefinitely.

DO JOBS WITH THE EARLIEST DUE DATE FIRST   This is the first rule that assigns priorities by due dates. It is also easy to apply in practice. The major shortcoming is that this rule does not examine the amount of work remaining. For example, a job due in three days may have a good deal of work left to do in other areas after we finish with it. That job should be given a higher priority than a job due in two days, but which is all done when we complete our step.

MINIMIZE THE NUMBER OF LATE JOBS   A variation of doing jobs with the earliest due date first, this rule follows a four-step process to minimize the number of jobs that are late:

Step 1:   Schedule the job with the earliest due date first.

Step 2:   Determine if this job will be completed on time. If the answer is "yes," skip to step 4. If the answer is "no," go to step 3.

Step 3:   Examine the list of all the jobs scheduled so far, and remove the one with the longest processing time. This job will be done after everything else is complete. Adjust the completion times of the remaining jobs, and go to step 4.

Step 4:   If there are no jobs left, the scheduling is finished. If there are some jobs left, schedule the one with the earliest due date next. Go to step 2.

Example 19-1 illustrates this process.

USE THE CRITICAL RATIO TO SCHEDULE JOBS   The critical ratio is defined as:

$$\frac{\text{Time remaining}}{\text{Work remaining}}$$

If the critical ratio is large, the job has a good deal of time left or only a small amount of work remaining. Thus it need not be done immediately. If the critical ratio is small, there is little time left and a good deal of work remaining, so the job is urgent. The smaller the critical ratio, the more urgent the job. The critical ratio is widely used in practice, since it is easy to understand and compute, and because it considers both due dates and the amount of work left.

To illustrate the use of the various scheduling rules, Example 19-2 (see page 610) shows the schedules resulting from applying each rule to the data indicated. Each rule gives a different sequence, and no one sequence is best in all circumstances. In general, however, such overly simple rules as "first come first served" do not do as well as the more sophisticated methods.

Shop Floor Control

Once work is scheduled and planned, there must be a method of tracking and controlling work in process. An effective manager must ensure that scheduled work is actually performed, and that it is done on time and within budget.

The easiest method of controlling work in process is to use a **job traveller**, a form that lists each step in order. Spaces are provided for the worker performing each step to record the time started, time stopped, and the number of pieces successfully completed. Workers are often required to sign off each completed task, so problems can eventually be traced back to the responsible person.

Example 19-1

Jobs A through E require the following work time and due dates:

JOB	WORK TIME (DAYS)	DUE DATE (DAY)
A	4	11
B	5	16
C	6	8
D	3	13
E	2	14

Step 1   The job with the earliest due date is job C. The initial schedule is:

JOB	DAYS NEEDED	CALENDAR DATE	DUE DATE	ON TIME?
C	6	6	8	Yes

Step 2   Job C is completed on time, so we skip to step 4.

Step 4   Since jobs A, B, D, and E have not yet been scheduled, we schedule the one with the earliest due date next—job A—and return to step 2. The schedule now is:

JOB	DAYS NEEDED	CALENDAR DATE	DUE DATE	ON TIME?
C	6	6	8	Yes
A	4	10	11	Yes

Step 2   Job A is completed on time. Go to step 4.

Step 4   Schedule job D next and return to step 2. The new schedule is:

JOB	DAYS NEEDED	CALENDAR DATE	DUE DATE	ON TIME?
C	6	6	8	Yes
A	4	10	11	Yes
D	3	13	13	Yes

Step 2   Since job D is completed on time, skip to step 4.

Step 4   Schedule job E next and return to step 2. The new schedule is:

This information can be extremely useful in determining actual costs, in identifying sources of problems, and tracking effects of changes and improvements. There are, however, two important problems associated with job travellers. First, the data can be analyzed only after the work is done. Someone must first gather all the travellers and transfer the information to a computer—a process that can take several days—before we can see how well we did. Sometimes information that is several days

JOB	DAYS NEEDED	CALENDAR DATE	DUE DATE	ON TIME?
C	6	6	8	Yes
A	4	10	11	Yes
D	3	13	13	Yes
E	2	15	14	No

Step 2 Job E is late, so go to step 3.

Step 3 We need to select the job with the longest processing time from those already scheduled—C, A, D, and E. Job C has the longest processing time, so we schedule it after everything else, and adjust all the completion times. The revised schedule is:

JOB	DAYS NEEDED	CALENDAR DATE	DUE DATE	ON TIME?
A	4	4	11	Yes
D	3	7	13	Yes
E	2	9	14	Yes
	(Any remaining jobs to be scheduled will go here.)			
C	6	15	8	No

Step 4 The only job left is job B. Schedule it *before* job C but after the others, and go to step 2. The new schedule is:

JOB	DAYS NEEDED	CALENDAR DATE	DUE DATE	ON TIME?
A	4	4	11	Yes
D	3	7	13	Yes
E	2	9	14	Yes
B	5	14	16	Yes
C	6	20	8	No

Step 2 Job B was on time, so skip to step 4.

Step 4 Since all jobs are scheduled, we are through.

Note that job C will always be put last no matter how many additional jobs we schedule. Thus, we maximize the number of jobs which are on time, but those few that are late will be very late.

old is adequate, but in many instances it is important to have information that is up to the minute. Second, workers often manipulate the figures they write down. A person who has ruined several work pieces, or who took a few extra minutes for lunch will record numbers that will make him or her look better. Filling in forms is an unpleasant task, and workers sometimes forget to do so, or might simply wait until quitting time to fill in a whole day's worth of forms with guesses.

Example 19-2

Suppose the following jobs are all waiting to be done. Assume that they arrived in the order listed.

| | WORK TIME (DAYS) | | | |
JOB	AT THIS STATION	TOTAL ALL STATIONS	DUE DATE	CRITICAL RATIO
A	4	4	11	2.75
B	3	5	16	3.20
C	1	6	8	1.33
D	2	3	13.	4.33
E	1	2	14	7.00

Rule 1: First Come, First Served   The job schedule is A B C D E. Note that job B is done before job C, even though it is due much later.

Rule 2: Do the Shortest Jobs First   The job schedule is C E D B A. Jobs C and E tie for the shortest job, so C gets priority since it has the earlier due date. Note that E is done ahead of A, even though A has an earlier due date.

Rule 3: Do Jobs with the Earliest Due Date First   The job schedule is C A D E B. Note that A has priority over E. Although this might be appropriate, note that A has 4 days of work at this station, and that when we complete our work A is finished. E has only one day of work at this station, and has additional work elsewhere.

Rule 4: Minimize the Number of Late Jobs.   As discussed in Example 19-1, jobs will be done in the order A D E B C. Note that most jobs are done on time, but that job C is very late.

Rule 5: Use the Critical Ratio to Schedule Jobs   The schedule is C A B D E. Job A, which is quite long, is scheduled ahead of three shorter jobs, but its due date is earlier.

Both these problems can be largely overcome through **machine-readable labels**. If a form or label can be read directly by a computer, data can be gathered more accurately and inexpensively than by having workers fill out forms. **Bar coding** has recently become the most commonly used form of machine-readable labelling. A bar coded document has information coded in black-and-white "zebra" stripes of varying widths. The information can be read with a wand or with stationary scanners of various types.

Bar codes have become common in grocery stores. At the check stand each item is passed over a scanner that identifies the item, finds the price in a central computer file, computes the customer's bill—broken down into dairy, meats, groceries, etc.—and updates sales and inventory data for the store. In a manufacturing setting, each batch of parts has a traveller with bar-coded identification. When a worker begins work on the batch, she or he walks to a nearby terminal, puts a bar-coded identification badge into a reader so the computer knows which worker is entering data, runs a wand over the traveller to identify the parts, and indicates that he or she is about to begin working on the batch. Time and data information is recorded automatically by the computer. When the batch is finished, a similar process is used to credit the worker with completed work. The technology makes most types of data falsification quite difficult, and since this information can be used to compute the worker's pay, there is less incentive to cheat the system.

QUALITY CONTROL

It is probably safe to say that quality is the major business issue of the 1980s. **Quality control** is the process by which management assures itself that minimum quality standards are being met. The sheer size of the U.S. merchandise trade deficit and the loss of domestic market share to foreign competitors brought about a crisis that forced management to realize that much of the problem could be attributed to the perceived higher quality of foreign-produced goods, especially Japanese goods. The current popularity of such Japanese manufacturing techniques as just-in-time inventory systems and quality circles can largely be attributed to attempts to close this "quality gap."

It is also important to realize that high quality, while sometimes resulting in lower short-term profits, is equated with higher long-run profitability. As John F. Akers, President and CEO of IBM has said: "We believe quality improvement will reduce quality costs 50 percent over the coming years. For us, that translates into billions of dollars of added profit."[6]

The issues involved in quality control can best be seen by considering the following illustration. The materials following the illustration will attempt to address the issues raised.

CASE
Plane Disaster Caused by Poor Quality

Several years ago a jumbo jetliner crashed upon takeoff, killing several hundred people. Upon investigation, federal authorities found that a strut holding one of the engines on the wing had failed. As the engine broke away it ruptured fuel lines and control cables, leading to a fire and the crash. The airplane obviously had a quality problem. Whose fault was it? The answer depended on who you asked.

Poor quality control in the airline industry can easily result
in disaster.

- ◼ It was the aircraft designers' fault. They did not provide enough strength in the airplane's structure.
- ◼ It was the fault of the assembly engineers. To make production easier and cheaper, they had made some minor modifications to the strut design. Some of these may have weakened the strut.
- ◼ It was the purchasing department's fault. The strut materials were not of high enough quality.
- ◼ It was the fault of the assembly workers. They may not have secured the strut to the wing correctly.
- ◼ It was the fault of the airline that operated the plane. Evidence indicated that improper procedures were followed in removing and reinstalling engines. Proper maintenance procedures might also have discovered the problem.
- ◼ It was the fault of management of both the manufacturer and the airline. They should have had quality-assurance systems in place to detect and prevent such errors.
- ◼ It was the federal government's fault. They failed to adequately fulfill their responsibility to ensure safety in the aviation industry.

Which of the above "reasons" is the correct one? All are, to some extent. In quality control, quality is everyone's job. Like a chain, just one weak link in a whole sequence of events is enough to cause a quality problem. ▼

Instilling a Quality-Conscious Attitude

The primary responsibility of management in quality control is to instill a quality-conscious attitude among workers. Blaine Shull, senior vice-president for product operations at Hughes Aircraft, puts it this way: "There are three little items you must have to convince your people you're serious. First, you measure for improvement, not blame. Second, you have to be more interested in trends, not absolutes. Third, you fix the problem, not the blame."[7] While this can be a difficult job, the following principles and methods have proven useful in implementing these concepts.

QUALITY BEGINS AT THE TOP   In practice this means that it is essential to define an important formal role for quality assurance. Hospitals have formal review boards that regularly review medical records of patients who die, or whose treatments appear questionable. In manufacturing companies, quality-assurance departments should be at least at the same organizational level as manufacturing.

Review boards and quality-assurance departments are both charged with defining measures of quality and measuring the trend in the data. To be effective, they need to have management's ear when a problem arises. If manufacturing or operations management is at a higher organizational level than quality control, the temptation is to pay more attention to schedules than quality. The families of the dead passengers in the plane crash will not be consoled that the manufacturer delivered a defective plane on time or that the flight was on schedule.

TAKE THE LONG VIEW   Be willing to sacrifice short-term profits for long-run quality goals; in the long-run better quality results in higher profitability. For example, both McDonald's and Burger King have strict limits on how long a hamburger can be held in a warming bin. If the limit is exceeded, the hamburgers are thrown away. In addition to protecting customers from stale product, this policy is important as a highly visible signal to employees that the company is serious about quality. If too many hamburgers end up being thrown away, these companies analyze the flow of demand so as to prepare products only when needed, thus reducing waste; it is cheaper in the long-run to throw away a hamburger than to lose a customer.

In our airline example, a sacrifice of short-term profits might have meant using better materials or more careful procedures to mount the strut. It might also have meant accepting a penalty for late delivery to correct the problem. For the airline, it might have meant grounding the plane more often for service and closer checks on maintenance work.

GET EMPLOYEES INVOLVED   If given meaningful responsibility for addressing and recognition for solving quality problems, workers can be a critical part of quality solutions, rather than a potential source of quality problems. One of the attractions of just-in-time systems is that workers can shut down production to correct quality problems. On the other hand, if management focuses on fixing blame for quality problems, worker cooperation will be lost because workers will see quality assurance as a threat to their security.

GET SUPPLIERS INVOLVED   Many problems can be solved by requesting the input of suppliers. At Ford Motor Company the rejection rate on steel shipments was cut from 9 percent to 2 percent in three years and late deliveries of steel fell from 20 percent to 3 percent as a result of supplier input.[8] The company also recognizes suppliers who consistently meet high quality standards. Just as workers know more about the job they do than a manager can, suppliers are in a better position to solve quality problems with purchased parts and subassemblies. The key is obtaining their input.

Total Quality Control

Since quality problems have many sources, they also can be solved in several ways. To guard against further failures of the aircraft engine mounting strut, for example, the strut could be redesigned and strengthened. Alternatively, the company could have stricter quality checks during the assembly operation, or could require all airline maintenance personnel to pass a strict course on proper procedures. It might be useful to inspect struts on a regular basis to check for metal fatigue in key locations. Perhaps some combination of methods would be most effective. If you were the manager responsible for correcting the problem, you would need to identify each possible corrective method, then find the cost and effectiveness of each. The first idea that springs to mind might well not be the best. **Total quality control** is a term used to describe a comprehensive system of ensuring quality meets established standards. Total quality control involves more than inspection of products upon completion; it considers methods of building quality controls into the production system itself.

Inspections and Charts

In order for a control system to work, management must be able to measure and monitor results. Thus, **inspections** are critical in quality control. Two issues are important in finding a good inspection strategy—where inspections are held, and how data are gathered and reported.

Since inspecting costs money, it should be done in those places where it does the maximum amount of good. Some general rules are:[9]

Table 19-1
Patient Waiting Times

SAMPLE NUMBER	WAITING TIME FOR PATIENTS					AVERAGE	RANGE
	1	2	3	4	5		
1	7	3	5	12	8	7.00	9
2	4	6	5	9	9	6.60	5
3	1	9	13	5	11	7.80	12
4	2	5	12	2	14	7.00	12
5	14	3	7	8	8	8.00	11
6	9	10	3	5	4	6.20	7
7	15	14	5	7	4	9.00	11
8	5	9	9	12	8	8.60	7
9	16	5	14	6	6	9.40	11
10	10	21	9	15	9	12.80	12
11	17	7	12	9	15	12.00	10
12	11	23	18	7	8	13.40	16
13	6	14	13	24	14	14.20	18
14	12	7	15	15	23	14.40	16
15	19	18	8	16	10	14.20	11
16	21	9	21	10	14	15.00	12

- Inspect critical factors as early as possible.
- Inspect before steps that are expensive, where parts are fastened or mixed irreversibly, or where bad parts might damage machinery.
- Inspect after problem-prone steps to pull out bad parts before further processing, and to give immediate feedback to the problem step.
- Inspect before steps that mask defects (such as painting) or make parts inaccessible.
- Inspect first and last parts on automatic machines. If these are correct, the in-between parts are likely to be correct.
- Inspect finished parts before storage or shipment.

To be useful, quality data must be understood and used by managers and workers. Charts are widely used not only because they summarize data clearly and efficiently, but because they also show trends.

To illustrate, suppose one measure of service quality in a medical clinic is the time patients must wait before being examined. Each hour, records of the five most recent patients are examined to find waiting times. Table 19-1 shows results. For each

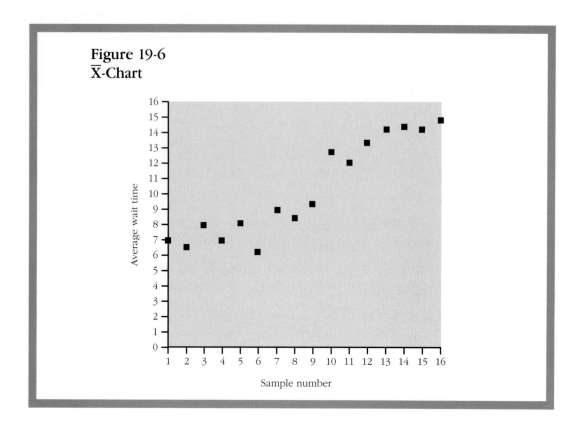

Figure 19-6
$\overline{X}$-Chart

set of five patients, the average and range of the observations is calculated. Figures 19-6 and 19-7 shows these results plotted over time. Note that the average waiting time was constant for the first few samples, but then began to increase steadily. The range likewise increases over time, indicating that consistency of service is also getting worse.

Figure 19-6 is called an **$\overline{X}$-chart**, while Figure 19-7 is an **R-chart**. These and similar charts are widely used in practice, since they show performance in a way that is easy to understand. Notice that the same charts show how much performance improves as corrective action is taken. Finally, it is easy to gather and plot the required information.

Quality Extends to All Functions

Finally, it should be noted that quality is a concept that extends much farther than just the manufacture of a product or the provision of a service. Many companies today are applying similar techniques to those discussed here to measure the quality of such

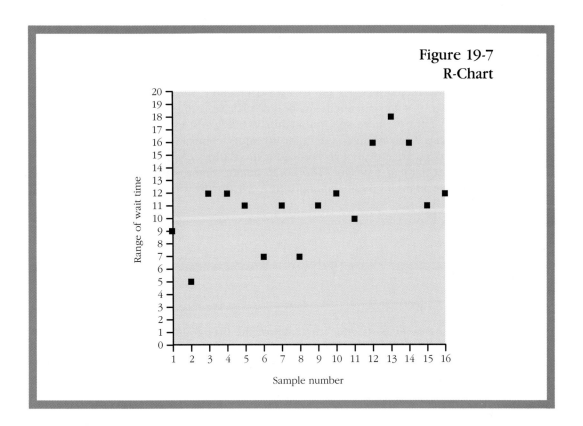

Figure 19-7
R-Chart

things as financial reports, internal communications, and customer service. Even employees who never see a customer and whose work never reaches a customer are told to treat those whom they deal with inside the company as customers whose needs for quality must be met. For such companies quality is a state of mind.

ENDING CASE
The Motorbike That Conquered Japan[10]

The most prestigious motorcycle you can buy in Japan these days is not a Kawasaki or a Honda—it's "Hari-Davidsonu," better known in English-speaking circles as the venerable Harley-Davidson. Although the basic Harley carries a price tag of around $12,000 in Tokyo, Japanese motorbike enthusiasts have been flocking to get one. The company now sells about 800 bikes a year in Japan.

Not a bad turnaround for a company that watched the Japanese share of the U.S. motorcycle market grow from zero to 90 percent in the late 1960s, while its own market share and reputation took a nosedive.

The reason for Harley's new success is a renewed emphasis on quality. A group of 13 investors, including CEO and Chairman Vaughn L. Beals, bought the 82-year-old company in 1981 and launched a major quality drive, using such techniques as statistical quality control, increased training for workers, just-in-time inventory, and even the Japanese "kanban" card system for inventory control.

"There's a great deal of reverence for the Harley-Davidson in Japan these days," says Robert H. Klein, manager of corporate affairs. "Some of the Japanese form Harley bike clubs and even buy police uniforms to wear when they're riding." ⓥ

SUMMARY

"Operations" is the part of the firm that provides the goods or services sold. As such it is a necessary part of every firm, even though the particular jobs done in the name of operations vary a good deal from company to company. Since operations usually include those parts of the firm that invest and spend most corporate resources, careful operations management can yield major increases in profitability.

The longest-term operations decision is to decide what product or service the company should offer, and how it should be designed. Then management must examine the overall demand pattern for the product, and decide on an aggregate production strategy. Some firms follow a chase strategy, in which production levels fluctuate to follow changing demand, while others try a level strategy—keeping production constant.

Inventory strategies require management to balance the investment in inventories with the expected return from that investment. ABC analysis helps separate items that can be managed by crude methods from those that must be managed carefully. When an item is expensive enough to justify careful management, the square-root lot size formula gives the best tradeoff between ordering and carrying costs.

In most manufacturing settings, dependent demand methods should be used in place of independent demand approaches. Material requirements planning is complex and requires complete accuracy in data records, but allows detailed planning of inventory levels and production schedules for dependent demand situations. Alternatively, just-in-time systems use simple management controls, small production lots, and rapid setup methods to control dependent demand right on the assembly floor.

Assembly-line planning consists of (1) finding the minimum number of work stations for the required production volume, (2) finding the cycle time at each station, and (3) assigning tasks to each station.

Scheduling consists of assigning priorities to each job at each work station in a facility. Several priority rules are used in practice, each leading to different overall system behavior. Jobs released to a production shop are often tracked and controlled through machine-readable labels and badges.

Quality is a concern throughout the planning/production cycle. The beginning point of effective quality control programs is worker and management attitude—quality must be regarded as everyone's job. Quality control data can be collected at strategic points in the process, and recorded on control charts. Both $\overline{X}$-Charts and R-Charts have found widespread application in practice.

KEY TERMS

Operations management
Operations
Aggregate planning
Chase strategy
Level strategy
Cycle stock
Safety stock
Work-in-process
Work-in-transit
ABC analysis
Ordering cost
Inventory holding cost
Economic order quantity
Dependent demand
Independent demand
MRP
Bill of materials

Lead time offsetting
Just-in-time (Kanban) system
Cycle time
Balance delay
First come, first served
Shortest job first
Earliest due date
Minimize late jobs
Critical ratio
Job traveller
Machine-readable labels
Bar coding
Quality control
Total quality control
Inspections
R-Chart
$\overline{X}$-Chart

REVIEW QUESTIONS

1. In what area of a firm is the largest portion of funds usually spent?

2. How does operations management differ between manufacturing and service businesses?

3. What functions were included in operations management at Priority One Electronics?

4. Why does a 10 percent increase in operating efficiency almost always produce a greater impact on profits than a 10 percent increase in sales?

5. What is the first task in operations management?

6. What time frame does aggregate planning concern itself with?

7. What are the differences between a chase and a level production strategy and in what circumstances would each be appropriate?

8. When is it appropriate to maintain safety stocks?

9. What is A inventory? B? C? Of what benefit is ABC analysis?

10. What does the formula for the best order size strike a balance between?

11. What are some of the limitations implicit in the formula for the best lot size?

12. What is dependent demand and how does it fit into MRP systems?

13. What is a bill of materials and why is it important to production scheduling?

14. Why is it important to know the lead times associated with the component parts in production scheduling?

15. In what circumstances is MRP most effective? What are the disadvantages associated with MRP systems?

16. How do just-in-time (Kanban) inventory systems differ from conventional inventory systems and what aspect of production costs do these systems significantly reduce?

17. What are two benefits associated with just-in-time as opposed to MRP?

18. What demands do just-in-time systems place on manufacturing design? In what ways are these significant?

19. Explain the concept of cycle time and why it is important in assembly-line management.

20. What is balance delay and what does it tell us about the production process?

21. Name five methods for assigning priority in work scheduling. Which would be the most effective to achieve the following goals?
   A. Maximize the number of jobs done quickly.
   B. Keep the most customers happy with their delivery date.
   C. Take into account due dates and amount of work.

22. What is the function performed by a job traveller?

23. How do bar codes work in a manufacturing setting?

24. Whose responsibility is quality control? Who should set the example?

25. While short-term profits must sometimes be sacrificed to achieve quality control, can you think of some reasons why manufacturing costs might be lowered by paying more attention to quality?

26. What are some rules of thumb for determining when it is best to conduct quality control inspections?

27. How are $\overline{X}$-charts and R-charts used? What information do they give us?

CHALLENGE QUESTIONS

1. How can a good product design help management achieve its goals of low cost and high quality? What does this suggest about the common practice of design-

ing a product first, then engineering it, and finally determining how it is to be produced?

2. How would poor information input affect an MRP system? How effective would an MRP system be in an environment where constant changes were made in the parts used and the lead times necessary to order parts?

3. What aspects of just-in-time inventory systems lend themselves to production of higher quality goods?

4. Why is so much time and effort put into cutting setup costs by firms which use just-in-time inventory systems?

5. How would a firm determine how many minutes it takes to assemble a single wagon? What would a drop in the number of minutes that it takes to assemble a wagon do to the minimum number of work stations required to produce a day's output?

6. What kind of measures would you use to determine whether quality standards are being met for the following?
   A. Tires
   B. Moving and storage service
   C. Jet engines
   D. Videocassette recorder

7. What would be an appropriate management signal of commitment to quality in the following case? You must decide which of two plants will be awarded the production of a new product. Plant A has an excellent quality record but sometimes fails to meet deadlines and labor costs are higher than average. Plant B has the advantage of the lowest labor and production costs in the company but its quality record is only mediocre. Deadlines are particularly important with regard to this product.

8. What impact does an organization's mission statement have on operations and operations management? Why is it important?

9. List five businesses that you would expect to employ a chase manufacturing strategy.

10. How can a service business attempt to overcome its inability to adopt a level-production strategy? What factors get in the way?

11. What costs do just-in-time systems help to reduce and why?

12. Name five scheduling methods. What are the strengths and weaknesses of each method?

13. What problems associated with job travellers do machine-readable labels solve? How does bar coding fit in?

14. How does total quality control differ from the old concept of quality control as an inspection process?

CASE AND RELATED QUESTIONS

1. Which of the inventory cost control systems discussed in the chapter was most applicable to Priority One Electronics? Why was this system particularly useful?

2. If Priority One's pretax profit margin is 10 percent, how much would the company have to increase sales to achieve the $60,000 per year improvement in pretax performance that was achieved through better control of operational costs?

3. How did a simple computer system help Priority One Electronics reduce its investment in inventory?

4. How might a system of total quality control have prevented the airline disaster mentioned in the case discussion? What advantages would such a system have over traditional quality control methods in the arline industry?

5. How might a job traveller assist the manufacturer of the jet that crashed to determine what might have gone wrong in the manufacture of the plane?

6. Political reactions to plane disasters are often focused on finding who was at fault. Why is such an approach likely not to result in improved performance?

7. Who should the relatives of a passenger killed in the jet crash sue? What does your answer suggest about the risks that a firm takes in producing potentially harmful products and services?

8. How did Harley-Davidson become the most prestigious bike to own in Japan? Is there any reason to conclude that the company's success could not be repeated here?

9. Why do just-in-time and Kanban systems lend themselves so well to improved quality? Are the principles involved in such systems applicable to all types of manufacturing? Why?

ENDNOTES

1. See Roger W. Schmenner, *Plant and Service Tours in Operations Management* 2nd ed. (Chicago: Science Research Associates, Inc., 1989). Chapter 10 has a thorough discussion of the issues in this section.

2. See William J. Sawaya and William C. Giauque, *Production and Operations Management* (San Diego: Harcourt Brace Jovanovich, Inc., 1986).

3. Oliver Wight, *Manufacturing Resource Planning—MRPII: Unlocking America's Productivity Potential* (Essex Junction, VT: Oliver Wight Limited Publications, Inc., 1981).

4. Richard J. Schonberger, *Japanese Manufacturing Techniques: Nine Hidden Lessons in Simplicity* (New York: The Free Press, 1982).

5. Rick Hesse and Gene Woolsey, *Applied Management Science* (Chicago: Science Research Associates, Inc., 1980). Chapter 2 covers techniques summarized in this section.

6. Excerpted from an advertisement of the American Society for Quality Control, "The Renaissance of American Quality," *Fortune*, October 14, 1985, p. 184.

7. Ibid., p. 168.

8. Ibid., p. 176.

9. See Sawaya and Giauque, Chapter 15.

10. "Harley-Davidson Takes Lessons from Arch-Rivals' Handbook," *International Management*, February 1985, pp. 46–48.

CHAPTER 20

COMPUTERS AND INFORMATION SYSTEMS

LEARNING OBJECTIVES

■ Develop an understanding of how computers and information systems enable managers to direct the activities of an organization more effectively.

■ Understand the basic concepts of information systems design.

■ Describe the basic types of information systems.

■ Trace the historical development of computerized data storage and the possibilities for future technologies.

■ Identify the functions of the components of computerized systems.

■ Identify the major uses of a personal computer and their limitations.

■ Understand the practical applications of system goals, system output, and the data base.

Managers at the Malouf Company knew that it was time to upgrade the quality and timeliness of their information systems. The company, a large manufacturer of women's and girls' clothing, had been feeling the effects of overseas competition. Despite an excellent reputation for quality and for on-time delivery, management knew that they had to oversee their manufacturing and inventory systems as efficiently as possible to compete with Taiwan, Korea, and other low-cost labor areas. Yet most management reports were available only monthly, and only after a two-week delay after the end of the month. Manufacturing planning, shipping, and accounting systems were essentially run by hand. Every second week, for example, the payroll department calculated pay and wrote out checks for nearly 1,000 employees—all by hand.

The answer seemed to be some sort of computerized system, but Malouf's only previous experience with computers had been a disaster, and was terminated after a few months. Despite this history, management knew that computerization was inevitable. Their major concerns were with timing and with how to avoid a repeat of their previous failure.

INTRODUCTION

The story of the Malouf Company is being repeated over and over in modern businesses. Probably no change has been so dramatic in recent years as advancements in information systems and computers. Technological advances do not change the basic nature of management, but radically alter the amount and quality of information available to managers. It is hard to conceive of a modern business competing effectively without the advantages offered by modern information systems. Yet, as Malouf's initial experience indicated, computers all too often only "Let us screw up ten times faster than we ever did before," as one manager wryly put it.

In this chapter we discuss basic concepts in information systems design and review various types of information systems. We then examine computerized information systems and introduce the important ideas and terminology in that field. Finally, we review systems design, and trace Malouf's subsequent experience with designing and implementing a computerized information system.

INFORMATION SYSTEMS

Defining Information Needs

The first step in designing an information system is to define what information management needs—both under current management practice and as it would be ideally. This is a surprisingly difficult task, as most managers are not used to thinking about what they wished they had. It is particularly difficult to define information needs for top management, since the roles of top managers are both more varied and more ambiguous than those of lower managers. Box 20-1 summarizes some of the differences in information needs of different levels of management. However, we can determine the general types of information various managers typically need. For example, a company president would be interested in overall profits, cash flows, and other financial information. He or she might track sales and manufacturing costs in order to measure how well managers in those areas were performing. A president might also have special projects to follow. If a new incentive plan was being tried in order to cut down on employee absenteeism, the president would be interested in tracking absentee rates to see how well the new plan was working. Other managers define the jobs that they are responsible for in a similar manner, and enumerate the information required to do each job properly.

Most managers can define information needs of their current jobs, but it is more challenging to try to define information they wished they had. Yet, it is this step that can lead to significant improvements. The business press abounds with articles indicating that information systems are not merely inexpensive ways to manage internal affairs, but are now powerful competitive weapons. For example, Wiseman and MacMillan[1] discuss a large clinical laboratory that has installed computer terminals in customers' offices to allow them to retrieve test results as soon as they are known. This allows the lab, Metpath, to gain an advantage over competition by providing a unique service. They can also build on this capability by offering a patient records filing service, and such financial services as billing and accounts payable.

Information services are now often part of the product itself. Porter and Millar[2] point out that most products have both a physical and an information component. A washing machine is a physical piece of equipment, but convenient, accessible information on how to use and maintain the washer is also an important part of the product. New information technologies have made it possible for General Electric to provide far more information with the product. For example, GE's appliance service data base supports a consumer hotline that helps differentiate their service support from that of the competition. Newer appliances often contain control systems that tell the user what is happening during a process cycle.

Clearly, computers have become pervasive in business practice. Not only do they allow more efficient management of traditional functions, but allow companies to offer services that would have been impossible several years ago. The starting point is

Box 20-1
Information Needs of Different Management Levels

LEVEL	ROLES	INFORMATION NEEDS
Top management	Strategy formulation	Mostly external—trends in markets, technology, and competition, changes in the economy and governmental policies
	Evaluate and reward subordinates	Performance of different areas of the company. Morale, competence, and productivity of various departments. In general, evaluation is more ambiguous at this level than at lower levels.
First-line management	Perform assigned responsibilities	Tasks are well-defined, with specific, measurable goals. First-line managers need internally generated information tied directly to those goals.
	Exercise operational control	Historical information on performance compared to goals. Ideally the information would be diagnostic, indicating sources of and corrections for problems.

defining the job to be done, and understanding how computers can provide information to help.

Data versus Information

As the examples above indicate, it is easy to generate enormous amounts of data by using modern technology. However, raw **data** becomes **information** only when combined with other data in the right way. For the General Electric Appliance Division, customer names and appliance maintenance histories are data. Those data become information when matched with historical data to give better service information to the customer. Similarly, data on sales, costs, and customers are useless by themselves. Data become useful, become information only when they are organized, compared against goals and standards, and combined with other data to help managers make decisions and give a better product or service.

In order to be most useful, information should be **accurate**, **timely**, and **complete**. Accuracy, the correctness of the information, can refer to either the accuracy of the underlying data or to the way it is packaged and presented for management attention. Information must also be timely if it is to be helpful. The best information in the world will not be useful if it arrives several days after a decision must be made. The value of information is also lessened if it is not complete. In evaluating the performance of a subordinate we would like to know how he or she did in every area of responsibility, not just a few.

INFORMATION SYSTEMS FOR MANAGEMENT

Obviously accurate, timely, and complete information is important to any manager. Let us examine the components of systems that generate information, and then review different ways of classifying and discussing information systems.

Basic Components of Information Systems

Any information system consists of four major components: **input**, **control**, **memory**, and **output**. These elements are always present, no matter whether the information system is run by hand or by computer.

In a manual system, such as a system that analyzes customer payments and produces analyses of accounts payable, customer payments are the inputs. A clerk examines each payment and determines which customer made the payment. This is one example of control, making decisions on how to record and summarize data. The clerk then pulls the customer file from a file cabinet—the memory—and records the payment. Control can also be exercised by examining the record for past-due payments and calculating interest charges. Finally, the clerk produces output by typing a letter to the customer giving the new balance on hand. The system could also produce other output, such as a summary of all accounts over thirty days past due.

In a computerized system the same functions exist, but the physical form of the system is very different from that of the manual system. Input, the customer checks, must be turned into a form the computer can read. Modern systems generally use television-like computer terminals. Most systems are designed to fill in blanks. A clerk indicates that she or he wants to record a customer payment, and the computer presents a form to be filled in on the screen. Control is built into the system in the form of computer programs (also called software, as opposed to the physical machinery known as hardware)—instructions that the machine uses to process the transaction correctly and update all of its records. Computer memory, which can take several different physical forms, is used to store all customer records. The computer can produce printed output, such as letters to customers or printed reports on overdue accounts, and can also produce output on terminals. For example, a computerized system can show a complete payment history of any customer on demand at a terminal. This capability can be useful in responding to customer inquiries, for example.

Transaction Reporting Systems

Information systems can be further classified by the level of information they provide. The simplest form is a **transaction reporting system**. Many tasks in a company are routine, repetitive, and predictable. A good example is computing the payroll each pay period. Work hours are collected, multiplied by the employee rate of pay, overtime and withholding computed, and checks written—all this every pay period for every employee. A transaction reporting system is one which handles such routine transactions. Typically, a transaction reporting system:

■ Creates a historical record of transactions.

■ Sorts, merges, and updates individual records.

■ Performs routine, well-defined processing tasks, such as calculating gross pay, withholding, and net pay.

■ Accumulates summary information.

■ Produces reports for employees, supervisors, and management.

Management Information Systems

A **management information system** (MIS) is one step up the evolutionary ladder from a transaction reporting system. An MIS allows information to be combined and retrieved in a variety of ways, rather than in the predefined, prespecified manner typical of a transaction reporting system. The additional complexity of an MIS requires more advanced hardware and software.

The flexibility required by an MIS normally requires that data be organized into a data base and administered by a **data base management system** (DBMS). In a data base, data can be found and summarized in several different ways, rather than just one way.

For example, if employee records are stored in consecutive order according to social security numbers, then in order to process the payroll we first must sort the timecards by social security number, then match the sorted timecard file with the employee file, computing salaries and printing paychecks as we go. This may be an excellent way to process the payroll, but what if we need to know how many employees worked overtime last month? What if we need to know how many employees under the level of supervisor have been with the company for at least ten years? A good MIS should be responsive to just these types of questions. But the only way to get this information from the social-security-sorted file is to examine every single employee record—a time-consuming process even for a computer. It would be much more efficient if we could find information by hours worked or time of employment, as well as by social security number. A DBMS allows that capability, but at the cost of significantly increased complexity in the way data are organized and stored.

Decision Support Systems

Decision support systems (DSS) offer yet another layer of sophistication in computerized information systems. A DSS is designed to help management with unstructured, unanticipated questions and decisions. They are also designed to be easy to communicate with and use, so relatively untrained managers could use them interactively. At top management levels, it is often difficult to articulate questions precisely, so it is important to have a tool that will allow users to explore various ideas, to try to make connections among disjointed pieces of information, and to follow hunches.

A DSS consists of the following pieces:

- An MIS to support several methods of accessing and summarizing data.
- Sophisticated and complex data bases, allowing information to be found in many different ways, some of which may be impossible to anticipate.
- A user interface, allowing the user to use natural, English-like commands rather than "computerese" to communicate with the system.
- Data drawn from both internal and external sources to allow managers to relate what is happening within the company to the economic and competitive environment.
- Rapid response, making the system easy and rewarding to use.

These characteristics are ideals, and while no actual system fully satisfies all of them at present, some extremely useful DSSs have been developed.

Through moving from manual to computer systems, then into a more sophisticated MIS and DSS, management at Southwestern Ohio Steel (SOS), a major midwestern steel service center (see the case below), found they had immediate access to order status information, resulting in far faster and cheaper customer service. Sales calls were more productive, since less salesperson time was spent answering customer queries about the status of their orders. In addition, SOS understood customer-buying patterns much better, and could do a better job of inventory control and production scheduling. Another critical benefit was understanding—understanding of the business, the customer, and the critical factors for success in this industry.

CASE
Southwestern Ohio Steel[3]

Southwestern Ohio Steel is one of the top three steel services centers in the United States, with sales of approximately $100 million. SOS is in the business of purchasing steel of various qualities, including primes, seconds, and overruns, from major steel companies and selling it directly to hundreds of customers throughout the Midwest. Most steel is processed to some extent—sheared, rolled, etc.—before resale. SOS has developed a reputation for high quality and excellent service with both its customers and suppliers. A key contributor to SOS's image is its capability to provide customized products quickly, resulting from extreme flexibility in production scheduling.

In early 1982, SOS faced an increasingly complex environment. At the same time, the management team was changing to a newer, younger group. Two of the younger managers were sons of the original top management, but there was still a need to pass on knowledge and to build systems to capture some of the expertise and perspectives the retiring generation had gained over the years. These trends led management to consider a major review of their information systems.

After two years, the payoffs were impressive. Major benefits of the new program included:

- **Immediate access to order status** Upon inquiry, it was possible to check order status immediately. In the past salespeople had to check with the plant, then make the long distance calls back to the customer. With the new system, what used to take an hour now takes only a minute or two.

- **Increase in salesperson effectiveness** Rather than constantly having to answer customer questions about order status, salespeople could spend their time selling. In addition, data available on inventories and customers enable salespeople to make "cold calls" more effectively.

- **Improved understanding of the customer** SOS could do a much better job of analyzing customer-order patterns and adjusting production schedules to those patterns.

- **Improved inventory control** Slow-moving items could be identified and moved out more quickly than in the past. In general, there was better control with fewer errors than with manual systems.

- **Improved production scheduling** One SOS manager commented, "The system allows us to foresee problems and react to them sooner. Before, we never knew where we would be in the future until we were there."

- **Reduction in plant personnel** With the introduction of the system, management was able to reduce staffing with no decrease in performance.

Box 20-2

Common Terms in the Computer Industry

ASCII This acronym (pronounced ask-ee) stands for the American Standard Code for Information Interchange. All computers store information in the form of a sequence of zeros and ones (see bit), so a code is needed to represent the numbers and letters. Most computer systems use the ASCII code.

Bit The smallest piece of information stored in a computer. All computers store information as a sequence of zeros and ones. A bit is a single zero or one.

Byte Computers generally group bits together into bytes for processing. The number of bits per byte varies from machine to machine. Many machines use eight bits per byte.

Cathode ray tube (CRT) A television-like screen used to communicate with the computer. The CRT almost always is accompanied by a keyboard, and perhaps other input devices (see mouse) for input. The CRT is also known as a terminal or a monitor.

Floppy disk A form of random-access memory, generally used in personal computers. Floppy disks can be inserted into and removed from the computer.

Hard disk A form of random-access memory built into the computer. Hard disks are used in large mainframe computers as well as personal computers. Hard disks generally hold much more information, and are much faster than floppy disks.

Hardware The physical mechanism, the machinery, of the computer.

Kilobyte (KB) Shorthand for 1,024 bytes. The capacity of storage devices and internal memory is often measured in kilobytes.

In addition, improved information led to sharper focus from all management on the few important things they must do well. They understood the business better, and could see how various parts of the enterprise interrelated. ▼

BASICS OF COMPUTERIZED INFORMATION SYSTEMS

Now that you have seen the potential of computer-based information systems, it makes sense to review some terms and concepts important in that field. Box 20-2 reviews some terms common in the computer industry.

Megabyte (MB, meg)   Shorthand for 1,024,000 bytes. Used to measure the capacity of computer memory and storage devices. Hard disks used for personal computers generally have at least 20MB of storage, while floppy disks generally come in capacities of 364KB to 1.44MB.

Microprocessor   The "brains" of the personal computer. The component that physically performs mathematics and exercises logical choices. The microprocessor also handles internal memory allocation, and retrieving and storing data from and to internal memory.

Modem   Short for "modulator, demodulator." A device to translate the electrical signals used inside of the computer to a form suitable for transmission on telephone lines, then back to computer format at the other end of the line.

Mouse   An input device for working with CRT terminals. A mouse, when moved over a desktop, causes an indicator on the CRT (a cursor or insertion point) to move in a similar direction.

Printer   A device to print output from a computer.

Random access   Able to get any piece of data from any point in a file. Floppy and hard disks are random access devices.

Sequential access   Able to get a specified piece of data only by reading all records before the desired data. Magnetic tape is a sequential access device.

Software   The instructions (programs) that enable computers to do useful work.

Data Storage in Computerized Systems

One of the most obvious differences between computerized and manual systems is the form in which data are stored. In a manual system information is stored on paper. Paper records are easy to read and understand, and it is a simple matter to visualize information flows by simply following each piece of paper through the system. In computerized systems, on the other hand, data must be stored in a form the computer can read. Over the years several different methods have been used to store computerized data. We will briefly review the most common methods of data storage, and then make some general comments about computer storage.

PUNCHED CARDS   In the 1950s and 1960s, data were generally stored on cards. Each alphabetic letter and numerical digit was represented by a pattern of punched

In the 1950s and 1960s the prevalent method of storing computerized data was by punched card.

holes that could be read by appropriate machines. Punched cards could also be read by people if required, and could be organized into files that would be stored in cabinets, much as manual records were stored. Cards were inexpensive, could be readily duplicated, and could be sorted to meet different needs.

Punched cards suffer from several disadvantages, however. They are easily damaged by heat, humidity, or careless handling. They are heavy, and take up a good deal of storage space. Machines that punch and read cards are large, slow, and relatively prone to breakdowns and errors. Finally, a punched card file can only be read sequentially. If the 5,000th record were needed, the only way to get to it is to read through the first 4,999 records.

Despite these problems, punched cards were the dominant method of storing information for many years, and are still found in some applications today.

MAGNETIC TAPE   Magnetic tape is a much more rugged and efficient medium than punched cards. Information that would fill several thousand punched cards can easily be stored on one reel of tape. Not only is it easier to store large amounts of data, but easier to transport it as well. A reel of tape can be carried or shipped to a distant location, say from branch plants to central headquarters. In addition, tape can be written to and read much faster than can cards. Since most business processing requires reading and writing vast volumes of data, increases in reading and writing speeds are critical to overall processing times. Tape is also very inexpensive, thus it remains in wide use even today as a means of storing large data files.

A major psychological problem in moving from punched cards to tape is that there is no longer a visible physical record for each data item. With cards there is a card representing each data item, but with tape the data appears to disappear into the computer, to reappear only when computer programmers and operators do their magic. The problem is compounded by the fact that "computer people" are not like ordinary managers. They do not come up through sales, production, or accounting, they use their own computer language, and they seem to spend most of their time telling us that simple information is either impossible to get or will cost several times more than we think it should. These issues also exist with punched cards, of course, but card systems seem to be somewhat less threatening to most managers.

There are more substantive disadvantages to tape. First, tape, like cards, is a sequential medium. The only way to read a tape file is from the beginning, reading each record in order. There are some limited methods for accessing tape files nonsequentially, but the physical characteristics of tape make it most suited for sequential files. Second, even though tape is more rugged than cards, it can still be damaged. If the damage is caused by electric or magnetic fields, it can easily go undetected until the tape is used.

MAGNETIC DISKS   A **magnetic disk** is a platter, shaped much like a phonograph record, coated (usually on both sides) with magnetic material. In use, a read/write head is moved to the proper position on the disk to read or write data. Thus, data can be read from the disk in any order we wish. A magnetic disk is a **random access** device, in contrast to punched cards and magnetic tapes, which are **sequential access** devices.

Through the 1960s and 1970s, disks were expensive relative to magnetic tapes and punched cards. However, prices have fallen dramatically in the past decade, and disks have come into wide use.

Disks and disk drives vary widely in cost and capacity. Floppy disk drives used in personal computers retailed for less than $200 in 1987, while the floppy diskettes themselves can be purchased in quantity for about $1. At the other extreme, disk drives used in mainframe computers cost as much as several hundred thousand dollars. Large drives such as these consist of several disks stacked on a common spindle that rotates rapidly. Since dust and smoke particles are large enough to plug the microscopic gap between the disk surface and the read/write head, drives are housed in sealed cabinets to avoid possible damage.

Historically, the major disadvantage of magnetic disks was cost, but current technology has advanced to the point that even very large data files can economically be kept on disk. Disks are not particularly damage prone, but modern disk drives store so much data that when there is a problem it is usually disastrous. Thus, good computer systems management requires that key data be copied, or backed up, frequently. Then if a problem does occur the files can easily be reconstructed from the backup data.

INTERNAL MEMORY   Although magnetic disks allow random access to data and have become relatively inexpensive, they are still slow compared to the internal computation speeds of most computers. Thus, nearly all computers also use **internal**

The random-access capability and cost-effectiveness of magnetic disks has led to their enormous popularity today.

memory (also called core memory) that works much faster than even the fastest mechanical devices. The computer reads a large block of data from a tape or a disk drive into internal memory, then does the processing for the entire block. In the meanwhile, another block is being read and stored in another section of internal memory, so it is ready when the first block is finished. In this manner the relatively slow speeds of disk and tape drives do not slow the computer too much. Internal memory formerly consisted of tiny magnetic donuts (cores, hence the term core memory) strung on fine wires, but this type of memory was extremely expensive. Currently, most internal memory is made of silicon semiconductor chips. Such memory chips can be made cheaply, and can pack incredible amounts of information in tiny bits of space.

OTHER DATA STORAGE DEVICES   In a field that is changing as rapidly as computers, it is hard to predict which new technologies will rise in the future. The most promising new data storage device at the moment is the optical disk. Like magnetic disks, optical disks are random access devices, but can store much more data than magnetic disks. One particular optical disk can store 256 megabytes, as much as 328 high-density floppy disks. The contents of a small library can be put onto a single compact disk, making this technology an ideal one for storing very large sets of data.

The primary historical disadvantage of optical disks is that they could not be erased and rewritten. However, this disadvantage has now been overcome. Some optical disks have been developed that can be written to once and then read as many times as wished (these are sometimes referred to as WORM disks—Write Once & Read Many times), and other technologies have been developed for erasable and reusable disks.

Continual advances in semiconductor technology are bringing the prices of internal memory lower and lower. As this trend continues, computers will undoubtedly have ever larger amounts of internal memory available. Such devices as tapes and disks will still be needed for permanent data storage, but may well become relatively less important as more and more data can be kept internally.

Other Components of Computerized Systems

So far, we have discussed only some of the components of a computer system, namely external storage devices and internal memory. Figure 20-1 indicates how these components are related to each other and to other parts of the computer system—the processor and communications devices.

THE PROCESSOR   The processor is the part of the computer that actually performs arithmetic. The processor contains the necessary electronics to add, subtract, and compare numbers, and special methods for multiplying and dividing. Modern computers use instructions, called a **program**, which tell the processor where to find data in memory, how it should be manipulated, and where results should be stored. For example, a program for processing a customer order record might contain the following steps:

1. Read the customer record into memory. Check the customer number against an active customer file to make sure that the number is valid, and that the customer's credit record is acceptable. If there is a problem, generate appropriate error messages and go on to the next customer.
2. Read the information on the first product. Make sure that the product number is a valid number, and that the price information is correct.
3. Multiply the amount ordered by the price per dozen to compute the total price.
4. Update records for this product number on the total amount ordered, and the colors and sizes ordered.
5. Update inventory records kept by product, size, and color, and if inventory is getting too low, generate a warning message for management attention.

Figure 20-1
Computer Components

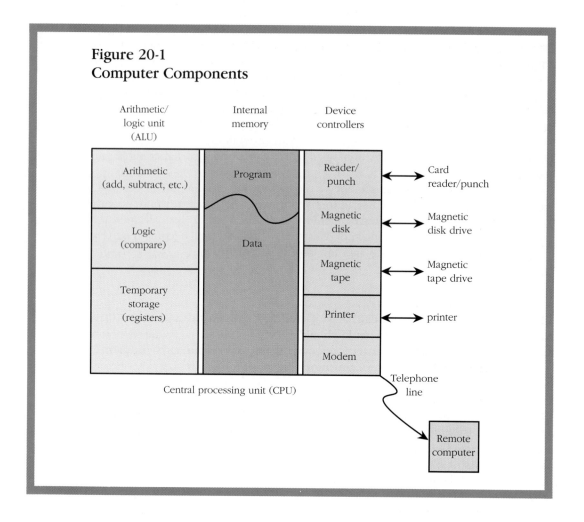

6. Update sales records for the customer.
7. Check to see if there are more products on the order form. If there are, return to step 2. If there are not, then compute the total price of the order, and print instructions to the shipping department to select and ship the order.

It is worth noting two important facets in the program outlined above. First, we are using the information on the order form to update at least three files—sales records by product, inventory records, and customer sales records. In addition, customer files and product files are used to check for possible errors and problems. In general, it is easy to set up programs to use and update several sets of records at the same time.

Second, the program uses a limited set of instructions to process large volumes of information. Steps 2 through 6, for example, are used to process each line of the order in turn. Rather than writing separate instructions for each line, we simply check in step 7 to see if there are more lines. If there are, we cycle through the identical steps to process each one. Likewise, we can process any number of customer orders by repeating steps 1 through 7 over and over. When step 7 is completed, we check to see if there are more orders to be processed. If there are, we go to step 1. If there are not, the computer can go on to other tasks. Programming loops, such as these, allow computers to process large amounts of data with simple sets of instructions.

COMMUNICATIONS DEVICES   Obviously the processor cannot do any useful work unless it can communicate with the external world. Data storage devices, which we have already examined, allow computers to communicate information to and from records and files. There are several other types of communications devices that are found in modern computer systems.

Terminals, usually cathode ray terminals (CRTs) look like small television sets. Terminals usually have keyboards as well, so they are used as both input and output devices—they can both display information and serve to enter data. When entering data on customer orders, for example, the terminal can display a form showing the information to record. Entering data is then just a matter of filling in the proper blanks. The computer can also check the information being entered for errors. Customer and style numbers, for example, should match valid numbers on file. The computer can be programmed so that the customer name and address is displayed as soon as the customer number is entered. It is quite easy then to verify whether the number is correct.

Some companies use optical character readers or magnetic character readers for data input. These technologies allow computers to read paper documents directly, bypassing the expensive and error-prone step of having an operator key in information on a terminal or other device. For example, bank checks are preprinted with numbers identifying the customer and the bank.

Printers are the most important output devices of a computer system. Often the packing slips that accompany customer shipments are printed by the computer. So are the invoices, bills, and checks mailed to customers and suppliers. Management uses printed daily summaries of order trends and inventory status for production planning and order shipping. Although many computer systems allow managers to retrieve information on a terminal, the vast majority of the information that is so vital to management in running an efficient business comes in the form of printed reports.

Printers are made in several price and speed ranges. Inexpensive printers might cost a few hundred dollars and be capable of printing one or two hundred characters per minute. Other machines cost hundreds of thousands of dollars, are capable of printing in any of several type sizes and fonts, and can print as fast as 25,000 lines per minute.

Voice synthesis is gaining popularity as an output device in some applications. For example, computers are frequently used to give the telephone numbers in directory assistance services.

Modems are not devices to allow computers to communicate with people, but to allow computers to communicate with each other over telephone lines. To transmit data, a computer sends information to a modem that translates the electronic signal to a form that can be sent over the telephone system. At the receiving end, another modem retranslates the telephone signal to the form the computer needs for internal processing. Modems also check for transmission errors and perform other "house-keeping" functions to make sure the signal is transmitted correctly.

Personal Computers

Until the 1980s computers were large, complex, and expensive. They required special cooling and air filtration. These considerations, plus the need for security, meant that computers were kept in specially built, central locations, and that separate data processing departments were generally responsible for operating and programming. There are several advantages to this arrangement that still hold true. In addition to the considerations mentioned above, centralized control encourages consistency and compatibility throughout the organization. The central staff can ensure that information from different parts of the company are stored consistently, so different departments can readily exchange data. New computing equipment will be purchased with an eye toward compatibility with existing systems. A central staff can design and enforce methods for ensuring data security.

However, centralized computer control has disadvantages too, primarily lack of responsiveness. Getting a new report designed and programmed could take weeks or months; this is terribly frustrating to an operating manager who needs answers immediately. The development of the **personal computer**, a desktop-sized machine costing a few thousand dollars, has opened new worlds in information processing. Managers can now have individual, personal machines with capacities significantly higher than mainframe computers of only twenty years ago.

The revolution in hardware has been accompanied by a revolution in software. Personal computer software falls into six major categories:

Word processing   Word processing is similar to typing, but with a major difference. A word processing program allows users to store, edit, and modify, as well as type documents. Modern word processors check spelling and even grammar, can use different type styles and sizes, and can incorporate charts and graphs, so even formal reports that once required professional typesetting can be composed and printed on word processors. **Desktop publishing** is a term used to describe computer packages with sophisticated layout and typography capabilities.

Spreadsheet analysis   A computer spreadsheet is an electronic version of an accounting pad. The spreadsheet is organized into rows and columns. Any cell, where a row and column intersects, can be used to hold numeric or alphabetic information. The electronic spreadsheet has easy-to-use and powerful methods for manipulating information entered into cells. The power and ease of using spreadsheets have made them useful in many areas. There are important applications in accounting and financial analysis, but spreadsheets are also used for inventory control, questionnaire analysis, mathematical modeling, data storage, and countless other applications. The development of VisiCalc, one of the earliest modern spreadsheet packages, is widely credited with creating the personal computer boom.

Data base usage Several powerful data base programs currently exist for personal computers, enabling these machines to keep track of information in a flexible and powerful format. Colleges and universities use data base programs on personal computers to maintain student and alumni records. Other businesses use them to track production information, customer and sales records, financial information, and other vital data.

Communications By using the appropriate software and hardware, computers can communicate over telephone lines. This provides a convenient and inexpensive method of sharing data among divisions or companies, but also opens worlds of wider possibilities. Several hundred private computer bulletin boards have sprung up across the country, offering programs, information, idea exchange, and several other services. Some for-profit bulletin boards offer extensive information services—indices and copies of newspapers and magazines, up-to-the-minute financial information, information search services, and similar data.

Graphics Personal computers are frequently used to produce attractive, sophisticated charts, graphs, and other visual aids. Many software packages have the capability of producing "slide shows," whereby several graphs are shown in sequence on the computer monitor. Nearly all graphics packages can use data from the most popular spreadsheets, and most spreadsheet programs also have at least rudimentary graphics capabilities.

There are other software categories as well, some of which are in wide use. For instance, there are several commercial programs to do project management, computer-aided-design and drafting, and accounting.

As liberating and productive as the personal computer has been, it also has problems. Security can be much more difficult. Important or confidential data can easily be copied or erased from personal computers. Human and mechanical failure can destroy vital records, and without strong central control, keeping good backup records is very much a hit-or-miss proposition. With the proliferation of machines and software on the market, maintaining compatibility across organizations is becoming difficult. If all managers and departments are allowed to make their own choices, it may become impossible to exchange information. Maintenance and training can also become unnecessarily expensive. It may also be difficult to ensure that computer purchases make sense. Personal computers have become status symbols, and some managers may want them even if there is no need for them.

The solution to most of these ills is to set up a central group to set standards for purchase, training, and use of personal computers, and to develop lists of approved hardware and software. However, this fights against some of the very freedoms that make the personal computer so attractive. On the balance, though, the alternative to strong central direction may be chaos.

Other Information Technologies

While computers form the basis of the information revolution, several other developments also are having an important effect on the way we work and manage.

Artificial intelligence (AI) refers to methods of teaching computers to "think." In reality computers do not think, of course, but merely follow specified instructions very rapidly. However, if the instructions are complex and complete enough, computers can appear to learn, exercise judgment, and show other "intelligent" characteristics.

AI has found several useful applications in medical diagnosis. Suppose you are a pediatrician, and have just finished examining Tammy Jones, an eight-year-old girl with a fever and sore throat. Your physical examination reveals that Tammy's fever is 102 degrees, she has been sick for one day, and that her older brother was down for a few days last week with the flu. Her throat is very red and obviously sore. What do you do next?

There are several possible causes for the sore throat. If Tammy has a strep throat—one possibility—you should start her on penicillin immediately. But she might be allergic to penicillin. What do you do then? It is also quite possible that she does not have a strep throat at all, and that her infection is caused by a virus. In that case penicillin would be of no help at all, and you should prescribe children's aspirin, rest, and plenty of fluids. There are other, less common, possibilities you also have to consider in diagnosing and treating Tammy.

Even for such a common and simple illness as this, it is difficult to decide how best to treat a patient. Suppose Tammy had a rare and potentially very serious illness. Clearly it is a difficult task to keep physicians fully informed of all the diseases in the world, particularly ones they may see only once or twice in their professional lives. AI could be of help if we could capture the methods expert physicians use in diagnosing and treating illnesses. However, most experts cannot fully explain how they reach decisions, so it takes a good deal of observation and interviewing to build a successful AI application. In those cases where the effort has been made, though, results can be impressive. Several medical AI systems have been developed that consistently outperform all but the best doctors in working with several types of diseases. AI has also been used to capture the knowledge of experts in maintenance, process design, and several other specialties.

The Office of the Future

The technology now exists to allow offices to be run virtually without paper. Personal computers can be linked together into networks, so people could examine central files or files of co-workers at the touch of a button. Reports and presentations can be presented on personal computers or computer terminals, in many cases much more easily and flexibly than in paper reports. Transactions with banks and customers can be made using current telecommunications hardware and software.

The so-called "**paperless office**" or "office of the future" has fascinated management thinkers for several years, and some parts of that potential have in fact been realized. Telecommuting, where an employee works at a computer at home connected to a central office, has emerged as a viable method of work for some people, particularly computer programmers and some clerical personnel. A good deal of banking and financial information is currently exchanged electronically between banks and client companies, yielding hundreds of thousands of dollars in additional interest earnings in some cases. However, a truly paperless office still remains a dream.

SYSTEMS DESIGN

The hardware discussed above forms the building blocks for a computerized information system. In systems design, we address the task of how the blocks should be put together to form a workable system—one that will handle the current needs of the company, that can grow and change as needs change, and that will make it easy to prevent and correct errors. Systems design is an art as well as a science. To do a good job, the systems designer must consider what computers, file storage, and communications devices are available, what level of expertise is available in the company, what costs the company can afford and justify, the kind of information management currently uses and will be likely to use in the future, and company size and growth. To illustrate the steps of successful systems design, we discuss a simplified version of the system that the Malouf Company designed and implemented.

System Goals

Malouf management began with only a strong feeling that it was time to upgrade from a manual to a computerized system. They were not entirely sure what a new system could do for the company, except that it would be faster.

The systems study began by documenting the current manual system. How were data gathered? What files were kept and why? What management reports were generated, and who did they go to? Most important, why were the reports generated? What decisions did they address, and how did the information help in managing the company? This part of the study served two major purposes—to document the parts of the system that were working well that should be preserved in the new system, and to encourage managers to think about their jobs and their needs.

System design is the process of determining the computer needs of a business.

In most companies payroll and accounting systems are among the first functions to be computerized since they are well-defined, standard applications. Malouf management guessed, before the study began, that these areas would probably be their first priorities as well. However, as the study progressed, it became increasingly obvious that the payroll and accounting systems were *not* the major problems in Malouf. In thinking through their problems, management came to the consensus that their needs should be ranked as follows:

Inventory status by size, style, and color   If Malouf ran out of even one popular size in one color for a style, either the production manager would have to schedule a new production run, or the style could no longer be sold through normal channels. In the latter case, all remaining stock would have to be sold as broken stock at substantially reduced prices. Unfortunately, new production runs were often impossible to schedule at the last minute because the style would often be seasonal, so even a few weeks delay in shipping would mean deliveries too late for the season. In addition, popular fabrics and trims were often in short supply. However, if a daily inventory report were available, some discretion could be used in most customer shipments to keep the stock in balance.

Sales figures by style, size, and color   The marketing manager, production manager, and president generally decided on production volumes and color mixes several months before customers started ordering. With their extensive experience in the industry they generally did an excellent job of guessing sales right on the money. However, every sales season seemed to bring its share of surprises too. One particular style of slacks, for example, started to sell very well in black and blue, but not at all in rust. Even as the early sales were coming in and the trend became apparent, Production was busy scheduling the final runs of rust-colored slacks. Malouf's manual system, which produced sales reports only monthly, was just too slow to adjust production plans in time. The president estimated that out-of-date information cost the company over $60,000 in this one instance alone.

Automate customer ordering, shipping, and billing systems   In order to accomplish the major goals listed above, it was clear that Malouf would have to enter all customer order information into the computer. It would then take very little extra effort to automate ordering, shipping, and invoicing totally.

Accounts receivable system   Malouf's major customer is the J. C. Penney Company. Penney stores order individually. The billings for each order are then consolidated by region by Penney's, so that when a check arrives it covers several individual orders. Malouf employed several clerks who did nothing but match checks with bills to make sure that payments were made correctly. In addition to being tedious and time consuming, this was a difficult job since returns, shipping charges, and similar incidentals also had to be accounted for.

Accounting   With the exception of Accounts Receivable, the accounting system was working well and generating reports in a timely manner. Although a computerized system would make life easier for the company accountants, the part of the system was not costing the company money through poor information. Thus, upgrading accounting systems received lower priority.

Payroll   Similar to accounting, a new payroll system would be useful, but the current system worked, was reliable, and was causing no major management problems.

Before continuing with Malouf's experience, let us summarize some general lessons. Note that systems design begins by defining managers' information needs. That requires managers to think about their responsibilities afresh—a process many people find difficult to do.

At Malouf, systems design began by documenting the current system, questioning the value of each report in the process. This was a useful method to get people to think constructively about information needs, but other approaches are also possible. Interviews, brainstorming sessions, examination of past management misjudgments—all are useful ways to define possible system goals.

System Output

The second step of a systems study is to define the **system output**—those reports that will address system goals. For Malouf, six reports were needed to address the first four goals defined above (the fifth and sixth goals were deferred until a future date).

Inventory status report   This report would report the amount of inventory left to be sold for every style. The report would show the total number of units left, the number of units of each color, and the breakdown of units left by size for each color. The data must be kept up-to-the-minute so management could use a CRT to get the latest status any time they wished. In addition, a summary report would be produced each week. The report could also be printed at any other time if needed.

Sales summary report   Incoming sales would be reported by style, by color within style, and by size breakdowns within color. As with the inventory status report, these data must be kept current so management could track sales at any time, either through a CRT or through special requests for printed reports. Again, a summary would be produced weekly.

Marketing felt that the raw sales data would be much more useful if they were somehow tracked over time so trends would be apparent. Many of Malouf's styles were sold only for a single season—for those styles a summary line was added that showed percentage breakdowns by color and size for the latest full day, the latest week, and total sales to date. For those styles that were sold for extended periods of time, breakdowns were provided for the latest full day, the latest week, and the latest month. The various summaries could easily be scanned for significant changes over time.

Summary of inventory versus sales   Since the major purpose of the inventory and sales summaries was to spot inventory imbalances, Marketing and Production felt that it would be extremely useful to have a report directly comparing the two. This report showed sales percentages by color and size for each style, and directly below showed both the number and percentage of each color and size in inventory. As with the inventory and sales summaries, this report was available at all times, and was routinely printed out weekly.

Customer orders   To automate the ordering system, the system would have to print copies of the customer order, after first checking to make sure that enough inventory was on hand and adjusting for items that could not be shipped. Styles ordered should be rearranged in a convenient sequence for pulling from inventory, and notes would be needed on items that were not in inventory and thus either could not be shipped or would be shipped later. The customer orders would obviously be printed daily, or perhaps even twice daily in order to even the workload in shipping.

The shipping department would then add information on shipping costs and dates after they had assembled and shipped the order. This information could be entered on a CRT terminal as each order was completed. The updated order information could then be used to prepare invoices and bills.

Accounts receivable summary and receivables analysis   Customer orders could be used as the basis for analyzing accounts receivable. A report showing outstanding bills, identified by customer and order number, would be needed weekly. The system would have to be able to credit payments against the proper outstanding invoices, allowing for such complications as returns, over- and undercharges, and penalty charges on late payments.

In addition to this detailed information, Malouf's accountant needed a Receivables Analysis—a summary of the total bills outstanding and information on how many were overdue. A monthly printout of this information would be adequate to collect overdue accounts and to project Malouf's cash needs.

Again, before proceeding with Malouf's story, let us pause to summarize some lessons. System goals are fulfilled by information in the form of reports. At this point we need not be concerned about the detailed appearance of the reports, but only what information is on them, and how frequently they will be needed. As we see from the Malouf case, reports sometimes contain only raw information—as in the inventory status report or the customer order. More often, reports also summarize historical trends or other comparison measures—as in the sales summary report. Many reports, such as the summary of inventory versus sales or the accounts receivable summary, pull together summary data, perhaps from different sources.

It is important to think about how each report will be used in order to define useful ways of summarizing and comparing information. The difference between data and information is that information is directly useful in making decisions, while data are simply the raw material from which information is derived. A good system eases the manager's job by providing information instead of simply data.

Designing the Data Base

System outputs cannot be computed unless the necessary data are stored in files. There are many different ways of structuring and organizing files; the decisions made at this point have a profound effect on the cost and time of producing various reports, and on future capabilities of the system. It is at this point that the systems designer must start making serious tradeoffs among cost, complexity, and capability.

To illustrate why file design decisions are so important, suppose a company decides to have a file of incoming customer orders, and decides to organize it in the following manner:

- Each record in the file will contain all the information on one customer order.
- The file will be stored on magnetic tape, sequenced by order date.
- Each new customer order will simply be added on to the end of the file.

This file structure has several advantages. It is simple, uses inexpensive and reliable storage devices, and is easy to back up. It is easy to update and maintain. Separate reels of tape could be used for each week's or each month's orders, making it simple to keep track of historical data. Finally, the file is perfectly adequate for many purposes, such as printing shipping and billing instructions.

In other ways, however, this file structure is inadequate. For example, suppose a customer calls with an inquiry about order number 12345, which was entered last Wednesday morning. Since the file is stored on magnetic tape—a sequential medium—the only way to find order 12345 is to mount the tape and read through every file until the proper one is found. If the file were stored on magnetic disks—a random access medium—then we could go directly to the proper record without reading everything that comes before. Thus, the choice of storage media has an important effect on the cost and ease of data retrieval.

In the example above we assume that we know the order number, and that the file is organized by order number. We say that order number is the key to the file. However, if we want to retrieve data by, say, style number rather than order number, we have a problem. We might simply search the entire file to find the order(s) for each style. Even at computer speeds this is expensive and time consuming, but if we retrieve data this way only rarely, it might be a reasonable choice.

Another option would be to construct a second file, this one organized by style number. This method obviously wastes a good deal of file space with duplicate information, but we can make matters somewhat better if one of the files does not need to store everything. For example, the style number file might contain only total sales by date and omit information on the customer. Duplicate files are also harder to maintain. Each incoming order now updates two separate files, and we must take care to ensure that information stays consistent between the two. For example, suppose there is a computer breakdown halfway through the file update. Is it possible to update one file and not the other? If so, we must provide methods to detect and correct the difference. What about data entry errors, cancelled orders, and orders that were refused because of a customer's poor credit record? We must make sure that both files are corrected in each case.

A third alternative is to set up a single file with both order numbers and style numbers as keys. There are several ways to do this. For example, we might have the computer construct an index relating order numbers to style number. For each style, the index would show all orders which specified that style. This method can also take a good deal of file space, but not as much as having duplicate files. It would also take longer to retrieve style data under this method than with duplicate files. To get the information for style number 6789, we would have to find and read the index for this style, then retrieve and summarize the appropriate information from each order number found in the index. Updating and maintaining the index also adds cost and complexity to the system, although not as much as maintaining duplicate files.

Yet another option is to design a data base to hold this and other information. As mentioned earlier, data bases allow systems designers to combine separate data files in one overall structure, and to specify several access keys to the data. In effect, data base design makes all the information in the data base accessible in many different ways. Although the design of data base systems is extremely complex, systems designers can use data base management systems to simplify the job. However, using a DBMS can still exact a significant penalty in the speed of the computer system.

Which of these methods is best? Unfortunately, there is no easy answer, and the systems designer must weigh such factors as expected file size, capacity and cost of different storage media, and the types of information management will want from the data. This is why it is so important to get a good handle on system outputs before we deal with file design. However, the analyst must also plan for growth, must provide room to add new customers and new methods of doing business, and try to anticipate the kinds of information management will need in the future. Once the corporate data are loaded into a particular file structure, it is very expensive to change it. The company will probably have to live with these files for several years.

Hardware and Software

When we reach this point, the major system design decisions have been made. Now we must decide on the computer equipment (**hardware**) we will need, and purchase or write the computer programs (**software**) needed to make the system work. Some hardware decisions come from the preceding steps. For example, the data design might require magnetic disks to store certain system files. However, the systems designer must examine such measures as the number of transactions expected per day, the number of files expected on the system, and the amount of historical data to be kept in order to decide the capacity needed in the hardware, and the number of terminals, disk drives, and printers needed.

Software also has to be designed and written. For example, suppose a company needs a program to read customer orders and to update the customer order and sales by style files. Suppose further that data entry clerks will enter customer orders at CRT terminals. The terminal should show a form with blank spaces where data should be entered, so the clerk simply fills in the form. In writing this program the programmer must know such details as how the entry form should be laid out. Since form layouts can affect how easy the system will be to use, management must remain closely involved with design work throughout this process.

Several other crucial design decisions must be made before programming can be completed. For example, the customer order form must show the customer's name and address. Unfortunately, some names and addresses are much longer than others. How much space should we allow for these data in the computer data file? Excessively large allowances waste too much file space, since we must provide the same amount of space for everyone, but small allowances require us to abbreviate or truncate long names and addresses. Is this acceptable to the customer? If the complete address cannot be entered, can we still deliver packages and mail to the correct location?

Another option might be to allow customer order records to be of different lengths. Note that some customer orders ask for only one product but others might request twenty, thirty, or even more individual products. Rather than allowing a fixed amount of space for information on products, we might be better off to have a variable length record so we could include information on precisely the number of products ordered. Variable length records are harder to store and manage efficiently, but are justified in such cases as these.

Even though it is not as exciting to make decisions on form design, field lengths, and whether records should be fixed or variable length as it was to think through system goals and system output, these issues are also crucial. Poor forms and records design can make a system clumsy, error prone, and difficult to work with. Management needs to pay as much attention and effort to these phases as the earlier ones in order to get an effective system.

What Happened at Malouf

Having lived with the Malouf Company through much of this chapter, you might be curious about the eventual outcome. There are also some additional lessons we can learn from their remaining experiences.

Malouf management devoted substantial time and effort to defining system goals and system output. Rather than trying to deal with the remaining technical issues themselves—file design, record layout, and so forth—Malouf management decided to turn to outside professionals. The company prepared a detailed document summarizing the system goals and output, outlining the current numbers of transactions processed and expected file sizes, and other pertinent data relating to the proposed systems design. This information was then sent to several companies specializing in **turnkey** computer systems, with a request for a bid on the system.

The term "turnkey" indicates that the outside firm takes full responsibility for hardware and software design and integration. In effect, they contract to deliver a complete system, ready to run, to the client. The client just needs to turn it on to be ready to go.

Some months later, after several conferences with potential bidders, Malouf received four serious bids. Total costs ranged from $128,950 to $205,000. One bidder proposed writing all the necessary software from scratch, so that the system would be custom-designed to meet Malouf's needs. Another bidder planned to use standard manufacturing systems software. There is a good deal of appeal to using standard software packages. They are already written, are nearly always cheaper than custom-written software since development costs are shared among several users, and are relatively free of errors, while with custom-written software one is almost sure to find several errors over time, some of which can be extremely serious. Furthermore, Malouf's information needs are not unique. Most manufacturers need to process customer orders, examine sales trends, and balance inventories, much as Malouf does. If Malouf's information needs are close enough to what is commonly seen in the industry, a standard package might be adequate.

Upon investigation, several important differences between clothing manufacturing and other manufacturing became obvious. Most manufacturing companies make a relatively small number of final products, but might use several levels of components, subcomponents, and sub-subcomponents to do so. In the clothing business, on the other hand, each style, color, and size combination is considered a separate product—which they are from a sales standpoint. Clothing manufacturers make an enormous number of final products but use only a limited number of raw materials—fabrics, thread, and trims—to do so. Thus, file and data structures appropriate for traditional manufacturers proved inappropriate for Malouf's needs.

Two bidders proposed using prewritten software packages designed specifically for clothing manufacturers. Both packages had been written from scratch several years ago by companies in Malouf's position. In the intervening years the packages had been refined and corrected, and the companies were now recouping part of their programming investment by selling the software. Malouf management spent several weeks investigating one of the packages. They were able to see a demonstration of the programs in operation, visit companies using it, and discuss technical matters with people knowledgeable with the industry. They found that the package satisfied each of the system goals, and went beyond Malouf's original planning in several areas. Malouf was impressed with the software design, the hardware package which would accompany it, and the support and service offered by the vendor. This system was purchased for $172,780.

After the first year of operation, the president reported that the system was working well, particularly in satisfying Malouf's original goals. There had been several implementation problems. For example, cables linking remote terminals to the computer had been stapled to the walls. The staples had damaged the wires inside the cables so that communication between the computer and the terminals was difficult and error prone. Another problem was that there was not enough magnetic disk space on the original system, and Malouf had to invest several thousand dollars in additional drives. Overall, however, the president felt that the move to computerization was timely, well thought out, and unquestionably successful. Company officials saw fewer inventory errors, stronger sales due to better inventory balance, and significantly better performance in the accounts receivables area. Estimated savings and additional profit were large enough that the computer system easily paid for itself in the first year of operation.

ENDING CASE
Mrs. Fields Cookies

A well-designed information system can open entire areas of possibility for a company. Mrs. Fields Cookies uses computers to monitor hourly sales progress in each of nearly 500 stores, and to make suggestions to improve performance. The computer forecasts sales, sets up production schedules, and serves as a communications center between each store and company headquarters. The computer suggests crew schedules, and helps schedule maintenance. Computers are even used to help interview and select employees, then to take care of the paperwork involved in adding new people! Clearly there are innovative and productive uses of computer systems that many companies barely even dream of.

Debbie Fields, 31, and Randy Fields, 40, run Mrs. Fields Cookies, of Park City, Utah. By the end of 1987 they projected that their business would run nearly 500 company-owned stores in 37 states and five other countries. Sales were $87 million in 1986, up from $72.6 million a year earlier.

Won't the cookie craze pass? people often ask Debbie. "I think that's very doubtful . . . I mean," she says, "if [they are] fresh, warm, and wonderful and make you feel good, are you going to stop buying cookies?"

Perhaps not, but the trick for her and her husband is to see that people keep buying them from Mrs. Fields, not David's Cookies, Blue Chip Cookies, The Original Great Chocolate Chip Cookie, or the dozens of other regional and local competitors. How do you keep cookies consistently warm, fresh, and wonderful at nearly 500 stores? Even more difficult, how do you keep nearly 4,500, mostly young, employees happy, productive, and honest?

On a typical morning, Richard Lui, who runs the Mrs. Fields store on Pier 39 in San Francisco, unlocks the store, then calls up the Day Planner Program on his Tandy computer, plugs in the day's sales projection, and answers a couple of questions the computer puts to him. What day of the week is it? What type of day: normal day, sale day, school day, or holiday? The computer then reviews historical data, and suggests what he will have to do today, hour by hour, product by product, to meet sales goals. It tells him how many batches of cookie dough he will need to meet demand and minimize leftovers. Each hour, as the day progresses, Lui keeps the computer informed of progress. The computer revises projections and makes suggestions on selling more effectively.

Several times a week Lui talks to Debbie Fields through a computerized message center. By the same token, if he has something to say to the boss, he calls up the system, types his message, and it is on Debbie's desk the next morning. Lui's computer also helps him with the following:

- Schedule crews, based on expected volume and productivity standards.
- Interview job applicants by having them work through a set of questions on the computer, then having the machine compare this person with prior applicants.
- Generate the personnel file, payroll entry, and remind Lui to do periodic evaluations for new employees.
- Help to repair broken machinery, by first going through a checklist with Lui to make sure the problem is not something simple, then for difficult problems, by keeping a maintenance history of the machine, generating repair requests, referring the problem to local vendors, and eventually paying the vendor's bill.

This is a lot of technology for a cookie store. Yet, in these and other ways, computer technology helps to multiply people's effectiveness, and to maintain control as business expands.[4]

SUMMARY

Information is an important competitive tool in modern management, and companies that have access to timely, accurate, detailed information have a major advantage over those that do not. The process of designing an information system begins with a definition of the information needs of the organization. The information needs determine what data is required and how it should be organized. Information systems can merely record and report transactions, can be structured as management information systems, or as decision support systems. Each layer offers additional management support and functionality.

In computerized systems, data can be stored on several different media, some are accessed sequentially and some randomly. Access method profoundly affects system design and data structures. Other major computer system components include the processor and several communications devices, notably terminals and printers. Personal computers have become increasingly important the past decade, and are now common in business. Several current technologies seem likely to affect office methods in the future.

Computer hardware and software components are assembled into systems. In systems design, management must work with technical experts to set up file structures, office procedures, and report strategies to accomplish work efficiently and accurately. There are several basic approaches to doing most jobs, and initial design decisions are critical in the flexibility, speed, and performance of the final system.

KEY TERMS

Information systems
Data versus Information
Accurate, timely, and complete
Input
Control
Memory
Output
Transaction reporting systems
Management information system
Data base management system
Decision support system
Magnetic disks
Random access
Sequential access

Internal memory
Program
Personal computer
Desktop publishing
Artificial intelligence
Paperless office
System goals
System output
Hardware
Software
Turnkey

REVIEW QUESTIONS

1. Why are information needs defined before designing an information system?
2. Of what importance is the identification of information that management wishes it had in the design of an information system?
3. What records can be abstracted from a customer order?
4. Of what importance is how files and records will eventually be used to their design?
5. What is the difference between data and information?
6. What deficiencies of manual systems do computer systems correct?
7. What deficiencies of punched cards are corrected by magnetic tape?
8. What deficiencies of punched cards are also possessed by magnetic tape?
9. What is a magnetic disk and what major access problem does it solve? What disadvantages does it possess and what trend is eliminating this disadvantage?
10. What operations does a computer perform in processing data?
11. What are the most important computer communications devices and why are they important?
12. Of what importance are system goals, output, and data base design to the design of a computerized information system?
13. What are some of the problems in designing a file structure and what relationship does file structure have to the data base?
14. What concerns are of importance before a decision is reached to make duplicate files in a data base system?
15. What are some of the advantages of customized software? When would customized software be more advantageous than commercially available software packages for certain applications (such as accounts receivable and billing packages)?
16. What are "turnkey" computer systems?

CHALLENGE QUESTIONS

1. What advantage does more accurate, up-to-date information present to organizations that have access to it?
2. How is a computer system better able to give a business information than a manual system?
3. How does a computer turn data into information? What impact does systems design have on this process?
4. What factors are important in deciding what type of printer to buy for a computer system?

5. What records and reports are commonly computerized? Should a firm computerize these items first? Why or why not?

6. Compare systems goals for a computer system with the mission statement of an organization. How do systems goals drive the operation of the system?

7. What factors would you consider in deciding whether to purchase a standardized software package versus a customized package?

8. What are the advantages of random access versus sequential access?

9. Given the dynamic nature of the computer industry, what factors should management consider when considering sources of supply for hardware and software? How do considerations such as compatibility and the ability of the operating system to facilitate communication within the system come into play?

10. What weight should a business firm give to the ability of its computer system to communicate with those of suppliers and customers?

CASE AND RELATED QUESTIONS

1. What information needs did Malouf's manual information system fail to supply? How did computerization help?

2. How was Malouf able to utilize customer orders to fulfill its own information needs?

3. What role did video display terminals have in Malouf's system?

4. What six reports did the Malouf management obtain from their new system? Were these choices wise uses of the resources available? Justify your answer.

5. What process did Malouf use in deciding on a software package? How was the company's final decision arrived at?

6. What services would you look for in a company providing turnkey computer installations? What kind of company are turnkey operations best suited to and why?

ENDNOTES

1. Charles Wiseman and Ian C. MacMillan, "Creating Competitive Weapons from Information Systems," *The Journal of Business Strategy*, Fall 1984.

2. Michael E. Porter and Victor E. Millar, "How Information Gives You Competitive Advantage," *Harvard Business Review*, July–August 1985.

3. John F. Rockart and Adam D. Crescenzi, "Engaging Top Management in Information Technology," *Sloan Management Review*, Summer 1984.

4. Tom Richman, "Mrs. Fields' Secret Ingredient," *Inc.*, October 1987.

PART VI

THE CHALLENGE OF THE FUTURE

CHAPTER 21

INTERNATIONAL DIMENSIONS OF MANAGEMENT

LEARNING OBJECTIVES

■ Develop an understanding of the wide range of challenges faced by the international manager.

■ Describe the ways that a business can become involved in international trade.

■ Understand how external environmental factors influence managerial decisions.

■ Describe the basic types of political and economic systems.

■ Understand the effect that differences in the human environment can have.

■ Describe some basic strategies for pursuing foreign trade.

■ Describe some basic global production strategies.

■ Understand the requirements for management success in an international business.

As war swept across Europe in 1939, Tom Bata had an important decision to make. His father, of the ninth generation of a family of shoemakers in Czechoslovakia, had built a worldwide shoe network in 28 countries, using machinery and the mass production technology of the 1920s. But now Tom was left with the responsibility of expanding that empire during a period of great uncertainty in the world. Because of the invasion of the Nazis and the uncertain future that occupation held, Bata took 100 Czech families and emigrated to Canada in order to preserve his father's business in a land of freedom.

Since that time, Bata's decision has been ratified through strong growth worldwide. Bata, Ltd. is a family-owned business that operates around the globe. Its production facilities produce hundreds of millions of shoes annually, and those shoes generate over $2 billion in revenues through sales in 6,000 Bata-owned retail outlets and 125 independent retailers in 115 nations. Its 85,000 employees work in over ninety factories and five engineering facilities, as well as the retail operations mentioned above. Bata's influence is so pervasive that it makes and sells one out of every three shoes manufactured and sold in the noncommunist world. In fact, the word for shoe in many parts of Africa is "bata."

Bata, Ltd. tends to operate as a decentralized operation that is free to adjust to the local environment, within parameters. Tom Bata travels extensively to check on quality control and to ensure good relations with the governments of the countries where Bata, Ltd. operates.

Although Bata, Ltd. has factories in more than ninety countries and operations of one form or another in over 100, it does not own all of those facilities. Where possible, it owns 100 percent of the operations. In some countries, however, the government requires less than majority ownership. In India, 60 percent of the stock of the local Bata operations trades on the Indian stock exchange, and in Japan, Bata, Ltd. owns only 9.9 percent of the operations. In some cases, Bata, Ltd. provides licensing, consulting, and technical assistance to companies in which it has no equity interest.

Bata, Ltd.'s strategy for servicing world markets is an interesting one. Some multinational businesses try to lower costs by achieving economies of scale in production. That means that they produce as much as they can in the most optimal-sized factory and then service markets around the world from that single production facility. Bata, Ltd. tries to service its different national markets by producing in a given market nearly everything it sells in that market. Part of the reason for this strategy is that Bata, Ltd. can achieve economies of scale very quickly, since it has a fairly large volume in the countries where it produces.

This may seem difficult to believe, especially when Bata, Ltd. has production facilities in some African nations where it is the only industry. However, Bata, Ltd. feels that it can achieve economies of scale very easily because it is a labor-intensive operation. Bata, Ltd. also tries to obtain all of its raw materials locally. This is not possible in some cases, especially in some of the poorer developing countries. However, it tries to have as much value-added as possible in those countries.

Another of Bata, Ltd.'s policies is that it prefers not to export production. It prefers to use local production to service the local market. Obviously, that rule is not a fixed one, since the company produces in only 90 countries but has distribution in over 100 countries. Sometimes, Bata, Ltd. runs into trouble with local governments when it imports raw materials but does not engage in exporting. Then it has to adjust to the local laws and requirements for operation.

One of the reasons why Bata, Ltd. avoids excessive reliance on exports is because of the risk. If an importing country were to restrict trade, Bata could possibly lose market opportunity and market share. In addition, Tom Bata noted the benefit to the developing country of not exposing itself to possible protectionism:

> We know very well what kind of a social shock it is when a plant closes in Canada. Yet in Canada we have unemployment insurance and all kinds of welfare operations, and there are many alternative jobs that people can usually go to. In most of the developing countries, on the other hand, it's a question of life and death for these people. They have uprooted themselves from an agricultural society. They've come to a town to work in an industry. They've brought their relatives with them because by working in industry their earnings are so much higher. Thus, a large group of their relatives have become dependent on them and have changed their lifestyle and standard of living. For these people it is a terrible thing to lose a job. And so we are very sensitive to that particular problem.

Bata, Ltd. operates in a variety of different types of economies. It has extensive operations in both the industrial democratic countries and in the developing countries. It has been soundly criticized (as have been most multinational businesses) for operating in South Africa and thus tacitly supporting the white minority political regime, and it has also been criticized for operating in other totalitarian regimes such as Chile. Bata counters by pointing out that the company has been operating in Chile for over forty years, during which a variety of political regimes have been in power. In 1986, however, Bata sold its South African operations to foreign investors. The Bata name and trademark will not be used by the new investors. A Bata spokesman said that the pullout was a result of adverse economic conditions in South Africa rather than apartheid, per se.

Although Bata's local operations have not been nationalized very many times, the company has had some interesting experiences. In Uganda, Bata's local operations were nationalized by Milton Obote, denationalized by Idi Amin, renationalized by Amin, and finally denationalized by Amin. During that time the factory continued to operate as if nothing had happened. Tom Bata's explanation for finally being left alone is that

> shoes had to be produced and sold, materials had to be bought and wages paid. Life went on. In most cases, the governments concluded it really wasn't in their interest to run businesses, so they cancelled the nationalization arrangements.

In spite of Bata's ability to operate in any type of political situation, Tom Bata prefers to operate in a democratic environment. He feels that democracies and totalitarian regimes both have bureaucracies, but in a democracy there is the potential to discuss and possibly change procedures. In a totalitarian regime it is sometimes wise not to say anything.

The impact of Bata, Ltd. on a country is multifaceted. The basic strategy of the company is to provide footwear at affordable prices for the largest possible segment of the population. So a basic product is being provided. It could be argued that the product is a necessity rather than a luxury. The production facilities are very labor-intensive, so jobs are created, which tends to increase the purchasing power of the economy. Although some top levels of management may come from outside of a country, there is a tendency to train local management as quickly as possible so that they can assume responsibility. Because the company tries to get most of its raw materials locally, suppliers are usually developed. Since Bata, Ltd. likes to diversify its purchases, it usually develops more than one supplier for a given product, leading to competition and efficiencies.

Bata, Ltd. usually brings in its own capital resources when it starts up a new operation, but it is also adroit in utilizing international capital markets. On more than one occasion, Bata, Ltd. has utilized the resources of the International Finance Corporation (IFC), a division of the World Bank that provides development financing for private enterprise projects in developing countries. One of Bata's most recent attempts at IFC financing was to expand a tannery in Bangladesh. The importance of getting IFC support is that Bata, Ltd. would be much more likely to attract other debt and equity capital once it had received IFC approval. All of the five previous Bata projects supported by the IFC have been successful, and the loans have been paid back. ▨

INTRODUCTION

The Nature and Scope of International Business

International business is defined as including all business transactions that involve two or more countries. These transactions can involve private businesses or those owned by governments. As noted in the Bata, Ltd. case, those transactions can occur in a variety of ways and in different types of economic and political environments.

A major problem for managers trying to manage a firm like Bata is that they are required to operate over great distances. It is one thing to oversee operations in the Canadian province of Ontario and quite another to monitor operations in India and Brazil. In spite of the distance problems, managers are better able to cope with the

International trade, such as with Hong Kong, challenges managers to understand the geography, political structure, and culture of a foreign country.

complexities because transportation has become quicker and communications—especially by satellite—allow managers to communicate with each other more easily.

The improvement of transportation and communication has also resulted in competition becoming truly global. For years, General Motors' major competition was Ford and Chrysler. Competition is now defined in terms of Toyota, Nissan, and Hyundai. New products can become global much more quickly than previously, firms can shift production from country to country, and new technology and ideas flow much more quickly.

The international challenges of the manager are interesting, because they draw on so many different disciplines. Because resources are not distributed evenly from country to country, it is important for the manager to understand world geography. History is another critical discipline, because it helps the manager understand the forces of society and the reasons why society reacts as it does to the foreign investor or foreign business person. Because the world is made up of nation states, the manager must have a good understanding of political science. Recent events in the Philippines, South Korea, and South Africa demonstrate how important it is to monitor political trends. Culture describes the values, attitudes, and beliefs of a people and influences nearly everything that a manager must do. Because cultures vary so much from country to country, the manager must be sensitive to these cultural differences.

Ways of Operating Abroad

MERCHANDISE TRADE   There are a variety of ways that firms can become involved in international business. Some of them require a commitment of capital abroad, whereas others do not. The first way that a firm usually becomes involved in international business is through exporting and/or importing. Merchandise exports are tangible goods that visibly leave a country, whereas merchandise imports are tangible goods that visibly enter a country. Merchandise flows constitute the largest volume of international transactions in the United States, with exports totaling $320 billion and imports totaling $446 billion in 1988.[2]

SERVICES TRADE   A second major way to become involved in international business is by providing a service abroad or receiving the benefit of someone from abroad performing a service for your firm. The service sector includes public utilities; communications; transportation; finance, insurance, and real estate; wholesale and retail trade; government; and other services (such as business services like advertising, public accounting, and legal work; personal services; and health services).[3] Although the service sector dominates the U.S. economy (67 percent of gross domestic product versus 22 percent for manufacturing and 11 percent for agriculture, mining, and construction), it is not quite as important in international trade. In 1988, service exports were $188 billion, and service imports were $183 billion.[4] It is more difficult to measure service transactions, however, so the numbers could be understated significantly. It is interesting to note that service transactions are called "invisibles" by economists and statisticians.

The payments for the performance of services are known as "fees." There are other forms of services income, however. For example, some firms will allow a foreign manufacturer to use a patent or a production process and will collect a royalty payment. The agreement that results in royalties being paid for the use of trademarks, copyrights, patents, or other know how is called a licensing agreement. It is a good way for a firm to become involved in international business without risking capital in a foreign location. A specialized form of a licensing agreement is a franchise. Fast-food companies such as McDonald's, Kentucky Fried Chicken, and Wendy's set up franchises abroad just as they do in the United States by providing a trademark, food components, and management services.

Construction firms will often design, build, and put into operation a sophisticated facility abroad for a foreign investor. The specific type of contract for that activity is called a turnkey contract, and the construction firm will generally collect a fee for the service.

Many hotel firms, such as Hilton or Marriott, will enter into a management contract to manage a hotel property in a foreign country for a local investor. The management contract will result in a management fee being paid to the hotel firm. These examples of merchandise and service exports and imports are just some of the ways that firms can get involved internationally without risking capital abroad.

DIRECT AND PORTFOLIO INVESTMENT   Many firms have decided that merchandise and services trade is not enough of a presence abroad. As a result, they decide to commit significant resources by investing overseas. If the investment is designed for a financial return without any management activity, it is called a **portfolio investment**. That would be similar to an individual buying some shares of stock in IBM in order to receive dividends and a capital appreciation in the stock. However, the individual is not really interested in running IBM. Securities in foreign companies are attractive because of their high returns and/or increase in the value of the securities over time. In addition, investors sometimes feel that they can diversify the risk in their investments by investing abroad where economies might not be affected in the same way as the U.S. economy.

A more significant form of investing abroad is known as **direct investment**. In this case, it is assumed that the investing company is devoting significant resources in order to gain some degree of management control. The motivations for direct investment will be discussed later in the chapter. However, when Ford opens a new plant in Europe and provides the capital for that plant, the investment is called a direct foreign investment.

Direct investment usually implies that the foreign investor organizes a corporation under the laws of the country in which the investment is located. The degree of investment is determined by the percentage of the shares of stock that the foreign investor owns. A wholly owned subsidiary is basically a corporation of which 100 percent of the stock is owned by the foreign investor. Sometimes, a foreign investor may not own 100 percent of the shares of stock. This could be due to government regulation, a desire to spread around risk or a lack of sufficient investment capital. If two or more organizations share in the ownership of the investment, the new firm is known as a joint venture. If one of the partners happens to be a government-owned firm, the new firm is known as a mixed venture.

MULTINATIONAL ENTERPRISE   In reality, firms that cross national boundaries usually become involved in international business in a variety of different ways. In fact, they usually get involved in everything—importing and exporting goods and services, entering into contractual relationships, and investing abroad, either alone or in combination with another firm.

A **multinational enterprise** (MNE) has a worldwide approach to foreign markets and production and has an integrated global philosophy encompassing both domestic and overseas operations.[5] MNEs are also known in the popular press as multinational corporations (MNCs) and transnational corporations (TNCs). There are a number of different kinds of business firms, such as public accounting firms, that are not corporations but operate all over the world. Thus the term MNE is slightly broader than MNC. The term TNC was coined by the United Nations and refers to firms owned and managed by nationals in different countries. However, that term is not used as much in popular discussion as is MNC.

An MNE cannot be precisely defined. However, its attributes can be described in such a way as to make it easily understood.[6] It may be obvious that IBM is an MNE, whereas the local hardware store is not. Why is that the case? First of all, an MNE must operate in a variety of different economic settings. Typically, an MNE must have operations in more than one country. The more countries in which a firm has operations, especially if those countries are in different types of economic environments, the greater the challenge to management and the more management is influenced by conditions beyond the domestic setting.

In addition, an MNE typically devotes a significant amount of its resources abroad. It should have more than 10 percent of corporate sales, earnings, assets, or employees abroad. Some feel that this degree of commitment should be even higher, for example 25 percent. However, the key is that significant resources must be at risk in the international environment.

It is obvious that operating in several different countries and investing significant resources to international operations implies that an MNE must have management that has a truly international attitude. An MNE is more than a domestic firm with an international hobby. Management must consider the entire world as a source of raw materials and components, a location for different aspects of the production process, and a market for final goods. The mentality of management of an MNE is very different from that of a predominantly domestic firm. In addition, an MNE will eventually end up with a management that is itself multinational, drawing on the best talent from around the world.

POLITICAL AND ECONOMIC ENVIRONMENT

It is obvious that management plays a key role in the success or failure of a firm. As managers travel from country to country, they find that it is not possible to do everything the same way in every country. Some practices have to be modified, others totally eliminated and replaced by what works in the specific country. The key for any manager is understanding the nature of the environment sufficiently to make the right decisions that will make the firm successful.

An Environmental Assessment Matrix

Farmer and Richman developed a framework that illustrates how external environmental factors (constraints) influence managers to change ways in which managerial decisions are made in order for the firm to be successful.[7] The framework is a matrix with critical elements of the management process on the vertical axis and environmental constraints on the horizontal axis. The elements of the management process are planning and innovation; control; organization; staffing; direction, leadership and motivation; marketing; production and procurement; research and development; finance; and public and external relations.

The environmental constraints, which are really the subject of this part of the chapter, are grouped into four categories: educational characteristics, sociological (or sociocultural) characteristics, political and legal characteristics, and economic characteristics. The educational characteristics include the level of literacy, the availability of specialized and higher education, the attitude toward education, and the education match with skill requirements in the economy. Sociocultural characteristics include the view toward managers and authority, interorganizational cooperation, the view toward achievement and work, class structure and individual mobility, the views toward wealth, rationality, risk taking and change.

Among the major political and legal characteristics are the relevant legal rules of the game and flexibility in their application, defense and foreign policy, political stability, and political organization. Key economic characteristics are the general economic framework, fiscal and monetary policy, economic stability, capital markets, factor endowments, and market size.

In Figure 21-1, these constraints are labeled C_1 (educational), C_2 (sociocultural), C_3 (legal-political), and C_4 (economic). The basic idea behind Figure 21-1 is that management operating in the home country makes operating decisions as influenced by the environmental constraints in that country. Any firm, domestic or foreign, needs to be aware of those constraints. When operations are set up in a foreign country, the constraints change. There may be economic constraints in both the home and foreign country, but those constraints may be different. For example, one of the economic constraints is the general economic framework. A firm that has operated in Hong Kong and decides to set up operations in Brazil will find a vast difference in the economic systems. Hong Kong is the epitome of free enteprise, whereas firms operating in Brazil are subject to significant government intervention. Thus, Hong Kong management would have to make some adjustments to management style to account for the different economic system in the foreign country.

The value of the framework is to allow management to anticipate ways that the environmental constraints might influence managerial decisions. The problem is that Farmer and Richman identified over 2,000 possible cells in their matrix of elements in the management process and environmental constraints. Thus, management needs to develop a feel for elements in the management process that are most important to the success of the organization and the aspects of the environment that could have the greatest influence on those elements.

As noted in Figure 21-1, there is also a list of international environmental constraints. Each country has its own unique set. Firms that cross national boundaries must adjust to the new set of environmental constraints in the host country. However, the mere crossing of boundaries introduces a different set of international environmental constraints. The sociological constraints (I_1) include national ideology, the view toward foreigners, and the nature and extent of nationalism. The attitude toward investments by U.S. MNEs may be very different in the United Kingdom than it would be in Iran. Important legal-political constraints (I_2) are relevant legal rules for foreign business, import-export restrictions, international investment restrictions, profit remission restrictions, and exchange control restrictions. Economic constraints (I_3)

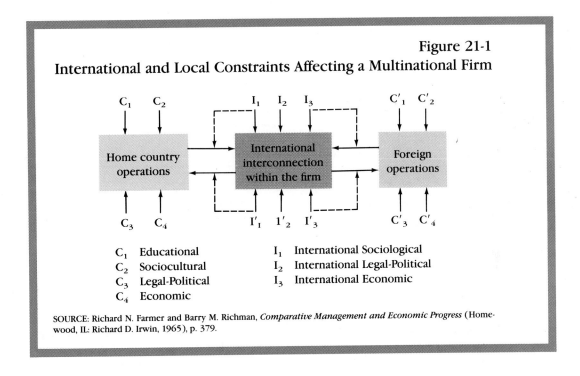

Figure 21-1
International and Local Constraints Affecting a Multinational Firm

C_1	Educational
C_2	Sociocultural
C_3	Legal-Political
C_4	Economic

I_1	International Sociological
I_2	International Legal-Political
I_3	International Economic

SOURCE: Richard N. Farmer and Barry M. Richman, *Comparative Management and Economic Progress* (Homewood, IL: Richard D. Irwin, 1965), p. 379.

include the general balance of payments position, international trade patterns, and membership and obligations in international financial organizations.

These constraints will exist for each country where a firm might set up operations, and the constraints differ country by country. It is obvious from this discussion that operating in different countries is complex and that anticipating variables or constraints that could influence management decisions is no easy matter. However, the Farmer-Richman matrix is useful in trying to identify the key interrelationships that might determine success or failure.

Political Systems

There are three major world economies in which the MNE may operate successfully. The First World is made up of the nonsocialist industrial countries, the Second World consists of the socialist countries, and the Third World is comprised of the developing countries. These three broad classifications will be broken down more finely in a later section of the chapter, but their general classification is useful for our purposes. The important thing to understand is that in each of these three worlds, there exists different political and economic systems, different levels of economic development, and a

Figure 21-2
The Political Spectrum

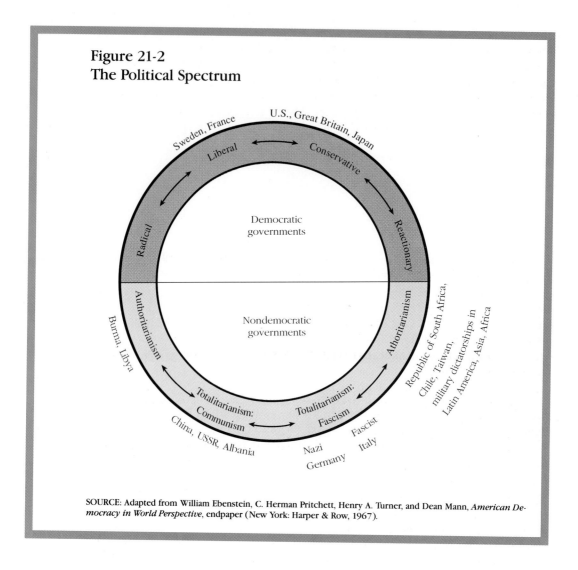

SOURCE: Adapted from William Ebenstein, C. Herman Pritchett, Henry A. Turner, and Dean Mann, *American Democracy in World Perspective*, endpaper (New York: Harper & Row, 1967).

variety of economic conditions. It is important for the MNE to analyze the interaction of its policies with these different political and economic conditions if it is to be successful.

A political system is designed to integrate the society into a viable, functioning unit. Most societies are pluralistic, that is different ideologies are held by numerous segments of the society rather than have one ideology held by everyone in the society. An example would be Angola. Three different ethnic and political groups formed a coalition government after independence from the Portuguese in 1975. However, the coalition broke apart shortly as the different factions refused to support each other. Italy is an industrial country comprised of many different political parties and is governed by compromise rather than clear consensus. The government is constantly being reorganized in an effort to build majority coalitions.

The two extremes in ideology are a democracy and totalitarianism. In a **democracy**, citizens are involved in the decision-making process through direct vote or elected representatives. In a **totalitarian** system, a single party, individual, or group of individuals holds a monopoly of political power and does not recognize or permit opposition. The opportunity to participate in decision making is restricted to a few individuals. Figure 21-2 illustrates the political spectrum that managers are faced with as they move from country to country.

Economic Systems

The economic system of a country is concerned with allocating scarce resources among competing users and involves two important matters: the control and coordination of resources and the ownership of property. Control and coordination is usually viewed in terms of a market economy on the one hand and a command economy on the other. Property can be owned by individuals in the private sector or by the government. In real life, it is difficult to look at any of these dimensions as discrete events. Instead, management needs to view them as a range or continuum in which all four elements are presented in various degrees. Figure 21-3 illustrates the different ways elements can interrelate with each other.

In a **market economy**, resources are owned and products consumed by individuals, whereas resources are used and products produced by firms. In a true market economy, there is little or no intervention by government in the exchanges that take place between firms and individuals. Some would point to Hong Kong as the ultimate market economy due to the lack of government intervention and control.

At the other end of the spectrum is the **command economy**. In this situation, the government harmonizes the activities of different economic sectors by setting goals, deciding prices of products to be sold and the quantity of goods to be produced. In essence, the individual has little or no say in what is produced and sold. At the same time, individual firms have no control over what is produced and sold either.

On the ownership side, property can be owned by governments or individuals in the private sector. Government ownership is especially helpful when governments also want to coordinate and control decisions made in the economy. However, countries basically adhering to a market economy can also have government ownership of some resources, such as utilities or housing. Government ownership can be justified on the basis of national security or the desire to promote the common good, especially of the economically disenfranchised. However, private ownership of resources is usually associated with a market economy since firms and households must have the freedom to determine prices.

It has been interesting to see how different countries have resolved the interrelationship of ownership and control in their own economies. Each country is unique, even though it may have elements similar to other countries. The U.S. often complains

Figure 21-3
Interrelationships between Control of Economic Activity and Ownership of Factors of Production

Control \ Ownership	Private	Mixed	Collective
Market	A	B	C
Mixed	D	E	F
Command	G	H	I

Control ownership	Control ownership	Control ownership
A. Market-Private	D. Mixed-Private	G. Command-Private
B. Market-Mixed	E. Mixed-Mixed	H. Command-Mixed
C. Market-Collective	F. Mixed-Collective	I. Command-Collective

SOURCE: John D. Daniels and Lee H. Radebaugh, *International Business: Environments and Operations*, 5th ed. (Reading, MA: Addison-Wesley, 1989), p. 42.

about heavy government intervention in the economy of Japan, whereas Hong Kong complains about the same issue when dealing with the U.S. Korea and Taiwan are two Asian countries that are industrializing at a rapid rate, but the governments deal with business in fundamentally different ways. The Korean government takes an active role in encouraging the development of large firms able to compete in world markets. The Taiwanese government takes more of a hands off approach that leans towards the Hong Kong model rather than the Korean model. The People's Republic of China is a strongly Marxist economy with heavy government ownership and control, but it is experimenting with significant decentralization of decision making and more private ownership of resources in some sectors of the economy. The Soviet Union, on the other hand, is still a traditional Marxist central command economy. Efforts to change the direction of the economy have met with significant resistance on the part of the entrenched bureaucracy.

Regional Economic Integration

A major hindrance to management of a global enterprise is the existence of national boundaries. Not only do laws and customs often differ in different countries, but restrictions usually exist on the movement of goods, services, people, and financial capital. As a result, it is difficult for a firm to achieve economies of scale in production. In order to counteract some of the barriers resulting from national boundaries, many countries have tried different forms of economic integration in order to abolish economic discrimination.

The most basic form of **economic integration** is the free trade area, which results in the elimination of tariffs on goods moving between countries. The European Free Trade Association, comprised of Austria, Finland, Iceland, Norway, Sweden, and Switzerland, is an example of a group of countries operating as a free trade area. A customs union combines the features of a free trade area with a common external tariff. That allows countries to decide on a unified policy toward the outside. The European Community (EC), also known as the European Economic Community, has taken the customs union concept one step further by forming a common market. The members of the EC are Belgium, Denmark, France, Greece, Ireland, Italy, Luxembourg, The Netherlands, Portugal, Spain, the United Kingdom, and West Germany. A common market builds on a customs union by allowing factor mobility—primarily capital and labor. In addition, the EC tries to formulate a harmonious economic and social policy.

When there are barriers to trade, consumers are forced to buy primarily locally produced goods, and producers are forced to serve the relatively small local market. Regional economic integration, however, results in having resources flow to the most efficient producers. Consumers are also allowed to purchase goods from participating countries at more competitive prices. As market size grows, firms are allowed to achieve economies of scale and therefore be more competitive worldwide.

Classification of Countries

As mentioned earlier, countries are often classified as First World, Second World, or Third World. However, this simple designation has tended to obscure complex relationships. As a result, the World Bank has refined its definitions. Table 21-1 illustrates those categories. First World countries are also known as industrial market economies. These are basically the industrial countries of Canada, the United States, Australia, New Zealand, and Western Europe.

Second World countries are more accurately described as East European nonmarket economies. Countries outside of East Europe that espouse a nonmarket economic approach are listed in other categories.

Table 21-1
World Bank Country Categories

INDUSTRIAL MARKET ECONOMIES*		
Australia	France	New Zealand
Austria	Iceland	Norway
Belgium	Ireland	Spain
Canada	Italy	Sweden
Denmark	Japan	Switzerland
Federal Republic of	Luxembourg	United Kingdom
Germany	The Netherlands	United States
Finland		

NONMARKET ECONOMIES		
Albania	Czechoslovakia	German Democratic
Angola	Democratic People's	Republic
Bulgaria	Republic of Korea	Mongolia
Cuba		Soviet Union

LOW-INCOME ECONOMIES
1985 annual per capita GNP of $400 or less

MIDDLE-INCOME ECONOMIES
1985 annual per capita GNP of $401 or more

The developing countries or Third World countries are broken down into several other categories. It is interesting to note that the presence or absence of oil seems to be the key that divides countries of the Third World into different categories. High-income oil exporters are countries with per capita incomes high enough to classify them as industrial countries. However, the one-dimensional nature of the economy is such that a separate classification seems more meaningful. Most of those countries are members of OPEC (Organization of Petroleum Exporting Countries).

The remaining countries are divided into low-income economies and middle-income economies. The low income economies have a per capita income of less than $400 per year. Although a list of countries is not provided in Table 21-1, the countries tend to be from Asia, Africa, and Latin America.

The middle-income countries are divided into net oil exporters and oil importers. Many of the net oil exporters are members of OPEC, but their per capita income is not high enough for them to be included in the high-income oil exporter

HIGH-INCOME OIL EXPORTERS	OIL EXPORTERS	EXPORTERS OF MANUFACTURES
Bahrain	Algeria†	Brazil
Brunei	Cameroon	China
Kuwait†	Congo	Hong Kong
Libya†	Ecuador†	Hungary
Qatar†	Egypt	India
Saudi Arabia†	Gabon†	Israel
United Arab Emirates†	Indonesia†	Republic of Korea
	Islamic Republic of Iran†	Poland
	Iraq†	Portugal
	Mexico	Romania
	Nigeria†	Singapore
	Oman	Yugoslavia
	Peru	
	Syria	
	Trinidad and Tobago	
	Venezuela†	

*These twenty-one countries plus Greece, Portugal, and Turkey comprise the Organization for Economic Cooperation and Development (OECD).
†Members of the Organization of Petroleum Exporting Countries (OPEC).
SOURCE: *World Development Report, 1987* (New York: Oxford University Press, 1987).

category. The oil importers are divided into those that are major exporters of manufactures and others. The exporters of manufactures are emerging developing countries that have diversified their production base rather than rely on a single crop or resource as is so often the case with the other developing countries. The countries in that group are also known as NICs (newly industrialized countries).

The developing countries present interesting challenges and opportunities. The challenges lie in the nature of the environment. Each of the constraints in Figure 21-1 could be discussed at length in terms of the problems for the manager of an MNE. However, the critical ones seem to be political and economic. Some of the most common problems that surface in the developing countries are hyperinflation, severe debt burdens, weakening currencies leading to currency controls, a shortage of skilled workers, political instability, war and insurrection, poverty, and weakening commodities prices. However, the major opportunity lies in the size of the market. The population of the industrialized world is less than 800 million, whereas the combined population of the low- and middle-income developing countries surpasses 3.5 billion. The population of the Third World is also increasing at a faster rate than that of the industrial world. Thus, the opportunities for production and marketing are infinite, even though they need to be tempered by the problems raised above.

Management Challenge and Opportunity

A manager that goes from an industrial market economy to a low-income developing country or an East European nonmarket economy is going to face some interesting challenges. Management practices need to be altered in order to adapt to the different social, political, and economic environments. The shift from Illinois to Iowa is not going to be as severe as the shift from Illinois to India. However, goods can be produced and sold in any economic environment. It would be good for the manager to answer some of the following questions:

1. What is the political structure of the country?
2. Under what type of economic system does the country operate?
3. Is my industry in the public or private sector?
4. If it is in the public sector, does the government also allow private competition in that sector?
5. If it is in the private sector, is there any tendency to move it toward public ownership?
6. Does the government view foreign capital as being in competition or in partnership with public or local private enterprises?
7. In what ways does the government control the nature and extent of private enterprise?
8. How much of a contribution is the private sector expected to make in helping the government formulate overall economic objectives?[8]

This last question is especially significant to the situation in developing countries. They are very sensitive to the impact of foreign investment and whether or not that investment is congruent with national goals.

THE HUMAN ENVIRONMENT

The essence of success for any manager is people. This book is based on the fact that people—both inside and outside of the firm—need to be molded and adapted to in order for the firm to succeed. In the international setting, the people issue becomes very complex. The human aspect can be viewed as physical and demographic on the one side and behavioral on the other. The concept of the nation-state implies that people are somehow different from one nation to another. Those differences are caused by geographic and economic barriers as well as linguistic, religious, and ethnic differences. However, these barriers and differences also occur within nation-states, which complicates the task of the manager even more. The manager of a manufacturing facility in West Germany, for example, might be confronted by workers from West Germany, Turkey, and Yugoslavia on the same shift.

Demographic Differences

Demographic differences are often divided into three different categories: population growth rates, education, and age distribution. It has already been alluded to earlier that population growth rates are higher in the developing countries than in the industrial market countries. Advances in medicine have helped reduced death rates, whereas cultural attitudes toward large families have not changed as quickly. Thus, population growth has become a significant issue in the Third World. It should be noted that there is substantial disagreement over the seriousness of population growth. Many experts feel that population growth is essential to economic growth. However, there is clear agreement that there are pockets of population growth around the world, such as Mexico City, that are creating serious social and political problems.

A second important dimension of human demography is education. Literacy rates vary widely around the world. Even in the Third World, for example, there are significant differences. In Zaire, only 54.5 percent of the population above the age of 15 is literate, compared with 92.6 percent in Argentina. The literacy level influences the nature of the work force as well as how a business reaches the consumer. In many countries, the level of education is not very high, and there tends to be a mismatch between the type of education people are receiving and the skills needed to make the economy grow.

A final demographic issue relates to the age distribution of the population. Economies with low rates of growth in the population tend to have an older population. Countries with rapid growth rates tend to have a younger population, which leads to a dynamic population.

Behavioral Differences

The culture of a country is based on attitudes, values, and beliefs. It is crucial for management to understand the nature of a country's culture and how that influences the management process.

People are arranged in countries by groups determined by birth based on sex, family, age, caste, and ethnic, racial, or national origin. Some group affiliations are made because of a conscious effort to join, such as religion, political affiliation, and associations. These groups, whether by birth or by choice, may reflect an individual's access to economic resources, power, and prestige. For example, blacks in South Africa have no political power and little economic power when compared with whites. Women in Saudi Arabia have very few economic rights compared with women in the United States.

Country attitudes vary significantly toward male versus female roles, the importance of youth versus older age, and the strength of group affiliations, such as the family. The manager needs to understand those relationships and take them into account, especially in the hiring process. Even if a person has the qualifications for a certain position, the manager needs to be aware of legal barriers for hiring as well as the more subtle cultural barriers.

Another important behavioral characteristic is the motivation for work. The reason for working and the relative importance of work among human activities may be explained largely by the interrelationship of the cultural and economic environment of the country in which one lives. The differences in motivation help to explain management styles, product demand, and levels of economic development. A number of studies have shown that there are significant differences among managers from different countries in areas such as achievement motivation, the importance of organizational goals, and the hierarchy of needs.[9]

Another area of frustration on the human side in international business relates to the importance of occupation. The feeling always is that the best people will gravitate to the best jobs. However, what is perceived as the "best job" in one country may not be the "best job" in another. In countries where the government plays an important role in the ownership and control of resources, good people may gravitate to the public sector. Private firms investing in the country may have trouble attracting the best people. There may also be a bias in favor of working for local firms rather than foreign firms. This can be seen in the Japanese environment where a lifetime linkage between the individual and a Japanese company is seen as important relative to the risks of working for a foreign firm that does not have the same attitude toward lifetime employment.

In some countries, workers are more self-reliant than they are in others. It is important for the manager to understand this attitude, especially when it comes to supervision. Autocratic leadership may be prized in Mexico or Malaysia, but that attitude would not go over well in the Scandinavian countries where a more consultative style is desirable.

A key cultural difference that influences managerial practices is communication. The most obvious communication difference is language. A common language can facilitate business ties significantly. It is no secret that language is an important reason why U.S. firms tend to invest in Canada and the United Kingdom before expanding into other countries. There are a number of countries that have serious internal difficulties because of language differences. The obvious example is India which has hundreds of languages and dialects. It also has a national language, but English tends to be the most common language because of the former colonial tie with Great Britain.

Even within the same language, such as English or Spanish, there can be significant differences in vocabulary from country to country. In contracts, correspondence, negotiations, advertisements, and social gatherings, a manager has to be very careful to ensure that what is intended is what is communicated.

In addition to the written and spoken language is the silent language.[10] Messages can often be transferred in things such as color, distance, time, and the status of the person. It is important to realize that these cues are perceived differently in different societies. A manager needs to be aware of the silent ways that communication takes place and the differences between what the manager is used to and what the local society perceives.

In spite of the many cultural differences that exist from country to country, cultures are becoming more similar than dissimilar. A big danger that a manager faces is to be so overwhelmed by cultural differences that he or she does not feel as if any management practices are transferable. This is the concept of polycentrism. If a company is too polycentric in its views, it stands the risk of being so overcautious that it shies away from certain areas or from transferring intact home country practices or resources that, in fact, may work well abroad. If an international firm is to have an advantage over local firms, it needs to do some things differently rather than simply conform to the national norm.

An equally dangerous attitude, however, is to be ethnocentric. Ethnocentrism describes the firm or individual so locked into the belief that what worked at home should work abroad that important cultural differences are ignored. A good international manager needs to follow a hybrid of home and foreign norms in order to adjust to the local environment but still introduce positive change. This may imply that change needs to occur more gradually in some countries, especially those with the greatest cultural differences from the home country of the investing firm. It is crucial to get local staff involved in the change process so that the manager can get some solid feedback on the potential impact of change and what is actually possible.

PENETRATING FOREIGN MARKETS

During the period of approximately 1500 to 1800, the dominant theory of economic activity between countries was mercantilism. The premise of mercantilism was that a country's wealth was dependent on its holdings of treasure, usually in the form of gold. Therefore, countries tended to restrict imports, subsidize exports, exploit colonies, and hoard gold. In the intervening years, however, imports have become strategically important, and firms have found ways other than the export and import of goods to become involved in international business. The purpose of this section is to examine a few of those strategies in more detail.

The Importance of Trade

Countries trade goods because of an absolute or comparative advantage that they have in production. **Absolute advantage** holds that different countries can produce different goods more efficiently than others. That advantage can be natural or acquired. A natural advantage refers primarily to climate and natural resources. Saudi Arabia has a natural advantage in the production of oil over Japan, and Honduras has a natural advantage in the production of bananas over Canada.

Acquired advantage implies that a country may develop an advantage in the production of certain goods due to product technology. Korea, for example, has become a key exporter of steel because of the application of new technology to its natural resources, especially relatively cheap labor. The theory of absolute advantage holds that countries would eventually specialize in the production of products for which they have a competitive advantage, and trade would result.

However, it is possible for countries to trade with each other even though they may not have an absolute advantage. That is because of the theory of **comparative advantage**. In that theory, countries tend to specialize in the production of products that they can produce most efficiently, even though they might not have an absolute advantage in the production of those products. The comparative advantage of a country is usually due to the abundance of certain factors of production. For example, a country with an abundance of cheap labor is usually better off producing labor-intensive products than it is capital-intensive ones.

There are a number of good reasons for exports to take place. Raw materials need to be exported to the manufacturer, components need to be exported to the assembly operation, and finished goods need to be exported to the consumer. Sometimes this process takes place within the confines of a vertically integrated company so that the exporter can sell directly to the next level through an intracompany transaction. However, the sale may be to an outsider. In that case the exporter may decide to sell directly to the buyer or indirectly through some sort of intermediary.

Firms often sell goods abroad because they need a larger market over which to spread costs. This may be because of high fixed costs or research and development costs—such as in aircraft production, large computers, or automobiles. The local market is just too small to achieve economies of scale. In other cases, firms sell goods abroad to get rid of excess production capacity. That is not a good long-run strategy, because the firm is not really looking at the global market as that important in overall success. Exporting is a good way to test a market without having to risk investing capital in that market. After seeing how the market reacts to the product, the firm can decide whether or not to expand production capacity in the home market to cover the expanded sales or to establish production facilities in the new market.

Many firms enter into exporting by accident rather than by design. When that happens, many problems often occur, and the firm may never get a chance to see how important exports could be. That is why it is important for management to develop a good export strategy.

Korea enjoys an acquired advantage in the production of steel due to low-cost labor.

EXPORT STRATEGY   The design of a strategy involves a series of steps. First, it is important for a firm to assess its export potential. That involves taking a look at opportunities and resources. It would not be a smart business decision to make commitments to export if the firm did not have the production capacity to deliver the product.

The next step is to select a market or markets. This step often occurs by default if the exporter is responding to requests from abroad that result from trade shows, advertisements, or articles in trade publications. However, it is important to pick a market or markets in which to concentrate sales.

Once the markets have been targeted and the decision has been made to expend corporate resources in the export effort, the firm should develop a more comprehensive market strategy involving export objectives, specific tactics that will be used, a schedule of activities, and the allocation of resources.

Finally, the firm needs to select a selling technique. The firm could sell directly to wholesalers, retailers, or consumers through its own sales staff abroad; select an independent distributor in the foreign country to sell the products; or operate through intermediaries in the home country by having them actually buy the goods or act as agents for the firm.

It is possible that the exporter could establish a staff to carry out all of its export functions. However, this would be impossible especially for a small exporter. In addition, new exporters, even if they are large, might not want to devote the resources to sales efforts that tend to fluctuate significantly. Therefore, exporters tend to use specialists. Freight forwarders are significant outside specialists used by exporters. Freight forwarders are responsible for moving the goods from the exporter to the buyer in the foreign country. Because of laws regulating commerce across national boundaries and the immense paperwork accompanying the goods, freight forwarders are indispensible. Even firms that have sophisticated export staffs use freight forwarders.

Freight forwarders also help firms with financial paperwork. International trade involves the use of specialized financial documents such as letters of credit, and freight forwarders can help exporters prepare documentation for the banks. Letters of credit are very specific instructions involving the shipment of goods and their payment. If those instructions are not adhered to exactly, it is possible that payment may not be made.

Besides freight forwarders and banks, exporters sometimes use export management companies. An **export management company** (EMC) is a firm that buys merchandise from manufacturers for international distribution or sometimes acts as an agent for the manufacturer. The difference between actually buying a product and acting as an agent is that the agent never really owns the goods, and it charges the exporter a fee for the sale of goods. When the EMC takes title to the goods, it keeps whatever it sells the goods for, but it also must absorb all of the risk. EMCs can be useful for exporters that do not have a large sales staff abroad.

Most of the same problems faced by exporters are also faced by importers. The key is to find a reliable source of supply and then make arrangements for financing and complying with customs regulations. Firms import goods for two major reasons: as primary or intermediate products used in the production process or as end use products for wholesalers, retailers, or final consumers.

GOVERNMENT INTERVENTION   Even though there are many reasons why countries should trade freely with each other, there are also many economic, social, and political objectives that countries have that cause them to intervene in the free flow of trade. Although there are many reasons for this intervention, the key ones are employment, infant industries, industrialization objectives, and general relationships with other countries.

The employment issue is particularly explosive because of its political ramifications. Mature industries that are no longer competitive, especially with low-wage countries, are the ones that typically seek protection in order to maintain employment.

The infant industry and industrialization arguments are closely related. Brazil, for example, has prohibited the sale of foreign-produced computers in order to develop a local computer industry. The basic idea is that infant industries should be sheltered from competition so that they can have a chance to develop economies of scale, cut costs, and raise quality to a level so they can compete internationally. The industrialization objective protects local industrial production in order to help diversify the economy and possibly attract investment abroad.

In 1987, the U.S. Congress was considering a number of measures to correct the imbalance in the balance of trade. In particular, it was singling out Japan because of Japan's large trade surplus with the U.S. Other countries were also being looked at individually because of their large trade surpluses with the U.S. In addition, countries may be singled out for other reasons. Trade with Cuba is virtually nonexistent because of the political tensions in Central America. Trade with the Soviet Union fluctuates, depending on the political tensions from year to year.

Intervention occurs through tariff or nontariff barriers. A tariff is a government tax levied on goods shipped internationally. There may be export tariffs, although the most common tariff is on imports. The tariff can be a set amount or a percentage amount levied on the cost of the product.

Nontariff barriers come in many forms. Governments have been known to talk down their exchange rate so that it takes more of the national currency to buy a unit of the foreign currency, thus making imports more expensive and hopefully reducing demand. Some countries have set different exchange rates for different types of transactions so that they can control demand better.

Another common form of nontariff barrier is a quota. This is a quantity control on the number of units or total value of a product that can be shipped into a country each year. A quota of zero, such as that described for Cuba, is an embargo. Governments often give preference to locally produced goods through "buy local" legislation. Governments can also delay goods coming in through licensing requirements or simple administrative delays in order to slow down the flow of imports.

It is difficult for management to work around some of these impediments to trade, and that often causes trade to stop and resources to be allocated unwisely. It may often force management to service the local market in ways other than export from the home country.

Foreign Investment

There are four major reasons why firms invest abroad. The first is to gain better access to foreign markets. Sometimes governments use trade restrictions as mentioned above to prevent access to local markets. The firm must either abandon the market or produce within the market in order to continue to sell there. Many Japanese firms are investing in the U.S. because of the fear of trade sanctions on exports from Japan. In addition, local production can help the firm respond more quickly to changes in consumer tastes and preferences.

A second reason is to achieve production efficiencies. Firms often invest in countries like Singapore, Taiwan, Korea, Malaysia, and Mexico in order to gain access to inexpensive local labor. The consumer electronics industry has basically shifted from the U.S. to the countries mentioned above due to the lower costs of production. The same can be said for parts of the computer industry, such as the manufacture of monitors. The production is undertaken in low-wage countries, not to gain access to the market, but to lower the cost of production.

A third reason is to gain access to raw materials. The investment of Gulf Oil in Angola is to gain access to oil, not to sell petroleum to the local market. Many mineral and food investments are undertaken because of unique natural resource endowments and climatic conditions.

A fourth reason for foreign investment is to gain access to knowledge. Many Japanese firms set up offices in the Silicon Valley in order to keep up to date on the latest technological developments in computers, software, and microchips. Advertising firms and market research firms set up offices around the region in order to gain access to valuable information that will help their multinational clients.

Although it may appear that investments can be categorized by separate motives, in reality most decisions to invest abroad are based on multiple motives. Political motives are seldom in isolation from economic motives. To encourage companies to invest abroad, governments must consider the objectives of potential investors. U.S. policy makers, for example, reasoned that many U.S. firms might find it advantageous to tap cheap labor sources in the Caribbean. Consequently, legislation was enacted to allow the Caribbean output to enter the U.S. virtually free of restrictions. Investors, acting purely on economic motives, were helping to achieve government objectives. This is also a good example of how government decisions can influence economic conditions to make investment feasible.

As mentioned earlier in the chapter, firms can invest in foreign markets in different degrees. A firm that has significant financial and managerial capital and needs strong control over production may choose to enter a market on a 100 percent ownership basis. The wholly owned subsidiary would be established as a corporation under the laws of the host country. However, total control would reside with the foreign investor. If management prefers to involve local ownership, spread risk and use scarce capital in a variety of locations, it may decide to enter into a joint venture with local investors and carry less than a 100 percent ownership.

Other Methods of Market Penetration

The two extremes for entering foreign markets have been described above. Exporting is a relatively risk-free way of entering into foreign markets, whereas investing abroad involves a significant commitment of resources. However, there are other ways to get involved abroad. One is to license technology to a foreign firm to produce your product in the foreign market. A licensing agreement involves trading technology for some type of return, known as a royalty payment, which is typically a percentage of sales or units produced. With a licensing agreement, a firm loses control over the quality of the product, may not have the market penetrated to the degree that it would like, and may even create a competitor for the future, but it does allow the firm to penetrate the market where exports might not be feasible and direct investment impossible.

Many firms, such as McDonald's and Kentucky Fried Chicken, have set up franchises all over the world. A franchise is similar to a licensing agreement in that the investor need not contribute capital abroad. Instead, local investors come up with the capital, and the franchising firm provides a trademark and the infusion of a necessary asset in order to keep the operation viable. In return, the franchisee is required to pay a fee.

Management contracts are popular with different types of firms, especially hotels. The property management company would not put up the capital for the facility, but it would manage the property for a fee. Sometimes, management contracts can be combined with licensing agreements or franchises.

It is important to realize that a large multinational firm is probably going to utilize every method possible of entering into international business. While it is possible to think of a natural progression from exports to partial investment to a wholly owned investment abroad, that does not always happen. Instead, a firm may be involved in exports to, investments in, and licensing agreements with local investors in the same country. The key is to use whatever form of international activity works.

The Impact of the MNC on Host Societies

Whether the MNC exports to or invests in a country, it will definitely have an impact. It is important for management to understand that impact in order to forecast how government may respond to any new form of economic activity. Those impacts can loosely be described as economic and political.

A major economic impact is through the flow of goods and capital. Any new investment will be positive to the country in the sense that financial capital will flow in. Over the long run, however, that capital will flow back out in the form of dividends, royalties, and other fees. Since goods will be produced locally rather than imported, the new investment will also save foreign exchange that would have been used to buy the imports. If the new investment results in products that can be exported, it will yield foreign exchange for the country.

Another major economic impact is on employment. In general, a new investment will result in a rise in employment. If the investment results from the acquisition of an existing firm, the employment impact could be mixed. On the one hand, it could be argued that if the acquisition had not been made, the local firm might have gone out of business, putting people out of work. If the new investor introduces capital intensity in the production process, the investment could result in unemployment. Management must be prepared to discuss the employment impact of an investment, because that is the most explosive political issue that it might face.

The political conflicts that arise from foreign investment are difficult to deal with. Foreign investors tend to be apolitical, able to deal with whatever political party or persuasion is in power at the time. However, the home government of the investor may have other ideas. U.S. companies operating in Angola have had a difficult time since the U.S. government is not especially supportive of the communist regime in Angola. Similar problems have been faced with firms operating in South Africa.

When governments extend the application of their laws to the foreign operations of companies, the term used to describe the situation is extraterritoriality. Host countries generally dislike these occurrences, since their own sovereignty over local business is weakened. Firms also fear situations in which the home and foreign laws are in conflict, since settlement must inevitably be between governments with companies caught in between.

Sometimes governments fear foreign investment over key sectors of the economy for fear that they will lose control of those sectors. This has resulted in the nationalization, or government takeover, of investments in areas such as transportation, communications, and utilities. Governments are sometimes afraid that key decisions will be made outside of the country rather than by local nationals. It is important for management to be aware of these potential conflicts in order to act responsibly and plan for interaction with local governments.

GLOBAL PRODUCTION STRATEGIES

For any given market, a firm can manufacture the product itself, or it can buy the product from someone else. If management decides to manufacture the product rather than purchase it from an outside supplier, it can either manufacture it in the local market or manufacture it in another country and import it into the market.

The decision on where to manufacture components and assemble final product is not an easy one. It depends on such factors as the cost of transportation, duties on components versus finished goods, the need to be close to the market, foreign exchange risk, economies of scale in the production process, and national image.

There are also a number of different production possibilities that a firm can choose. One way is to serve all markets from one single plant. Depending on the size of the markets being serviced, the single plant strategy would allow a firm to achieve economies of scale. However, beyond a certain point, the economies could begin to work against the firm. Smaller production facilities in several locations might be more cost effective than one large facility. Transportation costs could become significant, and tariffs on finished goods might make the product too expensive. Also, disruption in the production process in one location could be damaging to markets all around the world.

A multiple-plant strategy could solve many of the problems identified above. Being able to produce products in different locations would allow the firm to avoid heavy tariffs and be closer to the market so that it could react quicker to changes in market demands. The savings would have to be compared with the advantages of economies of scale and the relative importance of production costs. In a multiple-plant strategy, the firm can specialize production by product or process so that a particular plant produces a product or range of products or produces all products using a particular process and services all markets.

Obviously, there is no best way to set up the production process. For a particular product or line of products, a firm may use a single-plant strategy and depend on exports to serve world markets. This would essentially be a worldwide product and production strategy. For other products or groups of products a multiple-plant strategy might be more feasible.

Country Location

The choice of country for production is an interesting part of the production strategy. Many firms select countries as production locations because they have large markets. The Japanese are obviously producing in the U.S. in order to be close to the U.S. market and avoid possible protectionist measures rather than to get access to low-cost labor. Other firms produce in a specific country to get access to low-cost labor. These firms, considered production efficiency seekers, are those whose products require a high-labor content and do not necessarily require high-skill levels and significant amounts of capital and technology. As noted earlier, much of the investment in Asia in recent years has been to take advantage of low-cost labor in places like Korea, Taiwan, Malaysia, Singapore, and Thailand. Malaysia and Thailand are the newest of the Asian nations to receive significant amounts of foreign investment in production facilities, and they are likely to be followed closely by the People's Republic of China.

A great deal of off-shore production is beginning to take place in Latin America, principally Mexico and the Caribbean. In this new partnership with Latin America, U.S.-source components are shipped to Mexico duty-free, assembled by Mexican workers, and reexported to the United States under favorable tariff provisions. U.S. duties are levied on the imports only to the extent of the value added in Mexico. Since labor is so cheap, the value added is not great. This industry allows U.S. firms to assemble products more cheaply than would have been the case in the United States and provides employment for Mexicans.[11]

INTERNATIONAL MANAGERS

Most leading firms that expect to be competitive in world markets must develop a strategy for developing managers with an international perspective. Peter Drucker has remarked that a really multinational firm demands its people think and act as international businessmen in a world in which national passions are still very strong. Paul Oreffice, an Italian who moved to the U.S. when he was twelve but worked in both Europe and Latin America, became the chief executive of Dow Chemical in 1979. He commented that he would never have risen as far as he did in Dow without his foreign experience.

Key Requirements of Foreign Managers

Staffing a multinational corporation requires important decisions at two different levels. At the foreign subsidiary level, managers must be found that are able to adjust to the demands of the local environment and yet still keep in mind the pursuit of

Managers from multinational American firms meet with Tokyo officials to discuss business opportunities in Japan.

worldwide policies and practices. They must realize that an individual country's goals sometimes have to be sacrificed for the good of the corporation. At the home-office level, people must be hired who are equipped to coordinate and control the firm's various worldwide operations. They must be knowledgeable of and sensitive to the political, economic, and cultural differences in the firm's operations around the world.

A major decision that a firm has to make is whether or not it can introduce home country management practices in its foreign locations. It may face the dilemma that it has developed efficient technology, policies, and managerial style in one place that may be only partially applicable abroad. Thus, the manager needs to decide the types of policies and practices that may be transferred successfully, as well as the types of local adjustments that are necessary.

Top management in subsidiaries usually have broader duties than people with the same size operation at home. They often do not have the same time to gain the depth of experience that a counterpart in the home country might. The job tends to demand knowledge of more of the functions of business than would be the case at home. Management must spend more time in relations with government officials and be concerned with the impact of the operations on the local economy because of the high visibility that foreign ownership brings with it.

Communications in the foreign setting are more likely to be misunderstood than in the home country. A foreign manager needs to learn the local language or rely on the services of multilingual personnel or translators. Corporate policies and manuals are usually in the language of the home country, so personnel must be trained to use the foreign language manuals or learn the language. The problem of distance often makes communication difficult, as well as the language difficulties. The increased use of the facsimile machine and satellites to network computers has improved the communication between managers in the home country and the foreign location.

Finally, the manager in the foreign location can often feel isolated from the home office. That has good points as well as bad points. However, the isolation means that the manager will have less access to staff specialists that can help solve problems. Greater demands are also placed on headquarters personnel that travel to foreign locations to work with local managers. They have to cross often significant time zones, eat different foods, run the risk of health problems, and often spend a longer time away from home than would be the case in a comparable domestic setting.

Nationality Choice of Managers

If a U.S. firm were to set up a subsidiary in Brazil, it would have three nationality choices for its management team. A manager from Brazil would be considered a local national. A manager sent down to Brazil from the U.S. would be considered an expatriate. A manager sent to Brazil from any other country, such as Portugal, would be a special class of expatriate called third-country national.

There are strengths and weaknesses to each of the three possibilities. In making a choice, headquarters needs to consider a number of different factors. The first is knowledge of the environment. If the foreign operating environment is significantly different from that of the home country, management needs to be sensitive to those differences. A local national would be more accustomed to the local environment, but an expatriate could be successful depending on his or her background, experience, and ability to adapt.

A second factor is the importance of incentives to local nationals. A firm that constantly brings in expatriates will have trouble attracting and retaining good local nationals. For many years, Unilever, the British/Dutch consumer products firm, relied on expatriate managers for most of its top positions in Nigeria. It developed the reputation as a good firm to work for initially in order to get good marketing training, but it was not a firm that a local Nigerian wanted to consider over the long term, at least as far as management positions were concerned.

A third factor is the importance of developing a local image. In some cases, it might be best to have a local image. This is especially true in countries where the home country might be unpopular. In this case, the use of local nationals would be a good strategy. In other situations, it might be good to be known as a foreign firm. This would be true of high technology firms operating in a developing country. The use of expatriate personnel would help foster the foreign image.

A fourth factor is cost. It is definitely more expensive to bring in an expatriate and pay for all of the cost of living, housing, education, and hardship allowances. It is not uncommon for a firm to have to double the salary of an expatriate to induce him or her to work abroad.

A fifth factor relates to legal impediments to transfers abroad. Every government has laws favoring employment of its own citizens. These restrictions may simply prohibit foreign entry for specific jobs. Since government regulations and their enforcement may change drastically and quickly, considerable uncertainty is created. A visa may allow a manager to work in a country for a specific period of time—usually not very long.

The sixth factor is control. Managers transferred from headquarters are more likely to understand and accept headquarters policies. This enables the home office to make sure that its overall global objectives are not going to be slighted by a local manager who is only concerned with operations in the local country. However, local nationals can develop a global perspective by working on assignments in the home country periodically.

The final factor is management development. International assignments by expatriates can help those managers develop a more global perspective of the firm and prepare them for assignments where they are responsible for corporate strategy. In addition, expatriates can be sent to a foreign location to train local management and to prepare them for top-level assignments.

As can be seen, there are a variety of factors that must be considered when looking at the nationality choice of management. A local national has better knowledge of the environment, is a good incentive to other local nationals, promotes a local image, is less expensive, and does not have to worry about legal impediments to transfer. An expatriate provides a foreign image, is more likely to understand and implement corporate policy, and might be a good trainer for local management. A third-country national provides most of the advantages of the home country expatriate plus he or she has the experience of having worked in another location foreign to the home country.

Successful Managers

A great deal of research has been conducted on reasons for success and failure of managers in foreign assignments. The major factors associated with success are technical skills, managerial skills, and human skills. Knowledge of the local environment and the ability to speak the local language are not important if the manager does not have the technical skills to be successful. Those skills are developed through experience. Managerial skills are related to supervisory and organizing ability.

Human skills include the manager's ability to relate to people, especially in a different cultural situation. A foreign assignment requires a manager to not be judgmental and to tolerate ambiguity. Language ability, knowledge of culture, politics, and economics, and a healthy and supportive family are all critical elements in the human and personal side of the manager.

Even though a manager may have the experience and technical skills to cope with a foreign assignment, he or she might still not be successful. Some of the major causes for failure in a foreign assignment are intolerance, the inability to adjust, and a demeanor of superiority. Interestingly enough, those factors are primarily interpersonal. In addition, a family that has a difficult time adjusting is a major contributor to failure.

It is typical for a manager and his or her family to go through culture shock when going abroad. Culture shock is the trauma that one goes through in a new cultural setting when he or she discovers that old cultural cues and expectations do not fit the situation. No matter how many times one goes abroad, cultural shock can be experienced in a new country setting.

The home office needs to use a lot of care in selecting and training managers for foreign assignments. Many firms keep management inventories to help identify a pool of qualified personnel. Tests and interviews are often used to help screen qualified managers, but they are not foolproof. Thus, the training program can be crucial in preparing managers and their families for expatriate assignments. Some of the most successful programs focus on more than just the work requirements of the managers. They also deal with the language, culture, history, political system, and living conditions of the country. In addition, they include training for the families as well as for the managers. Some of the training occurs before the family relocates to the foreign setting, but good programs try to continue the training after relocation.

ENDING CASE
Black & Decker[12]

Black & Decker, once known almost exclusively as a manufacturer of power tools for professionals, is now involved in "the manufacturing, marketing, and servicing of a wide range of power tools, household products, and other labor-saving devices generally used in and around the home and by professional users." In the 1970s, before broadening its base to include a larger segment of the household market, B&D was flying high. It had captured a large share of the world's power tool market, and financial analysts were betting strongly on the future of the company.

By 1981, however, the picture began to change. Earnings had begun to slip, and a recession worldwide caused a significant downturn in the power tools segment of B&D's business, its bread and butter. In addition, other things were happening in the world economy that added to B&D's problems. After several years of relative weakness, the U.S. dollar began to strengthen. As the dollar strengthened, it took more units of foreign currencies to buy dollars and fewer dollars to buy foreign currencies, and thus foreign goods. As a result, the strengthening dollar eroded B&D's competitive position in export markets, and it also made B&D vulnerable to competition from abroad.

While these events were taking place, Japan's Makita Electric Works, Ltd. began to erode B&D's market share. Makita adopted a global strategy for its products that allowed it to become the low-cost producer in the world. It decided that consumers in different countries really did not need significantly different products. Then it combined its cost advantage with aggressive marketing, took advantage of the relatively weak yen compared with the U.S. dollar and B&D's mistakes to make serious inroads in the power tools market. By the late 1970s and early 1980s, Makita was able to nearly equal B&D's 20 percent market share in professional tools worldwide.

B&D's problems were partly a result of its own strategy. By 1982, B&D operated 25 plants in 13 countries on six continents. It had three operating groups as well as the headquarters in Maryland. Each group had its own staff, which led to a lot of duplication and overstaffing. In addition, B&D operated in more than 50 countries on a relatively autonomous basis. The philosophy had basically been to let each country adapt products and product lines to fit the unique characteristics of each market. The Italian firm produced power tools for Italians, the British subsidiary made power tools for Britons, etc.

As a result of this, countries did not really communicate well with each other. Successful products in one country often took years to introduce in others. For example, the highly successful Dustbuster, which was introduced in the U.S. in the late 1970s, was not introduced in Australia until 1983. When efforts were made to introduce B&D home products into European markets, the European managers refused to go along. Even though sales were stagnating, B&D held a large percentage of the power tools market in the early 1980s—over 50 percent on the Continent and 80 percent in the United Kingdom. They felt that home appliances and products were uniquely American and would not do well outside of the United States.

In order to meet the tailor-made specifications of different markets, design centers were not being used efficiently. At one point, eight design centers around the world had produced 260 different motors, even though it was determined that the firm needed fewer than 10 different models. Plant capacity utilization was quite low, employment levels were high, and output per employee left something to be desired.

For several years, B&D split its consumer and professional tools into two different groups. Because each group did not really work together to develop new product lines, Makita was able to spot a market niche that it could exploit—the mid-priced tools. In addition, B&D had begun to stagnate in new product development. It was almost as if it had decided to concentrate on its top lines and sell them aggressively.

As B&D moved into the mid-1980s, management realized that something had to be done. One area where the Japanese had not made significant inroads was the housewares and small appliances market. Japanese consumers were not big on those items, so Makita and other competitors had not really established a strong home market that it could use as an export base. B&D was having trouble introducing its own line of housewares because of everyone's perception of it as being a manufacturer of power tools. As a result, B&D considered acquiring the small appliances division of General Electric in order to give it more shelf space in housewares and also a large enough line of products to provide economies of scale in manufacturing. ∎

SUMMARY

According to Drucker, the world economy is in transition.[13] Many of the old theories and notions of how firms operate and countries interrelate are changing because of changing world conditions. The manager of today's firm cannot ignore the international environment and its impact on the national environment. A firm that is domestic today may be hit by international competition tomorrow. The manager needs to be aware of how the global economy fits together. The purpose of this chapter has been to identify some key elements of the international environment and how they influence the decisions of the manager. The manager of today's firm needs to be a political scientist, an economist, and a cultural anthropologist as well as a manager in the traditional setting. He or she needs to consider the entire world as a source of raw materials and components, a location for production, and a market for final products. In addition, its management pool must move beyond national boundaries in search of the best talent, especially talent that understands the global marketplace.

KEY TERMS

Merchandise trade
Services trade
Portfolio investment
Direct investment
Multinational enterprise
Environmental Assessment Matrix
Democracy
Totalitarianism
Market economy
Command economy
Economic integration

Demographic differences
Behavioral differences
Absolute advantage
Comparative advantage
Export strategy
Export management company
Government intervention
Foreign investment
Market penetration
Global production

REVIEW QUESTIONS

1. What disciplines should an international manager be familiar with in dealing with his/her company?
2. What do economists call service transactions?
3. What are some of the attributes of an MNE?
4. What are the three major world economies in which an MNE may operate?

5. What are the differences between a market economy and a command economy? What type of ownership usually characterizes each?

6. What are the characteristics of a newly industrialized country?

7. What are some of the demographic issues facing an international manager working with people from different nation-states?

8. What is the difference between absolute advantage and comparative advantage?

9. What are some of the reasons that firms sell goods abroad?

10. What are the steps in designing an export strategy?

11. What does a freight forwarder do?

12. What are some of the reasons that cause governments to intervene in the flow of trade?

13. What are some types of nontariff trade barriers?

14. What are the major reasons firms invest abroad?

15. What are some ways of getting involved abroad without exporting or investing?

16. What are some of the production possibilities that a firm can choose?

17. What are the factors that should be considered in choosing the nationality of managers?

CHALLENGE QUESTIONS

1. What are some of the main problems faced by multinational enterprises (MNEs)? Why?

2. Why is the management process so important to the success of multinational organizations?

3. Why are some countries pleased and others outraged by foreign ownership and control of their industry (economies)?

4. What are some of the barriers to trade, and why are they there?

5. What are some of the problems an industrialized country faces when investing in a country such as India? Why are they faced?

6. Why is it important to have an export strategy?

7. Describe an effective international manager.

CASE AND RELATED QUESTIONS

1. What is Bata, Ltd's strategy for servicing its world markets, and why is this strategy so successful?

2. What are the major reasons why Black & Decker had begun to lose its competitive position?

3. What are some strategies that B&D could pursue to improve its competitive position? Does the potential acquisition of GE's small appliance division make any sense in terms of the competitive position of B&D?

4. In 1985, the dollar began to weaken and continued to do so through the end of the decade. What impact might that have had on B&D's competitive position?

ENDNOTES

1. The case first appeared in the following book: John D. Daniels and Lee H. Radebaugh, *International Business Environments and Operations*, 4th ed. (Reading, MA: Addison-Wesley, 1986), pp. 77–80. The material was taken from the following sources: Dean Walker, "Shoemaker to the World," *Executive*, January 1981, pp. 63–69; Gary Vineberg, "Bata Favors Free Trade but Tempers Asia Stance," *Footwear News* 39, No. 24, (June 13, 1983), pp. 2+; Ira Breskin and Gary Vinesberg, "Parent Bata Looks after Farflung Footwear Family," *Footwear News* 39, No. 23, (June 6, 1983), pp. 1+; and Ira Breskin, "Globe-Trotting Bata, Ltd., A World Bank Customer," *Footwear News* 38, No. 38, (October 4, 1982), p. 23.

2. U.S. Department of Commerce, *Survey of Current Business*, Vol. 69, No. 3 (March 1989), p. 26.

3. Coalition of Services Industries, *The Service Economy* (Washington, D.C.: CSI, November 1986).

4. U.S. Department of Commerce, p. 26.

5. Daniels and Radebaugh, p. 16.

6. Ibid., pp. 10–11.

7. Richard N. Farmer and Barry M. Richman. *Comparative Management and Economic Progress* (Homewood, IL: Richard D. Irwin, 1965) and *International Business: An Operational Theory* (Bloomington, IL: Cedarwood Press, 1971).

8. Daniels and Radebaugh, p. 60.

9. David C. McClelland, "Business Drives and National Achievement," *Harvard Business Review*, July–August 1962, pp. 92–112; M. L. Maehr and J. G. Nicholls, "Culture and Achievement Motivations: A Second Look," in *Studies in Cross Cultural Psychology*, ed., Neil Warren (London: Academic Press, 1980), Vol. 2, Chapter 6; and George W. England and Raymond Lee, "Organizational Goals and Expected Behavior among American, Japanese and Korean Managers—A Comparative Study," *Academy of Management Journal*, December 1971, pp.425–38.

10. Edward T. Hall, "The Silent Language in Overseas Business," *Harvard Business Review*, May–June, 1960.

11. Roger Turner, "Mexico's In-Bond Industry Continues Its Dynamic Growth," *Business America*, November 26, 1984, p. 26.

12. Sources for this case are various issues of the Black & Decker annual report; Bill Saporito, "Black & Decker's Gamble on 'Globalization,'" *Fortune*, May 14, 1984, pp. 40–42, 44, 48; Christopher S. Eklund, "How Black & Decker Got Back in the Black," *Business Week*, July 13, 1987, pp. 86, 90; and "How Black & Decker Forged a Winning Brand Transfer Strategy," *Business International*, July 20, 1987, pp. 225, 227.

13. Peter F. Drucker, "The Changed World Economy," *Foreign Affairs*, Spring 1986, pp.768–91.

CHAPTER 22

MANAGEMENT IN THE TWENTY-FIRST CENTURY

CHAPTER OUTLINE

LEARNING OBJECTIVES

■ Recognize the major trends in management.

■ Develop an appreciation for a manager's ability to deal with an increasingly interdependent international business environment.

■ Identify major areas of innovation that future managers will be involved in.

■ Discuss the implications for managers of the interaction between government and the business community.

■ Explain the production and quality lessons learned by the U.S. auto industry in its competition with the Japanese.

■ Understand the idea of the transformational manager.

"To be trained as an *American* manager is to be trained for a world that is no longer there."[1]

By the time most of the students who read this text have graduated from college and have moved into positions of management, the twenty-first century will be close at hand. Will management in the future be any different than what is now found in current organizations? Will the issues be different? Will managers need new skills and knowledge not presented in today's courses on management? Fortunately, a number of writers and analysts have already addressed these questions, discovering future trends that have already started. It seems apparent that some of the directions can be understood now. This is all predicated on the assumption that there will not be a major earth-shaking crisis, such as World War III, a nuclear holocaust, a world famine, or an epidemic of world-wide proportions. Since there are some tremors in each of these possibilities (as evidenced as this is being written by the continuance of some type of warfare somewhere in the world, major famines in Africa, the threat of AIDS worldwide, and the continual jockeying of the superpowers for an advantage in nuclear warfare), you cannot automatically assume that the world will continue on its normal path. But assuming a future within a normal variance of problems and difficulties, the following trends seem to be already in progress.

COMPLEX BUSINESS ACTIVITIES IN THE INTERNATIONAL ARENA

Already a whole range of industries from automobiles and medicines to shoes and computers are being produced in a mix of international activities. Lester Thurow, Dean of MIT's Sloan School of Management, indicates that future managers "must have an understanding of how to manage in an international environment."[2]

In the automobile industry, all of the major American carmakers have affiliations with foreign manufacturers either to produce the entire car under the American label, or to produce a wide range of auto parts that are shipped to the United States to be assembled here. At the same time a number of foreign car companies, particularly Japanese, have built automobile factories in America. They use American personnel, produce cars, and sell them back in Japan. What then constitutes an American or a Japanese automobile? There are some products that are so international in scope that no one country can lay claim to have manufactured the product. Through a series of contractual arrangements a pair of shoes, for example, can be produced by buying hides in Argentina, processing them in Mexico, shipping them to be made into shoes in Taiwan, marketing them in America, and financing the whole thing in Tokyo. Such a range of activities in foreign countries will require the manager of the future to understand a wide range of cultures, languages, and business practices far different than those found at home.

Such a varied scene in the **international marketplace** makes it very difficult to determine what is a purely national product. This confusion makes it difficult to understand the issue of American companies applying political pressure to protect local interests from foreign companies by asking the government to establish quotas or restrictions on the importing of foreign goods. This has been called **protectionism**—protecting U.S. manufacturers against the importing of foreign products that often sell below the price of the same goods produced in America. There are strong political moves afoot to establish quotas or **trade restrictions** on the amount of goods that foreign countries can sell in this country. This is due, in part, to the wide disparity in the cost of labor for a product manufactured here and the same product produced in Korea or Taiwan. Some estimates show that labor in Korea in 1988 averages $3.00 per hour while in America the average is over $14.00 an hour. This has led to some companies wanting to push labor unions to cut back on union contracts that keep labor costs high. Labor leaders counter with showing that salaries and bonuses of top American executives have been as high as $12 million a year. Labor argues that if companies are making that kind of profit that the working person should benefit to some degree equal to the amount paid to management.

As a result of these concerns about profits, companies are more and more moving to **profit-sharing** programs where the gains of the company are shared with all members. This trend means that managers are going to need to know more about compensation systems of a new variety and not leave this area to staff people in the personnel area.

Management, unions, and government must work together. In the future, instead of these various groups fighting each other, there will be, almost of necessity, a movement towards increased **collaboration** to solve problems of mutual concern. This means that the future manager must know about the issues and learn to work in joint problem solving with individuals or groups that have in the past been seen as "the enemy."

BE PREPARED FOR INNOVATION

While the computer is already well-known throughout the world, the uses of this marvelous technology are just being uncovered. If upper managers are not clearly familiar with the uses of computers, they may lag behind in pushing ahead with new developments. One major bank in the 1980s knew that other financial institutions were becoming more and more computerized. Top management ordered a new computer system at a cost of millions of dollars, but when the system was installed, these same managers resisted its use because they did not understand how to use the new process or the data it produced. Computer literacy will be a must in the twenty-first century. This does not mean that managers will need to know how to program the computer, but they will need to know enough so they can talk knowledgeably with the experts they will hire and be open to the new uses that will surely be presented.

Since new technology can revolutionize an industry overnight, managers must keep abreast of innovations that may affect their businesses.

It is almost impossible to imagine the limits of the use of computer technology. It can be used to design and test complicated equipment and products without the enormous expense of building prototypes. Computers run robots, and this trend towards more and more computer-robot use to eliminate slow, routine work will continue. But while automation may eliminate some jobs, the manager will need to be sensitive to the human costs of automation and help in retraining displaced workers. There is an important interplay between the advancements of technology and the impact of these new innovations on human beings. Managers will have to help balance these two areas.

Technological innovations are only one of the possible new developments that will be available in the future. There will be new products, new marketing methods, new uses of television and the media, new ways to understand the customer.[3] The television industry now has a method of finding out from a sample of viewers with special equipment exactly what programs they watch during the week. This information is the basis for all future programming. A similar technique has not yet been developed in other areas—we rely on market surveys or polling techniques. But more sophisticated methods of tapping into customer responses will be developed, and customer preferences will be listened to very carefully.

New organization forms will also be present in the future. Some companies are already encouraging the development of new ventures, products, and ideas inside the larger company, trying to retain the flexibility and excitement of the smaller unit within the larger organization. The term "**intrapreneur**" is already in use. In contrast to the entrepreneur who is seen as the independent risk taker, the intrapreneur is one who is able to innovate inside the large organization.

GOVERNMENT RELATIONS

This has already been referred to in the above discussion, but managers in the twenty-first century certainly will be expected to be politically astute to understand the intricate relations between government and business. One of the reasons the Japanese have been so successful in recovering from almost total devastation following World War II has been the collaborative efforts between government and industry. Instead of having an adversarial relationship, government has cooperated clearly with industry to plan together for the revival of the industrial capability of the country. The Japanese leaders clearly saw that the whole country would benefit if the business capability of the country was enhanced. This has resulted in **joint planning**, favorable tax benefits, financial resources being made available, careful monitoring of the amount of foreign goods being allowed into the country, and a willingness to allow company control of unions.

The American system of interplay between government and industry has had a far different history. There has been a strong political issue around the amount of government "interference" that must be tolerated in the business arena. Some have felt that government in a free enterprise economy should stay out of the way and allow businesses to compete with each other in the marketplace with little interference from government. Others have felt that government must regulate or apply controls to business for the protection of the consumer, the public, and the unions. Very seldom has the United States seen joint planning between the various factions—government, unions, business, consumers—all working together for the common good. The future may begin to see more of such joint activities, and the manager of tomorrow will need to understand the political process and how to work effectively with government at the federal, state, and local levels (**government interface**). Just applying pressure through powerful lobbies will not be enough.

Future managers will need to be well grounded in the economic issues rising out of government and business activities. For example, the national debt has reached staggering proportions. Do managers clearly understand the impact the national debt has on the whole range of life in this country? Without examining this issue fully,

Managers will become more involved in the political process, as government and business engage in more joint planning.

companies for certain personal vested interests may still favor government contracts in a wide range of industries without looking at the consequences of an expanding national debt for the country as a whole.

The trend of government control or influence in certain human areas is probably going to increase. Already strong legislation has been passed to protect the interests of minorities, women, and the aging. No corporation can indiscriminately hire, fire, promote, or demote people. Government controls limit what can or cannot be done. A similar trend has taken place in terms of control inside organizations. The old pyramid form of organization with fixed positions and power located at the top is already being revised in new creative ways. Some companies have been experimenting with putting all personnel into a large labor pool. When someone comes up with a new product or service, those in the labor pool are reviewed, and a group of compatible resource people are allowed to form together to move the new idea ahead.

The issue for managers here is that they must be receptive to change, listen to new ideas, provide mechanisms for people at all levels to get their creative suggestions into the organization.

LONG-TERM VERSUS SHORT-TERM GOALS

One of the lessons America learned from the Japanese was that you cannot, without considerable cost, focus only on short-term profit and neglect longer-term goals. Robert Halberstam, among others, has pointed out that the Japanese strategy in the automobile field was different from American companies.[4] The U.S. automakers got possessed by the glitter of short-term profits, and the rapid increase in the price of the company stock. It was easier to get short-term profits by putting in expensive extras like radios, leather interiors, cruise control, electric equipment rather than putting money into improving quality or efficiency. The Japanese were equally possessed with changing the image of Japan as being the country of cheap, shoddy goods and wanted to have products of superior quality. They listened to an American, Edward Deming, who was a fanatic about quality, and who was virtually ignored in the U.S. Selling a quality product was also part of the Japanese marketing strategy. They wanted market share first—profits later. It was their contention that if they could get the customer to buy a quality product cheaper at first, they would remain a customer through future purchases. The Japanese could then raise the price and get a profit later. This strategy was eminently successful in cars and also with cameras, televisions, and a wide range of other products.

American managers have begun to learn this lesson. The slogan for several years for Ford Motor Company has been "Quality is Job One." The implication of this for managers is that they need to be more product-oriented and less financial manipulators for short-term gain (**immediate profit**). For many years in business schools the area of finance has attracted the most students because of the profit orientation of many companies. This is now beginning to change. Students are beginning to study production more and more. Students are combining technical fields like engineering with a degree in business or management.

MANAGEMENT PHILOSOPHY AND STYLE

This text has shown that the methods of management have changed through the years as working conditions have changed. Frederick Taylor and his scientific management had its place in a workplace of the 1920s where there were few standards for effective work. As the work force became better educated, the demand was for more consideration from management for recognition of the needs and abilities of employees. Their issue was involvement and participation. What will be the management philosophy of the twenty-first century? Already there are some inklings about this. The term **"transformational manager"** is just now coming into use. The term has a number of connotations. A manager who is transformationally oriented is interested in change.

The successful transformational manager of the twenty-first century will work in problem-solving teams.

Thus, a leader of this orientation will look at the ways to transform a limping or losing situation into one that is successful. It also implies that a major goal of the leader will be to help in the transformation of people—to provide opportunities for their growth and improvement. The leader will have a dual transformational task—to improve both the quality of the product or service and the people who are involved. This orientation requires more than just improving the concern for people by allowing more participation but includes such matters as career development, personal improvement, allowing for people at all levels to innovate and be rewarded.

As indicated above in the discussion of previous conditions, the twenty-first century will be a time of international agreements, collaborative problem solving with a variety of groups and organizations. These conditions will push managers to learn how to connect with people quickly and form effective problem-solving teams almost overnight—and with people with quite different cultures or points of view. Managers will have to learn to walk the fine line between being flexible and being too soft, between being sensitive to others and yet not abandoning principles, between understanding that cultures get work done differently and yet keeping personal ethical standards. Handling these different areas has never been easy and will continue to be a challenge, but that seems to be what the world will be like for people in management in the future.

KEY TERMS

International marketplace   Intrapreneur
Protectionism   Joint planning
Trade restrictions   Government interface
Profit sharing   Immediate profit
Collaboration   Transformational managers
Innovation

REVIEW QUESTIONS

1. Why is it important for a manager to have an international perspective?

2. What does the future imply for isolationist or protectionist attitudes?

3. Why must a manager be familiar with computers and computer technology?

4. What trend does an intrapreneur represent?

5. What is one reason for the success of Japanese industry after World War II? What place can this have in the American scene?

6. What is the role of government in relation to business?

7. Where has the U.S. auto industry traditionally concentrated its efforts? Was this good or bad? Why?

8. What does it mean to be a transformational manager?

ENDNOTES

1. "The 21st Century Executive," *U.S. News and World Report*, March 7, 1988.

2. Ibid., p. 23.

3. J. Naisbett and P. Aburdene, *Re-Inventing the Corporation* (New York: Warner Books, 1985).

4. R. Halberstam, *The Reckoning* (New York: Morrow, 1986).

GLOSSARY

ABC analysis A method of prioritizing inventories according to the price and usage of each item; items of higher price or higher usage are classified as A, and so on through C.

Absolute advantage The advantage a country holds when it can produce a good more efficiently than other countries.

Acid test ratio Similar to the current ratio (current assets to current liabilities), but it does not include inventory in the total current assets. (Also referred to as the quick ratio.)

Action planning The act of determining what, who, when, where, and how much is needed to achieve a given goal.

Adaptiveness The degree to which the organization adapts to forces that place demands on the organization.

Administrative system A network of policies and procedures, plus auditing, reporting, and formal structures that represents the system by which actions are assigned and controlled.

Affirmative action The government introduction of goals and timetables for the elimination of prejudice in the personnel practices of American companies.

Aggregate planning The act of looking into the intermediate-range future (generally a year or more in advance) to determine overall production levels and capacity requirements.

Alarm stage The alarm that is sounded when a "stressor" is encountered as the body prepares for conflict (fight or flight).

Allocate The process of dividing resources between departments and projects to achieve organizational goals.

Artifacts The "tangible" aspects of an organization's culture. Artifacts can be physical (office layout, company logo, employee dress), behavioral (rituals, ceremonies), and verbal (language, stories, and myths shared by members of an organization).

Artificial intelligence (AI) AI refers to methods of teaching computers to "think." In actuality computers do not think, but merely follow specified instructions very rapidly. However, if the instructions are complex and complete enough, computers can appear to learn, exercise judgment, and show other "intelligent" characteristics.

Assembly line A production technique where a product is assembled along a line—each station doing part of the work on each unit.

Asset turnover A measure of the effective use of assets using the ratio of sales to total assets.

Assumptions Beliefs group members hold about themselves, others, and the world in which they live.

Authoritarian leader A leader who leads by dominating and/or overpowering others.

Balance A compromise between conflicting factors. Balance is shown in the workplace when managers provide for both the needs of their work and of their families.

Balance delay The inefficiencies caused by imbalances in the amount of work to be done at different stations of an assembly line.

Balance sheet A statement that shows the assets, liabilities, and owners' equity at a specific time within a company.

Balance sheet budget A combination of all other financial budgets, it projects what the balance sheet will look like at the end of the budget period if actual results conform with planned for results.

Bar coding A type of machine-readable, "zebra-striped" label found on many products.

Behavioral differences The culture of a country is based on attitudes, values, and beliefs. Differences in such areas are known as behavioral differences.

Behaviorism A psychological approach with the central tenet that behavior is a direct result of the stimuli to which a person is subjected.

Benefits Supplementary rewards of employment, often including such things as health insurance, retirement, vacations, etc.

BFOQ Bona fide occupational qualifications constitute the use of a form of discrimination in order to fill a specific need.

Bill of materials A list of all materials going into a final product.

Bottom-up planning A planning structure where top management articulates what kinds of ideas it is interested in while middle managers and those who are closer to the operational problems formulate the actual plans.

Brainstorming The process of gathering key individuals together with the objective of generating alternative approaches to solving a given problem, regardless of how novel or unfamiliar they might be. One of the rules of a brainstorming session is that evaluation or criticism of suggestions is withheld so that participants feel free to offer their suggestions.

Break-even analysis A tool used by managers to indicate the profit and loss at various levels of production.

Budget Plans for allocating specific financial resources to organizational units or activities. Budgets itemize income and expenditures and thus provide targets for the purpose of controlling activities and/or units.

Bureaucracy An organizational system that is designed with a set of organizational rules and procedures, hierarchy of authority, and formal promotion rules.

Capital expenditure budget A budget that indicates future investments in capital equipment or fixed assets such as buildings, machinery, or land.

Capitalism The belief that profits are needed to reward innovation and risk-taking, which lead to entrepreneurship, employment, improvements, and ultimately, more prosperity for everyone.

Cash budget A projection of cash revenues and expenses for the budget period. They provide managers with information about the amount of cash flowing through the organization and the timing of the disbursements and receipts.

Cash cow A product that can generate a substantial cash flow.

Centralization The act of placing all functions in one location.

Change cycle A series of steps that can be followed to manage change.

Change strategy A long-term plan for planning and implementing changes.

Charisma Special gifts or powers that people possess.

Chase strategy A production plan when demand is seasonal, in which production levels vary with sales. *See* Level strategy.

Choice The prerogative to select the most advantageous behavior to achieve a desired outcome given the probability the desired outcome can be achieved.

Civility That conduct necessary for "civilized intercourse" among people.

Civil rights movement A movement initiated to eliminate the discriminatory policies in American business, etc.

Climate The prevailing emotional state shared by members in the system.

Coaching-training A method used by management to help subordinates reach better performance levels. After identifying current problems, the manager presents suggestions, ideas, and even role-play methods of dealing with the problems.

Cognitive insight The process of gaining knowledge from sources outside of oneself.

Cognitive skills Skills which deal with administrative matters such as determining the organization mission, seeing relationships with the external environment, and developing plans for markets, finances, and other resources and services.

Collaboration The pooling of efforts of individuals to meet a common goal.

Command economy An economic situation where the government harmonizes the activities of different economic sectors by setting goals, and deciding prices of products to be sold and the quantity of goods to be produced. In essence, the individual has little or no say in what is produced and sold.

Communication network Formal and informal patterns that determine who talks with whom, when, how often, and about what.

Communication strategy The steps used to achieve the desired outcome of communication.

Communication style Basic personal style, such as authoritarian or accepting, that influences communication patterns.

Communism The belief that a new man, free from corrupting influences (greed, exploitativeness) will emerge, as capitalism and its perpetrators are suppressed and "made impossible." Property belongs to society as a whole and private ownership is not appropriate. State control is necessary until the new man emerges and all ownership is abolished.

Comparative advantage The theory that countries tend to specialize in the production of products that they can produce most efficiently, even though they might not have an absolute advantage in the production of these products.

Competent communicator One who is capable of rather consistently achieving the impact intended.

Competitive advantage An advantage an organization has when it can do something better than its competitors.

Competitor analysis Analysis of strengths, weaknesses, opportunities, and characteristics of individual competitors.

Concurrent control measurements Control measures that are being performed as the work is being done. These control measures (also called screening control) relate not only to human performance but also to such items as departmental and machine performance.

Conflict-habituated relationship Chronic conflict, but under control, that seems to be the main basis of a relationship, constituting the cohesive factor for a couple.

Constraint Constraints exist when opportunities available in the environment do not match up with the resources of the organization. Additional resources will be required before opportunities can be exploited.

Contingency school Management approach that believes the type of management needed is contingent on the nature of the task, the kind of people involved, the time frame, and the goals.

Contingency theory This theory contends that there is no one leadership style that is effective in all situations—the nature of the task, the kind of people involved, the time frame, and the goals determine what leadership style would achieve the best results.

Contract A bargain struck between honorable individuals, wherein the conditions for work are laid down.

Control The activity of ensuring that activity and wants conform to plan.

Control system A system that permits top management to assess the organization's performance in meeting strategic objectives.

Critical path The sequence of processes within a PERT network that takes the most time.

Critical path method   *See* PERT.

Critical ratio   The ratio comparing total time before a job is due to the amount of work remaining.

Critical tasks   Tasks on the critical path.

Cultural change   A change that affects the cultural framework of the system—basic assumptions and values.

Culture   Shared assumptions, values, and artifacts that shape behavior.

Culture school   Management approach that looks at the organization as a small culture or subculture. This frame of reference examines the material and nonmaterial aspects of culture.

Current ratio   A ratio of the current assets to current liabilities.

Cycle   A predictable periodic fluctuation of a variable.

Cycle stock   The process of overstocking, usually to save ordering and shipping costs.

Cycle time   The time each unit spends at a station on the assembly line.

Data base   An approach to organizing and accessing data that allows systems designers to combine separate data files in one overall structure, and to specify several access keys to the data. In effect, data base design makes information in the data base accessible in many different ways.

Debt-to-assets ratio   A ratio of the total debt to total assets that measures the percentage of debt financing in the company.

Debt-to-equity ratio   The ratio of the long-term debt to total shareholders' equity.

Decisional roles   A set of key managerial activities that involve making decisions that will affect self, others, and the organization.

Decision analysis   A method of resolving problems using a structured approach. Four steps are involved in applying decision analysis: structuring the problem, assigning probabilities, measuring outcomes, and problem analysis.

Decision-making method   The method of formulating decisions within the firm.

Decision support systems   A decision support system (DSS) is designed to help management with unstructured, unanticipated questions and decisions. They are also designed to be easy to communicate with and use, so relatively untrained managers could use them interactively.

Decision tree   The decision tree shows how events may occur, where decisions have to be made, and how events and decisions interrelate.

Decision v. chance node   A decision node represents a point at which an individual must make a decision. A chance node represents a point at which the outcome is uncertain.

Decline stage   The stage in the life cycle when sales decline as the product becomes outdated and less desirable.

Defensive avoidance   The denial of the consequences of failure by passing the buck or avoiding the situation.

Democracy   The political system where citizens are involved in the decision-making process through direct vote or elected representatives.

Democratic leader   A leader who leads by sharing responsibility and decision making with others.

Demographic differences   Differences that occur between areas of the world. Demographic differences are often divided into three different categories: population growth rates, education, and age distribution.

Demotion   Usually a vertical move in the organization to a job with lower responsibility and pay.

Department   An organizational division that groups similar functions or tasks related to a single goal.

Dependent (derived) demand   Demand for an item directly determined by the demand for other items.

Derailment   The act of leaving the acceptable path for managerial advancement.

Devitalized relationship   A relationship that is characterized by the lack of real zest or vitality. The couple stays together out of legal or religious requirements.

Differentiation   The process of setting up separate departments to provide different services.

Direct investment   Direct investment assumes that the investing company is devoting significant resources in order to gain some degree of management control over the investment.

Discrimination   Biased behavior on the part of an individual.

Disparity models   Models based on the assumption that a change strategy must create a recognition of the difference between what an individual's ideal or objective is and what he or she is actually doing, thinking, or accomplishing.

Divisional structure   The structure an organization adopts to run the company in separate, autonomous divisions.

Division of labor   Functions that are divided between individuals in order to perform the task.

Dog   A weak product in a declining market.

Driving forces   Forces enhancing change within an environment.

Du Pont system   A method of analysis that identifies the factors that contribute to return on equity. (Return on equity equals profit margin times asset turnover times financial leverage.)

Earliest due date   In scheduling task completion, the method of giving the highest priority to the job with the earliest due date.

Early finish   The earliest time a task can be completed within the constraints of the prior activities.

Early start   The earliest time an activity can begin. The time is dependent on the completion of prior tasks.

Economic order quantity   The quantity that balances ordering and holding costs to provide the lowest total cost for procuring inventory. The quantity depends on the ordering costs, holding costs, and the demand for the item.

Edward Deming   An American pioneer of quality. Many of his ideas were adopted by the Japanese, but largely ignored by Americans.

Efficiency The art of accomplishing goals using as few resources as possible, and in the shortest time.

Entrepreneurial environment The conditions that allow a person the opportunity to create a new product or service and exploit the opportunities available to make a profit.

Environmental assessment matrix A matrix with critical elements of the management process on the vertical axis and environmental constraints on the horizontal axis. The elements of the management process are planning and innovation; control; organization; staffing; direction, leadership, and motivation; marketing; production and procurement; research and development; finance; and public and external relations. The environmental constraints are grouped into four categories: educational characteristics, sociological (or sociocultural) characteristics, political and legal characteristics, and economic characteristics.

Equal profit line The line along which the solutions provide the same profit level.

ERG theory A theory that is similar to Maslow's need theory and is based on three needs: existence (E), relatedness (R), and growth (G).

Ethics The fundamental values that should instruct the lives of individuals in a democratic society with a free enterprise system.

Exhaustion stage The situation when the body, faced with the same stressor too long, uses up the adaptive energy available and becomes exhausted.

Expansion stage The stage in the life cycle during which sales of the product increase with awareness and visibility.

Expected outcome The average outcome from an event.

Expense budget A budget that outlines the anticipated expenses of the organization in the coming time period.

Exponential smoothing The idea that data fluctuates randomly around some average figure, and that the best way to forecast is to find the average and not try to anticipate the random fluctuations. Exponential smoothing is an efficient, widely used technique to average past data, giving increasingly greater emphasis to more recent data.

Export management company A firm that buys merchandise from manufacturers for international distribution or sometimes acts as an agent for the manufacturer.

Export strategy A business plan designed to enter foreign markets, while maintaining production in the current market.

External audit Audits conducted by outside experts who are not employees of the organization. These examinations of an organization's financial records seek to determine the degree of accuracy and the extent to which financial statements reflect fairly what they are designed to represent.

Feasibility region The area within which solutions can be found given the constraints.

Feasible When there is an obtainable solution to a problem.

Feedback Information received from others about your own performance. Feedback obtained from suppliers, customers, subordinates, or supervisors can provide managers with evidence that problems exist and directions for change.

Feed forward Controls, sometimes called steering controls, that detect deviations from a standard before a major activity has begun.

Fight or flight The act of choosing between attacking a situation in order to resolve it, or avoiding the situation completely.

Filter system The perceptual screen people use to sort information. Filters are often made up of biases, prejudices, personal experiences and feelings.

Financial budget A budget that deals with how the organization is going to spend its cash during the coming period and where it expects to obtain its financial resources.

First come, first served A scheduling system in which the first job to arrive is the first job worked on.

Fixed budget A budget that is prepared for a fixed activity level.

Flat organization An organization with few levels of management.

Flexible scheduling The options for workers to set schedules more consistent with the demands of home and community.

Forecast error The actual result for the previous period minus the forecast for that period.

Foreign investment Investment in foreign countries by either direct investment or portfolio investment.

Form The structure used in organizations.

Foundation values The underlying values in the society as a whole, such as the beliefs that individuals are important, and individual rights and freedoms are fundamental.

Function Tasks performed by individuals, groups, and departments.

Generic strategies General business strategies developed by Michael Porter. Generic strategies are: (1) overall cost leadership, (2) differentiation, and (3) focus.

Global production Production in many areas and markets.

Goal conflict The occurrence when organizational goals and individual goals are not in harmony, resulting in trade-offs between the two and reduced commitment to at least one of the goals.

Government intervention Involvement of the government in the business sector of the economy usually as a protectionist measure.

GPSS An early simulation language.

Grapevine An informal channel of communication.

Great man theory An approach to leadership based on the assumption that certain people are either born to become leaders—or emerge at the right historical time—and events thrust them into the leadership positions.

Gresham's law of planning A theory that suggest that programmed activity tends to replace nonprogrammed activity. If a manager's job involves both kinds of decisions, the tendency is to emphasize programmed decisions at the expense of nonprogrammed decisions.

Group climate   The emotional climate or atmosphere existing within the group.

Group think   The situation when a group has a stronger desire for consensus and cohesiveness than for arriving at the best possible solution. Some causes of group think are: (1) the group is insulated from external pressures and information; (2) the group is led by a very forceful and dominant leader; and (3) the group lacks procedures for adequately searching for alternatives and ensuring that all points of view are considered.

Growth needs   The needs to be creative and to experience growth and development.

Guilt   A form of internal disparity. Guilt is sometimes used as a strategy to motivate others.

Hardware   The physical components of computers. Devices such as disk drives, monitors, and CPUs are classed as hardware.

Hierarchy   The number of levels within the organization.

High organization   An organization with many levels of management.

Human relations school   Management approach that emphasizes the importance of the relationship between management and workers in obtaining productivity.

Human resource accounting   Acknowledgment that human resources have a quantifiable value to an organization and should be considered in managerial decision making.

Human resource planning   A plan that covers both the short-term and long-term personnel needs of an organization.

Human skills   Skills that deal with the human aspects of the organization.

Hypervigilance   The buildup of a tremendous amount of stress when the inability to find a solution is coupled with a time deadline.

Immediate profit   Profits that are earned immediately, with little regard paid to the long-term consequences of the actions.

Imperfect competition   A competitive situation characterized by a single buyer or seller (or group of buyers or sellers) exerting disproportionate control over competitive conditions

Implementation   The act of putting a plan into action.

Income statement   A statement that shows the revenues and expenditures for a given period.

Independent demand   Demand for an item that is independent of demand for other goods.

Individual initiative   The right and obligation of individuals to develop their talents as far as they can.

Industry analysis   Analysis of the relative strengths and weaknesses, and threats and opportunities within an industry.

Informational roles   The role of the manager as a dispenser and receiver of information. Much of a manager's time is spent in getting or giving information.

Information systems   Systems designed to provide businesses with the information that they need.

Innovation   The means by which entrepreneurs can produce new products and services that others are not currently providing.

Input   The outside environment supplies inputs that are processed or converted by the organization, via its work, or throughput activities, into outputs. Input is also data that is fed into an information system.

Inspections   Formal evaluations of quality conducted at specified points in a production process.

Instrumentality   The perceived relationship between first- and second-level outcomes.

Instrumental values   A certain behavior that is appropriate in all situations. These values are known as instrumental values and are represented by such beliefs as honesty, love, and obedience.

Integration   The process of combining different departments to reach a common goal.

Intention to impact   The goal of personal communication to achieve the actual impact or result we intend.

Intermediate planning   Plans that generally have a planning horizon of one to three years. While long-range plans serve as general guidelines derived from the strategic planning process, intermediate plans are usually more detailed and relevant for middle and first-line management.

Internal audit   Audits that are conducted by employees of the organization and are frequently wider in scope than external audits. The internal audit is used to examine the effectiveness of the control system as well as to verify the accuracy of records.

Internal memory   Memory resident within the computer. This type of memory works much faster than external forms of data storage.

Internal resources   Resources owned or controlled directly by a company.

International businesses   Businesses that have sales in foreign countries

International marketplace   A business environment characterized by many different markets in different countries.

Interpersonal roles   A manager's interpersonal contact with others.

Intersystem planning   Plans that involve more than one system. Companies plan improvement programs taking the family and other external systems into account.

Intervention reinforcement   The need for reinforcements from all parts of the system when implementing changes in the system.

Interview   A question-and-answer session designed to show personal characteristics and qualifications, and evaluate potential employees.

Intrapreneur   One who is able to innovate inside the large organization.

Intuition   A hunch surrounding a decision or idea.

Inventory holding cost   The opportunity cost of tying up capital in inventory.

Inventory turnover   A ratio of the sales to inventory during each period.

Job definition   A description of a specific job and how it should be performed.

Job description   The detailed description of a position that includes both the requirements of the job and some assessment of the kind of skills needed to fulfill the job requirements.

Job enlargement   The act of making the task broader.

Job enrichment   The act of changing the requirements of a job to better suit the circumstances and improve the challenge for the employees.

Job redesign   The act of restructuring the organization, or parts of it, to attain efficiency and effectiveness.

Job rotation   Spending time in a variety of jobs to gain specific first-hand experience, often with coaching by a qualified person.

Job traveller   A paper generally outlining the tasks to be done, which travels with a job through a production process.

Johari window   A model that depicts the level of knowledge held between two people. The model separates things that are known to self and others from things not known.

Joint planning   Planning between the various factions—government, unions, business, consumers—all working together for the common good.

Just-in-time system   A production technique in which intermediate parts and materials arrive just as they are needed.

Kanban system   Another term for a just-in-time system.

Labor pool   The organization of workers in a "pool." When new projects arise, the workers form a group and pursue the task.

Lag   A predictable difference between a forecast and a variable. Lags often occur when there are cycles and trends in a variable.

Laissez-faire   The policy of allowing things to take their own course—giving free reign to people's actions.

Late finish   The latest time a task can be completed to meet the project deadline.

Late start   The latest time the task can commence to be completed by the required deadline.

Letter of reference   A letter from a previous employer or acquaintance listing personal characteristics and attributes that are beneficial to employers.

Level   The differentiation between managers at varying functions in the organization and how they fit in the hierarchy. All levels of management have important roles to play.

Level strategy   Planning for a constant production level, even though demand may be seasonal. *See* Chase strategy.

Leverage   Leverage comes into play when the internal strengths match or are consistent with opportunities found in the environmental analysis. The existence of this match would then support a strategy to take advantage of this opportunity. In financial terms, it refers to increasing profits through the use of debt: the cost of debt must be less than the expected return in order to achieve true leverage.

Linear programming   A method of finding the best combination of resources for achieving the desired goal.

Used to vary inputs and constraints to find the proportionate change in the output.

Line functions   Functions that are directly involved in operations of a business.

Liquidity   Liquidity is the ability of a firm to meet its financial liabilities.

Location of functions   Where each of the functions is physically performed.

Long-range planning   Plans that deal with the broad competitive, technological, and strategic aspects of managing an organization, including the necessary allocation of resources. Long-range planning usually encompasses research and development, capital expansion, organization and management development, and meeting organizational financial requirements.

Lost decisions   Decisions that get made but are not carried out. Nothing happens, and a few weeks later the same matter is raised again.

LP problem   A problem defined by linear constraints and objectives. Linear programming programs may be used to find solutions.

Machine-readable labels   Labels that can be read by a computer.

Magnetic disks   A platter, shaped much like a phonograph record, coated (usually on both sides) with magnetic material. A disk is a random-access storage device.

Management functions   Functions that managers are expected or need to do to meet corporate goals and what they actually do—how they really spend their time.

Management information systems   A management information system (MIS) allows information to be combined and retrieved in a variety of ways, rather than in the predefined, prespecified manner typical of a transaction reporting system.

Management of attention   The leader's ability to draw people by creating a vision, communicating that vision to others, and, through energy and commitment, making others want to join in trying to achieve the vision.

Management of meaning   The ability to communicate a vision to others so they can understand the meaning of the goals, directions, or issues.

Management of self   The self-understanding of effective leaders of their strengths and weaknesses that allows them to operate consistently within the bounds of their capabilities.

Management of trust   Management by creating trust with co-workers. A fundamental part of building trust is reliability or consistency.

Managerial grid   A model that measures a manager's attention to two essential activities: work results and the people who must do the work.

Margin   The point at which decision trade-offs are made.

Market economy   The economic situation where resources are owned and products consumed by individuals, whereas resources are used and products produced by firms. In a true market economy, there is little or no intervention by government in the exchanges that take place between firms and individuals.

Market penetration   The process of entering markets with the goal of doing business. Internationally, it is usually done by exporting to the market, or producing in the market.

Marxism   The belief that all productive goods are owned and shared equally by everyone. There are no classes— no aristocratic few, no starving masses. All donate to the common good according to ability, and all share in the common wealth according to need.

Matching analysis   The identification of the match, or gap, between opportunities/threats and the strengths/weaknesses coming from the internal resources. This integration of external and internal analysis allows managers to forecast the results of existing or contemplated strategies.

Mathematical school   Management approach that emphasizes the use of quantitative methods.

Matrix organization   An organizational structure where each person belongs to at least two groups at the same time.

Maturity stage   Stage in the life cycle when sales reach their peak as the product penetrates the whole market.

Maximize   Finding the maximum possible solution to the problem.

MBO   Management-By-Objectives (MBO) is one of the most widely used planning and control systems used in organizations. MBO consists of goal setting, planning to meet the goals set, a self-control process, a system of periodic review, and a performance appraisal.

Memory   The part of an information system that stores instructions and data. In a computer, memory usually refers to speed, internal (or core) memory.

Merchandise trade   The act of trading tangible goods. Merchandise exports are tangible goods that visibly leave a country, whereas merchandise imports are tangible goods that visibly enter a country.

Minimize late jobs   A scheduling system that minimizes the number of jobs that are late.

Mission statement   A statement that identifies and generates the organizational mission. A corporation's mission is more fundamental than a strategic plan because effective strategy depends on committing to essential strengths that stem from identity.

Modeling   The process of training employees by showing the employee an actual performance of a task, or a "staged" performance. This method of training is often done with the use of videotapes.

Monopoly power   The situation where one provider of a product or service is able to control the whole market.

Monopsony   Monopsonies are similar to monopolies, except they have one customer, rather than one supplier.

Moral entrepreneurism   A willingness to base all actions upon one's sense of virtue, and, even more difficultly, upon the sense of virtue of others. In this sense, the term "entrepreneur" applies not only to those individuals who are willing to risk money, but, more importantly, to those who are willing to risk all based upon their willingness to trust others.

Moral responsibility   The obligation of individuals to assume moral responsibility. When injustice is encountered, it cannot be passed off as the responsibility of institutions or other individuals.

MRP   Material requirements planning is a production plan that starts with the finished product requirements, and coordinates the purchases and production of raw materials of intermediate goods according to finished goods requirements.

Multinational businesses   Businesses that operate many of the organizational functions in many different countries.

Multinational enterprise   A multinational enterprise (MNE), has a worldwide approach to foreign markets and production and an integrated global philosophy encompassing both domestic and overseas operations.

Need theory   Social theory that postulates that humans have characteristic drives or needs. This theory says you can motivate people by providing something they need in exchange for effort.

9, 9 management   High concern for results integrated with high concern for people—best exemplified in an effective team.

Noblesse oblige   The obligation of the leaders to treat others as honorable men and women.

Norm   Predominant attitudes and habits of speech and behavior. Norms determine, among other things, the status of the various minority groups in a society and the comparative status of men and women.

Oligopoly   An economic situation characterized by a few dominant suppliers. The interdependencies and interactions among the supplying companies become important. Suppliers can act in concert to support high-price levels and profits, but the coalition is often a fragile one that can be destroyed by any of the participants.

Oligopsony   An oligopsony is similar to an oligopoly, except there are few customers rather than few suppliers.

Open door policy   A strategy that managers adopt to open the lines of communication. The manager "opens his/her door" to employees for discussion, problem solving, etc.

Open system   An organization that is continually interacting with its environment in a dynamic way.

Operating budget   A budget that focuses on the goods and services the organization intends to utilize during the budget period.

Operational planning   The day-to-day decision making done at lower levels in the organization.

Operational plans   Plans, sometimes referred to as tactical plans, that are focused on the day-to-day or month-to-month activities needed to execute strategic plans and achieve strategic goals.

Operations management   The field of management that encompasses the production of finished products.

Order cost   The costs incurred in ordering goods.

Organization design   How the organization is put together; from individual tasks to departmental structures within the company.

Orientation A process used to familiarize employees with job requirements, expectations, and programs of the company.

Outcome The result of an action taken.

Output Information communicated from an information system to a user or another system. Also, in operations, output refers to a product or service (output) that is returned to the outside environment.

Overdependency The situation when a team is overly dependent on a leader, usually becoming immobilized when the leader is not present.

Overlap Interaction between cultural change and systems change. Many areas can overlap depending on the nature of the change.

Paperless office An office where all paper is replaced with computer generated and transmitted information.

Passive-congenial relationship Relationship described as "comfortable adequacy." The couple shares interests in common that are not vital nor do they require much joint participation.

Path-goal model In this model the critical role of the leader is to understand the situation and the subordinates and to make sure the path to achieving goals is clear and to then supply rewards that are important to the subordinates.

Pattern of management The style of handling a subordinate action (authoritarian vs. participative).

Performance appraisal A meeting with supervisors and workers. The focus of this meeting should be on results and actual performance rather than on personalities or excuses.

Performance gap The gap between planned and actual performance.

Performance review A means of evaluating employees, by having an interview between boss and subordinate.

Personal computer A desk-sized relatively inexpensive computer system.

Personality test A test designed to find the personal characteristics of an individual.

Personal management interview A meeting between a manager and subordinate for planning or training.

Perspectives Shared ideas and actions that help people act "appropriately" in a given situation.

PERT Program Evaluation and Review Technique, also known as CPM (Critical Path Method), was developed as a method of managing complex projects.

Pioneer stage The development and introduction of a product into the market.

Planning An activity that focuses on the future. Specifically, it is the process of setting objectives and determining what needs to be done to accomplish them.

Pleasure-pain principle The belief that people will behave in ways to avoid pain and gain pleasure.

Policies Guidelines for decision making that set up boundaries around which decisions are made and generally flow from the organizations, goals, and strategies.

Portfolio investment Investment designed for financial return without any management control over it.

Power The ability to have people perform what you want to be performed.

Praise The acknowledgment of the moral worth of the individual in the esteem of loved others.

Praiseworthy The happiness that comes only from the knowledge that the praise is both earned and deserved—that one is praiseworthy.

Primary source data Information gathered first hand and best done by personal observation.

Probabilities Likelihoods of events and their likely payoffs and costs.

Probability The chance that an event will occur.

Problem An occurrence when one of the organization's weak points is in the same area as a threat being generated from the environment. This problem may be sufficiently large to endanger the existence of the organization or it may alter the strategies available for use until the problem is resolved.

Problem child A weak product in a strong market.

Problem-solving approach A widely used classic problem solving method applied to team problems. Either by use of interviews, surveys, or direct input by workers, data are gathered to address the question: "What keeps this unit from being as effective as it could be?" When a list of problems or barriers is developed, the next step is to engage in some type of action-taking or problem-solving behavior that removes the barriers.

Procedures Other forms of standing plans. A procedure precisely describes what actions are to be taken in specific situations and are the means by which policies are frequently implemented.

Process analysis A problem-solving approach that involves looking at the kinds of team interactions and the ways the team gets work done. Process analysis centers on watching the team work together and focuses on how the team works on problems.

Product liability suits Suits brought against companies for the damages, or injuries, caused by their products.

Product life cycle The life cycle consisting of the stages or periods most products experience—introduction, growth, maturity, and decline.

Product substitutes Products that are not identical to, but can be used in place of other products. For example, plastics compete with steel in automobile body manufacturing.

Profitability A measure of how company's revenues cover costs.

Profit budget A combination of the revenue and expense budget into one statement.

Profit margin The ratio of total income to total revenues.

Profit sharing The act of sharing the gains of the company with all members of the company.

Program Modern computers use instructions, called programs, to tell the processor where to find data in memory, how it should be manipulated, and where results should be stored.

Programmed decisions Decisions that are repetitive and routine. If a particular situation occurs frequently,

Programmed decisions *continued*
managers develop a habit, rule, or procedure for dealing with it.

Programs   A program is a single-use plan used for broad activities that include many different functions and interactions. New incentive programs and a plan for introducing a new product line are examples of programs.

Projects   A single-use plan that is much narrower in its focus than a program, but more complex.

Promotion   Usually a vertical move in the organization to a job with higher responsibility and pay.

Protectionism   The act of protecting U.S. manufacturers against the importing of foreign products that often sell below the price of the same goods produced in America.

Pruning the tree   The process of eliminating any obviously bad decisions from a decision tree, leaving only the prudent choices.

Psychological needs   A person's needs to fulfill his/her own mental desires, in order to become at ease.

Punishment   A negative outcome inflicted on people, sometimes used as negative reinforcement within an organization.

Quality circle   A group of people, often from different parts of the same organization, set up to examine and make recommendations for the improvement of work in the organization.

Quick ratio   Similar to the current ratio, but it does not include inventory in the total current assets. (Also referred to as the acid test ratio.)

Random fluctuation   Random deviations from the overall average of a process.

Random number   A number chosen completely at random without preference being given to any particular number.

Rational decision-making process   The steps that effective managers take, either formally or intuitively, to choose the alternative. A model of this process consists of five steps: (1) identifying the problem; (2) generating alternative solutions; (3) selecting the most beneficial alternative; (4) implementing the selected alternative; and (5) gathering feedback to see if the problem is being resolved.

Rational school   A school of thought that defines management as a rational system and that all business organizations have certain activities that need to be managed—technical, commercial, financial, security, and accounting. To handle these activities, managers needed to be aware of the basic principles of management.

R-Chart   A chart of the range of a series of observations.

Recruitment   A procedure for attracting qualified people to apply for positions in the organization.

Regional economic integration   The economic situation where resources flow to the most efficient producers. Consumers are also allowed to purchase goods from participating countries at more competitive prices.

Regression analysis   The main idea in regression analysis is to draw a straight line (or a curved line in more sophisticated applications) in such a manner that the line goes through past data points as closely as possible.

Regression constants   Constants that indicate how strongly the changes in the one variable or set of variables relate to changes in another variable.

Relaxation training   The process of teaching workers to relax; it removes some of the stress of work.

Relocation   A change in job responsibilities accompanied by a change of domicile.

Resistance stage   The stage when resistance to the stressor increases. The organ or system best able to deal with the threat is mobilized.

Restraining forces   Forces that resist change in an environment.

Resume   A written document listing qualifications and characteristics of an individual.

Return on assets   The ratio of net income to total assets.

Return on equity   The ratio of net income to total shareholders' equity.

Return on investment   The ratio of income to total investment (total equity plus debt minus other liabilities).

Revenue budget   A budget that focuses on the income that an organization expects to receive during the budgetary period.

Reward   A benefit for performing as desired. Rewards are often used to motivate people.

Right to privacy   The belief that government should not intrude upon personal affairs. In the true sense of the term, the right to privacy refers to all of the conditions necessary for the achievement of personal individuality.

Risk   Decisions that must be made on the basis of incomplete but factual information.

Role expectations   The demands other people place on you because of your relationship to them.

Root cause   The basic underlying cause of a problem or effect.

Rules   The specific form of all standing plans. A rule is not a guide to decision making, but a substitute for it.

Safety stock   Extra stock kept as a protection against running out of inventory.

Satisficing   The behavior of selecting the first course of action deemed "satisfactory" or "good enough" rather than examining the entire set of alternative preferences.

Schedule   The act of planning task completion within the time frame required.

Scientific school   Management approach that emphasizes the need for empirical observation (examination of real phenomena), analysis, and experimentation. The role of the manager is to discover the one best way to perform all work under the manager's direction.

Secondary source data   Anything other than direct observation, which sometimes produces inaccurate data.

Selection   The procedure used to determine the individuals who will actually perform the tasks of the organization—which applicants will be hired.

Selective perception   The perspective of seeing problems or conditions only in terms of one's own background and training.

Self-interest subgroup   A small subgroup which follows its own interests rather than the interests of the group as a whole.

Separate but equal   Policies instigated in the U.S. that separated blacks and whites, but declared equal treatment for both.

Services trade   The process of providing a service abroad or receiving the benefit of someone from abroad performing a service for your firm. The service sector includes public utilities; communications; transportation; finance, insurance, and real estate; wholesale and retail trade; government; and other services (such as business services like advertising, public accounting, legal work, etc.).

Shared assessment   A self-assessment of a manager's performance with others being asked to confirm or deny it, to share additional reactions, and to make suggestions for improvement.

Sharing meeting   An informative meeting held between a manager and subordinates. The meeting addresses what is happening in each area of the organization.

SIMSCRIPT   General-purpose simulation language designed to model manufacturing systems, financial systems, or other problems of special interest.

Shortest job first   Scheduling the job that requires the least amount of time first in the schedule

Short-term planning   Planning that involves taking steps to ensure that an organization functions to meet its objectives on a day-to-day basis. Short-term plans are generally made and carried out by lower-level managers and supervisors.

Simulation   A representation of reality through repeated trials, by which management can mathematically measure the outcome of proposed actions. Simulation is very flexible.

Single-use plans   Plans that are developed to carry out a course of action that is not likely to be repeated in the future.

Skill mix model   A model that treats management skills as a blend of technical, interpersonal, and cognitive skills.

Slack time   The difference between the early start and the late start of a task is slack time.

SLAM   General-purpose simulation language designed to model manufacturing systems, financial systems, or other problems of special interest.

Sloth   The tendency toward inertia that some believe all humans possess.

Smith's ideal society   A society where the necessary assistance is reciprocally afforded from love, gratitude, friendship, and esteem. The society flourishes and is happy.

Smith's minimal society   A society in which the necessary assistance is not afforded from generous and disinterested motives. Although among the different members of the society there is no mutual love and affection, the society, though less happy and agreeable, will not necessarily be dissolved.

Smoothing constant   A constant used in exponential smoothing.

Social responsibilities   The responsibilities that individuals should possess for the social well-being such as loyalty, trustworthiness, and kindness.

Social system   The dynamic condition made up of people in different positions interacting with each other.

Social system school   Management approach that suggests that managers must see the organization as a total system—an "open" system that interacts with the environment and has linked, internal subsystems.

Sociotechnical system   The system defining how people and technology interact.

Software   A series of instructions, organized into programs, used by the computer in order to perform specified tasks.

Span of control   The number of subordinates a manager directly supervises.

Spread effect   Effects of an action that are more widespread than was originally expected.

Square v. round node   Square nodes represent a decision in a decision tree. Round nodes indicate possible chance events.

Stable v. nervous   A term used in exponential smoothing in which small values of the smoothing constant give stable, smooth forecasts, whereas large values of the smoothing constant give greater fluctuations which respond to random fluctuations.

Staff   Employees generally not involved directly in producing or selling the firm's product.

Staffing   The process of procuring the necessary people for required positions: including a determination of how many people, with what needed skills, will be required at what particular time.

Staff functions   Functions that are support functions for the line.

Standards   Yardsticks to determine the adequacy of organizational performance.

Standing plans   Plans that are developed to direct activities that occur regularly. Because similar situations are handled in a predetermined and consistent manner, managers save time and energy in the decision-making process.

Star   A strong product in an expanding market.

Statement of changes in financial position   A statement that shows the financial changes that have occurred in a company between two periods.

Status-role structure   A system where some people, because of their function or position, have higher status, more power, and more influence than others.

Strategic planning   The act of understanding what business one wishes to be in, where one wants to be at some future date, and how to get there.

Strategic plans   Plans that address the mission and purpose of the organization and decide what the objectives of the organization should be.

Strategy   A vision that is directed at "what" the organization should be rather than "how" it will get there.

Stress   Tensions and pressures that affect individuals, both at work and at home.

Stressor   The causal factor of stress.

Subgoals Goals that are subordinate to the overall goals of the company.

Subgroup meetings Meetings in which smaller groups meet to discuss problems and concerns. This method often ensures more anonymity, and consequently, openness.

Subsystem A series of integrated parts or subsystems that must function together to allow the total system to operate adequately.

Supererogation Something above and beyond what is expected in human behavior.

Superior prudence The most perfect propriety in every possible circumstance and situation.

SWOT analysis The analysis of strengths, weaknesses, opportunities, and threats.

Sympathy The primary moral obligation of each individual to develop a feeling of love for all other individuals. All human relationships must be based upon a mutual sympathy of one for another, or else society will degenerate to the level of the Hobbesian war of "all against all."

System IV A managerial model developed by Likert dealing with different managerial styles. It also represents the participative group style.

System goals The intended purpose of a system.

System of enterprise of free individuals The key element in this economic system—that which justifies and defines it—must be the degree of freedom enjoyed by the individuals within this economic system.

System output Reports and information generated by an information system.

Systems change Changes implemented in the functioning of the organization that affect the structure, functions, or personnel of the organization.

Task Function performed by an individual or group of individuals.

Task dependence Relationships defining which tasks must be completed before other tasks can begin.

Task redesign The process of assessing and restructuring tasks, often because of stress factors.

Team development The stages in building unity, communications methods, internal controls, etc., within a team.

Teamness Amount of teamwork or collaboration within a group.

Technical or operating system A firm's method of getting work done—the equipment used, the raw materials, the arrangement of people.

Technical skills Skills that deal primarily with the technical nature of the organization.

Temporary structures New structures set up to meet current needs, often used for task forces and committees.

Terminal values Beliefs that a certain condition or state is worth striving for.

Theory X A belief that people are lazy, not trustworthy, and must be controlled. Managers holding Theory X assumptions often overcontrol subordinates, pay little attention to employee involvement, and exhibit low concern for employee growth and development.

Theory Y A belief that people are trustworthy, want to work, and to make a contribution. Managers holding Theory Y assumptions allow people more responsibility, involve them in goal setting and decision making, and show high concern for employee development.

Throughput Activities that occur within the system, turning inputs into outputs.

Time management The act of teaching people how to manage their time more effectively.

Times interest earned The ratio of gross income to interest charges. This ratio indicates the organization's ability to pay interest expenses directly from gross income.

Top-down planning Strategies by top-level managers that progress to people and/or units lower down in the organization.

Total group meetings Meetings with the entire staff, usually to solicit suggestions for improvement.

Totalitarianism A political system where a single party, individual, or group of individuals holds a monopoly of political power and does not recognize or permit opposition. The opportunity to participate in decision making is restricted to a few individuals.

Total quality control The process of examining all aspects of production for quality issues.

Total relationship A multifaceted, vital relationship, where the partners share a wide range of experiences together.

Trade restrictions Limits set on the amount of trade between the U.S. and other countries. Restrictions are often imposed to fight unfair trade practices.

Trailing spouse Someone who pulls up roots to follow a transplanted mate.

Training A means of improving the skill level of an individual.

Transaction reporting systems A system that handles routine transactions. Typically, a transaction reporting system creates a historical record of transactions; sorts, merges, and updates individual records; performs routine, well-defined processing tasks, such as calculating gross pay, withholding, and net pay; accumulates summary information; and produces reports for employees, supervisors, and management.

Transformational managers Managers who are interested in change. The term also implies that a major goal of the leader will be to help in the transformation of people—to provide opportunities for their growth and improvement. The leader will have a dual transformational task—to both improve the quality of the product or service and the people who are involved.

Trend A movement of a variable in a definite direction.

Trip to Abilene A behavior observed in groups: each member agrees to a suggestion or idea because he/she thinks it is what the others want. In fact no one may favor the idea, but each person thinks he/she is going along with the group's wishes.

Two-career family A family in which both parents actively pursue a career.

Type A A classification of individuals who are most likely to suffer from coronary disease.

Type B A classification of individuals who are least likely to suffer from coronary disease.

Unacted intentions Intentions that are not carried out because of many reasons: fear, inexperience, lack of skill, etc.

Uncertainty The unpredictability surrounding the possible outcomes of each decision alternative.

Unconflicted change The act of deciding to take action because the failure to do so will have serious repercussions. However, the first feasible low-risk alternative is usually taken.

Unconflicted inertia The state that occurs when a manager believes the consequences of the failure to act or decide are not very great. An operations manager may decide, for example, that a complaining customer is not in a position to complain much about inferior service.

Unintended communications Communications with a message that is different from the intended message.

Unity of purpose An ultimate goal shared by the entire group.

Utilitarianism The assumption that an individual or firm may use just about any tactics, fair or foul, to gain economic advantage over another, and that it is all justified in the name of "the bottom line."

Utility theory A body of theory examining how measures of desirability can be associated with specific outcomes.

Value context The set of values held by a majority of a group, the predominant set of values in which business decisions must operate.

Values Beliefs held by a group of people, society, company, etc.

Variable budget A budget that varies, depending on the activity level.

Virtuous qualities Qualities, such as honor, justice, courage, magnanimity, benevolence that are the necessary conditions for true happiness.

Vital relationship A relationship exhibiting a vitality based on the vibrant and exciting sharing of some important life experiences—children, work, or some creative activity.

Vroom-Yetton model A model that identifies five basic decision-making styles—each involving a different level of subordinate participation.

Vulnerability The state of a firm when an environmental condition poses a threat to an asset or strength. Even though an organization is doing something well, that strength may be threatened by events outside of the firm.

Win/win competition A competition in which all competitors can become winners.

Work A purely human endeavor that is achieved when we can embody that which is unique about the self upon something in the outside world. It requires, at the fundamental level, that individuals be able to comprehend their own uniqueness.

Worker autonomy The ability of workers to set bounds to their own work.

Work-in-process The amount of inventory that is still in the production phase. Upon completion it will enter finished goods.

Work-in-transit Stock that is in the process of being shipped from one location to another.

Work station A position on the assembly line where goods are worked on.

Written feedback technique A method that involves a request that the subject write down his or her recommendations about specific matters.

Wrongful dismissal The act of dismissing an employee from his/her position on grounds that are unfounded.

X-Chart A chart of the averages of a series of observations.

Zero-base budgeting A budget that is completely clear at the start of a new period, and the amounts are not dependent upon last period's budget.

COPYRIGHTS AND ACKNOWLEDGMENTS

328 Adapted from *Work, Mobility, and Participation: A Comparative Study of American and Japanese Industry*, by Robert Cole, published by the University of California Press. © 1979 The Regents of the University of California.

341–42 Adapted from *Team Building* by William Dyer, © 1987 Addison-Wesley Publishing Co., Inc., Reading, MA. Pages 3–5. Reprinted with permission of the publisher.

352 From "How Executive Team Training Can Help You," by R. R. Blake, J. S. Mouton, and M. G. Blansfield. Copyright © 1962, *Training and Development Journal*. American Society for Training and Development. Reprinted with Permission. All rights reserved.

392–97 Reprinted, by permission of publisher, from *Personnel* (February 1986), © 1986 by American Management Association, New York. All rights reserved.

411 Adapted, by permission of publisher, from *Organizational Dynamics* (Summer 1984). © 1984 by American Management Association, New York. All rights reserved.

412 From *A Passion for Excellence*, by Thomas J. Peters and Nancy K. Austin. Copyright © 1985 by Thomas J. Peters and Nancy K. Austin. Reprinted by permission of Random House, Inc.

418 Adapted from "To Achieve or Not: The Manager's Choice," by Jay Hall. © 1976 by the Regents of the University of California. Condensed from the *California Management Review*, vol. 18, no. 4. By permission of The Regents.

420–21 Taken from *The Managerial Grid III: The Key to Leadership Excellence*, by Robert R. Blake and Jane S. Mouton. Copyright © 1985 by Gulf Publishing Company. Reproduced with permission.

426, 428–29 Reprinted, by permission of publisher, from *Managerial Values and Expectations*, 1982. © 1982 by American Management Association, New York. All rights reserved.

442–44 Excerpts from *Motivation and Personality* by Abraham H. Maslow. Copyright 1954 by Harper & Row, Publishers, Inc. Copyright © 1970 by Abraham H. Maslow.

445–46 Adapted from *Work and Motivation* by Victor Vroom. Copyright © 1964 by John Wiley & Sons, Inc. Reprinted by permission of the publisher.

463 Adapted from *Communications and Interpersonal Relations* by William V. Haney. Copyright © 1985 by Richard D. Irwin, Inc.

495–96 Reprinted, by permission of publisher, from *Management Review* (August 1983). © 1983 by American Management Association, New York. All rights reserved.

500–501 Adapted from Thomas L. Moffatt, *Selection Interviewing for Managers*, © 1987 Science Tech Publishers.

528–30 Adapted from *Stress and Work: A Managerial Perspective* by John M. Ivancevich and Michael T. Matteson. Copyright © 1980 by Scott, Foresman and Company. Reprinted by permission.

533–34 From *Type A Behavior and Your Heart* by Meyer Friedman, M.D. and Ray Rosenman, M.D. Copyright © 1974 by Meyer Friedman. Reprinted by permission of Alfred A. Knopf, Inc. All rights reserved.

535 Reprinted by permission of Warner Books, New York from *Re-Inventing the Corporation* by John Naisbitt and Patricia Aburdene. Copyright © 1985 by Megatrends Ltd.

560–61 Excerpts from *Management: Tasks, Responsibilities and Practices* by Peter F. Drucker. Copyright © 1973, 1974 by the author.

602 Adapted from *Manufacturing Resource Planning—MRPII: Unlocking America's Productivity Potential*, by Oliver Wight. Oliver Wight Limited Publications, Inc., 5 Oliver Wight Drive, Essex Junction, VT 05452, (802) 878-8161 or (800) 343-0625. © 1981.

603 Reprinted with permission of The Free Press, a Division of Macmillan, Inc. from *Japanese Manufacturing Techniques*, by Richard Schonberger. Copyright © 1982 by Richard Schonberger.

611, 613, 614 Reprinted by permission from a paid advertising section prepared for the October 14, 1985 issue of *Fortune* magazine.

628 Reprinted with permission from *Journal of Business Strategy*, Summer 1984, vol. 5, no. 2, copyright © 1984. Warren Gorham & Lamont, Inc. 210 South Street, Boston, MA 02111. All rights reserved.

663–65 Adapted from *International Business: Environments and Operations* by J. Daniels and L. Radebaugh, © 1986, Addison-Wesley Publishing Co., Inc., Reading, MA. Pages 72–80. Reprinted with permission of the publisher.

667 Adapted from *International Business: Environments and Operations* by J. Daniels and L. Radebaugh, © 1986, Addison-Wesley Publishing Co., Inc., Reading, MA. Pages 13–15. Reprinted with permission of the publisher.

INDEX